Pro AngularJS

Adam Freeman

Apress·

Pro AngularJS

ISBN-13 (pbk): 978-1-4302-6448-4

ISBN-13 (electronic): 978-1-4302-6449-1

President and Publisher: Paul Manning
Lead Editor: James T. DeWolf
Development Editor: Douglas Pundick
Technical Reviewer: Fabio Claudio Ferracchiati
Editorial Board: Steve Anglin, Mark Beckner, Ewan Buckingham, Gary Cornell, Louise Corrigan, Jim DeWolf,
    Jonathan Gennick, Jonathan Hassell, Robert Hutchinson, Michelle Lowman, James Markham,
    Matthew Moodie, Jeff Olson, Jeffrey Pepper, Douglas Pundick, Ben Renow-Clarke, Dominic Shakeshaft,
    Gwenan Spearing, Matt Wade, Steve Weis
Coordinating Editor: Kevin Shea
Copy Editor: Kim Wimpsett
Compositor: SPi Global
Indexer: SPi Global
Artist: SPi Global
Cover Designer: Anna Ishchenko

Distributed to the book trade worldwide by Springer Science+Business Media New York, 233 Spring Street, 6th Floor, New York, NY 10013. Phone 1-800-SPRINGER, fax (201) 348-4505, e-mail orders-ny@springer-sbm.com, or visit www.springeronline.com. Apress Media, LLC is a California LLC and the sole member (owner) is Springer Science + Business Media Finance Inc (SSBM Finance Inc). SSBM Finance Inc is a Delaware corporation.

For information on translations, please e-mail rights@apress.com, or visit www.apress.com.

Apress and friends of ED books may be purchased in bulk for academic, corporate, or promotional use. eBook versions and licenses are also available for most titles. For more information, reference our Special Bulk Sales–eBook Licensing web page at www.apress.com/bulk-sales.

Any source code or other supplementary material referenced by the author in this text is available to readers at www.apress.com. For detailed information about how to locate your book's source code, go to www.apress.com/source-code/.

Dedicated to my lovely wife, Jacqui Griffyth.

Contents at a Glance

Contents

About the Author

Adam Freeman is an experienced IT professional who has held senior positions in a range of companies, most recently serving as chief technology officer and chief operating officer of a global bank. Now retired, he spends his time writing and running.

About the Technical Reviewer

Fabio Claudio Ferracchiati is a senior consultant and a senior analyst/developer using Microsoft technologies. He works for Brain Force (`www.brainforce.com`) in its Italian branch (`www.brainforce.it`). He is a Microsoft Certified Solution Developer for .NET, a Microsoft Certified Application Developer for .NET, a Microsoft Certified Professional, and a prolific author and technical reviewer. Over the past ten years, he's written articles for Italian and international magazines and coauthored more than ten books on a variety of computer topics.

Getting Ready

CHAPTER 1

■ ■ ■

Getting Ready

AngularJS taps into some of the best aspects of server-side development and uses them to enhance HTML in the browser, creating a foundation that makes building rich applications simpler and easier. AngularJS applications are built around a design pattern called Model-View-Controller (MVC), which places an emphasis on creating applications that are

- *Extendable*: It is easy to figure out how even a complex AngularJS app works once you understand the basics—and that means you can easily enhance applications to create new and useful features for your users.

- *Maintainable*: AngularJS apps are easy to debug and fix, which means that long-term maintenance is simplified.

- *Testable*: AngularJS has good support for unit and end-to-end testing, meaning that you can find and fix defects before your users do.

- *Standardized*: AngularJS builds on the innate capabilities of the web browser without getting in your way, allowing you to create standards-compliant web apps that take advantage of the latest features (such as HTML5 APIs) and popular tools and frameworks.

AngularJS is an open source JavaScript library that is sponsored and maintained by Google. It has been used in some of the largest and most complex web apps around. In this book, I show you everything you need to know to get the benefits of AngularJS in your own projects.

What Do You Need to Know?

Before reading this book, you should be familiar with the basics of web development, have an understanding of how HTML and CSS work, and, ideally, have a working knowledge of JavaScript. If you are a little hazy on some of these details, I provide refreshers for the HTML, CSS, and JavaScript I use in this book in Chapters 4 and 5. You won't find a comprehensive reference for HTML elements and CSS properties, though. There just isn't the space in a book about AngularJS to cover HTML in its entirety. If you want a complete reference for HTML and CSS, then I suggest another of my books, *The Definitive Guide to HTML5*, also published by Apress.

What Is the Structure of This Book?

This book is split into three parts, each of which covers a set of related topics.

Part 1: Getting Ready

Part 1 of this book provides the information you need to get ready for the rest of the book. It includes this chapter and primers/refreshers for HTML, CSS, and JavaScript. I also show you how to build your first AngularJS application and take you through the process of building a more realistic application, called SportsStore.

Part 2: Working with AngularJS

Part 2 of this book takes you through the features of the AngularJS library, starting with an overview of the different types of components in an AngularJS application and then working through each type in turn. AngularJS includes a lot of built-in functionality, which I describe in depth, and provides endless customization options, all of which I demonstrate.

Part 3: AngularJS Modules and Services

Part 3 of this book explains the roles that two important components play in AngularJS: modules and services. I show you the different ways you can create both components and explain the wide range of built-in services that AngularJS provides. This includes support for simplifying Single-Page Application development, Ajax and RESTful APIs, and unit testing.

Are There Lots of Examples?

There are *loads* of examples. The best way to learn AngularJS is by example, and I have packed as many of them as I can into this book. To maximize the number of examples in this book, I have adopted a simple convention to avoid listing the contents of files over and over again. The first time I use a file in a chapter, I'll list the complete contents, just as I have in Listing 1-1.

Listing 1-1. A Complete Example Document

```
<!DOCTYPE html>
<html ng-app="todoApp">
<head>
    <title>TO DO List</title>
    <link href="bootstrap.css" rel="stylesheet" />
    <link href="bootstrap-theme.css" rel="stylesheet" />
    <script src="angular.js"></script>
    <script>
        var model = {
            user: "Adam",
            items: [{ action: "Buy Flowers", done: false },
                    { action: "Get Shoes", done: false },
                    { action: "Collect Tickets", done: true },
                    { action: "Call Joe", done: false }]
        };

        var todoApp = angular.module("todoApp", []);
```

```
            todoApp.controller("ToDoCtrl", function ($scope) {
                $scope.todo = model;
            });

        </script>
    </head>
    <body ng-controller="ToDoCtrl">
        <div class="page-header">
            <h1>To Do List</h1>
        </div>
        <div class="panel">
            <div class="input-group">
                <input class="form-control" />
                <span class="input-group-btn">
                    <button class="btn btn-default">Add</button>
                </span>
            </div>
            <table class="table table-striped">
                <thead>
                    <tr>
                        <th>Description</th>
                        <th>Done</th>
                    </tr>
                </thead>
                <tbody></tbody>
            </table>
        </div>
    </body>
</html>
```

This listing is taken from Chapter 2. Don't worry about what it does; just be aware that the first time I use a file in each chapter there will be complete listing, similar to the one shown in Listing 1-1. For the second and subsequent examples, I just show you the elements that change, to create a *partial listing*. You can spot a partial listing because it starts and ends with ellipsis (. . .), as shown in Listing 1-2.

Listing 1-2. A Partial Listing

```
...
<body ng-controller="ToDoCtrl">
    <div class="page-header">
        <h1>
            {{todo.user}}'s To Do List
            <span class="label">{{todo.items.length}}</span>
        </h1>
    </div>
    <div class="panel">
        <div class="input-group">
            <input class="form-control" />
            <span class="input-group-btn">
                <button class="btn btn-default">Add</button>
            </span>
        </div>
```

```
        <table class="table table-striped">
            <thead>
                <tr>
                    <th>Description</th>
                    <th>Done</th>
                </tr>
            </thead>
            <tbody>
                <tr ng-repeat="item in todo.items">
                    <td>{{item.action}}</td>
                    <td>{{item.done}}</td>
                </tr>
            </tbody>
        </table>
    </div>
</body>
...
```

This is a subsequent listing from Chapter 2. You can see that just the body element, and its content, is shown and that I have highlighted a number of statements. This is how I draw your attention to the part of the example that shows the feature or technique I am describing. In a partial listing like this, only those parts shown have changed from the full listing earlier in the chapter. In some cases, I need to make changes to different parts of the same file, in which case I simply omit some elements or statements for brevity, as shown in Listing 1-3.

Listing 1-3. Omitting Elements for Brevity

```
<!DOCTYPE html>
<html ng-app="todoApp">
<head>
    <title>TO DO List</title>
    <link href="bootstrap.css" rel="stylesheet" />
    <script src="angular.js"></script>
    <script>

        var model = {
            user: "Adam",
            items: [{ action: "Buy Flowers", done: false },
                    { action: "Get Shoes", done: false },
                    { action: "Collect Tickets", done: true },
                    { action: "Call Joe", done: false }]
        };

        var todoApp = angular.module("todoApp", []);

        todoApp.controller("ToDoCtrl", function ($scope) {
            $scope.todo = model;
        });

    </script>
</head>
```

```
<body ng-controller="ToDoCtrl">

    <!-- ...elements omitted for brevity... -->

    <div class="panel">
        <div class="input-group">
            <input class="form-control" />
            <span class="input-group-btn">
                <button class="btn btn-default">Add</button>
            </span>
        </div>
        <table class="table table-striped">
            <thead>
                <tr>
                    <th>Description</th>
                    <th>Done</th>
                </tr>
            </thead>
            <tbody></tbody>
        </table>
    </div>
</body>
</html>
```

This convention lets me pack in more examples, but it does mean it can be hard to locate a specific technique. To this end, all of the chapters in which I describe AngularJS features in Parts 2 and 3 begin with a summary table that describes the techniques contained in the chapter and the listings that demonstrate how they are used.

Where Can You Get the Example Code?

You can download all the examples for all the chapters in this book from `www.apress.com`. The download is available without charge and includes all of the supporting resources that are required to re-create the examples without having to type them in. You don't have to download the code, but it is the easiest way of experimenting with the examples and cutting and pasting it into your own projects.

How Do You Set Up Your Development Environment?

You can get started with AngularJS development with a browser, a text editor, and a web server. One of the nice aspects of working on client-side web app development is that you can pick and mix from a wide range of development tools to create an environment that suits your working style and coding practice. In the sections that follow, I describe the environment I use so that you can re-create it on your own workstation. (You don't have use my tools, but doing so ensures that the examples work as expected. If you decide to use a different set of tools, then skip to the "Performing a Simple Test" section later in the chapter to make sure everything works.)

■ **Tip** A popular tool for client-side development is Yeoman (`http://yeoman.io`), which provides a tightly integrated development pipeline for client-side development. I don't get on with Yeoman: It has some issues on Windows (which I use for most of my development), and I find the overall approach to be a little too proscriptive. That said, it has some nice features and may well suit you better than it does me.

Choosing a Web Browser

AngularJS works in any modern web browser, and you should test your app in all of the browsers that your users are likely to use. You will need a go-to browser for development purposes, however, so that you can set up your development environment to show the current state of the application and perform basic testing.

I'll be using Google Chrome in this book, and I suggest you do the same. Not only is Chrome a solid browser, but it complies well with the latest W3C standards and has excellent F12 developer tools (so-called because you access them by pressing the F12 key).

The most compelling reason to use Chrome for development is that Google has created a Chrome extension that adds support for AngularJS to the F12 tools. It is a useful—if unpolished—tool, and I recommend you install it. The URL to the Chrome extension store is painfully long and impossible to type correctly, but you'll find the URL easily if you search for *Batarang AngularJS*.

■ **Caution** Like most JavaScript libraries, there are some compatibility issues with older versions of Internet Explorer. I'll show you how to resolve common problems in the appropriate chapters, but you can see a summary of the issues and how they can be addressed at `http://docs.angularjs.org/guide/ie`.

Choosing a Code Editor

You can use any text editor for AngularJS development. Two popular choices are WebStorm (`www.jetbrains.com/webstorm`) and Sublime Text (`www.sublimetext.com`). Both of these editors are paid-for products and are available for Windows, Linux, and Mac OS. Both offer enhancements over regular editors that make working with AngularJS easier.

Nothing polarizes developers like code editors, and I find that I am unable to work effectively with either WebStorm or Sublime Text, both of which constantly annoy me. Instead, I use Microsoft's Visual Studio Express 2013 for Web, which is available without charge and has built-in support for working with AngularJS (see `www.microsoft.com/visualstudio/express` for details and make sure you get the *Express for Web* edition). Visual Studio runs only on Windows, of course, but is an excellent IDE and has a code editor that I think is second-to-none.

■ **Tip** You can pick any editor to follow the examples in this book. As long as your preferred editor can write HTML and JavaScript files (both of which are plain text), then you will be able to follow along without any problems.

Installing Node.js

Many development tools that are commonly used for client-side web app development are written in JavaScript and rely on Node.js to run. Node.js is built from the same JavaScript engine that is used in the Google Chrome browser but has been adapted to work outside the browser, providing a general-purpose framework for writing JavaScript applications.

Go to `http://nodejs.org` and download and install the Node.js package for your platform (there are versions available for Windows, Linux, and Mac OS). Make sure you install the package manager and that the installation directory is added to your path.

To test the Node.js installation, open a command line and type node. Wait until the prompt changes and then enter the following (on a single line):

```
function testNode() {return "Node is working"}; testNode();
```

When used interactively, Node.js will evaluate input as JavaScript, and you will see the following output if the installation has been successful:

```
'Node is working'
```

■ **Note** There are lots of ways to configure Node.js and make a web server out of it. I am going to use the simplest and most reliable, which is to install the add-on modules I need locally within the Node.js installation directory. See `http://Nodejs.org` for other configuration options.

Installing the Web Server

A simple web server will suffice for development, and I create one using a Node.js module called Connect. From within the Node.js installation directory, run the following command:

```
npm install connect
```

NPM is the node package installer, and it will pull down the files required for the Connect module. Next, create a new file called `server.js` (still within the Node.js installation folder) and set the contents so they match those shown in Listing 1-4.

Listing 1-4. The Contents of the server.js File

```
var connect = require('connect');

connect.createServer(
    connect.static("../angularjs")

).listen(5000);
```

This simple file creates a basic web server that will respond to requests on port 5000 and serve up files contained in a folder called `angularjs`, which is at the same level as the Node.js installation folder on the disk.

Installing the Test System

One of the most important aspects of AngularJS is the support it has for unit testing. In this book, I'll be using the Karma test runner and the Jasmine test framework, both of which are widely used and easy to get along with. From within the Node.js installation directory, run the following command:

```
npm install -g karma
```

NPM will download and install all the files that Karma requires. There is no further configuration required in this chapter. I'll return to Karma in Chapter 25.

Creating the AngularJS Directory

The next step is to create a directory from which you will serve up your AngularJS applications during development. This allows you to check your progress as you code and organize all of your files consistently. Create a folder called angularjs at the same level on the disk as the Node.js installation folder. (You can use a different location, but remember to change the contents of the server.js file to match your choice.)

Getting the AngularJS Library

The next step is to download the latest stable release of AngularJS from http://angularjs.org. Click the Download link on the main page and ensure that the Stable and Uncompressed options are checked, as shown in Figure 1-1. As the figure shows, you can select an unstable (prerelease) version, get a minified version, or use a content distribution network (CDN), but for this book I am going to use a local copy of the uncompressed library. Save the file as angular.js in the angularjs directory.

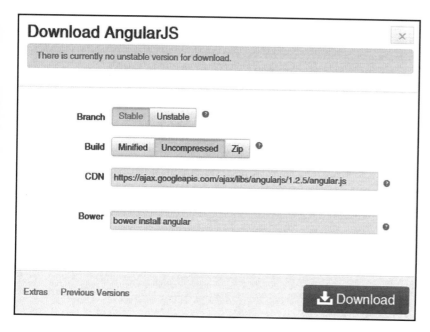

Figure 1-1. *Downloading the AngularJS library*

As I write this, the current stable version of AngularJS is 1.2.5, which I will be using throughout this book. It takes time for a book to be edited and published, so there may be a later version available by the time you read this; however, the AngularJS API for the stable releases doesn't change, so you should not encounter any problems using newer versions.

■ **Tip** There is a Previous Versions link on the download menu that will allow you to get exactly the same version I have used in the examples.

Getting the AngularJS Extras

If you look closely at Figure 1-1, you will see an Extras link in the bottom-left corner. This provides access to some additional files that extend the functionality of the core AngularJS library. I use some of the files in later chapters, and in Table 1-1 you can see a complete list of the extra files you will need and the chapters in which they are used.

Table 1-1. *The Types of Web Forms Code Nuggets*

File	Description	Used in Chapter
angular-touch.js	Provides touchscreen event support.	23
angular-animate.js	Provides animations when content changes.	23
angular-mocks.js	Provides mock objects for unit testing.	27
angular-route.js	Provides URL routing.	21
angular-sanitize.js	Provides escaping for dangerous content.	19
angular-locale-fr-fr.js	Provides localization details for French as it is spoken in France. This is one of a wide range of localization files found in the i18n folder.	14

Getting Bootstrap

I will be using the Bootstrap CSS framework to style the content in the examples throughout this book. Bootstrap isn't required when working with AngularJS, and there is no direct relationship between the two packages, but Bootstrap has a nice set of CSS styles that will let me create clear content layouts without having to define and endlessly redefine custom CSS styles.

Go to http://getbootstrap.com and click the Download Bootstrap button. You will receive an archive that contains JavaScript and CSS files. Copy the following files into the angularjs folder alongside the angularjs file:

- bootstrap-3.0.3/dist/css/bootstrap.css
- bootstrap-3.0.3/dist/css/bootstrap-theme.css

Don't re-create the file structure—copy the files into the angularjs folder. I introduce Bootstrap properly in Chapter 4. (As the file names suggest, the current version of Bootstrap as I write this is version 3.0.3.)

■ **Tip** Bootstrap consists of CSS files and a JavaScript file. I'll be using the CSS files in all of the examples in this book, but I don't use the JavaScript features at all since they are not required to explain how AngularJS works.

OPTIONAL: LIVERELOAD

AngularJS app development tends to be iterative, requiring lots of small changes that are then viewed in the browser. I use a tool called LiveReload (http://livereload.com) that monitors the files in a folder and automatically reloads the browser when a change is detected. This may seem like a small thing, but it is a huge timesaver, especially since you can have multiple browsers and browser windows updated simultaneously. As I write this, the Windows version is at an alpha release, but it works well. The Mac OS version is more mature and is available for $9.99. (To be clear, I don't have any relationship of any kind with any software company. All of the tools that I use for my books are provided by Apress, or I purchase them myself. When I recommend a tool, it is because I like working with it, and I receive no compensation or special treatment of any kind.)

Getting Deployd

In Chapter 6, I begin the process of creating a substantial example application, and for that I need a server to which I can send HTTP queries to obtain data. I also need this facility in Part 3, where I explain the AngularJS features for Ajax and for consuming RESTful web services.

The server that I have chosen for this task is called Deployd and is available from Deployd.com. Deployd is an excellent cross-platform tool for modeling APIs for web applications. It is built on top of Node.js and MongoDB, which allows it to store data as JSON (actually a close derivative of JSON, but the differences don't matter for this book), and server-side behaviors are written using JavaScript.

Sadly, the future of Deployd seems uncertain. The business model behind the project was to allow easy deployment of back-end services to cloud providers, but that doesn't seem to have caught on. As I write this, there hasn't been any active development on the project for a while and it is possible that the developers have moved on to other projects. The Deployd tools can still be downloaded and installed locally and, if you should want, deployed to any cloud provider that supports Node.js and MongoDB. Although active development of Deployd may have ceased, the project is open source. All of the source code, installers, and documentation are available at https://github.com/deployd/deployd as well as http://deployd.com. I have also included the Windows and Mac installers for Deployd in the source code download that accompanies this book, available from www.apress.com. Download and install Deployd for your platform. No further setup is required at the moment, and I'll show you how to use Deployd in Chapter 6.

Performing a Simple Test

To make sure everything is installed and working, create a new HTML file called test.html in the angularjs folder and set the contents to match Listing 1-5.

Listing 1-5. Testing for AngularJS and Bootstrap in the test.html File

```
<!DOCTYPE html>
<html ng-app>
<head>
    <title>First Test</title>
    <script src="angular.js"></script>
```

```
        <link href="bootstrap.css" rel="stylesheet" />
        <link href="bootstrap-theme.css" rel="stylesheet" />
</head>
<body>
        <div class="btn btn-default">{{"AngularJS"}}</div>
        <div class="btn btn-success">Bootstrap</div>
</body>
</html>
```

Some parts of this file may be new to you: the ng-app attribute on the html element and {{AngularJS}} in the body element come from AngularJS; the btn, btn-default, and btn-success classes are from Bootstrap. Don't worry about what these mean or do at the moment—the purpose of this HTML document is to check that the development environment is set up and working. I explain how Bootstrap works in Chapter 4 and, of course, explain everything you need to know about AngularJS throughout the rest of this book.

Starting the Web Server

To start the web server, run the following command from the Node.js installation directory:

```
node server.js
```

This will load the server.js file created earlier in the chapter and start listening for HTTP requests on port 5000.

Load the Test File

Start Chrome and navigate to the URL http://localhost:5000/test.html. You should see the result in Figure 1-2.

Figure 1-2. *Testing the development environment*

In Figure 1-3, you can see what happens if neither AngularJS nor Bootstrap works properly. Notice that you can see the brace characters ({ and }) in the AngularJS test and that the content isn't presented as buttons (which is performed by Bootstrap). Check the configuration of your web server, check that you have placed the correct files in the angularjs folder, and try again.

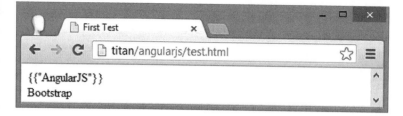

Figure 1-3. *Failing the basic tests*

Summary

In this chapter, I outlined the content and structure of this book and as well as the software that is required for AngularJS web development. As I said earlier, the best way to learn AngularJS development is by example, so in Chapter 2 I jump right in and show you how to create your first AngularJS application.

■ ■ ■

Your First AngularJS App

The best way to get started with AngularJS is to dive in and create a web application. In this chapter, I take you through a simple development process, starting with a static mock-up of the target application and applying AngularJS features to move to a dynamic web application, albeit a simple one. In Chapters 6–8, I show you how to create a more complex and realistic AngularJS application, but for now a simple example will suffice to demonstrate the major components of an AngularJS app and set the scene for the other chapters in this part of the book.

Preparing the Project

In Chapter 1, I showed you how to create and test the development environment that I use in this book. If you want to follow the examples, now is the time to get everything up and running.

I am going to start with a static HTML mock-up of my goal in this chapter, which is a simple to-do application. I created a new HTML file called todo.html in the angularjs folder. You can see the contents of the new file in Listing 2-1.

Listing 2-1. The Initial Contents of the todo.html File

```
<!DOCTYPE html>
<html data-ng-app>
<head>
    <title>TO DO List</title>
    <link href="bootstrap.css" rel="stylesheet" />
    <link href="bootstrap-theme.css" rel="stylesheet" />
</head>
<body>
    <div class="page-header">
        <h1>Adam's To Do List</h1>
    </div>
    <div class="panel">
        <div class="input-group">
            <input class="form-control" />
            <span class="input-group-btn">
                <button class="btn btn-default">Add</button>
            </span>
        </div>
```

```
        <table class="table table-striped">
            <thead>
                <tr>
                    <th>Description</th>
                    <th>Done</th>
                </tr>
            </thead>
            <tbody>
                <tr><td>Buy Flowers</td><td>No</td></tr>
                <tr><td>Get Shoes</td><td>No</td></tr>
                <tr><td>Collect Tickets</td><td>Yes</td></tr>
                <tr><td>Call Joe</td><td>No</td></tr>
            </tbody>
        </table>
    </div>
</body>
</html>
```

■ **Tip** From now on, unless I tell you otherwise, add all files to the `angularjs` folder that you created in the previous chapter. You don't have to re-create the examples by hand. Instead, you can download all of the examples without charge from Apress.com. The examples are complete and are organized by chapter, containing all of the files that I use to build and test the examples.

This file doesn't use AngularJS; in fact, there isn't even a `script` element to import the `angular.js` file at the moment. I'll add the JavaScript file and start applying AngularJS features shortly, but for now, the `todo.html` file contains static HTML elements that provide a skeletal mock-up of a to-do application: a header at the top of the page and a table that contains the to-do items. To see the effect I have created, use the browser to navigate to the `todo.html` file, as shown in Figure 2-1.

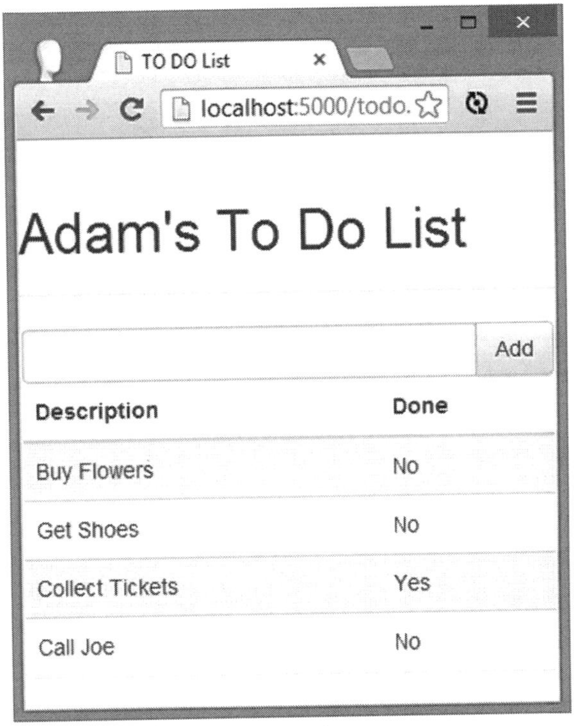

Figure 2-1. *The initial contents of the todo.html file*

■ **Note**   To keep the example in this chapter simple, I am going to do everything within the todo.html file. There is usually a carefully chosen structure for the files in an AngularJS application, but I won't be doing anything complicated enough to make that an issue; in Chapter 6, I start the process of building a more complex AngularJS application, and I'll talk about file structure in that context.

Using AngularJS

The static HTML in the todo.html file acts as a placeholder for the basic functionality that I want to create. The user should be able to see the list of to-do items, check off items that are complete, and create new items. In the sections that follow, I am going to add AngularJS and use some basic features to bring my to-do application to life. For simplicity I am going to assume that there is only one user and that I don't have to worry about preserving the state of the data in the application.

Applying AngularJS to the HTML File

It is easy to add AngularJS to an HTML file. Simply add a script element to import the angular.js file, create an AngularJS *module*, and apply an attribute to the html element, as shown in Listing 2-2.

Listing 2-2. Creating and Applying an AngularJS Module in the todo.html File

```
<!DOCTYPE html>
<html ng-app="todoApp">
<head>
    <title>TO DO List</title>
    <link href="bootstrap.css" rel="stylesheet" />
    <link href="bootstrap-theme.css" rel="stylesheet" />
    <script src="angular.js"></script>
    <script>
        var todoApp = angular.module("todoApp", []);
    </script>
</head>
<body>
    <div class="page-header">
        <h1>Adam's To Do List</h1>
    </div>
    <div class="panel">
        <div class="input-group">
            <input class="form-control" />
            <span class="input-group-btn">
                <button class="btn btn-default">Add</button>
            </span>
        </div>
        <table class="table table-striped">
            <thead>
                <tr>
                    <th>Description</th>
                    <th>Done</th>
                </tr>
            </thead>
            <tbody>
                <tr><td>Buy Flowers</td><td>No</td></tr>
                <tr><td>Get Shoes</td><td>No</td></tr>
                <tr><td>Collect Tickets</td><td>Yes</td></tr>
                <tr><td>Call Joe</td><td>No</td></tr>
            </tbody>
        </table>
    </div>
</body>
</html>
```

AngularJS apps are formed from one or more modules. Modules are created by calling the angular.module method, as follows:

```
...
var todoApp = angular.module("todoApp", []);
...
```

I describe modules properly in Chapters 9 and 18, but you can see how I create and apply a module for the example in Listing 2-2. The arguments to the angular.module method are the name of the module to create and an array of other modules that are going to be needed. I have created a module called todoApp, following the slightly confusing convention of appending App to application module names and telling AngularJS that I need no other modules by providing an empty array for the second argument. (Some AngularJS features are available in different modules, and I show you how to create your own modules in Chapter 18.)

■ **Caution** A common error is to omit the dependencies argument, which causes an error. You *must* supply a dependencies argument, using an empty array if there are no dependencies. I explain how to use dependencies in Chapter 18.

I tell AngularJS how to apply the module through the ng-app attribute. AngularJS works by extending HTML by adding new elements, attributes, classes, and (although rarely used) special comments. The AngularJS library dynamically *compiles* the HTML in a document in order to locate and process these additions and create an application. You can supplement the built-in functionality with JavaScript code to customize the behavior of the application and define your own additions to HTML.

■ **Note** AngularJS compilation isn't like the compilation you might have encountered in C# or Java projects, where the compiler has to process the source code in order to generate output that the runtime can execute. It would be more accurate to say that the AngularJS library evaluates the HTML elements when the browser has loaded the content and uses standard DOM API and JavaScript features to add and remove elements, sets up event handlers, and so on. There is no explicit compilation step in AngularJS development; just modify your HTML and JavaScript files and load them into the browser.

The most important AngularJS addition to HTML is the ng-app attribute, which specifies that the html element in the listing contains a module that should be compiled and processed by AngularJS. When AngularJS is the only JavaScript framework being used, the convention is to apply the ng-app attribute to the html element, as I have done in Listing 2-2. If you are mixing AngularJS with other technologies such as jQuery, you can narrow the boundaries of the AngularJS app by applying the ng-app attribute to an element within the document.

APPLYING ANGULARJS TO HTML

It can seem odd to add nonstandard attributes and elements to an HTML document, especially if you have been writing web apps for a while and have become accustomed to sticking to the HTML standard. There is an alternative approach you can use if you just can't get used to the idea of attributes like ng-app. You can use data attributes, prefixing the AngularJS directive with data-. I describe directives in detail in Part 2, but for the moment it is enough to know that ng-app is a directive and so can be applied like this:

```
...
<html data-ng-app="todoApp">
...
```

I am going to use the AngularJS convention and use the ng-app attribute and all of the other HTML enhancements that are available. I recommend you do the same, but you can use one of the other approaches if you prefer—or if your development tool chain can't process nonstandard HTML elements and attributes.

Creating a Data Model

AngularJS supports the *Model-View-Controller* (MVC) pattern, which I describe in Chapter 3. In short, following the MVC pattern requires you to break up the application into three distinct areas: the data in the application (the model), the logic that operates on that data (the controllers), and the logic that displays the data (the views).

The data in my to-do application is currently distributed across the HTML elements. The user's name is contained in the header, like this:

```
...
<h1>Adam's To Do List</h1>
...
```

and the details of the to-do items are contained within td elements in the table, like this:

```
...
<tr><td>Buy Flowers</td><td>No</td></tr>
...
```

My first task is to pull all of the data together and separate it from the HTML elements in order to create a model. Separating the data from the way that it is presented to the user is one of the key ideas in the MVC pattern, as I explain in Chapter 3. Since AngularJS applications exist in the browser, I need to define my data model using JavaScript within a script element, as shown in Listing 2-3.

Listing 2-3. Creating a Data Model in the todo.html File

```
<!DOCTYPE html>
<html ng-app="todoApp">
<head>
    <title>TO DO List</title>
    <link href="bootstrap.css" rel="stylesheet" />
    <link href="bootstrap-theme.css" rel="stylesheet" />
    <script src="angular.js"></script>
    <script>

        var model = {
            user: "Adam",
            items: [{ action: "Buy Flowers", done: false },
                    { action: "Get Shoes", done: false },
                    { action: "Collect Tickets", done: true },
                    { action: "Call Joe", done: false }]
        };

        var todoApp = angular.module("todoApp", []);

    </script>
</head>
<body>
    <div class="page-header">
        <h1>To Do List</h1>
    </div>
    <div class="panel">
        <div class="input-group">
            <input class="form-control" />
```

```
                <span class="input-group-btn">
                    <button class="btn btn-default">Add</button>
                </span>
            </div>
            <table class="table table-striped">
                <thead>
                    <tr>
                        <th>Description</th>
                        <th>Done</th>
                    </tr>
                </thead>
                <tbody>
                </tbody>
            </table>
        </div>
    </body>
</html>
```

■ **Tip**   I am simplifying here. The model can also contain the logic required to create, load, store, and modify data objects. In an AngularJS app, this logic is often at the server and is accessed by a web server. See Chapter 3 for further details.

I have defined a JavaScript object called model with properties that correspond to the data that was previously distributed among the HTML elements. The user property defines the name of the user, and the items property defines an array of objects that describe my to-do items.

You wouldn't usually define a model without also defining the other parts of the MVC pattern at the same time, but I want to demonstrate how I build up my simple AngularJS application. You can see the effect of this change in Figure 2-2.

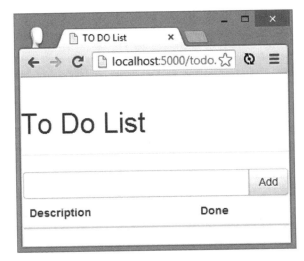

Figure 2-2. *The effect of creating the data model*

■ **Tip** In any AngularJS development project, there is a period where you have to define the main parts of the MVC pattern and plumb them together. During this period, it can feel like you have taken a step backward, especially if you are working from a static mock-up like I am in this chapter. This period of initial investment *will* ultimately pay off, I promise. You will see a larger example of this in Chapter 6 when I start to build a more complex and realistic AngularJS application; there is a lot of initial setup and configuration required, but then the features start to quickly snap into place.

Creating a Controller

The *controller* defines the business logic required to support a view, although the term *business logic* isn't helpful. The best way of describing a controller is to explain what kinds of logic it doesn't contain—and what's left goes into the controller.

Logic that deals with storing or retrieving data is part of the *model*. Logic that deals with formatting the data to display to the user is part of the *view*. The controller sits between the model and the view and connects them. The controller responds to user interaction, updating the data in the model and providing the view with the data that it requires.

It doesn't matter if this doesn't make sense at the moment; by the end of the book you'll be entirely comfortable with the MVC pattern and how it applies to AngularJS. I start getting into the details of the MVC pattern in Chapter 3, but you'll see this separation of components most clearly starting in Chapter 6, when I begin building a more realistic AngularJS web app.

■ **Tip** Don't worry if you are not a patterns person. The MVC pattern is largely common sense, and I apply it pretty loosely in this book. Patterns are simply tools to help developers, and you are free to adapt them to suit your needs. Once you get over the bump of the terminology associated with MVC, you can pick the bits that suit your needs and adapt MVC and AngularJS to your projects and preferred development style.

Controllers are created by calling the controller method on the Module object returned by calling angular.module, as demonstrated in the previous section. The arguments to the controller method are the name for the new controller and a function that will be invoked to define the controller functionality, as shown in Listing 2-4.

Listing 2-4. Creating a Controller in the todo.html File

```
<!DOCTYPE html>
<html ng-app="todoApp">
<head>
    <title>TO DO List</title>
    <link href="bootstrap.css" rel="stylesheet" />
    <link href="bootstrap-theme.css" rel="stylesheet" />
    <script src="angular.js"></script>
    <script>

        var model = {
            user: "Adam",
            items: [{ action: "Buy Flowers", done: false },
                    { action: "Get Shoes", done: false },
                    { action: "Collect Tickets", done: true },
                    { action: "Call Joe", done: false }]
        };
```

```
        var todoApp = angular.module("todoApp", []);

        todoApp.controller("ToDoCtrl", function ($scope) {
            $scope.todo = model;
        });

    </script>
</head>
<body ng-controller="ToDoCtrl">
    <div class="page-header">
        <h1>To Do List</h1>
    </div>
    <div class="panel">
        <div class="input-group">
            <input class="form-control" />
            <span class="input-group-btn">
                <button class="btn btn-default">Add</button>
            </span>
        </div>
        <table class="table table-striped">
            <thead>
                <tr>
                    <th>Description</th>
                    <th>Done</th>
                </tr>
            </thead>
            <tbody></tbody>
        </table>
    </div>
</body>
</html>
```

The convention is to name the controller <Name>Ctrl, where <Name> will help you recognize what the controller is responsible for in your application. Real applications will generally have several controllers, but I need only one for this example, which I have called ToDoCtrl.

■ **Tip** Naming controllers like this is just a convention, and you are free to use any name you like. The idea of following widely used conventions is that programmers who know AngularJS can quickly figure out the structure of your project.

I admit that the controller is underwhelming, but that's because I have created the simplest controller possible. One of the main purposes of the controller is to provide views with the data they require. You won't always want views to have access to the complete model, so you use the controller to explicitly select those portions of the data that are going to be available, known as the *scope*.

The argument to my controller function is called $scope—that is to say, the $ sign followed by the word scope. In an AngularJS app, variable names that start with $ represent built-in features that AngularJS provides. When you see the $ sign, it usually refers to a built-in *service*, which is a self-contained component that provides features to multiple controllers, but $scope is special and is used to expose data and functionality to views. I describe the scope in Chapter 13 and the built-in services in Chapter 18–25.

For this app, I want to work with the entire model in my views, so I have defined a property called todo on the $scope service object and assigned my complete model, as follows:

```
...
$scope.todo = model;
...
```

Doing this is a precursor to being able to work with the model data in views, which I demonstrate shortly. I also have to specify the region of the HTML document that the controller will be responsible for, which is done using the ng-controller attribute. Since I have only one controller—and since this is such a simple app—I have applied the ng-controller attribute to the body element, as follows:

```
...
<body ng-controller="ToDoCtrl">
...
```

The value of the ng-controller attribute is set to the name of the controller, which is ToDoCtrl in this example. I return to the topic of controllers in depth in Chapter 13.

Creating a View

Views are generated by combining data the controller provides with annotated HTML elements that produce content for the browser to display. In Listing 2-5, you can see how I have used one kind of annotation, known as a *data binding*, to populate the HTML document with the model data.

Listing 2-5. Displaying the Model Data with a View in the todo.html File

```
...
<body ng-controller="ToDoCtrl">
    <div class="page-header">
        <h1>
            {{todo.user}}'s To Do List
            <span class="label label-default">{{todo.items.length}}</span>
        </h1>
    </div>
    <div class="panel">
        <div class="input-group">
            <input class="form-control" />
            <span class="input-group-btn">
                <button class="btn btn-default">Add</button>
            </span>
        </div>
        <table class="table table-striped">
            <thead>
                <tr>
                    <th>Description</th>
                    <th>Done</th>
                </tr>
            </thead>
```

```
        <tbody>
            <tr ng-repeat="item in todo.items">
                <td>{{item.action}}</td>
                <td>{{item.done}}</td>
            </tr>
        </tbody>
    </table>
  </div>
</body>
...
```

You can see the effect of combining the model, controller, and view by using the browser to navigate to the todo.html file, as shown in Figure 2-3. I'll explain how the HTML was generated in the sections that follow.

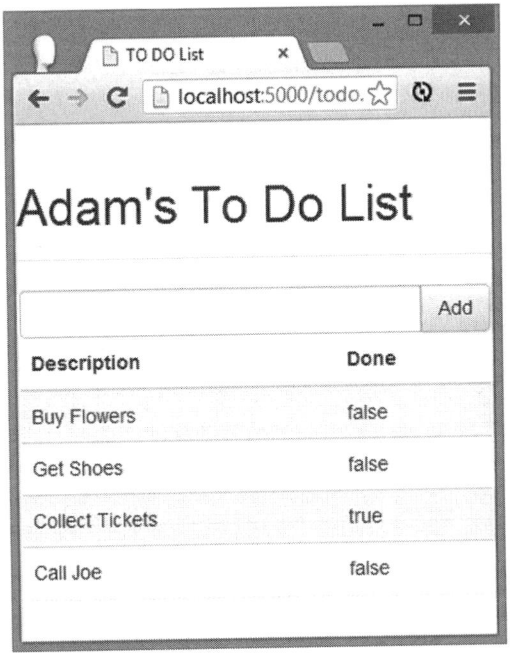

Figure 2-3. *The effect of applying a view to the todo.html file*

Inserting Model Values

AngularJS uses double-brace characters ({{ and }}) to denote a data binding expression. The content of the expression is evaluated as JavaScript, limited to the data and functions assigned to the scope by the controller. In this example, I can only access the parts of the model that I assigned to the $scope object when I defined the controller, using the names of the properties that I created on the $scope object.

This means, for example, that if I want to access the model.user property, I define a data binding expression that refers to todo.user; that's because I assigned the model object to the $scope.todo property.

AngularJS compiles the HTML in the document, discovers the `ng-controller` attribute, and invokes the ToDoCtrl function to set the scope that will be used to create the view. As each data binding expression is encountered, AngularJS looks up the specified value on the `$scope` object and inserts the value into the HTML document. As an example, this expression:

```
...
{{todo.user}}'s To Do List
...
```

is processed and transformed into the following string:

```
Adam's To Do List
```

This is known as *data binding* or *model binding*, where a value from the model is bound to the contents of an HTML element. There are a few different ways of creating data bindings, which I explain in Chapter 10.

Evaluating Expressions

The contents of a data binding expression can be any valid JavaScript statement, meaning that you can perform operations to create new data from the model. In Listing 2-5, I used this feature to display the number of to-do items in the list, as follows:

```
...
<div class="page-header">
    {{todo.user}}'s To Do List<span class="label label-default">{{todo.items.length}}</span>
</div>
...
```

AngularJS evaluates this expression and displays the number of items in the array to tell the user how many items are in the to-do list, which I show alongside the header in the HTML document (formatted with the Bootstrap `label` class for formatting).

■ **Tip** You should use expressions only to perform simple operations to prepare data values for display. Don't use data bindings to perform complex logic or to manipulate the model; that's the job of the controller. You will often encounter logic that is hard to classify as being suitable for the view or the controller, and it can be difficult to work out what to do. My advice is to not worry about it. Make a best guess in order to preserve development momentum and move the logic later if need be. If you really can't make a call, then put the logic in the controller; that will turn out to be the right decision about 60 percent of the time.

Using Directives

Expressions are also used with *directives*, which tell AngularJS how you want content to be processed. In the listing, I used the ng-repeat attribute, which applies a directive that tells AngularJS to generate the element it is applied to and its contents for each object in a collection, as follows:

```
...
<tr ng-repeat="item in todo.items">
    <td>{{item.action}}</td><td>{{item.done}}</td>
</tr>
...
```

The value of the ng-repeat attribute is in the format <name> in <collection>. I have specified item in todo.items, which means the following: Generate the tr element and the td elements it contains for each of the objects in the todo.items array and assign each object in the array to a variable called item.

Using the item variable, I am able to define binding expressions for the properties of each object in the array, producing the following HTML:

```
...
<tr ng-repeat="item in todo.items" class="ng-scope">
    <td class="ng-binding">Buy Flowers</td>
    <td class="ng-binding">false</td>
</tr>
<tr ng-repeat="item in todo.items" class="ng-scope">
    <td class="ng-binding">Get Shoes</td>
    <td class="ng-binding">false</td>
</tr>
<tr ng-repeat="item in todo.items" class="ng-scope">
    <td class="ng-binding">Collect Tickets</td>
    <td class="ng-binding">true</td>
</tr>
<tr ng-repeat="item in todo.items" class="ng-scope">
    <td class="ng-binding">Call Joe</td>
    <td class="ng-binding">false</td>
</tr>
...
```

As you'll learn in later chapters, directives are at the core of how AngularJS works, and the ng-repeat directive is one that you will use frequently.

Going Beyond the Basics

I have defined the basic MVC building blocks and, in doing so, have created a dynamic version of the static mock-up that I started the chapter with. Now that I have a solid foundation, I can use some more advanced techniques to add functionality and create a more complete app. In the sections that follow, I'll apply different AngularJS features to the to-do app and explain where in this book I describe those features in more detail.

Using Two-Way Model Binding

The bindings I used in the previous section are known as *one-way bindings*, where values are taken from the model and used to populate the elements in a template. This is pretty standard stuff and is a widely used technique in web app development. For example, I often use the Handlebars template package when I work with jQuery, which provides this kind of binding and is useful for generating HTML content from data objects.

AngularJS goes further and also provides *two-way bindings* as well, where the model is used to generate elements *and* changes in the element cause corresponding changes in the model. To demonstrate how two-way bindings are implemented, I have modified the todo.html file so that the status of each task is represented by a check box, as shown in Listing 2-6.

Listing 2-6. Adding Check Boxes to the todo.html File

```
...
<tr ng-repeat="item in todo.items">
    <td>{{item.action}}</td>
    <td><input type="checkbox" ng-model="item.done" /></td>
    <td>{{item.done}}</td>
</tr>
...
```

I have added a new td element to contain a check box input element. The important addition is the ng-model attribute, which tells AngularJS to create a two-way binding between the value of the input element and the done property of the corresponding data object (the one that the ng-repeat directive assigned to item when generating the elements).

When the HTML is first compiled, AngularJS will use the value of the done property to set the value of the input element, and since I am using a check box, a value of true causes the box to be checked, while a value of false causes the box to be unchecked. You can see the effect by using the browser to navigate to the todo.html file, as shown in Figure 2-4. You can see that the settings for the check boxes match the true/false values, which I have left in the table to help demonstrate the binding feature.

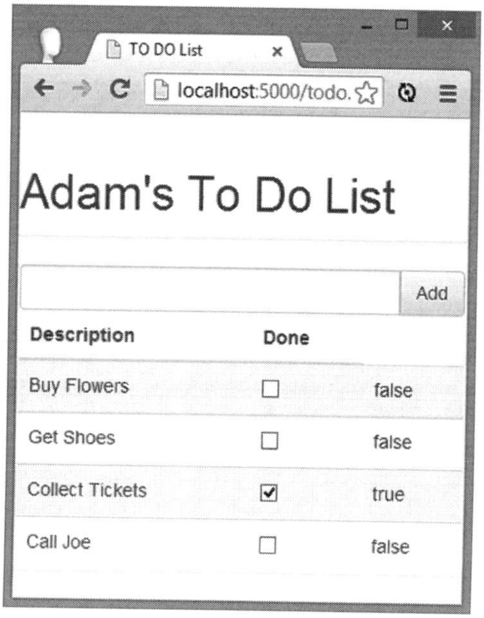

Figure 2-4. *Adding check box input elements*

The magic of a two-way binding becomes evident if you check and uncheck the box for the first item in the list; you will notice that the text value in the next column changes as well. AngularJS bindings are dynamic, and a two-way binding, such as the one I applied to the input element, updates the model, which, in turn, updates other elements that have related data bindings. In this case, the input element and the text in the rightmost column are kept seamlessly in sync, as Figure 2-5 illustrates.

Figure 2-5. *Using a two-way binding*

Two-way bindings can be applied to elements that take user input, which generally means elements associated with HTML form elements, a topic that I describe in depth in Chapter 12. Having a live and dynamic model makes creating complex applications easy with AngularJS, and you'll see examples of just how dynamic AngularJS is throughout this book.

■ **Tip** I left in the column of true/false values because they make it easy to see the effect of using a two-way data binding, but you wouldn't usually do this in a real development project. Fortunately, the Batarang extension for Google Chrome makes it easy to explore and monitor the model (and some other AngularJS features). See Chapter 1 for details of the Batarang extension.

Creating and Using Controller Behaviors

Controllers define *behaviors* on the scope. Behaviors are functions that operate on the data in the model to implement the business logic in the application. The behaviors defined by a controller support a view to display data to the user and to update the model based on user interactions.

To demonstrate a simple behavior, I am going to change the label displayed to the right of the header in todo.html so that it displays only the number of incomplete to-do items. You can see the changes required to do this in Listing 2-7. (I also removed the column that contains the true and false values, which I required only to demonstrate that data bindings reflected changes in the data model.)

Listing 2-7. Defining and Using a Controller Behavior in the todo.html File

```
<!DOCTYPE html>
<html ng-app="todoApp">
<head>
    <title>TO DO List</title>
    <link href="bootstrap.css" rel="stylesheet" />
    <link href="bootstrap-theme.css" rel="stylesheet" />
    <script src="angular.js"></script>
    <script>
```

```
        var model = {
            user: "Adam",
            items: [{ action: "Buy Flowers", done: false },
                    { action: "Get Shoes", done: false },
                    { action: "Collect Tickets", done: true },
                    { action: "Call Joe", done: false }]
        };

        var todoApp = angular.module("todoApp", []);

        todoApp.controller("ToDoCtrl", function ($scope) {
            $scope.todo = model;

            $scope.incompleteCount = function () {
                var count = 0;
                angular.forEach($scope.todo.items, function (item) {
                    if (!item.done) { count++ }
                });
                return count;
            }
        });

    </script>
</head>
<body ng-controller="ToDoCtrl">
    <div class="page-header">
        <h1>
            {{todo.user}}'s To Do List
            <span class="label label-default" ng-hide="incompleteCount() == 0">
                {{incompleteCount()}}
            </span>
        </h1>
    </div>
    <div class="panel">

        <div class="input-group">
            <input class="form-control" />
            <span class="input-group-btn">
                <button class="btn btn-default">Add</button>
            </span>
        </div>
        <table class="table table-striped">
            <thead>
                <tr>
                    <th>Description</th>
                    <th>Done</th>
                </tr>
            </thead>
            <tbody>
                <tr ng-repeat="item in todo.items">
                    <td>{{item.action}}</td>
```

```
            <td><input type="checkbox" ng-model="item.done" /></td>
         </tr>
      </tbody>
   </table>
</div>
</body>
</html>
```

Behaviors are defined by adding functions to the $scope object that is passed to the controller function. In the listing, I have defined a function that returns the number of incomplete items, which I determine by enumerating the objects in the $scope.todo.items array and counting the ones whose done property is false.

■ **Tip** I used the angular.forEach method to enumerate the contents of the data array. AngularJS includes some useful utility methods that supplement the JavaScript language. I describe the utility methods in Chapter 5.

The name of the property used to attach the function to the $scope object is used as the behavior name. My behavior is called incompleteCount, and I can invoke it within the scope of the ng-controller attribute, which applies the controller to the HTML elements that form the view.

I have used the incompleteCount behavior twice in Listing 2-7. The first is as a simple data binding to display the number of items, as follows:

```
...
<span class="label label-default" ng-hide="incompleteCount() == 0">
    {{incompleteCount()}}
</span>
...
```

Notice that I call the behavior using parentheses. You can pass objects as arguments to behaviors, which makes it possible to create general-purpose behaviors that can be used with different data objects. My application is sufficiently simple that I decided not to pass any arguments and instead get the data I require directly from the $scope object in the controller.

I also used the behavior in conjunction with a directive, like this:

```
...
<span class="label default" ng-hide="incompleteCount() == 0">
    {{incompleteCount()}}
</span>
...
```

The ng-hide directive will hide the element it is applied to—and its content elements—if the expression that is assigned as the attribute value evaluates to true. In this case, I call the incompleteCount behavior and check to see whether the number of incomplete items is zero; if it is, then the label that displays the number of items on the list is hidden from the user.

■ **Tip** The ng-hide directive is only one of a broad set of directives that manipulate the browser Document Object Model (DOM) automatically based on the state of the AngularJS model. I get into the detail of these directives in Chapter 11 and show you how to create your own directives in Chapters 15–17.

You can see the effect of the behavior and its application by using the browser to navigate to the todo.html file, as shown in Figure 2-6. Checking and unchecking items on the list changes the number of items displayed by the counter label, and checking all of the items causes the counter to be hidden.

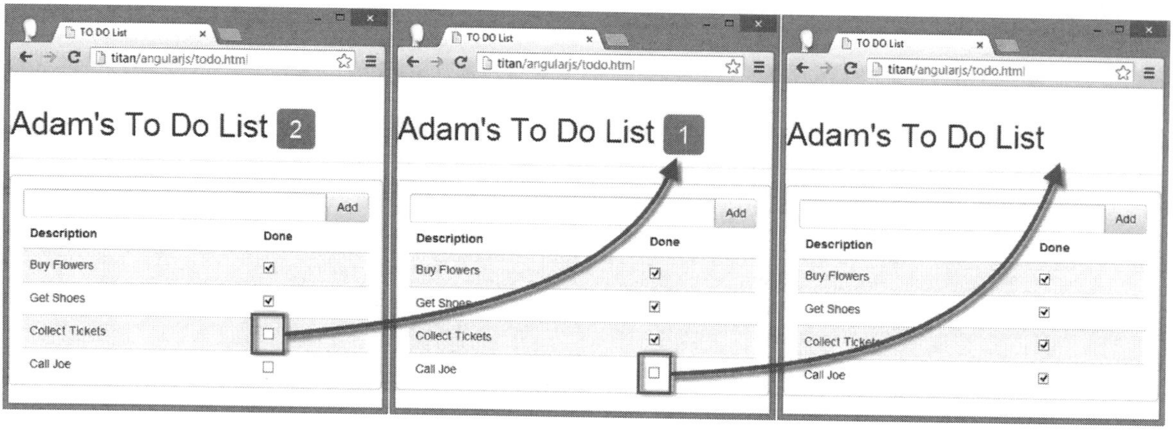

Figure 2-6. *Using a controller behavior*

Using Behaviors That Depend on Other Behaviors

One of the themes that runs through AngularJS is just how naturally the underlying characteristics of HTML, CSS, and JavaScript have been coopted for web application development. As an example, since behaviors are created using JavaScript functions, you can create behaviors that are built on the capabilities provided by other behaviors in the same controller. In Listing 2-8, I have created a behavior that selects a CSS class based on the number of incomplete items in the to-do list.

Listing 2-8. Building on Behaviors in the todo.html File

```
<!DOCTYPE html>
<html ng-app="todoApp">
<head>
    <title>TO DO List</title>
    <link href="bootstrap.css" rel="stylesheet" />
    <link href="bootstrap-theme.css" rel="stylesheet" />
    <script src="angular.js"></script>
    <script>

        var model = {
            user: "Adam",
            items: [{ action: "Buy Flowers", done: false },
                    { action: "Get Shoes", done: false },
                    { action: "Collect Tickets", done: true },
                    { action: "Call Joe", done: false }]
        };

        var todoApp = angular.module("todoApp", []);
```

```
        todoApp.controller("ToDoCtrl", function ($scope) {
            $scope.todo = model;

            $scope.incompleteCount = function () {
                var count = 0;
                angular.forEach($scope.todo.items, function (item) {
                    if (!item.done) { count++ }
                });
                return count;
            }

            $scope.warningLevel = function () {
                return $scope.incompleteCount() < 3 ? "label-success" : "label-warning";
            }
        });

    </script>
</head>
<body ng-controller="ToDoCtrl">
    <div class="page-header">
        <h1>
            {{todo.user}}'s To Do List
            <span class="label label-default" ng-class="warningLevel()"
                ng-hide="incompleteCount() == 0">
                {{incompleteCount()}}
            </span>
        </h1>
    </div>

    <!-- ...elements omitted for brevity... -->

</body>
</html>
```

I have defined a new behavior called warningLevel, which returns the name of a Bootstrap CSS class based on the number of incomplete to-do items, which is obtained by calling the incompleteCount behavior. This approach reduces the need to duplicate logic in the controller and, as you'll see in Chapter 25, can help simplify the process of unit testing.

I have applied the warningLevel behavior using the ng-class directive, as follows:

```
...
<span class="label" ng-class="warningLevel()" ng-hide="incompleteCount() == 0">
...
```

This directive applies the CSS class returned by the behavior, which has the effect of changing the color of the label in the HTML document, as shown in Figure 2-7. (I describe the complete set of AngularJS directives in Part 2 and show you how to create your own in Chapters 15–17.)

```
        <table class="table table-striped">
            <thead>
                <tr>
                    <th>Description</th>
                    <th>Done</th>
                </tr>
            </thead>
            <tbody>
                <tr ng-repeat="item in todo.items">
                    <td>{{item.action}}</td>
                    <td><input type="checkbox" ng-model="item.done" /></td>
                </tr>
            </tbody>
        </table>
    </div>
</body>
</html>
```

I have added a behavior called addNewItem that takes the text of a new to-do item and adds an object to the data model, using the text as the value for the action property and setting the done property to false, like this:

```
...
$scope.addNewItem = function(actionText) {
    $scope.todo.items.push({ action: actionText, done: false});
}
...
```

This is the first behavior I have shown you that modifies the model, but in a real project there is usually a much more even split between behaviors that obtain and prepare data for the view and those that respond to user interaction and update the model. Notice that my behavior is still defined as a standard JavaScript function and that I am able to update the model using the push method that JavaScript supports for arrays.

The magic in this example comes in the use of directives, of which there are two. Here is the first of them:

```
...
<input class="form-control" ng-model="actionText" />
...
```

This is the same ng-model directive that I used when I set up the check boxes, and you'll encounter this directive a lot when working with form elements. The point to note is that I have specified the name of a property for the directive to update that is not part of the model. The ng-model directive will dynamically create the property for me within the scope of the controller, effectively creating dynamic model properties that are used to handle user input. I use the dynamic property in the second directive I added to the example:

```
...
<button class="btn btn-default" ng-click="addNewItem(actionText)">Add</button>
...
```

The ng-click directive sets up a handler that evaluates the expression when the click event is triggered. In this case, the expression invokes the addNewItem behavior, passing the dynamic actionText property as the argument. This has the effect of adding a new to-do item that contains the text that the user entered into the input element, as shown in Figure 2-8.

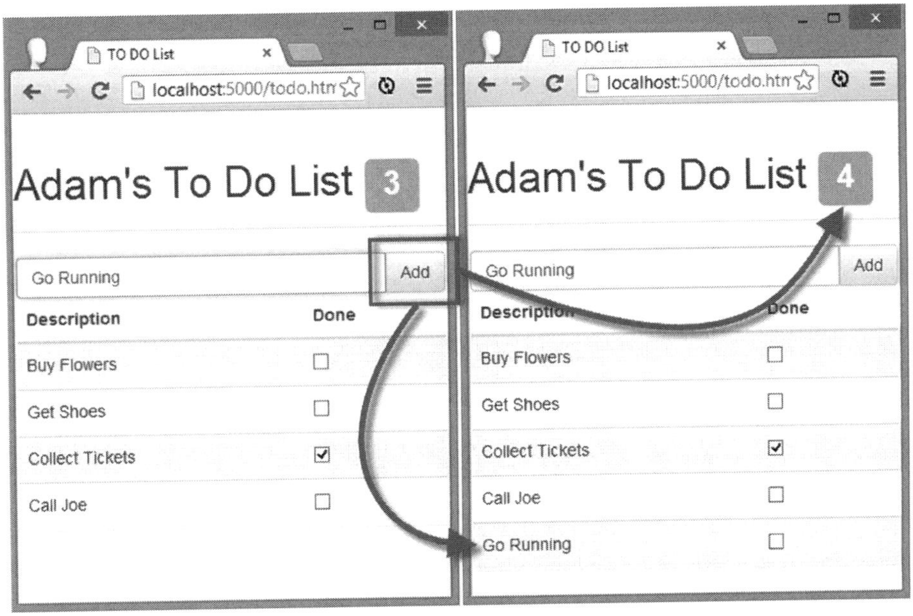

Figure 2-8. *Using behaviors and directives to create new to-do items*

■ **Tip**   You have probably been drilled not to add event handling code to individual elements, so it may seem odd to apply the ng-click directive to the button element. Don't worry—when AngularJS compiles the HTML file and encounters the directive, it sets up a handler following the unobtrusive JavaScript approach, such that the event handler code is separate from the element. It is important to differentiate between the AngularJS directives and the HTML and JavaScript that are generated from those directives during compilation.

Notice that the label that displays the number of incomplete to-do items updates automatically when you add a new item to the list. One of the benefits of the live model in AngularJS apps is that your bindings and behaviors create a foundation of features that work together.

Filtering and Ordering Model Data

In Chapter 14, I describe the AngularJS *filter* feature, which provides a nice way of preparing data in the model for display in views without having to create behaviors. There is nothing wrong with using behaviors, but filters tend to be more general-purpose and lend themselves to reuse across an application. Listing 2-10 shows the changes I made to the todo.html file to demonstrate filtering.

Listing 2-10. Adding Filtering to the todo.html File

```
...
<tbody>
    <tr ng-repeat="item in todo.items | filter:{done: false} | orderBy:'action'">
        <td>{{item.action}}</td>
        <td><input type="checkbox" ng-model="item.done" /></td>
    </tr>
</tbody>
...
```

Filtering can be applied to any part of the data model, and here you can see that I have used filters to control the data that is used by the ng-repeat directive that populates the table element with details of the to-do list items. I have used two filters: the filter filter (an annoying name for a useful component) and the orderBy filter.

The filter filter selects objects based on the criteria it is configured with. I have applied the filter such that it selects the items whose done property is false, which has the effect that any complete to-do item won't be shown to the user. The orderBy filter sorts the data items, and I have used it to sort by the value of the action property. I'll explain filters in detail in Chapter 14, but you can see the effect I have created by navigating the browser to the todo.html file, adding a new item, and then checking the Done box, as shown in Figure 2-9.

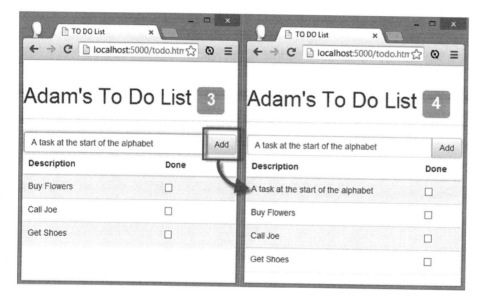

Figure 2-9. Using filtering and ordering

■ **Tip**   Notice that when using the orderBy filter, I specify the property I want to use for sorting as a string literal value, between single quote characters. By default, AngularJS assumes that everything is a property defined by the scope and without the quote characters, would look for a scope property called action. This is helpful when you want to define values programmatically but does mean you have to remember to use literal values when you want to specify a constant.

When you add a new item, it will be inserted into the list based on alphabetical order, and when you check the box, the item will be hidden. (The data in the model isn't sorted; the sort operation is performed when the ng-repeat directive is processed to create the rows in the table.)

Improving the Filter

The previous example demonstrates how the filter feature works, but the result is pretty useless because checked tasks are forever hidden from the user. Fortunately, it is a simple matter to create a custom filter, as shown in Listing 2-11.

Listing 2-11. Creating a Custom Filter in the todo.html File

```
...
<script>
    var model = {
        user: "Adam",
        items: [{ action: "Buy Flowers", done: false },
                { action: "Get Shoes", done: false },
                { action: "Collect Tickets", done: true },
                { action: "Call Joe", done: false }],

    };

    var todoApp = angular.module("todoApp", []);

    todoApp.filter("checkedItems", function () {
        return function (items, showComplete) {
            var resultArr = [];
            angular.forEach(items, function (item) {
                if (item.done == false || showComplete == true) {
                    resultArr.push(item);
                }
            });
            return resultArr;
        }
    });

    todoApp.controller("ToDoCtrl", function ($scope) {
        $scope.todo = model;

        // ...statements omitted for brevity...
    });
</script>
...
```

The `filter` method defined by the AngularJS module object is used to create a filter *factory*, which returns a function that is used to filter a set of data objects. Don't worry about the factory part for the moment; it is enough to know that using the `filter` method requires passing in a function that returns a function that returns the filtered data. The name I have given my filter is `checkedItems`, and the function that does the actual filtering has two arguments:

```
...
return function (items, showComplete) {
...
```

The `items` argument will be provided by AngularJS and will be the set of objects that should be filtered. I will provide a value for the `showComplete` argument when I apply the filter, and it is used to determine whether tasks that have been marked as done will be included in the filtered data. You can see how I have applied the custom filter in Listing 2-12.

Listing 2-12. Applying a Custom Filter in the todo.html File

```
...
<div class="panel">
    <div class="input-group">
        <input class="form-control" ng-model="actionText" />
        <span class="input-group-btn">
            <button class="btn btn-default"
                    ng-click="addNewItem(actionText)">Add</button>
        </span>
    </div>

    <table class="table table-striped">
        <thead>
            <tr>
                <th>Description</th>
                <th>Done</th>
            </tr>
        </thead>
        <tbody>
            <tr ng-repeat=
                    "item in todo.items | checkedItems:showComplete | orderBy:'action'">
                <td>{{item.action}}</td>
                <td><input type="checkbox" ng-model="item.done" /></td>
            </tr>
        </tbody>
    </table>

    <div class="checkbox-inline">
        <label><input type="checkbox" ng_model="showComplete"> Show Complete</label>
    </div>
</div>
...
```

I have added a check box that uses the ng-model directive to set a model value called showComplete, which I pass to my custom filter through the ng-repeat directive in the table:

```
...
<tr ng-repeat="item in todo.items | checkedItems:showComplete | orderBy:'action'">
...
```

The syntax for custom filters is the same as for the built-in filtering support. I specify the name of the filter I created with the filter method, followed by a colon (:), followed by the name of the model property that I want to pass to the filter function. I have specified the showComplete model property, which means that the state of the check box will be used to control the visibility of the checked items. You can see the effect in Figure 2-10.

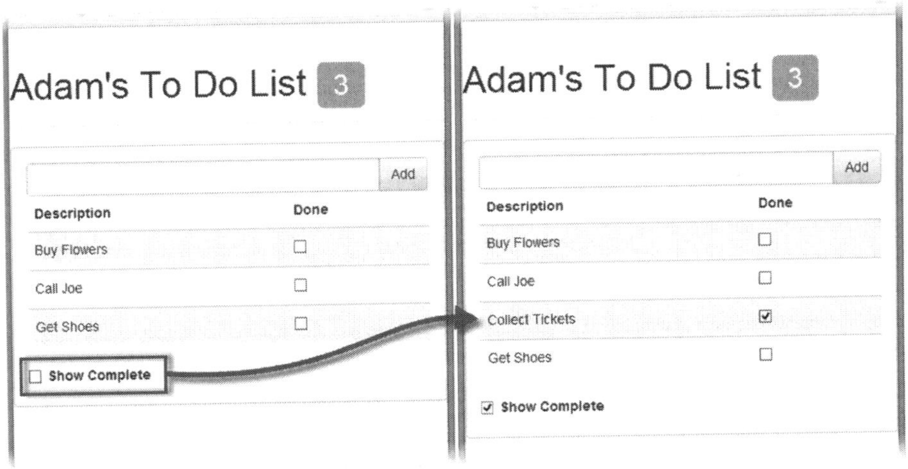

Figure 2-10. *Using a custom filter*

Getting the Data via Ajax

The last change I am going to make is to obtain the to-do list data as JSON data via an Ajax request. (I describe JSON in Chapter 5 if you are unfamiliar with it.) I created a file called todo.json in the angularjs folder; you can see the contents in Listing 2-13.

Listing 2-13. The Contents of the todo.json File

```
[{ "action": "Buy Flowers", "done": false },
 { "action": "Get Shoes", "done": false },
 { "action": "Collect Tickets", "done": true },
 { "action": "Call Joe", "done": false }]
```

As you can see, the JSON data format is similar to the way that literal JavaScript objects are declared, which is one of the reasons why JSON is a dominant data format for web apps. In Listing 2-14, you can see the changes that I made to the todo.html file to load the data from the todo.json file rather than using a locally declared array.

Listing 2-14. Making an Ajax Call for JSON Data in the todo.html File

```
...
<script>
    var model = {
        user: "Adam"
    };

    var todoApp = angular.module("todoApp", []);

    todoApp.run(function ($http) {
        $http.get("todo.json").success(function (data) {
            model.items = data;
        });
    });

    todoApp.filter("checkedItems", function () {
        return function (items, showComplete) {
            var resultArr = [];
            angular.forEach(items, function (item) {

                if (item.done == false || showComplete == true) {
                    resultArr.push(item);
                }
            });
            return resultArr;
        }
    });

    todoApp.controller("ToDoCtrl", function ($scope) {
        $scope.todo = model;

        $scope.incompleteCount = function () {
            var count = 0;
            angular.forEach($scope.todo.items, function (item) {
                if (!item.done) { count++ }
            });
            return count;
        }

        $scope.warningLevel = function () {
            return $scope.incompleteCount() < 3 ? "label-success" : "label-warning";
        }

        $scope.addNewItem = function(actionText) {
            $scope.todo.items.push({ action: actionText, done: false});
        }

    });
</script>
...
```

I removed the items array from the statically defined data model and added a call to the run method defined by the AngularJS module object. The run method takes a function that is executed once AngularJS has performed its initial setup and is used for one-off tasks.

I specified the $http argument for the function I passed to the run method, which tells AngularJS I want to use the service object that provides support for making Ajax calls. Using arguments to tell AngularJS what features you require is part of an approach known as *dependency injection*, which I describe in Chapter 9.

The $http service provides access to low-level Ajax requests. Low-level in this case really isn't that low at all, until compared with the $resources service that is used to interact with *RESTful* web services. (I describe REST in Chapter 3 and the $resource service object in Chapter 21.) I use the $http.get method to make an HTTP GET request to the server for the todo.json file:

```
...
$http.get("todo.json").success(function (data) {
    model.items = data;
});
...
```

The result from the get method is a *promise*, which is an object used to represent work that will complete in the future. I explain how promises work in Chapter 5 and get into the detail in Chapter 20, but for this chapter it is enough to know that calling the success method on the promise object lets me specify a function that will be invoked when the Ajax request to the server has completed and that the JSON data retrieved from the server will be parsed to create a JavaScript object and passed to my success function as the data argument. I take the data I receive and use it to update the model:

```
...
$http.get("todo.json").success(function (data) {
    model.items = data;
});
...
```

You won't notice any difference if you navigate to the todo.html file with the browser, but the data is being obtained from the server using a second HTTP request. You can see this using the F12 tools to report on network connections, as shown in Figure 2-11.

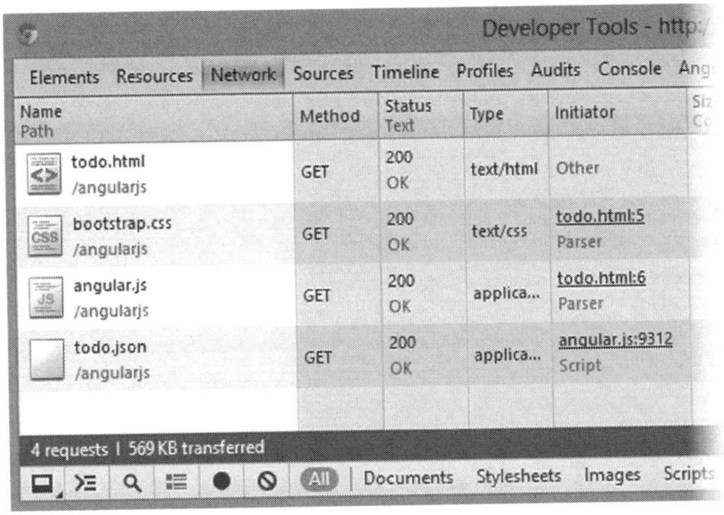

Figure 2-11. Checking that the data is being obtained via Ajax

The fact that I have to check the browser to prove that Ajax is being used demonstrates just how easy AngularJS makes it to work with remote files and data. This is a theme I will be returning to throughout the book because it underpins a lot of the features that AngularJS provides for creating more complex web apps.

Summary

In this chapter, I showed you how to create your first simple AngularJS app, moving from an HTML mock-up of the application to a dynamic app that implements the MVC pattern and obtains its data as JSON from the web server. Along the way, I touched on each of the major components and features that AngularJS provides to developers and pointed you to the part of the book in which you can find more information.

Now that you have seen how an AngularJS fits together, it is time to step back and provide some details about the context in which AngularJS exists, starting with the MVC pattern, which I describe in the next chapter.

CHAPTER 3

■ ■ ■

Putting AngularJS in Context

In this chapter, I put AngularJS in context within the world of web app development and set the foundation for the chapters that follow. The goal of AngularJS is to bring the tools and capabilities that have been available only for server-side development to the web client and, in doing so, make it easier to develop, test, and maintain rich and complex web applications.

AngularJS works by allowing you to *extend* HTML, which can seem like an odd idea until you get used to it. AngularJS applications express functionality through custom elements, attributes, classes, and comments; a complex application can produce an HTML document that contains a mix of standard and custom markup.

The style of development that AngularJS supports is derived through the use of the *Model-View-Controller* (MVC) pattern, although this is sometimes referred to as Model-View-*Whatever*, since there are countless variations on this pattern that can be adhered to when using AngularJS. I am going to focus on the standard MVC pattern in this book since it is the most established and widely used. In the sections that follow, I explain the characteristics of projects where AngularJS can deliver significant benefit (and those where better alternatives exist), describe the MVC pattern, and describe some common pitfalls.

Understanding Where AngularJS Excels

AngularJS isn't the solution to every problem, and it important to know when you should use AngularJS and when you should seek an alternative. AngularJS delivers the kind of functionality that used to be available only to server-side developers, but entirely in the browser. This means that AngularJS has a lot of work to do each time an HTML document to which AngularJS has been applied is loaded—the HTML elements have to be compiled, the data bindings have to be evaluated, directives need to be executed, and so on, building support for the features I described in Chapter 2 and those that are yet to come.

This kind of work takes time to perform, and the amount of time depends on the complexity of the HTML document, on the associated JavaScript code, and—critically—on quality of the browser and the processing capability of the device. You won't notice any delay when using the latest browsers on a capable desktop machine, but old browsers on underpowered smartphones can really slow down the initial setup of an AngularJS app.

The goal, therefore, is to perform this setup as infrequently as possible and deliver as much of the app as possible to the user when it is performed. This means giving careful thought to the kind of web application you build. In broad terms, there are two kinds of web application: *round-trip* and *single-page*.

Understanding Round-Trip and Single-Page Applications

For a long time, web apps were developed to follow a *round-trip* model. The browser requests an initial HTML document from the server. User interactions—such as clicking a link or submitting a form—led the browser to request and receive a completely new HTML document. In this kind of application, the browser is essentially a rending engine for HTML content, and all of the application logic and data resides on the server. The browser makes a series of stateless HTTP requests that the server handles by generating HTML documents dynamically.

A lot of current web development is still for round-trip applications, not least because they require little from the browser, which ensures the widest possible client support. But there are some serious drawbacks to round-trip applications: They make the user wait while the next HTML document is requested and loaded, they require a large server-side infrastructure to process all of the requests and manage all of the application state, and they require a lot of bandwidth because each HTML document has to be self-contained (leading to a lot of the same content being included in each response from the server).

Single-page applications take a different approach. An initial HTML document is sent to the browser, but user interactions lead to Ajax requests for small fragments of HTML or data inserted into the existing set of elements being displayed to the user. The initial HTML document is never reloaded or replaced, and the user can continue to interact with the existing HTML while the Ajax requests are being performed asynchronously, even if that just means seeing a "data loading" message.

Most current apps fall somewhere between the extremes, tending to use the basic round-trip model enhanced with JavaScript to reduce the number of complete page changes, although the emphasis is often on reducing the number of form errors by performing client-side validation.

AngularJS gives the greatest return from its initial workload as an application gets closer to the single-page model. That's not to say that you can't use AngularJS with round-trip applications—you can, of course—but there are other technologies that are simpler and better suit discrete HTML pages, such as jQuery. In Figure 3-1 you can see the spectrum of web application types and where AngularJS delivers benefit.

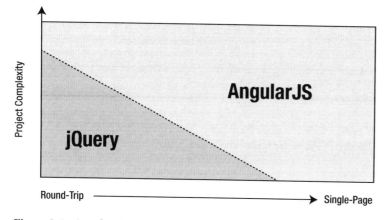

Figure 3-1. AngularJS is well-suited to single-page web apps

AngularJS excels in single-page applications and especially in complex round-trip applications. For simpler projects, jQuery or a similar alternative is generally a better choice, although nothing prevents you from using AngularJS in all of your projects.

There is a gradual tendency for current web app projects to move toward the single-page application model, and that's the sweet spot for AngularJS, not just because of the initialization process but because the benefits of using the MVC pattern (which I describe later in this chapter) really start to manifest themselves in larger and more complex projects, which are the ones pushing toward the single-page model.

▦ **Tip** This may seem like circular reasoning, but AngularJS and similar frameworks have arisen because complex web applications are difficult to write and maintain. The problems these projects face led to the development of industrial-strength tools like AngularJS, which then enable the next generation of complex projects. Think of it less as circular reasoning and more of a virtuous circle.

ANGULARJS AND JQUERY

AngularJS and jQuery take different approaches to web app development. jQuery is all about explicitly manipulating the browser's Document Object Model (DOM) to create an application. The approach that AngularJS takes is to coopt the browser into being the foundation for application development.

jQuery is, without any doubt, a powerful tool—and one I love to use. jQuery is robust and reliable, and you can get results pretty much immediately. I especially like the fluid API and the ease with which you can extend the core jQuery library. If you want more information about jQuery, then see my book *Pro jQuery 2.0*, which is published by Apress and provides detailed coverage of jQuery, jQuery UI, and jQuery Mobile.

But as much as I love jQuery, it isn't the right tool for every job any more than AngularJS is. It can be hard to write and manage large applications using jQuery, and thorough unit testing can be a challenge.

One of the reasons I like working with AngularJS is that it builds on the core functionality of jQuery. In fact, AngularJS contains a cut-down version of jQuery called *jqLite*, which is used when writing custom directives (and which I describe in Chapters 15–17). And, if you add the jQuery to an HTML document, AngularJS will detect it automatically and use jQuery in preference to jqLite, although this is something you rarely need to do.

The main drawback of AngularJS is that there is an up-front investment in development time before you start to see results—something that is common in any MVC-based development. This initial investment is worthwhile, however, for complex apps or those that are likely to require significant revision and maintenance.

So, in short, use jQuery for low-complexity web apps where unit testing isn't critical and you require immediate results. jQuery is also ideal for enhancing the HTML that is generated by round-trip web apps (where user interactions cause a new HTML document to be loaded) because you can easily apply jQuery without needing to modify the HTML content generated by the server. Use AngularJS for more complex single-page web apps, when you have time for careful design and planning and when you can easily control the HTML generated by the server.

Understanding the MVC Pattern

The term *Model-View-Controller* has been in use since the late 1970s and arose from the Smalltalk project at Xerox PARC where it was conceived as a way to organize some early GUI applications. Some of the fine detail of the original MVC pattern was tied to Smalltalk-specific concepts, such as *screens* and *tools*, but the broader ideas are still applicable to applications, and they are especially well-suited to web applications.

The MVC pattern first took hold in the server-side end of web development, through toolkits like Ruby on Rails and the ASP.NET MVC Framework. In recent years, the MVC pattern has been seen as a way to manage the growing richness and complexity of client-side web development as well, and it is in this environment that AngularJS has emerged.

The key to applying the MVC pattern is to implement the key premise of a *separation of concerns*, in which the data model in the application is decoupled from the business and presentation logic. In client-side web development, this means separating the data, the logic that operates on that data, and the HTML elements used to display the data. The result is a client-side application that is easier to develop, maintain, and test.

The three main building blocks are the *model*, the *controller*, and the *view*. In Figure 3-2, you can see the traditional exposition of the MVC pattern as it applies to server-side development.

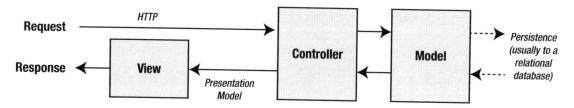

Figure 3-2. *The server-side implementation of the MVC pattern*

I took this figure from my *Pro ASP.NET MVC Framework* book, which describes Microsoft's server-side implementation of the MVC pattern. You can see that the expectation is that the model is obtained from a database and that the goal of the application is to service HTTP requests from the browser. This is the basis for round-trip web apps, which I described earlier.

Of course, AngularJS exists in the browser, which leads to a twist on the MVC theme, as illustrated in Figure 3-3.

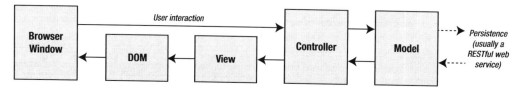

Figure 3-3. *The AngularJS implementation of the MVC pattern*

The client-side implementation of the MVC pattern gets its data from server-side components, usually via a RESTful web service, which I describe in Chapter 5. The goal of the controller and the view is to operate on the data in the model in order to perform DOM manipulation so as to create and manage HTML elements that the user can interact with. Those interactions are fed back to the controller, closing the loop to form an interactive application.

■ **Tip** Using an MVC framework like AngularJS in the client doesn't preclude using a server-side MVC framework, but you'll find that an AngularJS client takes on some of the complexity that would have otherwise existed at the server. This is generally a good thing because it offloads work from the server to the client, and that allows for more clients to be supported with less server capacity.

PATTERNS AND PATTERN ZEALOTS

A good pattern describes an approach to solving a problem that has worked for *other* people on *other* projects. Patterns are recipes, rather than rules, and you will need to adapt any pattern to suit your specific projects, just like a cook has to adapt a recipe to suit different ovens and ingredients.

The degree by which you depart from a pattern should be driven by experience. The time you have spent applying a pattern to similar projects will inform your knowledge about what does and doesn't work for you. If you are new to a pattern or you are embarking on a new kind of project, then you should stick as closely as possible to the pattern until you truly understand the benefits and pitfalls that await you. Be careful not to reform your entire development effort around a pattern, however, since wide-sweeping disruption usually causes productivity loses that undermine whatever outcome you were hoping the pattern would give.

Patterns are flexible tools and not fixed rules, but not all developers understand the difference, and some become *pattern zealots*. These are the people who spend more time talking about the pattern than applying it to projects and consider any deviation from their interpretation of the pattern to be a serious crime. My advice is to simply ignore this kind of person because any kind of engagement will just suck the life out of you, and you'll never be able to change their minds. Instead, just get on with some work and demonstrate how a flexible application of a pattern can produce good results through practical application and delivery.

With this in mind, you will see that I follow the broad concepts of the MVC pattern in the examples in this book but that I adapt the pattern to demonstrate different features and techniques. And this is how I work in my own projects—embracing the parts of patterns that provide value and setting aside those that do not.

Understanding Models

Models—the *M* in *MVC*—contain the data that users work with. There are two broad types of model: *view models*, which represent just data passed from the controller to the view, and *domain models*, which contain the data in a business domain, along with the operations, transformations, and rules for creating, storing, and manipulating that data, collectively referred to as the *model logic*.

■ **Tip**   Many developers new to the MVC pattern get confused with the idea of including logic in the data model, believing that the goal of the MVC pattern is to separate data from logic. This is a misapprehension: The goal of the MVC framework is to divide up an application into three functional areas, each of which may contain both logic *and* data. The goal isn't to eliminate logic from the model. Rather, it is to ensure that the model contains logic only for creating and managing the model data.

You can't read a definition of the MVC pattern without tripping over the word *business*, which is unfortunate because a lot of web development goes far beyond the line-of-business applications that led to this kind of terminology. Business applications are still a big chunk of the development world, however, and if you are writing, say, a sales accounting system, then your business domain would encompass the process related to sales accounting, and your domain model would contain the accounts data and the logic by which accounts are created, stored, and managed. If you are creating a cat video web site, then you still have a business domain; it is just that it might not fit within the structure of a corporation. Your domain model would contain the cat videos and the logic that will create, store, and manipulate those videos.

Many AngularJS models will effectively push the logic to the server side and invoke it via a RESTful web service because there is little support for data persistence within the browser and it is simply easier to get the data you require over Ajax. I describe the basic support that AngularJS provides for Ajax in Chapter 20 and for RESTful services in Chapter 21.

■ **Tip**   There *are* client-side persistence APIs defined as part of the HTML5 standard effort. The quality of these standards is currently mixed, and the implementations vary in quality. The main problem, however, is that most users still rely on browsers that don't implement the new APIs, and this is especially true in corporate environments, where Internet Explorer 6/7/8 are still widely used because of problems migrating line-of-business applications to standard versions of HTML.

For each component in the MVC pattern, I'll describe what should and should not be included. The model in an application built using the MVC pattern *should*

- Contain the domain data

- Contain the logic for creating, managing, and modifying the domain data (even if that means executing remote logic via web services)

- Provide a clean API that exposes the model data and operations on it

The model *should not*

- Expose details of how the model data is obtained or managed (in other words, details of the data storage mechanism or the remote web service should not be exposed to controllers and views)

- Contain logic that transforms the model based on user interaction (because this is the controller's job)

- Contain logic for displaying data to the user (this is the view's job)

The benefits of ensuring that the model is isolated from the controller and views are that you can test your logic more easily (I describe AngularJS unit testing in Chapter 25) and that enhancing and maintaining the overall application is simpler and easier.

The best domain models contain the logic for getting and storing data persistently and for create, read, update, and delete operations (known collectively as CRUD). This can mean the model contains the logic directly, but more often the model will contain the logic for calling RESTful web services to invoke server-side database operations (which I demonstrate in Chapter 8 when I built a realistic AngularJS application and which I describe in detail in Chapter 21).

Understanding Controllers

Controllers are the connective tissue in an AngularJS web app, acting as conduits between the data model and views. Controllers add business domain logic (known as *behaviors*) to *scopes*, which are subsets of the model.

■ **Tip** Other MVC frameworks use slightly different terminology. So, for example, if you are an ASP.NET MVC Framework developer (my preferred server-side framework), then you will be familiar with the idea of *action methods*, rather than *behaviors*. The intent and effect are the same, however, and any MVC skills you have developed through server-side development will help you with AngularJS development.

A controller built using the MVC *should*

- Contain the logic required to initialize the scope

- Contain the logic/behaviors required by the view to present data from the scope

- Contain the logic/behaviors required to update the scope based on user interaction

The controller *should not*

- Contain logic that manipulates the DOM (that is the job of the view)

- Contain logic that manages the persistence of data (that is the job of the model)

- Manipulate data outside of the scope

From these lists, you can tell that scopes have a big impact on the way that controllers are defined and used. I describe scopes and controllers in detail in Chapter 13.

Understanding View Data

The domain model isn't the only data in an AngularJS application. Controllers can create *view data* (also known as *view model data* or *view models*) to simplify the definition of views. View data is not persistent and is created either by synthesizing some aspect of the domain model data or in response to user interaction. You saw an example of view data in Chapter 2, when I used the ng-model directive to capture the text entered by the user in an input element. View data is usually created and accessed via the controller's scope, as I describe in Chapter 13.

Understanding Views

AngularJS views are defined using HTML elements that are enhanced and that generate HTML by the use of data bindings and directives. It is the AngularJS directives that make views so flexible, and they transform HTML elements into the foundation for dynamic web apps. I explain data bindings in detail in Chapter 10 and describe how to use built-in and custom directives in Chapters 10–17. Views *should*

- Contain the logic and markup required to present data to the user

Views *should not*

- Contain complex logic (this is better placed in a controller)
- Contain logic that creates, stores, or manipulates the domain model

Views *can* contain logic, but it should be simple and used sparingly. Putting anything but the simplest method calls or expressions in a view makes the overall application harder to test and maintain.

Understanding RESTful Services

As I explained in the previous chapter, the logic for domain models in AngularJS apps is often split between the client and the server. The server contains the persistent store, typically a database, and contains the logic for managing it. In the case of a SQL database, for example, the required logic would include opening connections to the database server, executing SQL queries, and processing the results so they can be sent to the client.

We don't want the client-side code accessing the data store directly—doing so would create a tight coupling between the client and the data store that would complicate unit testing and make it difficult to change the data store without also making changes to the client code as well.

By using the server to mediate access to the data store, we prevent tight coupling. The logic on the client is responsible for getting the data to and from the server and is unaware of the details of how that data is stored or accessed behind the scenes.

There are lots of ways of passing data between the client and the server. One of the most common is to use *Asynchronous JavaScript and XML* (Ajax) requests to call server-side code, getting the server to send JSON and making changes to data using HTML forms. (This is what I did at the end of Chapter 2 to get the to-do data from the server. I requested a URL that I knew would return the JSON content I required.)

■ **Tip** Don't worry if you are not familiar with JSON. I introduce it properly in Chapter 5.

This approach can work well and is the foundation of *RESTful web services,* which use the nature of HTTP requests to perform create, read, update, and delete (CRUD) operations on data.

■ **Note** REST is a style of API rather than a well-defined specification, and there is disagreement about what exactly makes a web service RESTful. One point of contention is that purists do not consider web services that return JSON to be RESTful. Like any disagreement about an architectural pattern, the reasons for the disagreement are arbitrary and dull and not at all worth worrying about. As far as I am concerned, JSON services *are* RESTful, and I treat them as such in this book.

In a RESTful web service, the operation that is being requested is expressed through a combination of the HTTP method and the URL. So, for example, imagine a URL like this one:

```
http://myserver.mydomain.com/people/bob
```

There is no standard URL specification for a RESTful web service, but the idea is to make the URL self-explanatory, such that it is obvious what the URL refers to. In this case, it is obvious that there is a collection of data objects called `people` and that the URL refers to the specific object within that collection whose identity is bob.

■ **Tip** It isn't always possible to create such self-evident URLs in a real project, but you should make a serious effort to keep things simple and not expose the internal structure of the data store through the URL (because this is just another kind of coupling between components). Keep your URLs as simple and clear as possible, and keep the mappings between the URL format and the data store structure within the server.

The URL identifies the data object that I want to operate on, and the HTTP method specifies what operation I want performed, as described in Table 3-1.

Table 3-1. *The Operations Commonly Performed in Response to HTTP Methods*

Method	Description
GET	Retrieves the data object specified by the URL
PUT	Updates the data object specified by the URL
POST	Creates a new data object, typically using form data values as the data fields
DELETE	Deletes the data object specified by the URL

You don't have to use the HTTP methods to perform the operations I describe in the table. A common variation is that the POST method is often used to serve double duty and will update an object if one exists and create one if not, meaning that the PUT method isn't used. I describe the support that AngularJS provides for Ajax in Chapter 20 and for easily working with RESTful services in Chapter 21.

IDEMPOTENT HTTP METHODS

You can implement any mapping between HTTP methods and operations on the data store, although I recommend you stick as closely as possible to the convention I describe in the table.

If you depart from the normal approach, make sure you honor the nature of the HTTP methods as defined in the HTTP specification. The GET method is *nullipotent*, which means that the operations you perform in response to this method should only retrieve data and not modify it. A browser (or any intermediate device, such as a proxy) expects to be able to repeatedly make a GET request without altering the state of the server (although this doesn't mean the state of the server won't change between identical GET requests because of requests from other clients).

The PUT and DELETE methods are *idempotent*, which means that multiple identical requests should have the same effect as a single request. So, for example, using the DELETE method with the `/people/bob` URL should delete the `bob` object from the `people` collection for the first request and then do nothing for subsequent requests. (Again, of course, this won't be true if another client re-creates the `bob` object.)

The POST method is neither nullipotent nor idempotent, which is why a common RESTful optimization is to handle object creation *and* updates. If there is no `bob` object, using the POST method will create one, and subsequent POST requests to the same URL will update the object that was created.

All of this is important only if you are implementing your own RESTful web service. If you are writing a client that consumes a RESTful service, then you just need to know what data operation each HTTP method corresponds to. I demonstrate consuming such a service in Chapter 6 and explain the AngularJS support for REST in detail in Chapter 21.

Common Design Pitfalls

In this section, I describe the three most common design pitfalls that I encounter in AngularJS projects. These are not coding errors but rather problems with the overall shape of the web app that prevent the project team from getting the benefits that AngularJS and the MVC pattern can provide.

Putting the Logic in the Wrong Place

The most common problem is logic put into the wrong component such that it undermines the MVC separation of concerns. Here are the three most common varieties of this problem:

- Putting business logic in views, rather than in controllers
- Putting domain logic in controllers, rather than in model
- Putting data store logic in the client model when using a RESTful service

These are tricky issues because they take a while to manifest themselves as problems. The application still runs, but it will become harder to enhance and maintain over time. In the case of the third variety, the problem will become apparent only when the data store is changed (which rarely happens until a project is mature and has grown beyond its initial user projections).

■ **Tip** Getting a feel for where logic should go takes some experience, but you'll spot problems earlier if you are using unit testing because the tests you have to write to cover the logic won't fit nicely into the MVC pattern. I describe the AngularJS support for unit testing in Chapter 25.

Knowing where to put logic becomes second nature as you get more experience in AngularJS development, but here are the three rules:

- View logic should prepare data only for display and never modify the model.

- Controller logic should never directly create, update, or delete data from the model.

- The client should never directly access the data store.

If you keep these in mind as you develop, you'll head off the most common problems.

Adopting the Data Store Data Format

The next problem arises when the development team builds an application that depends on the quirks of the server-side data store. I recently worked with a project team that had built their client so that it honored the data format quirks of their server-side SQL server. The problem they ran into—and the reason why I was involved—was they needed to upgrade to a more robust database, which used different representations for key data types.

In a well-designed AngularJS application that gets its data from a RESTful service, it is the job of the server to hide the data store implementation details and present the client with data in a suitable data format that favors simplicity in the client. Decide how the client needs to represent dates, for example, and then ensure you use that format within the data store—and if the data store can't support that format natively, then it is the job of the server to perform the translation.

Clinging to the Old Ways

One of the most powerful features of AngularJS is that it builds on jQuery, especially for its directives feature, which I describe in Chapter 15. The problem this presents, however, is that it makes it easy to notionally use AngularJS for a project but really end up using jQuery behind the scenes.

This may not seem like a design problem, but it ends up distorting the shape of the application because jQuery doesn't make it easy to separate the MVC components, and that makes it difficult to test, enhance, and maintain the web app you are creating. If you are manipulating the DOM directly from jQuery in an AngularJS app, then you have a problem.

As I explained earlier in the chapter, AngularJS isn't the right tool for every job, and it is important you decide at the start of the project which tools you are going to use. If you are going to use AngularJS, then you need to make sure you don't fall back to sneaky jQuery shortcuts that, in the end, will cause endless problems. I return to this topic in Chapter 15 when I introduce jqLite, the AngularJS jQuery implementation, and throughout Chapters 15–17, when I show you how to create custom directives.

Summary

In this chapter, I provided some context for AngularJS. I described the kinds of project where it makes sense to use AngularJS (and where it doesn't), I explained how AngularJS supports the MVC pattern for app development, and I gave a brief overview of REST and how it is used to express data operations over HTTP requests. I finished the chapter by describing the three most common design problems in AngularJS projects. In the next chapter, I provide a quick primer for HTML and the Bootstrap CSS framework that I use for examples throughout this book.

CHAPTER 4

■ ■ ■

HTML and Bootstrap CSS Primer

Developers come to the world of web app development via many paths and are not always grounded in the basic technologies that web apps rely on. In this chapter, I provide a brief primer for HTML and introduce the Bootstrap CSS library, which I use to style the examples in this book. In Chapter 5, I introduce the basics of JavaScript and give you the information you need to understand the examples I create in the rest of the book. If you are an experienced developer, you can skip these primer chapters and jump right to Chapter 6, where I use AngularJS to create a more complex and realistic web app. Table 4-1 summarizes this chapter.

Table 4-1. *Chapter Summary*

Problem	Solution	Listing
Declare content types in an HTML document.	Use HTML elements.	1
Configure an HTML element.	Use an attribute.	2, 3
Differentiate between content and metadata.	Use the head and body regions of the HTML document.	4
Apply Bootstrap styles to an HTML document.	Assign elements to Bootstrap CSS classes.	5
Style a table element.	Use the table and related CSS classes.	6, 7
Style form elements.	Use the form-group and form-control CSS classes.	8
Create a grid layout.	Use the Bootstrap 12-column grid.	9
Create a responsive grid.	Use the large and small grid classes.	10

■ **Tip**   I am not going to describe HTML in depth because it is a topic in its own right. See my book *The Definitive Guide to HTML5*, published by Apress, for complete details of HTML, CSS, and the JavaScript APIs that browsers support.

Understanding HTML

The best place to start is to look at an HTML document. From this, you can see the basic structure and hierarchy that all HTML documents follow. Listing 4-1 shows the simple HTML document that I used in Chapter 2. This isn't the first listing that I showed you in that chapter but comes a little later when I added the basic support for AngularJS. To prepare for this chapter, I saved the elements shown in the listing to the todo.html file in the angularjs directory set up in Chapter 2.

Listing 4-1. The Contents of the todo.html Document

```html
<!DOCTYPE html>
<html ng-app="todoApp">
<head>
    <title>TO DO List</title>
    <link href="bootstrap.css" rel="stylesheet" />
    <link href="bootstrap-theme.css" rel="stylesheet" />
    <script src="angular.js"></script>
    <script>
        var todoApp = angular.module("todoApp", []);
    </script>
</head>
<body>
    <div class="page-header">
        <h1>Adam's To Do List</h1>
    </div>
    <div class="panel">
        <div class="input-group">
            <input class="form-control" />
            <span class="input-group-btn">
                <button class="btn btn-default">Add</button>
            </span>
        </div>
        <table class="table table-striped">
            <thead>
                <tr>
                    <th>Description</th>
                    <th>Done</th>
                </tr>
            </thead>
            <tbody>
                <tr><td>Buy Flowers</td><td>No</td></tr>
                <tr><td>Get Shoes</td><td>No</td></tr>
                <tr><td>Collect Tickets</td><td>Yes</td></tr>
                <tr><td>Call Joe</td><td>No</td></tr>
            </tbody>
        </table>
    </div>
</body>
</html>
```

As a reminder, Figure 4-1 shows you how the browser displays the HTML elements that the document contains.

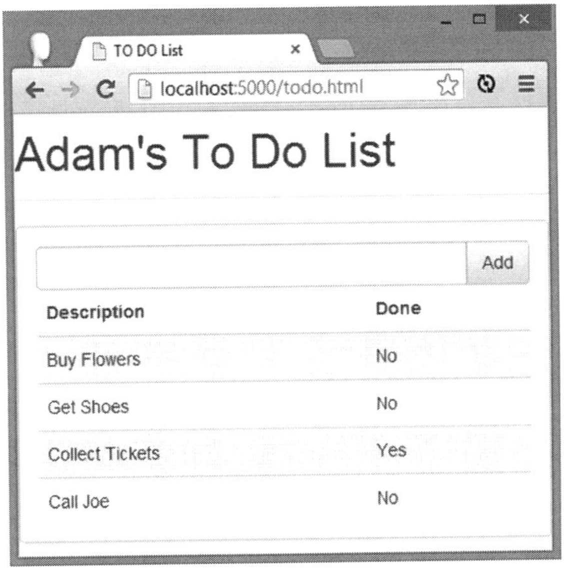

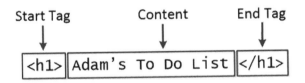

Figure 4-1. Displaying the todo.html file in the browser

Understanding the Anatomy of an HTML Element

At the heart of HTML is the *element,* which tells the browser what kind of content each part of an HTML document represents. Here is an element from the example:

```
...
<h1>Adam's To Do List</h1>
...
```

As illustrated by Figure 4-2, this element has three parts: the start tag, the end tag, and the content.

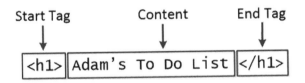

Figure 4-2. The anatomy of a simple HTML element

The *name* of this element (also referred to as the *tag name* or just the *tag*) is h1, and it tells the browser that the content between the tags should be treated as a top-level header. You start an element by placing the tag name in angle brackets (the < and > characters) and end an element by using the tag in a similar way, except that you also add a / character after the left-angle bracket (<).

Understanding Attributes

You can provide additional information to the browser by adding *attributes* to your elements. Listing 4-2 shows an element with an attribute from the example document.

Listing 4-2. Defining an Attribute

```
...
<link href="bootstrap.css" rel="stylesheet" />
...
```

This is a link element, and it imports content into the document. There are two attributes, which I have emphasized so they are easier to see. Attributes are always defined as part of the start tag and have a *name* and a *value*.

The names of the two attributes in this example are href and rel. For the link element, the href attribute specifies the content to import, and the rel attribute tells the browser what kind of content it is. The attributes on this link element tell the browser to import the bootstrap.css file and to treat it as a style sheet, which is a file that contains CSS styles.

Not all attributes require a value; just defining them sends a signal to the browser that you want a certain kind of behavior associated with the element. Listing 4-3 shows an example of an element with such an attribute (not from the example document; I just made up this example element).

Listing 4-3. Defining an Attribute That Requires No Value

```
...
<input name="snowdrop" value="0" required>
...
```

This element has three attributes. The first two, name and value, are assigned a value like with the previous example. (This can get a little confusing. The names of these attributes are name and value. The value of the name attribute is snowdrop, and the value of the value attribute is 0.) The third attribute is just the word required. This is an example of an attribute that doesn't need a value, although you can define one by setting the attribute value to its name (required="required") or by using the empty string (required="").

Understanding Element Content

Elements can contain text, but they can also contain other elements. Here is an example of an element that contains other elements:

```
...
<thead>
    <tr>
        <th>Description</th>
        <th>Done</th>
    </tr>
</thead>
...
```

The elements in an HTML document form a natural hierarchy. The html element contains the body element, which contains content elements, each of which can contain other elements, and so on. The thead element contains tr elements that, in turn, contain th elements. Nesting elements like this is a key concept in HTML because it imparts the significance of the outer element to those contained within.

Understanding Void Elements

The HTML specification includes elements that may not contain content. These are called *void* or *self-closing* elements, and they are written without a separate end tag. Here is an example of a void element:

```
...
<input class="form-control" />
...
```

A void element is defined in a single tag, and you add a / character before the last angle bracket (the > character).

Understanding the Document Structure

There are some key elements that define the basic structure of any HTML document: the DOCTYPE, html, head, and body elements. Listing 4-4 shows the relationship between these elements with the rest of the content removed.

Listing 4-4. The Basic Structure of an HTML Document

```
<!DOCTYPE html>
<html>
<head>
    ...head content...
</head>
<body>
    ...body content...
</body>
</html>
```

UNDERSTANDING THE DOCUMENT OBJECT MODEL

When the browser loads and processes an HTML document, it creates the *Document Object Model* (DOM). The DOM is a model in which JavaScript objects are used to represent each element in the document, and the DOM is the mechanism by which you can programmatically engage with the content of an HTML document.

You rarely work directly with the DOM in AngularJS—except when creating custom directives—but it is important to understand that the browser maintains a live model of the HTML document represented by JavaScript objects. When AngularJS modifies these objects, the browser updates the content it displays to reflect the modifications. This is one of the key foundations of web applications. If we were not able to modify the DOM, we would not be able to create client-side web apps.

Each of these elements has a specific role to play in an HTML document. The DOCTYPE element tells the browser that this is an HTML document and, more specifically, that this is an *HTML5* document. Earlier versions of HTML required additional information. For example, here is the DOCTYPE element for an HTML4 document:

```
...
<!DOCTYPE HTML PUBLIC "-//W3C//DTD HTML 4.01//EN"
    "http://www.w3.org/TR/html4/strict.dtd">
...
```

The html element denotes the region of the document that contains the HTML content. This element always contains the other two key structural elements: head and body. As I explained at the start of the chapter, I am not going to cover the individual HTML elements. There are too many of them, and describing HTML5 completely took me more than 1,000 pages in my HTML book. That said, I will provide brief descriptions of the elements I used in the todo.html file to help you understand how elements tell the browser what kind of content they represent. Table 4-2 summarizes the elements used in the example document from Listing 4-1.

Table 4-2. *HTML Elements Used in the Example Document*

Element	Description
DOCTYPE	Indicates the type of content in the document
body	Denotes the region of the document that contains content elements (described later in the chapter)
button	Denotes a button; often used to submit a form to the server
div	A generic element; often used to add structure to a document for presentation purposes
h1	Denotes a top-level header
head	Denotes the region of the document that contains metadata (described later in the chapter)
html	Denotes the region of the document that contains HTML (which is usually the entire document)
input	Denotes a field used to gather a single data item from the user
link	Imports content into the HTML document
script	Denotes a script, typically JavaScript, that will be executed as part of the document
span	A generic element; often used to add structure to a document for presentation purposes
style	Denotes a region of Cascading Style Sheet settings; see Chapter 3
table	Denotes a table, used to organize content into rows and columns
tbody	Denotes the body of the table (as opposed to the header or footer)
td	Denotes a content cell in a table row
th	Denotes a header cell in a table row
thead	Denotes the header of a table
tr	Denotes a row in a table
title	Denotes the title of the document; used by the browser to set the title of the window or tab

Understanding Bootstrap

HTML elements tell the browser what kind of content they represent, but they don't provide any information about how that content should be displayed. The information about how to display elements is provided using *Cascading Style Sheets* (CSS). CSS consists of a comprehensive set of *properties* that can be used to configure every aspect of an element's appearance and a set of *selectors* that allow those properties to be applied.

One of the main problems with CSS is that some browsers interpret properties slightly differently, which can lead to variations in the way that HTML content is displayed on different devices. It can be difficult to track down and correct these problems, and CSS frameworks have emerged to help web app developers style their HTML content in a simple and consistent way.

One CSS framework that has gained a lot of popularity recently is Bootstrap, which was originally developed at Twitter but has become a widely used open source project. Bootstrap consists of a set of CSS classes that can be applied to elements to style them consistently and some JavaScript code that performs additional enhancement. I use Bootstrap frequently in my own projects; it works well across browsers, it is simple to use, and it builds on jQuery (which, as we have already established, is something that I like a great deal, although I won't be using the features that rely on jQuery in this book).

I use the Bootstrap CSS styles in this book because they let me style my examples without having to define and then list my own custom CSS in each chapter. Bootstrap provides a lot more features than the ones I use and describe in this book; see http://getbootstrap.com for full details.

■ **Tip** I don't use the Bootstrap JavaScript components in this book. There is nothing wrong with them—in fact, they work well—but my focus is on AngularJS in this book, and I just need the basic CSS styles for my examples.

I don't want to get into too much detail about Bootstrap because it isn't the topic of this book, but I do want to give you just enough information so you can see which parts of an example are AngularJS features and which are Bootstrap styling. To help me demonstrate the basic Bootstrap features, I have created an HTML file called bootstrap.html in the angularjs folder, the contents of which you can see in Listing 4-5.

Listing 4-5. The Contents of the bootstrap.html File

```
<!DOCTYPE html>
<html xmlns="http://www.w3.org/1999/xhtml">
<head>
    <title>Bootstrap Examples</title>
    <link href="bootstrap.css" rel="stylesheet" />
    <link href="bootstrap-theme.css" rel="stylesheet" />
</head>
<body>
    <div class="panel">
        <h3 class="panel-heading">Button Styles</h3>
        <button class="btn">Basic Button</button>
        <button class="btn btn-primary">Primary</button>
        <button class="btn btn-success">Success</button>
        <button class="btn btn-warning">Warning</button>
        <button class="btn btn-info">Info</button>
        <button class="btn btn-danger">Danger</button>
    </div>
    <div class="well">
        <h3 class="panel-heading">Button Sizes</h3>
        <button class="btn btn-large btn-success">Large Success</button>
        <button class="btn btn-warning">Standard Warning</button>
        <button class="btn btn-small btn-danger">Small Danger</button>
    </div>
    <div class="well">
        <h3 class="panel-heading">Block Buttons</h3>
        <button class="btn btn-block btn-large btn-success">Large Block Success</button>
        <button class="btn btn-block btn-warning">Standard Block Warning</button>
        <button class="btn btn-block btn-small btn-info">Small Block Info</button>
    </div>
</body>
</html>
```

> ■ **Tip** The examples that follow rely on the `bootstrap.css` and `bootstrap-theme.css` files that were added to the `angularjs` folder in Chapter 1. If you have removed these file, then follow the instructions in Chapter 1 to download Bootstrap again and copy them into place.

This HTML demonstrates a number of different features that are typical of the way that Bootstrap works and of how I apply Bootstrap in this book. You can see the effect that the HTML creates in the browser in Figure 4-3; I explain the features I have used afterward.

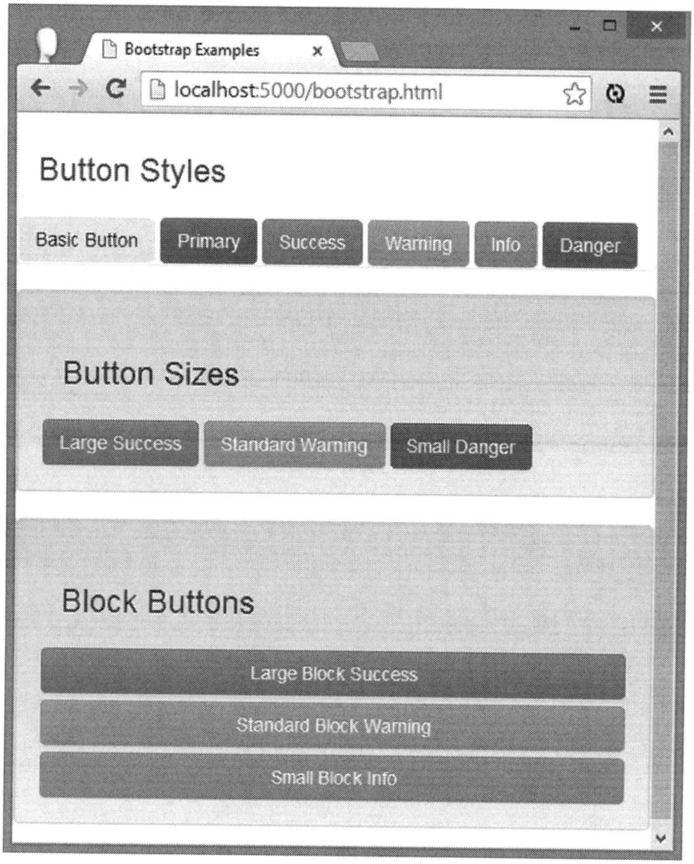

Figure 4-3. *Displaying the bootstrap.html file in the browser*

Applying Basic Bootstrap Classes

Bootstrap styles are applied via the `class` attribute, which is used to associate related elements. The `class` attribute isn't just used to apply CSS styles, but it is the most common use, and it underpins the way that Bootstrap and similar frameworks operate. Here is an example of an HTML element from the listing to which I have applied the `class` attribute:

```
...
<div class="panel">
...
```

I have set the class attribute to panel, which is one of the many CSS classes defined by Bootstrap. When I set the class attribute to the name of a Bootstrap class, CSS style properties defined by Bootstrap are applied by the browser to change the appearance of that element. There are three basic style classes in Listing 4-5, which I describe in Table 4-3.

Table 4-3. *The Basic Bootstrap Style Classes Used in the Example*

Bootstrap Class	Description
panel	Denotes a panel with a rounded border. A panel can have a header and a footer.
panel-heading	Creates a heading for a panel.
btn	Creates a button.
well	Groups elements with an inset effect.

■ **Tip** Not all Bootstrap styles require explicit use of the class attribute. The heading elements, h1–h6, are automatically styled whenever they are used.

Modifying Style Context

Bootstrap defines a set of *style context* classes that are applied to elements to signify their purpose. These classes are specified with the name created by combining a basic Bootstrap style class (such as btn), a hyphen, and one of primary, success, warning, info, or danger. Here is an example of applying a style context class:

```
...
<button class="btn btn-primary">Primary</button>
...
```

Context classes must be applied along with the basic class, which is why the button element has both the btn and btn-primary classes. (Multiple classes are separated using spaces.) You don't have to use a context class; they are entirely optional and are usually used just for emphasis.

Modifying Sizes

You can change the way that some elements are styled by using a size modification class. These are specified by combining a basic class name, a hyphen, and lg or sm. Here is an example from the listing of a size class:

```
...
<button class="btn btn-lg btn-success">Large Success</button>
...
```

Omitting a size class uses the default size for the element. Notice that I am able to combine a context class and a size class. Bootstrap class modifications work together to give you complete control over how elements are styled. For button elements, you can apply the btn-block class to create a button that fills the available horizontal space, as follows:

```
...
<button class="btn btn-block btn-lg btn-success">Large Block Success</button>
...
```

The btn-block class can be combined with size and context classes, as shown in Figure 4-3.

Using Bootstrap to Style Tables

Bootstrap also includes support for styling table elements—a feature I used for the example app in Chapter 2. Table 4-4 lists the CSS classes that Bootstrap includes for tables.

Table 4-4. *The Bootstrap CSS Classes for Tables*

Bootstrap Class	Description
table	Applies general styling to table elements and their contents
table-striped	Applies alternate-row striping to the rows in the table body
table-bordered	Applies borders to all rows and columns
table-hover	Displays a different style when the mouse hovers over a row in the table
table-condensed	Reduces the spacing in the table to create a more compact layout

All of these classes are applied directly to the table element. I modified the bootstrap.html file to demonstrate the Bootstrap styling for tables, as shown in Listing 4-6.

Listing 4-6. Adding Styled Tables to the bootstrap.html File

```
<!DOCTYPE html>
<html xmlns="http://www.w3.org/1999/xhtml">
<head>
    <title>Bootstrap Examples</title>
    <link href="bootstrap.css" rel="stylesheet" />
    <link href="bootstrap-theme.css" rel="stylesheet" />
</head>
<body>
    <div class="panel">
        <h3 class="panel-heading">Standard Table with Context</h3>
        <table class="table">
            <thead>
                <tr><th>Country</th><th>Capital City</th></tr>
            </thead>
            <tr class="success"><td>United Kingdom</td><td>London</td></tr>
            <tr class="danger"><td>France</td><td>Paris</td></tr>
            <tr><td>Spain</td><td class="warning">Madrid</td></tr>
        </table>
    </div>
```

```
<div class="panel">
    <h3 class="panel-heading">Striped, Bordered and Highlighted Table</h3>
    <table class="table table-striped table-bordered table-hover">
        <thead>
            <tr><th>Country</th><th>Capital City</th></tr>
        </thead>
        <tr><td>United Kingdom</td><td>London</td></tr>
        <tr><td>France</td><td>Paris</td></tr>
        <tr><td>Spain</td><td>Madrid</td></tr>
    </table>
</div>
</body>
</html>
```

I have used two table elements to show how different Bootstrap classes can be combined. You can see the result in Figure 4-4.

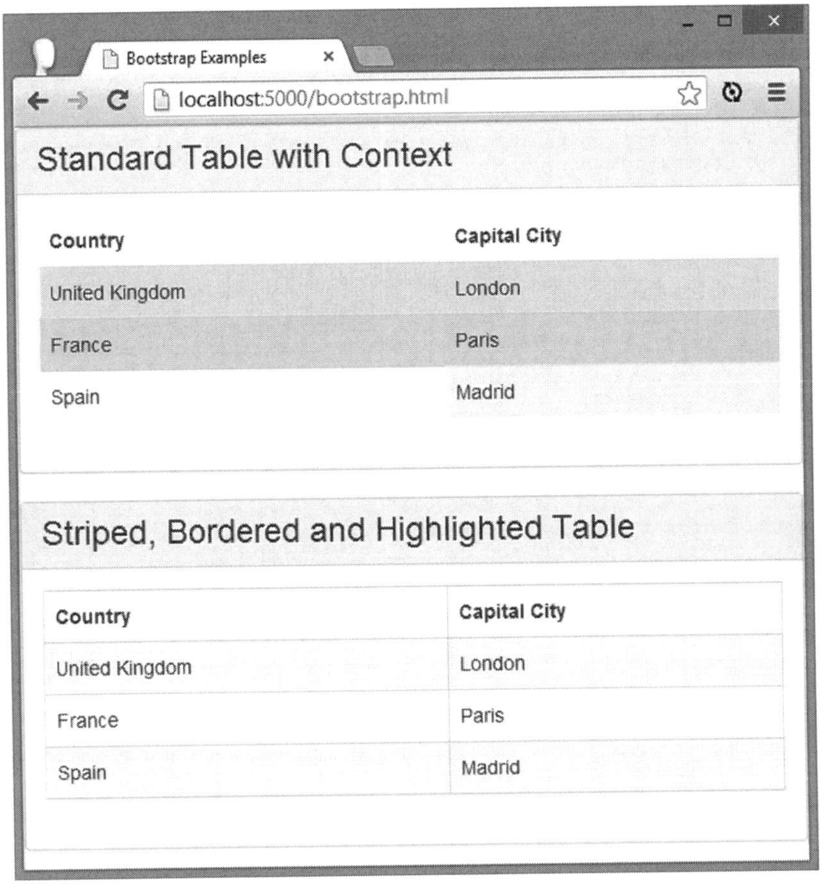

Figure 4-4. *Styling table elements with Bootstrap*

The first table element has just the table class, so only the basic Bootstrap styles for tables are applied. For variety, I have applied the context classes to two tr elements and one td element to show that context styles can be applied to individual rows and cells.

For the second table, I have applied the basic table class as well as the table-striped, table-bordered, and table-hover classes. This has the effect of alternating the styles used for table rows, adding borders for rows and cells, and—although it can't be seen in a static figure—highlighting rows as the mouse passes over them.

Ensuring the Correct Table Structure

Notice that I have used the thead element when defining the tables in Listing 4-6. Browsers will automatically add any tr elements that are direct descendants of table elements to a tbody element if one has not been used. You will get odd results if you rely on this behavior when working with Bootstrap because most of the CSS classes that are applied to the table element cause styles to be added to the descendants of the tbody element. Consider the table shown in Listing 4-7, which I have defined in the bootstrap.html file.

Listing 4-7. Defining a Table Without a Separate Header in the bootstrap.html File

```
<!DOCTYPE html>
<html xmlns="http://www.w3.org/1999/xhtml">
<head>
    <title>Bootstrap Examples</title>
    <link href="bootstrap.css" rel="stylesheet" />
    <link href="bootstrap-theme.css" rel="stylesheet" />
</head>
<body>
    <div class="panel">
        <h3 class="panel-heading">Striped, Bordered and Highlighted Table</h3>
        <table class="table table-striped table-bordered table-hover">
            <tr><th>Country</th><th>Capital City</th></tr>
            <tr><td>United Kingdom</td><td>London</td></tr>
            <tr><td>France</td><td>Paris</td></tr>
            <tr><td>Spain</td><td>Madrid</td></tr>
        </table>
    </div>
</body>
</html>
```

There is no thead element in the table element, which means that the header row is added to the tbody element that the browser creates automatically. This has a subtle but important effect on the way that the content is displayed, as shown in Figure 4-5.

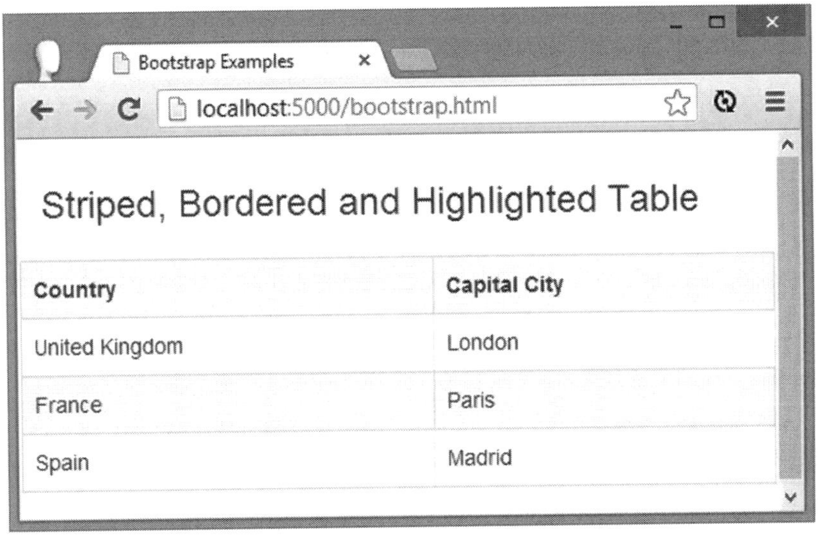

Figure 4-5. *The effect of combining header and body rows in a table*

Notice that the striping of the rows now starts with the header. This may not seem like a big deal, but if you run this example yourself and move the mouse over the table rows, you will see that the header row is included in the highlighting, something that is rarely desirable since it will confuse the user.

Using Bootstrap to Create Forms

Bootstrap includes styling for form elements, allowing them to be styled consistently with other elements in the application, as illustrated by Listing 4-8.

Listing 4-8. Styling Form Elements in the bootstrap.html File

```
<!DOCTYPE html>
<html xmlns="http://www.w3.org/1999/xhtml">
<head>
    <title>Bootstrap Examples</title>
    <link href="bootstrap.css" rel="stylesheet" />
    <link href="bootstrap-theme.css" rel="stylesheet" />
</head>
<body>
    <div class="panel">
        <h3 class="panel-header">
            Form Elements
        </h3>
```

```
        <div class="form-group">
            <label>Name:</label>
            <input name="name" class="form-control" />
        </div>

        <div class="form-group">
            <label>Email:</label>
            <input name="email" class="form-control" />
        </div>

        <div class="radio">
            <label>
                <input type="radio" name="junkmail" value="yes" checked />
                Yes, send me endless junk mail
            </label>
        </div>
        <div class="radio">
            <label>
                <input type="radio" name="junkmail" value="no" />
                No, I never want to hear from you again
            </label>
        </div>

        <div class="checkbox">
            <label>
                <input type="checkbox" />
                I agree to the terms and conditions.
            </label>
        </div>

        <input type="button" class="btn btn-primary" value="Subscribe" />
    </div>
</body>
</html>
```

This HTML file contains a number of form elements that gather data from the user. I explain the AngularJS support for forms in Chapter 12, but this example is just to show how Bootstrap can be used to style form elements; you can see the result in Figure 4-6.

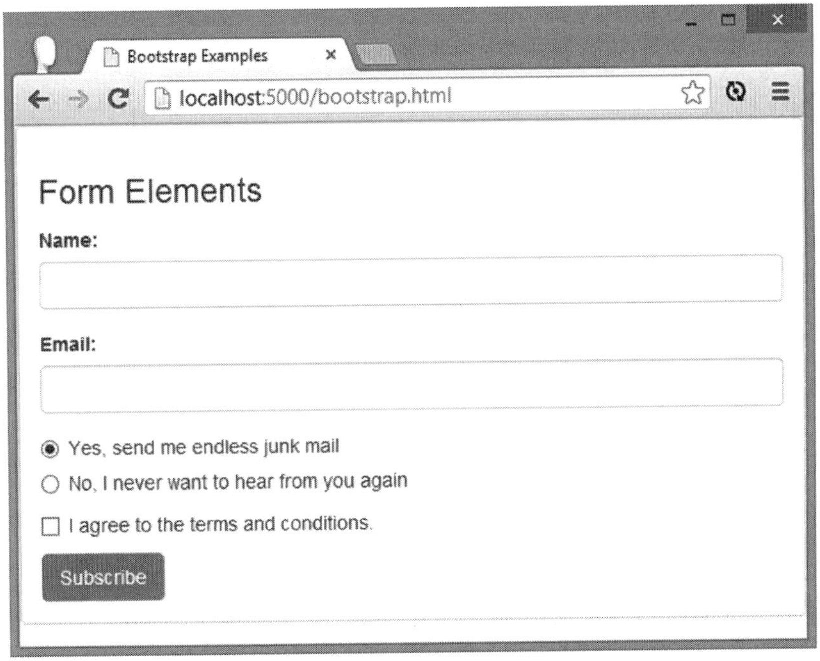

Figure 4-6. *Styling form elements with Bootstrap*

The basic styling for forms is achieved by applying the `form-group` class to a `div` element that contains a `label` and an `input` element, as follow:

```
...
<div class="form-group">
    <label>Email:</label>
    <input name="email" class="form-control" />
</div>
...
```

Bootstrap styles the elements so that the `label` is shown above the `input` element and the `input` element occupies 100 percent of the available horizontal space.

There are different classes for other form elements. In the example, I have used the `checkbox` class, which is also applied to `div` elements, for `input` elements whose type is set to, obviously enough, checkbox, as follows:

```
...
<div class="checkbox">
    <label>
        <input type="checkbox" />
        I agree to the terms and conditions.
    </label>
</div>
...
```

■ **Tip**   Notice that the `label` element is used to contain the descriptive text and the `input` element, which is a different structure from the one used for other types of `input` element.

Using Bootstrap to Create Grids

Bootstrap provides style classes that can be used to create different kinds of grid layout, ranging from one to twelve columns and with support for responsive layouts (where the layout of the grid changes based on the width of the screen, allowing the same content to be laid out on mobile and desktop devices). In Listing 4-9, I have used the bootstrap.html file to create a grid layout.

Listing 4-9. Creating a Grid Layout in the bootstrap.html File

```
<!DOCTYPE html>
<html xmlns="http://www.w3.org/1999/xhtml">
<head>
    <title>Bootstrap Examples</title>
    <link href="bootstrap.css" rel="stylesheet" />
    <link href="bootstrap-theme.css" rel="stylesheet" />
    <style>
        #gridContainer {padding: 20px;}
        .grid-row > div { border: 1px solid lightgrey; padding: 10px;
                          background-color: aliceblue; margin: 5px 0; }
    </style>
</head>
<body>
    <div class="panel">

        <h3 class="panel-header">
            Grid Layout
        </h3>

        <div id="gridContainer">

            <div class="row grid-row">
                <div class="col-xs-1">1</div>
                <div class="col-xs-1">1</div>
                <div class="col-xs-2">2</div>
                <div class="col-xs-2">2</div>
                <div class="col-xs-6">6</div>
            </div>

            <div class="row grid-row">
                <div class="col-xs-3">3</div>
                <div class="col-xs-4">4</div>
                <div class="col-xs-5">5</div>
            </div>
```

```
        <div class="row grid-row">
            <div class="col-xs-6">6</div>
            <div class="col-xs-6">6</div>
        </div>

        <div class="row grid-row">
            <div class="col-xs-11">11</div>
            <div class="col-xs-1">1</div>
        </div>

        <div class="row grid-row">
            <div class="col-xs-12">12</div>
        </div>
      </div>
    </div>
</body>
</html>
```

TABLES VS. GRIDS

The `table` element denotes tabular data, but it is often used to lay out content in a grid. In general, you should use CSS to lay out content in grids because using a table goes against the principle of separating content from the way it is presented. CSS3 includes grid layouts as part of the specification, but they are still not consistently implemented even in the mainstream browsers. The best option, therefore, is to use a CSS framework like Bootstrap.

This is another pattern that I adhere to right up until I have a problem to solve. In my own projects there are sometimes reasons why CSS frameworks are not acceptable to the client and the web app will be running on devices that don't support the latest CSS3 layouts. In these situations, I use a `table` element to create a grid layout because doing it manually with CSS2 creates an unmanageable mess of styles that requires constant tweaking and adjustment. As ever, my advice is to stick to the pattern of separating element types from layouts when you can, but don't be afraid to use `table` elements as grids when you find yourself stuck without a better alternative.

The Bootstrap grid layout system is simple to use. You specify a column by applying the `row` class to a `div` element, which has the effect of setting up the grid layout for the content that the `div` element contains.

Each row defines 12 columns, and you specify how many columns each child element will occupy by assigning a class whose name is `col-xs` followed by the number of columns. For example, the class `col-xs-1` specifies that an element occupies one column, `col-xs-2` specifies two columns, and so on, right through to `col-xs-12`, which specifies that an element fills the entire row. In the listing, I have created a series of `div` elements with the `row` class, each of which contains further `div` elements to which I have applied `col-xs-*` classes. You can see the effect in the browser in Figure 4-7.

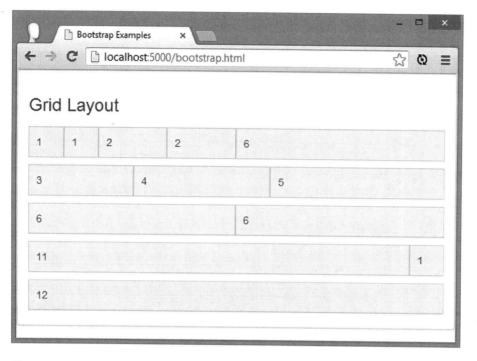

Figure 4-7. *Creating a Bootstrap grid layout*

Bootstrap doesn't apply any styling to the elements within a row, which I why I have used a `style` element to create a custom CSS style that sets a background color, sets up some spacing between rows, and adds a border. This is the `grid-row` class that you can see applied alongside the `row` class:

```
...
<div class="row grid-row">
...
```

Creating Responsive Grids

Responsive grids adapt their layout based on the size of the browser window. The main use for responsive grids is to allow mobile devices and desktops to display the same content, taking advantage of whatever screen space is available. To create a responsive grid, replace the `col-*` class on individual cells with one of the classes shown in Table 4-5.

Table 4-5. *The Bootstrap CSS Classes for Responsive Grids*

Bootstrap Class	Description
`col-sm-*`	Grid cells are displayed horizontally when the screen width is greater than 768 pixels.
`col-md-*`	Grid cells are displayed horizontally when the screen width is greater than 940 pixels.
`col-lg-*`	Grid cells are displayed horizontally when the screen width is greater than 1170 pixels.

When the width of the screen is less than the class supports, the cells in the grid row are stacked vertically rather than horizontally. As a demonstration, I have created a responsive grid on the bootstrap.html file, as shown in Listing 4-10.

Listing 4-10. Creating a Responsive Grid in the bootstrap.html File

```
<!DOCTYPE html>
<html xmlns="http://www.w3.org/1999/xhtml">
<head>
    <title>Bootstrap Examples</title>
    <meta name="viewport" content="width=device-width, initial-scale=1">
    <link href="bootstrap.css" rel="stylesheet" />
    <link href="bootstrap-theme.css" rel="stylesheet" />
    <style>
        #gridContainer { padding: 20px; }
        .grid-row > div { border: 1px solid lightgrey;
                        padding: 10px; background-color: aliceblue; margin: 5px 0; }
    </style>
</head>
<body>
    <div class="panel">

        <h3 class="panel-header">
            Grid Layout
        </h3>
        <div id="gridContainer">

            <div class="row grid-row">
                <div class="col-sm-3">3</div>
                <div class="col-sm-4">4</div>
                <div class="col-sm-5">5</div>
            </div>

            <div class="row grid-row">
                <div class="col-sm-6">6</div>
                <div class="col-sm-6">6</div>
            </div>

            <div class="row grid-row">
                <div class="col-sm-11">11</div>
                <div class="col-sm-1">1</div>
            </div>

        </div>
    </div>
</body>
</html>
```

I removed some grid rows from the previous example and replaced the col-xs* classes with col-sm-*. The effect is that the cells in the row will be stacked horizontally when the browser window is greater than 768 pixels wide and stacked horizontally when it is smaller. You can see the effect in Figure 4-8, which shows the listing displayed in Chrome and an iPhone emulator.

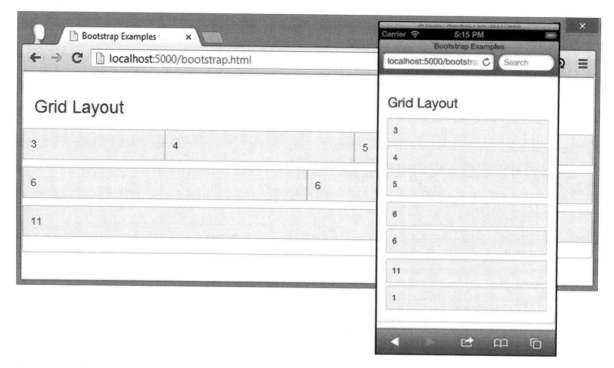

Figure 4-8. *Creating a responsive grid layout*

■ **Tip**   Notice that I added a meta element to this example. This element tells mobile browsers to display the content actual size. Without the meta element, many mobile browsers will display the content as though it were intended only for a desktop and expect the user to zoom in to see any detail. In short, you should always add a meta element like the one in the listing when targeting mobile devices. See my *The Definitive Guide to HTML5* book, also published by Apress, for full details.

Summary

In this chapter, I provided a brief overview of HTML and the Bootstrap CSS framework. You need to have a good grasp of HTML and CSS to be truly effective in web application development, but the best way to learn is by first-hand experience, and the descriptions and examples in this chapter will be enough to get you started and provide just enough background information for the examples ahead. In the next chapter, I continue the primer theme and introduce the basic features of JavaScript that I use in this book and some of the language enhancements that AngularJS provides.

CHAPTER 5

■ ■ ■

JavaScript Primer

In this chapter I provide a quick tour of the most important features of the JavaScript language, as they apply to this book. I don't have the space to describe JavaScript completely, but I have focused on the essentials that you'll need to get up to speed and follow the examples in this book. In addition to the most important core JavaScript language features, I describe the set of utility methods that AngularJS provides.

I finish this chapter by demonstrating how JavaScript *promises* work. A promise represents an asynchronous task, such as an Ajax request, and they are widely used in AngularJS apps, which is a topic I return to in Chapter 21. I also describe the AngularJS support for working with JSON data, which is the most widely used format for dealing with data in AngularJS. Table 5-1 summarizes this chapter.

Table 5-1. Chapter Summary

Problem	Solution	Listing
Add JavaScript to an HTML document.	Use the `script` element.	1
Create JavaScript functionality.	Use JavaScript statements.	3
Create groups of statements that are executed on command.	Use functions.	4–6
Detect a function.	Use the `angular.isFunction` method.	7
Store values and objects for later use.	Use variables.	8
Store different kinds of data.	Use types.	9, 10, 12
Detect and manipulate strings.	Use the `angular.isString`, `angular.uppercase`, and `anguler.lowercase` methods.	11
Define custom data types.	Create objects.	13–23
Control the flow of JavaScript code.	Use conditional statements.	24
Determine whether two objects or values are the same.	Use the quality and identity operators.	25–28
Explicitly convert types.	Use the `to<type>` methods.	29–31
Store related objects or values together in sequence.	Use an array.	32–37
Determine whether a variable has been defined and if it has been assigned a value.	Check for the `null` and `undefined` values.	38–41
Receive a notification when an asynchronous task completes.	Use a promise object.	42, 43
Encode and decode JSON data.	Use the `angular.toJson` and `angular.fromJson` methods.	44

Preparing the Example Project

For this chapter, I will be demonstrating some basic JavaScript techniques and some helpful general-purpose utility methods that AngularJS provides to supplement the JavaScript language.

Ensure that the angular.js, bootstrap.css, and bootstrap-theme.css files are in the web server angularjs folder, and create a new HTML file called jsdemo.html. Set the contents of the HTML file to match those in Listing 5-1.

Listing 5-1. The Initial Contents of the jsdemo.html File

```
<!DOCTYPE html>
<html>
<head>
    <title>Example</title>
    <script src="angular.js"></script>
    <script type="text/javascript">
        console.log("Hello");
    </script>
</head>
<body>
    This is a simple example
</body>
</html>
```

If you use the browser to navigate to the jsdemo.html file, you will see the result shown in Figure 5-1. In this chapter, my emphasis is on the JavaScript language, and the content displayed by the browser isn't important.

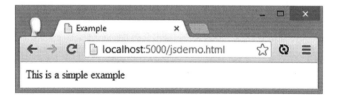

Figure 5-1. Testing the example HTML file

I'll also be using the todo.json file that I created in Chapter 2. You can copy this file from your previous example or re-create it so that it contains the content shown in Listing 5-2.

Listing 5-2. The Contents of the todo.json File

```
[{ "action": "Buy Flowers", "done": false },
 { "action": "Get Shoes", "done": false },
 { "action": "Collect Tickets", "done": true },
 { "action": "Call Joe", "done": false }]
```

Understanding the Script Element

JavaScript code is added to an HTML document using the `script` element. There are two ways to use the `script` element, and you can see both of them in Listing 5-1. The first way is to apply the `src` attribute and import a separate file that contains JavaScript statements. This is what I did with the AngularJS library file, like this:

```
...
<script src="angular.js"></script>
...
```

You can also create *inline* scripts by putting JavaScript statements between the `script` element tags, like this:

```
...
<script type="text/javascript">
    console.log("Hello");
</script>
...
```

For real projects, you will usually use external files because they are easier to manage, but for the examples I create in this book it is often more convenient for me to be able to demonstrate the HTML and the JavaScript in the same file.

The inline script in this example contains a statement that calls the `console.log` method, which writes a message to the *JavaScript console*. The console is a basic (but useful) tool that the browser provides that lets you display debugging information as your script is executed. Each browser has a different way of showing the console. For Google Chrome, you select JavaScript console from the Tools menu. You can see how the console is displayed in Chrome in Figure 5-2.

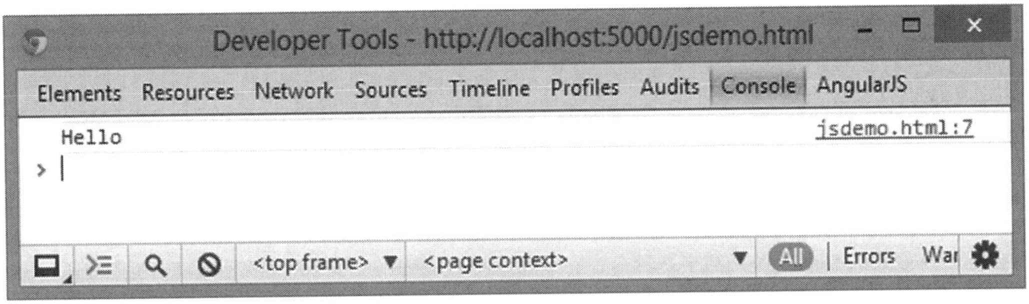

Figure 5-2. *The Google Chrome JavaScript console*

▓ **Tip**   Notice that the Chrome window shown in the figure has an AngularJS tab. This is added by the Batarang extension that I described in Chapter 1 and is useful for debugging AngularJS apps.

You can see that the output from calling the `console.log` method is displayed in the console window, along with the details of where the message originated (in this case on line 7 of the `jsdemo.html` file). In this chapter, I won't show screenshots; I'll show just the results from the examples. So, for example, for Listing 5-1, the output is as follows:

```
Hello
```

I have formatted some of the results later in the chapter to make them easier to read. In the sections that follow, I'll show you the core features of the JavaScript language. If you have had any experience programming in any other modern language, you will find the JavaScript syntax and style familiar.

Using Statements

The basic JavaScript building block is the *statement*. Each statement represents a single command, and statements are usually terminated by a semicolon (;). The semicolon is optional, but using them makes your code easier to read and allows for multiple statements on a single line. Listing 5-3 shows a pair of statements in a script that is defined using a script element.

Listing 5-3. Using JavaScript Statements in the jsdemo.html File

```
<!DOCTYPE HTML>
<html>
    <head>
        <title>Example</title>
        <script src="angular.js"></script>
        <script type="text/javascript">
            console.log("This is a statement");
            console.log("This is also a statement");
        </script>
    </head>
    <body>
        This is a simple example
    </body>
</html>
```

The browser executes each statement in turn. In this example, I simply write a pair of messages to the console. The results are as follows:

```
This is a statement
This is also a statement
```

Defining and Using Functions

When the browser processes an HTML document, it looks at the elements one by one. When it encounters a script element, it immediately executes the JavaScript statements it contains in the sequence in which they are defined.

This is what happened in the previous example. The browser processed the HTML document, found the script element, and executed the two statements that it encountered, both of which wrote a message to the console. You can also package multiple statements into a *function*, which won't be executed until the browser encounters a statement that *invokes* the function, as shown in Listing 5-4.

Listing 5-4. Defining a JavaScript Function in the jsdemo.html File

```html
<!DOCTYPE HTML>
<html>
<head>
    <title>Example</title>
    <script src="angular.js"></script>
    <script type="text/javascript">
        function myFunc() {
            console.log("This is a statement");
        };

        myFunc();
    </script>
</head>
<body>
    This is a simple example
</body>
</html>
```

Defining a `function` is simple: Use the `function` keyword followed by the name you want to give the function, followed by parentheses (the (and) characters). The statements you want the function to contain are enclosed between braces (the { and } characters).

In the listing I used the name `myFunc`, and the function contains a single statement that writes a message to the JavaScript console. The statement in the function won't be executed until the browser reaches another statement that calls the `myFunc` function, like this:

```
...
myFunc();
...
```

Executing the statement in the function produces the following output:

```
This is a statement
```

Other than demonstrating how functions are defined, this example isn't especially useful because the function is invoked immediately after it has been defined. Functions are much more useful when they are invoked in response to some kind of change or event, such as user interaction.

Defining Functions with Parameters

JavaScript allows you to define parameters for functions, as shown in Listing 5-5.

Listing 5-5. Defining Functions with Parameters in the jsdemo.html File

```html
<!DOCTYPE HTML>
<html>
<head>
    <title>Example</title>
    <script src="angular.js"></script>
    <script type="text/javascript">
```

```
        function myFunc(name, weather) {
            console.log("Hello " + name + ".");
            console.log("It is " + weather + " today");
        };

        myFunc("Adam", "sunny");
    </script>
</head>
<body>
    This is a simple example
</body>
</html>
```

I added two parameters to the myFunc function, called name and weather. JavaScript is a dynamically typed language, which means you don't have to declare the data type of the parameters when you define the function. I'll come back to dynamic typing later in the chapter when I cover JavaScript variables. To invoke a function with parameters, you provide values as arguments when you invoke the function, like this:

```
...
myFunc("Adam", "sunny");
...
```

The results from this listing are as follows:

```
Hello Adam.
It is sunny today
```

The number of arguments you provide when you invoke a function doesn't need to match the number of parameters in the function. If you call the function with fewer arguments than it has parameters, then the value of any parameters you have not supplied values for is undefined, which is a special JavaScript value. If you call the function with more arguments than there are parameters, then the additional arguments are ignored.

The consequence of this is that you can't create two functions with the same name and different parameters and expect JavaScript to differentiate between them based on the arguments you provide when invoking the function. This is called *polymorphism*, and although it is supported in languages such as Java and C#, it isn't available in JavaScript. Instead, if you define two functions with the same name, then the second definition replaces the first.

■ **Tip**   The closest you can come to polymorphism in JavaScript is to define a single function to act differently based on the number and the types of the arguments. Doing this requires careful testing, can result in an awkward API, and is generally best avoided.

Defining Functions That Return Results

You can return results from functions using the return keyword. Listing 5-6 shows a function that returns a result.

Listing 5-6. Returning a Result from a Function in the jsdemo.html File

```
<!DOCTYPE HTML>
<html>
<head>
    <title>Example</title>
    <script src="angular.js"></script>
    <script type="text/javascript">
        function myFunc(name) {
            return ("Hello " + name + ".");
        };

        console.log(myFunc("Adam"));
    </script>
</head>
<body>
    This is a simple example
</body>
</html>
```

This function defines one parameter and uses it to produce a result. I invoke the function and pass the result as the argument to the `console.log` function, like this:

```
...
console.log(myFunc("Adam"));
...
```

Notice that you don't have to declare that the function will return a result or denote the data type of the result. The result from this listing is as follows:

```
Hello Adam.
```

Detecting Functions

Functions can be passed around as objects within JavaScript, and it can be useful to be able to tell whether an object is a function. AngularJS provides the `angular.isFunction` method for this purpose, as demonstrated in Listing 5-7.

■ **Note** All of the AngularJS utility methods are accessed via the global `angular` object, such as `angular.isFunction`, which is the subject of this example. The `angular` object is created automatically when you add `angular.js` to an HTML file using a `script` element.

Listing 5-7. Detecting Functions in the jsdemo.html File in the jsdemo.html File

```html
<!DOCTYPE html>
<html>
<head>
    <title>Example</title>
    <script src="angular.js"></script>
    <script type="text/javascript">

        function printMessage(unknownObject) {
            if (angular.isFunction(unknownObject)) {
                unknownObject();
            } else {
                console.log(unknownObject);
            }
        }

        var variable1 = function sayHello() {
            console.log("Hello!");
        };

        var variable2 = "Goodbye!";

        printMessage(variable1);
        printMessage(variable2);

    </script>
</head>
<body>
    This is a simple example
</body>
</html>
```

This example is made more complex because it doesn't have the context of a real project. I defined a function called printMessage that expects to receive different types of argument. I use the angular.isFunction method to check whether the object I am processing is a function and—if it is—then I invoke the function, like this:

```
...
unknownObject();
...
```

If the isFunction method takes an object as an argument and returns true if the argument is a function and false otherwise. For objects that are not functions, I pass the object to the console.log method.

I created two variables to demonstrate the printMessage function: variable1 is a function, and variable2 is a string. I pass both to the printMessage function; variable1 is identified as a function and invoked, and variable2 is written to the console. When variable1 is invoked, it writes to the console anyway, producing the following results:

```
Hello!
Goodbye!
```

Using Variables and Types

You saw how to define variables in the previous example: You use the var keyword and, optionally, assign a value to the variable in a single statement. Variables that are defined within a function are *local variables* and are available for use only within that function. Variables that are defined directly in the script element are *global variables* and can be accessed anywhere, including other scripts in the same HTML document. Listing 5-8 demonstrates the use of local and global variables.

Listing 5-8. Using Local and Global Variables in the jsdemo.html File

```
<!DOCTYPE HTML>
<html>
    <head>
        <title>Example</title>
        <script src="angular.js"></script>
        <script type="text/javascript">
            var myGlobalVar = "apples";

            function myFunc(name) {
                var myLocalVar = "sunny";
                return ("Hello " + name + ". Today is " + myLocalVar + ".");
            };
            console.log(myFunc("Adam"));
        </script>
        <script type="text/javascript">
            console.log("I like " + myGlobalVar);
        </script>
    </head>
    <body>
        This is a simple example
    </body>
</html>
```

JavaScript is a dynamically typed language. This doesn't mean JavaScript doesn't have types. It just means you don't have to explicitly declare the type of a variable and that you can assign different types to the same variable without any difficulty. JavaScript will determine the type based on the value you assign to a variable and will freely convert between types based on the context in which they are used. The result from Listing 5-8 is as follows:

```
Hello Adam. Today is sunny.
I like apples
```

Using global variables in AngularJS development is frowned upon because it undermines the separation of concerns (which I described in Chapter 3) and makes it harder to perform unit testing (which I describe in Chapter 25). As a rule of thumb, if you have to use a global variable to get two components to talk to one another, then something has gone wrong with the application design.

Using the Primitive Types

JavaScript defines a set of primitive types: string, number, and boolean. This may seem like a short list, but JavaScript manages to fit a lot of flexibility into these three types.

Working with Booleans

The boolean type has two values: `true` and `false`. Listing 5-9 shows both values being used, but this type is most useful when used in conditional statements, such as an `if` statement. There is no console output from this listing.

Listing 5-9. Defining boolean Values in the jsdemo.html File

```html
<!DOCTYPE HTML>
<html>
<head>
    <title>Example</title>
    <script src="angular.js"></script>
    <script type="text/javascript">
        var firstBool = true;
        var secondBool = false;
    </script>
</head>
<body>
    This is a simple example
</body>
</html>
```

Working with Strings

You define `string` values using either the double quote or single quote characters, as shown in Listing 5-10.

Listing 5-10. Defining string Variables in the jsdemo.html File

```html
<!DOCTYPE HTML>
<html>
<head>
    <title>Example</title>
    <script src="angular.js"></script>
    <script type="text/javascript">
        var firstString = "This is a string";
        var secondString = 'And so is this';
    </script>
</head>
<body>
    This is a simple example
</body>
</html>
```

The quote characters you use must match. You can't start a string with a single quote and finish with a double quote, for example. There is no console output for this listing. AngularJS includes three utility methods that make working with `string` values a little easier, as described in Table 5-2.

Table 5-2. *The AngularJS Methods for Working with Strings*

Name	Description
angular.isString(object)	Returns true if the argument is a string, false otherwise
angular.lowercase(string)	Converts the argument to lowercase
angular.uppercase(string)	Converts the argument to uppercase

You can see all three AngularJS string-related methods in Listing 5-11.

Listing 5-11. Using the AngularJS String-Related Methods in the jsdemo.html File

```
<!DOCTYPE html>
<html>
<head>
    <title>Example</title>
    <script src="angular.js"></script>
    <script type="text/javascript">
        console.log(angular.isString("Hello") + " " + angular.isArray(23));
        console.log("I am " + angular.uppercase("shouting"));
        console.log("I am " + angular.lowercase("WhiSpeRing"));
    </script>
</head>
<body>
    This is a simple example
</body>
</html>
```

The angular.isString method is useful when you are dealing with an object whose type you are unsure of. This is one of a number of related methods that AngularJS provides for typing objects, described throughout this chapter. The angular.uppercase and angular.lowercase methods do exactly as you might imagine, and the statements in the listing produce the following output in the JavaScript console:

```
true false
I am SHOUTING
I am whispering
```

Working with Numbers

The number type is used to represent both *integer* and *floating-point* numbers (also known as *real numbers*). Listing 5-12 provides a demonstration.

Listing 5-12. Defining number Values in the jsdemo.html File

```
<!DOCTYPE html>
<html>
<head>
    <title>Example</title>
```

```
    <script src="angular.js"></script>
    <script type="text/javascript">
        var daysInWeek = 7;
        var pi = 3.14;
        var hexValue = 0xFFFF;

        console.log(angular.isNumber(7) + " " + angular.isNumber("Hello"));
    </script>
</head>
<body>
    This is a simple example
</body>
</html>
```

You don't have to specify which kind of number you are using. You just express the value you require, and JavaScript will act accordingly. In the listing, I have defined an integer value, defined a floating-point value, and prefixed a value with 0x to denote a hexadecimal value.

AngularJS supplements the standard JavaScript functionality with the angular.isNumber method, which is passed an object or value and returns true if it is a number and false otherwise. This example produces the following output to the console:

```
true false
```

Creating Objects

There are different ways to create JavaScript objects. Listing 5-13 gives a simple example.

■ **Tip** JavaScript provides support for prototype inheritance, which allows new objects to inherit functionality. This isn't widely used in JavaScript, but I describe it briefly in Chapter 18 because it underpins one of the ways in which AngularJS services can be created.

Listing 5-13. Creating an Object in the jsdemo.html File

```
<!DOCTYPE HTML>
<html>
<head>
    <title>Example</title>
    <script src="angular.js"></script>
    <script type="text/javascript">
        var myData = new Object();
        myData.name = "Adam";
        myData.weather = "sunny";

        console.log("Hello " + myData.name + ". ");
        console.log("Today is " + myData.weather + ".");
```

```
    </script>
</head>
<body>
    This is a simple example
</body>
</html>
```

I create an object by calling new Object(), and I assign the result (the newly created object) to a variable called myData. Once the object is created, I can define properties on the object just by assigning values, like this:

```
...
myData.name = "Adam";
...
```

Prior to this statement, my object doesn't have a property called name. After the statement has executed, the property does exist, and it has been assigned the value Adam. You can read the value of a property by combining the variable name and the property name with a period, like this:

```
...
console.log("Hello " + myData.name + ". ");
...
```

The result from the listing is as follows:

```
Hello Adam.
Today is sunny.
```

Using Object Literals

You can define an object and its properties in a single step using the *object literal* format. Listing 5-14 shows how this is done.

Listing 5-14. Using the Object Literal Format in the jsdemo.html File

```
<!DOCTYPE HTML>
<html>
<head>
    <title>Example</title>
    <script src="angular.js"></script>
    <script type="text/javascript">
        var myData = {
            name: "Adam",
            weather: "sunny"
        };
        console.log("Hello " + myData.name + ". ");
        console.log("Today is " + myData.weather + ".");
    </script>
</head>
<body>
```

```
        This is a simple example
    </body>
    </html>
```

Each property that you want to define is separated from its value using a colon (:), and properties are separated using a comma (,). The effect is the same as in the previous example, and the result from the listing is as follows:

```
Hello Adam.
Today is sunny.
```

Using Functions as Methods

One of the features that I like most about JavaScript is the way you can add functions to objects. A function defined on an object is called a *method*. Listing 5-15 shows how you can add methods in this manner.

Listing 5-15. Adding Methods to an Object in the jsdemo.html File

```html
<!DOCTYPE HTML>
<html>
<head>
    <title>Example</title>
    <script src="angular.js"></script>
    <script type="text/javascript">
        var myData = {
            name: "Adam",
            weather: "sunny",
            printMessages: function() {
                console.log("Hello " + this.name + ". ");
                console.log("Today is " + this.weather + ".");
            }
        };
        myData.printMessages();
    </script>
</head>
<body>
    This is a simple example
</body>
</html>
```

In this example, I have used a function to create a method called printMessages. Notice that to refer to the properties defined by the object, I have to use the this keyword. When a function is used as a method, the function is implicitly passed the object on which the method has been called as an argument through the special variable this. The output from the listing is as follows:

```
Hello Adam.
Today is sunny.
```

Extending Objects

AngularJS makes it easy to copy methods and properties from one object to another through the `angular.extend` method, which I have demonstrated in Listing 5-16.

Listing 5-16. Extending Objects in the jsdemo.html File

```html
<!DOCTYPE html>
<html>
<head>
    <title>Example</title>
    <script src="angular.js"></script>
    <script type="text/javascript">
        var myData = {
            name: "Adam",
            weather: "sunny",
            printMessages: function () {
                console.log("Hello " + this.name + ". ");
                console.log("Today is " + this.weather + ".");
            }
        };

        var myExtendedObject = {
            city: "London"
        };

        angular.extend(myExtendedObject, myData);

        console.log(myExtendedObject.name);
        console.log(myExtendedObject.city);

    </script>
</head>
<body>
    This is a simple example
</body>
</html>
```

In this example I create an object with a `city` property and assign it to the variable called `myExtendedObject`. I then use the `angular.extend` method to copy all of the properties and functions from the `myData` object to `myExtendedObject`. Finally, to demonstrate the mix of original and copied properties, I use the `console.log` method to write out the values of the `name` and `city` properties, producing the following console output:

```
Adam
London
```

■ **Tip** The extend method preserves any properties and methods on the target object. If you want to create a copy of an object without this preservation, then you can use the angular.copy method instead.

Working with Objects

Once you have created objects, you can do a number of things with them. In the following sections, I'll describe the activities that will be useful later in this book.

Detecting Objects

AngularJS provides the angular.isObject method, which returns true if the argument it is called with is an object and false otherwise, as demonstrated in Listing 5-17.

Listing 5-17. Detecting Objects in the jsdemo.html File

```
<!DOCTYPE html>
<html>
<head>
    <title>Example</title>
    <script src="angular.js"></script>
    <script type="text/javascript">
        var myObject = {
            name: "Adam",
            weather: "sunny",
        };

        var myName = "Adam";
        var myNumber = 23;

        console.log("myObject: " + angular.isObject(myObject));
        console.log("myName: " + angular.isObject(myName));
        console.log("myNumber: " + angular.isObject(myNumber));
    </script>
</head>
<body>
    This is a simple example
</body>
</html>
```

I have defined an object, a string, and a number, and I assess them all using the angular.isObject method, producing the following output to the console:

```
myObject: true
myName: false
myNumber: false
```

Reading and Modifying the Property Values

The most obvious thing to do with an object is to read or modify the values assigned to the properties that the object defines. There are two different syntax styles you can use, both of which are shown in Listing 5-18.

Listing 5-18. Reading and Modifying Object Properties in the jsdemo.html File

```html
<!DOCTYPE HTML>
<html>
<head>
    <title>Example</title>
    <script src="angular.js"></script>
    <script type="text/javascript">
        var myData = {
            name: "Adam",
            weather: "sunny",
        };

        myData.name = "Joe";
        myData["weather"] = "raining";

        console.log("Hello " + myData.name + ".");
        console.log("It is " + myData["weather"]);
    </script>
</head>
<body>
    This is a simple example
</body>
</html>
```

The first style is the one that most programmers with be familiar with and that I used in earlier examples. You concatenate the object name and the property name together with a period, like this:

```
...
myData.name = "Joe";
...
```

You can assign a new value to the property by using the equal sign (=) or read the current value by omitting it. The second style is an array-style index, like this:

```
...
myData["weather"] = "raining";
...
```

In this style, you specify the name of the property you want between square braces ([and]). This can be a convenient way to access a property because you can pass the name of the property you are interested as a variable, like this:

```
...
var myData = {
    name: "Adam",
    weather: "sunny",
};
```

```
var propName = "weather";
myData[propName] = "raining";
...
```

This is the basis for how you enumerate the properties of an object, which I describe next. Here is the console output from the listing:

```
Hello Joe.
It is raining
```

Enumerating an Object's Properties

You enumerate the properties that an object has using the for...in statement. Listing 5-19 shows how you can use this statement.

Listing 5-19. Enumerating an Object's Properties in the jsdemo.html File

```
<!DOCTYPE html>
<html>
<head>
    <title>Example</title>
    <script src="angular.js"></script>
    <script type="text/javascript">
        var myData = {
            name: "Adam",
            weather: "sunny",
            printMessages: function () {
                console.log("Hello " + this.name + ". ");
                console.log("Today is " + this.weather + ".");
            }
        };

        for (var prop in myData) {
            console.log("Name: " + prop + " Value: " + myData[prop]);
        }

        console.log("---");

        angular.forEach(myData, function (value, key) {
            console.log("Name: " + key + " Value: " + value);
        });

    </script>
</head>
<body>
    This is a simple example
</body>
</html>
```

The for...in loop is a standard JavaScript feature and performs the statement in the code block for each property in the myData object. The prop variable is assigned the name of the property being processed in each iteration. I use an array-index style to retrieve the value of the property from the object.

AngularJS provides an alternative through the angular.forEach method, which takes the object and a function that will be executed for each property. The function is passed the value of the current property and its name through the value and key parameters. The result is the same as when using the for...in loop, as the following console output shows:

```
Name: name Value: Adam
Name: weather Value: sunny
Name: printMessages Value: function () {
    console.log("Hello " + this.name + ". ");
    console.log("Today is " + this.weather + ".");
}
---
Name: name Value: Adam
Name: weather Value: sunny
Name: printMessages Value: function () {
    console.log("Hello " + this.name + ". ");
    console.log("Today is " + this.weather + ".");
}
```

From the result, you can see that the function I defined as a method on the myData object is also enumerated in both cases. This is as a result of the flexible way that JavaScript handles functions, but it is something to be aware of when you are new to JavaScript.

Adding and Deleting Properties and Methods

You can still define new properties on an object even if it has been defined using the object literal style. Listing 5-20 gives a demonstration. (The listings in this section do not produce any console output.)

Listing 5-20. Adding a New Property to an Object in the jsdemo.html File

```
<!DOCTYPE HTML>
<html>
<head>
    <title>Example</title>
    <script src="angular.js"></script>
    <script type="text/javascript">
        var myData = {
            name: "Adam",
            weather: "sunny",
        };

        myData.dayOfWeek = "Monday";
    </script>
</head>
<body>
    This is a simple example
</body>
</html>
```

Table 5-3. *Useful JavaScript Operators*

Operator	Description
++, --	Pre- or post-increment and decrement
+, -, *, /, %	Addition, subtraction, multiplication, division, remainder
<, <=, >, >=	Less than, less than or equal to, more than, more than or equal to
==, !=	Equality and inequality tests
===, !==	Identity and nonidentity tests
&&, ||	Logical AND and OR (|| is used to coalesce null values)
=	Assignment
+	String concatenation
?:	Three operand conditional statement

Using Conditional Statements

Many of the JavaScript operators are used in conjunction with conditional statements. In this book, I tend to use the if/else and switch statements. Listing 5-24 shows the use of both (which will be familiar if you have worked with pretty much any programming language).

Listing 5-24. Using the if/else and switch Conditional Statements in the jsdemo.html File

```
<!DOCTYPE HTML>
<html>
<head>
    <title>Example</title>
    <script src="angular.js"></script>
    <script type="text/javascript">

        var name = "Adam";

        if (name == "Adam") {
            console.log("Name is Adam");
        } else if (name == "Jacqui") {
            console.log("Name is Jacqui");
        } else {
            console.log("Name is neither Adam or Jacqui");
        }

        switch (name) {
            case "Adam":
                console.log("Name is Adam");
                break;
            case "Jacqui":
                console.log("Name is Jacqui");
                break;
```

```
        default:
            console.log("Name is neither Adam or Jacqui");
            break;
        }
    </script>
</head>
<body>
    This is a simple example
</body>
</html>
```

The results from the listing are as follows:

```
Name is Adam
Name is Adam
```

The Equality Operator vs. the Identity Operator

The equality and identity operators are of particular note. The equality operator will attempt to coerce operands to the same type in order to assess equality. This is a handy feature, as long as you are aware it is happening. Listing 5-25 shows the equality operator in action.

Listing 5-25. Using the Equality Operator in the jsdemo.html File

```
<!DOCTYPE HTML>
<html>
<head>
    <title>Example</title>
    <script src="angular.js"></script>
    <script type="text/javascript">

        var firstVal = 5;
        var secondVal = "5";

        if (firstVal == secondVal) {
            console.log("They are the same");
        } else {
            console.log("They are NOT the same");
        }
    </script>
</head>
<body>
    This is a simple example
</body>
</html>
```

The output from this script is as follows:

```
They are the same
```

JavaScript is converting the two operands into the same type and comparing them. In essence, the equality operator tests that values are the same irrespective of their type. If you want to test to ensure that the values *and* the types are the same, then you need to use the identity operator (===, three equals signs, rather than the two of the equality operator), as shown in Listing 5-26.

Listing 5-26. Using the Identity Operator in the jsdemo.html File

```html
<!DOCTYPE HTML>
<html>
<head>
    <title>Example</title>
    <script src="angular.js"></script>
    <script type="text/javascript">

        var firstVal = 5;
        var secondVal = "5";

        if (firstVal === secondVal) {
            console.log("They are the same");
        } else {
            console.log("They are NOT the same");
        }
    </script>
</head>
<body>
    This is a simple example
</body>
</html>
```

In this example, the identity operator will consider the two variables to be different. This operator doesn't coerce types. The result from this script is as follows:

```
They are NOT the same
```

JavaScript primitives are compared by value, but JavaScript objects are compared by reference. Listing 5-27 shows how JavaScript handles equality and identity tests for objects.

Listing 5-27. Performing Equality and Identity Tests on Objects in the jsdemo.html File

```html
<!DOCTYPE HTML>
<html>
<head>
    <title>Example</title>
    <script src="angular.js"></script>
    <script type="text/javascript">

        var myData1 = {
            name: "Adam",
            weather: "sunny",
        };
```

```
        var myData2 = {
            name: "Adam",
            weather: "sunny",
        };

        var myData3 = myData2;

        var test1 = myData1 == myData2;
        var test2 = myData2 == myData3;
        var test3 = myData1 === myData2;
        var test4 = myData2 === myData3;

        console.log("Test 1: " + test1 + " Test 2: " + test2);
        console.log("Test 3: " + test3 + " Test 4: " + test4);
    </script>
</head>
<body>
    This is a simple example
</body>
</html>
```

The results from this script are as follows:

```
Test 1: false Test 2: true
Test 3: false Test 4: true
```

Listing 5-28 shows the same tests performed on primitives.

Listing 5-28. Performing Equality and Identity Tests on Objects in the jsdemo.html File

```
<!DOCTYPE HTML>
<html>
<head>
    <title>Example</title>
    <script src="angular.js"></script>
    <script type="text/javascript">

        var myData1 = 5;
        var myData2 = "5";
        var myData3 = myData2;

        var test1 = myData1 == myData2;
        var test2 = myData2 == myData3;
        var test3 = myData1 === myData2;
        var test4 = myData2 === myData3;

        console.log("Test 1: " + test1 + " Test 2: " + test2);
        console.log("Test 3: " + test3 + " Test 4: " + test4);
    </script>
</head>
<body>
```

Table 5-4. *Useful Number-to-String Methods*

Method	Description	Returns
toString()	Represents a number in base 10	string
toString(2)toString(8)toString(16)	Represent a number in binary, octal, or hexadecimal notation	string
toFixed(n)	Represents a real number with the n digits after the decimal point	string
toExponential(n)	Represents a number using exponential notation with one digit before the decimal point and n digits after	string
toPrecision(n)	Represents a number with n significant digits, using exponential notation if required	string

Converting Strings to Numbers

The complementary technique is to convert strings to numbers so that you can perform addition rather than concatenation. You can do this with the Number function, as shown in Listing 5-31.

Listing 5-31. Converting Strings to Numbers in the jsdemo.html File

```
<!DOCTYPE HTML>
<html>
<head>
    <title>Example</title>
    <script src="angular.js"></script>
    <script type="text/javascript">

        var firstVal = "5";
        var secondVal = "5";

        var result = Number(firstVal) + Number(secondVal);

        console.log("Result: " + result);
    </script>
</head>
<body>
    This is a simple example
</body>
</html>
```

The output from this script is as follows:

```
Result: 10
```

The Number method is strict in the way that is parses string values, but there are two other functions you can use that are more flexible and will ignore trailing non-number characters. These functions are parseInt and parseFloat. I have described all three methods in Table 5-5.

Table 5-5. *Useful String to Number Methods*

Method	Description
Number(str)	Parses the specified string to create an integer or real value
parseInt(str)	Parses the specified string to create an integer value
parseFloat(str)	Parses the specified string to create an integer or real value

Working with Arrays

JavaScript arrays work like arrays in most other programming languages. Listing 5-32 shows how you can create and populate an array.

Listing 5-32. Creating and Populating an Array in the jsdemo.html File

```
<!DOCTYPE HTML>
<html>
<head>
    <title>Example</title>
    <script src="angular.js"></script>
    <script type="text/javascript">

        var myArray = new Array();
        myArray[0] = 100;
        myArray[1] = "Adam";
        myArray[2] = true;

    </script>
</head>
<body>
    This is a simple example
</body>
</html>
```

I have created a new array by calling new Array(). This creates an empty array, which I assign to the variable myArray. In the subsequent statements, I assign values to various index positions in the array. (There is no console output from this listing.)

There are a couple of things to note in this example. First, I didn't need to declare the number of items in the array when I created it. JavaScript arrays will resize themselves to hold any number of items. The second point is that I didn't have to declare the data types that the array will hold. Any JavaScript array can hold any mix of data types. In the example, I have assigned three items to the array: a number, a string, and a boolean.

Using an Array Literal

The array literal style lets you create and populate an array in a single statement, as shown in Listing 5-33.

Listing 5-33. Using the Array Literal Style in the jsdemo.html File

```
<!DOCTYPE HTML>
<html>
<head>
    <title>Example</title>
    <script src="angular.js"></script>
    <script type="text/javascript">

    var myArray = [100, "Adam", true];

    </script>
</head>
<body>
    This is a simple example
</body>
</html>
```

In this example, I specified that the myArray variable should be assigned a new array by specifying the items I wanted in the array between square brackets ([and]). (There is no console output from this listing.)

Detecting an Array

AngularJS provides the angular.isArray method, which returns true if the argument it is called with is an array, as illustrated by Listing 5-34.

Listing 5-34. Detecting Arrays in the jsdemo.html File

```
<!DOCTYPE html>
<html>
<head>
    <title>Example</title>
    <script src="angular.js"></script>
    <script type="text/javascript">

        console.log(angular.isArray([100, "Adam", true]));
        console.log(angular.isArray("Adam"));
        console.log(angular.isArray(23));

    </script>
</head>
<body>
    This is a simple example
</body>
</html>
```

This example produces the following console output:

```
true
False
False
```

Reading and Modifying the Contents of an Array

You read the value at a given index using square braces ([and]), placing the index you require between the braces, as shown in Listing 5-35.

Listing 5-35. Reading the Data from an Array Index in the jsdemo.html File

```
<!DOCTYPE HTML>
<html>
<head>
    <title>Example</title>
    <script src="angular.js"></script>
    <script type="text/javascript">
        var myArray = [100, "Adam", true];
        console.log("Index 0: " + myArray[0]);
    </script>
</head>
<body>
    This is a simple example
</body>
</html>
```

You can modify the data held in any position in a JavaScript array simply by assigning a new value to the index. Just as with regular variables, you can switch the data type at an index without any problems. The output from the listing is as follows:

```
Index 0: 100
```

Listing 5-36 demonstrates modifying the contents of an array.

Listing 5-36. Modifying the Contents of an Array in the jsdemo.html File

```
<!DOCTYPE HTML>
<html>
<head>
    <title>Example</title>
    <script src="angular.js"></script>
    <script type="text/javascript">
        var myArray = [100, "Adam", true];
        myArray[0] = "Tuesday";
        console.log("Index 0: " + myArray[0]);
    </script>
</head>
<body>
    This is a simple example
</body>
</html>
```

In this example, I have assigned a `string` to position 0 in the array, a position that was previously held by a number and produces this output:

```
Index 0: Tuesday
```

Enumerating the Contents of an Array

You enumerate the content of an array using a `for` loop or the AngularJS `angular.forEach` method, both of which are demonstrated in Listing 5-37.

Listing 5-37. Enumerating the Contents of an Array in the jsdemo.html File

```html
<!DOCTYPE html>
<html>
<head>
    <title>Example</title>
    <script src="angular.js"></script>
    <script type="text/javascript">
        var myArray = [100, "Adam", true];

        for (var i = 0; i < myArray.length; i++) {
            console.log("Index " + i + ": " + myArray[i]);
        }

        console.log("---");

        angular.forEach(myArray, function (value, key) {
            console.log(key + ": " + value);
        });

    </script>
</head>
<body>
    This is a simple example
</body>
</html>
```

The JavaScript `for` loop works just the same way as loops in many other languages. You determine how many elements there are in the array by using the `length` property. The `angular.forEach` method doesn't require array bounds to work but doesn't provide the index of the currently array item. The output from the listing is as follows:

```
Index 0: 100
Index 1: Adam
Index 2: true
---
0: 100
1: Adam
2: true
```

Using the Built-in Array Methods

The JavaScript `Array` object defines a number of methods that you can use to work with arrays. Table 5-6 describes the most useful of these methods.

Table 5-6. *Useful Array Methods*

Method	Description	Returns
concat(otherArray)	Concatenates the contents of the array with the array specified by the argument. Multiple arrays can be specified.	Array
join(separator)	Joins all of the elements in the array to form a string. The argument specifies the character used to delimit the items.	string
pop()	Treats an array like a stack and removes and returns the last item in the array.	object
push(item)	Treats an array like a stack and appends the specified item to the array.	void
reverse()	Reverses the order of the items in the array.	Array
shift()	Like pop, but operates on the first element in the array.	object
slice(start,end)	Returns a section of the array.	Array
sort()	Sorts the items in the array.	Array
splice(index, count)	Removes count items from the array, starting at the specified index.	Array
unshift(item)	Like push, but inserts the new element at the start of the array.	void

Comparing undefined and null Values

JavaScript defines a couple of special values that you need to be careful with when you compare them: undefined and null. The undefined value is returned when you read a variable that hasn't had a value assigned to it or try to read an object property that doesn't exist. Listing 5-38 shows how undefined is used in JavaScript.

Listing 5-38. The undefined Special Value in the jsdemo.html File

```
<!DOCTYPE HTML>
<html>
<head>
    <title>Example</title>
    <script src="angular.js"></script>
    <script type="text/javascript">
        var myData = {
            name: "Adam",
            weather: "sunny",
        };
        console.log("Prop: " + myData.doesntexist);
    </script>
</head>
<body>
    This is a simple example
</body>
</html>
```

The output from this listing is as follows:

```
Prop: undefined
```

JavaScript is unusual in that it *also* defines null, another special value. The null value is slightly different from undefined. The undefined value is returned when no value is defined, and null is used when you want to indicate that you have assigned a value but that value is not a valid object, string, number, or boolean; that is, you have defined a value of *no value*. To help clarify this, Listing 5-39 shows the transition from undefined to null.

Listing 5-39. Using undefined and null in the jsdemo.html File

```
<!DOCTYPE HTML>
<html>
<head>
    <title>Example</title>
    <script src="angular.js"></script>
    <script type="text/javascript">

        var myData = {
            name: "Adam",
        };

        console.log("Var: " + myData.weather);
        console.log("Prop: " + ("weather" in myData));

        myData.weather = "sunny";
        console.log("Var: " + myData.weather);
        console.log("Prop: " + ("weather" in myData));

        myData.weather = null;
        console.log("Var: " + myData.weather);
        console.log("Prop: " + ("weather" in myData));

    </script>
</head>
<body>
    This is a simple example
</body>
</html>
```

I create an object and then try to read the value of the weather property, which is not defined:

```
...
console.log("Var: " + myData.weather);
console.log("Prop: " + ("weather" in myData));
...
```

There is no weather property, so the value returned by calling myData.weather is undefined, and using the in keyword to determine whether the object contains the property returns false. The output from these two statements is as follows:

```
Var: undefined
Prop: false
```

Next, I assign a value to the weather property, which has the effect of adding the property to the object:

```
...
myData.weather = "sunny";
console.log("Var: " + myData.weather);
console.log("Prop: " + ("weather" in myData));
...
```

I read the value of the property and check to see whether the property exists in the object again. As you might expect, the object *does* define the property, and its value is sunny:

```
Var: sunny
Prop: true
```

Now I set the value of the property to null, like this:

```
...
myData.weather = null;
...
```

This has a specific effect. The property is still defined by the object, but I have indicated it doesn't contain a value. When I perform my checks again, I get the following results:

```
Var: null
Prop: true
```

This distinction is important when it comes to comparing undefined and null values because null is an object and undefined is a type in its own right.

Checking for null or undefined

If you want to check to see whether a property is null or undefined (and you don't care which), then you can simply use an if statement and the negation operator (!), as shown in Listing 5-40.

Listing 5-40. Checking to See Whether a Property Is null or undefined in the jsdemo.html File

```
<!DOCTYPE HTML>
<html>
<head>
    <title>Example</title>
    <script src="angular.js"></script>
    <script type="text/javascript">
```

```
        var myData = {
            name: "Adam",
            city: null
        };

        if (!myData.name) {
            console.log("name IS null or undefined");
        } else {
            console.log("name is NOT null or undefined");
        }

        if (!myData.city) {
            console.log("city IS null or undefined");
        } else {
            console.log("city is NOT null or undefined");
        }

    </script>
</head>
<body>
    This is a simple example
</body>
</html>
```

This technique relies on the type coercion that JavaScript performs such that the values you are checking are treated as boolean values. If a variable or property is null or undefined, then the coerced boolean value is false. The listing produces this output:

```
name is NOT null or undefined
city IS null or undefined
```

■ **Tip** You can use the || operator to coalesce null values and can see this technique demonstrated in Chapter 9.

You can also use the AngularJS angular.isDefined and angular.isUndefined methods, as shown in Listing 5-41.

Listing 5-41. Using the AngularJS Methods for Testing Defined Values in the jsdemo.html File

```
<!DOCTYPE html>
<html>
<head>
    <title>Example</title>
    <script src="angular.js"></script>
    <script type="text/javascript">
```

```
    var myData = {
        name: "Adam",
        city: null
    };


    console.log("name: " + angular.isDefined(myData.name));
    console.log("city: " + angular.isDefined(myData.city));
    console.log("country: " + angular.isDefined(myData.country));

    </script>
</head>
<body>
    This is a simple example
</body>
</html>
```

These methods check only whether a value has been defined, not whether it is null, and this can be useful for differentiating between null and undefined values. In the listing I have used the angular.isDefined method to check a property that has been defined and assigned a value, a property that has been defined but is null, and an undefined value. The example produces the following console output:

```
name: true
city: true
country: false
```

Working with Promises

Promises are the JavaScript way of representing an item of work that will be performed asynchronously and that will be completed at some point in the future. The most common way to encounter promises is by making Ajax requests; the browser makes the HTTP request behind the scenes and uses a promise to notify your application when the request has completed. In Listing 5-42, I have created a minimal AngularJS application that makes an Ajax request.

■ **Note** This example relies on the todo.json file that I created at the start of the chapter.

Listing 5-42. Creating a Minimal AngularJS Application in the jsdemo.html File

```
<!DOCTYPE html>
<html ng-app="demo">
<head>
    <title>Example</title>
    <script src="angular.js"></script>
    <link href="bootstrap.css" rel="stylesheet" />
    <link href="bootstrap-theme.css" rel="stylesheet" />
    <script type="text/javascript">
```

```
        var myApp = angular.module("demo", []);

        myApp.controller("demoCtrl", function ($scope, $http) {
            var promise = $http.get("todo.json");
            promise.success(function (data) {
                $scope.todos = data;
            });
        });

    </script>
</head>
<body ng-controller="demoCtrl">
    <div class="panel">
        <h1>To Do</h1>
        <table class="table">
            <tr><td>Action</td><td>Done</td></tr>
            <tr ng-repeat="item in todos">
                <td>{{item.action}}</td>
                <td>{{item.done}}</td>
            </tr>
        </table>
    </div>
</body>
</html>
```

The AngularJS features that I have used in this listing will be familiar from Chapter 2. I have created am AngularJS module and given it a controller called demoCtrl. The controller uses the $scope object to provide data to a view that populates a table using data bindings and the ng-repeat directive. You can see how the browser displays this example in Figure 5-3.

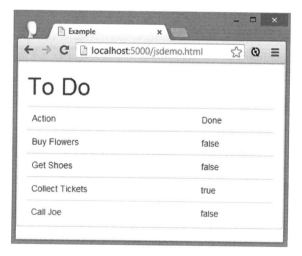

Figure 5-3. *A simple AngularJS app*

JAVASCRIPT AND ASYNCHRONOUS PROGRAMMING

If you have come to JavaScript from a language like C# or Java, you may be surprised by the lack of keywords to control asynchronous execution of code, such as `lock` or `synchronized`. JavaScript does not support these kinds of flow control or provide support for setting priorities. This makes a simpler developer experience, albeit one in which it is easy to create unintended side effects. I'll return to this topic in Chapter 20, when I describe the AngularJS support for creating custom promises.

The module, controller, and view are all AngularJS plumbing that I need to set up to show you how promises work. The key part of the listing is here:

```
...
var promise = $http.get("todo.json");
promise.success(function (data) {
    $scope.todos = data;
});
...
```

The $http service (which I describe in Chapter 20) is used for making Ajax requests, and the get method takes the URL of the file that you want to retrieve from the server. (By just specifying the file name, I am telling the browser that the file I want is located alongside the currently displayed HTML document.)

The Ajax request is performed asynchronously, and the browser continues to run my simple application while the request is being made. The $http.get method returns a promise object that I can use to receive notifications about the Ajax request. In this example, I used the success method to register a callback function that will be invoked when the request has been completed. The callback function receives the data retrieved from the server, which I use to assign a property to the $scope, and this, in turn, gives the ng-repeat directive the content to populate the table with to-do items. The success method is one of three that promise objects define, as described in Table 5-7.

Table 5-7. The Methods Defined by a Promise Object

Name	Description
error(callback)	Specifies a callback function that is invoked if the work represented by the Promise cannot be completed
success(callback)	Specifies a callback function that is invoked when the work represented by the Promise is completed
then(success, err)	Specifies callbacks that will be invoked if the Promise succeeds or fails

All three methods take functions as arguments and invoke them based on the outcome of the promise. The success callback function is passed the data retrieved from the server, and the error callback receives details of the problem that was encountered.

■ **Tip** Another way to think about the methods defined by a promise is that they are like events. In the same way that a callback function can be invoked when a user clicks a button and triggers an event, a promise will invoke a callback function when work has been completed.

All three promise methods return other promise objects, allowing asynchronous tasks to be chained together in sequence. Listing 5-43 contains a simple example.

Listing 5-43. Chaining Promises in the jsdemo.html File

```
<!DOCTYPE html>
<html ng-app="demo">
<head>
    <title>Example</title>
    <script src="angular.js"></script>
    <link href="bootstrap.css" rel="stylesheet" />
    <link href="bootstrap-theme.css" rel="stylesheet" />
    <script type="text/javascript">

        var myApp = angular.module("demo", []);

        myApp.controller("demoCtrl", function ($scope, $http) {
            $http.get("todo.json").then(function (response) {
                $scope.todos = response.data;
            }, function () {
                $scope.todos = [{action: "Error"}];
            }).then(function () {
                $scope.todos.push({action: "Request Complete"});
            });
        });

    </script>
</head>
<body ng-controller="demoCtrl">
    <div class="panel">
        <h1>To Do</h1>
        <table class="table">
            <tr><td>Action</td><td>Done</td></tr>
            <tr ng-repeat="item in todos">
                <td>{{item.action}}</td>
                <td>{{item.done}}</td>
            </tr>
        </table>
    </div>
</body>
</html>
```

Here I have used the then method twice, the first time to handle the response from the call to the $http.get method and again to register a function that will be invoked afterward. It can be hard to read this kind of code, so I'll use highlighting to show the sequence. First, I call the get method to create the Ajax request:

```
...
$http.get("todo.json").then(function (response) {
    $scope.todos = response.data;
}, function () {
    $scope.todos = [{action: "Error"}];
```

```
}).then(function () {
    $scope.todos.push({action: "Request Complete"});
});
...
```

I used the then method to provide functions that will be called when the Ajax request completes. The first function is called when the request succeeds and the second when the request fails:

```
...
$http.get("todo.json").then(function (response) {
    $scope.todos = response.data;
}, function () {
    $scope.todos = [{action: "Error"}];
}).then(function () {
    $scope.todos.push({action: "Request Complete"});
});
...
```

The promise guarantees that one of these functions will be invoked but not until the Ajax request has completed or failed. I use the then method again to add a further function:

```
...
$http.get("todo.json").then(function (response) {
    $scope.todos = response.data;
}, function () {
    $scope.todos = [{action: "Error"}];
}).then(function () {
    $scope.todos.push({action: "Request Complete"});
});
...
```

This time I have passed only one function to the then method, meaning that I don't want a notification if there is a problem. This final function adds an item to the data model irrespective of the preceding function that was invoked. You can see the effect of a successful Ajax request in Figure 5-4.

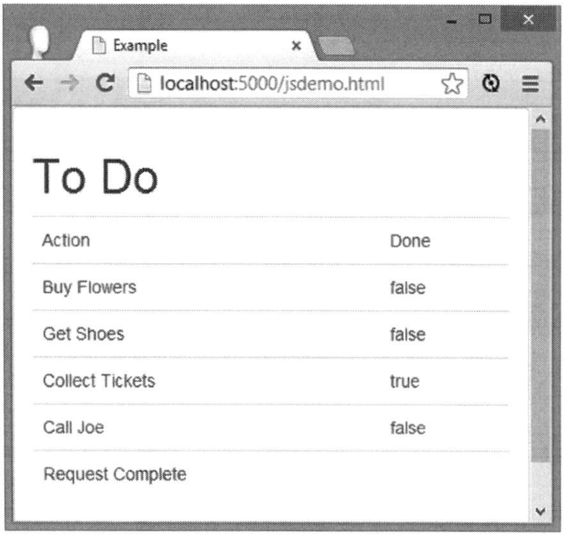

Figure 5-4. *Chaining promises*

■ **Tip**   Don't worry if chaining doesn't make sense at the moment. You'll quickly get the idea when you start to use promises in your own projects, and you'll see more promise examples in Chapter 20 (when I describe AngularJS Ajax support) and in Chapter 21 (when I describe RESTful web services).

Working with JSON

The JavaScript Object Notation (JSON) has become the de facto data format for web apps. JSON is simple and easy to work with in JavaScript code, which is why it has become so popular. JSON supports some basic data types, which neatly align with those of JavaScript: Number, String, Boolean, Array, Object, and the special type null.

As a reminder, here is the content of the todo.json file, which contains a simple JSON string:

```
[{ "action": "Buy Flowers", "done": false },
 { "action": "Get Shoes", "done": false },
 { "action": "Collect Tickets", "done": true },
 { "action": "Call Joe", "done": false }]
```

The JSON data looks similar to the literal formats used to declare arrays and objects in JavaScript. The only difference is that the property names of the objects are enclosed in quotes.

■ **Tip** JSON is easy to work with, but you can still get into trouble because JSON libraries encode and decode JSON slightly differently—a problem that can manifest itself when the web app and the servers that support it are written in different programming languages. A common problem is dates, which are hard to work with at the best of times because of all of the regional calendars and notational forms. JSON doesn't have a native definition for dates, and that gives JSON libraries the kind of latitude that leads to different encoding styles. It is important to test your JSON data thoroughly to ensure that the data is encoded consistently throughout your end-to-end application.

AngularJS makes working with JSON simple. When you request JSON data via Ajax, the response will be parsed automatically into JavaScript objects and passed to the success function, as demonstrated in the previous example when I used the `$http.get` method to get a JSON file from the web server.

AngularJS supplements this with two methods that explicitly encode and decode JSON: `angular.fromJson` and `angular.toJson`. You can see both demonstrated in Listing 5-44.

Listing 5-44. Encoding and Decoding JSON Data in the jsdemo.html File

```
<!DOCTYPE html>
<html ng-app="demo">
<head>
    <title>Example</title>
    <script src="angular.js"></script>
    <link href="bootstrap.css" rel="stylesheet" />
    <link href="bootstrap-theme.css" rel="stylesheet" />
    <script type="text/javascript">

        var myApp = angular.module("demo", []);

        myApp.controller("demoCtrl", function ($scope, $http) {
            $http.get("todo.json").success(function (data) {
                var jsonString = angular.toJson(data);
                console.log(jsonString);
                $scope.todos = angular.fromJson(jsonString);
            });
        });

    </script>
</head>
<body ng-controller="demoCtrl">
    <div class="panel">
        <h1>To Do</h1>
        <table class="table">
            <tr><td>Action</td><td>Done</td></tr>
            <tr ng-repeat="item in todos">
                <td>{{item.action}}</td>
                <td>{{item.done}}</td>
            </tr>
        </table>
    </div>
</body>
</html>
```

In this example, I operate on the data object that is passed to the promise success function. This was received as JSON data from the web server and automatically parsed into a JavaScript array by AngularJS. I then call the angular.toJson method to encode the array as JSON again and write it to the console. Finally, I take the JSON that I have created and call the angular.fromJson method to create another JavaScript object, which I use to populate the data model in the AngularJS controller and populate the table element via the ng-repeat directive.

■ **Tip**   Many of the most common AngularJS features that need JSON data will encode and decode data automatically, so you won't often need to use these methods.

Summary

In this chapter I provided a brief primer on the JavaScript language and the utility methods that AngularJS provides to supplement the core language features. I also introduced promises and the AngularJS support for JSON, both of which are essential for working with Ajax and implementing the single-page application model that I described in Chapter 3. I am not able to provide a complete description of JavaScript in this book, but the features I have described here are the ones that I use most often in the examples in this book and should be enough for you to follow along as I describe different aspects of AngularJS development. In Chapter 6, I provide a more in-depth example of an AngularJS web app as I start to build a more realistic development example.

CHAPTER 6

■ ■ ■

SportsStore: A Real Application

In the previous chapters, I built quick and simple AngularJS applications. Small and focused examples allow me to demonstrate specific AngularJS features, but they can lack context. To help overcome this problem, I am going to create a simple but realistic e-commerce application.

My application, called SportsStore, will follow the classic approach taken by online stores everywhere. I will create an online product catalog that customers can browse by category and page, a shopping cart where users can add and remove products, and a checkout where customers can enter their shipping details and place their orders. I will also create an administration area that includes create, read, update, and delete (CRUD) facilities for managing the catalog—and I will protect it so that only logged-in administrators can make changes.

My goal in this chapter and those that follow is to give you a sense of what real AngularJS development is like by creating as realistic an example as possible. I want to focus on AngularJS, of course, so I have simplified the integration with external systems, such as the data store, and have omitted others entirely, such as payment processing.

The SportsStore example is one that I use in a few of my books, not least because it demonstrates the ways in which different frameworks, languages, and development styles can be used to achieve the same result. You don't need to have read any of my other books to follow this chapter, but you will find the contrasts interesting if you already own my *Pro ASP.NET* and *Pro ASP.NET MVC* books.

The AngularJS features that I use in the SportsStore application are covered in depth in later chapters. Rather than duplicate everything here, I tell you just enough to make sense for the example application and refer you to other chapters for in-depth information. You can either read the SportsStore chapters end to end and get a sense of how AngularJS works or jump to and from the details chapter to get into the depth. Either way, don't expect to understand everything right away—AngularJS has a lot of moving parts and the SportsStore application is intended to show you how they fit together without diving too deeply into the details that I spend the rest of the book covering.

UNIT TESTING

One of the reasons that I use the SportsStore application in different books is because it makes it easy to introduce unit testing early. AngularJS provides some excellent support for unit testing, but I don't describe it until the final chapter in the book. That's because you really need to understand how AngularJS works before you can write comprehensive unit tests, and I don't want to include all of the required information and then duplicate it throughout the rest of the book.

That's not to say that unit testing with AngularJS is difficult or that you need to be an expert in AngularJS to write a unit test. Rather, the features that make unit testing simple depend on some key concepts that I don't describe until Parts 2 and 3. You can skip ahead to Chapter 25 now if you want to get an early start on unit testing, but my advice is to read the book in sequence so that you understand the foundation on which the unit test features are built.

Getting Started

There is some basic preparation required before I start on the application. The instructions in the following sections install some optional AngularJS features to set up the server that will deliver the data.

Preparing the Data

The first step is to create a new Deployd application. You will need to create a directory to hold the files that are generated (it doesn't matter where you create the directory). I called my directory deployd, and I put it at the same level as the angularjs folder that will hold the application files.

■ **Note**   I asked you to download and install Deployd in Chapter 1. If you have not done so, then refer to that chapter for details of all the software that will be required.

Change to the new directory and enter the following at the command line:

```
dpd create sportsstore
```

To start the new server, enter the following commands:

```
dpd -p 5500 sportsstore\app.dpd
dashboard
```

■ **Tip**   This is the Windows style of file separator. You'll need to use sportsstore/app.dpd on other platforms.

The Deployd dashboard, which is used to configure the service, will be displayed in the browser, as shown in Figure 6-1.

Figure 6-1. The initial state of the Deployd dashboard

Creating the Data Structure

The next step is to tell Deployd about the structure of the data it will be storing. Click the large green button in the dashboard and select Collection from the pop-up menu. Set the name of the collection to /products, as shown in Figure 6-2.

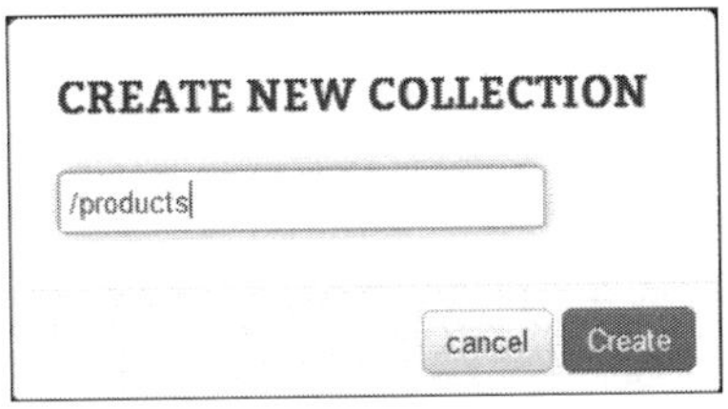

Figure 6-2. *Creating the products collection*

Deployd will prompt you to create the properties of the JSON objects it will store in the collection. Enter the properties listed in Table 6-1.

Table 6-1. *The Properties Required for the Products Collection*

Name	Type	Required?
name	string	Yes
description	string	Yes
category	string	Yes
price	number	Yes

When you have finished adding the properties, the dashboard should match Figure 6-3. Make sure you have entered the property names correctly and have selected the right type for each property.

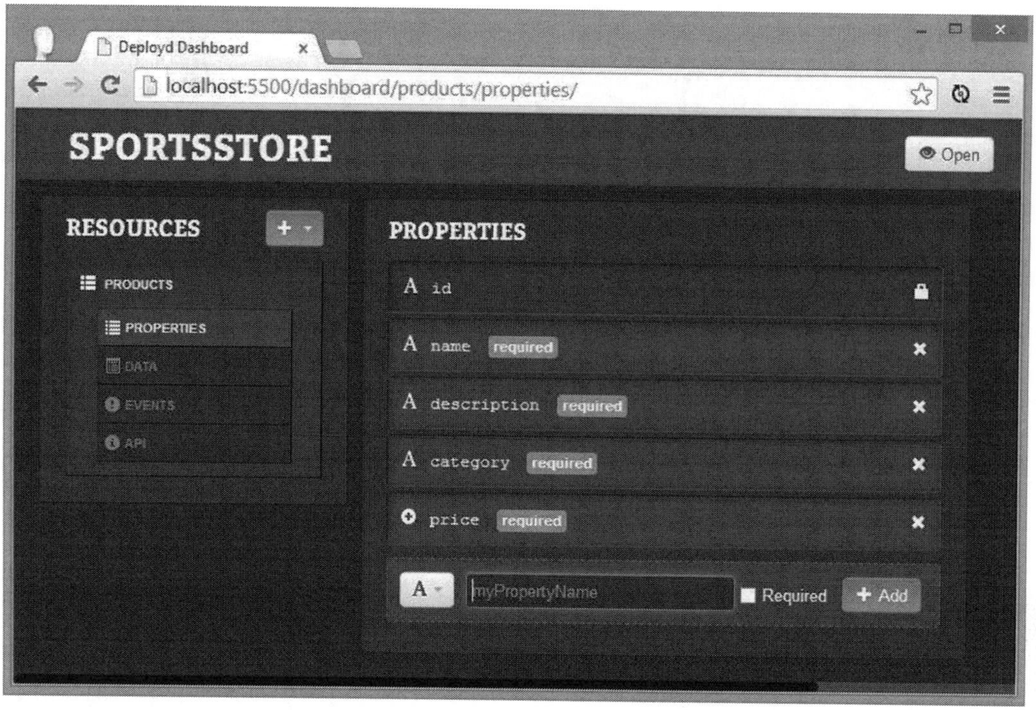

Figure 6-3. *The set of properties in the Deployd dashboard*

■ **Tip**   Notice that Deployd has added an `id` property. This will be used to uniquely identify objects in the database. Deployd will assign unique values to the `id` property automatically, and I'll be relying on these values when I implement the administration functions in Chapter 8.

Adding the Data

Now that I have defined the structure of the objects that Deployd will store, I can add details of the products that the SportsStore will offer to customers. Click the Data link, which is on the left side of the dashboard. This will display an editor grid into which you can enter values for object properties and so populate the database.

Use the grid to create the data items I have described in Table 6-2. Don't worry about assigning values for the `id` property because Deployd will generate them automatically as each object is stored.

Table 6-2. *The Data for the Products Table*

Name	Description	Category	Price
Kayak	A boat for one person	Watersports	275
Lifejacket	Protective and fashionable	Watersports	48.95
Soccer Ball	FIFA-approved size and weight	Soccer	19.5
Corner Flags	Give your playing field a professional touch	Soccer	34.95

(continued)

Table 6-2. (*continued*)

Name	Description	Category	Price
Stadium	Flat-packed 35,000-seat stadium	Soccer	79500.00
Thinking Cap	Improve your brain efficiency by 75%	Chess	16
Unsteady Chair	Secretly give your opponent a disadvantage	Chess	29.95
Human Chess Board	A fun game for the family	Chess	75
Bling-Bling King	Gold-plated, diamond-studded King	Chess	1200

■ **Tip** Deployd displays an odd behavior when entering values with a decimal point into `number` fields. The first period you enter is, for some reason, deleted, and you need to enter another period to enter a decimal value.

When you have finished entering the data, the Deployd dashboard should look like Figure 6-4.

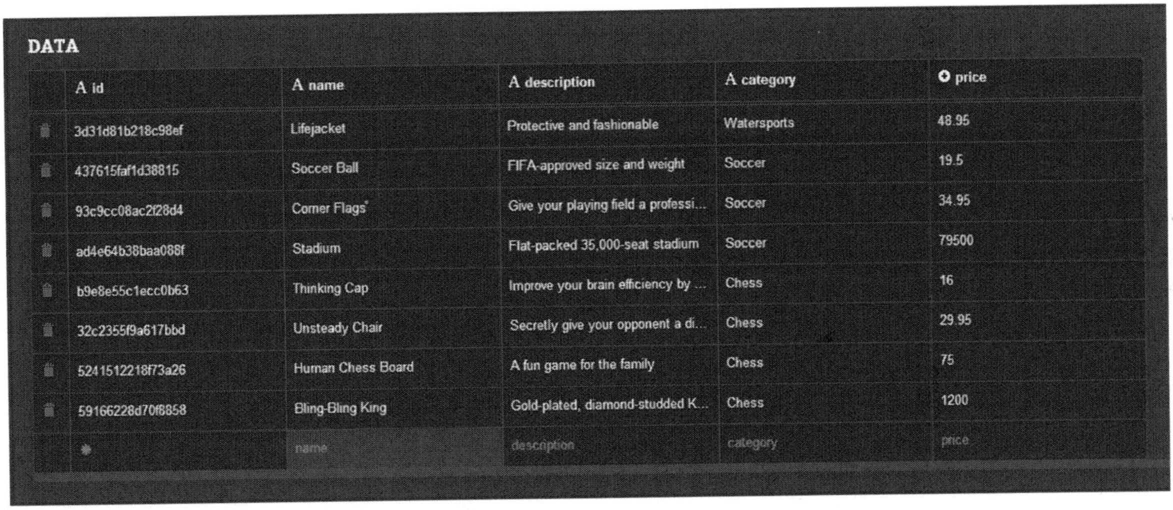

Figure 6-4. *Entering the product data into the SportsStore dashboard*

Testing the Data Service

To test that Deployd is correctly configured and working, open a browser window and navigate to the following URL:

```
http://localhost:5500/products
```

This URL assumes you installed Deployd on the local machine and that you didn't change the port number when starting Deployd. The /products URL is interpreted by Deployd as a request for the contents of the /products collection, expressed as a JSON string. Some browsers, such as Google Chrome, will display the JSON response directly in the browser window, but others, such as Microsoft Internet Explorer, require you to download the JSON to a file. Either way, you should see the following data, which I have formatted to help clarity, although the value of the id fields will be different:

```
[{"category":"Watersports","description":"A boat for one person","name":"Kayak",
    "price":275,"id":"05af70919155f8fc"},
 {"category":"Watersports", "description":"Protective and fashionable",
    "name":"Lifejacket","price":48.95,"id":"3d31d81b218c98ef"},
 {"category":"Soccer","description":"FIFA-approved size and weight",
    "name":"Soccer Ball","price":19.5,"id":"437615faf1d38815"},
 {"category":"Soccer","description":"Give your playing field a professional touch",
    "name":"Corner Flags","price":34.95,"id":"93c9cc08ac2f28d4"},
 {"category":"Soccer","description":"Flat-packed 35,000-seat stadium",
    "name":"Stadium","price":79500,"id":"ad4e64b38baa088f"},
 {"category":"Chess","description":"Improve your brain efficiency by 75%",
    "name":"Thinking Cap","price":16,"id":"b9e8e55c1ecc0b63"},
 {"category":"Chess","description":"Secretly give your opponent a disadvantage",
    "name":"Unsteady Chair","price":29.95,"id":"32c2355f9a617bbd"},
 {"category":"Chess","description":"A fun game for the family",
    "name":"Human Chess Board","price":75,"id":"5241512218f73a26"},
 {"category":"Chess","description":"Gold-plated, diamond-studded King",
    "name":"Bling-Bling King","price":1200,"id":"59166228d70f8858"}]
```

Preparing the Application

Before I start writing the application, I need to prepare the angularjs folder by creating a directory structure for the files that will make up the application and downloading the AngularJS and Bootstrap files that I will need.

Creating the Directory Structure

You can arrange the files that make up an AngularJS application in any way you like. You can even use predefined templates with some client-side development tools, but I am going to keep things simple and follow the basic layout that I use for most AngularJS projects. This isn't always the layout that I finish with, because I tend to move and regroup files as a project grows in complexity, but this is where I usually start. Create the directories described in Table 6-3 within the angularjs folder.

Table 6-3. *The Folders Required for the SportsStore Application*

Name	Description
components	Contains self-contained custom AngularJS components.
controllers	Contains the application's controllers. I describe controllers in Chapter 13.
filters	Contains custom *filters*. I describe filters in depth in Chapter 14.
ngmodules	Contains optional AngularJS modules. I describe the optional modules throughout this book and will give references for each of them as I apply them to the SportsStore application.
views	Contains the partial views for the SportsStore application. Views contain a mix of directives and filters, which I described in Chapters 10–17.

Installing the AngularJS and Bootstrap Files

My preference, without any real foundation in reason, is to put the main AngularJS JavaScript file and the Bootstrap CSS files into the main angularjs directory and put the optional AngularJS modules that I use into the ngmodules folder. I can't explain why I do this, but it has become a habit. Following the instructions in Chapter 1, copy the files I listed in Table 6-4 into the angularjs folder.

Table 6-4. *The Files to Be Installed in the angularjs Folder*

Name	Description
angular.js	The main AngularJS functionality
bootstrap.css	The Bootstrap CSS styles
bootstrap-theme.css	The default theme for the Bootstrap CSS files

Not all AngularJS functionality comes in the angular.js file. For the SportsStore application I will require some additional features that are available in optional modules. These are the files that I keep in the ngmodules folder. Following the instructions in Chapter 1, download the files described in Table 6-5 and place them in the angularjs/ngmodules folder.

Table 6-5. *The Optional Module Files to Be Installed in the ngmodules Folder*

Name	Description
angular-route.js	Adds support for URL routing. See Chapter 7 for URL routing in the SportsStore application, and see Chapter 22 for full details of this module.
angular-resource.js	Adds support for working with RESTful APIs. See Chapter 8 for REST in the SportsStore application, and see Chapter 21 for full details of this module.

Building the Basic Outline

I like to start a new AngularJS application by mocking up the basic structure with placeholder content and then filling in each part in turn. The basic layout of the SportsStore application is the classic two-column layout that you will find in many web stores—a set of categories in the first column that is used to filter the set of products displayed in the second column. Figure 6-5 shows the effect I am aiming for.

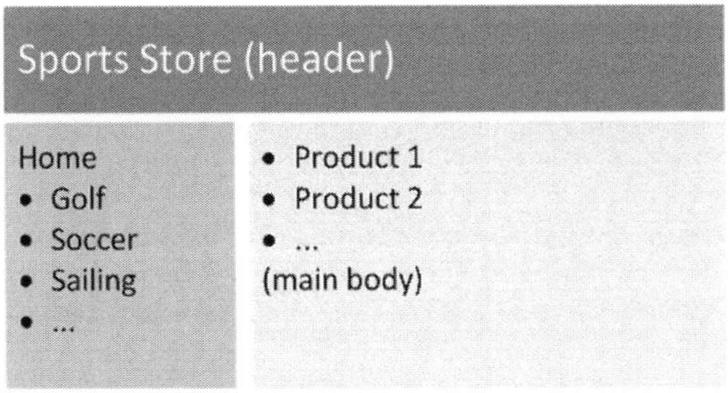

Figure 6-5. *The two-column SportsStore layout*

I'll add some additional features as I build the application, but the figure shows the initial functionality I will create. The first step is to create the top-level HTML file that will contain the structural markup and the script and link elements for the JavaScript and CSS files I will be using. Listing 6-1 shows the contents of the app.html file, which I created in the angularjs folder.

Listing 6-1. The Contents of the app.html File

```
<!DOCTYPE html>
<html ng-app="sportsStore">
<head>
    <title>SportsStore</title>
    <script src="angular.js"></script>
    <link href="bootstrap.css" rel="stylesheet" />
    <link href="bootstrap-theme.css" rel="stylesheet" />
    <script>
        angular.module("sportsStore", []);
    </script>
</head>
<body>
    <div class="navbar navbar-inverse">
        <a class="navbar-brand" href="#">SPORTS STORE</a>
    </div>
    <div class="panel panel-default row">
        <div class="col-xs-3">
            Categories go here
        </div>
        <div class="col-xs-8">
            Products go here
        </div>
    </div>
</body>
</html>
```

This file contains HTML elements that define the basic layout, styled using Bootstrap into a table structure, as described in Chapter 4. There are two AngularJS-specific aspects to this file. The first is the script element in which I call the angular.module method, as follows:

```
...
<script>
    angular.module("sportsStore", []);
</script>
...
```

Modules are the top-level building block in an AngularJS application, and this method call creates a new module called sportsStore. I don't do anything with the module other than create it at the moment, but I'll be using it to define functionality for the application later.

The second aspect is that I have applied the ng-app directive to the html element, like this:

```
...
<html ng-app="sportsStore">
...
```

The ng-app directive makes the functionality defined within the sportsStore module available within the HTML. I like to apply the ng-app directive to the html element, but you can be more specific, and a common alternative is to apply it to the body element instead.

Despite creating and applying an AngularJS module, the contents app.html file are simple and merely lay out the basic structure of the application, styled using Bootstrap. You can see how the browser displays the app.html file in Figure 6-6.

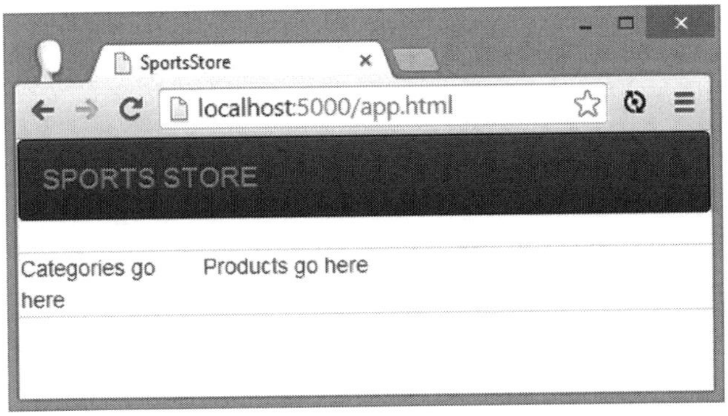

Figure 6-6. *The initial layout of the SportsStore application*

■ **Tip** To request the app.html file, I asked the browser to display the URL http://localhost:5000/app.html. I am using the Node.js web server that I introduced in Chapter 1, running on port 5000 of my local machine. This is separate from the Deployd server I created at the start of this chapter, which I have set up to run on port 5500.

It doesn't look like much at the moment, but the application will start to take shape pretty quickly once the plumbing is in place and I start using AngularJS to build the application functionality.

Displaying the (Fake) Product Data

I am going to start by adding support for displaying the product data. I want to focus on one area of functionality at a time, so I am going to define fake local data initially, which I will then replace with data obtained from the Deployd server in Chapter 7.

Creating the Controller

I need to start with a controller, which, as I explained in Chapter 3, defines the logic and data required to support a view on its scope. The controller I am going to create will be used throughout the application—something I refer to as the *top-level controller*, although this is a term of my own invention—and I define this controller in its own file. Later, I'll start to group multiple related controllers in a file, but I put the top-level controller in its own file. Listing 6-2 shows the contents of the controllers/sportsStore.js file, which I created for this purpose.

■ **Tip** The reason I keep the top-level controller in a separate file is so that I can keep an eye on it when it changes in a revision control system. The top-level controller tends to change a lot during the early stages of development, when the application is taking shape, and I don't want the avalanche of change notifications to mask when other controllers are being altered. Later in the project, when the main functionality is complete, the top-level controller changes infrequently, but when it does change, there is a potential for breaking pretty much everything else in the application. At that point in the development cycle, I want to know when someone alters the top-level controller so that I can ensure that the changes have been thought through and fully tested.

Listing 6-2. The Contents of the sportsStore.js File

```
angular.module("sportsStore")
.controller("sportsStoreCtrl", function ($scope) {

    $scope.data = {
        products: [
            { name: "Product #1", description: "A product",
                category: "Category #1", price: 100 },
            { name: "Product #2", description: "A product",
                category: "Category #1", price: 110 },
            { name: "Product #3", description: "A product",
                category: "Category #2", price: 210 },
            { name: "Product #4", description: "A product",
                category: "Category #3", price: 202 }]
    };
});
```

Notice that the first statement in this file is a call to the angular.module method. This is the same method call that I made in the app.html file to define the main module for the SportsStore application. The difference is that when I defined the module, I provided an additional argument, like this:

```
...
angular.module("sportsStore", []);
...
```

The second argument is an array, which is currently empty, that lists the modules on which the sportsStore module depends and tells AngularJS to locate and provide the functionality that these modules contain. I'll be adding elements to this array later, but for now it is important to know that when you supply the array—empty or otherwise—you are telling AngularJS to *create* a new module. AngularJS will report an error if you try to create a module that already exists, so you need to make sure your module names are unique.

By contrast, the call to the angular.module method in the sportsStore.js file doesn't have the second argument:

```
...
angular.module("sportsStore")
...
```

Omitting the second argument tells AngularJS that you want to locate a module that has already been defined. In this situation, AngularJS will report an error if the module specified doesn't exist, so you need to make sure the module has already been created.

Both uses of the angular.module method return a Module object that can be used to define application functionality. I have used the controller method that, as its name suggests, defines a controller, but I describe the full set of methods available—and the components they create—in Chapters 9 and 18. You will also see me use some of these methods as I build the SportsStore application.

■ **Note** I wouldn't usually put the call to create the main application module in the HTML file like this because it is simpler to put everything in the JavaScript file. The reason I split up the statements is because the dual uses of the angular.module method cause endless confusion and I wanted to draw your attention to it, even if that means putting a JavaScript statement in the HTML file that could be omitted.

The main role of the top-level controller in the SportsStore application is to define the data that will be used in the different views that the application will display. As you will see—and as I describe in detail in Chapter 13—an AngularJS can have multiple controllers arranged in a hierarchy. Controllers arranged in this way can inherit data and logic from controllers above them, and by defining the data in the top-level controller, I can make it easily available to the controllers that I will be defining later.

The data I have defined is an array of objects that have the same properties as the data that is stored by Deployd, which allows me to get started before I start making Ajax requests to get the real product information.

■ **Caution**   Notice that when I define the data on the controller's scope, I define the data objects in an array that I assign to a property called products on an object called data, which in turn is attached to the scope. You have to be careful when you define data you want to be inherited because if you assign properties directly to the scope (that is, $scope.products = [data]) because other controllers can read, but not always modify, the data. I explain this in detail in Chapter 13.

Displaying the Product Details

To display details of the products, I need to add some HTML markup to the app.html file. AngularJS makes it easy to display data, as Listing 6-3 shows.

Listing 6-3. Displaying Product Details in the app.html File

```
<!DOCTYPE html>
<html ng-app="sportsStore">
<head>
    <title>SportsStore</title>
    <script src="angular.js"></script>
    <link href="bootstrap.css" rel="stylesheet" />
    <link href="bootstrap-theme.css" rel="stylesheet" />
    <script>
        angular.module("sportsStore", []);
    </script>
    <script src="controllers/sportsStore.js"></script>
</head>
<body ng-controller="sportsStoreCtrl">
    <div class="navbar navbar-inverse">
        <a class="navbar-brand" href="#">SPORTS STORE</a>
    </div>
    <div class="panel panel-default row">
        <div class="col-xs-3">
            Categories go here
        </div>
        <div class="col-xs-8">
            <div class="well" ng-repeat="item in data.products">
                <h3>
                    <strong>{{item.name}}</strong>
                    <span class="pull-right label label-primary">
                        {{item.price | currency}}
                    </span>
                </h3>
```

```
            <span class="lead">{{item.description}}</span>
        </div>
    </div>
</div>
</body>
</html>
```

There are three different kinds of changes highlighted in this listing. The first is that I have added a `script` element that imports the `sportsStore.js` file from the `controllers` folder. This is the file that contains the `sportsStoreCtrl` controller. Because I defined the `sportsStore` module in the `app.html` file and then located and used it in the `sportsStore.js` file, I need to make sure the inline `script` element (the one that *defines* the module) appears before the one that imports the file (which *extends* the module).

The next change is to apply the controller to its view using the `ng-controller` directive, like this:

```
...
<body ng-controller="sportsStoreCtrl">
...
```

I will be using the `sportsStoreCtrl` controller to support the entire application, so I have applied it to the body element so that the view it supports is the entire set of content elements. This will start to make more sense when I begin to add other controllers to support specific features.

Generating the Content Elements

The last set of changes in Listing 6-3 creates the elements to display details of the products for sale in the SportsStore. One of the most useful directives that AngularJS provides is `ng-repeat`, which generates elements for each object in an array of data. The `ng-repeat` directive is applied as an attribute whose value creates a local variable that is used for each data object in a specified array, like this:

```
...
<div class="well" ng-repeat="item in data.products">
...
```

The value I have used tells the `ng-repeat` directive to enumerate the objects in the `data.products` array applied to the scope by the controller for the view and assign each object to a variable called `item`. I can then refer to the current object in *data binding* expressions, which are denoted with the {{ and }} characters, like this:

```
...
<div class="well" ng-repeat="item in data.products">
    <h3>
        <strong>{{item.name}}</strong>
        <span class="pull-right label label-primary">{{item.price | currency}}</span>
    </h3>
    <span class="lead">{{item.description}}</span>
</div>
...
```

The `ng-repeat` directive duplicates the element to which it is applied (and any descendant elements) for each data object. That data object is assigned to the variable `item`, which allows me to insert the values of the `name`, `price`, and `description` properties as required.

The `name` and `description` values are inserted as-is in the HTML elements, but I have done something different with the `price` property: I have applied a *filter*. A filter formats or orders data values for display in a view. AngularJS comes with some built-in filters, including the `currency` filter, which formats numeric values as currency amounts. Filters are applied by using the | character, followed by the name of the filter, such that the expression `item.price |` `currency` tells AngularJS to pass the value of the `price` property of the `item` object through the `currency` filter.

The `currency` filter formats amounts as U.S. dollars by default, but, as I explain in Chapter 14, you can use some AngularJS localization filters to display other currency formats. I describe the built-in filters and show you how to create your own in Chapter 14. I will also create a custom filter in the next section. The result is that a set of elements like this one is generated for each element:

```
<div class="well ng-scope" ng-repeat="item in data.products">
    <h3>
        <strong class="ng-binding">Product #1</strong>
        <span class="pull-right label label-primary ng-binding">$100.00</span>
    </h3>
    <span class="lead ng-binding">A product</span>
</div>
```

Notice now AngularJS has annotated the elements with classes that begin with `ng-`. These are an artifact of AngularJS processing the elements and resolving data bindings, and you should not attempt to change them. You can see the visual effect changes in Listing 6-3 by loading the `app.html` file in the browser, as shown in Figure 6-7. I have shown only the first couple of products, but all of the details are displayed in a single list (something I will address by adding pagination later in this chapter).

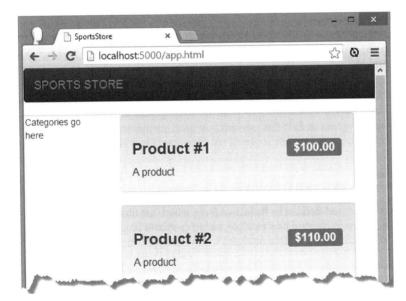

Figure 6-7. *Generating the product detail elements*

```
<body ng-controller="sportsStoreCtrl">
    <div class="navbar navbar-inverse">
        <a class="navbar-brand" href="#">SPORTS STORE</a>
    </div>
    <div class="panel panel-default row">
        <div class="col-xs-3">
            <a ng-click="selectCategory()"
                class="btn btn-block btn-default btn-lg">Home</a>
            <a ng-repeat="item in data.products | orderBy:'category' | unique:'category'"
                ng-click="selectCategory(item)" class=" btn btn-block btn-default btn-lg">
                 {{item}}
            </a>
        </div>
        <div class="col-xs-8">
            <div class="well" ng-repeat="item in data.products">
                <h3>
                    <strong>{{item.name}}</strong>
                    <span class="pull-right label label-primary">
                         {{item.price | currency}}
                    </span>
                </h3>
                <span class="lead">{{item.description}}</span>
            </div>
        </div>
    </div>
</body>
</html>
```

The first change that I made in this listing was to update the definition of the sportsStore module to declare a dependency on the customFilters module that I created in Listing 6-4 and that contains the unique filter:

```
...
angular.module("sportsStore", ["customFilters"]);
...
```

This is known as *declaring a dependency*. In this case, I am declaring that the sportsStore module depends on the functionality in the customFilters module. This causes AngularJS to locate the customFilters module and make it available so that I can refer to the components it contains, such as filters and controllers—a process known as *resolving the dependency*.

■ **Tip** The process of declaring and managing dependencies between modules and other kinds of components—known as *dependency injection*—is central to AngularJS. I explain the process in Chapter 9.

I also have to add a script element that loads the contents of the file that contains the customFilters module, as follows:

```
...
<script>
    angular.module("sportsStore", ["customFilters"]);
</script>
```

```
<script src="controllers/sportsStore.js"></script>
<script src="filters/customFilters.js"></script>
...
```

Notice that I am able to define the script element for the customFilters.js file *after* the one that creates the sportsStore module and declares a dependency on the customFilters module. This is because AngularJS loads all of the modules before using them to resolve dependencies. The effect can be confusing: The order of the script elements is important when you are *extending* a module (because the module must already have been defined) but not when *defining* a new module or declaring a dependency on one. The final set of changes in Listing 6-5 generates the category selection elements. There is quite a lot going on in these elements, and it will be easier to understand if you know what the result looks like—the addition of the category buttons—shown in Figure 6-8.

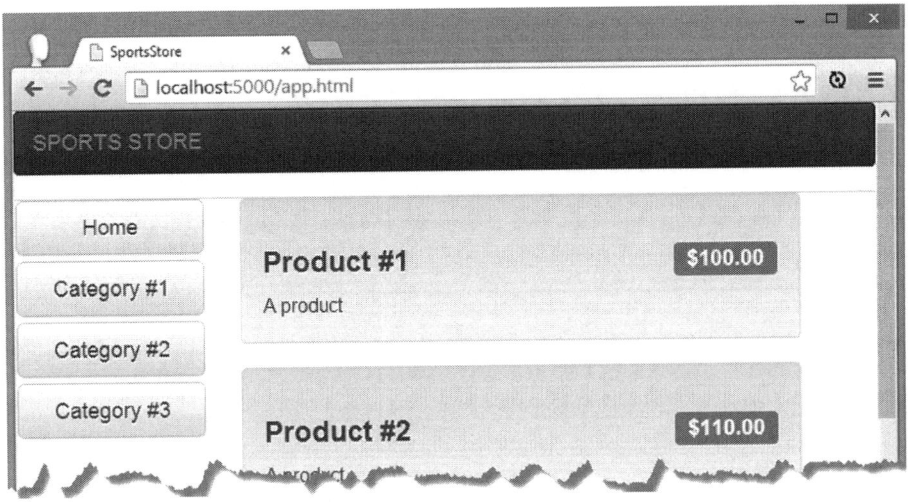

Figure 6-8. *The category navigation buttons*

Generating the Navigation Elements

The most interesting part of the markup is the use of the ng-repeat element to generate an a element for each product category, as follows:

```
...
<a ng-click="selectCategory()" class="btn btn-block btn-default btn-lg">Home</a>
<a ng-repeat="item in data.products | orderBy:'category' | unique:'category'"
    ng-click="selectCategory(item)" class=" btn btn-block btn-default btn-lg">
        {{item}}
</a>
...
```

The first part of the ng-repeat attribute value is the same as the one I used when generating the product details, item in data.products, and tells the ng-repeat directive that it should enumerate the objects in the data.products array, assign the current object to a variable called item, and duplicate the a element to which the directive has been applied.

The second part of the attribute value tells AngularJS to pass the data.products array to a built-in filter called orderBy, which is used to sort arrays. The orderBy filter takes an argument that specifies which property the objects will be sorted by, which I specify by placing a colon (the : character) after the filter name and then the argument value. In this example, I have specified that the category property be used. (I describe the orderBy filter fully in Chapter 14.)

▪ **Tip** Notice that I have specified the name of the property between single quotes (the ' character). By default, AngularJS assumes that names in expression refer to variables defined on the scope. To specify a static value, I have to use a string literal, which requires the single quote characters in JavaScript. (I could have used double quotes, but I already used them to demark the start and end of the ng-repeat directive attribute value.)

The use of the orderBy filter puts the product objects in order, sorted by the value of their category property. But one of the nice features of filters is that you can chain several together by using the bar symbol (the | character) and the name of another filter. In this case, I have used the unique filter that I developed earlier in the chapter. AngularJS applies filters in the order in which they are applied, which means that the objects are sorted by the category property and only then passed to the unique filter, which generates the set of unique category values. You can see how I have specified the property the unique filter will operate on:

```
...
<a ng-repeat="item in data.products | orderBy:'category' | unique:'category'"
...
```

The effect is that the data.products array is passed to the orderBy filter, which sorts the objects based on the value of the category property. The sorted array is then passed to the unique array, which returns a string array that contains the set of unique category values—and since the unique filter doesn't change the order of the values it processes, the results remain sorted by the previous filter.

Or, to put it more directly, this is an instruction to the ng-repeat directive to generate a set of unique category names, enumerate each of them, assign the current value to a variable called item, and generate an a element for each value.

▪ **Tip** I could have reversed the filters and achieved the same effect. The difference would be that the orderBy filter would be operating on an array of strings, rather than product objects (because that's what the unique filter produces as its result). The orderBy filter is designed to operate on objects, but you can sort strings by using this incantation: orderBy:'toString()'. Don't forget the quotes; otherwise, AngularJS will look for a scope property called toString, rather than invoking the toString method.

Handling the Click Event

I used the ng-click directive on the a elements so that I can respond when the user clicks of the buttons. AngularJS provides a set of built-in directives, which I describe in Chapter 11, that make it easy to call controller behaviors in response to events. As its name suggests, the ng-click directive specifies what AngularJS should do when the click event is triggered, as follows:

```
...
<a ng-click="selectCategory()" class="btn btn-block btn-default btn-lg">Home</a>
<a ng-repeat="item in data.products | orderBy:'category' | unique:'category'"
    ng-click="selectCategory(item)" class=" btn btn-block btn-default btn-lg">
        {{item}}
</a>
...
```

There are two a elements in the app.html file. The first is static and creates the Home button, which I will use to display all of the products in all of the categories. For this element, I have set the ng-click directive so that it calls a controller behavior called selectCategory with no arguments. I'll create the behavior shortly, but for now, the important thing to note is that for the other a element—the one to which the ng-repeat directive has been applied—I have set up the ng-click directive so that it calls the selectCategory behavior with the value of the item variable as the argument. When the ng-repeat directive generates an a element for each unique category, the ng-click directive will be automatically configured such that the selectCategory behavior will be passed the category for the button, such as selectCategory('Category #1'), for example.

Selecting the Category

Clicking the category buttons in the browser doesn't have any effect at the moment because the ng-click directive on the a elements is set up to call a controller behavior that isn't defined. AngularJS doesn't complain when you try to access a nonexistent behavior or data value on the scope on the basis that it might be defined at some point in the future. This can make debugging a little frustrating because typos don't result in errors, but the flexibility that this approach gives is generally useful, as I explain in Chapter 13 when I describe how controllers and their scopes work in more depth.

Defining the Controller

I need to define a controller behavior called selectCategory in order to respond to the user clicking the category buttons. I don't want to add the behavior to the top-level sportsStoreCtrl controller, which I am reserving for behaviors and data that are required for the entire application. Instead, I am going to create a new controller that will be used just by the product listing and category views. Listing 6-6 shows the contents of the controllers/ productListControllers.js file, which I added to the project in order to define the new controller.

■ **Tip** You may be wondering why I used a more specific name for the controller's file than for the one that contains filters. The reason is that filters are more generic and readily reused in other parts of the application or even other applications, whereas the kind of controller I am creating in this section tends to be tied to specific functionality. (This isn't true for all controllers, however, as you'll see in Chapters 15–17 when I show you how to create custom directives.)

Listing 6-6. The Contents of the productListControllers.js File

```
angular.module("sportsStore")
    .controller("productListCtrl", function ($scope, $filter) {

        var selectedCategory = null;

        $scope.selectCategory = function (newCategory) {
            selectedCategory = newCategory;
        }

        $scope.categoryFilterFn = function (product) {
            return selectedCategory == null ||
                product.category == selectedCategory;
        }
    });
```

I call the controller method on the sportsStore module that is defined in the app.html file (remember that one argument to the angular.module method means find an existing module, while two arguments means create a new one).

The controller is called productListCtrl, and it defines a behavior called selectCategory, matching the name of the behavior that the ng-click directives in Listing 6-5. The controller also defines categoryFilterFn, which takes a product object as its argument and returns true if no category has been selected or if a category has been selected and the product belongs to it—this will be useful shortly when I add the controller to the view.

■ **Tip** Notice that the selectedCategory variable is not defined on the scope. It is just a regular JavaScript variable, and that means it cannot be accessed from directives or data bindings in the view. The effect I have created is that the selectCategory behavior can be called to set the category, and the categoryFilterFn can be used to filter the product objects, but details of which category has been selected remains private. I won't be relying on this feature in the SportsStore applications—I just wanted to draw your attention to how controllers (and most other kinds of AngularJS components) can be selective about what public services and data they provide.

Applying the Controller and Filtering the Products

I have to apply the controller to the view using the ng-controller directive so that the ng-click directive is able to invoke the selectCategory behavior. Otherwise, the scope for the elements that contain the ng-click directive would be the one created by the top-level sportsStoreCtrl controller that doesn't contain the behavior. You can see the changes I have made to do this in Listing 6-7.

Listing 6-7. Applying a Controller in the app.html File

```
<!DOCTYPE html>
<html ng-app="sportsStore">
<head>
    <title>SportsStore</title>
    <script src="angular.js"></script>
    <link href="bootstrap.css" rel="stylesheet" />
    <link href="bootstrap-theme.css" rel="stylesheet" />
```

```
    <script>
        angular.module("sportsStore", ["customFilters"]);
    </script>
    <script src="controllers/sportsStore.js"></script>
    <script src="filters/customFilters.js"></script>
    <script src="controllers/productListControllers.js"></script>
</head>
<body ng-controller="sportsStoreCtrl">
    <div class="navbar navbar-inverse">
        <a class="navbar-brand" href="#">SPORTS STORE</a>
    </div>
    <div class="panel panel-default row" ng-controller="productListCtrl">
        <div class="col-xs-3">
            <a ng-click="selectCategory()"
                class="btn btn-block btn-default btn-lg">Home</a>
            <a ng-repeat="item in data.products | orderBy:'category' | unique:'category'"
                ng-click="selectCategory(item)" class=" btn btn-block btn-default btn-lg">
                {{item}}
            </a>
        </div>
        <div class="col-xs-8">
            <div class="well"
                ng-repeat="item in data.products | filter:categoryFilterFn">
                <h3>
                    <strong>{{item.name}}</strong>
                    <span class="pull-right label label-primary">
                        {{item.price | currency}}
                    </span>
                </h3>
                <span class="lead">{{item.description}}</span>
            </div>
        </div>
    </div>
</body>
</html>
```

I have added a `script` element to import the `productListControllers.js` file and applied the `ng-controller` directive for the `productListCtrl` controller on the part of the view that contains both the list of categories and the list of products.

Placing the `ng-controller` directive for the `productListCtrl` controller within the scope of the one for the `sportsStoreCtrl` controller means I can take advantage of *controller scope inheritance*, which I explain in detail in Chapter 13. The short version is the scope for the `productListCtrl` inherits the `data.products` array and any other data and behaviors that `sportsStoreCtrl` defines, which are then passed on to the view for the `productListCtrl` controller, along with any data or behaviors that it defines. The benefit of using this technique is that it allows you to limit the scope of controller functionality to the part of the application where it will be used, which makes it easier to perform good unit tests (as described in Chapter 25) and prevents unexpected dependencies between components in the application.

There is one other change in Listing 6-7: I changed the configuration of the ng-repeat directive that generates the product details, like this:

```
...
<div class="well" ng-repeat="item in data.products | filter:categoryFilterFn">
...
```

One of the built-in filters that AngularJS provides is called, confusingly, filter. It processes a collection and selects a subset of the objects it contains. I describe filters in Chapter 14, but the technique I am using here is to specify the name of the function defined by the productListCtrl controller. By applying the filter to the ng-repeat directive that creates the product details, I ensure that only the products in the currently selected category are displayed, as illustrated by Figure 6-9.

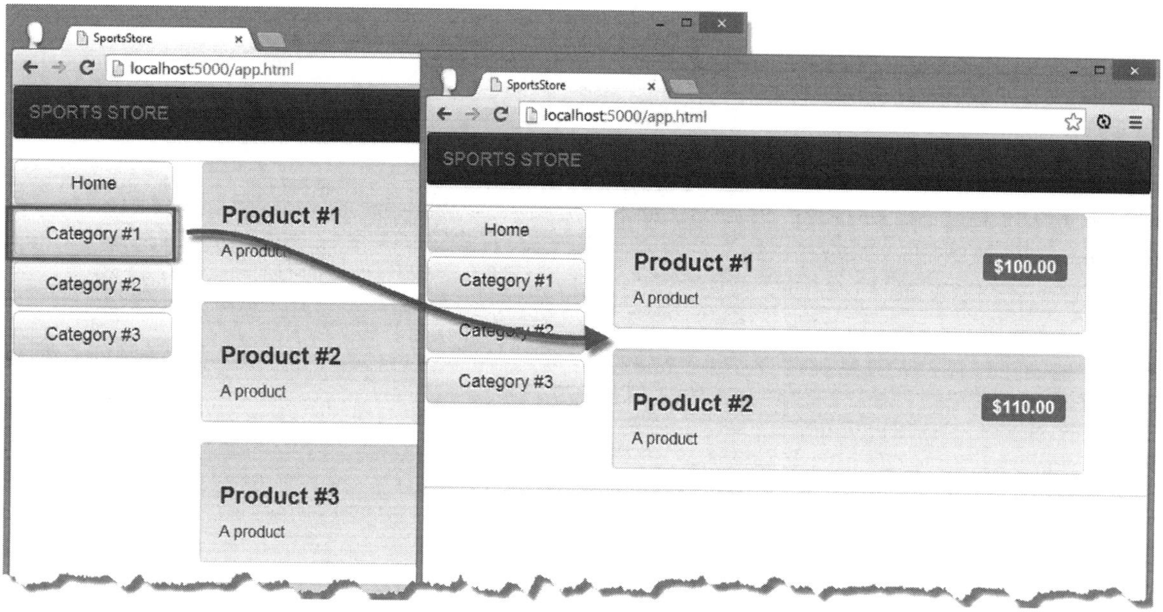

Figure 6-9. *Selecting a category*

Highlighting the Selected Category

The user can click the category buttons to filter the products, but there is no visual feedback to show which category has been selected. To address this, I am going to selectively apply the Bootstrap btn-primary CSS class to the category button that corresponds to the selected category. The first step is to add a behavior to the controller that will accept a category and, if it is the selected category, return the CSS class name, as shown in Listing 6-8.

■ **Tip**   Notice how I am able to chain together method calls on an AngularJS module. This is because the methods defined by the Module return the Module, creating what is commonly referred to as a *fluent API*.

Listing 6-8. Returning the Bootstrap Class Name in the productListControllers.js File

```
angular.module("sportsStore")
    .constant("productListActiveClass", "btn-primary")
    .controller("productListCtrl", function ($scope, $filter, productListActiveClass) {

        var selectedCategory = null;

        $scope.selectCategory = function (newCategory) {
            selectedCategory = newCategory;
        }

        $scope.categoryFilterFn = function (product) {
            return selectedCategory == null ||
                product.category == selectedCategory;
        }

        $scope.getCategoryClass = function (category) {
            return selectedCategory == category ? productListActiveClass : "";
        }
    });
```

I don't want to embed the name of the class in the behavior code, so I have used the constant method on the Module object to define a fixed value called productListActiveClass. This will allow me to change the class that is used in one place and have the change take effect wherever it is used. To access the value in the controller, I have to declare the constant name as a dependency, like this:

```
...
.controller("productListCtrl", function ($scope, $filter, productListActiveClass) {
...
```

I can then use the productListActiveClass value in the getCategoryClass behavior, which simply checks the category it receives as an argument and returns either the class name or the empty string.

The getCategoryClass behavior may seem a little odd, but it is going to be called by each of the category navigation buttons, each of which will pass the name of the category it represents as the argument. To apply the CSS class, I use the ng-class directive, which I have applied to the app.html file in Listing 6-9.

Listing 6-9. Applying the ng-class Directive to the app.html File

```
...
<div class="col-xs-3">
    <a ng-click="selectCategory()"
        class="btn btn-block btn-default btn-lg">Home</a>
    <a ng-repeat="item in data.products | orderBy:'category' | unique:'category'"
        ng-click="selectCategory(item)" class=" btn btn-block btn-default btn-lg"
        ng-class="getCategoryClass(item)">
        {{item}}
    </a>
</div>
...
```

The ng-class attribute, which I describe in Chapter 11, will add the element to which it has been applied to the classes returned by the getCategoryClass behavior. You can see the effect this creates in Figure 6-10.

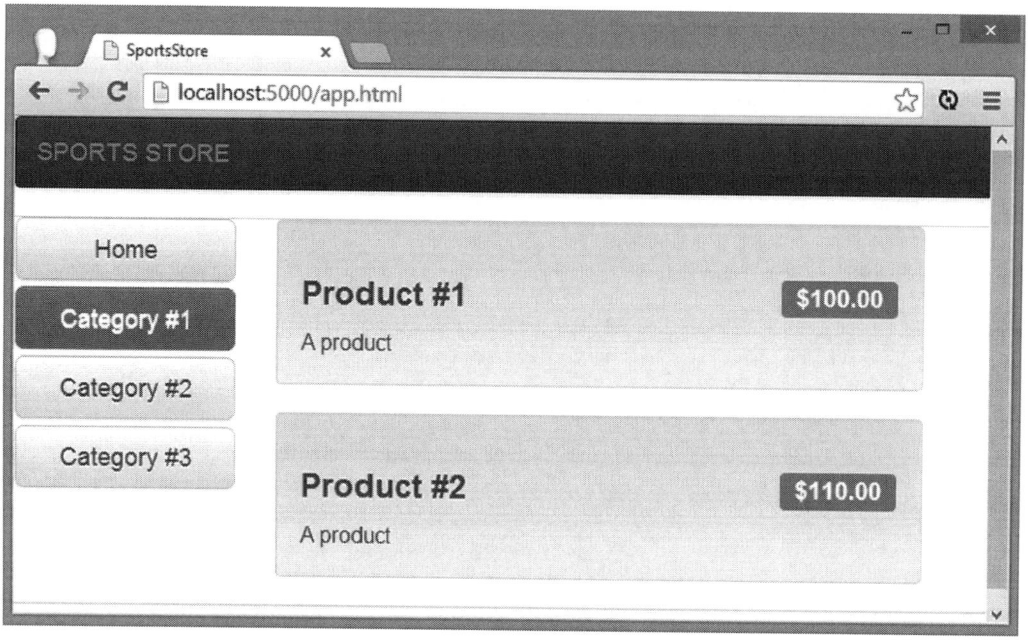

Figure 6-10. *Highlighting the selected category*

Adding Pagination

The last feature I am going to add in this chapter is *pagination*, such that only a certain number of product details are displayed at once. I don't really have enough data to make pagination terribly important, but it is a common requirement and worth demonstrating. There are three steps to implementing pagination: modify the controller so that the scope tracks the pagination state, implement filters, and update the view. I explain each step in the sections that follow.

Updating the Controller

I have updated the productListCtrl controller to support pagination, as shown in Listing 6-10.

Listing 6-10. Updating the Controller to Track Pagination in the productListControllers.js File

```
angular.module("sportsStore")
    .constant("productListActiveClass", "btn-primary")
    .constant("productListPageCount", 3)
    .controller("productListCtrl", function ($scope, $filter,
        productListActiveClass, productListPageCount) {

        var selectedCategory = null;

        $scope.selectedPage = 1;
        $scope.pageSize = productListPageCount;
```

```
    $scope.selectCategory = function (newCategory) {
        selectedCategory = newCategory;
        $scope.selectedPage = 1;
    }

    $scope.selectPage = function (newPage) {
        $scope.selectedPage = newPage;
    }

    $scope.categoryFilterFn = function (product) {
        return selectedCategory == null ||
            product.category == selectedCategory;
    }

    $scope.getCategoryClass = function (category) {
        return selectedCategory == category ? productListActiveClass : "";
    }

    $scope.getPageClass = function (page) {
        return $scope.selectedPage == page ? productListActiveClass : "";
    }
});
```

The number of products shown on a page is defined as a constant called productListPageCount, which I have declared as a dependency of the controller. Within the controller I define variables on the scope that expose the constant value (so I can access it in the view) and the currently selected page. I have defined a behavior, selectPage, that allows the selected page to be changed and another, getPageClass, that is designed for use with the ng-class directive to highlight the selected page, much as I did with the selected category earlier.

■ **Tip** You might be wondering why the view can't access the constant values directly, instead of requiring everything to be explicitly exposed via the scope. The answer is that AngularJS tries to prevent tightly coupled components, which I described in Chapter 3. If views could access services and constant values directly, then it would be easy to end up with endless couplings and dependencies that are hard to test and hard to maintain.

Implementing the Filters

I have created two new filters to support pagination, both of which I have added to the customFilters.js file, as shown in Listing 6-11.

Listing 6-11. Adding Filters to the customFilters.js File

```
angular.module("customFilters", [])
.filter("unique", function () {
    return function (data, propertyName) {
        if (angular.isArray(data) && angular.isString(propertyName)) {
            var results = [];
            var keys = {};
            for (var i = 0; i < data.length; i++) {
                var val = data[i][propertyName];
```

```
                    if (angular.isUndefined(keys[val])) {
                        keys[val] = true;
                        results.push(val);
                    }
                }
                return results;
            } else {
                return data;
            }
        }
    }
})
.filter("range", function ($filter) {
    return function (data, page, size) {
        if (angular.isArray(data) && angular.isNumber(page) && angular.isNumber(size)) {
            var start_index = (page - 1) * size;
            if (data.length < start_index) {
                return [];
            } else {
                return $filter("limitTo")(data.splice(start_index), size);
            }
        } else {
            return data;
        }
    }
})
.filter("pageCount", function () {
    return function (data, size) {
        if (angular.isArray(data)) {
            var result = [];
            for (var i = 0; i < Math.ceil(data.length / size) ; i++) {
                result.push(i);
            }
            return result;
        } else {
            return data;
        }
    }
});
```

The first new filter, called range, returns a range of elements from an array, corresponding to a page of products. The filter accepts arguments for the currently selected page (which is used to determine the start index of range) and the page size (which is used to determine the end index).

The range filter isn't especially interesting, other than I have built on the functionality provided by one of the built-in filters, called limitTo, which returns up to a specified number of items from an array. To use this filter, I have declared a dependency on the $filter service, which lets me create and use instances of filter. I explain how this works in detail in Chapter 14, but the key statement from the listing is this one:

```
...
return $filter("limitTo")(data.splice(start_index), size);
...
```

The result is that I use the standard JavaScript `splice` method to select part of the data array and then pass it to the `limitTo` filter to select no more than the number of items that can be displayed on the page. The `limitTo` filter ensures that there are no problems stepping over the end of the array and will return fewer items if the specified number isn't available.

The second filter, pageCount, is a dirty—but convenient—hack. The ng-repeat directive makes it easy to generate content, but it works only on data arrays. You can't, for example, have it repeat a specified number of times. My filter works out how many pages an array can be displayed in and then creates an array with that many numeric values. So, for example, if a data array can be displayed in three pages, then the result from the pageCount filter would be an array containing the values 1, 2, and 3. You'll see why this is useful in the next section.

■ **Caution**   I am abusing the filter functionality to get around a limitation of the ng-repeat directive. This is a bad thing, but it is expedient and, as you will see, allows me to build on some of the functionality I created for related features. The better alternative would be to create a custom replacement for the ng-repeat directive that will generate elements a specified number of times. I explain the techniques required to do this—which are rather advanced—in Chapters 16 and 17.

Updating the View

The last step to implement pagination is to update the view so that only one page of products is displayed and to provide the user with buttons to move from one page to another. You can see the changes I have made to the app.html file in Listing 6-12.

Listing 6-12. Adding Pagination to the app.html File

```
<!DOCTYPE html>
<html ng-app="sportsStore">
<head>
    <title>SportsStore</title>
    <script src="angular.js"></script>
    <link href="bootstrap.css" rel="stylesheet" />
    <link href="bootstrap-theme.css" rel="stylesheet" />
    <script>
        angular.module("sportsStore", ["customFilters"]);
    </script>
    <script src="controllers/sportsStore.js"></script>
    <script src="filters/customFilters.js"></script>
    <script src="controllers/productListControllers.js"></script>
</head>
<body ng-controller="sportsStoreCtrl">
    <div class="navbar navbar-inverse">
        <a class="navbar-brand" href="#">SPORTS STORE</a>
    </div>
    <div class="panel panel-default row" ng-controller="productListCtrl">
        <div class="col-xs-3">
            <a ng-click="selectCategory()"
                class="btn btn-block btn-default btn-lg">Home</a>
```

```
            <a ng-repeat="item in data.products | orderBy:'category' | unique:'category'"
                ng-click="selectCategory(item)" class=" btn btn-block btn-default btn-lg"
                ng-class="getCategoryClass(item)">
                {{item}}
            </a>
        </div>
        <div class="col-xs-8">
            <div class="well"
                    ng-repeat=
             "item in data.products | filter:categoryFilterFn | range:selectedPage:pageSize">
                <h3>
                    <strong>{{item.name}}</strong>
                    <span class="pull-right label label-primary">
                        {{item.price | currency}}
                    </span>
                </h3>
                <span class="lead">{{item.description}}</span>
            </div>
            <div class="pull-right btn-group">
                <a ng-repeat=
                    "page in data.products | filter:categoryFilterFn | pageCount:pageSize"
                    ng-click="selectPage($index + 1)" class="btn btn-default"
                    ng-class="getPageClass($index + 1)">
                    {{$index + 1}}
                </a>
            </div>
        </div>
    </div>
</body>
</html>
```

The first change is to the ng-repeat directive that generates the product list so that the data is passed through the range filter to select the products for the current page. The details of the current page and the number of products per page are passed to the filter as arguments using the values I defined on the controller scope.

The second change is the addition of the page navigation buttons. I use the ng-repeat directive to work out how many pages the products in the currently selected category requires and pass the result to the pageCount filter, which then causes the ng-repeat directive to generate the right number of page navigation buttons. The currently selected page is indicated through the ng-class directive, and the page is changed through the ng-click directive.

You can see the result in Figure 6-11, which shows the two pages required to display all of the products. There are not enough items in the fake data for any one category to require multiple pages, but the effect is evident.

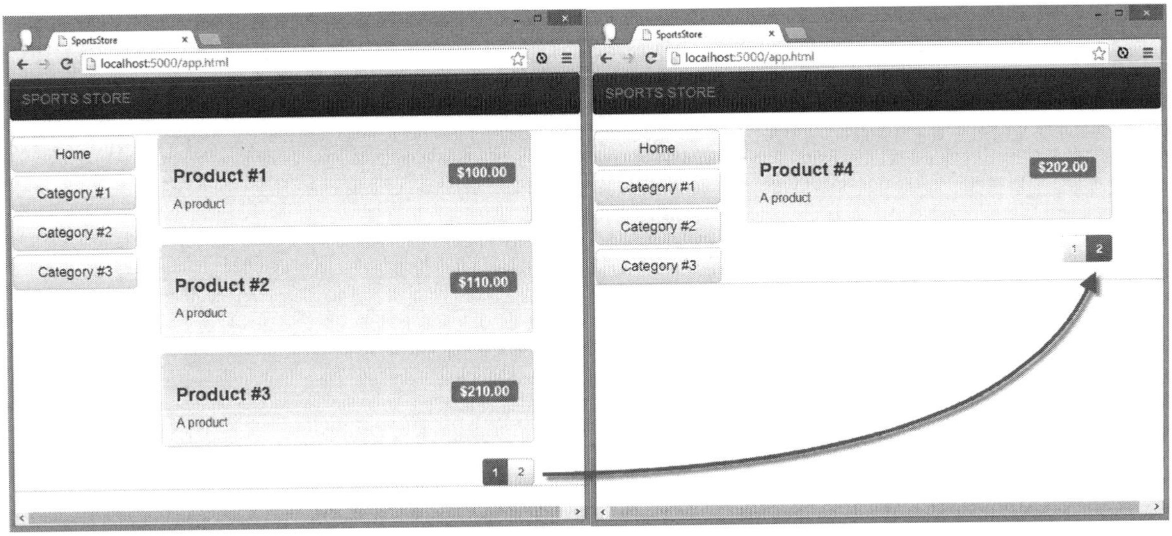

Figure 6-11. *Paginating the product details*

Summary

In this chapter, I started the process of developing the SportsStore application. All development frameworks that follow the MVC pattern have a common characteristic, which is that there is a lot of seemingly slow preparation and then, all of a sudden, features start to fall into place. AngularJS is no exception, and you can get a sense of the quickening pace throughout this chapter, to the point where adding pagination took longer for me to explain than to actually do. Now that the basic plumbing is in place, the pace will continue to crack along in the next chapter, where I will start using the real data from the Deployd server, implement the shopping cart, and start the checkout process.

CHAPTER 7

SportsStore: Navigation and Checkout

In this chapter, I will continue the development of the SportsStore application by adding support for working with the real data, by implementing the cart, and by beginning work on the order checkout process.

Preparing the Example Project

I am going to continue building the project I started in Chapter 6. You can download the source code from Chapter 6 from www.apress.com if you want to follow along with the examples but don't want to have to build the project from scratch.

Using the Real Product Data

In Chapter 6, I put all of the features in place for displaying the product data to the user, but I did so using dummy data so that I could focus on building the basic plumbing of the application. It is now time to switch over to using the real data, which I will obtain from the Deployd server that I set up right at the start of Chapter 6.

AngularJS provides support for making Ajax requests through a service called $http. I describe how services work in detail in Part 3 and the $http service itself in Chapter 23, but you can get a sense of how it works through the changes I made to the top-level sportsStoreCtrl controller, as shown in Listing 7-1.

Listing 7-1. Making an Ajax Request in the sportsStore.js File

```
angular.module("sportsStore")
    .constant("dataUrl", "http://localhost:5500/products")
    .controller("sportsStoreCtrl", function ($scope, $http, dataUrl) {

        $scope.data = {};

        $http.get(dataUrl)
            .success(function (data) {
                $scope.data.products = data;
            })
            .error(function (error) {
                $scope.data.error = error;
            });
    });
```

Most JavaScript methods calls, including those made on AngularJS components, are *synchronous*, which means that execution doesn't move on to the next statement until the current one has been completed. That doesn't work when making network requests in web applications because we want the user to be able to interact with the application while the request is being made in the background.

I am going to obtain the data I need using an Ajax request. Ajax stands for *Asynchronous JavaScript and XML*, where the important word is *asynchronous*. An Ajax request is a regular HTTP request that happens asynchronously, in other words, in the background. AngularJS represents asynchronous operations using *promises*, which will be familiar to you if you have used libraries such as jQuery (and which I introduced in Chapter 5 and explain in detail in Chapter 20).

The $http service defines methods for making different kinds of Ajax request. The get method, which is the one I have used here, uses the HTTP GET method to request the URL passed as an argument. I have defined the URL as a constant called dataUrl and used the URL from Chapter 6 with which I tested the Deployd server.

The $http.get method starts the Ajax request, and execution of the application continues, even though the request has yet to be completed. AngularJS needs a way to notify me when the server has responded to the request, which is where the promise comes in. The $http.get method returns an object that defines success and error methods. I pass functions to these methods, and AngularJS *promises* to call one of them to tell me how the request turns out.

AngularJS will invoke the function I passed to the success method if everything with the HTTP request went well and—as a bonus—will automatically convert JSON data to JavaScript objects and pass them as the argument to the success function. If there is a problem with the Ajax HTTP request, then AngularJS will invoke the function I passed to the error method.

■ **Tip**   JSON stands for *JavaScript Object Notation* and is a data exchange format that is widely used in web applications. JSON represents data in a way that is similar to JavaScript, which makes it easy to operate on JSON data in JavaScript applications. JSON has largely displaced XML, the *X* in Ajax, because it is human-readable and easy to implement. I introduced JSON in Chapter 5, and you can learn about the details of it at
http://en.wikipedia.org/wiki/Json.

The success function I have used in the listing is simple because it relies on the automatic conversion that AngularJS performs for JSON data. I just assign the data that is obtained from the server to the data.products variable on the controller scope. The error function assigns the object passed by AngularJS to describe the problem to the data.error variable on the scope. (I'll return to the error in the next section.)

You can see the effect of making the Ajax request in Figure 7-1. When AngularJS creates its instance of the sportsStore controller, the HTTP request is started, and then the scope is updated with the data when it arrives. The product detail, category, and page features that I created in Chapter 6 operate just as they did before, but with the product data delivered from the Deployd server.

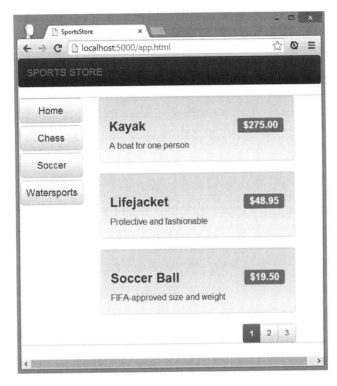

Figure 7-1. *Obtaining product data via Ajax*

UNDERSTANDING THE SCOPE

It may not be obvious when testing the changes, but obtaining the data via Ajax highlights one of the most important aspects of AngularJS development, which is the dynamic nature of scopes. When the application first starts, the HTML content is generated and displayed to the user even though there is no product information available.

At some point after the content has been rendered, the data will arrive from the server and be assigned to the data.products variable in the scope. When this happens, AngularJS updates all of the bindings and the output from behaviors that depend on the product data, ensuring that the new data is propagated throughout the application. In essence, AngularJS scopes are *live* data stores, which respond and propagate changes. You will see countless examples of this propagation of changes throughout the book.

Handling Ajax Errors

Dealing with successful Ajax requests is easy because I just assign the data to the scope and let AngularJS update all of the bindings and directives in the views. I have to work a little harder to deal with errors and add some new elements to the view that I will display when there is a problem. In Listing 7-2, you can see the changes that I have made to the app.html file to display errors to the user.

Listing 7-2. Displaying Errors in the app.html File

```html
<!DOCTYPE html>
<html ng-app="sportsStore">
<head>
    <title>SportsStore</title>
    <script src="angular.js"></script>
    <link href="bootstrap.css" rel="stylesheet" />
    <link href="bootstrap-theme.css" rel="stylesheet" />
    <script>
        angular.module("sportsStore", ["customFilters"]);
    </script>
    <script src="controllers/sportsStore.js"></script>
    <script src="filters/customFilters.js"></script>
    <script src="controllers/productListControllers.js"></script>
</head>
<body ng-controller="sportsStoreCtrl">
    <div class="navbar navbar-inverse">
        <a class="navbar-brand" href="#">SPORTS STORE</a>
    </div>

    <div class="alert alert-danger" ng-show="data.error">
        Error ({{data.error.status}}). The product data was not loaded.
        <a href="/app.html" class="alert-link">Click here to try again</a>
    </div>

    <div class="panel panel-default row" ng-controller="productListCtrl"
        ng-hide="data.error">
        <div class="col-xs-3">
            <a ng-click="selectCategory()"
               class="btn btn-block btn-default btn-lg">Home</a>
            <a ng-repeat="item in data.products | orderBy:'category' | unique:'category'"
               ng-click="selectCategory(item)" class=" btn btn-block btn-default btn-lg"
               ng-class="getCategoryClass(item)">
                {{item}}
            </a>
        </div>
        <div class="col-xs-8">
            <div class="well"
                 ng-repeat=
          "item in data.products | filter:categoryFilterFn | range:selectedPage:pageSize">
                <h3>
                    <strong>{{item.name}}</strong>
                    <span class="pull-right label label-primary">
                        {{item.price | currency}}
                    </span>
                </h3>
                <span class="lead">{{item.description}}</span>
            </div>
            <div class="pull-right btn-group">
                <a ng-repeat=
                  "page in data.products | filter:categoryFilterFn | pageCount:pageSize"
```

```
                    ng-click="selectPage($index + 1)" class="btn btn-default"
                    ng-class="getPageClass($index + 1)">
                        {{$index + 1}}
                </a>
            </div>
        </div>
    </div>
</body>
</html>
```

I have added a new div element to the view, which shows an error to the user. I have used the ng-show directive, which hides the element it applied to until the expression specified in the attribute value evaluates to true. I have specified the data.error property, which AngularJS takes as an instruction to show the div element when the property has been assigned a value. Since the data.error property is undefined until an Ajax error occurs, the visibility of the div element is tied to the outcome of the $http.get method in the controller.

The counterpart to the ng-show directive is ng-hide, which I have applied to the div element that contains the category buttons and the product details. The ng-hide directive will show an element and its contents until its expression evaluates to true, at which point they will be hidden. The overall effect is that when there is an Ajax error, the normal content is hidden and replaced with the error, as shown in Figure 7-2.

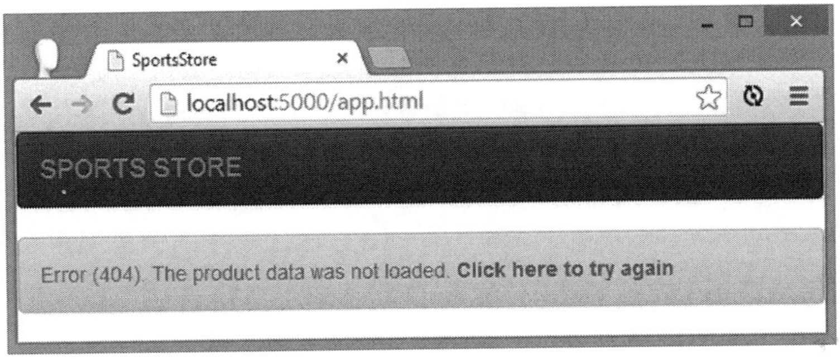

Figure 7-2. *Displaying an error to the user*

■ **Tip**　I describe the ng-show and ng-hide directives in detail in Chapter 10.

I created this screenshot by changing the value of the dataUrl in the sportsStore.js file to one that doesn't exist, such as http://localhost:5500/doesNotExist.

The object passed to the error function defines status and message properties. The status property is set to the HTTP error code, and the message property returns a string that describes the problem. I included the status property in the message that I show to the user, along with a link that lets them reload the application and, implicitly, try to load the data again.

Creating Partial Views

The HTML in the app.html file is approaching the point of complexity where it isn't immediately obvious what every element does—something that will get worse as I add further features to the SportsStore application.

Fortunately, I can break up the markup into separate files and use the ng-include directive to import those files at runtime. To that end, I created the views/productList.html file, the contents of which are shown in Listing 7-3.

Listing 7-3. The Contents of the productList.html File

```
<div class="panel panel-default row" ng-controller="productListCtrl"
        ng-hide="data.error">
    <div class="col-xs-3">
        <a ng-click="selectCategory()"
            class="btn btn-block btn-default btn-lg">Home</a>
        <a ng-repeat="item in data.products | orderBy:'category' | unique:'category'"
            ng-click="selectCategory(item)" class=" btn btn-block btn-default btn-lg"
            ng-class="getCategoryClass(item)">
            {{item}}
        </a>
    </div>
    <div class="col-xs-8">
        <div class="well"
            ng-repeat=
          "item in data.products | filter:categoryFilterFn | range:selectedPage:pageSize">
            <h3>
                <strong>{{item.name}}</strong>
                <span class="pull-right label label-primary">
                    {{item.price | currency}}
                </span>
            </h3>
            <span class="lead">{{item.description}}</span>
        </div>
        <div class="pull-right btn-group">
            <a ng-repeat=
                "page in data.products | filter:categoryFilterFn | pageCount:pageSize"
                ng-click="selectPage($index + 1)" class="btn btn-default"
                ng-class="getPageClass($index + 1)">
                {{$index + 1}}
            </a>
        </div>
    </div>
</div>
```

I have copied the elements that define the product and category lists into the HTML file. Partial views are fragments of HTML, which means that they do not require html, head, and body elements in the way that a complete HTML document does. In Listing 7-4, you can see how I have removed these elements from the app.html file and replaced them with the ng-include directive.

Listing 7-4. Importing a Partial View in the app.html File

```html
<!DOCTYPE html>
<html ng-app="sportsStore">
<head>
    <title>SportsStore</title>
    <script src="angular.js"></script>
    <link href="bootstrap.css" rel="stylesheet" />
    <link href="bootstrap-theme.css" rel="stylesheet" />
    <script>
        angular.module("sportsStore", ["customFilters"]);
    </script>
    <script src="controllers/sportsStore.js"></script>
    <script src="filters/customFilters.js"></script>
    <script src="controllers/productListControllers.js"></script>
</head>
<body ng-controller="sportsStoreCtrl">
    <div class="navbar navbar-inverse">
        <a class="navbar-brand" href="#">SPORTS STORE</a>
    </div>

    <div class="alert alert-danger" ng-show="data.error">
        Error ({{data.error.status}}). The product data was not loaded.
        <a href="/app.html" class="alert-link">Click here to try again</a>
    </div>

    <ng-include src="'views/productList.html'"></ng-include>

</body>
</html>
```

■ **Tip**   There are three benefits to using partial views. The first is to break up the application into manageable chunks, as I have done here. The second is to create fragments of HTML that can be used repeatedly in an application. The third is to make it easier to show different areas of functionality to the user as they use the application—I'll return to this benefit in the "Defining URL Routes" section later in the chapter.

The creator of a directive can specify how it can be applied: as an element, as an attribute, as a class, or even as an HTML comment. I explain how this is done in Chapter 16, but the ng-include directive has been set up so that it can be applied as an element and as the more conventional attribute, and I have used it in this way solely for variety. When AngularJS encounters the ng-include directive, it makes an Ajax request, loads the file specified by the src attribute, and inserts the contents in place of the element. There is no visible difference in the content presented to the user, but I have simplified the markup in the app.html file and put all the product list–related HTML in a separate file.

■ **Tip**   When using the ng-include directive, I specified the name of the file as a literal value in single quotes. If I had not done this, then the directive would have looked for a scope property to get the name of the file.

Creating the Cart

The user can see the products that I have available, but I can't sell anything without a shopping cart. In this section, I will build the cart functionality that will be familiar to anyone who has used an e-commerce site, the basic flow of which is illustrated by Figure 7-3.

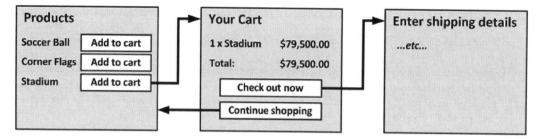

Figure 7-3. *The basic flow of the shopping cart*

As you will see in the following sections, several sets of changes are required to implement the cart feature, including creating a custom AngularJS component.

Defining the Cart Module and Service

So far, I have been organizing the files in my project based on the type of component they contain: Filters are defined in the `filters` folder, views in the `views` folder, and so on. This makes sense when building the basic features of an application, but there will always be some functionality in a project that is relatively self-contained but requires a mix of AngularJS components. You can continue to organize the files by component type, but I find it more useful to order the files by the function that they collectively represent, for which I use the `components` folder. The cart functionality is suitable for this kind of organization because, as you will see, I am going to need partial views and several components to get the effect I require. I started by creating the `components/cart` folder and adding a new JavaScript file to it called `cart.js`. You can see the contents of this file in Listing 7-5.

Listing 7-5. The Contents of the cart.js File

```
angular.module("cart", [])
.factory("cart", function () {

    var cartData = [];

    return {

        addProduct: function (id, name, price) {
            var addedToExistingItem = false;
            for (var i = 0; i < cartData.length; i++) {
                if (cartData[i].id == id) {
                    cartData[i].count++;
                    addedToExistingItem = true;
                    break;
                }
            }
            if (!addedToExistingItem) {
```

```
                    cartData.push({
                        count: 1, id: id, price: price, name: name
                    });
                }
        },

        removeProduct: function (id) {
            for (var i = 0; i < cartData.length; i++) {
                if (cartData[i].id == id) {
                    cartData.splice(i, 1);
                    break;
                }
            }
        },

        getProducts: function () {
            return cartData;
        }
    }
});
```

I started by creating a custom service in a new module called cart. AngularJS provides a lot of its functionality through services, but they are simply singleton objects that are accessible throughout an application. (*Singleton* just means that only one object will be created and shared by all of the components that depend on the service.)

Not only does using a service allow me to demonstrate an important AngularJS feature, but implementing the cart this way works well because having a shared instance ensures that every component can access the cart and have the same view of the user's product selections.

As I explain in Chapter 18, there are different ways to create services depending on what you are trying to achieve. I have used the simplest in Listing 7-5, which is to call the Module.factory method and pass in the name of the service (which is cart, in this case) and a factory function. The factory function will be invoked when AngularJS needs the service and is responsible for creating the service object; since one service object is used throughout the application, the factory function will be called only once.

My cart service factory function returns an object with three methods that operate on a data array that is not exposed directly through the service, which I did to demonstrate that you don't have to expose all of the workings in a service. The cart service object defines the three methods described in Table 7-1. I represent products in the cart with objects that define id, name, and price properties to describe the product and a count property to record the number the user has added to the basket.

Table 7-1. *The Methods Defined by the Cart Service*

Method	Description
addProduct(id, name, price)	Adds the specified product to the cart or increments the number required if the cart already contains the product
removeProduct(id)	Removes the product with the specified ID
getProducts()	Returns the array of objects in the cart

Creating a Cart Widget

My next step is to create a widget that will summarize the contents of the cart and provide the user with the means to begin the checkout process, which I am going to do by creating a custom directive. *Directives* are self-contained, reusable units of functionality that sit at the heart of AngularJS development. As you start with AngularJS, you will rely on the many built-in directives (which I describe in Chapters 9–12), but as you gain confidence, you will find yourself creating custom directives to tailor functionality to suit your applications.

You can do a lot with directives, which is why it takes me six chapters to describe them fully later in the book. They even support a cut-down version of jQuery, called *jqLite*, to manipulate elements in the DOM. In short, directives allow you to write anything from simple helpers to complex features and to decide whether the result is tightly woven into the current application or completely reusable in other applications. Listing 7-6 shows the additions I made to the cart.js file to create the widget directive, which is at the simpler end of what you can do with directives.

Listing 7-6. Adding a Directive to the cart.js File

```
angular.module("cart", [])
.factory("cart", function () {

    var cartData = [];

    return {
        // ...service statements omitted for brevity...
    }
})
.directive("cartSummary", function (cart) {
    return {
        restrict: "E",
        templateUrl: "components/cart/cartSummary.html",
        controller: function ($scope) {

            var cartData = cart.getProducts();

            $scope.total = function () {
                var total = 0;
                for (var i = 0; i < cartData.length; i++) {
                    total += (cartData[i].price * cartData[i].count);
                }
                return total;
            }

            $scope.itemCount = function () {
                var total = 0;
                for (var i = 0; i < cartData.length; i++) {
                    total += cartData[i].count;
                }
                return total;
            }
        }
    };
});
```

Directives are created by calling the `directive` method on an AngularJS module and passing in the name of the directive (`cartSummary` in this case) and a factory function that returns a *directive definition object*. The definition object defines properties that tell AngularJS what your directive does and how it does it. I have specified three properties when defining the `cartSummary` directive, and I have described them briefly in Table 7-2. (I describe and demonstrate the complete set of properties in Chapters 16 and 17.)

Table 7-2. *The Definition Properties Used for the cartSummary Directive*

Name	Description
restrict	Specifies how the directive can be applied. I have used a value of E, which means that this directive can be applied only as an element. The most common value is EA, which means that the directive can be applied as an element or as an attribute.
templateUrl	Specifies the URL of a partial view whose contents will be inserted into the directive's element.
controller	Specifies a controller that will provide data and behaviors to the partial view.

■ **Tip** Although my directive is rather basic, it isn't the simplest approach you can use to create a directive. In Chapter 15, I show you how to create directives that use jqLite, the AngularJS version of jQuery to manipulate existing content. The kind of directive that I have created here, which specifies a template and a controller and restricts how it can be applied, is covered in Chapter 16 and Chapter 17.

In short, my directive definition defines a controller, tells AngularJS to use the `components/cart/cartSummary.html` view, and restricts the directive so that it can be applied only as an element. Notice that the controller in Listing 7-6 declares a dependency on the `cart` service, which is defined in the same module. This allows me to define the `total` and `itemCount` behaviors that consume the methods provided by the service to operate on the cart contents. The behaviors defined by the controller are available to the partial view, which is shown in Listing 7-7.

Listing 7-7. The Contents of the cartSummary.html File

```
<style>
    .navbar-right { float: right !important; margin-right: 5px;}
    .navbar-text { margin-right: 10px; }
</style>

<div class="navbar-right">
    <div class="navbar-text">
        <b>Your cart:</b>
        {{itemCount()}} item(s),
        {{total() | currency}}
    </div>
    <a class="btn btn-default navbar-btn">Checkout</a>
</div>
```

■ **Tip**   This partial view contains a `style` element to redefine some of the Bootstrap CSS for the navigation bar that runs across the top of the SportsStore layout. I don't usually like embedding `style` elements in partial views, but I do so when the changes affect only that view and there is a small amount of CSS. In all other situations, I would define a separate CSS file and import it into the application's main HTML file.

The partial view uses the controller behaviors to display the number of items and the total value of those items. There is also an a element that is labeled Checkout; clicking the button doesn't do anything at the moment, but I'll wire it up later in the chapter.

Applying the Cart Widget

Applying the cart widget to the application requires three steps: adding a `script` element to import the contents of the JavaScript file, adding a dependency for the `cart` module, and adding the directive element to the markup. Listing 7-8 shows all three changes applied to the `app.html` file.

Listing 7-8. Adding the Cart Widget to the app.html File

```
<!DOCTYPE html>
<html ng-app="sportsStore">
<head>
    <title>SportsStore</title>
    <script src="angular.js"></script>
    <link href="bootstrap.css" rel="stylesheet" />
    <link href="bootstrap-theme.css" rel="stylesheet" />
    <script>
        angular.module("sportsStore", ["customFilters", "cart"]);
    </script>
    <script src="controllers/sportsStore.js"></script>
    <script src="filters/customFilters.js"></script>
    <script src="controllers/productListControllers.js"></script>
    <script src="components/cart/cart.js"></script>
</head>
<body ng-controller="sportsStoreCtrl">
    <div class="navbar navbar-inverse">
        <a class="navbar-brand" href="#">SPORTS STORE</a>
        <cart-summary />
    </div>
    <div class="alert alert-danger" ng-show="data.error">
        Error ({{data.error.status}}). The product data was not loaded.
        <a href="/app.html" class="alert-link">Click here to try again</a>
    </div>
    <ng-include src="'views/productList.html'"></ng-include>
</body>
</html>
```

Notice that although I used the name cartSummary when I defined the directive in Listing 7-8, the element I added to the app.html file is cart-summary. AngularJS *normalizes* component names to map between these formats, as I explain in Chapter 15. You can see the effect of the cart summary widget in Figure 7-4. The widget doesn't do much at the moment, but I'll start adding other features that will drive its behavior in the following sections.

Figure 7-4. *The cart summary widget*

Adding Product Selection Buttons

As with all AngularJS development, there is some up-front effort to develop the foundations and then other features start to snap into place—something that holds true for the cart as much as another part of the application. My next step is to add buttons to the product details so that the user can add products to the cart. First, I need to add a behavior to the controller for the product list view to operate on the cart. Listing 7-9 shows the changes I have made to the `controllers/productListController.js` file.

Listing 7-9. Adding Support for the Cart to the productListControllers.js File

```
angular.module("sportsStore")
    .constant("productListActiveClass", "btn-primary")
    .constant("productListPageCount", 3)
    .controller("productListCtrl", function ($scope, $filter,
        productListActiveClass, productListPageCount, cart) {

        var selectedCategory = null;

        $scope.selectedPage = 1;
        $scope.pageSize = productListPageCount;

        $scope.selectCategory = function (newCategory) {
            selectedCategory = newCategory;
            $scope.selectedPage = 1;
        }

        $scope.selectPage = function (newPage) {
            $scope.selectedPage = newPage;
        }

        $scope.categoryFilterFn = function (product) {
            return selectedCategory == null ||
                product.category == selectedCategory;
        }
```

```
    $scope.getCategoryClass = function (category) {
        return selectedCategory == category ? productListActiveClass : "";
    }

    $scope.getPageClass = function (page) {
        return $scope.selectedPage == page ? productListActiveClass : "";
    }

    $scope.addProductToCart = function (product) {
        cart.addProduct(product.id, product.name, product.price);
    }
});
```

I have declared a dependency on the cart service and defined a behavior called addProductToCart that takes a product object and uses it to call the addProduct method on the cart service.

■ **Tip**   This pattern of declaring a dependency on a service and then selectively exposing its functionality through the scope is one you will encounter a lot in AngularJS development. Views can access only the data and behaviors that are available through the scope—although, as I demonstrated in Chapter 6 (and explain in depth in Chapter 13), scopes can inherit from one another when controllers are nested or (as I explain in Chapter 17) when directives are defined.

I can then add button elements to the partial view that displays the product details and invokes the addProductToCart behavior, as shown in Listing 7-10.

Listing 7-10. Adding Buttons to the productList.html File

```
<div class="panel panel-default row" ng-controller="productListCtrl"
        ng-hide="data.error">
    <div class="col-xs-3">
        <a ng-click="selectCategory()"
            class="btn btn-block btn-default btn-lg">Home</a>
        <a ng-repeat="item in data.products | orderBy:'category' | unique:'category'"
            ng-click="selectCategory(item)" class=" btn btn-block btn-default btn-lg"
            ng-class="getCategoryClass(item)">
              {{item}}
        </a>
    </div>
    <div class="col-xs-8">
        <div class="well"
             ng-repeat=
          "item in data.products | filter:categoryFilterFn | range:selectedPage:pageSize">
            <h3>
                <strong>{{item.name}}</strong>
                <span class="pull-right label label-primary">
                    {{item.price | currency}}
                </span>
            </h3>
            <button ng-click="addProductToCart(item)"
                    class="btn btn-success pull-right">
```

```
          Add to cart
        </button>
        <span class="lead">{{item.description}}</span>
    </div>
    <div class="pull-right btn-group">
        <a ng-repeat=
            "page in data.products | filter:categoryFilterFn | pageCount:pageSize"
          ng-click="selectPage($index + 1)" class="btn btn-default"
          ng-class="getPageClass($index + 1)">
            {{$index + 1}}
        </a>
    </div>
  </div>
</div>
```

■ **Tip** Bootstrap lets me style a and button elements so they have the same appearance; as a consequence, I tend to use them interchangeably. That said, a elements are more useful when using *URL routing*, which I describe later in this chapter.

You can see the buttons and the effect they have in Figure 7-5. Clicking one of the Add to cart buttons invokes the controller behavior, which invokes the service methods, which then causes the cart summary widget to update.

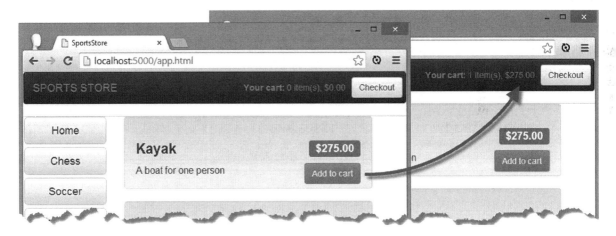

Figure 7-5. *Adding products to the cart*

Adding URL Navigation

Before I go any further and add support for checking out, I am going to enhance the infrastructure of the SportsStore application by adding support for *URL routing*. I describe URL routing in detail in Chapter 22, but the short version is that it allows for different partial views to be displayed automatically based on the current URL. This makes it easier to build larger applications that the user can navigate freely around, and I will use it as the foundation for displaying the views that the user needs to complete their purchase and submit an order to the server.

To get started, I need to create a view that I will display when the user begins the checkout process. Listing 7-11 shows the contents of the views/checkoutSummary.html file, which contains some placeholder content for the moment. I'll return to this file and add the real content once I have set up the URL routing feature.

Listing 7-11. The Contents of the checkoutSummary.html File

```
<div class="lead">
    This is the checkout summary view
</div>
<a href="#/products" class="btn btn-primary">Back</a>
```

Defining URL Routes

I am going to start by defining the *routes* I require, which are the mappings between specific URLs and the views that should be displayed when the browser navigates to that URL. The first two will map the /product and /checkout URLs to the productList.html and checkoutSummary.html views, respectively. The other will be a catchall route that will display the productList.html view by default. Listing 7-12 shows the changes I have made to implement routing in the app.html file.

Listing 7-12. Adding Support for URL Routing in the app.html File

```
<!DOCTYPE html>
<html ng-app="sportsStore">
<head>
    <title>SportsStore</title>
    <script src="angular.js"></script>
    <link href="bootstrap.css" rel="stylesheet" />
    <link href="bootstrap-theme.css" rel="stylesheet" />
    <script>
        angular.module("sportsStore", ["customFilters", "cart", "ngRoute"])
        .config(function ($routeProvider) {

            $routeProvider.when("/checkout", {
                templateUrl: "/views/checkoutSummary.html"
            });

            $routeProvider.when("/products", {
                templateUrl: "/views/productList.html"
            });

            $routeProvider.otherwise({
                templateUrl: "/views/productList.html"
            });
        });
    </script>
    <script src="controllers/sportsStore.js"></script>
    <script src="filters/customFilters.js"></script>
    <script src="controllers/productListControllers.js"></script>
    <script src="components/cart/cart.js"></script>
    <script src="ngmodules/angular-route.js"></script>
</head>
```

```
<body ng-controller="sportsStoreCtrl">
    <div class="navbar navbar-inverse">
        <a class="navbar-brand" href="#">SPORTS STORE</a>
        <cart-summary />
    </div>
    <div class="alert alert-danger" ng-show="data.error">
        Error ({{data.error.status}}). The product data was not loaded.
        <a href="/app.html" class="alert-link">Click here to try again</a>
    </div>
    <ng-view />
</body>
</html>
```

I have added a script element to import the angular-route.js file into the application. The functionality that this file provides is defined in a module called ngRoute, which I have declared as a dependency of the sportsStore module.

To set up my routes, I have called the config method on the module object. The config method takes a function as its argument, which is executed when the module is loaded but before the application is executed, providing an opportunity for any one-off configuration tasks.

The function that I passed to the config method declares a dependency on a *provider*. As I mentioned earlier, there are different ways to create AngularJS services, and one of them creates a service that can be configured through a *provider object*, whose name is the concatenation of the service name and Provider. The $routeProvider that I have declared a dependency on is the provider for the $route service and is used to set up the URL routing in an application.

▓ **Tip** I explain how to create services with providers in Chapter 18 and how to use the $route service and the $routeProvider in Chapter 22.

I use two methods defined by the $routeProvider object to set up the routes I require. The when method allows me to match a URL to a view, like this:

```
...
$routeProvider.when("/checkout", {
    templateUrl: "/views/checkoutSummary.html"
});
...
```

This statement tells AngularJS that when the URL is /checkout, I want the /views/checkoutSummary.html file to be displayed. The otherwise method specifies the view that should be used when the URL doesn't match one of those defined by the when method. It is always sensible to define such a fallback route, and mine specifies the /views/ProductList.html view file.

URL routes are matched against the *path* section of the current URL and *not* the complete URL. Here is a URL that would match the route shown earlier:

---

http://localhost:5000/app.html#**/checkout**

I have highlighted the path, which follows the # character in the URL. AngularJS doesn't monitor the whole URL because a URL such as http://localhost:5000/checkout would cause the browser to dump the AngularJS application and try to load a different document from the server—something that is rarely required. This point causes a lot of confusion, so I have summarized the effect of my URL routing policy in Table 7-3.

Table 7-3. The Effect of the URL Routing Policy

URL	Effect
http://localhost:5000/app.html#**/checkout**	Displays the checkoutSummary.html view
http://localhost:5000/app.html#**/products**	Displays the productList.html view
http://localhost:5000/app.html#**/other**	Displays the productList.html view (because of the fallback route defined by the otherwise method)
http://localhost:5000/app.html	Displays the productList.html view (because of the fallback route defined by the otherwise method)

■ **Tip** As I describe in Chapter 22, you can enable support for using the HTML5 History API, which changes the way URLs are monitored so that something like http://localhost:5000/checkout will work. Caution is required because browser implementations differ, and it is easy to confuse the user because the browser will attempt to load a different document if they try to edit the URL manually.

Displaying the Routed View

The routing policy defines which views should be displayed for given URL paths, but it doesn't tell AngularJS *where* to display them. For that I need the ng-view directive, which is defined in the ngRoute module along with the other routing features. In Listing 7-12, I replaced the ng-include directive with ng-view, as follows:

```
...
<body ng-controller="sportsStoreCtrl">
    <div class="navbar navbar-inverse">
        <a class="navbar-brand" href="#">SPORTS STORE</a>
        <cart-summary />
    </div>
    <div class="alert alert-danger" ng-show="data.error">
        Error ({{data.error.status}}). The product data was not loaded.
        <a href="/app.html" class="alert-link">Click here to try again</a>
    </div>
    <ng-view />
</body>
...
```

There are no configuration options or settings required; just adding the directive tells AngularJS where it should insert the content of the currently selected view.

Using URL Routing to Navigate

Having defined my URL routes and applied the ng-view directive, I can change the URL path to navigate through the application. My first change is to the Checkout button displayed by the cart summary widget that I created earlier in the chapter. Listing 7-13 shows the change I made to the cartSummary.html file.

Listing 7-13. Using URL Path Navigation to the cartSummary.html File

```
<style>
    .navbar-right { float: right !important; margin-right: 5px;}
    .navbar-text { margin-right: 10px; }
</style>

<div class="navbar-right">
    <div class="navbar-text">
        <b>Your cart:</b>
        {{itemCount()}} item(s),
        {{total() | currency}}
    </div>
    <a href="#/checkout" class="btn btn-default navbar-btn">Checkout</a>
</div>
```

I updated the a element to add an href attribute whose value changes the path. Clicking the element will cause the browser to navigate to the new URL (which is local to the already-loaded document). The navigation change is detected by the AngularJS routing service, which causes the ng-view directive to display the checkoutSummary.html view, as illustrated by Figure 7-6.

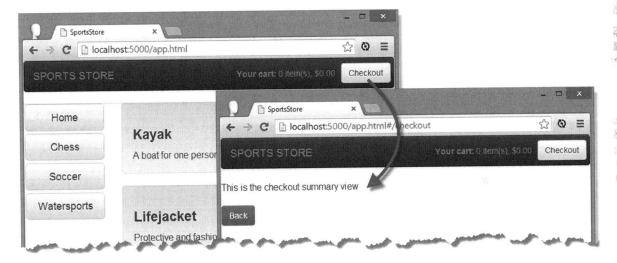

Figure 7-6. *Navigating to the checkout summary*

Notice that the URL displayed by the browser changes from the initial starting point of http://localhost:5000/app.html to http://localhost:5000/app.html#/checkout. You can click the Back button displayed by the checkoutSummary.html view, which I configured in Listing 7-12 to move to the /products path, as follows:

```
...
<a href="#/products" class="btn btn-primary">Back</a>
...
```

167

The main benefit of using URL routing is that components can change the layout shown by the ng-view directive without having any prior knowledge of the view that will be shown, the location or disposition of the ng-view directive, or sharing components (such as controllers or services) with the view that will be displayed. This makes it easier to scale up complex applications and makes it possible to change the behavior of the application just by changing the URL routing configuration.

▪ **Tip** You can also return to the products listing by manually editing the URL to be http://localhost:5000/app. html#/products or http://localhost:5000/app.html#. Note the trailing # character in that last URL. If you omit it, the browser will interpret the URL as a request to load the app.html page, which will cause any unsaved state to be lost. For the SportsStore application, that means the contents of the cart will be lost. The finicky nature of the URLs means that the user can edit them directly but that the results can be unexpected with even the slightest error.

Starting the Checkout Process

Now that the routing configuration is in place, I am going to turn to the checkout process. My first task is to define a new controller called cartSummaryController, which I have placed in a new file called controllers/ checkoutControllers.js. Listing 7-14 shows the contents of the new file.

Listing 7-14. The Contents of the checkoutControllers.js File

```
angular.module("sportsStore")
.controller("cartSummaryController", function($scope, cart) {

    $scope.cartData = cart.getProducts();

    $scope.total = function () {
        var total = 0;
        for (var i = 0; i < $scope.cartData.length; i++) {
            total += ($scope.cartData[i].price * $scope.cartData[i].count);
        }
        return total;
    }

    $scope.remove = function (id) {
        cart.removeProduct(id);
    }
});
```

The new controller is added to the sportsStore module and depends on the cart service. It exposes the contents of the cart through a scope property called cartData and defines behaviors to calculate the total value of the products in the cart and to remove a product from the cart. Using the features created by the controller, I can replace the temporary content in the checkoutSummary.html file with a summary of the cart. Listing 7-15 shows the changes I have made.

Listing 7-15. Revising the Contents of the checkoutSummary.html File

```html
<h2>Your cart</h2>

<div ng-controller="cartSummaryController">

    <div class="alert alert-warning" ng-show="cartData.length == 0">
        There are no products in your shopping cart.
        <a href="#/products" class="alert-link">Click here to return to the catalogue</a>
    </div>

    <div ng-hide="cartData.length == 0">
        <table class="table">
            <thead>
                <tr>
                    <th>Quantity</th>
                    <th>Item</th>
                    <th class="text-right">Price</th>
                    <th class="text-right">Subtotal</th>
                </tr>
            </thead>
            <tbody>
                <tr ng-repeat="item in cartData">
                    <td class="text-center">{{item.count}}</td>
                    <td class="text-left">{{item.name}}</td>
                    <td class="text-right">{{item.price | currency}}</td>
                    <td class="text-right">{{ (item.price * item.count) | currency}}</td>
                    <td>
                        <button ng-click="remove(item.id)"
                                class="btn btn-sm btn-warning">Remove</button>
                    </td>
                </tr>
            </tbody>
            <tfoot>
                <tr>
                    <td colspan="3" class="text-right">Total:</td>
                    <td class="text-right">
                        {{total() | currency}}
                    </td>
                </tr>
            </tfoot>
        </table>

        <div class="text-center">
            <a class="btn btn-primary" href="#/products">Continue shopping</a>
            <a class="btn btn-primary" href="#/placeorder">Place order now</a>
        </div>
    </div>
</div>
```

There are no new techniques in this view. The controller is specified using the ng-controller directive, and I use the ng-show and ng-hide directives to show a warning when there are no items in the cart and a summary when there are. The ng-repeat directive is used to generate rows in a table for each product in the cart, and the details are displayed using data bindings. Each row contains unit and total pricing and a button that uses the ng-click directive to invoke the remove controller behavior and remove an item from the cart.

The two a elements at the end of the view allow the user to navigate elsewhere in the application:

```
...
<a class="btn btn-primary" href="#/products">Continue shopping</a>
<a class="btn btn-primary" href="#/placeorder">Place order now</a>
...
```

The Continue shopping button returns the user to the product list by navigating to the #/products path, and the Place order button navigates to a new URL path, #/placeorder, which I will configure in the next section.

Applying the Checkout Summary

The next step is to add a script element to the app.html file and define the additional routes that I will need to complete the checkout process, as shown in Listing 7-16.

Listing 7-16. Applying the Checkout Summary to the app.html File

```
<!DOCTYPE html>
<html ng-app="sportsStore">
<head>
    <title>SportsStore</title>
    <script src="angular.js"></script>
    <link href="bootstrap.css" rel="stylesheet" />
    <link href="bootstrap-theme.css" rel="stylesheet" />
    <script>
        angular.module("sportsStore", ["customFilters", "cart", "ngRoute"])
        .config(function ($routeProvider) {
            $routeProvider.when("/complete", {
                templateUrl: "/views/thankYou.html"
            });

            $routeProvider.when("/placeorder", {
                templateUrl: "/views/placeOrder.html"
            });

            $routeProvider.when("/checkout", {
                templateUrl: "/views/checkoutSummary.html"
            });

            $routeProvider.when("/products", {
                templateUrl: "/views/productList.html"
            });
```

```
            $routeProvider.otherwise({
                templateUrl: "/views/productList.html"
            });
        });
    </script>
    <script src="controllers/sportsStore.js"></script>
    <script src="filters/customFilters.js"></script>
    <script src="controllers/productListControllers.js"></script>
    <script src="components/cart/cart.js"></script>
    <script src="ngmodules/angular-route.js"></script>
    <script src="controllers/checkoutControllers.js"></script>
</head>
<body ng-controller="sportsStoreCtrl">
    <div class="navbar navbar-inverse">
        <a class="navbar-brand" href="#">SPORTS STORE</a>
        <cart-summary />
    </div>
    <div class="alert alert-danger" ng-show="data.error">
        Error ({{data.error.status}}). The product data was not loaded.
        <a href="/app.html" class="alert-link">Click here to try again</a>
    </div>
    <ng-view />
</body>
</html>
```

The new routes associate URLs with views that I will create in the next chapter. Figure 7-7 shows the cart summary that is now presented when the user clicks the Checkout button on the cart widget.

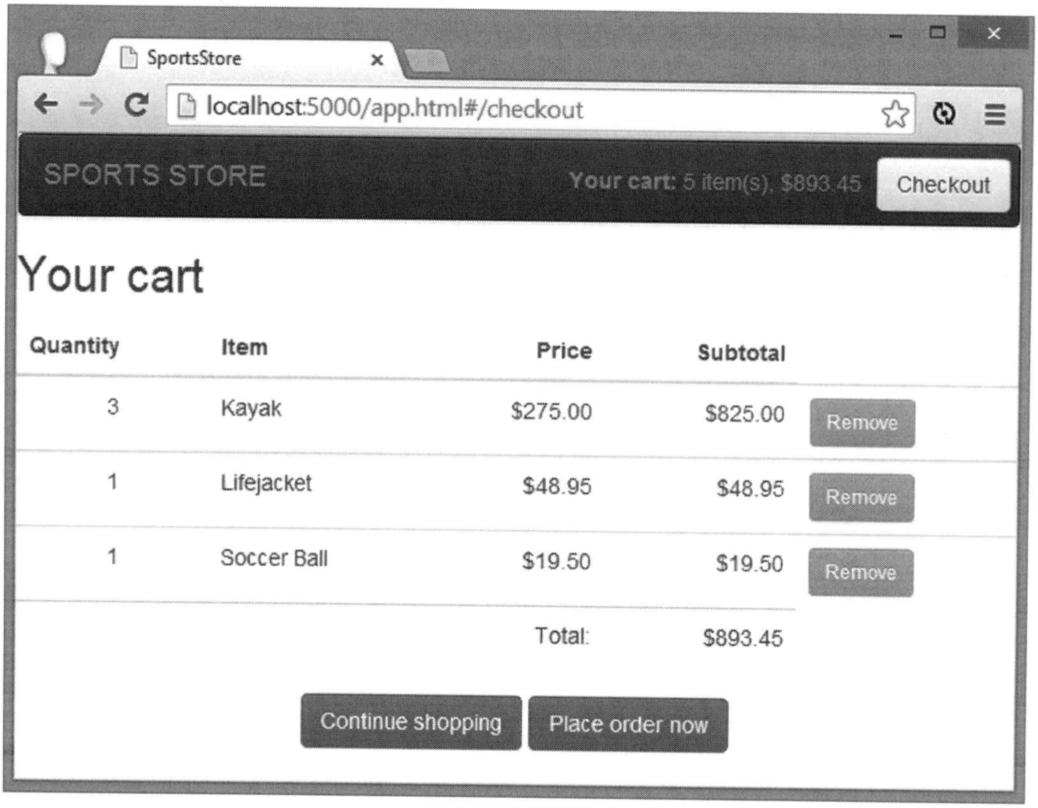

Figure 7-7. *Summarizing the contents of the shopping cart*

Summary

In this chapter, I continued the development of the SportsStore application to obtain the product data from the Deployd server, to add support for working with partial views, and to implement a custom directive. I also set up URL routing and started adding the functionality that will allow the user to place an order. In the next chapter, I will complete the SportsStore application and add support for administration.

■ ■ ■

CHAPTER 8

SportsStore: Orders and Administration

In this chapter, I complete the SportsStore application by collecting and validating shipping details and storing the order on the Deployd server. I also build an administration application that allows authenticated users to see the set of orders and manage the product catalog.

Preparing the Example Project

I am going to continue to build on the project that I started in Chapter 6 and extended in Chapter 7. You can download the source code from Chapter 7 from www.apress.com if you want to follow along with the examples but don't want to have to build the project from scratch.

In Chapter 7, I started the checkout process by displaying a summary of the cart to the user. That summary included an a element that navigated to the /placeorder URL path, for which I added a URL route to the app.html file. In fact, I defined two routes, both of which I will need to complete the checkout process in this chapter:

```
...
$routeProvider.when("/complete", {
    templateUrl: "/views/thankYou.html"
});

$routeProvider.when("/placeorder", {
    templateUrl: "/views/placeOrder.html"
});
...
```

In this chapter I am going to create the views named in the URL routes and create the components required to complete the checkout process.

Getting Shipping Details

After showing the user a summary of the products in the cart, I want to capture the shipping details for the order. That takes me to the AngularJS features for working with forms, which you are likely to require in most web applications. I have created the views/placeOrder.html file to capture the user's shipping details, which is the view named in one of the routing URLs shown earlier. I am going to introduce a number of form-related features, and to avoid having to repeat largely similar code, I am going to start working with a couple of data properties (for the user's name and street address) and then add other properties when I have introduced the features I will be using. Listing 8-1 shows the initial content of the placeOrder.html view file.

Listing 8-1. The Contents of the placeOrder.html File

```html
<h2>Check out now</h2>
<p>Please enter your details, and we'll ship your goods right away!</p>

<div class="well">
    <h3>Ship to</h3>
    <div class="form-group">
        <label>Name</label>
        <input class="form-control" ng-model="data.shipping.name" />
    </div>

    <h3>Address</h3>

    <div class="form-group">
        <label>Street Address</label>
        <input class="form-control" ng-model="data.shipping.street" />
    </div>

    <div class="text-center">
        <button class="btn btn-primary">Complete order</button>
    </div>
</div>
```

The first thing to notice about this view is that I have not used the ng-controller directive to specify a controller. That means the view will be supported by the top-level controller, sportsStoreCrtl, which manages the view that contains the ng-view directive (which I introduced in Chapter 7). I make this point because you don't *have* to define controllers for partial views, which is convenient when the view doesn't require any additional behaviors, as is the case here.

The important AngularJS feature in the listing is the use of the ng-model directive on the input elements, like this:

```html
...
<input class="form-control" ng-model="data.shipping.name" />
...
```

The ng-model directive sets up a *two-way data binding*. I explain data bindings in depth in Chapter 10, but the short version is that the kind of data binding I have been using so far in the SportsStore application—the ones that use the {{ and }} characters—are *one-way bindings*, which means they simply display a value from the scope. The value a one-way binding displays can be filtered, or it can be an expression rather than just a data value, but it a read-only relationship. The value displayed by the binding will be updated if the corresponding value on the scope changes, but that's the only direction that updates flow in—from the scope to the binding.

Two-way data bindings are used on form elements to allow the user to enter values that change the scope, rather than just displaying them. Updates flow in both directions between the scope and the data binding. An update to the scope data property performed through a JavaScript function, for example, will cause an input element to display the new value, and a new value entered by the user into the input element will update the scope. I explain the use of the ng-model directive in Chapter 10 and the broader AngularJS support for forms in Chapter 12. For this chapter it is enough to know that when the user enters a value into an input element, that value is assigned to the scope property specified by the ng-model directive—either the data.shipping.name property or the data.shipping.street property in this example. You can see how the form looks in the browser in Figure 8-1.

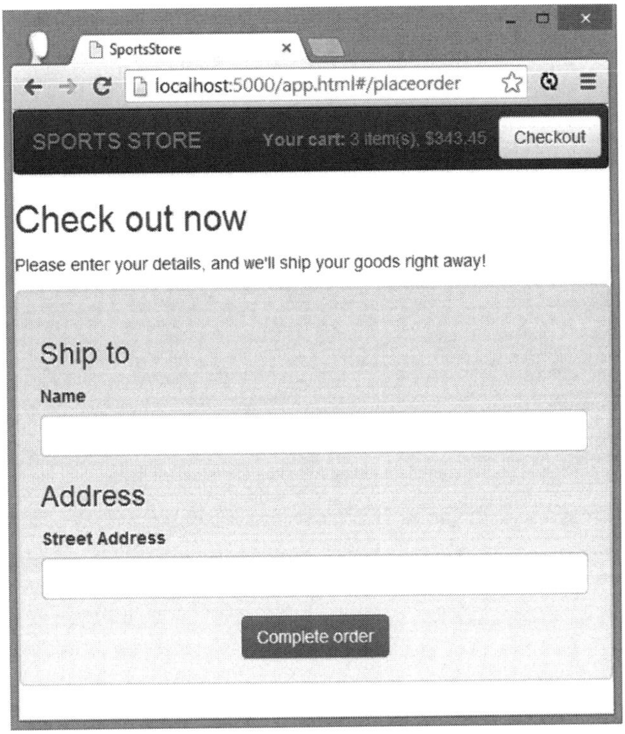

Figure 8-1. *The short version of the shipping details form*

■ **Tip** Notice that I don't have to update the controller so that it defines a `data.shipping` object on its scope or the individual `name` or `street` properties. AngularJS scopes are remarkably flexible and assume that you want to define a property dynamically if it isn't already defined. I explain this in more detail in Chapter 13.

Adding Form Validation

If you have written any kind of web application that uses form elements, then you will already know that users will put just about anything in an `input` field and that it is unwise to assume that users will have provided meaningful and useful data. To ensure you get the data you expect, AngularJS supports *form validation*, which allows values to be checked for suitability.

AngularJS form validation is based on honoring standard HTML attributes applied to form elements, such as `type` and `required`. Form validation is performed automatically, but some work is required to display validation feedback to the user and to integrate the overall validation results into an application.

■ **Tip** HTML5 defined a new set of values for the `type` attribute on `input` elements, which can be used to specify that a value should be an e-mail address or a number, for example. As I explain in Chapter 12, AngularJS can validate some of these new values.

Preparing for Validation

The first step in setting up form validation is to add a form element to the view and add the validation attributes to my input elements. Listing 8-2 shows the changes to the placeOrder.html file.

Listing 8-2. Preparing the placeOrder.html File for Validation

```
<h2>Check out now</h2>
<p>Please enter your details, and we'll ship your goods right away!</p>

<form name="shippingForm" novalidate>
    <div class="well">
        <h3>Ship to</h3>
        <div class="form-group">
            <label>Name</label>
            <input class="form-control" ng-model="data.shipping.name" required />
        </div>

        <h3>Address</h3>

        <div class="form-group">
            <label>Street Address</label>
            <input class="form-control" ng-model="data.shipping.street" required />
        </div>

        <div class="text-center">
            <button class="btn btn-primary">Complete order</button>
        </div>
    </div>
</form>
```

The form element has three purposes, even though I won't be using the browser's built-in support for submitting forms in the SportsStore application.

The first purpose is to enable validation. AngularJS redefines some HTML elements with custom directives to enable special features, and one such element is form. Without a form element, AngularJS won't validate the contents of elements such as input, select, textarea, and so on.

The second purpose of the form element is to disable any validation that the browser might try to perform, which is done through the application of the novalidate attribute. This attribute is a standard HTML5 feature, and it ensures that only AngularJS is checking the data that the user provides. If you omit the novalidate attribute, then the user may get conflicting or duplicated validation feedback, depending on the browser being used.

The final purpose of the form element is to define a variable that will be used to report on the form validity. This is done through the name attribute, which I have set to shippingForm. You'll see how this value is used later in this chapter when I display validation feedback and when I wire up the button element so that the user can place the order only when the contents of the form are valid.

In addition to the form element, I have applied the required attribute to the input elements. This is one of the simplest validation attributes that AngularJS recognizes, and it means that the user has to provide a value—any value—for the input element to be valid. See Chapter 12 for details of the other ways in which you can validate form elements.

Displaying Validation Feedback

Once the form element and the validation attributes are in place, AngularJS starts to validate the data that the user provides, but I have to do a little more work to give the user any feedback. I get into the details in Chapter 12, but there are two kinds of feedback I can use: I can define CSS styles to take advantage of classes that AngularJS assigns valid and invalid form elements to, and I can use scope variables to control the visibility of targeted feedback messages for specific elements. Listing 8-3 shows both kinds of changes.

Listing 8-3. Applying Validation Feedback to the placeOrder.html File

```
<style>
    .ng-invalid { background-color: lightpink; }
    .ng-valid { background-color: lightgreen; }
    span.error { color: red; font-weight: bold; }
</style>

<h2>Check out now</h2>
<p>Please enter your details, and we'll ship your goods right away!</p>

<form name="shippingForm" novalidate>
    <div class="well">
        <h3>Ship to</h3>
        <div class="form-group">
            <label>Name</label>
            <input name="name" class="form-control"
                ng-model="data.shipping.name" required />
            <span class="error" ng-show="shippingForm.name.$error.required">
                Please enter a name
            </span>
        </div>

        <h3>Address</h3>

        <div class="form-group">
            <label>Street Address</label>
            <input name="street" class="form-control"
                ng-model="data.shipping.street" required />
            <span class="error" ng-show="shippingForm.street.$error.required">
                Please enter a street address
            </span>
        </div>

        <div class="text-center">
            <button class="btn btn-primary">Complete order</button>
        </div>
    </div>
</form>
```

AngularJS assigns form elements to the ng-valid and ng-invalid classes, so I started by defining a style element that contains CSS styles that target those classes. Form elements are always in one of these classes, such that one of these styles is always applied.

■ **Tip**   I am setting up a simple validation configuration for the SportsStore application, the effect of which is that the form is invalid from the moment that it is shown to the user. This isn't always acceptable, and in Chapter 12 I describe some additional features that AngularJS provides to control when validation messages are displayed.

The CSS styles have the effect of indicating when there is a problem with an input element but provide no indication what the problem is. For that I have to add a name attribute to each element and use some validation data that AngularJS adds to the scope to control the visibility of error messages, like this:

```
...
<input name="street" class="form-control" ng-model="data.shipping.street" required />
<span class="error" ng-show="shippingForm.street.$error.required">
    Please enter a street address
</span>
...
```

In this fragment, I have shown the input element that captures the user's street address, which I have assigned the name value of street. AngularJS creates a shippingForm.street object on the scope (which is the combination of the name of the form element and the name of the input element). This object defines a $error property, which itself is an object that has properties for each of the validation attributes that the contents of the input element fail to satisfy. Or, to put it another way, if the shippingForm.street.$error.required property is true, then I know that the contents of the street input element are invalid, which I use to display an error message to the user through the application of the ng-show directive. (I explain the validation properties fully in Chapter 12 and the ng-show directive in Chapter 11.) You can see the initial state of the form in Figure 8-2.

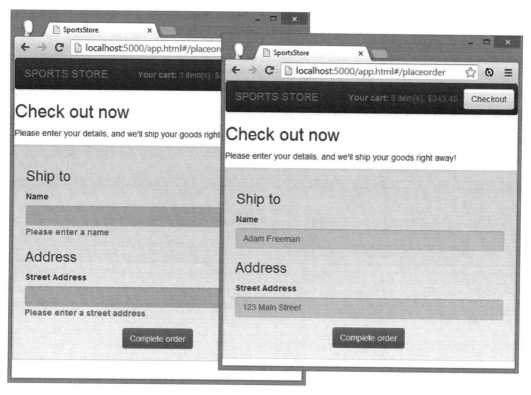

Figure 8-2. *The initial (invalid) form*

I satisfy the `required` attribute as I enter details into the `input` elements, which has the effect of switching the color applied to the element from red to green and hiding the error message.

■ **Note**   I am deliberately simplifying the way I apply validation in this chapter, but AngularJS can be used to create much more subtle and pleasing validation configurations, as I describe in Chapter 12.

Linking the Button to Validity

In most web applications, the user shouldn't be able to move to the next step in a process until all the form data has been provided and is valid. To that end, I want to disable the Complete order button when the form is invalid and automatically enable it when the user has completed the form properly.

To do this, I can take advantage of the validation information that AngularJS adds to the scope. In addition to the per-field information that I used in the previous section to display per-element messages, I can get information about the overall state of the form as well. The `shippingForm.$invalid` property will be set to `true` when one or more of the `input` elements is invalid, and I can combine this with the `ng-disabled` directive to manage the state of the `button` element. I describe the `ng-disabled` directive in Chapter 11, but it adds and removes the `disabled` attribute from the element it has been applied to based on the scope property or expression it is configured with. Listing 8-4 shows how I can tie the state of the `button` to form validation.

Listing 8-4. Setting the State of the Button in the placeOrder.html File

```
...
<div class="text-center">
    <button ng-disabled="shippingForm.$invalid"
        class="btn btn-primary">Complete order</button>
</div>
...
```

You can see the effect that the `ng-disabled` directive has on the `button` element in Figure 8-3.

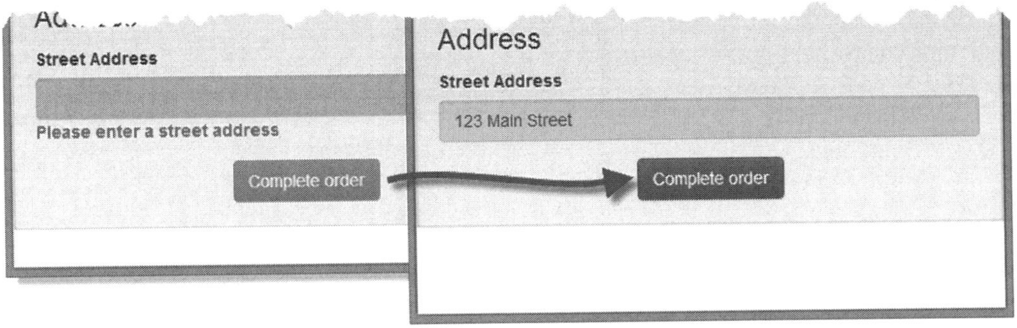

Figure 8-3. Controlling the state of a button based on form validation

Adding the Remaining Form Fields

Now that you have seen how AngularJS form validation works, I am going to add the remaining input elements to the form. I avoided this earlier because I wanted to show you the individual validation features without listing duplicate markup, but I can't go any further without the completed form. Listing 8-5 shows the addition of the remaining input elements and their associated validation messages.

Listing 8-5. Adding the Remaining Form Fields to the placeOrder.html File

```
<style>
    .ng-invalid { background-color: lightpink; }
    .ng-valid { background-color: lightgreen; }
    span.error { color: red; font-weight: bold; }
</style>

<h2>Check out now</h2>
<p>Please enter your details, and we'll ship your goods right away!</p>

<form name="shippingForm" novalidate>
    <div class="well">
        <h3>Ship to</h3>
        <div class="form-group">
            <label>Name</label>
            <input name="name" class="form-control"
                ng-model="data.shipping.name" required />
            <span class="error" ng-show="shippingForm.name.$error.required">
                Please enter a name
            </span>

        </div>

        <h3>Address</h3>

        <div class="form-group">
            <label>Street Address</label>
            <input name="street" class="form-control"
                ng-model="data.shipping.street" required />
            <span class="error" ng-show="shippingForm.street.$error.required">
                Please enter a street address
            </span>
        </div>

        <div class="form-group">
            <label>City</label>
            <input name="city" class="form-control"
                ng-model="data.shipping.city" required />
            <span class="error" ng-show="shippingForm.city.$error.required">
                Please enter a city
            </span>
        </div>
```

```
<div class="form-group">
    <label>State</label>
    <input name="state" class="form-control"
        ng-model="data.shipping.state" required />
    <span class="error" ng-show="shippingForm.state.$error.required">
        Please enter a state
    </span>
</div>

<div class="form-group">
    <label>Zip</label>
    <input name="zip" class="form-control"
        ng-model="data.shipping.zip" required />
    <span class="error" ng-show="shippingForm.zip.$error.required">
        Please enter a zip code
    </span>
</div>

<div class="form-group">
    <label>Country</label>
    <input name="country" class="form-control"
        ng-model="data.shipping.country" required />
    <span class="error" ng-show="shippingForm.country.$error.required">
        Please enter a country
    </span>
</div>

<h3>Options</h3>
<div class="checkbox">
    <label>
        <input name="giftwrap" type="checkbox"
            ng-model="data.shipping.giftwrap" />
        Gift wrap these items
    </label>
</div>

<div class="text-center">
    <button ng-disabled="shippingForm.$invalid"
            class="btn btn-primary">Complete order</button>
</div>
    </div>
</form>
```

■ **Tip**   The markup shown in Listing 8-5 is highly duplicative and is the sort of thing that attracts typos. You might be tempted to try to use the ng-repeat directive to generate the input elements from an array of objects that describes each field. This doesn't work well because of the way that the attribute values for directives like ng-model and ng-show are evaluated within the scope of the ng-repeat directive. My advice is to simply accept the duplication in the markup, but if you do want a more elegant technique, then read Chapters 15–17, which describe the ways in which you can create custom directives.

Placing Orders

Even though the state of the button element is controlled by form validation, clicking the button has no effect, and that's because I need to finish off the SportsStore application by allowing the user to submit orders. In the sections that follow, I'll extend the database provided by the Deployd server, send order data to the server using an Ajax request, and display a final thank-you message to complete the process.

Extending the Deployd Server

I need to extend the Deployd configuration to capture the orders that the SportsStore application will submit. Using the Deployd dashboard (which I first used in Chapter 6), click the large green plus button and select Collection, as shown in Figure 8-4.

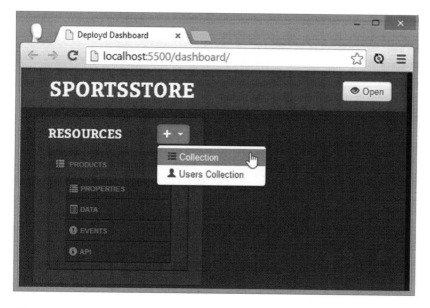

Figure 8-4. *Adding a new collection to Deployd*

Set the name of the new collection to /orders and click the Create button. The Deployd dashboard will display the property editor that I described in Chapter 6 when creating the products collection. Define the properties shown in Table 8-1.

Table 8-1. *The Properties Required for the Orders Collection*

Name	Type	Required
name	string	Yes
street	string	Yes
city	string	Yes
state	string	Yes
zip	string	Yes
country	string	Yes
giftwrap	boolean	No
products	array	Yes

Pay particular attention to the type of the giftwrap and products properties—they are not the same type as the other properties, and you'll get some odd results if you don't define them correctly. When you are finished, the property list for the orders collection should match that shown in Figure 8-5.

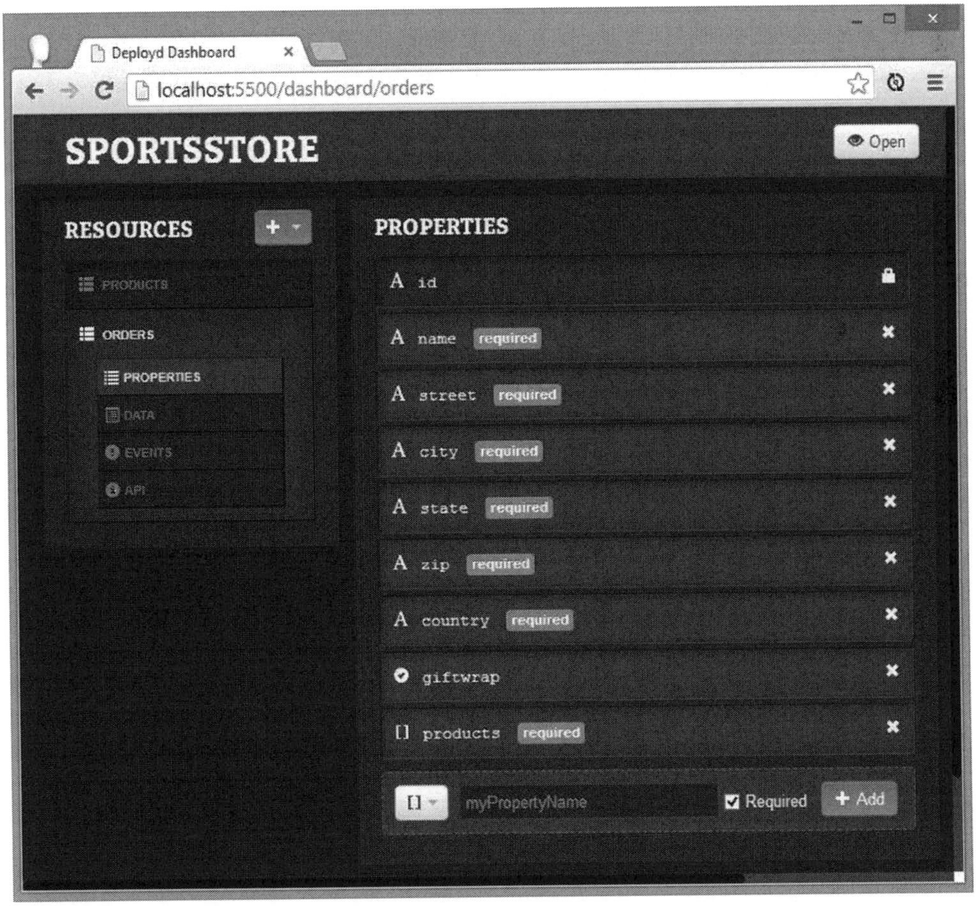

Figure 8-5. *Adding properties to the Deployd orders collection*

Defining the Controller Behavior

The next step is to define the controller behavior that will send details of an order to the Deployd server using an Ajax request. I could define this functionality in a number of different ways—as a service or in a new controller, for example. This flexibility is one of the hallmarks of working with AngularJS. There is no absolute right or wrong when it comes to the structure of an AngularJS application, and you will develop your own style and set of preferences as your experience builds. I am going to keep things simple and add the behavior I need to the top-level sportsStore controller, which already contains the code that makes the Ajax request to load the product data. Listing 8-6 shows the changes I have made.

Listing 8-6. Sending the Order to the Server in the sportsStore.js File

```
angular.module("sportsStore")
    .constant("dataUrl", "http://localhost:5500/products")
    .constant("orderUrl", "http://localhost:5500/orders")
    .controller("sportsStoreCtrl", function ($scope, $http, $location,
        dataUrl, orderUrl, cart) {

        $scope.data = {
        };

        $http.get(dataUrl)
            .success(function (data) {
                $scope.data.products = data;
            })
            .error(function (error) {
                $scope.data.error = error;
            });

        $scope.sendOrder = function (shippingDetails) {
            var order = angular.copy(shippingDetails);
            order.products = cart.getProducts();
            $http.post(orderUrl, order)
                .success(function (data) {
                    $scope.data.orderId = data.id;
                    cart.getProducts().length = 0;
                })
                .error(function (error) {
                    $scope.data.orderError = error;
                }).finally(function () {
                    $location.path("/complete");
                });
        }
    });
```

Deployd will create a new object in the database in response to a POST request and will return the object that it has created in the response, including the id attribute that has been generated to reference the new object.

Knowing this, you can see how the new additions to the controller operate. I have defined a new constant that specifies the URL that I will use for the POST request and added a dependency for the cart service so that I can get details of the products that the user requires. The behavior I added to the controller is called sendOrder, and it receives the shipping details for the user as its argument.

I use the angular.copy utility method, which I describe in Chapter 5, to create a copy of the shipping details object so that I can safely manipulate it without affecting other parts of the application. The properties of the shipping details object—which are created by the ng-model directives in the previous section—correspond to the properties that I defined for the orders Deployd collection, and all I have to do is define a products property that references the array of products in the cart.

I use the $http.post method, which creates an Ajax POST request to the specified URL and data, and I use the success and error methods that I introduced in Chapter 5 (and which I describe fully in Chapter 20) to respond to the outcomes from the request. For a successful request, I assign the id of the newly created order object to a scope property and clear the contents of the cart. If there is a problem, I assign the error object to the scope so that I can refer to it later.

I also use the then method on the promise returned by the $http.post method. The then method takes a function that is invoked whatever the outcome of the Ajax request. I want to display the same view to the user whatever happens, so I use the then method to call the $location.path method. This is how the path component of the URL is set programmatically, and it will trigger a change of view through the URL configuration that I created in Chapter 7. (I describe the $location service in Chapter 11 and demonstrate its use with URL routing in Chapter 22.)

Calling the Controller Behavior

To invoke the new controller behavior, I need to add the ng-click directive to the button element in the shipping details view, as shown in Listing 8-7.

Listing 8-7. Adding a Directive to the placeOrder.html File

```
...
<div class="text-center">
    <button ng-disabled="shippingForm.$invalid"
            ng-click="sendOrder(data.shipping)"
            class="btn btn-primary">
        Complete order
    </button>
</div>
...
```

Defining the View

The URL path that I specify after the Ajax request has completed is /complete, which the URL routing configuration maps to the file /views/thankYou.html. I created this file, and you can see the contents of it in Listing 8-8.

Listing 8-8. The Contents of the thankYou.html File

```
<div class="alert alert-danger" ng-show="data.orderError">
    Error ({{data.orderError.status}}). The order could not be placed.
    <a href="#/placeorder" class="alert-link">Click here to try again</a>
</div>

<div class="well" ng-hide="data.orderError">
    <h2>Thanks!</h2>
    Thanks for placing your order. We'll ship your goods as soon as possible.
    If you need to contact us, use reference {{data.orderId}}.
</div>
```

This view defines two different blocks of content to deal with success and unsuccessful Ajax requests. If there has been an error, then details of the error are displayed, along with a link that takes the user back to the shipping details view so they can try again. If the request is successful, then the user is shown a thank-you message that contains the id of the new order object. You can see the successful outcome in Figure 8-6.

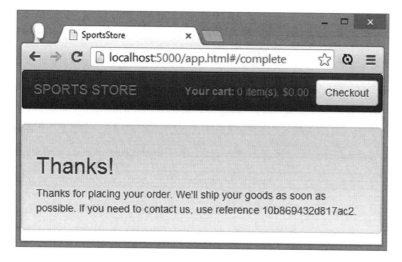

Figure 8-6. *Displaying feedback to the user when an order is placed*

Making Improvements

In building the user side of the SportsStore application, I took a couple of shortcuts that could be improved upon with techniques that I describe in later chapters but that depend on some concepts that I didn't want to introduce here.

First, when you load the app.html file into the browser, you may notice a small delay between the view being displayed and the elements for the products and categories being generated. This is because the Ajax request that gets the data is happening in the background, and while waiting for the server to return the data, AngularJS carries on executing the application and displaying the views, which are then updated when the data arrives. In Chapter 22, I describe how you can use the URL routing feature to prevent AngularJS from displaying the view until the Ajax request has been completed.

Next, I process the product data to extract the set of categories for the navigation and pagination features. In a real project, I would consider generating this information once when the product data first arrives and then reusing it thereafter. In Chapter 20, I describe how you can use promises to build chains of behavior, which is ideally suited to this kind of task.

Finally, I would have used the $animate service, which I describe in Chapter 23, to display short, focused animations to ease the transition from one view to another when the URL path changes.

AVOIDING OPTIMIZATION PITFALLS

You will notice that I say that I could *consider* reusing the category and pagination data, not that I would definitely do so. That's because any kind of optimization should be carefully assessed to ensure it is sensible and that it avoids two main pitfalls that dog optimization efforts.

The first pitfall is *premature optimization*, which is where a developer sees an opportunity to optimize an operation or task before the current implementation causes any problems or breaks a contract in the nonfunctional specification. This kind of optimization tends to make code more specific in its nature that it would otherwise be, and that can kill the easy movement of functionality from one component to another that is typical of AngularJS (and is one of the most enjoyable aspects of AngularJS development). Further, by optimizing code that hasn't been identified as a problem, you are spending time solving a (*potential*) problem that no one cares about—time that could equally be spent fixing real problems or building features that users require.

The second pitfall is *translation optimization*, where the optimization simply changes the nature of the problem rather than offers a real solution. The main issue with the way that the category and pagination data is generated is that it requires computation that could be avoided by caching the information. This seems like a good idea, but caching requires memory, which is often in short supply in mobile devices. The same kinds of devices that would benefit from not having to process a few data records are the same ones that lack the capacity to store some additional data to avoid that computation. And, if you are sending the client so much data that the user has to wait while the processing is performed, then the problems are more fundamental, and you should consider the way you have designed your application—perhaps obtaining and processing data in smaller chunks would be a more sensible solution.

I am not saying that you should not optimize your applications, but I *am* saying that you should not do so until you have a real problem to solve and that your optimizations should be a solution to the problem. Don't let an abhorrence of inefficiency prevent you from seeing that your development time is important and should only be spent solving real issues.

Administering the Product Catalog

To complete the SportsStore application, I am going to create an application that will allow the administrator to manage the contents of the product catalog and the order queue. This will allow me to demonstrate how AngularJS can be used to perform *create, read, update,* and *delete* (CRUD) operations and reinforce the use of some key features from the main SportsStore application.

■ **Note** Every back-end service implements authentication in a slightly different way, but the basic premise is the same: Send a request with the user's credentials to a specific URL, and if the request is successful, the browser will return a cookie that the browser will automatically send with subsequent requests to identify the user. The examples in this section are specific to Deployd, but they will translate easily to most platforms.

Preparing Deployd

Making changes to the database is something that only administrators should be able to do. To that end, I am going to use Deployd to define an administrator user and create the access policy described by Table 8-2.

Table 8-2. *The Access Control Policy for the Deployd Collections*

Collection	Admin	User
products	create, read, update, delete	read
orders	create, read, update, delete	create

In short, the administrator should be able to perform any operation on any collection. The normal users should be able to read (but not modify) the products collection and create new objects in the orders collection (but not be able to see, modify, or delete them).

Click the large green button in the Deployd dashboard and select Users Collection from the pop-up menu. Set the name of the new collection to be /users, as shown in Figure 8-7.

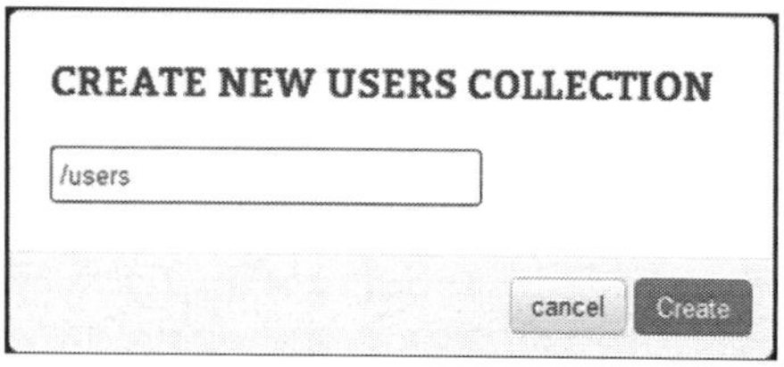

Figure 8-7. *Creating a users collection*

Click the Create button. Deployd will create the collection and display the property editor that I used to define the objects in the other collections. User collections are defined with id, username, and password properties, which are all that I need for this application. Click the Data button for the /users collection and create a new object with a username value of admin and a password of secret, as shown in Figure 8-8.

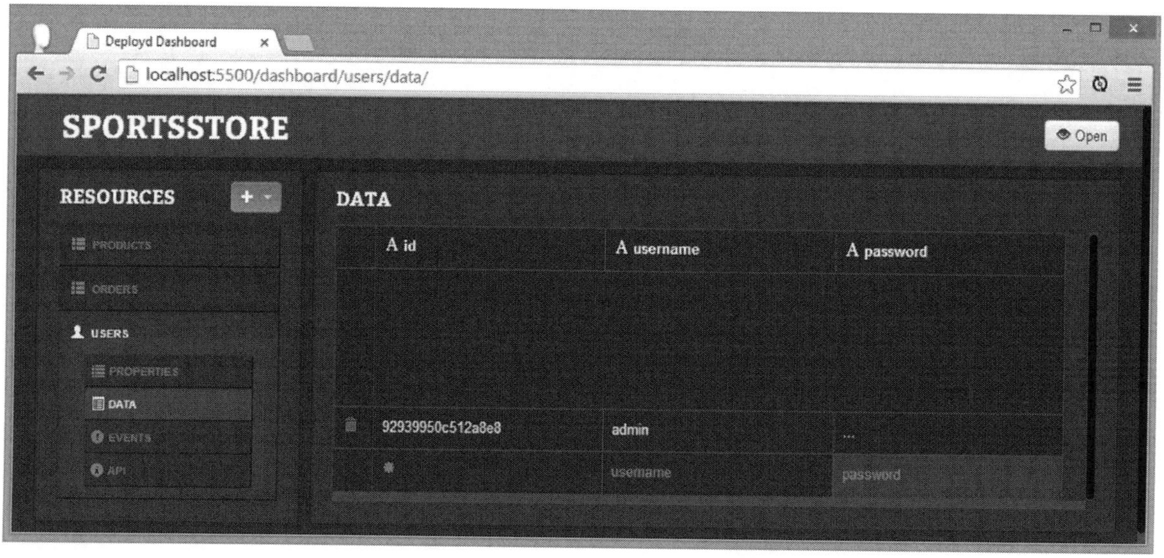

Figure 8-8. *Creating the admin user*

Securing the Collections

One of the features that I like about Deployd is that it defines a simple JavaScript API that can be used to implement server-side functionality, a series of events that are triggered when operations are performed on a collection. Click the products collection in the console and then click Events. You will see a series of tabs that represent different collection events: On Get, On Validate, On Post, On Put, and On Delete. These events are defined for all collections, and one of the many things you can do is use JavaScript to enforce an authorization policy. Enter the following JavaScript into the On Put and On Delete tabs:

```
if (me === undefined || me.username != "admin") {
    cancel("No authorization", 401);
}
```

In the Deployd API, the variable me represents the current user, and the cancel function terminates a request with the specified message and HTTP status code. This code allows access when there is an authenticated user and when that user is admin but terminates all other requests with a 401 status code, which indicates that the client is unauthorized to make the request.

■ **Tip** Don't worry about what the On XXX tabs relate to at the moment; it will become clear when I start making Ajax requests to the server.

Repeat the process for all the Events tabs in the orders collection, except for the On Post and On Validate tabs. Table 8-3 summarizes which collection tabs require the code shown earlier. The other tabs should be empty.

Table 8-3. *The Event Tabs That Require the JavaScript Code to Enforce Authentication Control*

Collection	Description
products	On Put, On Delete
orders	On Get, On Put, On Delete
users	None

Creating the Admin Application

I am going to create a separate AngularJS application for the administration tasks. I could integrate these features into the main application, but that would mean all users would be required to download the code for the admin functions, even though most of them would never use it. I added a new file called admin.html to the angularjs folder, the contents of which are shown in Listing 8-9.

Listing 8-9. The Contents of the admin.html File

```
<!DOCTYPE html>
<html ng-app="sportsStoreAdmin">
<head>
    <title>Administration</title>
    <script src="angular.js"></script>
    <script src="ngmodules/angular-route.js"></script>
```

```
<link href="bootstrap.css" rel="stylesheet" />
<link href="bootstrap-theme.css" rel="stylesheet" />
<script>
    angular.module("sportsStoreAdmin", ["ngRoute"])
        .config(function ($routeProvider) {

            $routeProvider.when("/login", {
                templateUrl: "/views/adminLogin.html"
            });

            $routeProvider.when("/main", {
                templateUrl: "/views/adminMain.html"
            });

            $routeProvider.otherwise({
                redirectTo: "/login"
            });
        });
</script>
</head>
<body>
    <ng-view />
</body>
</html>
```

This HTML file contains the script and link elements required for the AngularJS and Bootstrap files and an inline script element that defines the sportsStoreAdmin module, which will contain the application functionality (and which I have applied to the html element using the ng-app directive). I have used the Module.config method to create three routes for the application, which drive the ng-view directive in the body element. Table 8-4 summarizes the paths that the URLs match and the view files that they load.

Table 8-4. *The URL Paths in the admin.html File*

URL Path	View
/login	/views/adminLogin.html
/main	/views/adminMain.html
All others	Redirects to /login

For the route defined with the otherwise method, I used the redirectTo option, which changes the URL path to another route. This has the effect of moving the browser to the /login path, which is the one that I will use to authenticate the user. I describe the complete set of configuration options that you can use with URL routes in Chapter 22.

Adding the Placeholder View

I am going to implement the authentication feature first, but I need to create some placeholder content for the /views/adminMain.html view file so that I have something to show when authentication is successful. Listing 8-10 shows the (temporary) contents of the file.

Listing 8-10. The Contents of the adminMain.html File

```
<div class="well">
    This is the main view
</div>
```

I'll replace this placeholder with useful content once the application is able to authenticate users.

Implementing Authentication

Deployd authenticates users using standard HTTP requests. The application sends a POST request to the /users/login URL, which includes username and password values for the authenticating user. The server responds with status code 200 if the authentication attempt is successful and code 401 when the user cannot be authenticated. To implement authentication, I started by defining a controller that makes the Ajax calls and deals with the response. Listing 8-11 shows the contents of the controllers/adminControllers.js file, which I created for this purpose.

Listing 8-11. The Contents of the adminControllers.js File

```
angular.module("sportsStoreAdmin")
.constant("authUrl", "http://localhost:5500/users/login")
.controller("authCtrl", function($scope, $http, $location, authUrl) {

    $scope.authenticate = function (user, pass) {
        $http.post(authUrl, {
            username: user,
            password: pass
        }, {
            withCredentials: true
        }).success(function (data) {
            $location.path("/main");
        }).error(function (error) {
            $scope.authenticationError = error;
        });
    }
});
```

I use the angular.module method to extend the sportsStoreAdmin module that is created in the admin.html file. I use the constant method to specify the URL that will be used for authentication and create an authCtrl controller that defines a behavior called authenticate that receives the username and password values as arguments and makes an Ajax request to the Deployd server with the $http.post method (which I describe in Chapter 20). I use the $location service, which I describe in Chapter 11, to programmatically change the path displayed by the browser (and so trigger a URL route change) if the Ajax request is successful.

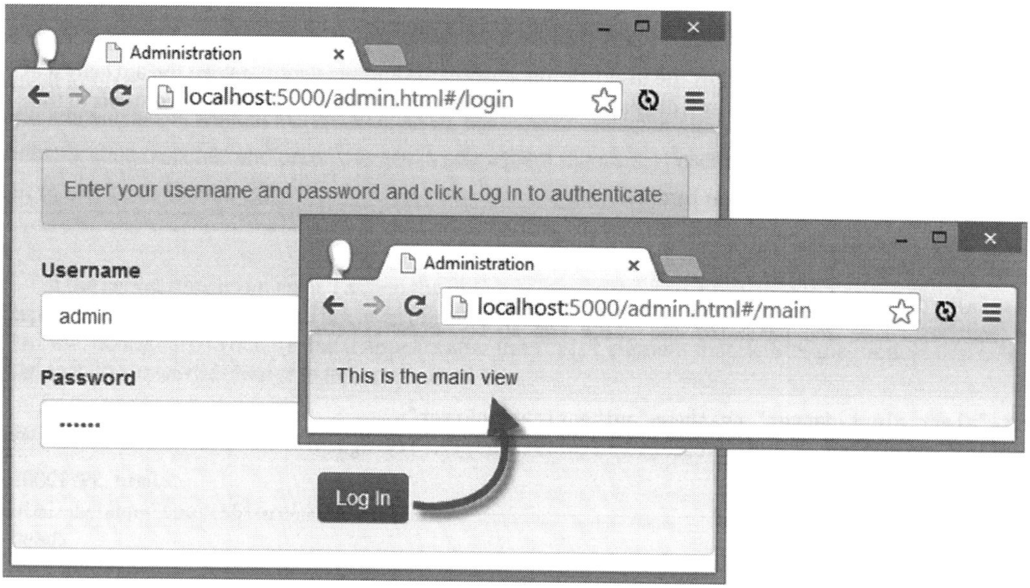

Figure 8-9. *Authenticating the user*

Defining the Main View and Controller

Once the user is authenticated, the `ng-view` directive displays the `adminMain.html` view. This view will be responsible for allowing the administrator to manage the contents of the product catalog and see the queue of orders.

Before I start to define the functionality that will drive the application, I need to define placeholder content for the views that will display the list of products and orders. First, I created `views/adminProducts.html`, the content of which is shown in Listing 8-14.

Listing 8-14. The Contents of the adminProducts.html File

```
<div class="well">
    This is the product view
</div>
```

Next, I create the `views/adminOrders.html` file, for which I have defined a similar placeholder, as shown in Listing 8-15.

Listing 8-15. The Contents of the adminOrders.html File

```
<div class="well">
    This is the order view
</div>
```

I need the placeholders so I can demonstrate the flow of views in the admin application. The URL routing feature has a serious limitation: You can't nest multiple instances of the `ng-view` directive, which makes it slightly more difficult to arrange to display different views within the scope of `ng-view`. I am going to demonstrate how to address this using the `ng-include` directive as a slightly less elegant—but perfectly functional—alternative. I started by defining a new controller in the `adminControllers.js` file, as shown in Listing 8-16.

Listing 8-16. Adding a New Controller in the adminControllers.js File

```
angular.module("sportsStoreAdmin")
.constant("authUrl", "http://localhost:5500/users/login")
.controller("authCtrl", function($scope, $http, $location, authUrl) {

    $scope.authenticate = function (user, pass) {
        $http.post(authUrl, {
            username: user,
            password: pass
        }, {
            withCredentials: true
        }).success(function (data) {
            $location.path("/main");
        }).error(function (error) {
            $scope.authenticationError = error;
        });
    }
})
.controller("mainCtrl", function($scope) {

    $scope.screens = ["Products", "Orders"];
    $scope.current = $scope.screens[0];

    $scope.setScreen = function (index) {
        $scope.current = $scope.screens[index];
    };

    $scope.getScreen = function () {
        return $scope.current == "Products"
            ? "/views/adminProducts.html" : "/views/adminOrders.html";
    };
});
```

The new controller is called mainCtrl, and it provides the behaviors and data I need to use the ng-include directive to manage views, as well as generate the navigation buttons that will switch between the views. The setScreen behavior is used to change the displayed view, which is exposed through the getScreen behavior.

You can see how the controller functionality is consumed in Listing 8-17, which shows how I have revised the adminMain.html file to remove the placeholder functionality.

Listing 8-17. Revising the adminMain.html File

```
<div class="panel panel-default row" ng-controller="mainCtrl">
    <div class="col-xs-3 panel-body">
        <a ng-repeat="item in screens" class="btn btn-block btn-default"
            ng-class="{'btn-primary': item == current }" ng-click="setScreen($index)">
            {{item}}
        </a>
    </div>
    <div class="col-xs-8 panel-body" >
        <div ng-include="getScreen()" />
    </div>
</div>
```

Listing 8-19. The Contents of the adminOrders.html File

```
<div ng-controller="ordersCtrl">

    <table class="table table-striped table-bordered">
        <tr><th>Name</th><th>City</th><th>Value</th><th></th></tr>
        <tr ng-repeat="order in orders">
            <td>{{order.name}}</td>
            <td>{{order.city}}</td>
            <td>{{calcTotal(order) | currency}}</td>
            <td>
                <button ng-click="selectOrder(order)" class="btn btn-xs btn-primary">
                    Details
                </button>
            </td>
        </tr>
    </table>

    <div ng-show="selectedOrder">
        <h3>Order Details</h3>

        <table class="table table-striped table-bordered">
            <tr><th>Name</th><th>Count</th><th>Price</th></tr>
            <tr ng-repeat="item in selectedOrder.products">
                <td>{{item.name}}</td>
                <td>{{item.count}}</td>
                <td>{{item.price| currency}} </td>
            </tr>
        </table>
    </div>
</div>
```

The view consists of two table elements. The first table shows a summary of the orders, along with a button element that invokes the selectOrder behavior to focus on the order. The second table is visible only once an order has been selected and displays details of the products that have been ordered. You can see the result in Figure 8-11.

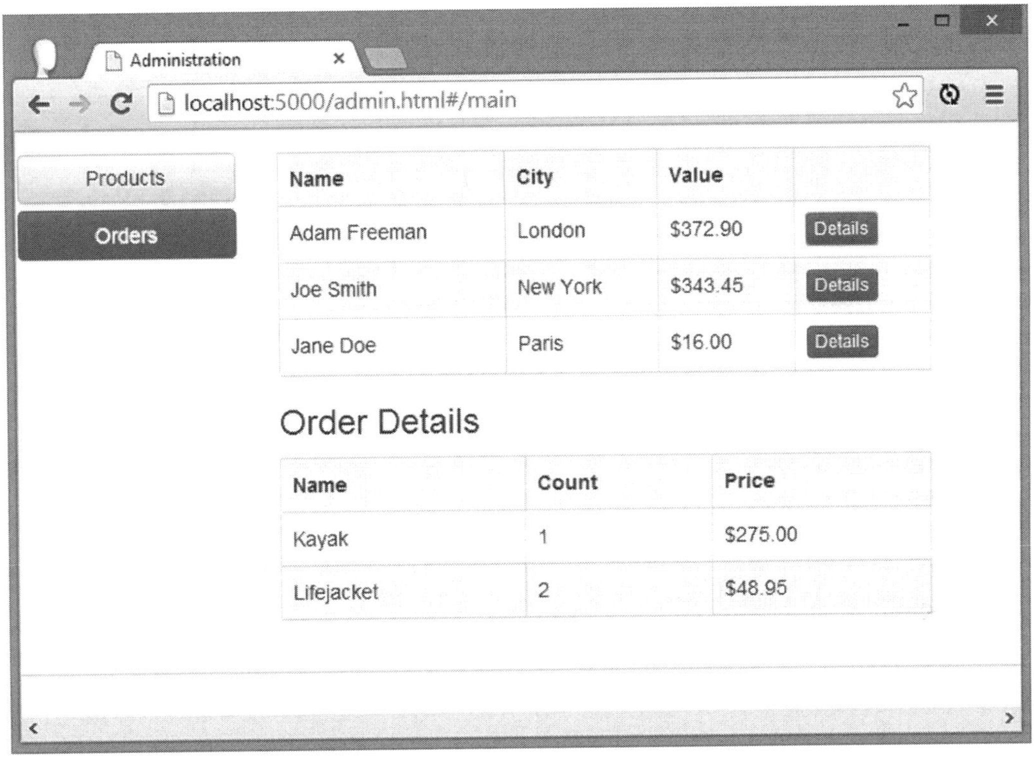

Figure 8-11. Viewing the SportsStore orders

Implementing the Products Feature

For the products feature, I am going to perform a full range of operations on the data so that the administrator not only can see the products but create new ones and edit and delete existing ones. If you turn to the Deployd dashboard, select the Products collection, and click the API button, you will see details of the RESTful API that Deployd provides for working with data using HTTP requests. I get into the details of RESTful APIs properly in Chapter 21, but the short version is that the data object you want is specified using the URL, and the operation you want to perform is specified by the HTTP method of the request sent to the server. So, for example, if I want to delete the object whose id attribute is 100, I would sent a request to the server using the DELETE HTTP method and the URL /products/100.

You can use the $http service to work with a RESTful API, but doing so means you have to expose the complete set of URLs that are used to perform operations throughout the application. You can do this by defining a service that performs the operations for you, but a more elegant alternative is to use the $resource service, defined in the optional ngResource module, which also has a nice way of dealing with defining the URLs that are used to send requests to the server.

Defining the RESTful Controller

I am going to start by defining the controller that will provide access to the Deployd RESTful API via the AngularJS $resource service. I created a new file called adminProductController.js in the controllers folder and used it to define the controller shown in Listing 8-20.

Listing 8-20. The Contents of the adminProductController.js File

```
angular.module("sportsStoreAdmin")
.constant("productUrl", "http://localhost:5500/products/")
.config(function($httpProvider) {
    $httpProvider.defaults.withCredentials = true;
})
.controller("productCtrl", function ($scope, $resource, productUrl) {

    $scope.productsResource = $resource(productUrl + ":id", { id: "@id" });

    $scope.listProducts = function () {
        $scope.products = $scope.productsResource.query();
    }

    $scope.deleteProduct = function (product) {
        product.$delete().then(function () {
            $scope.products.splice($scope.products.indexOf(product), 1);
        });
    }

    $scope.createProduct = function (product) {
        new $scope.productsResource(product).$save().then(function (newProduct) {
            $scope.products.push(newProduct);
            $scope.editedProduct = null;
        });
    }

    $scope.updateProduct = function (product) {
        product.$save();
        $scope.editedProduct = null;
    }

    $scope.startEdit = function (product) {
        $scope.editedProduct = product;
    }

    $scope.cancelEdit = function () {
        $scope.editedProduct = null;
    }

    $scope.listProducts();
});
```

I am not going to go too deeply into the code for this listing because I cover the topic fully in Chapter 21. But there some important themes that are worth explaining now, so I'll cover just the highlights.

First, the $resource service is built on top of the features provided by the $http service, and that means I need to enable the withCredentials option that I used earlier to get authentication to work properly. I don't have access to the requests made by the $http service, but I can change the default settings for all Ajax requests by calling the config method on the module and declaring a dependency on the *provider* for the $http service, like this:

```
...
.config(function($httpProvider) {
    $httpProvider.defaults.withCredentials = true;
})
...
```

As I explain in Chapter 18, services can be created in several different ways, and one option includes defining a provider object that can be used to change the way that the service works. In this case, the provider for the $http service, which is called $httpProvider, defines a defaults property that can be used to configure settings for all Ajax requests. See Chapter 20 for details of the default values that can be set through the $httpProvider object.

The most important part of this example, however, is the statement that creates the *access object* that provides access to the RESTful API:

```
...
$scope.productsResource = $resource(productUrl + ":id", { id: "@id" });
...
```

The first argument passed into the $resource call defines the URL format that will be used to make queries. The :id part, which corresponds to the map object that is the second argument, tells AngularJS that if the data object it is working with has an id property, then it should be appended to the URL used for the Ajax request.

The URLs and HTTP methods that are used to access the RESTful API are inferred from these two arguments, which means I don't have to make individual Ajax calls using the $http service.

The access object that is the result from using the $resource service has query, get, delete, remove, and save methods that are used to obtain and operate on the data from the server (methods are also defined on individual data objects, as I explain in Chapter 21). Calling these methods triggers the Ajax request that performs the required operation.

■ **Tip**   The methods defined by the access object don't quite correspond to the API defined by Deployd, although Deployd is flexible enough to accept the requests that the $resource service makes. In Chapter 21, I show you how you can change the $resource configuration to fully map onto any RESTful API.

Most of the code in the controller presents these methods to the view in a useful way that works around a wrinkle in the $resource implementation. The collection of data objects returned by the query method isn't automatically updated when objects are created or deleted, so I have to include code to take care of keeping the local collection in sync with the remote changes.

■ **Tip**   The access object doesn't automatically load the data from the server, which is why I call the query method directly at the end of the controller function.

Defining the View

To take advantage of the functionality defined by the controller, I have replaced the placeholder content in the adminProducts.html view with the markup shown in Listing 8-21.

Listing 8-21. The Contents of the adminProduct.html File

```html
<style>
    #productTable { width: auto; }
    #productTable td { max-width: 150px; text-overflow: ellipsis;
                      overflow: hidden; white-space: nowrap; }
    #productTable td input { max-width: 125px; }
</style>

<div ng-controller="productCtrl">
    <table id="productTable" class="table table-striped table-bordered">
        <tr>
            <th>Name</th><th>Description</th><th>Category</th><th>Price</th><th></th>
        </tr>
        <tr ng-repeat="item in products" ng-hide="item.id == editedProduct.id">
            <td>{{item.name}}</td>
            <td class="description">{{item.description}}</td>
            <td>{{item.category}}</td>
            <td>{{item.price | currency}}</td>
            <td>
                <button ng-click="startEdit(item)" class="btn btn-xs btn-primary">
                    Edit
                </button>
                <button ng-click="deleteProduct(item)" class="btn btn-xs btn-primary">
                    Delete
                </button>
            </td>
        </tr>
        <tr ng-class="{danger: editedProduct}">
            <td><input ng-model="editedProduct.name" required /></td>
            <td><input ng-model="editedProduct.description" required /></td>
            <td><input ng-model="editedProduct.category" required /></td>
            <td><input ng-model="editedProduct.price" required /></td>
            <td>
                <button ng-hide="editedProduct.id"
                        ng-click="createProduct(editedProduct)"
                        class="btn btn-xs btn-primary">
                    Create
                </button>
                <button ng-show="editedProduct.id"
                        ng-click="updateProduct(editedProduct)"
                        class="btn btn-xs btn-primary">
                    Save
                </button>
                <button ng-show="editedProduct"
                        ng-click="cancelEdit()" class="btn btn-xs btn-primary">
                    Cancel
                </button>
            </td>
        </tr>
    </table>
</div>
```

There are no new techniques in this view, but it shows how AngularJS directives can be used to manage a stateful editor view. The elements in the view use the controller behaviors to manipulate the collection of product objects, allowing the user to create new products and edit or delete existing products.

Adding the References to the HTML File

All that remains is to add script elements to the admin.html file to import the new module and the new controller and to update the main application module so that it declares a dependency on ngResource, as shown in Listing 8-22.

Listing 8-22. Adding the References to the admin.html File

```
<!DOCTYPE html>
<html ng-app="sportsStoreAdmin">
<head>
    <title>Administration</title>
    <script src="angular.js"></script>
    <script src="ngmodules/angular-route.js"></script>
    <script src="ngmodules/angular-resource.js"></script>
    <link href="bootstrap.css" rel="stylesheet" />
    <link href="bootstrap-theme.css" rel="stylesheet" />
    <script>
        angular.module("sportsStoreAdmin", ["ngRoute", "ngResource"])
            .config(function ($routeProvider) {

                $routeProvider.when("/login", {
                    templateUrl: "/views/adminLogin.html"
                });

                $routeProvider.when("/main", {
                    templateUrl: "/views/adminMain.html"
                });

                $routeProvider.otherwise({
                    redirectTo: "/login"
                });
            });
    </script>
    <script src="controllers/adminControllers.js"></script>
    <script src="controllers/adminProductController.js"></script>
</head>
<body>
    <ng-view />
</body>
</html>
```

You can see the effect in Figure 8-12. The user creates a new product by filling in the input elements and clicking the Create button, modifies a product by clicking one of the Edit buttons, and removes a product using one of the Delete buttons.

Table 9-1. (*continued*)

Problem	Solution	Listing
Define a service.	Use the Module.service, Module.factory, or Module.provider method.	12
Define a service from an existing object or value.	Use the Module.value method.	13
Add structure to the code in an application.	Create multiple modules and declare dependencies from the module referenced by the ng-app attribute.	14–16
Register functions that are called when modules are loaded.	Use the Module.config and Module.run methods.	17

Preparing the Example Project

I am going to return to a simple project structure for the examples in this part of the book. Remove the contents of the angularjs folder and add the angular.js, bootstrap.css, and bootstrap-theme.css files as described in Chapter 1. Create an HTML file called example.html and set the content to match Listing 9-1.

Listing 9-1. The Contents of the example.html File

```
<!DOCTYPE html>
<html ng-app="exampleApp" >
<head>
    <title>AngularJS Demo</title>
    <link href="bootstrap.css" rel="stylesheet" />
    <link href="bootstrap-theme.css" rel="stylesheet" />
    <script src="angular.js"></script>
    <script>

        var myApp = angular.module("exampleApp", []);

        myApp.controller("dayCtrl", function ($scope) {
            // controller statements will go here
        });

    </script>
</head>
<body>
    <div class="panel" ng-controller="dayCtrl">
        <div class="page-header">
            <h3>AngularJS App</h3>
        </div>
        <h4>Today is {{day || "(unknown)"}}</h4>
    </div>
</body>
</html>
```

The listing contains the plumbing for a minimal AngularJS app, which I'll explain in the sections that follow. The view for this app contains a data binding expression that isn't set up at the moment, so I have used the JavaScript || operator, which I described in Chapter 5, to display the value of the day variable if it is defined and the string (unknown) otherwise. Figure 9-1 shows how this HTML document is displayed by the browser.

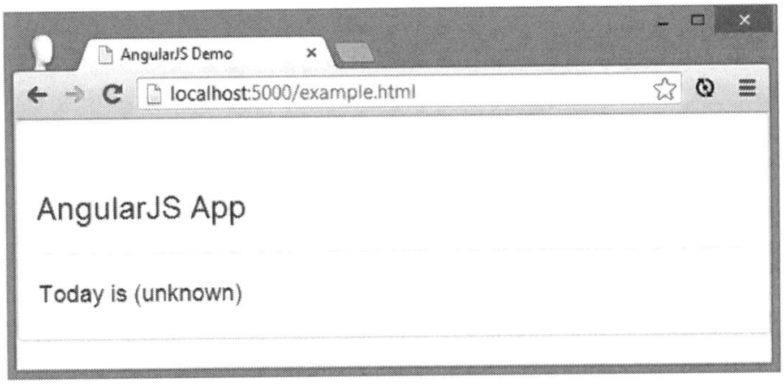

Figure 9-1. *Displaying the example HTML document in the browser*

Working with Modules

Modules are the top-level components for AngularJS applications. You can actually build simple AngularJS apps without needing to reference modules at all, but I don't recommend doing so because simple applications become complex applications over time, and you'll just end up having to rewrite the application when it becomes unmanageable. Working with modules is easy, and the handful of additional JavaScript statements that you need to set up and manage modules is a worthwhile investment. Modules have three main roles in an AngularJS app:

- To associate an AngularJS application with a region of an HTML document

- To act as a gateway to key AngularJS framework features

- To help organize the code and components in an AngularJS application

I explain each of these functions in the sections that follow.

Setting the Boundaries of an AngularJS Application

The first step when creating an AngularJS app is to define a module and associate it with a region of the HTML document. Modules are defined with the angular.module method. Listing 9-2 shows the statement from the example that creates the module for the example app.

Listing 9-2. Creating a Module

```
...
var myApp = angular.module("exampleApp", []);
...
```

The module method supports the three arguments described in Table 9-2, although it is common to use only the first two.

Table 9-2. *The Arguments Accepted by the angular.module Method*

Name	Description
name	The name of the new module
requires	The set of modules that this module depends on
config	The configuration for the module, equivalent to calling the Module.config method—see the "Working with the Module Life Cycle" section

When creating a module that will be associated with an HTML document (as opposed to organizing code, which I describe shortly), the convention is to give the module a name with the suffix App. In the example, I used the name exampleApp for my module, and the benefit of this convention is that it makes it clear which module represents the top-level AngularJS application in your code structure—something that can be useful in complex apps that can contain multiple modules.

Defining a module in JavaScript is only part of the process; the module must also be applied to the HTML content using the ng-app attribute. When AngularJS is the only web framework being used, the convention is to apply the ng-app attribute to the html element, as illustrated by Listing 9-3, which shows the element from the example.html file to which the ng-app element has been applied.

Listing 9-3. Applying the **ng-app** Attribute in the example.html File

```
...
<html ng-app="exampleApp">
...
```

The ng-app attribute is used during the *bootstrap* phase of the AngularJS life cycle, which I describe later in this chapter (and which is not to be confused with the Bootstrap CSS framework that I described in Chapter 4).

AVOIDING THE MODULE CREATE/LOOKUP TRAP

When creating a module, you must specify the name and requires arguments, even if your module has no dependencies. I explain how dependencies work later in this chapter, but a common mistake is to omit the requires argument, like this:

```
...
var myApp = angular.module("exampleApp");
...
```

This has the effect of trying to locate a previously created module called exampleApp, rather than creating one, and will usually result in an error (unless there is already a module by that name, in which case you will usually get some unexpected behavior).

Using Modules to Define AngularJS Components

The angular.module method returns a Module object that provides access to the most important features that AngularJS provides via the properties and methods I have described in Table 9-3. As I explained at the start of this chapter, the features that the Module object provides access to are the features that I spend a lot of this book describing. I provide a brief demonstration and explanation of the most important features in the section and include references to the chapters in which you can find more details.

Table 9-3. *The Members of the Module Object*

Name	Description
animation(name, factory)	Supports the animation feature, which I describe in Chapter 23.
config(callback)	Registers a function that can be used to configure a module when it is loaded. See the "Working with the Module Life Cycle" section for details.
constant(key, value)	Defines a service that returns a constant value. See the "Working with the Module Life Cycle" section later in this chapter.
controller(name, constructor)	Creates a controller. See Chapter 13 for details.
directive(name, factory)	Creates a directive, which extends the standard HTML vocabulary. See Chapters 15–17.
factory(name, provider)	Creates a service. See Chapter 18 for details and an explanation of how this method differs from the provider and service methods.
filter(name, factory)	Creates a filter that formats data for display to the user. See Chapter 14 for details.
provider(name, type)	Creates a service. See Chapter 18 for details and an explaination of how this method differs from the service and factory methods.
name	Returns the name of the module.
run(callback)	Registers a function that is invoked after AngularJS has loaded and configured all of the modules. See the "Working with the Module Life Cycle" section for details.
service(name, constructor)	Creates a service. See Chapter 18 for details and an explanation of how this method differs from the provider and factory methods.
value(name, value)	Defines a service that returns a constant value; see the "Defining Values" section later in this chapter.

The methods defined by the Module object fall into three broad categories: those that define components for an AngularJS application, those that make it easier to create those building blocks, and those that help manage the AngularJS life cycle. I'll start by introducing the building blocks and then talk about the other features that are available.

Defining Controllers

Controllers are one of the big building blocks of an AngularJS application, and they act as a conduit between the model and the views. Most AngularJS projects will have multiple controllers, each of which delivers the data and logic required for one aspect of the application. I describe controllers in depth in Chapter 13.

Controllers are defined using the Module.controller method, which takes two arguments: the name of the controller and a *factory* function, which is used to set up the controller and get it ready for use (see the "Factory and Worker Functions" sidebar later in the chapter for more details). Listing 9-4 shows the statements from the example.html file that create the controller.

Listing 9-4. Creating a Controller in the example.html File

```
...
myApp.controller("dayCtrl", function ($scope) {
    // controller statements will go here
});
...
```

The convention for controller names is to use the suffix Ctrl. The statement in the listing creates a new controller called dayCtrl. The function passed to the Module.controller method is used to declare the controller's *dependencies*, which are the AngularJS components that the controller requires. AngularJS provides some built-in services and features that are specified using argument names that start with the $ symbol. In the listing you can see that I have specified the $scope, which asks AngularJS to provide the scope for the controller. To declare a dependency on $scope, I just have to use the name as an argument to the factory function, like this:

```
...
myApp.controller("dayCtrl", function (**$scope**) {
...
```

This is an example of *dependency injection* (DI), where AngularJS inspects the arguments that are specified for a function and locates the components they correspond to; see the "Understanding Dependency Injection" sidebar for details. The function I passed to the controller method has an argument called x, and AngularJS will automatically pass in the scope object when the function is called. I explain how services work in Chapter 18 and show you how scopes work in Chapter 13.

UNDERSTANDING DEPENDENCY INJECTION

One of the AngularJS features that causes the most confusion is dependency injection (DI). It can be hard to figure out what DI is, how it works, and why it is useful. Even if you have encountered dependency injection in other frameworks, AngularJS takes an unusual approach and mixes in some features that are distinct from other languages.

As you will learn as you read this chapter, an AngularJS application consists of different components: controllers, directives, filters, and so on. I describe each of them and give a little example.

The place to start is to understand the problem that DI sets out to solve. Some of the components in an AngularJS application will depend on others. In Listing 9-4, my controller needs to use the $scope component, which allows it to pass data to the view. This is an example of a *dependency*—my controller *depends* on the $scope component to perform its work.

Dependency injection simplifies the process of dealing with dependencies—known as *resolving a dependency*—between components. Without DI, I would have to locate $scope myself somehow, probably using global variables. It would work, but it wouldn't be as simple as the AngularJS technique.

A component in an AngularJS application *declares its dependencies* by defining arguments on its factory function whose names match the components it depends on. In this example, AngularJS inspects the arguments of my controller function, determines that it depends on the $scope component, locates $scope for me, and passes it as an argument to the factory function when it is invoked.

To put it another way, DI changes the purpose of function arguments. Without DI, arguments are used to *receive* whatever objects the caller wants to pass, but with DI, the function uses arguments to make *demands*, telling AngularJS what building blocks it needs.

One of the interesting side effects of the way that DI works in AngularJS is that the order of the arguments always matches the order in which the dependencies are declared. Consider this function:

```
...
myApp.controller("dayCtrl", function ($scope, $filter) {
...
```

The first argument passed to the function will be the $scope component, and the second will be the $filter service object. Don't worry about what the $filter object does for the moment. I introduce it later in this chapter. What's important is that the order in which you declare dependencies is honored by AngularJS. If I change the order of my dependencies, like this:

```
...
myApp.controller("dayCtrl", function ($filter, $scope) {
...
```

then AngularJS will pass me the $filter object as the first argument and the $scope object as the second. In short, it doesn't matter what order you define dependency-injected arguments. This may seem obvious, but it isn't the way that JavaScript usually works, and it can take some time to get used to. You may already have seen a similar technique used in other programming languages—this is known as *named parameters* in C#, for example.

The main benefit of using dependency injection during development is that AngularJS takes care of managing component and feeding them to your functions when they are needed. DI also provides benefits when testing your code, because it allows you to easily replace real building blocks with *fake* or *mock objects* that let you focus on specific parts of your code; I explain how this works in Chapter 25.

Applying Controllers to Views

Defining controllers is only part of the process—they must also be applied to HTML elements so that AngularJS knows which part of an HTML document forms the view for a given controller. This is done through the ng-controller attribute, and Listing 9-5 shows the HTML elements from the example.html file that apply the dayCtrl controller to the HTML document.

Listing 9-5. Defining Views in the example.html File

```
...
<body>
    <div class="panel" ng-controller="dayCtrl">
        <div class="page-header">
            <h3>AngularJS App</h3>
        </div>
        <h4>Today is {{day || "(unknown)"}}</h4>
    </div>
</body>
...
```

The view in this example is the div element and its contents—in other words, the element to which the ng-controller attribute has been applied and the elements it contains.

The $scope component that I specified as an argument when I created the controller is used to provide the view with data, and only the data configured via $scope can be used in expressions and data bindings. At the moment,

213

when you navigate to the example.html file with the browser, the data binding generates the string (unknown) because I have used the || operator to coalesce null values, like this:

```
...
<h4>Today is {{day || "(unknown)"}}</h4>
...
```

A nice feature of AngularJS data bindings is that you can use them to evaluate JavaScript expressions. This binding will display the value of the day property provided by the $scope component unless it is null, in which case (unknown) will be displayed instead. To provide a value for the day property, I must assign it to the $scope in the controller setup function, as shown in Listing 9-6.

Listing 9-6. Defining a Model Data Value in the example.html File

```
...
<script>

    var myApp = angular.module("exampleApp", []);

    myApp.controller("dayCtrl", function ($scope) {
        var dayNames = ["Sunday", "Monday", "Tuesday", "Wednesday",
            "Thursday", "Friday", "Saturday"];
        $scope.day = dayNames[new Date().getDay()];
    });

</script>
...
```

I create a new Date, call the getDay method to get the numeric day of the week, and look up the day name from an array of string values. As soon as I make this addition to the script element, the value I have specified is available to the view and is used in the HTML output, as shown in Figure 9-2.

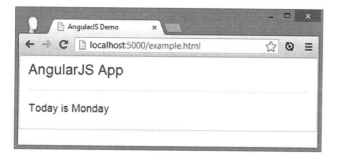

Figure 9-2. The effect of defining a variable using the $scope service

Creating Multiple Views

Each controller can support multiple views, which allows the same data to be presented in different ways or for closely related data to be created and managed efficiently. In Listing 9-7, you can see how I have added a data property to $scope and created a second view that takes advantage of it.

Listing 9-7. Adding a Second View to the example.html File

```
<!DOCTYPE html>
<html ng-app="exampleApp">
<head>
    <title>AngularJS Demo</title>
    <link href="bootstrap.css" rel="stylesheet" />
    <link href="bootstrap-theme.css" rel="stylesheet" />
    <script src="angular.js"></script>
    <script>

        var myApp = angular.module("exampleApp", []);

        myApp.controller("dayCtrl", function ($scope) {
            var dayNames = ["Sunday", "Monday", "Tuesday", "Wednesday",
                "Thursday", "Friday", "Saturday"];
            $scope.day = dayNames[new Date().getDay()];
            $scope.tomorrow = dayNames[(new Date().getDay() + 1) % 7];
        });

    </script>
</head>
<body>
    <div class="panel">
        <div class="page-header">
            <h3>AngularJS App</h3>
        </div>
        <h4 ng-controller="dayCtrl">Today is {{day || "(unknown)"}}</h4>
        <h4 ng-controller="dayCtrl">Tomorrow is {{tomorrow || "(unknown)"}}</h4>
    </div>
</body>
</html>
```

I have moved the ng-controller attribute so that I can create two simple views side-by-side in the HTML document; you can see the effect in Figure 9-3.

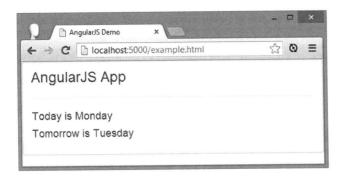

Figure 9-3. Adding a controller

I could have achieved the same result within a single view, of course, but I want to demonstrate different ways in which controllers and views can be used.

Creating Multiple Controllers

All but the simplest applications will contain multiple controllers, each of which will be responsible for a different aspect of the application functionality. Listing 9-8 shows how I have added a second controller to the example.html file.

Listing 9-8. Adding a Second Controller to the example.html File

```
<!DOCTYPE html>
<html ng-app="exampleApp">
<head>
    <title>AngularJS Demo</title>
    <link href="bootstrap.css" rel="stylesheet" />
    <link href="bootstrap-theme.css" rel="stylesheet" />
    <script src="angular.js"></script>
    <script>

        var myApp = angular.module("exampleApp", []);

        myApp.controller("dayCtrl", function ($scope) {
            var dayNames = ["Sunday", "Monday", "Tuesday", "Wednesday",
                "Thursday", "Friday", "Saturday"];
            $scope.day = dayNames[new Date().getDay()];
        });

        myApp.controller("tomorrowCtrl", function ($scope) {
            var dayNames = ["Sunday", "Monday", "Tuesday", "Wednesday",
                "Thursday", "Friday", "Saturday"];
            $scope.day = dayNames[(new Date().getDay() + 1) % 7];
        });

    </script>
</head>
<body>
    <div class="panel">
        <div class="page-header">
            <h3>AngularJS App</h3>
        </div>
        <h4 ng-controller="dayCtrl">Today is {{day || "(unknown)"}}</h4>
         <h4 ng-controller="tomorrowCtrl">Tomorrow is {{day || "(unknown)"}}</h4>
    </div>
</body>
</html>
```

I have added a controller called tomorrowCtrl that works out tomorrow's name. I have also edited the HTML markup so that each controller has its own view. The result of these changes is the same as shown in Figure 9-3—only the way the content is generated differs.

■ **Tip** Notice how I am able to use the `day` property in both views without the values interfering with each other. Each controller has its own part of the overall application scope, and the `day` property of the `dayCtrl` controller is isolated from the one defined by the `tomorrowCtrl` controller. I describe scopes in Chapter 13.

You would not create two controllers and two views for such a simple app in the real world, but I want to demonstrate the different features of modules, and this is a good foundation for doing so.

USING THE FLUENT API

The result of the methods defined by the `Module` object is the `Module` object itself. This is an odd-sounding but neat trick that allows for a *fluent API*, where multiple calls to methods are chained together. As a simple example, I can rewrite the script element from Listing 9-8 without needing to define the `myApp` variable, as follows:

```
...
<script>

    angular.module("exampleApp", [])
        .controller("dayCtrl", function ($scope) {
            var dayNames = ["Sunday", "Monday", "Tuesday", "Wednesday",
                "Thursday", "Friday", "Saturday"];
            $scope.day = dayNames[new Date().getDay()];
        })
        .controller("tomorrowCtrl", function ($scope) {
            var dayNames = ["Sunday", "Monday", "Tuesday", "Wednesday",
                "Thursday", "Friday", "Saturday"];
            $scope.day = dayNames[(new Date().getDay() + 1) % 7];
        });

</script>
...
```

I call the `angular.module` method and get a `Module` object as the result, on which I immediately call the `controller` method to set up the `dayCtrl` controller. The result from the `controller` method is the same `Module` object that I got when I called the `angular.module` method, so I can use it again to call the `controller` method to set up `tomorrowCtrl`.

Defining Directives

Directives are the most powerful AngularJS feature because they extend and enhance HTML to create rich web applications. There are lots of features to like in AngularJS, but directives are the most enjoyable and flexible to create. I describe the built-in directives that come with AngularJS in Chapters 10–12, but you can also create your own custom directives when the built-in ones don't meet your needs. I explain this process in detail in Chapters 15–17, but the short version is that custom directives are created via the `Module.directive` method. You can see a simple example of a custom directive in Listing 9-9.

Listing 9-9. Creating a Custom Directive in the example.html File

```html
<!DOCTYPE html>
<html ng-app="exampleApp">
<head>
    <title>AngularJS Demo</title>
    <link href="bootstrap.css" rel="stylesheet" />
    <link href="bootstrap-theme.css" rel="stylesheet" />
    <script src="angular.js"></script>
    <script>

        var myApp = angular.module("exampleApp", []);

        myApp.controller("dayCtrl", function ($scope) {
            var dayNames = ["Sunday", "Monday", "Tuesday", "Wednesday",
                "Thursday", "Friday", "Saturday"];
            $scope.day = dayNames[new Date().getDay()];
        });

        myApp.controller("tomorrowCtrl", function ($scope) {
            var dayNames = ["Sunday", "Monday", "Tuesday", "Wednesday",
                "Thursday", "Friday", "Saturday"];
            $scope.day = dayNames[(new Date().getDay() + 1) % 7];
        });

        myApp.directive("highlight", function () {
            return function (scope, element, attrs) {
                if (scope.day == attrs["highlight"]) {
                    element.css("color", "red");
                }
            }
        });

    </script>
</head>
<body>
    <div class="panel">
        <div class="page-header">
            <h3>AngularJS App</h3>
        </div>
        <h4 ng-controller="dayCtrl" highlight="Monday">
            Today is {{day || "(unknown)"}}
        </h4>
        <h4 ng-controller="tomorrowCtrl">Tomorrow is {{day || "(unknown)"}}</h4>
    </div>
</body>
</html>
```

There are different ways to create a custom directive, and the listing shows one of the simplest. I have called the `Module.directive` method, providing the name of the directive I want to create and a factory function that creates the directive.

FACTORY AND WORKER FUNCTIONS

All of the `Module` methods that create AngularJS building blocks accept functions as arguments. These are often *factory functions*, so called because they are responsible for creating the object that AngularJS will employ to perform the work itself. Often, factory functions will return a *worker function*, which is to say that the object that AngularJS will use to perform some work is a function, too. You can see an example of this when I call the `directive` method in Listing 9-9. The second argument to the directive method is a factory function, as follows:

```
...
myApp.directive("highlight", function () {
    return function (scope, element, attrs) {
        if (scope.day == attrs["highlight"]) {
            element.css("color", "red");
        }
    }
});
...
```

The `return` statement in the factory function returns another function, which AngularJS will invoke each time it needs to apply the directive, and this is the *worker function*:

```
...
myApp.directive("highlight", function () {
    return function (scope, element, attrs) {
        if (scope.day == attrs["highlight"]) {
            element.css("color", "red");
        }
    }
});
...
```

It is important to understand that you can't rely on either the factory or worker function being called at a specific time. You call the `Module` method—`directive` in this case—when you want to register a building block. AngularJS will call the factory function when it wants to set up the building block and then calls the worker function when it needs to apply the building block, and these three events won't occur in an immediate sequence (in other words, other `Module` methods will be called before your factory function is invoked, and other factory functions will be invoked before your worker function is called).

Applying Directives to HTML Elements

The factory function in this example is responsible for creating a directive, which is a worker function that AngularJS calls when it encounters the directive in the HTML. To understand how a custom directive works, it helps to start with the way it is applied to an HTML element, as follows:

```
...
<h4 ng-controller="dayCtrl" highlight="Monday">
...
```

My custom directive is called `highlight`, and it is applied as an attribute (although there are other options—such as custom HTML elements—as I describe in Chapter 16). I have set the value of the `highlight` attribute to be Monday. The purpose of my custom directive is to highlight the contents of the element that it is applied to if the day model property corresponds to the attribute value.

The factory function I passed to the `directive` method is called when AngularJS encounters the `highlight` attribute in the HTML. The directive function that the factory function creates is invoked by AngularJS and is passed three arguments: the scope for the view, the element to which the directive has been applied, and the attributes of that element.

■ **Tip**   Notice that the argument for the directive function is `scope` and not `$scope`. I explain why there is no $ sign and what the difference is in Chapter 15.

The `scope` argument lets me inspect the data that is available in the view; in this case, it allows me to get the value of the day property. The `attrs` argument provides me with a complete set of the attributes that have been applied to the element, including the attribute that applies the directive: I use this to get the value of the `highlight` attribute. If the value of the `highlight` attribute and the day value from the scope match, then I use the `element` argument to configure the HTML content.

The `element` argument is a jqLite object, which is the cut-down version of jQuery that is included with AngularJS. The method I used in this example—`css`—sets the value of a CSS property. By setting the `color` property, I change the color of the text for the element. I explain the complete set of jqLite methods in Chapter 15. You can see the effect of the directive in Figure 9-4 (although you will have to change the value of the `highlight` attribute if you are not running the example on a Monday).

Figure 9-4. *The effect of a custom directive*

Defining Filters

Filters are used in views to format the data displayed to the user. Once defined, filters can be used throughout a module, which means you can use them to ensure consistency in data presentation across multiple controllers and views. In Listing 9-10, you can see how I have updated the example.html file to include a filter, and in Chapter 14, I explain the different ways that filters can be used, including using the built-in filters that come with AngularJS.

Listing 9-10. Adding a Filter to the example.html File

```
<!DOCTYPE html>
<html ng-app="exampleApp">
<head>
    <title>AngularJS Demo</title>
    <link href="bootstrap.css" rel="stylesheet" />
    <link href="bootstrap-theme.css" rel="stylesheet" />
    <script src="angular.js"></script>
    <script>

        var myApp = angular.module("exampleApp", []);

        myApp.controller("dayCtrl", function ($scope) {
            $scope.day = new Date().getDay();
        });

        myApp.controller("tomorrowCtrl", function ($scope) {
            $scope.day = new Date().getDay() + 1;
        });

        myApp.directive("highlight", function () {
            return function (scope, element, attrs) {
                if (scope.day == attrs["highlight"]) {
                    element.css("color", "red");
                }
            }
        });

        myApp.filter("dayName", function () {
            var dayNames = ["Sunday", "Monday", "Tuesday", "Wednesday",
                            "Thursday", "Friday", "Saturday"];
            return function (input) {
                return angular.isNumber(input) ? dayNames[input] : input;
            };
        });

    </script>
</head>
<body>
    <div class="panel">
        <div class="page-header">
            <h3>AngularJS App</h3>
        </div>
```

```
        <h4 ng-controller="dayCtrl" highlight="Monday">
            Today is {{day || "(unknown)" | dayName}}
        </h4>
        <h4 ng-controller="tomorrowCtrl">
            Tomorrow is {{day || "(unknown)" | dayName}}
        </h4>
    </div>
</body>
</html>
```

The filter method is used to define a filter, and the arguments are the name of the new filter and a factory function that will create the filter when invoked. Filters are themselves functions, which receive a data value and format it so it can be displayed.

My filter is called dayName, and I have used it to consolidate the code that transforms the numeric day of the week that I get from the Date objects into a name. My factory function defines the array of weekday names and returns a function that uses that array to transform numeric values:

```
...
return function (input) {
    return angular.isNumber(input) ? dayNames[input] : input;
};
...
```

I use the angular.isNumber method that I described in Chapter 5 to check that I am dealing with a numeric value and return the day name if I am. (To keep the example simple, I am not checking for values that are out of bounds.)

Applying Filters

Filters are applied in template expressions contained in views. The data binding or expression is followed by a bar (the | character) and then the name of the filter, as follows:

```
...
<h4 ng-controller="dayCtrl" highlight="Monday">
    Today is {{day || "(unknown)" | dayName}}
</h4>
...
```

Filters are applied after JavaScript expressions are evaluated, which allows me to use the || operator to check for null values and then the | operator to apply the filter. The result of this is that the value of the day property will be passed to the filter function if it is not null, and if it is, then (unknown) will be passed instead, which is why I used the isNumber method.

Fixing the Directive

If you have sharp eyes, you may have noticed when I added the filter, I managed to break the directive I created earlier. This is because my controllers now add a numeric representation of the current day to their scopes, rather than the formatted name. My directive checks for the value Monday, but it will only ever find 1, 2, and so on, and so will never highlight the date.

AngularJS development is full of little challenges like this because you will often refactor your code to move functionality from one component to another, just as I removed the name formatting from the controllers to a filter. There are several ways to solve this problem—including updating the directive to use numeric values as well—but the solution I want to demonstrate is a little more complex. In Listing 9-11, you can see the modifications I made to the definition of the directive.

Listing 9-11. Changing the Directive in the example.html File

```
...
myApp.directive("highlight", function ($filter) {

    var dayFilter = $filter("dayName");

    return function (scope, element, attrs) {
        if (dayFilter(scope.day) == attrs["highlight"]) {
            element.css("color", "red");
        }
    }
});
...
```

What I want to demonstrate with this example is that the building blocks that you create in an AngularJS application are not just limited to use on HTML elements; you can also use them in your JavaScript code.

In this case, I have added a `$filter` argument to my directive factory function, which tells AngularJS that I want to receive the filter service object when my function is called. The `$filter` service gives me access to all of the filters that have been defined, including my custom addition from the previous example. I obtain my filter by name, like this:

```
...
var dayFilter = $filter("dayName");
...
```

I receive the filter function that my factory creates, and I can then call that function to transform my numeric value to a name:

```
...
if (dayFilter(scope.day) == attrs["highlight"]) {
...
```

With this change, my directive works again. There are two important points to note in this example. The first is that refactoring code is a natural part of the AngularJS development process, and the second is that AngularJS makes refactoring easier by providing both declarative (via HTML) and imperative (via JavaScript) access to the building blocks you create.

Defining Services

Services are *singleton* objects that provide any functionality that you want to use throughout an application. There are some useful built-in services that come with AngularJS for common tasks such as making HTTP requests. Some key AngularJS are delivered as services, including the `$scope` and `$filter` objects that I used in the earlier example. Since this is AngularJS, you can create your own services, a process that I demonstrate briefly here and describe in depth in Chapter 18.

Three of the methods defined by the Module object are used to create services in different ways: service, factory, and provider. All three are closely related, and I'll explain the differences between them in Chapter 18. For this chapter, I am going to use the service method to create a basic service to consolidate some of the logic in my example, as shown in Listing 9-12.

Listing 9-12. Creating a Simple Service in the example.html File

```
<!DOCTYPE html>
<html ng-app="exampleApp">
<head>
    <title>AngularJS Demo</title>
    <link href="bootstrap.css" rel="stylesheet" />
    <link href="bootstrap-theme.css" rel="stylesheet" />
    <script src="angular.js"></script>
    <script>

        var myApp = angular.module("exampleApp", []);

        myApp.controller("dayCtrl", function ($scope, days) {
            $scope.day = days.today;
        });

        myApp.controller("tomorrowCtrl", function ($scope, days) {
            $scope.day = days.tomorrow;
        });

        myApp.directive("highlight", function ($filter) {

            var dayFilter = $filter("dayName");

            return function (scope, element, attrs) {
                if (dayFilter(scope.day) == attrs["highlight"]) {
                    element.css("color", "red");
                }
            }
        });

        myApp.filter("dayName", function () {
            var dayNames = ["Sunday", "Monday", "Tuesday", "Wednesday",
                            "Thursday", "Friday", "Saturday"];
            return function (input) {
                return angular.isNumber(input) ? dayNames[input] : input;
            };
        });
```

```
        myApp.service("days", function () {
            this.today = new Date().getDay();
            this.tomorrow = this.today + 1;
        });

    </script>
</head>
<body>
    <div class="panel">
        <div class="page-header">
            <h3>AngularJS App</h3>
        </div>
        <h4 ng-controller="dayCtrl" highlight="Monday">
            Today is {{day || "(unknown)" | dayName}}
        </h4>
        <h4 ng-controller="tomorrowCtrl">
            Tomorrow is {{day || "(unknown)" | dayName}}
        </h4>
    </div>
</body>
</html>
```

The service method takes two arguments: the name of the service and a factory function that is called to create the service object. When AngularJS calls the factory function, it assigns a new object that is accessible via the this keyword, and I use this object to define today and tomorrow properties. This is a simple service, but it means I can access the today and tomorrow values via my service anywhere in my AngularJS code—something that helps simplify the development process when creating more complex applications.

■ **Tip** Notice that I am able to use the server from within the controllers, even though I call the service method after I call the controller method. You can create your component in any order, and AngularJS will ensure that everything is set up correctly before it starts calling factory functions and performing dependency injection. See the "Working with the AngularJS Life Cycle" section later in this chapter for more details.

I access my service by declaring a dependency for my days service, like this:

```
...
myApp.controller("tomorrowCtrl", function ($scope, days) {
...
```

AngularJS uses dependency injection to locate the days service and pass it as an argument to the factory function, which means I can then get the value of the today and tomorrow properties and use the $scope service to pass them to the view:

```
...
myApp.controller("tomorrowCtrl", function ($scope, days) {
    $scope.day = days.tomorrow;
});
...
```

I show you the other ways of creating services—including how to use the `service` method to take advantage JavaScript prototypes—in Chapter 18.

Defining Values

The `Module.value` method lets you create services that return fixed values and objects. This may seem like an odd thing to do, but it means you can use dependency injection for any value or object, not just the ones you create using module methods like `service` and `filter`. It makes for a more consistent development experience, simplifies unit testing, and allows you to use some advanced features, like *decoration*, which I describe in Chapter 24. In Listing 9-13, you can see how I have modified the `example.html` file to use a value.

Listing 9-13. Defining a Value in the example.html File

```
...
<script>

    var myApp = angular.module("exampleApp", []);

    // ...statements omitted for brevity...

    var now = new Date();
    myApp.value("nowValue", now);

    myApp.service("days", function (nowValue) {
        this.today = nowValue.getDay();
        this.tomorrow = this.today + 1;
    });

</script>
...
```

In this listing I have defined a variable called now. I have assigned a new `Date` to the variable and then called the `Module.value` method to create the value service, which I called `nowValue`. I then declared a dependency on the `nowValue` service when I created my days service.

USING OBJECTS WITHOUT VALUES

Using values may seem like an unnecessary complication, and you may not be persuaded by the argument for unit testing. Even so, you will find that creating AngularJS values is just simpler than *not* using them because AngularJS assumes any argument to a factory function declares a dependency that it needs to resolve. Developers who are new to AngularJS will often try to write code like this, which doesn't use a value:

```
...
var now = new Date();

myApp.service("days", function (now) {
    this.today = now.getDay();
    this.tomorrow = this.today + 1;
});
...
```

If you try to run this code, you will see an error like this one in the browser JavaScript console:

Error: Unknown provider: nowProvider <- now <- days

The problem here is that AngularJS won't use the local variable as the value for the now parameter when it calls the factory function, and the now variable will no longer be in scope when it is required.

If you are determined that you don't want to create AngularJS values—and most developers go through a phase of feeling this way—then you can rely on the JavaScript *closure* feature, which will let you reference variables from within functions when they are defined, like this:

```
...
var now = new Date();

myApp.service("days", function () {
    this.today = now.getDay();
    this.tomorrow = this.today + 1;
});
...
```

I removed the argument from the factory function, which means that AngularJS won't find a dependency to resolve. This code works, but it makes the days service harder to test, and my advice is to follow the AngularJS approach of creating value services.

Using Modules to Organize Code

In previous examples, I showed you how AngularJS uses dependency injection with factory functions when you create components such as controllers, filters, and services. Right at the start of the chapter, I explained that the second argument to the angular.module method, used to create modules, was an array of the module's dependencies:

```
...
var myApp = angular.module("exampleApp", []);
...
```

Any AngularJS module can rely on components defined in other modules, and this is a feature that makes it easier to organize the code in a complex application. To demonstrate how this works, I have added a JavaScript file called controllers.js to the angularjs folder. You can see the contents of the new file in Listing 9-14.

Listing 9-14. The Contents of the controller.js File

```
var controllersModule = angular.module("exampleApp.Controllers", [])

controllersModule.controller("dayCtrl", function ($scope, days) {
    $scope.day = days.today;
});

controllersModule.controller("tomorrowCtrl", function ($scope, days) {
    $scope.day = days.tomorrow;
});
```

You can put as much or as little functionality in other modules as you like. I have defined four modules in this example but left the value in the main module. I could have created a module just for values, a module that combined services and values, or a module with any other combination that suited my development style.

Working with the Module Life Cycle

The Module.config and Module.run methods register functions that are invoked at key moments in the life cycle of an AngularJS app. A function passed to the config method is invoked when the current module has been loaded, and a function passed to the run method is invoked when *all* modules have been loaded. You can see an example of both methods in use in Listing 9-17.

Listing 9-17. Using the config and run Methods in the example.html File

```
...
<script>

    var myApp = angular.module("exampleApp",
        ["exampleApp.Controllers", "exampleApp.Filters",
            "exampleApp.Services", "exampleApp.Directives"]);

    myApp.constant("startTime", new Date().toLocaleTimeString());
    myApp.config(function (startTime) {
        console.log("Main module config: " + startTime);
    });
    myApp.run(function (startTime) {
        console.log("Main module run: " + startTime);
    });

    angular.module("exampleApp.Directives", [])
        .directive("highlight", function ($filter) {

            var dayFilter = $filter("dayName");

            return function (scope, element, attrs) {
                if (dayFilter(scope.day) == attrs["highlight"]) {
                    element.css("color", "red");
                }
            }
        });

    var now = new Date();
    myApp.value("nowValue", now);

    angular.module("exampleApp.Services", [])
        .service("days", function (nowValue) {
            this.today = nowValue.getDay();
            this.tomorrow = this.today + 1;
        })
```

```
    .config(function() {
        console.log("Services module config: (no time)");
    })
    .run(function (startTime) {
        console.log("Services module run: " + startTime);
    });
```

```
</script>
...
```

My first change in this listing is to use the constant method, which is similar to the value method but creates a service that can be declared as a dependency by the config method (which you can't do when you create values).

The config method accepts a function that is invoked after the module on which the method is called is loaded. The config method is used to configure a module, usually by injecting values that have been obtained from the server, such as connection details or user credentials.

The run method also accepts a function, but it will be invoked only when all of the modules have been loaded and their dependencies have been resolved. Here is the sequence in which the callback functions are invoked:

1. The config callback on the exampleApp.Services module

2. The config callback on the exampleApp module

3. The run callback on the exampleApp.Services module

4. The run callback on the exampleApp module

AngularJS does something clever, which is to ensure that modules on which there are dependencies have their callbacks invoked first. You can see this in the way that the callbacks for the exampleApp.Services module are made before those for the main exampleApp module. This allows modules to configure themselves before they are used to resolve module dependencies. If you run the example, you will see JavaScript console output like the following:

```
Services module config: (no time)
Main module config: 16:57:28
Services module run: 16:57:28
Main module run: 16:57:28
```

I am able to use the startTime constant in three of the four callbacks, but I can't use in the config callback for the exampleApp.Services module because the module dependencies have yet to be resolved. At the moment the config callback is invoked, the startTime constant is unavailable.

Summary

In this chapter, I explained the basic structure of an AngularJS application from the perspective of the module. I demonstrated how to create modules; how to use them to create key building blocks like controllers, services, and filters; and how these building blocks can be used to organize the code in an application and respond to two key moments in the application life cycle. As I explained at the start of the chapter, the information I have presented here is intended to give you somewhere to refer to in order to put individual features described in the following chapters in a broader context and to point you to where you can find more details. In the next chapter, I start digging into the details, beginning with the built-in directives.

CHAPTER 10

■ ■ ■

Using Binding and Template Directives

In the previous chapter, I briefly described the range of components that can be used to create an AngularJS application. You may have found the variety of these components overwhelming and, even with the examples, struggled to understand what they are all for. Don't worry—as I explained at the start of that chapter, those descriptions and examples are intended to provide context for the detailed information that follows, starting with this chapter, in which I describe *directives*.

Directives are the most powerful AngularJS feature; they allow you to extend HTML to create the foundation for rich and complex web applications in a way that is naturally expressive. AngularJS includes a wide range of built-in directives, and you can get a surprising amount done by ignoring every other aspect of AngularJS and just relying on them. There are a lot of built-in directives to describe, which I start to do in this chapter and continue in Chapter 11 and Chapter 12. You can also create your own custom directives, and I describe the process for doing this in Chapters 15–17, after describing some of the features that are required for writing custom directives.

The directives I describe in this chapter are the ones you will use most often at the start of a new AngularJS project, but they are also the most complex and can be used in several ways. The directives I describe in the chapters that follow are simpler, so, once again, don't worry if you don't take in all of the details in one go. Table 10-1 summarizes this chapter.

Table 10-1. *Chapter Summary*

Problem	Solution	Listing
Create a one-way binding.	Define properties on the controller $scope and use the ng-bind or ng-bind-template directive or inline expressions (denoted by the {{ and }} characters).	1–2
Prevent AngularJS from processing inline binding expressions.	Use the ng-non-bindable directive.	2
Create two-way data bindings.	Use the ng-model directive.	3
Generate repeated elements.	Use the ng-repeat directive.	4–6
Get context information about the current object in an ng-repeat directive.	Use the built-in variables provided by the ng-repeat directive, such as $first or $last.	7–9
Repeat multiple top-level attributes.	Use the ng-repeat-start and ng-repeat-end directives.	10
Load a partial view.	Use the ng-include directive.	11–16
Conditionally display elements.	Use the ng-switch directive.	17
Hide inline template expressions while AngularJS is processing content.	Use the ng-cloak directive.	18

Why and When to Use Directives

Directives are the signature feature of AngularJS, setting the overall style of AngularJS development and the shape of an AngularJS application. Other JavaScript libraries—including the much-loved jQuery—treat the elements in an HTML document as a problem to be overcome, requiring manipulation and correction before they can be used to create a web application.

The AngularJS approach is different: You create AngularJS web apps by embracing and enhancing HTML and treating it not as a problem but a *foundation* on which to build application features. It can take a little while to get used to the way that directives work—especially when you start to create your own custom HTML elements, a process I describe in Chapter 16—but it becomes second nature, and the result is a pleasing mix of standard HTML mixed with custom elements and attributes.

AngularJS comes with more than 50 built-in directives that provide access to core features that are useful in almost every web application including data binding, form validation, template generation, event handling, and manipulating HTML elements. And, as I already mentioned, you use custom directives to apply your application's capabilities. Table 10-2 summarizes why and when to use directives in an AngularJS application.

Table 10-2. *Why and When to Use Directives*

Why	When
Directives expose core AngularJS functionality such as event handling, form validation, and templates. You use custom directives to apply your application features to views.	Directives are used throughout an AngularJS application.

Preparing the Example Project

To prepare for this chapter, I deleted the contents of the angularjs web server folder and installed the angular.js, bootstrap.css, and bootstrap-theme.css files, as described in Chapter 1. I then created a file called directives.html, which you can see in Listing 10-1.

Listing 10-1. The Contents of the directives.html File

```
<!DOCTYPE html>
<html ng-app="exampleApp">
<head>
    <title>Directives</title>
    <script src="angular.js"></script>
    <link href="bootstrap.css" rel="stylesheet" />
    <link href="bootstrap-theme.css" rel="stylesheet" />
    <script>
        angular.module("exampleApp", [])
            .controller("defaultCtrl", function ($scope) {
                $scope.todos = [
                    { action: "Get groceries", complete: false },
                    { action: "Call plumber", complete: false },
                    { action: "Buy running shoes", complete: true },
                    { action: "Buy flowers", complete: false },
                    { action: "Call family", complete: false }];
            });
    </script>
</head>
```

```
<body>
    <div id="todoPanel" class="panel" ng-controller="defaultCtrl">
        <h3 class="panel-header">To Do List</h3>
        Data items will go here...
    </div>
</body>
</html>
```

This is a skeletal outline for the classic to-do list application (one of the reasons that so many web app examples are based on to-do lists is because lists of data objects are perfect for demonstrating template techniques).

You will recognize some of the AngularJS components that I described in Chapter 9. I created a module called exampleApp using the angular.module method and then used the fluent API to define a controller called defaultCtrl. The controller uses the $scope service to add some data items to the data model, and the module and the controller are applied to HTML elements with the ng-app and ng-controller directives. You can see how the initial content in the directives.html file is displayed by the browser in Figure 10-1.

Figure 10-1. *The initial contents of the directives.html file*

■ **Tip**   You can treat the content of Listing 10-1 as a black box for the moment, get a brief description about each component from Chapter 9, or consult the chapters later in the book where I describe these building blocks in detail.

Using the Data Binding Directives

The first category of built-in directives is responsible for performing *data binding*, which is one of the features that elevates AngularJS from a template package into a full-fledged application development framework. Data binding uses values from the model and inserts them into the HTML document. Table 10-3 describes the directives in this category, and I demonstrate their use in the sections that follow.

Table 10-3. *The Data Binding Directives*

Directive	Applied As	Description
ng-bind	Attribute, class	Binds the innerText property of an HTML element.
ng-bind-html	Attribute, class	Creates data bindings using the innerHTML property of an HTML element. This is potentially dangerous because it means that the browser will interpret the content as HTML, rather than content. See Chapter 19 for details of how to use this directive and the service that supports it.
ng-bind-template	Attribute, class	Similar to the ng-bind directive but allows for multiple template expressions to be specified in the attribute value.
ng-model	Attribute, class	Creates a two-way data binding.
ng-non-bindable	Attribute, class	Declares a region of content for which data binding will not be performed.

Data binding is incredibly important in AngularJS development, and you will rarely encounter any substantial fragment of HTML in an AngularJS application that doesn't have some kind of data binding applied to it, and as you'll learn in the next section, the functionality provided by the ng-bind directive is so central to AngularJS that it has an alternative notation so you can create data bindings more easily.

APPLYING DIRECTIVES

Table 10-3 contains an Applied As column that tells you how you can use each directive. All of the data binding directives can be applied as an attribute or as a class. Later in this chsapter, I describe a directive that can be applied as a custom HTML element.

The way you apply a directive is generally a matter of style preferences combined with a consideration for your development toolset. I generally prefer to apply directives as attributes, as follows:

```
...
There are <span ng-bind="todos.length"></span> items
...
```

The directive is specified as the attribute name, ng-bind in this case, and the configuration for the directive is set as the attribute value. This fragment comes from Listing 10-2 and sets up a one-way data binding on the todos.length property, which I explain in the following section.

Some developers don't like the attribute approach, and—surprisingly often—attributes cause problems in development tool chains. Some JavaScript libraries make assumptions about attribute names, and some restrictive revision control systems won't let HTML content be committed with nonstandard attributes. (I encounter this most often in large corporations where the revision control system is managed by a central group that lags far behind the needs of the development teams it supports.) If you can't or won't use custom attributes, then you can configure directives using the standard class attribute, as follows:

```
...
There are <span class="ng-bind: todos.length"></span> items
...
```

The value of the class attribute is the name of the directive, followed by a colon, followed by the configuration for the directive. This statement has the same effect as the last one: It creates a one-way data binding on the todos.length property. Some directives can be applied as custom AngularJS elements. You can see an example of this in the "Working with Partial Views" section when I demonstrate the ng-include directive.

Not all directives can be applied in every way; most of them can be applied as attributes or classes, but only some can be applied as custom elements. The information in the tables I provide for each category of directive explains how each can be used. I explain how to create custom directives in Chapter 16, and you can specify how you want new directives to be applied as part of this process.

Note that older versions of Internet Explorer don't support custom HTML elements by default. See http://docs.angularjs.org/guide/ie for information and workarounds.

Performing One-Way Bindings (and Preventing Them)

AngularJS supports two kinds of data binding. The first, *one-way* binding, means a value is taken from the data model and inserted into an HTML element. AngularJS bindings are *live*, which means that when the value associated with the binding is changed in the data model, the HTML element will be updated to display the new value.

The ng-bind directive is responsible for creating one-way data bindings, but it is rarely used directly because AngularJS will also create this kind of binding whenever it encounters the {{ and }} characters in the HTML document. Listing 10-2 shows the different ways you can create one-way data bindings.

Listing 10-2. Creating One-Way Data Bindings in the directives.html File

```html
<!DOCTYPE html>
<html ng-app="exampleApp">
<head>
    <title>Directives</title>
    <script src="angular.js"></script>
    <link href="bootstrap.css" rel="stylesheet" />
    <link href="bootstrap-theme.css" rel="stylesheet" />
    <script>
        angular.module("exampleApp", [])
            .controller("defaultCtrl", function ($scope) {
                $scope.todos = [
                    { action: "Get groceries", complete: false },
                    { action: "Call plumber", complete: false },
                    { action: "Buy running shoes", complete: true },
                    { action: "Buy flowers", complete: false },
                    { action: "Call family", complete: false }];
            });
    </script>
</head>
<body>
    <div id="todoPanel" class="panel" ng-controller="defaultCtrl">
        <h3 class="panel-header">To Do List</h3>

        <div>There are {{todos.length}} items</div>

        <div>
            There are <span ng-bind="todos.length"></span> items
        </div>
```

237

```
        <div ng-bind-template=
            "First: {{todos[0].action}}. Second: {{todos[1].action}}">
        </div>

        <div ng-non-bindable>
            AngularJS uses {{ and }} characters for templates
        </div>
    </div>
</body>
</html>
```

You can see the result of navigating to the directives.html file with the browser in Figure 10-2. The effect isn't the most visually striking, but the directives in the example are doing some interesting things.

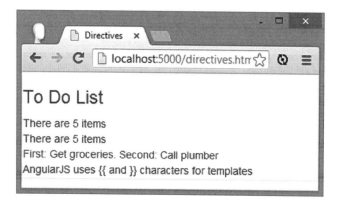

Figure 10-2. *Creating one-way data bindings*

■ **Tip**   AngularJS isn't the only JavaScript package that uses the {{ and }} characters, which can be a problem if you are trying to make multiple libraries work together. AngularJS allows you to change the characters used for inline bindings; I explain the process in Chapter 19.

The first two data bindings in this example are equivalent. I have used {{ and }} to denote a one-way binding for the number of items in the $scope.todos collection:

```
...
<div>There are {{todos.length}} items</div>
...
```

This is the most natural and expressive way of creating data bindings: The bindings are easy to read and fit naturally into the content of HTML elements. The second data binding uses the ng-bind directive, which has the same effect but requires an additional element:

```
...
There are <span ng-bind="todos.length"></span> items
...
```

The ng-bind directive replaces the content of the element that it is applied to, which means I have to add a span element to create the effect I want. I don't use the ng-bind directive in my own projects; I prefer the inline bindings.

The ng-bind directive *does* allow you to hide your template markup when the HTML content is shown to the user before it is processed by AngularJS (because browsers don't display attribute values to users), but this is rarely a problem and is addressed by the ng-cloak directive, which I describe later in this chapter.

■ **Caution**   You can create bindings only for data values that are added to the $scope object by the controller. I explain how $scope works in Chapter 13.

Aside from being a little awkward to use, the ng-bind directive is limited to being able to process a single data binding expression. If you need to create multiple data bindings, then you should use the ng-bind-template directive, which is more flexible, as follows:

```
...
<div ng-bind-template="First: {{todos[0].action}}. Second: {{todos[1].action}}"></div>
...
```

The value I specified for the directive contains two data bindings, which the ng-bind directive would not be able to process. I have never used this directive in a real project, and I suspect I never will. I include this directive here for completeness only.

Preventing Inline Data Binding

The drawback of the inline bindings is that AngularJS will find and process every set of {{ and }} characters in your content. This can be a problem, especially if you are mixing and matching JavaScript toolkits and want to use some other template system on a region of HTML (or if you just want to use double-brace characters in your text). The solution is to use the ng-non-bindable directive, which prevents AngularJS from processing inline bindings:

```
...
<div ng-non-bindable>
    AngularJS uses {{ and }} characters for templates
</div>
...
```

If I had not applied the directive, AngularJS would have processed the contents of the div element and then tried to bind to a model property called and. AngularJS doesn't complain when it is asked to bind to a nonexisting model property because it assumes it will be created later (as I explain when I describe the ng-model directive later in this chapter). Instead, it inserts no content at all, which means that instead of the output I wanted:

```
AngularJS uses {{ and }} characters for templates
```

I would instead produce this:

```
AngularJS uses  characters for templates
```

Creating Two-Way Data Bindings

Two-way data bindings track changes in both directions, allowing elements that gather data from the user to modify the state of the application. Two-way bindings are created with the ng-model directive, and as Listing 10-3 demonstrates, a single data model property can be used for both one- and two-way bindings.

Listing 10-3. Creating Two-Way Bindings in the directives.html File

```
...
<body>
    <div id="todoPanel" class="panel" ng-controller="defaultCtrl">
        <h3 class="panel-header">To Do List</h3>
        <div class="well">
            <div>The first item is: {{todos[0].action}}</div>
        </div>

        <div class="form-group well">
            <label for="firstItem">Set First Item:</label>
            <input name="firstItem" class="form-control" ng-model="todos[0].action" />
        </div>
    </div>
</body>
...
```

There are two data bindings in this listing, both of which are applied to the action property of the first object in the todos data array (which I set up using the $scope object in the controller and reference in bindings as todos[0].action). The first binding is an inline one-way binding that simply displays the value of the data property, just as I did in the previous example. The second binding is applied via the input element and is a two-way binding:

```
...
<input name="firstItem" class="form-control" ng-model="todos[0].action" />
...
```

Two-way bindings can be applied only to elements that allow the user to provide a data value, which means the input, textarea, and select elements. The ng-model directive sets the content of the element it is applied to and then responds to changes that the user makes by updating the data model.

■ **Tip**   The ng-model directive provides additional features for working with HTML forms and even for creating custom form directives. See Chapters 12 and 17 for details.

Changes to data model properties are disseminated to all of the relevant bindings, ensuring that the application is kept in sync. For my example, this means that changes to the input element update the data model, which then causes the update to be shown in the inline one-way binding.

To see the effect, use the browser to navigate to the directives.html document and edit the text in the input element; you will see that the one-way binding is kept in sync with the contents of the input element, all through the magic of the two-way binding. The best way to experience this effect is by re-creating the example and experiencing it first hand, but you can get a sense of what happens in Figure 10-3.

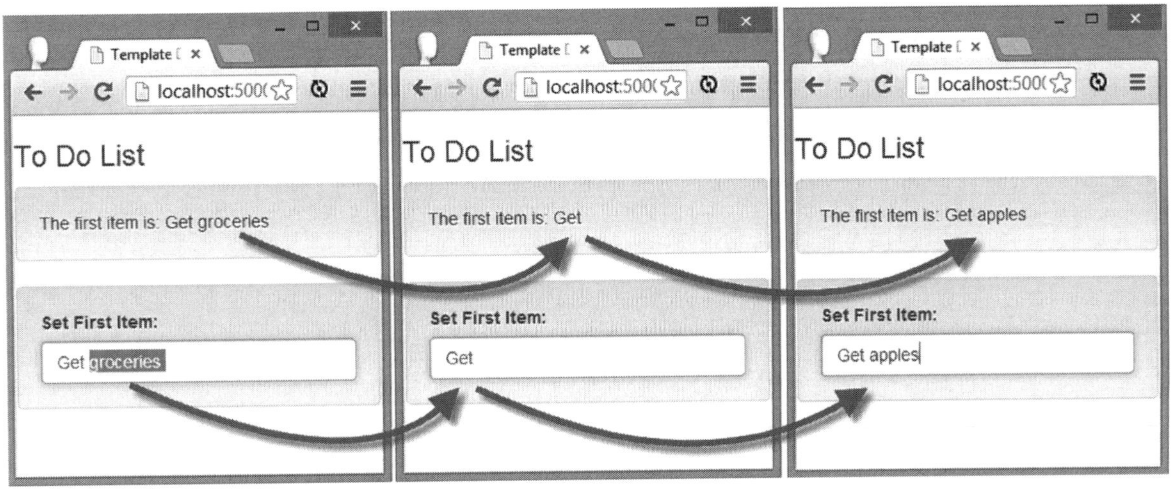

Figure 10-3. *Using two-way data bindings*

■ **Note**　OK, two-way bindings are not really magic. AngularJS uses standard JavaScript events to receive notifications from the `input` element when its content changes and propagates these changes via the `$scope` service. You can see the event handler that AngularJS sets up through the F12 developer tools, and I explain how the `$scope` service detects and disseminates changes in Chapter 13.

■ **Tip**　In this example, I used properties that had been explicitly added to the data model through the `$scope` service in the controller factory method. One nice feature of data binding is that AngularJS will dynamically create model properties as they are needed, which means you don't have to laboriously define all of the properties you use to glue views together. You can see further examples of this technique in Chapter 12 when I describe the AngularJS support for working with form elements.

Using the Template Directives

Data bindings are the core feature of AngularJS views, but on their own they are pretty limited. Web applications—or *any* kind of application for that matter—tend to operate on collections of similar data objects and vary the view they present to the user based on different data values.

　　Fortunately, AngularJS includes a set of directives that can be used to generate HTML elements using templates, making it easy to work with data collections and to add basic logic to a template that responds to the state of the data. I have summarized the template directives in Table 10-4.

Table 10-4. *The Template Directives*

Directive	Applied As	Description
ng-cloak	Attribute, class	Applies a CSS style that hides inline binding expressions, which can be briefly visible when the document first loads
ng-include	Element, attribute, class	Loads, processes, and inserts a fragment of HTML into the Document Object Model
ng-repeat	Attribute, class	Generates new copies of a single element and its contents for each object in an array or property on an object
ng-repeat-start	Attribute, class	Denotes the start of a repeating section with multiple top-level elements
ng-repeat-end	Attribute, class	Denotes the end of a repeating section with multiple top-level elements
ng-switch	Element, attribute	Changes the elements in the Document Object Model based on the value of data bindings

These directives help you put simple logic into views without having to write any JavaScript code. As I explained in Chapter 3, the logic in views should be restricted to generating the content required to display data, and these directives all fit into that definition.

Generating Elements Repeatedly

One of the most common tasks in any view is to generate the same content for each item in a collection of data. In AngularJS this is done with the ng-repeat directive, which is applied to the element that should be duplicated. Listing 10-4 contains a simple example of using the ng-repeat directive.

Listing 10-4. Using the ng-repeat Directive in the directives.html File

```
...
<body>
    <div id="todoPanel" class="panel" ng-controller="defaultCtrl">
        <h3 class="panel-header">To Do List</h3>

        <table class="table">
            <thead>
                <tr>
                    <th>Action</th>
                    <th>Done</th>
                </tr>
            </thead>
            <tbody>
                <tr ng-repeat="item in todos">
                    <td>{{item.action}}</td>
                    <td>{{item.complete}}</td>
                </tr>
            </tbody>
        </table>
    </div>
</body>
...
```

This is the simplest and most common way of using the ng-repeat directive: to generate rows for a table element using a collection of objects. There are two parts to using the ng-repeat directive. The first is to specify the source of the data objects and the name by which you want to refer to the object that is being processed from within the template:

```
...
<tr ng-repeat="item in todos">
...
```

The basic format of the value for the ng-repeat directive attribute is <variable> in <source>, where source is an object or array defined by the controller $scope, in this example the todos array. The directive iterates through the objects in the array, creates a new instance of the element and its content, and then processes the templates it contains. The <variable> name assigned in the directive attribute value can be used to refer to the current data object. In my example, I used the variable name item:

```
...
<tr ng-repeat="item in todos">
    <td>{{item.action}}</td>
    <td>{{item.complete}}</td>
</tr>
...
```

In my example, I generate a tr element that contains td elements that, in turn, contain inline data bindings that refer to the action and complete properties of the current object. If you navigate to the directives.html file in the browser, AngularJS will process the directive and generate the following HTML elements:

```
...
<tbody>
    <!-- ngRepeat: item in todos -->
    <tr ng-repeat="item in todos" class="ng-scope">
        <td class="ng-binding">Get groceries</td>
        <td class="ng-binding">false</td>
    </tr>
    <tr ng-repeat="item in todos" class="ng-scope">
        <td class="ng-binding">Call plumber</td>
        <td class="ng-binding">false</td>
    </tr>
    <tr ng-repeat="item in todos" class="ng-scope">
        <td class="ng-binding">Buy running shoes</td>
        <td class="ng-binding">true</td>
    </tr>
    <tr ng-repeat="item in todos" class="ng-scope">
        <td class="ng-binding">Buy flowers</td>
        <td class="ng-binding">false</td>
    </tr>
    <tr ng-repeat="item in todos" class="ng-scope">
        <td class="ng-binding">Call family</td>
        <td class="ng-binding">false</td>
    </tr>
</tbody>
...
```

You will see that AngularJS has generated a comment to make it easier to see which directive generated the elements and has added the generated elements to some classes (these are used internally by AngularJS). Figure 10-4 illustrates the effect of this HTML in the browser window.

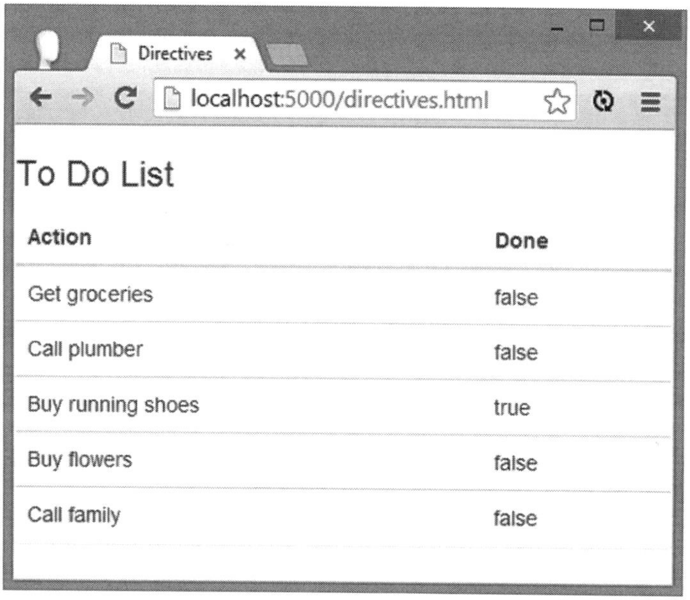

Figure 10-4. *Generating HTML elements with the ng-repeat directive*

■ **Tip**   You will need to use your browser's F12 developer tools to see these elements, rather than the View HTML or View Page Source menu. Most browsers will display the HTML they receive from the server only through the View Page Source menu, which won't contain the elements that AngularJS generates from templates. The developer tools show you the live Document Object Model, which reflects the changes that AngularJS makes.

Repeating for Object Properties

The previous example used the ng-repeat directive to enumerate the objects in an array, but you can also enumerate the properties of an object. The ng-repeat directive can also be nested, and you can see how I have combined these features to simplify my template in Listing 10-5.

Listing 10-5. Repeating Object Properties and Nesting the ng-repeat Directive in the directives.html File

```
...
<table class="table">
    <thead>
        <tr>
            <th>Action</th>
            <th>Done</th>
        </tr>
    </thead>
```

```
    <tbody>
        <tr ng-repeat="item in todos">
            <td ng-repeat="prop in item">{{prop}}</td>
        </tr>
    </tbody>
</table>
...
```

The outer ng-repeat directive generates a tr element for each object in the todos array, and each object is assigned to the item variable. The inner ng-repeat directive generates a td element for each property of the item object and assigns the value of the property to the prop variable. Finally, the prop variable is used for a one-way data binding as the contents of the td element. This produces the same result as the previous example but will adapt fluidly to generate td elements for any new properties that are defined on the data objects. This is a simple example, but it gives a sense of the flexibility available when working with AngularJS templates.

Working with Data Object Keys

There is an alternative syntax for the ng-repeat directive configuration that allows you to receive a key with each property or data object that is processed. You can see an example of this syntax in Listing 10-6.

Listing 10-6. Receiving a Key Along with a Data Value in the directives.html File

```
...
<tr ng-repeat="item in todos">
    <td ng-repeat="(key, value) in item">
        {{key}}={{value}}
    </td>
</tr>
...
```

Instead of a single variable name, I have specified two names separated by a comma within parentheses. For each object or property that the ng-repeat directive enumerates, the second variable will be assigned the data object or property value. The way the first variable is used depends on the source of the data. For objects, the key is the current property name, and for collections the key is the position of the current object. I am enumerating the properties of an object in the listing, so the value of key will be the property name, and value will be assigned the property value. Here is an example of the HTML element that this ng-repeat directive will generate, with the values inserted by the data bindings to the key and value variables emphasized:

```
...
<tr ng-repeat="item in todos" class="ng-scope">
    <!-- ngRepeat: (key, value) in item -->
    <td ng-repeat="(key, value) in item" class="ng-scope ng-binding">
        action=Get groceries
    </td>
    <td ng-repeat="(key, value) in item" class="ng-scope ng-binding">
        complete=false
    </td>
</tr>
...
```

Working with the Built-in Variables

The ng-repeat directive assigns the current object or property to the variable you specify, but there is also a set of built-in variables that provide context for the data being processed. You can see an example of one of them applied in Listing 10-7.

Listing 10-7. Using a Built-in ng-repeat Variable in the directives.html File

```
...
<table class="table">
    <thead>
        <tr>
            <th>#</th>
            <th>Action</th>
            <th>Done</th>
        </tr>
    </thead>
    <tr ng-repeat="item in todos">
        <td>{{$index + 1}}</td>
        <td ng-repeat="prop in item">
            {{prop}}
        </td>
    </tr>
</table>
...
```

I added a new column to the table that contains the to-do items and used the $index variable, which is provided by the ng-repeat directive, to display the position of each item in the array. Since JavaScript collection indexes are zero-based, I simply add one to $index, relying on the fact that AngularJS will evaluate JavaScript expressions in data bindings. You can see the effect in Figure 10-5.

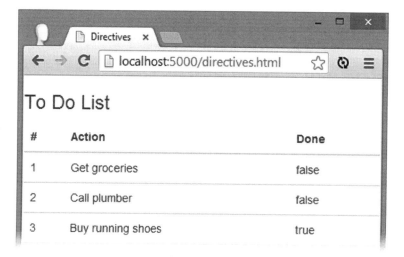

Figure 10-5. Using the built-in variables provided by the ng-repeat directive

The $index variable is the one that I find most useful, but I have described the complete set in Table 10-5.

Table 10-5. *The Built-in ng-repeat Variables*

Variable	Description
$index	Returns the position of the current object or property
$first	Returns true if the current object is the first in the collection
$middle	Returns true if the current object is neither the first nor last in the collection
$last	Returns true if the current object is the last in the collection
$even	Returns true for the even-numbered objects in a collection
$odd	Returns true for the odd-numbered objects in a collection

You can use these variables to control the elements you generate. A typical use of these variables is to create the classic striping effect for table elements, which I have shown in Listing 10-8.

Listing 10-8. Creating a Striped Table Using the ng-repeat Directive in the directives.html File

```
<!DOCTYPE html>
<html ng-app="exampleApp">
<head>
    <title>Directives</title>
    <script src="angular.js"></script>
    <link href="bootstrap.css" rel="stylesheet" />
    <link href="bootstrap-theme.css" rel="stylesheet" />
    <script>
        angular.module("exampleApp", [])
            .controller("defaultCtrl", function ($scope) {
                $scope.todos = [
                    { action: "Get groceries", complete: false },
                    { action: "Call plumber", complete: false },
                    { action: "Buy running shoes", complete: true },
                    { action: "Buy flowers", complete: false },
                    { action: "Call family", complete: false }];
            });
    </script>
    <style>
        .odd { background-color: lightcoral}
        .even { background-color: lavenderblush}
    </style>
</head>
<body>
    <div id="todoPanel" class="panel" ng-controller="defaultCtrl">
        <h3 class="panel-header">To Do List</h3>
```

```
        <table class="table">
            <thead>
                <tr>
                    <th>#</th>
                    <th>Action</th>
                    <th>Done</th>
                </tr>
            </thead>
            <tr ng-repeat="item in todos" ng-class="$odd ? 'odd' : 'even'">
                <td>{{$index + 1}}</td>
                <td ng-repeat="prop in item">{{prop}}</td>
            </tr>
        </table>
    </div>
</body>
</html>
```

I have used the ng-class directive, which sets the class attribute of an element using a data binding. I use a JavaScript ternary expression to assign elements to either the odd or even class based on the value of the $odd variable. You can see the result in Figure 10-6.

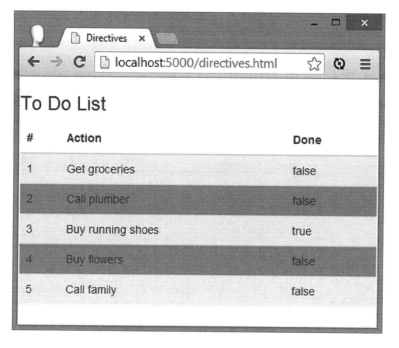

Figure 10-6. Varying content styling based on the ng-repeat variables

---

■ **Tip**   I explain the ng-class directive in Chapter 11, along with two related directives that are often used with ng-repeat: ng-class-even and ng-class-odd. As their names suggest, these directives set the value of the class attribute based on the $odd and $even variables defined by the ng-repeat directive.

Although this is the standard demonstration for the ng-repeat variables, most CSS frameworks can stripe tables, and this includes Bootstrap, as I demonstrated in Chapter 4. The real power of these variables comes when they are used in conjunction with other, more complex directives. Listing 10-9 provides a demonstration.

Listing 10-9. A More Complex ng-repeat Variable Example in the directives.html File

```
...
<table class="table">
    <thead>
        <tr>
            <th>#</th>
            <th>Action</th>
            <th>Done</th>
        </tr>
    </thead>
    <tr ng-repeat="item in todos" ng-class="$odd ? 'odd' : 'even'">
        <td>{{$index + 1}}</td>
        <td>{{item.action}}</td>
        <td><span ng-if="$first || $last">{{item.complete}}</span></td>
    </tr>
</table>
...
```

I have used the ng-if directive in this example, which I describe properly in Chapter 11. For now, it is enough to know that the ng-if directive will remove the element it is applied to if the expression it evaluates is false. I used this directive to control the presence of a span element in the Done column of the table, ensuring that it is displayed for only the first and last items.

Repeating Multiple Top-Level Elements

The ng-repeat directive repeats a single top-level element and its contents for each object or property that it processes. There are times, however, when you need to repeat *multiple* top-level elements for each data object. I encounter this problem most often when I need to generate multiple table rows for each data item that I am processing—something that is difficult to achieve with ng-repeat because no intermediate elements are allowed between tr elements and their parents. To address this problem, I can use the ng-repeat-start and ng-repeat-end directives, as shown in Listing 10-10.

Listing 10-10. Using the ng-repeat-start and ng-repeat-end Directives in the directives.html File

```
...
<table class="table">
    <tbody>
        <tr ng-repeat-start="item in todos">
            <td>This is item {{$index}}</td>
        </tr>
        <tr>
            <td>The action is: {{item.action}}</td>
        </tr>
        <tr ng-repeat-end>
            <td>Item {{$index}} is {{$item.complete? '' : "not "}} complete</td>
        </tr>
    </tbody>
</table>
...
```

The ng-repeat-start directive is configured just like ng-repeat, but it repeats all of the top-level elements (and their contents) until (but including) the element to which the ng-repeat-end attribute has been applied. In this example, it means I am able to generate three tr elements for each object in the todos array.

Working with Partial Views

The ng-include directive retrieves a fragment of HTML content from the server, compiles it to process any directives that it might contain, and adds it to the Document Object Model. These fragments are known as *partial views*. To demonstrate how this works, I have added an HTML file called table.html to the web server angularjs folder. You can see the contents of the new file in Listing 10-11.

Listing 10-11. The Contents of the table.html File

```
<table class="table">
    <thead>
        <tr>
            <th>#</th>
            <th>Action</th>
            <th>Done</th>
        </tr>
    </thead>
    <tr ng-repeat="item in todos" ng-class="$odd ? 'odd' : 'even'">
        <td>{{$index + 1}}</td>
        <td ng-repeat="prop in item">{{prop}}</td>
    </tr>
</table>
```

This file contains the fragment of HTML that defines the table element from earlier examples, complete with data bindings and directives—a simple partial view. In Listing 10-12, you can see how I can use the ng-include directive to load, process, and insert the table.html file into the main document.

Listing 10-12. Using the ng-include Directive in the directives.html File

```
<!DOCTYPE html>
<html ng-app="exampleApp">
<head>
    <title>Directives</title>
    <script src="angular.js"></script>
    <link href="bootstrap.css" rel="stylesheet" />
    <link href="bootstrap-theme.css" rel="stylesheet" />
    <script>
        angular.module("exampleApp", [])
            .controller("defaultCtrl", function ($scope) {
                $scope.todos = [
                    { action: "Get groceries", complete: false },
                    { action: "Call plumber", complete: false },
                    { action: "Buy running shoes", complete: true },
                    { action: "Buy flowers", complete: false },
                    { action: "Call family", complete: false }];
            });
    </script>
</head>
```

```
<body>
    <div id="todoPanel" class="panel" ng-controller="defaultCtrl">
        <h3 class="panel-header">To Do List</h3>
        <ng-include src="'table.html'"></ng-include>
    </div>
</body>
</html>
```

This is the first of the built-in directives that can be used as an HTML element as well as an attribute or class. As the listing illustrates, the name of the directive is used as the element tag name, like this:

```
...
<ng-include src="'table.html'"></ng-include>
...
```

The custom element is used just like any of the standard ones. The ng-include directive supports three configuration parameters, and when used like an element, they are applied as attributes.

■ **Caution**   Don't try to use apply the ng-include directive as a void element (in other words, <ng-include src="'table.html'" />). The content that follows the ng-include element will be removed from the DOM. You must always specify open and close tags, as I have shown in the example.

You can see the first of these parameters in the listing: The src attribute sets the location of the partial view file I want loaded, processed, and added to the document. For this example, I have specified the table.html file. When AngularJS processes the directive.html file, it encounters the ng-include directive and automatically makes an Ajax request for the table.html file, processes the file contents, and adds them to the document. I have described the three configuration parameters in Table 10-6, although it is src that interests us in this chapter.

Table 10-6. *The Configuration Parameters of the ng-include Directive*

Name	Description
src	Specifies the URL of the content to load
onload	Specifies an expression to be evaluated when the content is loaded
autoscroll	Specifies whether AngularJS should scroll the viewport when the content is loaded

The contents of files loaded by the ng-include directive are processed as though they were defined in situ, meaning you have access to the data model and behaviors defined by the controller and, if you use the ng-include directive within the ng-repeat directive, the special variables such as $index and $first that I described earlier in this chapter.

Selecting Partial Views Dynamically

My previous example demonstrated how the ng-include directive can be used to break a view into multiple partial view files. This is, in and of itself, a useful feature, and it allows you to create reusable partial views that can be applied throughout an application to avoid duplication and ensure consistent presentation of data.

That's all well and good, but you may have noticed something a little odd in the way that I specified which file the ng-include directive should request from the server:

```
...
<ng-include src="'table.html'"></ng-include>
...
```

I specified the table.html file as a string literal, denoted by the single-quote characters. I had to do this because the src attribute is evaluated as a JavaScript expression, and to statically define a file, I have to surround the file name with single quotes.

The real power of the ng-include directive comes from the way that the src setting is evaluated. To demonstrate how this works, I have created a new partial view file called list.html in the web server angularjs folder. You can see the content of the new file in Listing 10-13.

Listing 10-13. The Contents of the list.html File

```
<ol>
    <li ng-repeat="item in todos">
        {{item.action}}
        <span ng-if="item.complete"> (Done)</span>
    </li>
</ol>
```

This file contains a fragment of new markup that I have not used in previous examples. I use an ol element to denote an ordered list and use the ng-repeat directive on an li element to generate list items for each to-do. I use the ng-if directive, which I applied in a previous example (and explain fully in Chapter 11) to control the inclusion of a span element for those to-do items that are complete. Now that I have two partial views that can display the to-do items, I can use the ng-include directive to switch between them, as shown in Listing 10-14.

Listing 10-14. Using the ng-include Directive to Process Fragments Dynamically in the directives.html File

```
<!DOCTYPE html>
<html ng-app="exampleApp">
<head>
    <title>Directives</title>
    <script src="angular.js"></script>
    <link href="bootstrap.css" rel="stylesheet" />
    <link href="bootstrap-theme.css" rel="stylesheet" />
    <script>
        angular.module("exampleApp", [])
            .controller("defaultCtrl", function ($scope) {
                $scope.todos = [
                    { action: "Get groceries", complete: false },
                    { action: "Call plumber", complete: false },
                    { action: "Buy running shoes", complete: true },
                    { action: "Buy flowers", complete: false },
                    { action: "Call family", complete: false }];
```

```
                    $scope.viewFile = function () {
                        return $scope.showList ? "list.html" : "table.html";
                    };
                });
        </script>
    </head>
    <body>
        <div id="todoPanel" class="panel" ng-controller="defaultCtrl">
            <h3 class="panel-header">To Do List</h3>

            <div class="well">
                <div class="checkbox">
                    <label>
                        <input type="checkbox" ng-model="showList">
                        Use the list view
                    </label>
                </div>
            </div>

            <ng-include src="viewFile()"></ng-include>

        </div>
    </body>
</html>
```

I have defined a behavior called viewFile in the controller that returns the name of one of the two fragment files I created based on the value of a variable called showList. If showList is true, then the viewFile behavior returns the name of the list.html file; if showList is false or undefined, then the behavior returns the name of the table.html file.

The showList variable is initially undefined, but I have added a check box input element that sets the variable when it is checked using the ng-model directive, which I described earlier in this chapter. The user can change the value of the showList variable by checking or unchecking the element.

The final link in this chain is to change the way I apply the ng-include directive so that the src attribute gets its value from the controller behavior, which I do as follows:

```
...
<ng-include src="viewFile()"></ng-include>
...
```

The AngularJS data binding feature will keep the check box and the value of the showList variable synchronized, and the ng-include directive will change the content it loads and displays in concert with the showList value. You can see the effect of checking and unchecking the box in Figure 10-7.

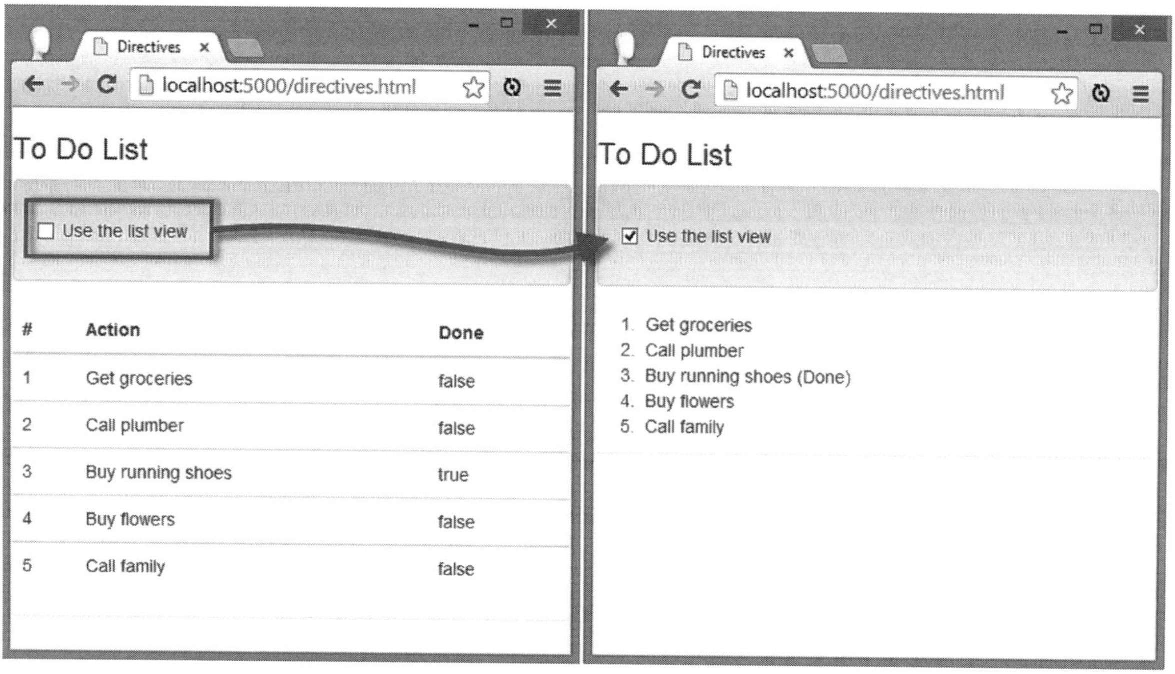

Figure 10-7. *Using the ng-include directive to display content based on a model property*

Using the ng-include Directive as an Attribute

Since this is the first directive I have described that can be expressed as an element, I am going to take a moment and show you how can achieve the same effect using an attribute. To start with, Listing 10-15 shows the ng-include directive applied as an element with the src and onload attributes set. You have seen src used in the previous examples. The onload attribute is used to specify an expression that will be evaluated when content is loaded; I have specified a call to the reportChange behavior that I added to the example and that writes a message to the JavaScript console reporting the name of the content file used. The onload attribute isn't especially interesting, but I want to use multiple configuration options to show you.

Listing 10-15. Using the ng-include Directive as an Element with Multiple Options in the directives.html File

```
<!DOCTYPE html>
<html ng-app="exampleApp">
<head>
    <title>Directives</title>
    <script src="angular.js"></script>
    <link href="bootstrap.css" rel="stylesheet" />
    <link href="bootstrap-theme.css" rel="stylesheet" />
    <script>
        angular.module("exampleApp", [])
            .controller("defaultCtrl", function ($scope) {
                $scope.todos = [
                    { action: "Get groceries", complete: false },
                    { action: "Call plumber", complete: false },
```

```
                        { action: "Buy running shoes", complete: true },
                        { action: "Buy flowers", complete: false },
                        { action: "Call family", complete: false }];

                $scope.viewFile = function () {
                    return $scope.showList ? "list.html" : "table.html";
                };

                $scope.reportChange = function () {
                    console.log("Displayed content: " + $scope.viewFile());
                }

            });
    </script>
</head>
<body>
    <div id="todoPanel" class="panel" ng-controller="defaultCtrl">
        <h3 class="panel-header">To Do List</h3>

        <div class="well">
            <div class="checkbox">
                <label>
                    <input type="checkbox" ng-model="showList">
                    Use the list view
                </label>
            </div>
        </div>

        <ng-include src="viewFile()" onload="reportChange()"></ng-include>
    </div>
</body>
</html>
```

Now, assuming I cannot use a custom element—or that I just prefer not to—I can rewrite this example to apply the ng-include directive as a custom attribute on a standard HTML element, as shown in Listing 10-16.

Listing 10-16. Applying the ng-include Directive as an Attribute in the directives.html File

```
...
<div ng-include="viewFile()" onload="reportChange()"></div>
...
```

The ng-include attribute can be applied to any HTML element, and the value of the src parameter is taken from the attribute value, which is viewFile() in this case. The other directive configuration parameters are expressed as separate attributes, which you can see with the onload attribute. This application of the ng-include directive has *exactly* the same effect as using the custom element.

Conditionally Swapping Elements

The ng-include directive is excellent for managing more significant fragments of content in partial, but often you need to switch between smaller chucks of content that are already within the document—and for this, AngularJS provides the ng-switch directive. You can see how I have applied this directive in Listing 10-17.

Listing 10-17. Using the ng-switch Directive in the directives.html File

```html
<!DOCTYPE html>
<html ng-app="exampleApp">
<head>
    <title>Directives</title>
    <script src="angular.js"></script>
    <link href="bootstrap.css" rel="stylesheet" />
    <link href="bootstrap-theme.css" rel="stylesheet" />
    <script>
        angular.module("exampleApp", [])
            .controller("defaultCtrl", function ($scope) {

                $scope.data = {};

                $scope.todos = [
                    { action: "Get groceries", complete: false },
                    { action: "Call plumber", complete: false },
                    { action: "Buy running shoes", complete: true },
                    { action: "Buy flowers", complete: false },
                    { action: "Call family", complete: false }];
            });
    </script>
</head>
<body>
    <div id="todoPanel" class="panel" ng-controller="defaultCtrl">

        <h3 class="panel-header">To Do List</h3>

        <div class="well">
            <div class="radio" ng-repeat="button in ['None', 'Table', 'List']">
                <label>
                    <input type="radio" ng-model="data.mode"
                            value="{{button}}" ng-checked="$first" />
                    {{button}}
                </label>
            </div>
        </div>

        <div ng-switch on="data.mode">
            <div ng-switch-when="Table">
                <table class="table">
                    <thead>
                        <tr><th>#</th><th>Action</th><th>Done</th></tr>
                    </thead>
                    <tr ng-repeat="item in todos" ng-class="$odd ? 'odd' : 'even'">
                        <td>{{$index + 1}}</td>
                        <td ng-repeat="prop in item">{{prop}}</td>
                    </tr>
                </table>
            </div>
```

```
        <div ng-switch-when="List">
            <ol>
                <li ng-repeat="item in todos">
                    {{item.action}}<span ng-if="item.complete"> (Done)</span>
                </li>
            </ol>
        </div>
        <div ng-switch-default>
            Select another option to display a layout
        </div>
    </div>

</div>
</body>
</html>
```

I start this example by using the ng-repeat directive to generate a set of radio buttons that use two-way data bindings to set the value of a model property called data.mode. The three values defined by the radio buttons are None, Table, and List and use each to represent a layout to display the to-do items.

■ **Tip** Notice that I have defined the scope property mode as a property on an object called data. This is required because of the way that AngularJS scopes inherit from one another and how some directives—including ng-model—create their own scopes. I explain how this works in Chapter 13.

The rest of the example demonstrates the ng-switch directive, which lets me display a different set of elements for each value that the data.mode property will be set to. You can see the result in Figure 10-8, and I explain the different parts of the directive after the figure.

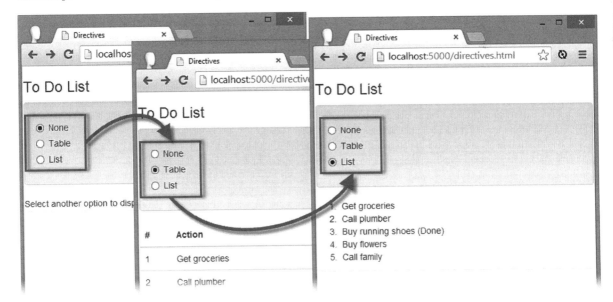

Figure 10-8. *Using the ng-switch directive*

■ **Tip** The ng-switch directive can be applied as an element, but the ng-switch-when and ng-switch-default sections have to be applied as attributes. Because of this, I tend to use ng-switch as an attribute as well for consistency.

The ng-switch directive is applied with an on attribute that specifies the expression that will be evaluated to decide which region of content will be displayed, as follows:

```
...
<div ng-switch on="data.mode">
...
```

In this example, I have specified that the value of the data.mode model property—the one that the radio buttons manage—will be used. You then use the ng-switch-when directive to denote a region of content that will be associated with a specific value, like this:

```
...
<div ng-switch-when="Table">
    <table class="table">
        <!-- elements omitted for brevity -->
    </table>
</div>
<div ng-switch-when="List">
    <ol>
        <!-- elements omitted for brevity -->
    </ol>
</div>
...
```

AngularJS will show the element to which the ng-switch-when directive has been applied when the attribute value matches the expression defined by the on attribute. The other elements within the ng-switch directive block are removed. The ng-switch-default directive is used to specify content that should be displayed when none of the ng-switch-when sections matches, as follows:

```
...
<div ng-switch-default>
    Select another option to display a layout
</div>
...
```

The ng-switch directive responds to changes in the value of its data binding, which is why clicking a radio button in the example causes the layout to change.

CHOOSING BETWEEN THE NG-INCLUDE AND NG-SWITCH DIRECTIVES

The ng-include and ng-switch directives can be used to create the same effects, and it can be difficult to figure out when to use each of them to best effect.

Use ng-switch when you need to alternate between smaller, simpler blocks of content and that there is a good chance the user will be shown most or all of those blocks in the normal execution of the web app. This is because you have to deliver all the content that the ng-switch directive needs as part of the HTML document, and that's a waste of bandwidth and loading time for content that is unlikely to be used.

The ng-include attribute is better suited for more complex content or content that you need to use repeatedly throughout an application. Partial views can help reduce the amount of duplication in a project when you need to include the same content in different places, but you must bear in mind that partial views are not requested until the first time they are required, and this can cause delays while the browser makes the Ajax request and receives the response from the server.

If in doubt, start with ng-switch. It is simpler and easier to work with, and you can always change to ng-include if your content gets too complex to easily manage or if you need to use the same content elsewhere in the same app.

Hiding Unprocessed Inline Template Binding Expressions

When working with complex content on slow devices, there can be a moment when the browser displays the HTML in the document while AngularJS is still parsing the HTML, processing the directives, and generally getting ready. In this interval, any inline template expressions you have defined will be visible to the user, as I have illustrated in Figure 10-9.

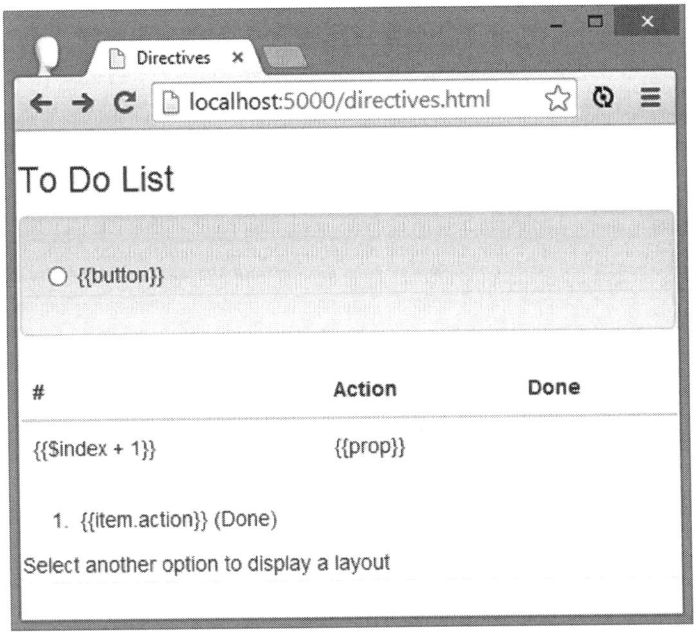

Figure 10-9. The template expressions displayed to the user while AngularJS is getting ready

Most devices have pretty good browsers these days with JavaScript implementations that are quick enough to prevent this from being a problem; in fact, I had to work pretty hard to capture the screenshot shown in the figure because desktop browsers are so fast that the situation doesn't arise.

But it does happen—especially if you are targeting older devices/browsers—and there are two ways to solve the problem. The first is to avoid using inline template expressions and stick with the ng-bind directive. I described this directive at the start of the chapter and made the point that it is ungainly when compared to inline expressions.

A better alternative is to use the ng-cloak directive, which has the effect of hiding content until AngularJS has finished processing it. The ng-cloak directive uses CSS to hide the elements to which it is applied, and the AngularJS library removes the CSS class when the content has been processed, ensuring that the user never sees the {{ and }} characters of a template expression. You can apply the ng-cloak directive as broadly or selectively as you want. A common approach is to apply the directive to the body element, but that just means that the user sees an empty browser window while AngularJS processes the content. I prefer to be more selective and apply the directive only to the parts of the document where there are inline expressions, as shown in Listing 10-18.

Listing 10-18. Selectively Applying the ng-cloak Directive to the directives.html File

```
...
<body>
    <div id="todoPanel" class="panel" ng-controller="defaultCtrl">
        <h3 class="panel-header">To Do List</h3>

        <div class="well">
            <div class="radio" ng-repeat="button in ['None', 'Table', 'List']">
                <label ng-cloak>
                    <input type="radio" ng-model="data.mode"
                        value="{{button}}" ng-checked="$first">
                    {{button}}
                </label>
            </div>
        </div>

        <div ng-switch on="data.mode" ng-cloak>
            <div ng-switch-when="Table">
                <table class="table">
                    <thead>
                        <tr><th>#</th><th>Action</th><th>Done</th></tr>
                    </thead>
                    <tr ng-repeat="item in todos" ng-class="$odd ? 'odd' : 'even'">
                        <td>{{$index + 1}}</td>
                        <td ng-repeat="prop in item">{{prop}}</td>
                    </tr>
                </table>
            </div>
            <div ng-switch-when="List">
                <ol>
                    <li ng-repeat="item in todos">
                        {{item.action}}<span ng-if="item.complete"> (Done)</span>
                    </li>
                </ol>
            </div>
        </div>
```

```
        <div ng-switch-default>
            Select another option to display a layout
        </div>
    </div>
  </div>
</body>
...
```

Applying the directive to the sections of the document that contain template expressions leaves the user able to see the static structure of a page, which still isn't ideal but is a lot better than just an empty window. You can see the effect the directive creates in Figure 10-10 (and, of course, the full app layout is revealed to the user when AngularJS finishes processing the content).

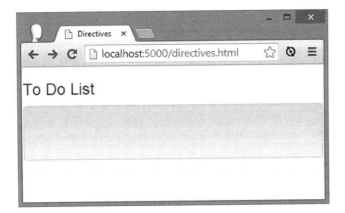

Figure 10-10. *Showing static content without template expressions*

Summary

In this chapter, I introduced you to AngularJS directives and described the directives that are used for data binding and managing templates. These are the most powerful and complex of the built-in templates, and they are the ones that underpin the early phases of development in an AngularJS project. In Chapter 11, I continue describing and demonstrating the built-in directives, focusing on the ones that manipulate elements and respond to events.

CHAPTER 11

∎ ∎ ∎

Using Element and Event Directives

In this chapter I continue to describe the directives that AngularJS provides. I describe the directives that you use to add, remove, hide, and show elements in the Document Object Model (DOM); the directives that add and remove elements from classes and set individual CSS style properties; the directives for handling events; and the directives that map between the way that AngularJS relies on data bindings and an HTML feature called Boolean attributes.

Along the way, I show you how to create custom directives to respond to events for which AngularJS doesn't provide built-in support. I don't get into the detail of creating custom directives until Chapter 15, but this is such a common task that it makes sense to describe it in this chapter, even though it requires AngularJS features that I don't describe until later chapters. Table 11-1 summarizes this chapter.

Table 11-1. *Chapter Summary*

Problem	Solution	Listing
Show or hide elements.	Use the ng-show and ng-hide directives.	1, 2
Remove elements from the DOM.	Use the ng-if directive.	3
Avoid the transclusion problem when generating elements that can't have an intermediate parent element.	Use the ng-repeat directive with a filter.	4, 5
Assign elements to classes or set individual CSS style properties.	Use the ng-class or ng-style directive.	6
Assign different classes to odd and even elements generated by the ng-repeat directive.	Use the ng-class-odd and ng-class-even directives.	7
Define behavior to be performed when an event is triggered.	Use an event directive such as ng-click (you can see a full list of the event directives in Table 11-3).	8
Handle an event for which AngularJS does not provide a directive.	Create a custom event directive.	9
Apply Boolean attributes to elements.	Use one of the Boolean attribute directives, such as ng-checked. (You can see a complete list of Boolean attribute directives in Table 11-4.)	10

Preparing the Example Project

I am going to continue working with the `directives.html` file in this example. In Listing 11-1, you can see that I have removed some of the markup from the previous chapter in order to simplify the example and prepare for the directives that I am going describe in this one.

Listing 11-1. The Contents of the directives.html File

```html
<!DOCTYPE html>
<html ng-app="exampleApp">
<head>
    <title>Directives</title>
    <script src="angular.js"></script>
    <link href="bootstrap.css" rel="stylesheet" />
    <link href="bootstrap-theme.css" rel="stylesheet" />
    <script>
        angular.module("exampleApp", [])
            .controller("defaultCtrl", function ($scope) {
                $scope.todos = [
                    { action: "Get groceries", complete: false },
                    { action: "Call plumber", complete: false },
                    { action: "Buy running shoes", complete: true },
                    { action: "Buy flowers", complete: false },
                    { action: "Call family", complete: false }];
            });
    </script>
</head>
<body>
    <div id="todoPanel" class="panel" ng-controller="defaultCtrl">
        <h3 class="panel-header">To Do List</h3>

        <table class="table">
            <thead>
                <tr><th>#</th><th>Action</th><th>Done</th></tr>
            </thead>
            <tr ng-repeat="item in todos">
                <td>{{$index + 1}}</td>
                <td ng-repeat="prop in item">{{prop}}</td>
            </tr>
        </table>
    </div>
</body>
</html>
```

All of the content from the previous chapter that controlled how the to-do items were laid out has been removed, and I have returned to using a simple table. You can see how the browser displays the `directives.html` file in Figure 11-1.

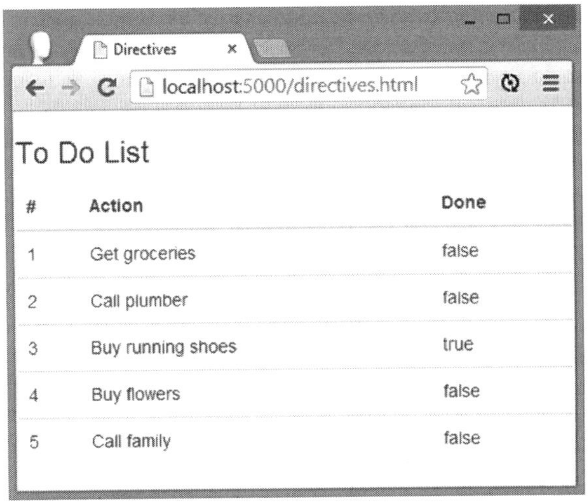

Figure 11-1. Displaying the directives.html file in the browser

Using the Element Directives

The first set of directives that I describe in this chapter are used to configure and style elements in the Document Object Model (DOM). These directives are useful for managing the way that an application displays content and data and, since this is AngularJS, for using bindings to change the HTML document dynamically when the data model changes. I have listed the element directives in Table 11-2. I describe each of these directives and demonstrate their use in the sections that follow.

Table 11-2. The Element Directives

Directive	Applied As	Description
ng-if	Attribute	Adds and removes elements from the DOM
ng-class	Attribute, class	Sets the class attribute for an element
ng-class-even	Attribute, class	Sets the class attribute for even-numbered elements generated within the ng-repeat directive
ng-class-odd	Attribute, class	Sets the class attribute for odd-numbered elements generated within the ng-repeat directive
ng-hide	Attribute, class	Shows and hides elements in the DOM
ng-show	Attribute, class	Shows and hides elements in the DOM
ng-style	Attribute, class	Sets one or more CSS properties

Showing, Hiding, and Removing Elements

Many of the directives in this category control whether elements are visible to the user, either by hiding them or by removing them completely from the DOM. Listing 11-2 shows the basic techniques for managing element visibility.

Listing 11-3. Using the ng-if Directive in the directives.html File

```
...
<td>
    <span ng-if="!item.complete">(Incomplete)</span>
    <span ng-if="item.complete">(Done)</span>
</td>
...
```

There is no convenient inverted directive that corresponds to ng-if, so I have to take responsibility for negating the value of the data-bound property to create the effect of the ng-hide directive. As Figure 11-3 shows, using the ng-if directive addresses the issue of the CSS style.

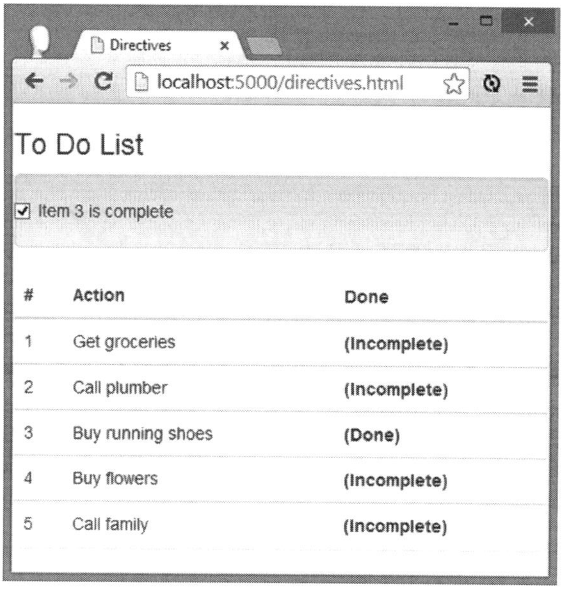

Figure 11-3. Using the ng-if directive

Avoiding Table Striping Problems and Conflicts with ng-repeat

The ng-show, ng-hide, and ng-if directives all have problems when they are applied to the elements that make up tables, which is a shame because new AngularJS developers often try to use the directives to manage the contents displayed by tables.

First, the way that ng-show and ng-hide work means they cannot be easily used in striped tables. This is just a restatement of the problem I showed you earlier, but it bears demonstration because it is such a common cause of confusion. In Listing 11-4, you can see how I have applied the ng-hide directive to the tr element so that only incomplete items are displayed. I have added the table element to the Bootstrap table-striped class to create the striping effect, as described in Chapter 4.

Listing 11-4. Using ng-hide on the Table Rows in the directives.html File

```
...
<table class="table table-striped">
    <thead>
        <tr><th>#</th><th>Action</th><th>Done</th></tr>
    </thead>
    <tr ng-repeat="item in todos" ng-hide="item.complete">
        <td>{{$index + 1}}</td>
        <td>{{item.action}}</td>
        <td>{{item.complete}}</td>
    </tr>
</table>
...
```

AngularJS will process the directives, but since the elements are hidden and not removed, the result is inconsistent striping, as shown in Figure 11-4. Notice that the coloring for rows has not been applied in rotation.

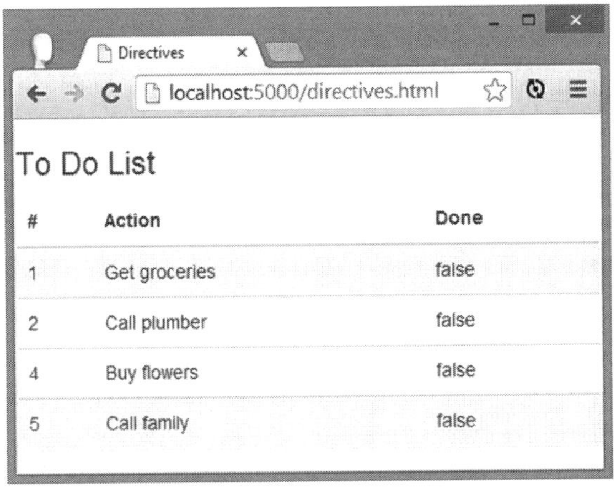

Figure 11-4. Inconsistent striping caused by the ng-hide directive

This may seem like a problem that the ng-if directive can solve, but you can't use the ng-if directive on the same element as the ng-repeat directive, like this:

```
...
<tr ng-repeat="item in todos" ng-if="!item.complete">
    <td>{{$index + 1}}</td>
    <td>{{item.action}}</td>
    <td>{{item.complete}}</td>
</tr>
...
```

Both the ng-repeat and ng-if directives rely on a technique called *transclusion*, which I describe in Chapter 17 but which essentially means that both directives want to modify the child elements and AngularJS doesn't know how to allow both to do so. If you try to apply both of these directives to an element, you will see an error similar to this one in the JavaScript console:

```
Error: [$compile:multidir] Multiple directives [ngRepeat, ngIf] asking for transclusion on:
<!-- ngRepeat: item in todos -->
```

This is a rare example where you can't wire up multiple AngularJS features to solve a problem. But that doesn't mean the problem can't be solved—just that it can't be solved by applying the ng-repeat and ng-if directives together. The answer is to use a filter, which I describe fully in Chapter 14 but which you can see demonstrated in Listing 11-5.

Listing 11-5. Using a Filter to Resolve the Transclusion Problem in the directives.html File

```
...
<table class="table table-striped">
    <thead>
        <tr><th>#</th><th>Action</th><th>Done</th></tr>
    </thead>
    <tr ng-repeat="item in todos | filter: {complete: 'false'}">
        <td>{{$index + 1}}</td>
        <td>{{item.action}}</td>
        <td>{{item.complete}}</td>
    </tr>
</table>
...
```

This is an example of a filter that uses an object to match properties on the source items. It selects those to-do items whose complete property is false. As Figure 11-5 shows, this creates a result that works with table striping because elements are created only for those objects that pass through the filter. (Filters, like so much else in AngularJS, are linked to the data model and will dynamically reflect changes in the data array.)

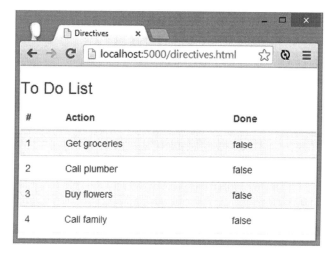

Figure 11-5. *Using a filter to preserve table striping*

Managing Classes and CSS

AngularJS provides a set of directives that are used to assign elements to classes and set individual CSS properties. You can see the first two of these directives—ng-class and ng-style—used in Listing 11-6.

Listing 11-6. Using the ng-class and ng-style Directives in the directives.html File

```
<!DOCTYPE html>
<html ng-app="exampleApp">
<head>
    <title>Directives</title>
    <script src="angular.js"></script>
    <link href="bootstrap.css" rel="stylesheet" />
    <link href="bootstrap-theme.css" rel="stylesheet" />
    <script>
        angular.module("exampleApp", [])
            .controller("defaultCtrl", function ($scope) {
                $scope.todos = [
                    { action: "Get groceries", complete: false },
                    { action: "Call plumber", complete: false },
                    { action: "Buy running shoes", complete: true },
                    { action: "Buy flowers", complete: false },
                    { action: "Call family", complete: false }];

                $scope.buttonNames = ["Red", "Green", "Blue"];

                $scope.settings = {
                    Rows: "Red",
                    Columns: "Green"
                };
            });
    </script>
    <style>
        tr.Red { background-color: lightcoral; }
        tr.Green { background-color: lightgreen;}
        tr.Blue { background-color: lightblue; }
    </style>
</head>
<body>
    <div id="todoPanel" class="panel" ng-controller="defaultCtrl">
        <h3 class="panel-header">To Do List</h3>

        <div class="row well">
            <div class="col-xs-6" ng-repeat="(key, val) in settings">
                <h4>{{key}}</h4>
                <div class="radio" ng-repeat="button in buttonNames">
                    <label>
                        <input type="radio" ng-model="settings[key]"
                            value="{{button}}">{{button}}
                    </label>
                </div>
            </div>
        </div>
```

```
            <table class="table">
                <thead>
                    <tr><th>#</th><th>Action</th><th>Done</th></tr>
                </thead>
                <tr ng-repeat="item in todos" ng-class="settings.Rows">
                    <td>{{$index + 1}}</td>
                    <td>{{item.action}}</td>
                    <td ng-style="{'background-color': settings.Columns}">
                        {{item.complete}}
                    </td>
                </tr>
            </table>
        </div>
    </body>
</html>
```

I have used a fair number of directives just to get to the point in this example where I can meaningfully apply the ng-class and ng-style directives. At the heart of this example is a simple object that I added to the controller scope:

```
...
$scope.settings = {
    Rows: "Red",
    Columns: "Green"
};
...
```

I will use the Rows property to set the background color of the tr elements in the table and the Columns property to set the background color of the Done column. To let the user set these values, I have used the ng-repeat directive to create two sets of radio buttons, laid out using a Bootstrap grid (as described in Chapter 4). I have used the ng-class directive to set the colors for the tr elements, like this:

```
...
<tr ng-repeat="item in todos" ng-class="settings.Rows">
...
```

The ng-class directive manages the class attribute of an element. In this example, the tr elements will be assigned to a class based on the value of the Rows property, corresponding to one of the CSS styles I defined:

```
...
<style>
    tr.Red { background-color: lightcoral; }
    tr.Green { background-color: lightgreen;}
    tr.Blue { background-color: lightblue; }
</style>
...
```

■ **Tip** You can specify multiple CSS classes using a map object, where the properties refer to the CSS classes and the values are the expressions that control whether the classes are applied. You can see this use of the ng-class directive in Chapter 8, where I used it in the SportsStore administration application.

I use the ng-style property to set CSS properties directly, rather than through a class:

```
...
<td ng-style="{'background-color': settings.Columns}">{{item.complete}}</td>
...
```

The ng-style directive is configured using an object whose properties correspond to the CSS properties that should be set—in this case, the background-color property, which will be set to the current value of the Columns model property.

■ **Tip**   It is generally considered poor technique to apply individual CSS properties to elements. When working with static content, styles applied through classes are much easier to work with, not least because a single change to the style definition will be applied wherever the style has been used. The situation is slightly different when using the ng-style directive because the value for the properties is obtained via a data binding and the usual guidance doesn't apply. My advice is to use classes when you can, but there is no need to avoid using the ng-style directive.

The result is that you can change the background color for the rows and one column in the table through the radio buttons, as shown in Figure 11-6. The effect is the same, but the rows are configured with classes (and the ng-class directive), and the column is configured by setting the CSS property directly via the ng-style directive.

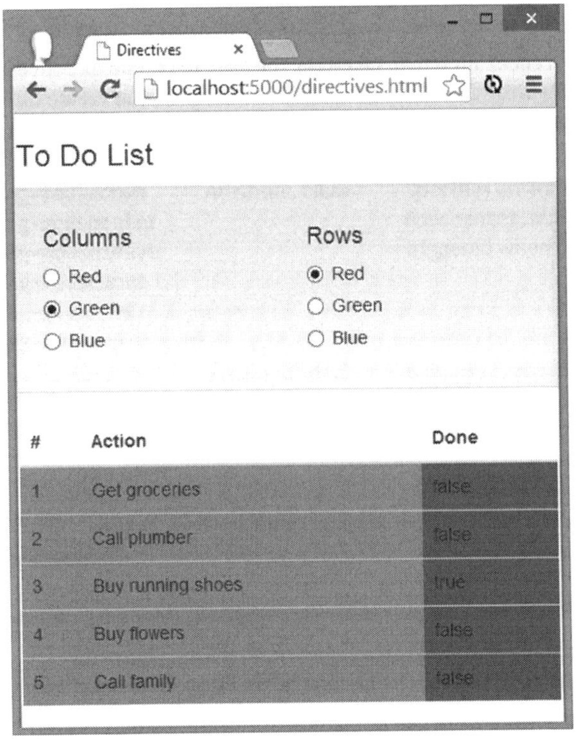

Figure 11-6. *Using the ng-class and ng-style directives*

You must be careful when handling events in behaviors because there is a mismatch between the event names that AngularJS uses for the names of the directives and the value of the type property of the underlying events. In this example, I have added directives to handle the mouseenter and mouseleave events, but I receive different events in the behavior function:

```
...
$scope.handleEvent = function (e) {
    console.log("Event type: " + e.type);
    $scope.data.columnColor = e.type == "mouseover" ? "Green" : "Blue";
}
...
```

The safest way to figure out which events you will receive in the behavior is to set up the function and use console.log to write the value of the type property to the console. In this way, I am able to tell that the mouseenter event will really be presented as mouseover and that the mouseleave event will be represented by mouseout. I check the type of the event I received and set the value of the data.columnColor model property to either Green or Blue. This value is used by the ng-class directive I applied to one of the td elements in the table, which has the effect of changing the color of the final table column when the mouse enters and leaves table rows.

■ **Note** This mismatch isn't really the fault of AngularJS. The world of browser events, especially when it comes to dealing with the mouse or pointer, is a mess. AngularJS relies on jQuery, which takes care of some of the complexity, but it isn't a perfect solution, and thorough testing is essential to make sure you are getting and handling the right events.

UNDERSTANDING EVENTS IN ANGULARJS

Although AngularJS provides a set of event directives, you will find that you create fewer event handlers than you would with, say, jQuery. This is because a lot of interesting events in web apps arise when the user changes the state of form elements, such as input and select. You don't need to use events to respond to these changes with AngularJS because you can use the ng-model directive instead. Event handlers are still used behind the scenes by AngularJS, but you don't have to write and manage them yourselves.

Some developers are uncomfortable with the idea of applying event directives directly to elements, especially when they contain inline expressions. There are two reasons for this discomfort; one is just habit, and one has some merit.

The habitual discomfort comes from the way web developers are frequently drilled to use unobtrusive JavaScript to create event handlers, rather than adding code directly to elements. This isn't a concern for AngularJS, which uses jQuery to create unobtrusive handlers behind the scenes. Applying event directives to elements *feels* a little odd, but it won't lead to the maintenance problems that unobtrusive JavaScript sets out to avoid.

The concern that has merit is the idea of using expressions with directives, rather than relying on controller behaviors. I don't like to see anything but the simplest logic contained in a view (see Chapter 3 for details), and I tend to use controller behaviors for preference. In defense of expressions, one has to understand that there are far fewer of them in an AngularJS view because of the heavy reliance on directives like ng-repeat to generate elements, but it is still an easy path to create code that is hard to test and maintain. My recommendation is to embrace the event directives wholeheartedly but rely on controller behaviors to contain the logic that is executed when the event is triggered.

Creating a Custom Event Directive

I explain the different ways you can create custom directives in Chapter 15–17. It can be a complex process, and there are lots of features to understand and use. But for this chapter, I am going to show you how to create a simple directive that you can use in your own projects to handle events for which AngularJS doesn't provide a built-in directive. I am going to give you only a cursory explanation of how it works, but it is such a common requirement that it is worth showing you the technique in the context of this chapter. In Listing 11-9, I have created a directive that handles the touchstart and touchend events, which are trigged by touch-enabled devices when the user taps and releases the screen.

Listing 11-9. Creating a Custom Event Directive in the directives.html File

```
<!DOCTYPE html>
<html ng-app="exampleApp">
<head>
    <title>Directives</title>
    <script src="angular.js"></script>
    <link href="bootstrap.css" rel="stylesheet" />
    <link href="bootstrap-theme.css" rel="stylesheet" />
    <script>
        angular.module("exampleApp", [])
            .controller("defaultCtrl", function ($scope, $location) {

                $scope.message = "Tap Me!";

            }).directive("tap", function () {
                return function (scope, elem, attrs) {
                    elem.on("touchstart touchend", function () {
                        scope.$apply(attrs["tap"]);
                    });
                }
            });
    </script>
</head>
<body>
    <div id="todoPanel" class="panel" ng-controller="defaultCtrl">
        <div class="well" tap="message = 'Tapped!'">
            {{message}}
        </div>
    </div>
</body>
</html>
```

I create the directive using the Module.directive method that I introduced in Chapter 9. The directive is called tap, and it returns a factory function that, in turn, creates a worker function to process the element to which the directive has been applied. The arguments to the worker function are the scope in which the directive is operating (I describe scopes in Chapter 13), the jqLite or jQuery representation of the element to which the directive has been applied, and a collection of the attributes applied to the element.

I use the jqLite on method (which is derived from the jQuery method of the same name) to register a handler function for the touchstart and touchend events. My handler function calls the scope.$apply method to evaluate whatever expression has been defined as the value for the directive attribute, which I obtain from the attribute collection.

I describe jqLite in Chapter 15 and the scope $apply method in Chapter 13. I have applied the directive to the div element as I would any other directive, and my expression in this case modifies the message model property:

```
...
<div class="well" tap="message = 'Tapped!'">
...
```

You will need to enable touch event emulation in Google Chrome to test this example (or use a device or emulator that supports touch) because the touchstart and touchend events are not triggered on mouse-only platforms. When you tap the div element, the contents will change, as illustrated in Figure 11-8.

Figure 11-8. *Creating a custom event handling directive*

Managing Special Attributes

For the most part, AngularJS works neatly with HTML, seamlessly building on the standard elements and attributes. There are, however, quirks in HTML in the way that some attributes work that cause AngularJS some problems and require the use of directives. I describe the two categories of attributes that cause AngularJS problems in the sections that follow.

Managing Boolean Attributes

The significance of most HTML attributes is driven by the value assigned to the attribute, but some HTML attributes have an effect by their presence on an element, irrespective of their value. These are known as *Boolean attributes*. A good example is the disabled attribute; a button element, for instance, is disabled when the disabled attribute is applied, even when the attribute has no value, like this:

```
...
<button class="btn" disabled>My Button</button>
...
```

The only values that can be set for the disabled attribute are the empty string, like this:

```
...
<button class="btn" disabled="">My Button</button>
...
```

or disabled, like this:

```
...
<button class="btn" disabled="disabled">My Button</button>
...
```

What you can't do is set the disabled attribute to false in order to enable a button. This kind of attribute runs counter to the data binding approach that AngularJS uses. To solve this problem, AngularJS contains a number of directives that can be used to manage Boolean attributes, as described in Table 11-4.

Table 11-4. *The Boolean Attribute Directives*

Directive	Applied As	Description
ng-checked	Attribute	Manages the checked attribute (used on input elements)
ng-disabled	Attribute	Manages the disabled attribute (used on input and button elements)
ng-open	Attribute	Manages the open attribute (used on details elements)
ng-readonly	Attribute	Manages the readonly attribute (used on input elements)
ng-selected	Attribute	Manages the selected attribute (used on option elements)

I am not going to demonstrate all of these directives because they work in the same way, but in Listing 11-10, I have applied the ng-disabled directive.

Listing 11-10. Managing Boolean Attributes in the directives.html File

```
<!DOCTYPE html>
<html ng-app="exampleApp">
<head>
    <title>Directives</title>
    <script src="angular.js"></script>
    <link href="bootstrap.css" rel="stylesheet" />
    <link href="bootstrap-theme.css" rel="stylesheet" />
    <script>
        angular.module("exampleApp", [])
            .controller("defaultCtrl", function ($scope) {
                $scope.dataValue = false;
            });
    </script>
</head>
```

```
<body>
    <div id="todoPanel" class="panel" ng-controller="defaultCtrl">
        <h3 class="panel-header">To Do List</h3>

        <div class="checkbox well">
            <label>
                <input type="checkbox" ng-model="dataValue">
                Set the Data Value
            </label>
        </div>

        <button class="btn btn-success" ng-disabled="dataValue">My Button</button>
    </div>
</body>
</html>
```

I defined a model property called dataValue that I will use to control the state of a button element. The example contains a check box that uses the ng-model directive to create a two-way data binding with the dataValue property (as described in Chapter 10), and I have applied the ng-disabled directive to the button element as follows:

```
...
<button class="btn btn-success" ng-disabled="dataValue">My Button</button>
...
```

Notice that I don't set the disabled attribute directly. This is the responsibility of the ng-disabled directive based on the value of the expression it is given, which in this case is just the value of the dataValue property. When the dataValue property is true, the ng-disabled directive will add the disabled attribute to the element in the DOM, like this:

```
...
<button class="btn btn-success" ng-disabled="dataValue" disabled="disabled">
    My Button
</button>
...
```

The disabled directive is removed when the data property is false. You can see the effect of checking and unchecking the box in Figure 11-9.

Figure 11-9. *Using the ng-disabled directive to manage the disabled attribute*

Managing Other Attributes

There are three directives that are used to work with other attributes that AngularJS can't operate on directly, as described in Table 11-5.

Table 11-5. *The Boolean Attribute Directives*

Directive	Applied As	Description
ng-href	Attribute	Sets the href attribute on a elements.
ng-src	Attribute	Sets the src attribute on img elements.
ng-srcset	Attribute	Sets the srcset attribute on img elements. The srcset attribute is a draft standard to extend HTML5, allowing for multiple images to be specified for different display sizes and pixel densities. Browser support is limited as I write this.

These directives allow AngularJS data bindings to be used to set the value of the attribute they correspond to and, in the case of the ng-href directive, prevent the user from being able to navigate to the wrong destination by clicking the link before AngularJS has processed the element.

Summary

In this chapter, I described the directives that AngularJS provides for manipulating elements and handling events. I showed you how to show, hide, add, and remove elements from the DOM; how to add and remove elements from classes; how to set individual CSS style properties on elements; and how to handle events, including creating a simple custom directive that can be used to handle events for which AngularJS doesn't provide built-in support. I finished this chapter with the directives that are used to manage attributes that don't fit neatly into the AngularJS model. In the next chapter, I describe the AngularJS features for working with forms.

```
                    <div class="form-group row">
                        <label for="actionLocation">Location:</label>
                        <select id="actionLocation" class="form-control"
                                ng-model="newTodo.location">
                            <option>Home</option>
                            <option>Office</option>
                            <option>Mall</option>
                        </select>
                    </div>
                    <button class="btn btn-primary btn-block"
                            ng-click="addNewItem(newTodo)">
                        Add
                    </button>
                </div>
            </div>

            <div class="col-xs-6">
                <table class="table">
                    <thead>
                        <tr><th>#</th><th>Action</th><th>Done</th></tr>
                    </thead>
                    <tr ng-repeat="item in todos">
                        <td>{{$index + 1}}</td>
                        <td>{{item.action}}</td>
                        <td>
                            <input type="checkbox" ng-model="item.complete">
                        </td>
                    </tr>
                </table>
            </div>
        </div>
    </div>
</body>
</html>
```

The new HTML elements in this example look more complicated than they really are because of the Bootstrap classes I have applied to get the layout I want. In fact, all we care about is this input element:

```
...
<input id="actionText" class="form-control" ng-model="newTodo.action">
...
```

and this select element:

```
...
<select id="actionLocation" class="form-control" ng-model="newTodo.location">
    <option>Home</option>
    <option>Office</option>
    <option>Mall</option>
</select>
...
```

They both use the ng-model directive, configured to update model properties that I have not explicitly defined: the newTodo.action and newTodo.location properties. These properties are not part of my domain model, but I need to access the value that the user enters for use in the addNewItem behavior I defined in the controller and that I invoke when the user clicks the button element:

```
...
$scope.addNewItem = function (newItem) {
    $scope.todos.push({action: newItem.action + " (" + newItem.location + ")",
        complete: false
    });
};
...
```

The controller behavior is a function that takes an object with action and location properties and adds a new object to the array of to-do items. You can see how I pass the newTodo object to the behavior in the ng-click directive I applied to the button element:

```
...
<button class="btn btn-primary btn-block" ng-click="addNewItem(newTodo)">
    Add
</button>
...
```

■ **Tip** I could have written this behavior so that it works on the $scope.newTodo object directly, rather than accepting an object as an argument, but this approach allows a behavior to be used in multiple places in a view, which becomes important when considering controller inheritance, as described in Chapter 13.

The newTodo object and its action and location properties don't exist when the forms.html page is first loaded by the browser; the only data in the model is the set of existing to-do items that I have hard-coded in the controller factory function. AngularJS will create the newTodo object automatically when the input or select element is changed and assign a value to its action or location properties based on which element the user is working with.

Because of this flexibility, AngularJS takes a relaxed view of the state of the data model. There are no errors when you retrieve a nonexistent object or property, and when you assign a value to an object or property that doesn't exist, AngularJS will simply create it for you—producing what is known as an *implicitly defined* value or object.

■ **Tip** I have used the newTodo object to group related properties, but you can also implicitly define properties directly on the $scope object. This is what I did in Chapter 2 when I created the first AngularJS example in this book.

To see the effect, enter some text in the input element, select a value in the select element, and click the Add button. Your interactions with the input and select elements will have created the newTodo object and its properties, and the ng-click directive applied to the button element will invoke the controller behavior that uses these values to create a new to-do item in the list, as shown in Figure 12-3.

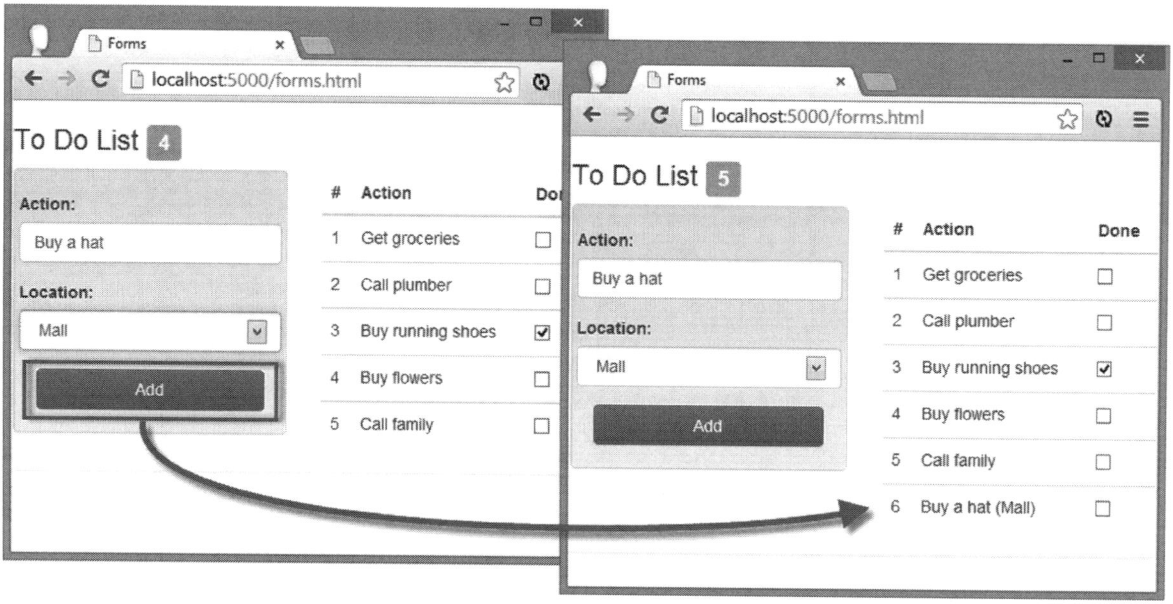

Figure 12-3. *Using implicitly defined model properties*

Checking That the Data Model Object Has Been Created

Using an implicitly defined object on which properties are defined has some benefits, such as being able to call the behavior that processes the data in a clean and simple way. But it has a drawback as well, which you can see if you reload the forms.html file in the browser and click the Add button without editing the input element or selecting an option for the select element. The interface won't change when you click the button, but you'll see an error message like this one in the JavaScript console:

```
TypeError: Cannot read property 'action' of undefined
```

The problem is that my controller behavior is trying to access properties on an object that AngularJS won't create until the one of the form controls has been modified, triggering the ng-model directive.

When relying on implicit definition, it is important to write your code to cater for the possibility that the objects or properties you are going to use do not yet exist. I have made this a separate example because it is a common problem when coming to grips with AngularJS. In Listing 12-4, you can see how I have modified my behavior so that it checks for the object and its properties.

Listing 12-4. Checking That Implicitly Defined Objects and Properties Exist in the forms.html File

```
...
$scope.addNewItem = function (newItem) {
    if (angular.isDefined(newItem) && angular.isDefined(newItem.action)
            && angular.isDefined(newItem.location)) {
```

```
        $scope.todos.push({
            action: newItem.action + " (" + newItem.location + ")",
            complete: false
        });
    }
};
...
```

I have used the `angular.isDefined` method to check that the `newItem` object and both of its properties have been defined before I add a new item to the set of to-dos.

Validating Forms

The change I made in the previous section prevents a JavaScript error, but it has the effect of allowing the user to interact with the application without producing a result or an error. I have fixed one problem, the JavaScript error, and introduced another: a confused user.

I wanted to show you the need to check for the existence of the data object because it is a common problem, but the underlying issue is that my simple example app has a constraint, which is that I need to receive an action and a location from the user before creating a new to-do item. I have enforced this constraint in my code, but I really need to tell the user about it as well—and that leads neatly into the world of *form validation*.

Most web applications need to receive data from the user. Users dislike forms, especially on touch-enabled devices, and even the best-intentioned users will enter unexpected data. There are some good reasons for this—see the "Are My Users Stupid?" sidebar for a summary—but the result is that you will need to check the data that users provide before using it. AngularJS provides comprehensive support for validating form data, which I describe in the sections that follow.

ARE MY USERS STUPID?

Web application developers wonder why they get all the stupid users—the ones who enter nonsense into form fields and manage to mess up their accounts. There *are* stupid users, of course, but most of the problems with form data are caused by a much more pernicious problem: developers. There are four common reasons why users give bad data values, and all can be mitigated to some extent by careful design and development.

The first reason is that the user doesn't understand what they are being asked for, either because the cues they are given are confusing or because they just aren't paying attention. If you are building an application that takes credit card details, for example, take a look at the failed attempts—many of them will be caused by the user entering their credit card number in the field for their name, and vice versa. A user sees two long `input` elements and has been trained by every other web application in the world that one of them will be for the card number and one will be for their name. A *distracted* user sees the same cues but doesn't take the time to read the labels for each `input` element and provides the information in the wrong fields. Distractions come in many forms, most of which are beyond your control, but a certain amount of inattention arises when the user has completed the part of the process that interests *them* (selecting a new shirt or a pair of running shoes, for example) and now has to grind through the part of the process that interests *you* (providing a shipping address, payment details, and so on). There are some useful steps you can take to reduce user confusion and inattention. Ask for the information that causes the most errors as early in the process as you can. For example, ask for credit card details before you have the user fill out a lengthy shipping details form. You can also structure your forms to reduce confusion: Make the labels clearer and follow a conventional order for the form elements, for example.

The second reason users give bad data is that they don't want to provide the information you are asking for. In this situation, the user is trying to get through the form process as quickly as possible, and they will enter the minimum amount of data to get to the end. If you have a lot of users whose e-mail addresses are a@a.com, then you are suffering from this problem. Ask yourself *why* users don't want to give accurate data—are you asking for too much information or for details that are too personal, for example?

The third reason is that the user doesn't have what you are asking for. I live in the United Kingdom, which means that I have problems with address forms that require me to pick a U.S. state. There are no states in the United Kingdom, and making a value mandatory just means you'll get bad data or that users won't complete the process you are leading them through. (This is why NPR doesn't get donations from me; I like *This American Life*, but I can't complete the donation process.)

The final reason is the simplest: The user has made a mistake. I am a quick but inaccurate typist, and I often type my surname as *Freman* instead of *Freeman*, missing an *e*. There is little you can do about errors, other than to minimize the amount of free-form text the user has to enter. Wherever possible, offer the user a list of options to pick from.

I don't want to get into a long lecture about the design of web forms, but I do want to say that the best way of approaching this issue is to focus on what the *user* is trying to achieve. And when things go wrong, you should try to see the problem (and the required resolution) the way the user sees it. Your users don't know about how you have built your systems, and they don't care about your business processes; they just want to get something done. Everyone can be happy if you keep the focus on the task the *user* is trying to complete and strip everything else out of the process.

Performing Basic Form Validation

AngularJS provides basic form validation by honoring the standard HTML element attributes, such as type and required, and adding some directives. In Listing 12-5, I have simplified the forms.html file to focus on the form elements in order to demonstrate the basic validation support.

Listing 12-5. Performing Basic Form Validation in the forms.html File

```
<!DOCTYPE html>
<html ng-app="exampleApp">
<head>
    <title>Forms</title>
    <script src="angular.js"></script>
    <link href="bootstrap.css" rel="stylesheet" />
    <link href="bootstrap-theme.css" rel="stylesheet" />
    <script>
        angular.module("exampleApp", [])
            .controller("defaultCtrl", function ($scope) {
                $scope.addUser = function (userDetails) {
                    $scope.message = userDetails.name
                        + " (" + userDetails.email + ") (" + userDetails.agreed + ")";
                }

                $scope.message = "Ready";
            });
    </script>
</head>
```

```
<body>
    <div id="todoPanel" class="panel" ng-controller="defaultCtrl">
        <form name="myForm" novalidate ng-submit="addUser(newUser)">
            <div class="well">
                <div class="form-group">
                    <label>Name:</label>
                    <input name="userName" type="text" class="form-control"
                            required ng-model="newUser.name">
                </div>
                <div class="form-group">
                    <label>Email:</label>
                    <input name="userEmail" type="email" class="form-control"
                            required ng-model="newUser.email">
                </div>
                <div class="checkbox">
                    <label>
                        <input name="agreed" type="checkbox"
                                ng-model="newUser.agreed" required>
                        I agree to the terms and conditions
                    </label>
                </div>
                <button type="submit" class="btn btn-primary btn-block"
                        ng-disabled="myForm.$invalid">
                    OK
                </button>
            </div>
            <div class="well">
                Message: {{message}}
                <div>
                    Valid: {{myForm.$valid}}
                </div>
            </div>
        </form>
    </div>
</body>
</html>
```

There is a lot going on in this example, and the best place to start is by showing you the overall effect before digging into the detail. In Figure 12-4, I have shown the initial state of the HTML document when it is loaded by the browser. There are three input elements and an OK button that is disabled and cannot be clicked.

Table 12-2. *The type Attribute Values for Input Elements*

Type Value	Description
checkbox	Creates a check box (pre-dates HTML5)
email	Creates a text input that accepts an e-mail address (new in HTML5)
number	Creates a text input that accepts a number address (new in HTML5)
radio	Creates a radio button (pre-dates HTML5)
text	Creates a standard text input that accepts any value (pre-dates HTML5)
url	Creates a text input that accepts a URL (new in HTML5)

In addition to the formats specified by the type attribute, I can apply further constraints through a mix of standard attributes and AngularJS directives. In the example, I have used the required attribute, which specifies that the user must provide a value for the form to be valid. When this is combined with the type attribute value, the effect is to tell AngularJS that the user must provide a value and that value must be formatted as an e-mail address.

■ **Caution**   The validation of e-mail addresses and URLs checks the formatting, not whether the address or URL exists and is in use.

There are different attributes for each type of input element, and AngularJS defines a set of optional directives for each element type that can be used to customize the validation. I describe each element and the attributes and directives available later in this chapter.

For the other input elements in the example, I have specified only the required attribute. For the text type input element, this just means that the user is required to enter a value but without any specific format validation:

```
...
<input name="userName" type="text" class="form-control" required ng-model="newUser.name">
...
```

I have specified the type attribute for this input element, but omitting it has the same effect as setting it to text, as I have done here. The final input element in this example is a check box:

```
...
<input name="agreed" type="checkbox" ng-model="newUser.agreed" required>
...
```

Each of the input elements uses the ng-model directive to set a property on the implicitly defined newUser object, and since all of the elements have the required attribute, the result is that the form will be valid only when the user has entered a name and a well-formatted e-mail address and checked the box.

Monitoring the Validity of the Form

The directives that AngularJS uses to replace the standard form elements define special variables that you can use to check the validation state of individual elements or the form as a whole. Table 12-3 describes the variables that are available.

Table 12-3. *The Validation Variables Defined by the Form Directives*

Variable	Description
$pristine	Returns true if the user has not interacted with the element/form
$dirty	Returns true if the user has interacted with the element/form
$valid	Returns true if the contents of the element/form are valid
$invalid	Returns true if the contents of the element/form are invalid
$error	Provides details of validation errors—see the "Providing Form Validation Feedback" section for details

As I'll demonstrate later in this chapter, these variables can be used in combination to present the user with feedback about validation errors. For my current example, I used two of the special variables. The first use is through an inline data binding, like this:

```
...
<div>Valid: {{myForm.$valid}}</div>
...
```

This expression displays the $valid variable to represent the overall validity of the form element. I explained earlier in the chapter that it is important to use the name attribute on the elements that you want to validate, and this is why: AngularJS exposes the properties in the table via an object with the name value for each element, in this case myForm. The second variable I used was $invalid, and I used it in combination with another AngularJS directive, as follows:

```
...
<button type="submit" class="btn btn-primary btn-block" ng-disabled="myForm.$invalid">
    OK
</button>
...
```

The $invalid property will return true if any of the elements in the form are not valid, and using this value as the expression for the ng-disabled directive ensures that the OK button is disabled until the form is valid.

Providing Form Validation Feedback

The overall effect of the example in the previous section was simple: The OK button is disabled until all of the input elements are valid, preventing the user from providing badly formatted or incomplete data. Behind the scenes, AngularJS performs validation checks as the user is interacting with the form elements, and we can use the information that these checks provide to give the user meaningful feedback in real time, rather than waiting until they are ready to submit the data. In the sections that follow, I demonstrate the two mechanisms that AngularJS provides for reporting real-time validation: classes and variables.

Using CSS to Provide Feedback

Each time the user interacts with an element that is being validated, AngularJS checks its state to see whether it is valid. The validity checks depend on the element type and how it has been configured. For a check box, for example, the check is generally as simple as checking to see that the user has checked the box. An example for an input element whose type is email might be the user has provided a value, that the value is formatted as a valid e-mail address, and that the e-mail address is within a specific domain.

AngularJS reports on the outcome of these validation checks by adding and removing the elements it validates from a set of classes, which can be combined with CSS to provide feedback to the user by styling the element. AngularJS uses four basic classes, which I have listed in Table 12-4.

Table 12-4. *The Classes Used by AngularJS Validation*

Variable	Description
ng-pristine	Elements that the user has not interacted are added to this class.
ng-dirty	Elements that the user has interacted are added to this class.
ng-valid	Elements that are valid are in this class.
ng-invalid	Elements that are not valid are in this class.

AngularJS adds and removes elements that are being validated from these classes after every interaction, which means you can use these classes to give keystroke-by-keystroke, click-by-click feedback to the user, both for the overall form and for individual elements. Listing 12-6 shows the use of these classes.

Listing 12-6. Using the Validation Classes to Provide Feedback in the forms.html File

```
<!DOCTYPE html>
<html ng-app="exampleApp">
<head>
    <title>Forms</title>
    <script src="angular.js"></script>
    <link href="bootstrap.css" rel="stylesheet" />
    <link href="bootstrap-theme.css" rel="stylesheet" />
    <script>
        angular.module("exampleApp", [])
            .controller("defaultCtrl", function ($scope) {
                $scope.addUser = function (userDetails) {
                    $scope.message = userDetails.name
                        + " (" + userDetails.email + ") (" + userDetails.agreed + ")";
                }

                $scope.message = "Ready";
            });
    </script>
    <style>
        form .ng-invalid.ng-dirty { background-color: lightpink; }
        form .ng-valid.ng-dirty { background-color: lightgreen; }
        span.summary.ng-invalid { color: red; font-weight: bold; }
        span.summary.ng-valid { color: green; }
    </style>
</head>
```

```
<body>
    <div id="todoPanel" class="panel" ng-controller="defaultCtrl">
        <form name="myForm" novalidate ng-submit="addUser(newUser)">
            <div class="well">
                <div class="form-group">
                    <label>Name:</label>
                    <input name="userName" type="text" class="form-control"
                            required ng-model="newUser.name">
                </div>
                <div class="form-group">
                    <label>Email:</label>
                    <input name="userEmail" type="email" class="form-control"
                            required ng-model="newUser.email">
                </div>
                <div class="checkbox">
                    <label>
                        <input name="agreed" type="checkbox"
                                ng-model="newUser.agreed" required>
                        I agree to the terms and conditions
                    </label>
                </div>
                <button type="submit" class="btn btn-primary btn-block"
                        ng-disabled="myForm.$invalid">OK</button>
            </div>
            <div class="well">
                Message: {{message}}
                <div>
                    Valid:
                    <span class="summary"
                            ng-class="myForm.$valid ? 'ng-valid' : 'ng-invalid'">
                        {{myForm.$valid}}
                    </span>
                </div>
            </div>
        </form>
    </div>
</body>
</html>
```

I have defined four CSS styles that select elements that belong to the classes I described in Table 12-4. The first two styles select elements that are members of the ng-dirty class, which is applied to elements only after the user has interacted with them. (Before the interaction, elements are members of the ng-pristine class.) Elements that have valid content are members of the ng-valid class and are shaded a light green color. Elements that have invalid content are members of the ng-invalid class and are shaded in light pink (which is as close to a light red shade as I can easily get). Combining the ng-valid and ng-valid classes with ng-dirty in the CSS selector means that the real-time feedback about element validity doesn't begin until the user starts interacting with the element. The best way of seeing how this works is to load the forms.html file into the browser and start entering an e-mail address into the input element whose type is email. Before you start typing, the input element will be in the ng-pristine class, and none of the CSS styles I have defined will be applied, as shown in Figure 12-5.

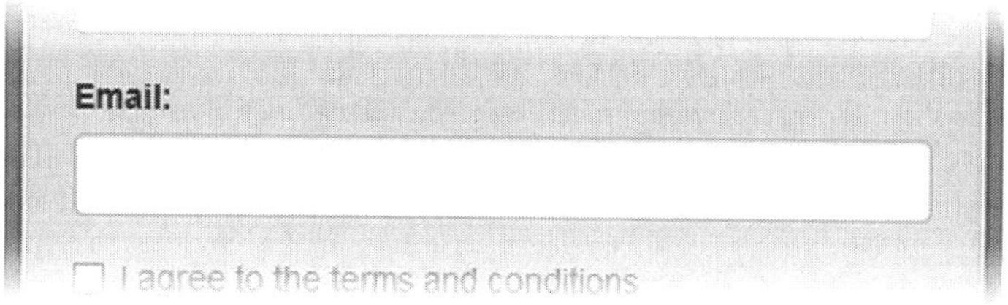

Figure 12-5. The pristine state of the input element

As you start to type, AngularJS moves the element from the ng-pristine class, adds it to the ng-dirty class, and starts validating the content. In Figure 12-6, you can see the effect of the first few characters of an e-mail address. The element was added to the ng-invalid class after the first character was entered because the content isn't in the right format for an e-mail address.

Figure 12-6. The invalid state of the input element

Finally, as I complete the e-mail address, AngularJS removes the element from the ng-invalid class and adds it to ng-valid, reflecting the fact that I have provided a properly formatted e-mail address, as shown in Figure 12-7. The element is still in the ng-dirty class: There is no going back to ng-pristine once you have changed the element.

Figure 12-7. The valid state of the input element

You can, of course, use the special variables that AngularJS provides to add and remove elements from these classes yourself. This is what I have done with the span element that I added in Listing 12-6:

```
...
<div>
    Valid: <span class="summary" ng-class="myForm.$valid ? 'ng-valid' : 'ng-invalid'">
        {{myForm.$valid}}
    </span>
</div>
...
```

I used the ng-class directive, which I described in Chapter 11, to add and remove the span element from the ng-valid and ng-invalid classes based on the validation status of the complete form. The styles that I defined for the span element set the color to red when the form is invalid and green otherwise. (The text itself is set using a data binding to the $valid variable that AngularJS associates with the form element, which I introduced in the basic validation section and describe in detail later in this chapter.)

Providing Feedback for Specific Validation Constraints

The classes that I listed in Table 12-4 give an overall indication of the validation state of an element, but AngularJS also adds elements to classes to give specific information about each of the validation constraints that apply to an element. The name of the class that is used is based on the corresponding attribute, as demonstrated in Listing 12-7.

Listing 12-7. Providing Feedback About Specific Constraints in the forms.html File

```
...
<style>
    form .ng-invalid-required.ng-dirty { background-color: lightpink; }
    form .ng-invalid-email.ng-dirty { background-color: lightgoldenrodyellow; }
    form .ng-valid.ng-dirty { background-color: lightgreen; }
    span.summary.ng-invalid {color: red; font-weight: bold; }
    span.summary.ng-valid { color: green }
</style>
...
```

In the highlighted styles, I have changed the selectors so that they are applied to specific validation problems. I applied two validation constraints to one of the input elements in the example: using the required attribute to mandate a value and setting the type attribute to email, requiring that value to be formatted as an e-mail address.

AngularJS will add the element to the ng-valid-required and ng-invalid-required classes to signal compliance with the required attribute and use the ng-valid-email and ng-invalid-email classes to single compliance with the formatting constraint.

You need to be careful when working with these classes because it is possible for an element to be valid for one constraint but not another. For example, an element whose type attribute is email will be valid when the input is empty, meaning that the element will be in the ng-valid-email class and the ng-invalid-required class at the same time. This is an artifact of the HTML specification, and thorough testing is required to make sure you don't give the user nonsensical feedback (although this can be addressed by showing text cues, which I describe in the next section).

Using the Special Variables to Provide Feedback

As I described in Table 12-3 earlier in the chapter, AngularJS provides a set of special variables for form validation that you can use in views to check the validation status of individual elements and of the form as a whole. I used these variables to control the disabled state of a button in earlier examples by applying the ng-disabled directive, but they can also be used to control visibility of elements that give feedback to the user by applying them with the ng-show directive, as illustrated in Listing 12-8. For this example, I removed some of the elements from previous examples so I can keep the listing simple.

Listing 12-8. Using Validation Variables to Control Element Visibility in the forms.html File

```
<!DOCTYPE html>
<html ng-app="exampleApp">
<head>
    <title>Forms</title>
    <script src="angular.js"></script>
```

```
<link href="bootstrap.css" rel="stylesheet" />
<link href="bootstrap-theme.css" rel="stylesheet" />
<script>
    angular.module("exampleApp", [])
        .controller("defaultCtrl", function ($scope) {
            $scope.addUser = function (userDetails) {
                $scope.message = userDetails.name
                    + " (" + userDetails.email + ") (" + userDetails.agreed + ")";
            }

            $scope.message = "Ready";
        });
</script>
<style>
    form .ng-invalid-required.ng-dirty { background-color: lightpink; }
    form .ng-invalid-email.ng-dirty { background-color: lightgoldenrodyellow; }
    form .ng-valid.ng-dirty { background-color: lightgreen; }
    span.summary.ng-invalid { color: red; font-weight: bold; }
    span.summary.ng-valid { color: green; }
    div.error {color: red; font-weight: bold;}
</style>
</head>
<body>
    <div id="todoPanel" class="panel" ng-controller="defaultCtrl">
        <form name="myForm" novalidate ng-submit="addUser(newUser)">
            <div class="well">
                <div class="form-group">
                    <label>Email:</label>
                    <input name="userEmail" type="email" class="form-control"
                        required ng-model="newUser.email">
                    <div class="error"
                        ng-show="myForm.userEmail.$invalid && myForm.userEmail.$dirty">
                        <span ng-show="myForm.userEmail.$error.email">
                            Please enter a valid email address
                        </span>
                        <span ng-show="myForm.userEmail.$error.required">
                            Please enter a value
                        </span>
                    </div>
                </div>
                <button type="submit" class="btn btn-primary btn-block"
                    ng-disabled="myForm.$invalid">OK</button>
            </div>
        </form>
    </div>
</body>
</html>
```

I have added a new div element to display validation messages to the user. The visibility of the div element is controlled by the ng-show directive, which will display the element if the input element has not passed its validation checks and if it is dirty.

> ■ **Tip** The continuous nature of AngularJS validation means that an empty, pristine `input` element with the `required` attribute is invalid, because it contains no value. I don't want to display an error message before the user has started to even enter data, so I check that `$dirty` is `true`, indicating that the user has interacted with the element, before displaying the error message.

Notice how I refer to the input element in order to access the special validation variables:

```
...
<div class="error" ng-show="myForm.userEmail.$invalid && myForm.userEmail.$dirty">
...
```

I refer to the element via the name value of the `form` element combined with the name of the `input` element, separated by a period: `myForm.userEmail`. It is for this reason that I have emphasized the importance of applying the name attribute to elements that are being validated.

Within the `div` element, I have defined an error message contained in a `span` element for both of the validation constraints I applied to the `input` element. I control the visibility of these elements by using the special `$error` variable, which returns an object with properties representing the validation constraints. I can tell whether the `required` constraint has not been met by checking if `$error.required` is `true` and checking the formatting of the value the user has entered by seeing whether `$error.email` is `true`. The `$error` object will contain properties for all the constraints applied to an element; you can see the effect I have created in Figure 12-8. (To create the first panel in the figure, I typed a character and then deleted it to switch the element from pristine to dirty.)

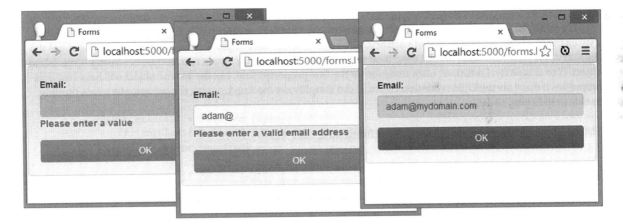

Figure 12-8. *Displaying contextual validation error messages*

Reducing the Number of Feedback Elements

The previous example neatly demonstrates the way that the special validation variables can be combined with other directives in order to improve the user experience, but you can end up with a lot of elements in your markup that duplicate the same messages. As Listing 12-9 shows, it is a simple matter to consolidate these messages into a controller behavior.

```
<body>
    <div id="todoPanel" class="panel" ng-controller="defaultCtrl">
        <form name="myForm" novalidate ng-submit="addUser(newUser)"
                ng-class="showValidation ? 'validate' : ''">
            <div class="well">
                <div class="form-group">
                    <label>Email:</label>
                    <input name="userEmail" type="email" class="form-control"
                            required ng-model="newUser.email">
                    <div class="error" ng-show="showValidation">
                        {{getError(myForm.userEmail.$error)}}
                    </div>
                </div>
                <button type="submit" class="btn btn-primary btn-block">OK</button>
            </div>
        </form>
    </div>
</body>
</html>
```

With an example like this, you can really see how the generic functionality offered by each directive can be combined to create custom interactions in a web app. I have modified my addUser behavior so that it checks the validity of the whole form and sets an implicitly defined model property to true if validation feedback should be displayed. The addUser behavior is not called until the form is submitted, which means that the user can enter anything they like into the input element without getting feedback.

If the form is submitted and has validation errors, setting the model property to true reveals the validation feedback, which I control through a class that I applied to the form element and that I target with my CSS selectors. I use the same model property on the div element that contains the text feedback, although just to simplify the view logic. The result is that validation feedback isn't displayed to the user until the form is first submitted, as illustrated in Figure 12-9, after which the normal real-time feedback is provided.

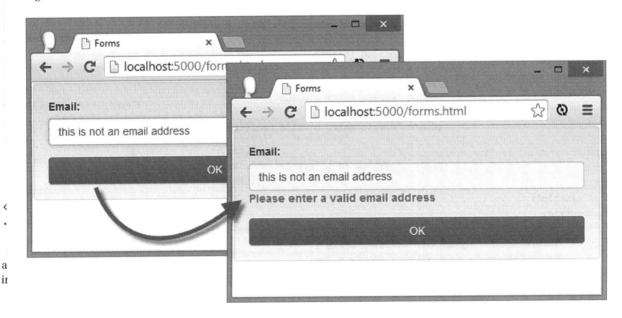

Figure 12-9. Deferring validation feedback

Using the Form Directive Attributes

As I explained earlier in this chapter, AngularJS provides its form features using directives that replace the standard form elements, such as form, input, and select. These directives support optional attributes that can be used to integrate form elements more closely into the AngularJS style of application development. In the sections that follow, I detail each of the form elements for which there are AngularJS replacement directives and describe the additional attributes you can use to fine-tune the way forms work.

Using Input Elements

The directive that AngularJS uses for input elements provides some additional attributes that can be used to improve integration with the data model, as described in Table 12-5. These attributes are available only when the input element does not have a type attribute or when the type attribute is text, url, email, or number.

Table 12-5. *The Attributes That Can Be Used for an input Element*

Name	Description
ng-model	Specifies a two-model binding, as described earlier in this chapter
ng-change	Specifies an expression that is evaluated when the contents of the element are changed, as described in Chapter 11
ng-minlength	Sets a minimum number of characters required for the element to be valid
ng-maxlength	Sets a maximum number of characters required for the element to be valid
ng-pattern	Sets a regular expression. The contents of the element must match this pattern in order to be valid
ng-required	Sets the value of the required attribute with a data binding

Some of these attributes are described elsewhere, but in Listing 12-12 you can see how the others are applied to perform validation.

Listing 12-12. Using the Attributes for input Elements in the forms.html File

```
<!DOCTYPE html>
<html ng-app="exampleApp">
<head>
    <title>Forms</title>
    <script src="angular.js"></script>
    <link href="bootstrap.css" rel="stylesheet" />
    <link href="bootstrap-theme.css" rel="stylesheet" />
    <script>
        angular.module("exampleApp", [])
            .controller("defaultCtrl", function ($scope) {
                $scope.requireValue = true;
                $scope.matchPattern = new RegExp("^[a-z]");
            });
    </script>
</head>
```

```
<body>
    <div id="todoPanel" class="panel" ng-controller="defaultCtrl">
        <form name="myForm" novalidate>
            <div class="well">
                <div class="form-group">
                    <label>Text:</label>
                    <input name="sample" class="form-control" ng-model="inputValue"
                            ng-required="requireValue" ng-minlength="3"
                            ng-maxlength="10" ng-pattern="matchPattern">
                </div>
            </div>

            <div class="well">
                <p>Required Error: {{myForm.sample.$error.required}}</p>
                <p>Min Length Error: {{myForm.sample.$error.minlength}}</p>
                <p>Max Length Error: {{myForm.sample.$error.maxlength}}</p>
                <p>Pattern Error: {{myForm.sample.$error.pattern}}</p>
                <p>Element Valid: {{myForm.sample.$valid}}</p>
            </div>
        </form>
    </div>
</body>
</html>
```

I have used the ng-required, ng-minlength, ng-maxlength, and ng-pattern attributes, all of which apply validation constraints. The effect is that I have created an element that is valid only if the user has supplied a value and that value starts with a lowercase letter and is between three and ten characters long. I have added a set of data bindings that display the validation status for the individual constraints and the input element overall, as shown in Figure 12-10.

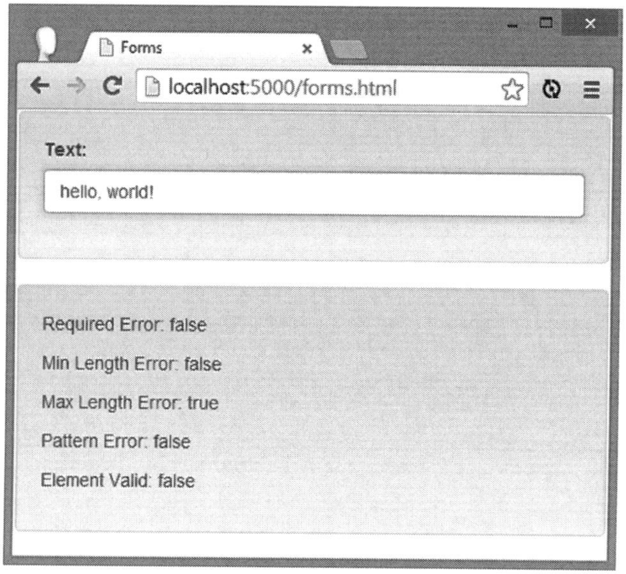

Figure 12-10. *Using the additional attributes on the input element*

■ **Note**   When the type attribute is email, url, or number, AngularJS sets the ng-pattern automatically to check the formatting. You should not set the ng-pattern attribute on these types of input element.

Using Checkboxes

Table 12-6 shows the additional attributes that are available when you use an input element whose type attribute is set to checkbox.

Table 12-6. *The Attributes That Can Be Used for an input Element Whose type Attribute Is checkbox*

Name	Description
ng-model	Specifies a two-model binding, as described earlier in this chapter
ng-change	Specifies an expression that is evaluated when the contents of the element are changed, as described in Chapter 11
ng-true-value	Specifies the value that the model binding expression will be set to when the element is checked
ng-false-value	Specifies the value that the model binding expression will be set to when the element is unchecked

You can see a simple example of using the ng-true-value and ng-false-value attributes in Listing 12-13.

Listing 12-13. Using the Additional Attributes for Check Boxes in the forms.html File

```
<!DOCTYPE html>
<html ng-app="exampleApp">
<head>
    <title>Forms</title>
    <script src="angular.js"></script>
    <link href="bootstrap.css" rel="stylesheet" />
    <link href="bootstrap-theme.css" rel="stylesheet" />
    <script>
        angular.module("exampleApp", [])
            .controller("defaultCtrl", function ($scope) {});
    </script>
</head>
<body>
    <div id="todoPanel" class="panel" ng-controller="defaultCtrl">
        <form name="myForm" novalidate>
            <div class="well">
                <div class="checkbox">
                    <label>
                        <input name="sample" type="checkbox" ng-model="inputValue"
                                ng-true-value="Hurrah!" ng-false-value="Boo!">
                        This is a checkbox
                    </label>
                </div>
            </div>
```

```
                <div class="well">
                    <p>Model Value: {{inputValue}}</p>
                </div>
            </form>
        </div>
    </body>
</html>
```

The values of the ng-true-value and ng-false-value attributes will be used to set the model binding expression, but only when the state of the check box changes. This means that the model property—if implicitly defined—will not be created until the user interacts with the element. See the "Implicitly Creating Model Properties" section earlier in this chapter for further details.

Using Text Areas

AngularJS includes a directive for the textarea element, which supports the same attributes as described in Table 12-5. You can see a simple example of applying some of these attributes in Listing 12-14. This is the same basic example I used in Listing 12-12 but with a textarea instead of an input element.

Listing 12-14. Using the Additional Attributes for the textarea Element in the forms.html File

```
<!DOCTYPE html>
<html ng-app="exampleApp">
<head>
    <title>Forms</title>
    <script src="angular.js"></script>
    <link href="bootstrap.css" rel="stylesheet" />
    <link href="bootstrap-theme.css" rel="stylesheet" />
    <script>
        angular.module("exampleApp", [])
            .controller("defaultCtrl", function ($scope) {
                $scope.requireValue = true;
                $scope.matchPattern = new RegExp("^[a-z]");
            });
    </script>
</head>
<body>
    <div id="todoPanel" class="panel" ng-controller="defaultCtrl">
        <form name="myForm" novalidate>
            <div class="well">
                <div class="form-group">
                    <textarea name="sample" cols="40" rows="3"
                        ng-model="textValue"
                        ng-required="requireValue" ng-minlength="3"
                        ng-maxlength="10" ng-pattern="matchPattern">
                    </textarea>
                </div>
            </div>
            <div class="well">
                <p>Required Error: {{myForm.sample.$error.required}}</p>
                <p>Min Length Error: {{myForm.sample.$error.minlength}}</p>
                <p>Max Length Error: {{myForm.sample.$error.maxlength}}</p>
```

```
                <p>Pattern Error: {{myForm.sample.$error.pattern}}</p>
                <p>Element Valid: {{myForm.sample.$valid}}</p>
            </div>
        </form>
    </div>
</body>
</html>
```

Using Select Elements

The directive that AngularJS uses for select elements defined the ng-required attribute that is available for input elements and an ng-options attribute that can be used to generate option elements from arrays and objects. Listing 12-15 provides an example of using the ng-options attribute.

Listing 12-15. Using the ng-options Attribute on a select Element in the forms.html File

```
<!DOCTYPE html>
<html ng-app="exampleApp">
<head>
    <title>Forms</title>
    <script src="angular.js"></script>
    <link href="bootstrap.css" rel="stylesheet" />
    <link href="bootstrap-theme.css" rel="stylesheet" />
    <script>
        angular.module("exampleApp", [])
            .controller("defaultCtrl", function ($scope) {
                $scope.todos = [
                    { id: 100, action: "Get groceries", complete: false },
                    { id: 200, action: "Call plumber", complete: false },
                    { id: 300, action: "Buy running shoes", complete: true }];
            });
    </script>
</head>
<body>
    <div id="todoPanel" class="panel" ng-controller="defaultCtrl">
        <form name="myForm" novalidate>
            <div class="well">
                <div class="form-group">
                    <label>Select an Action:</label>
                    <select ng-model="selectValue"
                            ng-options="item.action for item in todos">
                    </select>
                </div>
            </div>

            <div class="well">
                <p>Selected: {{selectValue || 'None'}}</p>
            </div>
        </form>
    </div>
</body>
</html>
```

For this example, I have defined a data model that contains three to-do items and, in addition to the `action` and `complete` properties that I have been using in earlier example, I have defined an id attribute.

For the `select` element, I have set the `ng-options` attribute so that `option` elements are generated for each of the to-do items, as follows:

```
...
<select ng-model="selectValue" ng-options="item.action for item in todos">
...
```

This is the basic `ng-options` expression, and it is in the format `<label> for <variable> in <array>`. AngularJS will generate an `option` element for each object in the array and set the contents to be the label. For this listing, the `select` element generates the following HTML:

```
...
<select ng-model="selectValue" ng-options="item.action for item in todos"
        class="ng-pristine ng-valid">
    <option value="?" selected="selected"></option>
    <option value="0">Get groceries</option>
    <option value="1">Call plumber</option>
    <option value="2">Buy running shoes</option>
</select>
...
```

Using the `ng-options` attribute is similar to using the `ng-repeat` directive, but with some additions and quirks that are particular to `select` elements.

Changing the First Option Element

Notice that the output from the `select` element contains an `option` element whose `value` attribute is a question mark and that has no content. AngularJS generates this when the property specified by the `ng-model` attribute is undefined. I can replace this default `option` element by adding my own with an empty `value` attribute, as shown in Listing 12-16.

Listing 12-16. Replacing the Default Option Element in the forms.html File

```
...
<select ng-model="selectValue" ng-options="item.action for item in todos">
    <option value="">(Pick One)</option>
</select>
...
```

This produces the following HTML:

```
...
<select ng-model="selectValue" ng-options="item.action for item in todos"
        class="ng-pristine ng-valid">
    <option value="" class="">(Pick One)</option>
    <option value="0">Get groceries</option>
```

```
    <option value="1">Call plumber</option>
    <option value="2">Buy running shoes</option>
</select>
...
```

Changing the Selection Value

By default, picking an option element in a select element causes the ng-model expression to be updated with the object in the collection. You can see this by loading forms.html in the browser and making a selection. There is a data binding at the bottom of the page that shows the selectValue model property, which is implicitly defined by the select element, as Figure 12-11 illustrates.

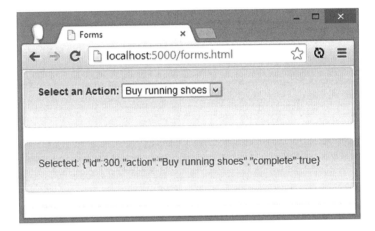

Figure 12-11. *Selecting an object with an select element*

You won't always want to use the complete source object to set the ng-model value; you can use a slightly different expression for the ng-options attribute to specify one of the properties from the object, as shown in Listing 12-17.

Listing 12-17. Specifying a Property as the ng-model Value in the forms.html File

```
...
<select ng-model="selectValue"
        ng-options="item.id as item.action for item in todos">
    <option value="">(Pick One)</option>
</select>
...
```

The expression is in the form <selected property> as <label> for <variable> in <array>, and in the listing, I have specified that the item.id is the value I want used when the user picks an option element. You can see the effect of this change in Figure 12-12.

315

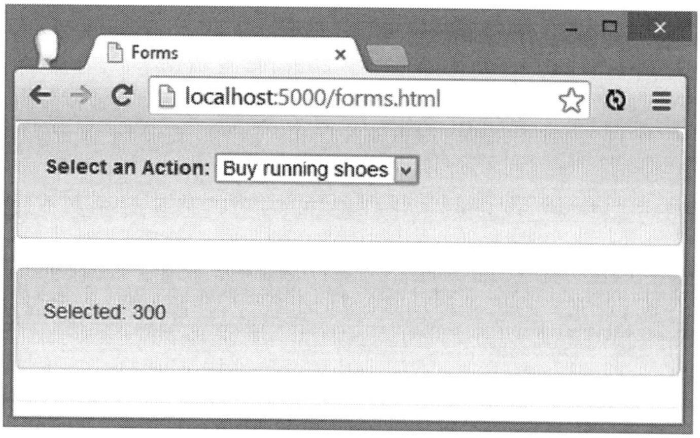

Figure 12-12. Specifying a property that will be used for the ng-model value

Creating optgroup Elements

The ng-options attribute can be used to group items together based on the value of a property, generating a set of optgroup elements for each value that is encountered. Listing 12-18 provides an example, in which I have added a place property to the to-do object in the model.

Listing 12-18. Generating optgroup Elements in the forms.html File

```
<!DOCTYPE html>
<html ng-app="exampleApp">
<head>
    <title>Forms</title>
    <script src="angular.js"></script>
    <link href="bootstrap.css" rel="stylesheet" />
    <link href="bootstrap-theme.css" rel="stylesheet" />
    <script>
        angular.module("exampleApp", [])
            .controller("defaultCtrl", function ($scope) {
                $scope.todos = [
                  { id: 100, place: "Store", action: "Get groceries", complete: false },
                  { id: 200, place: "Home", action: "Call plumber", complete: false },
                  { id: 300, place: "Store", action: "Buy running shoes", complete: true }];
            });
    </script>
</head>
<body>
    <div id="todoPanel" class="panel" ng-controller="defaultCtrl">
        <form name="myForm" novalidate>

            <div class="well">
                <div class="form-group">
                    <label>Select an Action:</label>
                    <select ng-model="selectValue"
                        ng-options="item.action group by item.place for item in todos">
```

```
                    <option value="">(Pick One)</option>
                </select>
            </div>
        </div>

        <div class="well">
            <p>Selected: {{selectValue || 'None'}}</p>
        </div>
    </form>
</div>
</body>
</html>
```

The property that is used to group objects together is specified with group by in the ng-options expression. In this example, I have specified that the place property should be used to group elements, which causes the following HTML to be generated:

```
...
<select ng-model="selectValue"
        ng-options="item.action group by item.place for item in todos"
        class="ng-pristine ng-valid">
    <option value="" class="">(Pick One)</option>
    <optgroup label="Store">
        <option value="0">Get groceries</option>
        <option value="2">Buy running shoes</option>
    </optgroup>
    <optgroup label="Home">
        <option value="1">Call plumber</option>
    </optgroup>
</select>
...
```

You can see how the browser uses the optgroup element to add structure to the select element menu in Figure 12-13.

Figure 12-13. *Generating optgroup elements*

■ **Tip**   You can combine the selection value and grouping features by using an expression such as `item.id as`
`item.action group by item.place for item in todos`.

Summary

In this chapter, I explained how AngularJS uses directives to seamlessly replace and enhance the standard form elements. I describe how `ng-model` is used to create two-way data bindings and how model values can be explicitly and implicitly defined. I showed you how AngularJS provides real-time form validation and demonstrated how you can respond to this information using CSS or special variables that can be used with directives such as `ng-show`. I also showed you how to can defer validation to dial down the AngularJS approach, which can be overwhelming for users. I finished this chapter by describing the additional attributes for integrating form elements into AngularJS by enhancing the validation checks that are performed, making it easier to control model binding or by generating elements from collections. In the next chapter, I describe the relationship between two key AngularJS components: controllers and scopes.

CHAPTER 13

Using Controllers and Scopes

In this chapter, I describe the relationship between controllers and scopes and demonstrate how to use both to best effect. Scopes are more complex than they first appear and—as you'll learn—form a hierarchy that can be used to communicate between controllers. I'll also show you how can create controllers that don't use scopes and how you can use scopes to integrate AngularJS with other JavaScript frameworks. Table 13-1 summarizes this chapter.

Table 13-1. *Chapter Summary*

Problem	Solution	Listing
Create a controller.	Use the `Module.controller` method to define a controller and apply it to an HTML element using the `ng-controller` directive.	1–2, 13
Add data and behavior to the controller scope.	Declare a dependency on the `$scope` service and assign properties to it within the controller factory function.	3-4
Create a monolithic controller.	Apply the `ng-controller` directive to the body element and use the factory function to define all the data and behaviors that the application requires.	5
Reuse a controller.	Apply the `ng-controller` directive to multiple HTML elements.	6
Communicate between controllers.	Send events via the root scope or via a service.	7, 8
Inherit behaviors and data from another controller.	Nest `ng-controller` directives.	9–12
Create controllers without scopes.	Use scope-less controllers.	14
Notify the scope that there has been a change.	Use the `$apply`, `$watch`, and `$watchCollection` methods to inject changes into a scope or to monitor a scope for changes.	15–17

Why and When to Use Controllers and Scopes

Controllers act as the link between the domain model and the view; they provide data and services to the view and define the business logic required to translate user actions into changes in the model.

You can't build an AngularJS application without a controller; it is one of the fundamental building blocks of the MVC model, as described in Chapter 3. You *can*, however, decide how many controllers your application has, how they are organized, and how they expose data and functionality to the views they support.

Controllers provide data and logic to views through *scopes*, which underpin the data binding techniques I demonstrated in earlier chapters and which are a signature feature of AngularJS development. Knowing how scopes work will give you a greater understanding of how AngularJS is designed, even though there are quirks and gotchas that lie on the path to comprehension. Table 13-2 summarizes why and when controllers are used in AngularJS.

Table 13-2. *Why and When to Use Controllers and Scopes*

Why	When
Controllers are the link between the model and views. They use scopes to expose data from the model to views and the logic required to make changes to the model based on user interactions with the view.	Controllers are used throughout an AngularJS application and provide scopes to the views they support.

Preparing the Example Project

For this chapter I created an HTML file called `controllers.html` in the web server `angularjs` directory. You can see the initial contents of the new file in Listing 13-1.

Listing 13-1. The Contents of the controllers.html File

```
<!DOCTYPE html>
<html ng-app="exampleApp">
<head>
    <title>Controllers</title>
    <script src="angular.js"></script>
    <link href="bootstrap.css" rel="stylesheet" />
    <link href="bootstrap-theme.css" rel="stylesheet" />
    <script>
        angular.module("exampleApp", []);
    </script>
</head>
<body>
    <div class="well">
        Content will go here.
    </div>
</body>
</html>
```

The file contains a minimal AngularJS application with a module—but nothing else. You can see the effect of displaying the `controllers.html` file in the browser in Figure 13-1.

Figure 13-1. *Displaying the controllers.html file*

Understanding the Basics

You can get a lot done in AngularJS by sticking to some basic controller and scope techniques, and it is only as the complexity of your application grows that you will need more advanced features. In this section, I describe the fundamentals. I show you how to create and apply a simple controller, how to define data and logic in a scope, and how to modify the scope. Later in the chapter, I'll move on to more advanced techniques and features.

Creating and Applying Controllers

Controllers are created through the `controller` method provided by the AngularJS `Module` object. The arguments to the controller method are the name for the new controller and a function that will create the controller. The function is properly known as the *constructor*, but I will refer to it as the *factory function* because many of the method calls required to create AngularJS components are expressed as one function (the factory) that is used to create another function (the *worker functions*). The factory/worker function approach is a little odd at first, but you'll soon get used to it.

The factory function can use the dependency injection feature to declare dependencies on AngularJS services. Almost every controller will request the `$scope` service, which is used to provide the view with its scope, defining the data and logic that can be used in the view. You can see how I have created a simple controller in Listing 13-2.

Listing 13-2. Creating a Simple Controller in the controllers.html File

```
<!DOCTYPE html>
<html ng-app="exampleApp">
<head>
    <title>Controllers</title>
    <script src="angular.js"></script>
    <link href="bootstrap.css" rel="stylesheet" />
    <link href="bootstrap-theme.css" rel="stylesheet" />
    <script>
        angular.module("exampleApp", [])
            .controller("simpleCtrl", function ($scope) {

            });
    </script>
</head>
<body>
    <div class="well" ng-controller="simpleCtrl">
        Content will go here.
    </div>
</body>
</html>
```

■ **Tip** Strictly speaking, `$scope` isn't a service but is an object provided by a service called `$rootScope`, which I introduce later in this chapter. For all practical purposes, `$scope` is used like a service, so I am going to refer to it as though it were one for simplicity.

Not only do you have to create the controller, but you also have to demark the views that the controller will support, which is done through the application of the `ng-controller` directive. The value of the directive must match the name used to create the controller, which is `simpleCtrl` in this example. The convention when using AngularJS is to use the suffix `Ctrl` for the name of the controller, but this is not a requirement. At the moment, the controller I have defined doesn't *do* anything; it doesn't provide the view with any data or logic. I'll populate the controller in the sections that follow.

Setting Up the Scope

Controllers provide capabilities to their views through their *scope*, which is what the controller in Listing 13-2 asked AngularJS to provide when it declared its dependency on the $scope service. Scopes not only define the relationship between controllers and views but also provide the mechanism for many of the most important AngularJS features, such as data binding.

There are two ways to use a scope within a controller. You can define *data*, and you can define *behaviors*, which are JavaScript functions that can be called from binding expressions or directives in the view.

Creating the initial data and setting up behaviors is simple. You just create properties on the $scope object that is passed to the controller factory function and assign them data values or functions. Listing 13-3 provides a demonstration.

Listing 13-3. Adding Data and Logic to a Scope in the controller.html File

```html
<!DOCTYPE html>
<html ng-app="exampleApp">
<head>
    <title>Controllers</title>
    <script src="angular.js"></script>
    <link href="bootstrap.css" rel="stylesheet" />
    <link href="bootstrap-theme.css" rel="stylesheet" />
    <script>
        angular.module("exampleApp", [])
            .controller("simpleCtrl", function ($scope) {

                $scope.city = "London";

                $scope.getCountry = function (city) {
                    switch (city) {
                        case "London":
                            return "UK";
                        case "New York":
                            return "USA";
                    }
                }
            });
    </script>
</head>
<body>
    <div class="well" ng-controller="simpleCtrl">
        <p>The city is: {{city}}</p>
        <p>The country is: {{getCountry(city) || "Unknown"}}</p>
    </div>
</body>
</html>
```

I have set up the controller's scope by defining a `city` property, to which I have assigned a string value, and by defining a getCountry behavior, which is a simple function that takes a city and returns the country in which it can be found. I use the data value and the behavior through data bindings. I can access any data variable directly by its name and call any behavior just as I would a regular JavaScript function. You can see the effect of these changes in Figure 13-2.

Figure 13-2. *Adding data and variables to the scope*

PASSING ARGUMENTS TO CONTROLLER BEHAVIORS

In Listing 13-3, I created the getCountry behavior so that it receives a `city` argument, which is then processed to generate the associated country. This may have struck you as a little odd, given that I invoked the behavior from the data binding, like this:

```
...
<p>The country is: {{getCountry(city) || "Unknown"}}</p>
...
```

I am passing the value of the `city` property from the scope as the argument to the behavior, which is, of course, also part of the scope. I could have written the behavior like this:

```
...
$scope.getCountry = function () {
    switch ($scope.city) {
        case "London":
            return "UK";
        case "New York":
            return "USA";
    }
}
...
```

In this implementation of the behavior, I have removed the argument and get the city directly from the scope. This would allow me to simplify my data binding, like this:

```
...
<p>The country is: {{getCountry() || "Unknown"}}</p>
...
```

There are two reasons why I took the approach in Listing 13-3. The first is that it means my behavior can be used with any city value, rather than just the one defined in the same scope. This can be useful when using *controller inheritance*, which I describe later in this chapter. The second reason is that accepting an argument makes unit testing a little easier because the behavior is self-contained. I explain the AngularJS support for unit testing in Chapter 25. You don't *have* to use arguments for your controller behaviors, and nothing terrible will happen if you don't—but this is a convention I like and recommend you adopt.

Modifying the Scope

The most important aspect of scopes is that changes ripple through, automatically updating all of the dependent data values even when they are produced through a behavior. Listing 13-4 shows how a modification made using the ng-model directive causes the data bindings to be updated.

Listing 13-4. Making an Update to the Scope in the controllers.html File

```
<!DOCTYPE html>
<html ng-app="exampleApp">
<head>
    <title>Controllers</title>
    <script src="angular.js"></script>
    <link href="bootstrap.css" rel="stylesheet" />
    <link href="bootstrap-theme.css" rel="stylesheet" />
    <script>
        angular.module("exampleApp", [])
            .controller("simpleCtrl", function ($scope) {

                $scope.cities = ["London", "New York", "Paris"];

                $scope.city = "London";

                $scope.getCountry = function (city) {
                    switch (city) {
                        case "London":
                            return "UK";
                        case "New York":
                            return "USA";
                    }
                }
            });
    </script>
</head>
<body ng-controller="simpleCtrl">

    <div class="well">
        <label>Select a City:</label>
        <select ng-options="city for city in cities" ng-model="city">
        </select>
    </div>
```

```
    <div class="well">
        <p>The city is: {{city}}</p>
        <p>The country is: {{getCountry(city) || "Unknown"}}</p>
    </div>
</body>
</html>
```

I have added an array of city names and used them with the ng-options attribute on the select element to generate a set of option elements. The ng-model directive means that the city model property in the scope is changed when the user picks a value from the select element.

Notice that I have changed where I apply the ng-controller directive so that it contains both the select elements and the data bindings. Each instance of a controller has its *own* scope, and by ensuring all of the directives and bindings are in the same view (meaning applied to children of the element to which the ng-controller directive is applied to), I ensure that I am working with a single set of data values. This one-scope-per-controller-instance concept is important, and I'll return to it later in this chapter.

The result of adding the select element is exactly what you would expect from having seen earlier examples: Picking a value with the select element causes the updated value to be used in the data bindings, as shown in Figure 13-3.

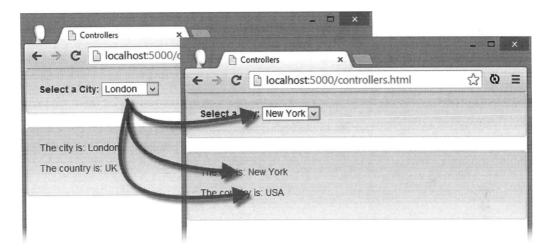

***Figure 13-3.** The effect of changing a value in the scope*

Of particular note, it isn't just the data binding that displays the selected city name that has been changed. The data binding that displays the result from invoking the controller behavior has also been updated. This is one of the great AngularJS strengths and—as you will learn—the cause of a lot of potential problems.

Organizing Controllers

In Listing 13-4, I have a single controller that supports all of the content in the body element. This is perfectly reasonable for small applications, but it gets unwieldy as the complexity of the project grows, and it can make using some features difficult, such as partial views (which I touched on with the ng-include directive in Chapter 10 and return to in more depth in Chapter 22). There are several different ways in which you can organize the controllers in your application, and I describe them in the sections that follow.

■ **Tip**   It can be difficult to decide which approach to take in an application, so I provide some general guidance about when each technique should be applied. But, as with so much in AngularJS development, I suggest you start with my recommendations but also try each approach and see what suits you and your project best.

Using a Monolithic Controller

The first approach is the one that I used in Listing 13-4: one controller that is applied to all HTML elements in the application by using the ng-controller directive on the body element (or at least on some element that encompasses all of your data bindings and directives).

There are some benefits to this approach: It is simple, you don't have to worry about communication between scopes (a topic I introduce later in this chapter), and your behaviors are available for use throughout your HTML. When you use a monolithic controller, you effectively create one view for the entire application, as illustrated by Figure 13-4.

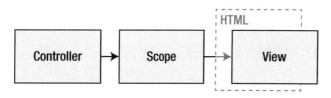

Figure 13-4. *Using a monolithic controller*

There are drawbacks to this approach: It is fine for simple applications—such as the examples I have been using to demonstrate AngularJS features—but you can easily end up with a mass of code as you add the behaviors required to deliver your application functionality. This makes maintaining the project more difficult and can complicate the testing process. It is also counter to the broad AngularJS philosophy of lots of small, focused building blocks, but that's just a matter of style rather than a technical requirement. In Listing 13-5, you can see an example of a monolithic controller and a single view used to obtain simple shipping and billing details. I have included only a single data field for each address in this example because my focus is on the relationship between the controller and the view. I rework this example in the sections that follow as I describe the different kinds of relationship you can create.

Listing 13-5. Creating a Monolithic Controller in the controllers.html File

```
<!DOCTYPE html>
<html ng-app="exampleApp">
<head>
    <title>Controllers</title>
    <script src="angular.js"></script>
    <link href="bootstrap.css" rel="stylesheet" />
    <link href="bootstrap-theme.css" rel="stylesheet" />
    <script>
        angular.module("exampleApp", [])
            .controller("simpleCtrl", function ($scope) {

                $scope.addresses = {};
```

```
                $scope.setAddress = function (type, zip) {
                    console.log("Type: " + type + " " + zip);
                    $scope.addresses[type] = zip;
                }

                $scope.copyAddress = function () {
                    $scope.shippingZip = $scope.billingZip;
                }
            });
    </script>
</head>
<body ng-controller="simpleCtrl">

    <div class="well">
        <h4>Billing Zip Code</h4>
        <div class="form-group">
            <input class="form-control" ng-model="billingZip">
        </div>
        <button class="btn btn-primary" ng-click="setAddress('billingZip', billingZip)">
            Save Billing
        </button>
    </div>

    <div class="well">
        <h4>Shipping Zip Code</h4>
        <div class="form-group">
            <input class="form-control" ng-model="shippingZip">
        </div>
        <button class="btn btn-primary" ng-click="copyAddress()">
            Use Billing
        </button>
        <button class="btn btn-primary"
                ng-click="setAddress('shippingZip', shippingZip)">
            Save Shipping
        </button>
    </div>
</body>
</html>
```

The controller in this example defines an addresses object that I will use to gather my ZIP codes and behaviors called setAddress and copyAddress. The setAddress behavior prints out one of the ZIP code values, and the copyAddress copies one implicitly defined ZIP code behavior to another. The data and the behavior are wired up to the HTML elements using standard AngularJS directives and model bindings. You can see how the example is displayed in the browser in Figure 13-5.

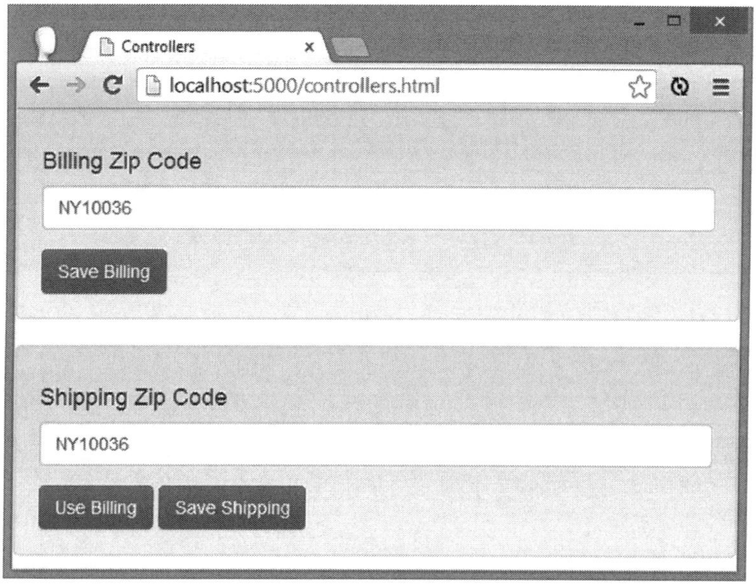

Figure 13-5. *Using a monolithic controller*

You can enter ZIP codes directly into the input elements, and you can copy the billing ZIP code to the shipping input element by clicking the Use Billing button. Copying data values like this is simple because there is only one scope to worry about and every data value is immediately available.

This is the controller organization you should start with if you are new to AngularJS, if you are creating a simple application, or if you don't have a clear design in mind when you start development. You can get up and running quickly, and you can adopt one of the other approaches I describe as you progress.

Reusing a Controller

You can reuse a controller to create several views in the same application. AngularJS will call the factory function each time you apply the controller, with the result that each instance will have its own scope. This may seem like an odd thing to do, but this approach allows for simpler controllers because it only has to manage a subset of the data values that a monolithic controller has to deal with. This works because the way that the MVC pattern separates functionality means that different views can present the same data and functionality in different ways. In Listing 13-6, you can see how I have reworked the example to simplify the controller and consume it through two different views.

Listing 13-6. Reusing a Controller in the controllers.html File

```
<!DOCTYPE html>
<html ng-app="exampleApp">
<head>
    <title>Controllers</title>
    <script src="angular.js"></script>
    <link href="bootstrap.css" rel="stylesheet" />
    <link href="bootstrap-theme.css" rel="stylesheet" />
```

```
<script>
    angular.module("exampleApp", [])
        .controller("simpleCtrl", function ($scope) {

            $scope.setAddress = function (type, zip) {
                console.log("Type: " + type + " " + zip);
            }

            $scope.copyAddress = function () {
                $scope.shippingZip = $scope.billingZip;
            }
        });
</script>
</head>
<body>
    <div class="well" ng-controller="simpleCtrl">
        <h4>Billing Zip Code</h4>
        <div class="form-group">
            <input class="form-control" ng-model="zip">
        </div>
        <button class="btn btn-primary" ng-click="setAddress('billingZip', zip)">
            Save Billing
        </button>
    </div>
    <div class="well" ng-controller="simpleCtrl">
        <h4>Shipping Zip Code</h4>
        <div class="form-group">
            <input class="form-control" ng-model="zip">
        </div>
        <button class="btn btn-primary" ng-click="copyAddress()">
            Use Billing
        </button>
        <button class="btn btn-primary" ng-click="setAddress('shippingZip', zip)">
            Save Shipping
        </button>
    </div>
</body>
</html>
```

In this example, I have removed the ng-controller directive from the body element and instead applied it to two identical regions of content, each supported by the simpleCtrl controller. This has the effect of creating two controllers and two views. AngularJS calls the controller factory function for each of the views, which has the effect of giving each view its own scope. You can see the effect of this technique in Figure 13-6.

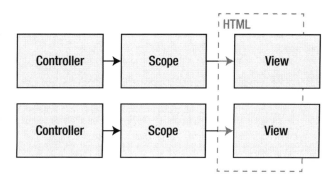

Figure 13-6. *Creating multiple instances of the same controller*

The data and behaviors provided by each controller to its scope are independent from the other scope in the application, and this allows me to simplify the controllers and the views. Each controller has to worry only about gathering a single ZIP code, and this allows me to simplify the code (although only slightly because this is already a simple example—the effect is more pronounced in a real application).

Communicating Between Scopes

The downside of this approach is that my `copyAddress` behavior no longer works because each ZIP code is stored in a variable called `zip` in a different scope. Fortunately, AngularJS provides mechanisms for sharing data between scopes. First, however, I have to confess that Figure 13-6 contains a simplification of the way that scopes work.

Scopes are really organized in a hierarchy, starting with the *root scope*. Each controller is given a new scope that is a child of the root scope, which means that Figure 13-7 presents a more accurate representation of how multiple controllers work.

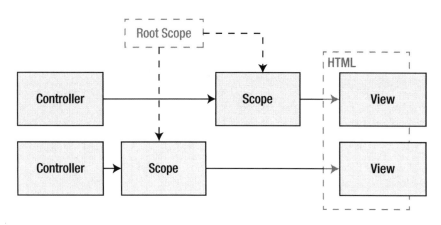

Figure 13-7. *The hierarchy of scopes when multiple controllers are applied*

The root scope provides the means for sending events between scopes and, by implication, allowing communication between controllers. You can see how I have used the root scope in Listing 13-7.

Listing 13-7. Using the Root Scope to Communicate Between Controllers

```
...
<script>
    angular.module("exampleApp", [])
        .controller("simpleCtrl", function ($scope, $rootScope) {

            $scope.$on("zipCodeUpdated", function (event, args) {
                $scope[args.type] = args.zipCode;
            });

            $scope.setAddress = function (type, zip) {
                $rootScope.$broadcast("zipCodeUpdated", {
                    type: type, zipCode: zip
                });
                console.log("Type: " + type + " " + zip);
            }

            $scope.copyAddress = function () {
                $scope.zip = $scope.billingZip;
            }
        });
</script>
...
```

The root scope is available as a service, so I declare a dependency on it on my controller using the name $rootScope (this is one of the built-in AngularJS services, and I describe the others in Chapter 18). All scopes, including the $rootScope service, define a number of methods that are used to send and receive events, as described in Table 13-3.

Table 13-3. The Scope Methods for Sending and Receiving Events

Method	Description
$broadcast(name, args)	Sends an event from the current scope down to all of the child scopes. The arguments are the name of the event and an object used to provide supplementary data with the event.
$emit(name, args)	Sends an event from the current scope up to the root scope.
$on(name, handler)	Registers a handler function that is invoked when the specified event is received by the scope.

The $broadcast and $emit events are *directional* and send an event up through the scope hierarchy until it reaches the root scope or down through the hierarchy to each of the child scopes. This seems like overkill at the moment, but as you'll see, different arrangements of controllers can result in more complex scope hierarchies, which I describe later in this chapter.

In the example, I call the $on method on the current scope to set up a handler function for an event called zipCodeUpdated. The handler function for scope events receives an Event object and an argument's object—my argument object will define type and zipCode properties, and I use them to define a property on the local scope, like this:

```
...
$scope.$on("zipCodeUpdated", function (event, args) {
    $scope[args.type] = args.zipCode;
});
...
```

■ **Tip**   I defined the property on the $scope object using the array-style notation. The name of the $scope property is set to the value of the args.type property from the method argument. Placing args.type between the [and] characters causes the args.type property to be evaluated, and its value is used as the name of the scope property.

I will use this event to keep both scopes in sync so that each has both ZIP codes that the user has provided. I achieve the other side of this synchronization by calling the $broadcast method on the $rootScope object, passing in an object with the type and zipCode properties that my event handler function expects:

```
...
$rootScope.$broadcast("zipCodeUpdated", {
    type: type, zipCode: zip
});
...
```

To summarize, when the Save Billing button is clicked, the $broadcast method is called on the root scope, which sends a zipCodeUpdated event down through the scope hierarchy. This has the effect of triggering my handler for the event, ensuring that the scope associated with the controller collecting the shipping ZIP code knows what the billing ZIP code is. This allows me to reinstate the Use Billing button, like this:

```
...
$scope.copyAddress = function () {
    $scope.zip = $scope.billingZip;
}
...
```

Setting the value of $scope.zip updates the input element, which has the binding to the property through the ng-model directive.

Using a Service to Mediate Scope Events

The convention in AngularJS is to use a service to mediate communication between scopes. I don't cover services in depth until Chapter 18, but I wanted to show you the convention in context so you can decide whether to adopt it.

The convention doesn't have a huge impact in this example because I am working with only a single controller, but it can reduce duplication if there are multiple controllers, all of which need to send the same kind of event. In Listing 13-8 you can see how I have used the Module.service method to create a service object that my controllers use to send and receive events, without directly interacting with the scope event methods.

Listing 13-8. Using a Service to Mediate Scope Events

```
...
<script>
    angular.module("exampleApp", [])
        .service("ZipCodes", function($rootScope) {
            return {
                setZipCode: function(type, zip) {
                    this[type] = zip;
                    $rootScope.$broadcast("zipCodeUpdated", {
                        type: type, zipCode: zip
                    });
                }
            }
        })
        .controller("simpleCtrl", function ($scope, ZipCodes) {

            $scope.$on("zipCodeUpdated", function (event, args) {
                $scope[args.type] = args.zipCode;
            });

            $scope.setAddress = function (type, zip) {
                ZipCodes.setZipCode(type, zip);
                console.log("Type: " + type + " " + zip);
            }

            $scope.copyAddress = function () {
                $scope.zip = $scope.billingZip;
            }
        });
</script>
...
```

The ZipCodes service declares a dependency on the $rootScope service and uses it within the setZipCode method to call the $broadcast event. The controllers declare a dependency on the ZipCodes service and call the setZipCode method rather than operate directly on $rootScope. There is no change in the functionality—this convention is about reducing duplication by putting code that is likely to be required by different controllers in a single location.

Using Controller Inheritance

The ng-controller directive can nested in HTML elements to create an effect known as *controller inheritance*. This is a feature that aims to reduce code duplication by letting you define common functionality in a *parent controller* and use it in one or more *child controllers*. The best way to explain is with an example, such as the one in Listing 13-9.

Listing 13-9. Using Controller Inheritance in the controllers.html File

```
<!DOCTYPE html>
<html ng-app="exampleApp">
<head>
    <title>Controllers</title>
    <script src="angular.js"></script>
```

```html
    <script src="controllers.js"></script>
    <link href="bootstrap.css" rel="stylesheet" />
    <link href="bootstrap-theme.css" rel="stylesheet" />
</head>
<body ng-controller="topLevelCtrl">

    <div class="well">
        <h4>Top Level Controller</h4>
        <div class="input-group">
            <span class="input-group-btn">
                <button class="btn btn-default" type="button"
                        ng-click="reverseText()">Reverse</button>
                <button class="btn btn-default" type="button"
                        ng-click="changeCase()">Case</button>
            </span>
            <input class="form-control" ng-model="dataValue">
        </div>
    </div>

    <div class="well" ng-controller="firstChildCtrl">
        <h4>First Child Controller</h4>
        <div class="input-group">
            <span class="input-group-btn">
                <button class="btn btn-default" type="button"
                        ng-click="reverseText()">Reverse</button>
                <button class="btn btn-default" type="button"
                        ng-click="changeCase()">Case</button>
            </span>
            <input class="form-control" ng-model="dataValue">
        </div>
    </div>

    <div class="well" ng-controller="secondChildCtrl">
        <h4>Second Child Controller</h4>
        <div class="input-group">
            <span class="input-group-btn">
                <button class="btn btn-default" type="button"
                        ng-click="reverseText()">Reverse</button>
                <button class="btn btn-default" type="button"
                        ng-click="changeCase()">Case</button>
                <button class="btn btn-default" type="button"
                        ng-click="shiftFour()">Shift</button>
            </span>
            <input class="form-control" ng-model="dataValue">
        </div>
    </div>
</body>
</html>
```

■ **Caution** This listing won't work until you create the `controllers.js` file that I describe next.

There are three controllers at work in this example, each of which has been applied to a region of markup using the `ng-controller` directive. The controller called `topLevelCtrl` is applied to the body element, and two child controllers, `firstChildCtrl` and `secondChildCtrl`, are nested within it. In addition to the child controllers, the top-level controller contains its own elements, and all three controllers present an `input` element with some inline buttons that invoke controller behaviors.

To reduce the amount of markup and code I have to duplicate for this example, I have moved the contents of the `script` element to a separate file called `controllers.js`. This file contains the code to set up the AngularJS application and define the controllers, as shown in Listing 13-10.

Listing 13-10. The Contents of the controllers.js File

```
var app = angular.module("exampleApp", []);

app.controller("topLevelCtrl", function ($scope) {

    $scope.dataValue = "Hello, Adam";

    $scope.reverseText = function () {
        $scope.dataValue = $scope.dataValue.split("").reverse().join("");
    }

    $scope.changeCase = function () {
        var result = [];
        angular.forEach($scope.dataValue.split(""), function (char, index) {
            result.push(index % 2 == 1
                    ? char.toString().toUpperCase() : char.toString().toLowerCase());
        });
        $scope.dataValue = result.join("");
    };
});

app.controller("firstChildCtrl", function ($scope) {

    $scope.changeCase = function () {
        $scope.dataValue = $scope.dataValue.toUpperCase();
    };
});

app.controller("secondChildCtrl", function ($scope) {

    $scope.changeCase = function () {
        $scope.dataValue = $scope.dataValue.toLowerCase();
    };
```

```
        $scope.shiftFour = function () {
            var result = [];
            angular.forEach($scope.dataValue.split(""), function (char, index) {
                result.push(index < 4 ? char.toUpperCase() : char);
            });
            $scope.dataValue = result.join("");
        }
});
```

You can see how the browser displays the example in Figure 13-8. I have applied header elements and Bootstrap styles to emphasize each controller. All three controllers present a Reverse button that reverses the order of the characters in the input element.

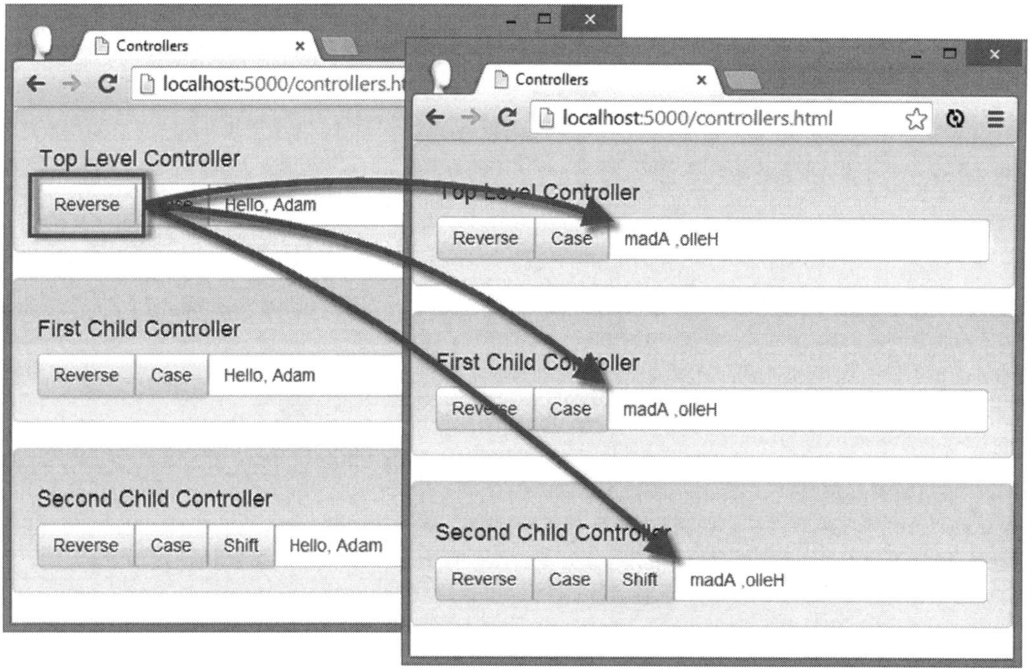

Figure 13-8. Using an inherited controller behavior

When you nest controllers through the ng-controller directive, the scopes of the child controllers inherit the data and behaviors of the parent controller scope. (I have shown only one level of parent-child relationship in this example, but you can nest controllers as deeply as you want.) Each controller in this example has its own scope, but the scopes for the child controllers contain the data values and behaviors of the parent controller, as shown in Figure 13-9.

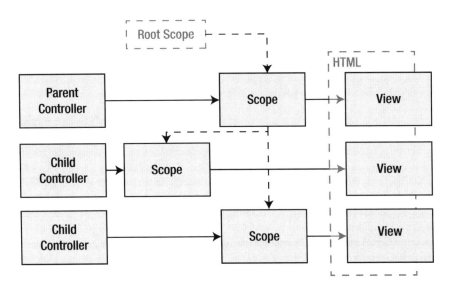

Figure 13-9. *The hierarchy of scopes when child controllers are used*

You can see how this works you click the Reverse button. The input elements are all wired up to manage the dataValue property, and the Reverse buttons all call the reverseText behavior, both of which are defined by the top-level controller. The child controllers inherit the data value and the behavior, which is why all of the input elements change when you click any of the Reverse buttons, even those implemented by the child controllers.

Adding to the Inherited Data and Behaviors

The main benefit of using controller inheritance is the ability to mix functionality that is inherited from the parent scope with locally defined additions. You can see an example of this in the secondChildCtrl controller, which defines a behavior called shiftFour that makes the first four characters of the dataValue property uppercase, as follows:

```
...
$scope.shiftFour = function () {
    var result = [];
    angular.forEach($scope.dataValue.split(""), function (char, index) {
        result.push(index < 4 ? char.toUpperCase() : char);
    });
    $scope.dataValue = result.join("");
}
...
```

This behavior is available only in the scope of the secondChildCtrl controller—but notice that even here, I am able to use an inherited feature as I perform my changes on the dataValue property defined by the parent scope. You use this feature to build on the functionality of existing controllers, without having to duplicate behaviors and data.

Overriding Inherited Data and Behaviors

Child controllers can *override* the data and behaviors of their parents, which means that data values and behaviors can be replaced with local versions that have the same name. In Listing 13-9 you can see that each of the child controllers defines a behavior called changeCase on its scope. Each implementation of this behavior is different and changes the dataValue property in a different way, but they are all invoked in the same way through the ng-click directive:

```
...
<button class="btn btn-default" type="button" ng-click="changeCase()">Case</button>
...
```

When looking for a behavior, AngularJS starts with the scope of the controller in which the directive has been applied. If such a behavior exists, then it will be executed. If not, AngularJS moves up to the next level in the scope hierarchy and continues looking until a behavior with the specified name is found.

You use this feature to use *most* of the functionality provided by a parent controller, overriding just the parts you need to customize. This allows you to build controllers that are tailored to different parts of your application without needing to duplicate the code and data in the parent controller.

Understanding Data Inheritance

I included a common trap in Listing 13-10 that affects just about everyone who uses controller inheritance for the first time. To see the problem, load the controllers.html file into the browser and click each of the Reverse buttons in turn (it doesn't matter which order you click them in).

This is the behavior that you would expect given my description so far. The Reverse button invokes the reverseText behavior, which operates on the dataValue property. The behavior and data are defined by the parent controller and inherited by the children, which is why the contents of all three input elements change together.

Now change the contents of the input element associated with the second child controller. It doesn't matter what you enter, just as long as you change the text. Now click all three Reverse buttons in turn again, and you'll see a different behavior. All three buttons operate on the first two input elements, and the input element that you edited remains unchanged. To dig deeper into the problem, click the Case and Shift buttons for the second child controller; these *do* change the final input element.

Before I explain why this happens, I am going to show you the solution. Listing 13-11 shows the changes I have made to the controllers.js file.

Listing 13-11. Solving the Inheritance Problem in the controllers.js File

```
var app = angular.module("exampleApp", []);

app.controller("topLevelCtrl", function ($scope) {

    $scope.data = {
        dataValue: "Hello, Adam"
    }

    $scope.reverseText = function () {
        $scope.data.dataValue = $scope.data.dataValue.split("").reverse().join("");
    }
```

```
    $scope.changeCase = function () {
        var result = [];
        angular.forEach($scope.data.dataValue.split(""), function (char, index) {
            result.push(index % 2 == 1
                ? char.toString().toUpperCase() : char.toString().toLowerCase());
        });
        $scope.data.dataValue = result.join("");
    };
});

app.controller("firstChildCtrl", function ($scope) {

    $scope.changeCase = function () {
        $scope.data.dataValue = $scope.data.dataValue.toUpperCase();
    };
});

app.controller("secondChildCtrl", function ($scope) {

    $scope.changeCase = function () {
        $scope.data.dataValue = $scope.data.dataValue.toLowerCase();
    };

    $scope.shiftFour = function () {
        var result = [];
        angular.forEach($scope.data.dataValue.split(""), function (char, index) {
            result.push(index < 4 ? char.toUpperCase() : char);
        });
        $scope.data.dataValue = result.join("");
    }
});
```

Instead of defining dataValue as a property directly on the scope of the parent controller, I have defined it as a property of an object called data. The other changes in this file update the reference to the dataValue property to access it via the data object. In Listing 13-12, you can see how I have reflected this change in the ng-model directives that link the input elements with the dataValue property in the controllers.html file.

Listing 13-12. Solving the Inheritance Problem in the controllers.html File

```
<!DOCTYPE html>
<html ng-app="exampleApp">
<head>
    <title>Controllers</title>
    <script src="angular.js"></script>
    <script src="controllers.js"></script>
    <link href="bootstrap.css" rel="stylesheet" />
    <link href="bootstrap-theme.css" rel="stylesheet" />
</head>
```

```
<body ng-controller="topLevelCtrl">

    <div class="well">
        <h4>Top Level Controller</h4>
        <div class="input-group">
            <span class="input-group-btn">
                <button class="btn btn-default" type="button"
                        ng-click="reverseText()">Reverse</button>
                <button class="btn btn-default" type="button"
                        ng-click="changeCase()">Case</button>
            </span>
            <input class="form-control" ng-model="data.dataValue">
        </div>
    </div>

    <div class="well" ng-controller="firstChildCtrl">
        <h4>First Child Controller</h4>
        <div class="input-group">
            <span class="input-group-btn">
                <button class="btn btn-default" type="button"
                        ng-click="reverseText()">Reverse</button>
                <button class="btn btn-default" type="button"
                        ng-click="changeCase()">Case</button>
            </span>
            <input class="form-control" ng-model="data.dataValue">
        </div>
    </div>

    <div class="well" ng-controller="secondChildCtrl">
        <h4>Second Child Controller</h4>
        <div class="input-group">
            <span class="input-group-btn">
                <button class="btn btn-default" type="button"
                        ng-click="reverseText()">Reverse</button>
                <button class="btn btn-default" type="button"
                        ng-click="changeCase()">Case</button>
                <button class="btn btn-default" type="button"
                        ng-click="shiftFour()">Shift</button>
            </span>
            <input class="form-control" ng-model="data.dataValue">
        </div>
    </div>
</body>
</html>
```

If you load the new version of the controllers.html file into the browser, you will see that all of the buttons affect the contents of the input elements and that editing the input element content doesn't stop subsequent changes from taking effect.

To understand what's happening, we need to look at the way that AngularJS deals with inheritances of data values in scopes and how this is affected by the ng-model directive.

When you read the value of a property that is defined directly on the scope, AngularJS checks to see whether there is a local property in the controller's scope and, if not, starts working its way up the scope hierarchy to see whether it has inherited one. However, when you use the ng-model directive to *modify* such a property, AngularJS checks to see whether the scope has a property of the right name and, if not, assumes you want to implicitly define it. The effect is to *override* the property value, much as I did with the behavior in the previous section. The reason that editing the contents of a child input element prevents the Reverse button from working is that there are now two dataValue properties—one defined by the top-level controller and one by the child you edited. The reverseText behavior is defined by the top-level controller, and it operates on the dataValue defined in the top-level scope, leaving the child's dataValue property unaltered.

This doesn't happen when you assign an object to the scope and then define your data properties on that object. This is because JavaScript implements what is known as *prototype inheritance*—a topic so dry and confusing that I am not going to attempt to explain it here, although I describe the basics in Chapter 18. What is important is the knowledge that defining properties directly on the scope like this:

```
...
$scope.dataValue = "Hello, Adam";
...
```

means that using the ng-model directive will create local variables, while using an object as an intermediary, like this:

```
...
$scope.data = {
    dataValue: "Hello, Adam"
}
...
```

ensures that ng-model will update the data values defined in the parent scope. This is not a bug. It is a deliberate feature that allows you to decide how your controller and its scope will work, and you can mix and match both techniques in the same scope. If you want a value that is initially shared but will be copied when modified, then define your data properties directly on the scope. To ensure that there is only one value, then define your data properties via an object.

■ **Note**   The controller behaviors that I used to demonstrate inheritance all operate directly on values defined on their scopes. I did this to make the problems that can arise with inheritance more obvious, but the convention in AngularJS development is to have behaviors receive arguments. This doesn't change the way that inheritance works—or the confusion that it can cause—because AngularJS has to perform the same sequence of steps to locate values whether they are accessed directly from the behavior or passed in as an argument.

Using Multiple Controllers

An application can contain as many controllers as you need. Don't worry about figuring out the right number of controllers when you start working with AngularJS. You'll know it is time to split up your monolithic controllers when you struggle to find particular data values or behaviors in the code file.

My approach—which is pretty common and far from unique to me—is to create a new controller for each major view in the application, although this is only a rule of thumb, and I often reuse controllers or rely on controller inheritance. There are no hard-and-fast rules, and you will naturally develop you own set of techniques. In Listing 13-13, you can see how I have reworked the example so that there are two distinct controllers—one for each of the ZIP codes that I want to capture.

Listing 13-13. Creating Multiple Distinct Controllers in the controllers.html File

```
<!DOCTYPE html>
<html ng-app="exampleApp">
<head>
    <title>Controllers</title>
    <script src="angular.js"></script>
    <link href="bootstrap.css" rel="stylesheet" />
    <link href="bootstrap-theme.css" rel="stylesheet" />
    <script>
        var app = angular.module("exampleApp", []);

        app.controller("firstController", function ($scope) {

            $scope.dataValue = "Hello, Adam";

            $scope.reverseText = function () {
                $scope.dataValue = $scope.dataValue.split("").reverse().join("");
            }
        });

        app.controller("secondController", function ($scope) {

            $scope.dataValue = "Hello, Jacqui";

            $scope.changeCase = function () {
                $scope.dataValue = $scope.dataValue.toUpperCase();
            };
        });
    </script>
</head>
<body>
    <div class="well" ng-controller="firstController">
        <h4>First Controller</h4>
        <div class="input-group">
            <span class="input-group-btn">
                <button class="btn btn-default" type="button"
                        ng-click="reverseText()">Reverse</button>
            </span>
            <input class="form-control" ng-model="dataValue">
        </div>
    </div>

    <div class="well" ng-controller="secondController">
        <h4>Second Controller</h4>
        <div class="input-group">
            <span class="input-group-btn">
                <button class="btn btn-default" type="button"
                        ng-click="changeCase()">
                    Case
                </button>
            </span>
```

```
            <input class="form-control" ng-model="dataValue">
        </div>
    </div>
</body>
</html>
```

There are two controllers defined in this example, and each has been applied to separate HTML elements. This means that the controllers operate independently and don't share scopes or inherit data or behaviors, as shown in Figure 13-10.

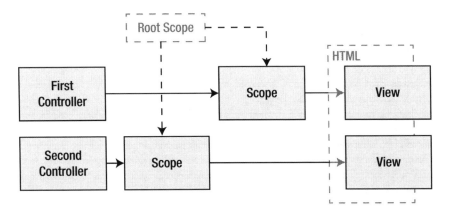

Figure 13-10. *The hierarchy of scopes when separate controllers are used*

You will notice that this is the same arrangement I showed you in Figure 13-6 when describing the use of multiple instances of the same controller; the only difference is that I have since revealed the existence of the root scope, which must be used if you want to communicate between the scopes set up by each controller.

Using Scope-less Controllers

If scopes seem unnecessarily complex and your application doesn't benefit from inheritance or need to communicate between controllers, then you can use *scope-less controllers*. These are controllers that provide data and behaviors to views without using scopes at all. Instead, the view is provided with a special variable that represents the controller, as shown in Listing 13-14.

Listing 13-14. Using a Scope-less Controller in the controllers.html File

```
<!DOCTYPE html>
<html ng-app="exampleApp">
<head>
    <title>Controllers</title>
    <script src="angular.js"></script>
    <link href="bootstrap.css" rel="stylesheet" />
    <link href="bootstrap-theme.css" rel="stylesheet" />
```

```
    <script>
        var app = angular.module("exampleApp", [])
            .controller("simpleCtrl", function () {
                this.dataValue = "Hello, Adam";

                this.reverseText = function () {
                    this.dataValue = this.dataValue.split("").reverse().join("");
                }
            });
    </script>
</head>
<body>
    <div class="well" ng-controller="simpleCtrl as ctrl">
        <h4>Top Level Controller</h4>
        <div class="input-group">
            <span class="input-group-btn">
                <button class="btn btn-default" type="button"
                        ng-click="ctrl.reverseText()">Reverse</button>
            </span>
            <input class="form-control" ng-model="ctrl.dataValue">
        </div>
    </div>
</body>
</html>
```

The controller in this example doesn't declare a dependency on $scope and defines its data values and behaviors using the JavaScript this keyword, as follows:

```
...
this.dataValue = "Hello, Adam";
...
```

When applying a scope-less controller, the expression used for the ng-controller directive takes a different form, specifying the name of a variable by which the controller will be accessible in the view:

```
...
<div class="well" ng-controller="simpleCtrl as ctrl">
...
```

The format of this expression is <controller to apply> as <variable name>, and this example applies the simpleCtrl controller to the div element and creates a variable called ctrl. I then use the ctrl variable to access the data and behaviors in the view, like this:

```
...
<input class="form-control" ng-model="ctrl.dataValue">
...
```

Scope-less controllers allow you to avoid the complexities of scopes, but they are a relatively new addition to AngularJS and are not widely used. My advice is to take the time to master the way that scopes operate so that you can take full advantage of the features that AngularJS offers—not just in terms of working with controllers but also when you create custom directives using the techniques that I describe in Chapters 15–17.

Explicitly Updating the Scope

For the most part, AngularJS is pretty good at keeping the scope up-to-date automatically, but there are times when you need to take more direct control of the process, such as when integrating AngularJS with another JavaScript framework. You won't always be able to use AngularJS throughout an application, especially when you are integrating new functionality into an existing product or service that was built using a different client-side framework.

You can integrate AngularJS with other frameworks using three methods that are defined on scope objects. These methods, which I have described in Table 13-4, allow you to register handler functions to respond to changes in the scope and to inject changes in the scope from outside of AngularJS code.

Table 13-4. *The Scope Integration Methods*

Method	Description
`$apply(expression)`	Applies a change to the scope
`$watch(expression, handler)`	Registers a handler that will be notified when the value referred to by the expression changes
`$watchCollection(object, handler)`	Registers a handler that will be notified when any of the properties of the specified object change

I am going to use jQuery UI to demonstrate how these methods work. jQuery UI is the UI toolkit from the jQuery team and provides an excellent set of widgets that are built on jQuery and that work across a wide range of browsers.

■ **Tip** You can also pass functions, rather than expressions, to the `$apply` method, which can be useful when creating custom directives and allows you to define updates to the scope in response to user interaction with the elements that the directive manages. I explain how to create custom directives in Chapters 15–17, and you can see an example of using a function with the `$apply` method in Chapter 18.

Setting Up jQuery UI

I am not going to go into details about how jQuery UI works; see my *Pro jQuery 2* book, also published by Apress, for full details if you are interested. I am going to obtain the jQuery and jQuery UI files I need from the Google content delivery network (CDN) so that I don't have to download and install any files locally. In Listing 13-15, you can see a simple example application that contains a jQuery UI button—one of the simplest UI components that jQuery UI provides.

Listing 13-15. Defining a jQuery UI Button in the controllers.html File

```
<!DOCTYPE html>
<html ng-app="exampleApp">
<head>
    <title>Controllers</title>
    <script src="angular.js"></script>
    <link href="bootstrap.css" rel="stylesheet" />
    <link href="bootstrap-theme.css" rel="stylesheet" />
    <script src="//ajax.googleapis.com/ajax/libs/jquery/1.10.2/jquery.min.js"></script>
    <script src="//ajax.googleapis.com/ajax/libs/jqueryui/1.10.3/jquery-ui.min.js">
        </script>
```

```
    <link rel="stylesheet" href=
    "http://ajax.googleapis.com/ajax/libs/jqueryui/1.10.3/themes/sunny/jquery-ui.min.css">
     <script>

        $(document).ready(function () {
            $('#jqui button').button().click(function (e) {
                alert("jQuery UI Button was clicked");
            });
        });

        var app = angular.module("exampleApp", [])
            .controller("simpleCtrl", function ($scope) {

                $scope.buttonEnabled = true;
                $scope.clickCounter = 0;

                $scope.handleClick = function () {
                    $scope.clickCounter++;
                }
            });
    </script>
</head>
<body>
    <div id="angularRegion" class="well" ng-controller="simpleCtrl">
        <h4>AngularJS</h4>
        <div class="checkbox">
            <label>
                <input type="checkbox" ng-model="buttonEnabled"> Enable Button
            </label>
        </div>
        Click counter: {{clickCounter}}
    </div>
    <div id="jqui" class="well">
        <h4>jQuery UI</h4>
        <button>Click Me!</button>
    </div>
</body>
</html>
```

I have defined two sections of content, one of which contains AngularJS directives and data bindings. The other section contains a jQuery UI button, and the important point is the way that jQuery UI widgets are set up, which is through method calls, as follows:

```
...
$('#jqui button').button().click(function (e) {
    alert("jQuery UI Button was clicked");
});
...
```

This statement selects the button element, applies jQuery UI to it, and sets up an event handler that will be invoked when the button is clicked. As I explained, I don't want to get bogged down in the details of jQuery UI in this book, but you can see that this is a different approach to the directives used by AngularJS. At the moment, clicking the button will display an alert, but that's just a placeholder until I integrate jQuery UI and AngularJS together.

The AngularJS section of this example contains a check box that I will use to enable and disable the jQuery UI button and a variable and behavior that I will use to count the number of times that the button is clicked. You can see how the browser displays this example in Figure 13-11.

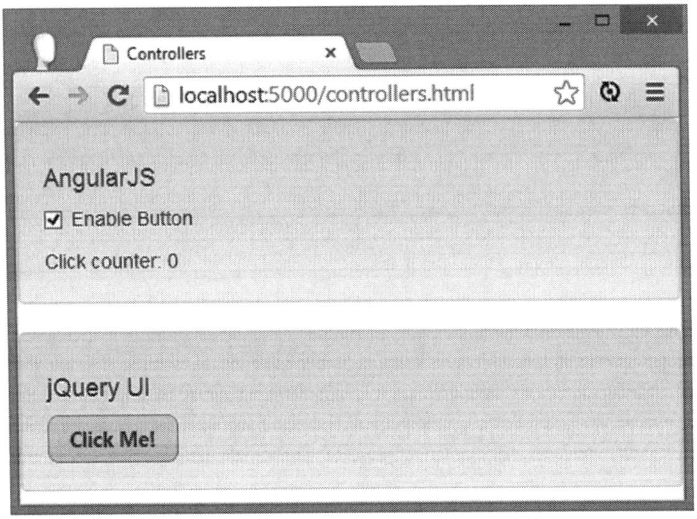

Figure 13-11. *An example containing a jQuery UI button*

Controlling the Button State

The first integration task is to respond to the AngularJS check box by enabling and disabling the jQuery UI button. You can see how I have done this in Listing 13-16.

Listing 13-16. Controlling the jQuery UI Button State from AngularJS in the controllers.html File

```
...
<script>
    $(document).ready(function () {
        $('#jqui button').button().click(function (e) {
            alert("jQuery UI Button was clicked");
        });
    });

    var app = angular.module("exampleApp", [])
        .controller("simpleCtrl", function ($scope) {

            $scope.buttonEnabled = true;
            $scope.clickCounter = 0;
```

```
        $scope.handleClick = function () {
            $scope.clickCounter++;
        }

        $scope.$watch('buttonEnabled', function (newValue) {
            $('#jqui button').button({
                disabled: !newValue
            });
        });
    });
</script>
...
```

The $watch method registers a handler function that is invoked when a value in the scope changes. In this case, I have specified the buttonEnabled property. The handler function that I have created receives the new value of the property and the previous property. I use the new property to change the state of the jQuery UI button, which requires a method call.

The $watch method provides the means for *outgoing* integration, in which a change in the scope can be the trigger for invoking some corresponding change in the other framework—in this case, changing the state of the button.

■ **Tip**   The first argument to the $watch method is an expression, which AngularJS evaluates to figure out what you want to monitor. This means you can call a function that generates a property name, but it also means that you have to use a string literal if you want to specify a property name directly, as I have done in this example.

Counting the Button Clicks

The $apply method provides the means for *incoming* integration so that a change in the other framework causes a corresponding change in AngularJS. In Listing 13-17, you can see how I have modified the event handlers for the jQuery UI button to call the handleClick behavior defined by my AngularJS controller.

Listing 13-17. Updating the AngularJS scope in Response to the jQuery UI Click in the controllers.html File

```
...
$(document).ready(function () {
    $('#jqui button').button().click(function (e) {
        angular.element(angularRegion).scope().$apply('handleClick()');
    });
});
...
```

This is a densely packed statement. The first thing it does is locate the scope associated with the element to which I have applied the AngularJS controller. Remember that this JavaScript code isn't part of the AngularJS world and so it can't declare a dependency on $scope to get what it needs.

AngularJS provides the angular.element method as part of its lightweight implementation of jQuery, and passing the id attribute value of the element I am interested in to this method gives me an object that defines a scope method that returns the scope I need.

Having located the scope, I call the $apply method to invoke the handleClick behavior. Notice that I don't call the handleClick behavior directly. I must specify an expression through the $apply method so that the scope is aware of the change and propagates it to binding expressions. Calling the handleClick behavior updates the clickCounter variable, which I display in the HTML via a one-way data binding. I could have modified the clickCounter variable directly using an expression like this:

```
...
angular.element(angularRegion).scope().$apply('clickCounter = clickCounter + 1');
...
```

but I prefer to define behaviors because they allow me to keep the logic that updates the scope in one place and within the AngularJS code. I recommend you follow the same approach.

Summary

In this chapter I described the role that controllers and scopes play in an AngularJS application. I explained how to use scopes in controller factory functions, how to arrange controllers in an application and the effect this has on the scope hierarchy, and even how to create controllers that don't use scopes. I finished this chapter by demonstrating how you can use scopes to integrate AngularJS with other JavaScript frameworks, which is an invaluable technique when you are retrofitting AngularJS to an existing project. In the next chapter, I describe AngularJS filters, which format or transform data for display in views.

■ ■ ■

CHAPTER 14

Using Filters

Filters transform the data before it is processed by a directive and displayed in a view without modifying the original data in the scope, allowing the same data to be displayed in different ways in different parts of the application. Filters can perform any kind of transformation, but for the most part they are used to format or sort the data in some way. In this chapter, I explain the role that filters play in an AngularJS application, describe the built-in AngularJS filters, and demonstrate how to create and apply custom filters. Table 14-1 summarizes this chapter.

Table 14-1. *Chapter Summary*

Problem	Solution	Listing
Format a currency value.	Use the currency filter.	1–3
Format a general numeric value.	Use the number filter.	4
Format a date.	Use the date filter.	5
Change the case of a string.	Use the uppercase or lowercase filter.	6
Generate a JSON representation of a JavaScript object.	Use the json filter.	7
Localize the formatting produced by the currency, number, and date filters.	Add an AngularJS localization file to the HTML document via a script element.	8
Select a limited number of objects from an array.	Use the limitTo filter.	9
Select objects in an array.	Use the filter filter.	10, 11
Sort the objects in an array.	Use the orderBy filter.	12–16
Combine multiple filters.	Use filter chaining.	17
Create a custom filter.	Use the Module.filter method to specify a factory function that generates a worker function that will perform the data formatting or transformation.	18–22
Create a filter that uses other filters.	Declare a dependency on the $filter service in the custom filter factory function and use the service to access and invoke the filters you require.	23, 24

Why and When to Use Filters

Filters let you define commonly used data transformations so that they can be applied throughout an application, without being tied to a specific controller or type of data. Filters transform the data as it passes from the scope to the directive but don't change the source data, allowing you to flexibly format or transform data for display in views.

You could include the transformation logic in your controller behaviors or in custom directives, but separating transformation into reusable filters increases the flexibility of the application by allowing you to apply different filters to the same behaviors and directives and display data in different ways, either within the same view or in different views. Table 14-2 summarizes why and when to use filters in an AngularJS application.

Table 14-2. *Why and When to Use Filters*

Why	When
Filters contain transformation logic that can be applied to any data in the application for presentation in a view.	Filters are used to format data before it is processed by a directive and displayed in a view.

Preparing the Example Project

To prepare for this chapter, I deleted the contents of the angularjs web server folder and installed the angular.js, bootstrap.css, and bootstrap-theme.css files, as described in Chapter 1. I then created a file called filters.html, which you can see in Listing 14-1.

Listing 14-1. The Contents of the filters.html File

```
<html ng-app="exampleApp">
<head>
    <title>Filters</title>
    <script src="angular.js"></script>
    <link href="bootstrap.css" rel="stylesheet" />
    <link href="bootstrap-theme.css" rel="stylesheet" />
    <script>
        angular.module("exampleApp", [])
            .controller("defaultCtrl", function ($scope) {
                $scope.products = [
                    { name: "Apples", category: "Fruit", price: 1.20, expiry: 10 },
                    { name: "Bananas", category: "Fruit", price: 2.42, expiry: 7 },
                    { name: "Pears", category: "Fruit", price: 2.02, expiry: 6 },

                    { name: "Tuna", category: "Fish", price: 20.45, expiry: 3 },
                    { name: "Salmon", category: "Fish", price: 17.93, expiry: 2 },
                    { name: "Trout", category: "Fish", price: 12.93, expiry: 4 },

                    { name: "Beer", category: "Drinks", price: 2.99, expiry: 365 },
                    { name: "Wine", category: "Drinks", price: 8.99, expiry: 365 },
                    { name: "Whiskey", category: "Drinks", price: 45.99, expiry: 365 }
                ];
            });
    </script>
</head>
```

```
<body ng-controller="defaultCtrl">
    <div class="panel panel-default">
        <div class="panel-heading">
            <h3>
                Products
                <span class="label label-primary">{{products.length}}</span>
            </h3>
        </div>
        <div class="panel-body">
            <table class="table table-striped table-bordered table-condensed">
                <thead>
                    <tr>
                        <td>Name</td>
                        <td>Category</td>
                        <td>Expiry</td>
                        <td class="text-right">Price</td>
                    </tr>
                </thead>
                <tbody>
                    <tr ng-repeat="p in products">
                        <td>{{p.name}}</td>
                        <td>{{p.category}}</td>
                        <td>{{p.expiry}}</td>
                        <td class="text-right">{{p.price}}</td>
                    </tr>
                </tbody>
            </table>
        </div>
    </div>
</body>
</html>
```

I defined a controller whose scope contains a products array of objects that describe a set of products you might find in a supermarket. The data itself isn't important, other than there are enough items with shared characteristics to allow me to demonstrate different filtering techniques. I have used the ng-repeat directive to generate rows in a table element to display the product objects, and you can see how the browser displays the filters.html file in Figure 14-1.

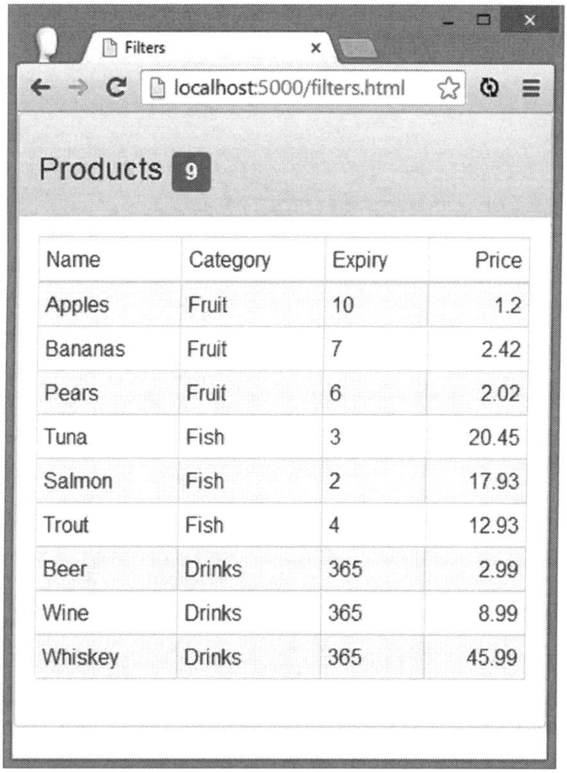

Figure 14-1. *Displaying the initial version of the filters.html file*

■ **Note** For most of the figures in this chapter, I am going to show you only a few rows from the table; that's because all of the rows are formatted the same, and I don't want to waste pages showing you repeating data.

Downloading the Localization File

Some of the built-in filters that I describe in this chapter are capable of formatting data values using localized rules. To demonstrate how this works, I need to use a file that specifies the rules for a given file.

Go to angularjs.org, click the Download button, and click the Extras link. This will display a list of the files available for AngularJS in an unformatted list. Click the i18n link and locate and save the angular-locale_fr-fr.js file into the angularjs folder. This is the locale file for the French language as used in France (I picked it because it is different enough from the default locale—English as used in the United States—to be obvious in the examples). You don't need to do anything with this file at the moment, other than to download it.

Filtering Single Data Values

AngularJS comes with two kinds of built-in filters: those that operate on single values and those that operate on collections. I am going to start with those that work on a single value because they are the easiest to work with and provide a gentle introduction to the world of filters. I have listed the single-value filters in Table 14-3. I describe each of these filters in the sections that follow.

Table 14-3. *The Built-in Filters for Single Values*

Name	Description
currency	This filter formats currency values.
date	This filter formats date values.
json	This filter generates an object from a JSON string.
number	This filter formats a numeric value.
uppercase lowercase	These filters format a string into all uppercase or lowercase letters.

■ **Tip** One of the most useful things you can do with filters is *chain* them together so that multiple filters operate in sequence on the same data. I am going to demonstrate how the built-in filters work—especially those that operate on collections—before demonstrating how this feature works. See the "Chaining Filters" section later in the chapter for a demonstration.

Formatting Currency Values

The currency filter formats numeric values so they represent currency amounts—so that 1.2, for example, becomes $1.20. You can see how I have applied the currency filter to the Price column in the example table in Listing 14-2.

Listing 14-2. Applying the currency Filter in the filters.html File

```
...
<tr ng-repeat="p in products">
    <td>{{p.name}}</td>
    <td>{{p.category}}</td>
    <td>{{p.expiry}}</td>
    <td class="text-right">{{p.price | currency}}</td>
</tr>
...
```

You can see how easy it is to apply the filter to the data binding. I append the bar symbol (the | character) to the binding source (p.price in this case) followed by the filter name. This is the way that all filters are applied, and you can see the effect in Figure 14-2.

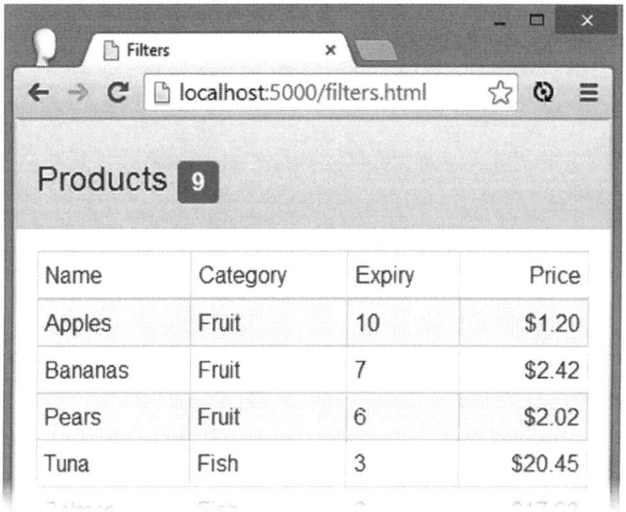

Figure 14-2. *The effect of the currency filter*

WHY NOT FORMAT DATA IN THE CONTROLLER?

You might be wondering why I don't just format the currency amounts in the source data, rather than applying the currency filter in the data binding. After all, it would be a trivial matter to update the controller factory function, like this:

```
...
<script>
    angular.module("exampleApp", [])
        .controller("defaultCtrl", function ($scope) {
            $scope.products = [
                { name: "Apples", category: "Fruit", price: 1.20 },
                { name: "Bananas", category: "Fruit", price: 2.42 },
                { name: "Pears", category: "Fruit", price: 2.02 },
                // ...other data objects omitted for brevity...
            ];

            for (var i = 0; i < $scope.products.length; i++) {
                $scope.products[i].price =
                    "$" + Number($scope.products[i].price).toFixed(2);
            }
        });
</script>
...
```

This approach may seem appealing, but it restricts the way that you work with the data. By using the JavaScript Number.toFixed method, I round the numeric values and lose resolution. This isn't a problem in my example, but it does preventing me from performing accurate calculations using the source data, and that can be important when dealing with more precise values.

I also lose the ability to transform the data in different ways. If I want to calculate an average of the `price` property values or display only whole dollar amounts, for example, I have to parse my currency strings to extract the numbers before I can perform the calculation or create the new display values.

Not only do filters help preserve the integrity of the data in the scope, but, as you'll learn, keeping the formatting logic out of the controller means that it can be applied throughout an application, which helps create reusable formatting logic that is easy to test and maintain.

The numeric value is adjusted and rounded to show two decimal places and prefixed with the currency symbol. The default currency symbol is $, but you can specify an alternative, as shown in Listing 14-3.

Listing 14-3. Using a Different Symbol for the currency Filter in the filters.html File

```
...
<tr ng-repeat="p in products">
    <td>{{p.name}}</td>
    <td>{{p.category}}</td>
    <td>{{p.expiry}}</td>
    <td class="text-right">{{p.price | currency:"£" }}</td>
</tr>
...
```

I have followed the name of the filter with a colon (the : character) and then the symbol I want expressed as a literal string. This example uses the symbol for the British pound, and you can see the effect in Figure 14-3.

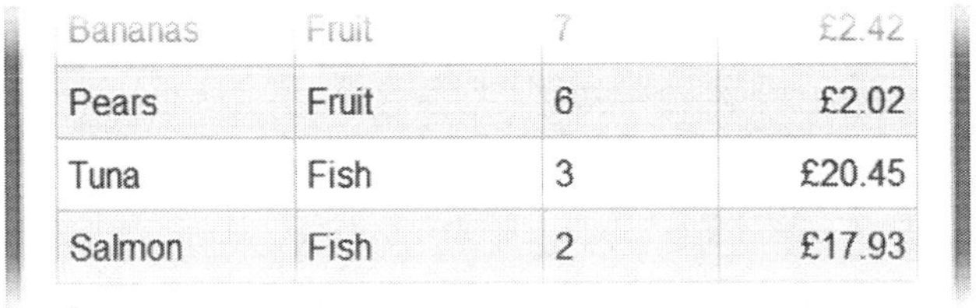

Bananas	Fruit	7	£2.42
Pears	Fruit	6	£2.02
Tuna	Fish	3	£20.45
Salmon	Fish	2	£17.93

Figure 14-3. *Specifying an alternative currency symbol*

Formatting Other Numeric Values

The number filter formats numeric data values to fix the number of decimal places displayed, rounding the value as required. You can see how I have used the number filter to display only whole-dollar amounts in the Price column of the example table in Listing 14-4.

Listing 14-4. Applying the number Filter in the filters.html File

```
...
<tr ng-repeat="p in products">
    <td>{{p.name}}</td>
    <td>{{p.category}}</td>
    <td>{{p.expiry}}</td>
    <td class="text-right">${{p.price | number:0 }}</td>
</tr>
...
```

I apply the filter using the bar character and the filter name, followed by a colon and then the number of decimal places I want to display. I have specified zero decimal places, which creates the effect shown in Figure 14-4.

Apples	Fruit	10	$1
Bananas	Fruit	7	$2
Pears	Fruit	6	$2
Tuna	Fish	3	$20
Salmon	Fish	2	$18

Figure 14-4. *Using the number filter*

■ **Caution**   The number filter will automatically insert commas to separate thousands so that a value such as 12345 will be transformed to 12,345.

Formatting Dates

The date filter formats dates, which can be expressed as strings, JavaScript Date objects, or numbers of milliseconds. To demonstrate the use of the date filter, I have added a behavior to the controller in the example that returns a Date object, which is a number of days into the future. I then used this behavior to prepare the expiry property of each data object for use with the date filter, as shown in Listing 14-5.

Listing 14-5. Using the date Filter in the filters.html File

```
<html ng-app="exampleApp">
<head>
    <title>Filters</title>
    <script src="angular.js"></script>
    <link href="bootstrap.css" rel="stylesheet" />
    <link href="bootstrap-theme.css" rel="stylesheet" />
    <script>
        angular.module("exampleApp", [])
            .controller("defaultCtrl", function ($scope) {
                $scope.products = [
                    { name: "Apples", category: "Fruit", price: 1.20, expiry: 10 },
                    { name: "Bananas", category: "Fruit", price: 2.42, expiry: 7 },
                    { name: "Pears", category: "Fruit", price: 2.02, expiry: 6 },

                    // ...other data objects omitted for brevity...
                ];

                $scope.getExpiryDate = function (days) {
                    var now = new Date();
                    return now.setDate(now.getDate() + days);
                }
            });
    </script>
</head>
```

```
<body ng-controller="defaultCtrl">
    <div class="panel panel-default">
        <div class="panel-heading">
            <h3>
                Products
                <span class="label label-primary">{{products.length}}</span>
            </h3>
        </div>
        <div class="panel-body">
            <table class="table table-striped table-bordered table-condensed">
                <thead>
                    <tr>
                        <td>Name</td><td>Category</td>
                        <td>Expiry</td><td class="text-right">Price</td>
                    </tr>
                </thead>
                <tbody>
                    <tr ng-repeat="p in products">
                        <td>{{p.name}}</td>
                        <td>{{p.category}}</td>
                        <td>{{getExpiryDate(p.expiry) | date:"dd MMM yy"}}</td>
                        <td class="text-right">${{p.price | number:0 }}</td>
                    </tr>
                </tbody>
            </table>
        </div>
    </div>
</body>
</html>
```

To use the filter, I specify date, followed by a colon, followed by a formatting string that consists of the date components you want to display. In the listing I have used three date components in my formatting string: d, MMM, and yy. I have listed the full set of date components in Table 14-4.

Table 14-4. *The Formatting String Components Supported by the date Filter*

Component	Description
yyyy	A four-digit representation of the year (e.g., 2050)
yy	A two-digit representation of the year (e.g., 50)
MMMM	The full month name (e.g., January)
MMM	Short representation of the month (e.g., Jan)
MM	Numeric month, padded to two characters (e.g., 01)
M	Numeric month, without padding (e.g., 1)
dd	Day of month, padded to two characters (e.g., 02)
d	Day of month, no padding (e.g., 2)
EEEE	Full name of day of week (e.g., Tuesday)

(continued)

Table 14-4. (*continued*)

Component	Description
EEE	Short name of day of week (e.g., Tue)
HH	Hour in day, 24-hour clock with padding to two characters (e.g., 02)
H	Hour in day, 24-hour clock without padding (e.g., 2)
hh	Hour in day, 12-hour clock with padding to two characters (e.g., 02)
h	Hour in day, 12-hour clock without padding (e.g., 2)
mm	Minute in hour, padded to two characters (e.g., 02)
m	Minute in hour without padding (e.g., 2)
ss	Second in minute, padded to two characters (e.g., 02)
s	Second in minute without padding (e.g., 2)
a	Marker for a.m./p.m.
Z	Four-character representation of time zone

You can see from the table that the formatting string I used in the listing produces a date like 05 Mar 15, and you can see the effect on the product table in Figure 14-5.

Bananas	Fruit	02 Mar 15	$2
Pears	Fruit	01 Mar 15	$2
Tuna	Fish	26 Feb 15	$20
Salmon	Fish	25 Feb 15	$18

Figure 14-5. *Formatting dates with the date filter*

■ **Caution**   The expression of dates varies significantly in different parts of the world, and you must try to use formatting strings that make sense to the user. For example, a date like 1/9/2015 represents the 9th of January in the United States but would be interpreted as the 1st of September in other regions. The date filter provides support for predefined localized formatting strings, which I describe in the "Localizing Filter Output" section later in this chapter.

Changing String Case

The uppercase and lowercase filters transform strings so that the characters are all uppercase or lowercase. I don't often use the uppercase filter, but I find that the lowercase filter is useful for mapping between strings that are capitalized for display in the HTML layout and property names. In Listing 14-6, you can see how I have applied the uppercase filter to the Name column and the lowercase to the Category column in the example. There are no configuration options for these filters.

Listing 14-6. Applying the uppercase and lowercase Filters in the filters.html File

```
...
<tr ng-repeat="p in products">
    <td>{{p.name | uppercase }}</td>
    <td>{{p.category | lowercase }}</td>
    <td>{{getExpiryDate(p.expiry) | date:"dd MMM yy"}}</td>
    <td class="text-right">${{p.price | number:0 }}</td>
</tr>
...
```

These filters do exactly what you would expect, and you can see the result of these changes in Figure 14-6.

BANANAS	fruit	02 Mar 15	$2
PEARS	fruit	01 Mar 15	$2
TUNA	fish	26 Feb 15	$20
SALMON	fish	25 Feb 15	$18

Figure 14-6. Using the uppercase and lowercase filters

Generating JSON

The json filter creates a JSON string from a JavaScript object. I have included this filter for completeness, but it is one that I have never found a use for, given how easy it is to work with JSON data in JavaScript anyway. In Listing 14-7, you can see how I have changed the ng-repeat directive in the example to include a JSON representation of each data object.

Listing 14-7. Applying the json Filter in the filters.html File

```
...
<tr ng-repeat="p in products">
    <td colspan="4">{{p | json}}</td>
</tr>
...
```

I replaced the original table cells with one that spans all of the columns and contains the data object, filtered by the json filter. You can see the result in Figure 14-7.

{ "name": "Apples", "category": "Fruit", "price": 1.2, "expiry": 10 }
{ "name": "Bananas", "category": "Fruit", "price": 2.42, "expiry": 7 }
{ "name": "Pears", "category": "Fruit", "price": 2.02, "expiry": 6 }
{ "name": "Tuna", "category": "Fish", "price": 20.45, "expiry": 3 }

Figure 14-7. Generating JSON representations of JavaScript objects using the json filter

Localizing Filter Output

The currency, number, and date filters all have support for formatting values using localization rules, which are defined in localization files such as the one that I downloaded at the start of the chapter. You can see how I have used the localization file to generate localized formatting in Listing 14-8.

Listing 14-8. Using Localized Filter Formatting in the filters.html File

```html
<html ng-app="exampleApp">
<head>
    <title>Filters</title>
    <script src="angular.js"></script>
    <script src="angular-locale_fr-fr.js"></script>
    <link href="bootstrap.css" rel="stylesheet" />
    <link href="bootstrap-theme.css" rel="stylesheet" />
    <script>
        angular.module("exampleApp", [])
            .controller("defaultCtrl", function ($scope) {
                $scope.products = [
                    { name: "Apples", category: "Fruit", price: 1.20, expiry: 10 },
                    { name: "Bananas", category: "Fruit", price: 2.42, expiry: 7 },
                    { name: "Pears", category: "Fruit", price: 2.02, expiry: 6 },

                    { name: "Tuna", category: "Fish", price: 20.45, expiry: 3 },
                    { name: "Salmon", category: "Fish", price: 17.93, expiry: 2 },
                    { name: "Trout", category: "Fish", price: 12.93, expiry: 4 },

                    { name: "Beer", category: "Drinks", price: 2.99, expiry: 365 },
                    { name: "Wine", category: "Drinks", price: 8.99, expiry: 365 },
                    { name: "Whiskey", category: "Drinks", price: 45.99, expiry: 365 }
                ];

                $scope.getExpiryDate = function (days) {
                    var now = new Date();
                    return now.setDate(now.getDate() + days);
                }
            });
    </script>
</head>
<body ng-controller="defaultCtrl">
    <div class="panel panel-default">
        <div class="panel-heading">
            <h3>
                Products
                <span class="label label-primary">{{products.length}}</span>
            </h3>
        </div>
```

```
        <div class="panel-body">
            <table class="table table-striped table-bordered table-condensed">
                <thead>
                    <tr>
                        <td>Name</td>
                        <td>Category</td>
                        <td>Expiry</td>
                        <td class="text-right">Price</td>
                    </tr>
                </thead>
                <tbody>
                    <tr ng-repeat="p in products">
                        <td>{{p.name}}</td>
                        <td>{{p.category}}</td>
                        <td>{{getExpiryDate(p.expiry) | date:"shortDate"}}</td>
                        <td class="text-right">{{p.price | currency }}</td>
                    </tr>
                </tbody>
            </table>
        </div>
    </div>
</body>
</html>
```

I have added a script element to import the angular-locale_fr-fr.js file into the HTML document and restored the table cells for the individual model object properties. The name and category properties are not filtered, but I have used the date and currency filters for the expiry and price properties, respectively.

Notice that I have specified shortDate for the date filter formatting string. This is one of a number of shortcut formats that the date filter supports for common date expressions. Table 14-5 shows the complete set of these shortcuts. The output generated by these shortcuts is, of course, locale-specific, but I have shown the equivalent format string for the en-US locale, which represents English as used in the United States.

Table 14-5. *The Shortcut Formatting Strings Supported by the date Filter*

Formatting String	Description
medium	Equivalent to MMM d, y h:mm:ss a
short	Equivalent to M/d/yy h:mm a
fullDate	Equivalent to EEEE, MMMM d,y
longDate	Equivalent to MMMM d, y
mediumDate	Equivalent to MMM d, y
shortDate	Equivalent to M/d/yy
mediumTime	Equivalent to h:mm:ss a
shortTime	Equivalent to h:mm a

In Figure 14-8, I show some of the table rows with and without the script element for the angular-locale_fr-fr.js file so that you can see the impact of using localized formatting.

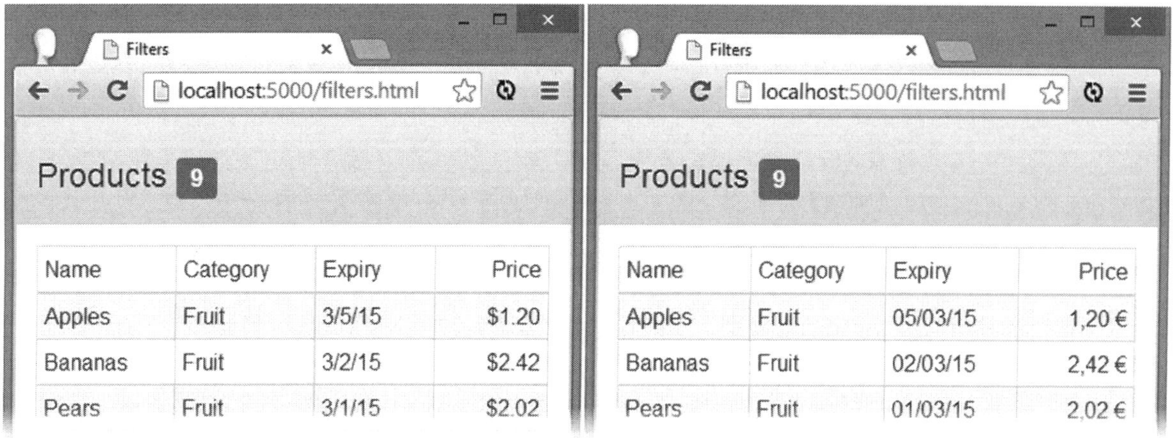

Figure 14-8. *The effect of localized formatting*

There are some obvious differences between the formatting in the default and `fr-fr` locales: The order of the month and day is reversed, the currency symbol and position have changed, and a comma is used to separate the whole and fractional elements of the numbers (3,41 rather than 3.41).

THE DANGERS OF LOCALIZATION-LITE

The AngularJS support for localization is pretty standard for client-side development frameworks. It is functional, but its use doesn't produce a localized application. Differences between locales go deeper than date, number, and currency formats, and you will need to plan carefully and seek expert advice to create a truly localized application, taking into account everything from local business conventions and regulation, idiom, and religious beliefs.

My advice is to target just the en-US locale if you can't commit the time, effort, and resources required for a fully localized application. A web app that is specific to English as it is used in the United States and that follows North American business and language conventions is relatively easy to create for English speakers (which I assume you are given that this is an English-language book), and the U.S.-centric nature of the Internet means that en-US conventions are widely understood. This approach will exclude any potential customers who do not speak English or do not understand U.S. conventions, but this is often a better outcome than a poorly localized application will produce anyway.

To be clear, the better outcome is usually a properly localized application for each region that you want to service, but you will only get into trouble if you don't localize any further than dates and currency symbols.

Filtering Collections

Filtering collections works by using the same basic techniques as filtering single data values but generally requires more care and consideration to get the right result. The AngularJS library includes three built-in collection filters—which I describe in the following sections—and, of course, you can create your own custom filters, a process that I describe in the "Creating Custom Filters" section later in this chapter.

Limiting the Number of Items

The limitTo filter restricts the number of items taken from an array of data objects, which can be useful when working with a layout that can accommodate only a certain number of items. Listing 14-9 shows the changes I made to the filters.html file to demonstrate the limitTo filter.

Listing 14-9. Using the limitTo Filter in the filters.html File

```html
<html ng-app="exampleApp">
<head>
    <title>Filters</title>
    <script src="angular.js"></script>
    <link href="bootstrap.css" rel="stylesheet" />
    <link href="bootstrap-theme.css" rel="stylesheet" />
    <script>
        angular.module("exampleApp", [])
            .controller("defaultCtrl", function ($scope) {
                $scope.products = [
                    { name: "Apples", category: "Fruit", price: 1.20, expiry: 10 },
                    { name: "Bananas", category: "Fruit", price: 2.42, expiry: 7 },
                    { name: "Pears", category: "Fruit", price: 2.02, expiry: 6 },

                    { name: "Tuna", category: "Fish", price: 20.45, expiry: 3 },
                    { name: "Salmon", category: "Fish", price: 17.93, expiry: 2 },
                    { name: "Trout", category: "Fish", price: 12.93, expiry: 4 },

                    { name: "Beer", category: "Drinks", price: 2.99, expiry: 365 },
                    { name: "Wine", category: "Drinks", price: 8.99, expiry: 365 },
                    { name: "Whiskey", category: "Drinks", price: 45.99, expiry: 365 }
                ];

                $scope.limitVal = "5";
                $scope.limitRange = [];
                for (var i = (0 - $scope.products.length);
                        i <= $scope.products.length; i++) {
                    $scope.limitRange.push(i.toString());
                }
            });
    </script>
</head>
<body ng-controller="defaultCtrl">
    <div class="panel panel-default">
        <div class="panel-heading">
            <h3>
                Products
                <span class="label label-primary">{{products.length}}</span>
            </h3>
        </div>
        <div class="panel-body">
            Limit: <select ng-model="limitVal"
                ng-options="item for item in limitRange"></select>
        </div>
```

```
        <div class="panel-body">
            <table class="table table-striped table-bordered table-condensed">
                <thead>
                    <tr>
                        <td>Name</td>
                        <td>Category</td>
                        <td>Expiry</td>
                        <td class="text-right">Price</td>
                    </tr>
                </thead>
                <tbody>
                    <tr ng-repeat="p in products | limitTo:limitVal">
                        <td>{{p.name}}</td>
                        <td>{{p.category}}</td>
                        <td>{{p.expiry}}</td>
                        <td class="text-right">{{p.price | currency }}</td>
                    </tr>
                </tbody>
            </table>
        </div>
    </div>
</body>
</html>
```

■ **Tip**   Notice that I have removed the localization file for this example for brevity.

The most important change in the filters.html file is the application of the limitTo filter to the products array in the expression I defined for the ng-repeat directive, as follows:

```
...
<tr ng-repeat="p in products | limitTo:limitVal">
...
```

The collections that operate on filters are applied in the same way as those applied to single values. The limitTo filter is configured by specifying the number of items that should be used from the source array. In this example, I have specified that the limit is set by the value of the limitVal property, which is defined in the controller factory function:

```
...
$scope.limitVal = "5";
...
```

In other words, I have used the limitTo filter to restrict the ng-repeat directive so that it operates only on the first five objects in the products array, as illustrated by Figure 14-9.

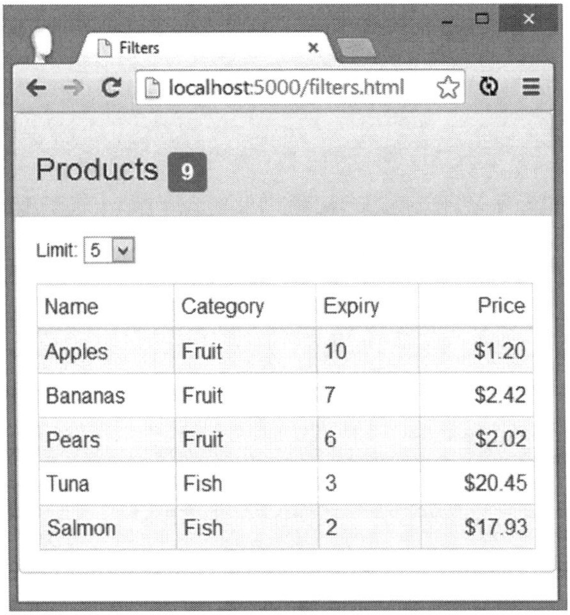

Figure 14-9. *Using the limitTo filter*

Like all filters, limitTo doesn't modify the data in the scope; it affects only the data that is passed to the ng-repeat directive. You can see this in the figure where the counter next to the Products title still reads 9 (because it is generated through an inline binding to products.length) even though the ng-repeat directive has received only five objects from the array.

■ **Tip**   The limitTo filter will also operate on string values, treating each character as an object in an array.

I specified the value for the limitTo filter as a variable to demonstrate what happens when you specify negative values. To that end, the filters.html markup contains a select element whose ng-options attribute is set to an array of values that I create like this:

```
...
for (var i = (0 - $scope.products.length); i <= $scope.products.length; i++) {
    $scope.limitRange.push(i.toString());
}
...
```

There are nine data objects in the products array, which means that the select element contains option elements from -9 through to 9. If you configure the limitTo filter with a positive number—such as 5, in the figure—then the filter selects the first five objects from the array. However, if you select a negative value, such as -5, for example, then the filter selects the last five objects in the array. You can see the effect in Figure 14-10.

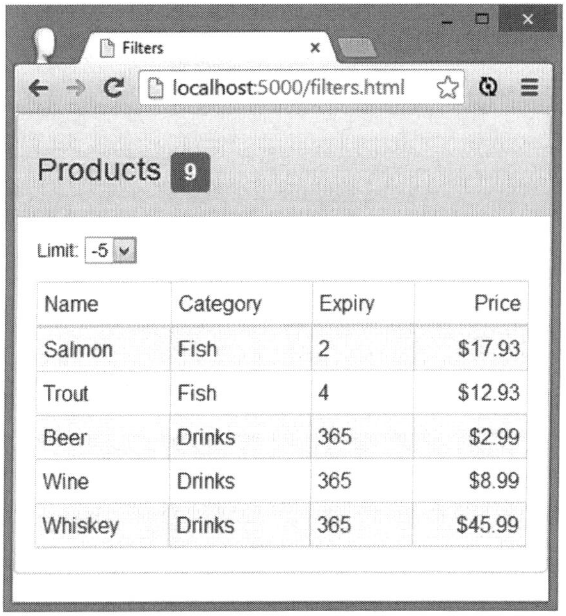

Figure 14-10. *Using negative values for the limitTo filter*

■ **Tip** You don't have to worry about going out of bounds. The limitTo filter will return all of the objects in the array if you specify a number that is greater than the size of the array.

Selecting Items

The confusingly named filter filter is used to select objects from an array. The selection criteria can be specified as an expression, as a map object used to match property values, or using a function. Listing 14-10 shows a simple selection.

Listing 14-10. Selecting items in the filters.html file

```
...
<tr ng-repeat="p in products | filter:{category: 'Fish'}">
    <td>{{p.name}}</td>
    <td>{{p.category}}</td>
    <td>{{p.expiry}}</td>
    <td class="text-right">{{p.price | currency }}</td>
</tr>
...
```

I have used the map object approach in this example, specifying that I want to select those items whose category property is Fish. If you filter using a function, the selected items will be those for which the function returns true, as shown in Listing 14-11.

Listing 14-11. Selecting Items in the filters.html File

```html
<html ng-app="exampleApp">
<head>
    <title>Filters</title>
    <script src="angular.js"></script>
    <link href="bootstrap.css" rel="stylesheet" />
    <link href="bootstrap-theme.css" rel="stylesheet" />
    <script>
        angular.module("exampleApp", [])
            .controller("defaultCtrl", function ($scope) {
                $scope.products = [
                    { name: "Apples", category: "Fruit", price: 1.20, expiry: 10 },
                    { name: "Bananas", category: "Fruit", price: 2.42, expiry: 7 },
                    { name: "Pears", category: "Fruit", price: 2.02, expiry: 6 },

                    { name: "Tuna", category: "Fish", price: 20.45, expiry: 3 },
                    { name: "Salmon", category: "Fish", price: 17.93, expiry: 2 },
                    { name: "Trout", category: "Fish", price: 12.93, expiry: 4 },

                    { name: "Beer", category: "Drinks", price: 2.99, expiry: 365 },
                    { name: "Wine", category: "Drinks", price: 8.99, expiry: 365 },
                    { name: "Whiskey", category: "Drinks", price: 45.99, expiry: 365 }
                ];

                $scope.limitVal = "5";
                $scope.limitRange = [];
                for (var i = (0 - $scope.products.length) ;
                        i <= $scope.products.length; i++) {
                    $scope.limitRange.push(i.toString());
                }

                $scope.selectItems = function (item) {
                    return item.category == "Fish" || item.name == "Beer";
                };
            });
    </script>
</head>
<body ng-controller="defaultCtrl">
    <div class="panel panel-default">
        <div class="panel-heading">
            <h3>
                Products
                <span class="label label-primary">{{products.length}}</span>
            </h3>
        </div>
        <div class="panel-body">
            Limit: <select ng-model="limitVal"
                        ng-options="item for item in limitRange"></select>
        </div>
```

```
        <div class="panel-body">
            <table class="table table-striped table-bordered table-condensed">
                <thead>
                    <tr>
                        <td>Name</td>
                        <td>Category</td>
                        <td>Expiry</td>
                        <td class="text-right">Price</td>
                    </tr>
                </thead>
                <tbody>
                    <tr ng-repeat="p in products | filter:selectItems">
                        <td>{{p.name}}</td>
                        <td>{{p.category}}</td>
                        <td>{{p.expiry}}</td>
                        <td class="text-right">{{p.price | currency }}</td>
                    </tr>
                </tbody>
            </table>
        </div>
    </div>
</body>
</html>
```

In this example, I defined a scope behavior called selectItems. This behavior is invoked for each item in the collection and is passed each object in turn. My implementation returns true if the category property is Fish or if the name property is Beer. Using a behavior to provide the filter with a function allows for more complex selections than is possible using an expression.

Sorting Items

The most complex built-in filter is orderBy, which sorts the objects in an array. In Listing 14-12, you can see how I have applied the orderBy filter to the example.

Listing 14-12. Applying the orderBy Filter in the filters.html File

```
...
<tr ng-repeat="p in products | orderBy:'price'">
    <td>{{p.name}}</td>
    <td>{{p.category}}</td>
    <td>{{p.expiry}}</td>
    <td class="text-right">{{p.price | currency }}</td>
</tr>
...
```

This is the simplest way to order objects—by specifying the name of a property by which the objects should be sorted. In this case I have specified the price property, which has the effect shown in Figure 14-11.

Name	Category	Expiry	Price
Apples	Fruit	10	$1.20
Pears	Fruit	6	$2.02
Bananas	Fruit	7	$2.42
Beer	Drinks	365	$2.99
Wine	Drinks	365	$8.99
Trout	Fish	4	$12.93
Salmon	Fish	2	$17.93
Tuna	Fish	3	$20.45
Whiskey	Drinks	365	$45.99

Figure 14-11. *Sorting objects by price*

▪ **Caution**   Notice that I have surrounded the property name with quotes: `'price'` and not just `price`. The `orderBy` filter will quietly fail if you forget the quotes when hardwiring a property name into a directive expression. Without the quotes, the filter assumes you want to use a scope variable or a controller variable called `price` and figures that you'll get around to defining it at some point in the future.

Setting the Sort Direction

By specifying just a property name, I am implicitly asking the filter to sort the objects in ascending order. I can make the order explicit by using the + or – character, as shown in Listing 14-13.

Listing 14-13. Explicitly Setting the Sort Direction in the filters.html File

```
...
<tr ng-repeat="p in products | orderBy:'-price'">
...
```

By prefixing the property name with a minus sign (-) I specify that the objects should be sorted in descending order of their price property, as shown in Figure 14-12. Specifying a plus sign (+) is equivalent to no prefix at all and has the effect of applying an ascending sort.

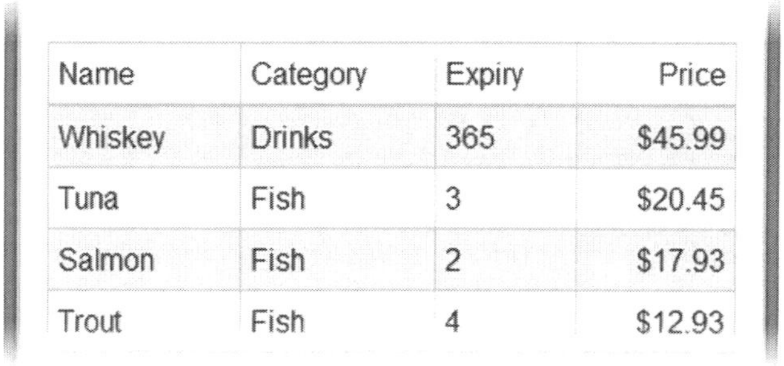

Name	Category	Expiry	Price
Whiskey	Drinks	365	$45.99
Tuna	Fish	3	$20.45
Salmon	Fish	2	$17.93
Trout	Fish	4	$12.93

Figure 14-12. *Performing a descending sort*

Sorting by Function

The reason you have to be careful when specifying a property name as a literal string is because the orderBy filter will also sort using a function, which allows for sorting in ways that are not directly tied to single property values. In Listing 14-14, you can see how I have defined such a function, which performs a sort based on multiple properties.

Listing 14-14. Defining a Sorting Function in the filters.html File

```
...
<script>
    angular.module("exampleApp", [])
        .controller("defaultCtrl", function ($scope) {
            $scope.products = [
                { name: "Apples", category: "Fruit", price: 1.20, expiry: 10 },
                { name: "Bananas", category: "Fruit", price: 2.42, expiry: 7 },
                { name: "Pears", category: "Fruit", price: 2.02, expiry: 6 },

                { name: "Tuna", category: "Fish", price: 20.45, expiry: 3 },
                { name: "Salmon", category: "Fish", price: 17.93, expiry: 2 },
                { name: "Trout", category: "Fish", price: 12.93, expiry: 4 },

                { name: "Beer", category: "Drinks", price: 2.99, expiry: 365 },
                { name: "Wine", category: "Drinks", price: 8.99, expiry: 365 },
                { name: "Whiskey", category: "Drinks", price: 45.99, expiry: 365 }
            ];

            $scope.myCustomSorter = function (item) {
                return item.expiry < 5 ? 0 : item.price;
            }
        });
</script>
...
```

Functions used for sorting are passed an object from the data array and return an object or value that will be used for comparison during sorting. In this function, I return the value of the price property unless the value of the expiry property is less than 5, in which case I return zero. The effect of this function is that items with a small expiry value will be placed near the start of the data array for ascending sorts. In Listing 14-15, you can see how I have applied the function to the orderBy filter.

Listing 14-15. Applying the Search Function in the filters.html File

```
...
<tr ng-repeat="p in products | orderBy:myCustomSorter">
    <td>{{p.name}}</td>
    <td>{{p.category}}</td>
    <td>{{p.expiry}}</td>
    <td class="text-right">{{p.price | currency }}</td>
</tr>
...
```

Notice that I don't surround the name of the function with quotes, as I did when I specified a property name as a literal string. You can see the effect the function has in Figure 14-13.

Name	Category	Expiry	Price
Tuna	Fish	3	$20.45
Salmon	Fish	2	$17.93
Trout	Fish	4	$12.93
Apples	Fruit	10	$1.20
Pears	Fruit	6	$2.02
Bananas	Fruit	7	$2.42
Beer	Drinks	365	$2.99
Wine	Drinks	365	$8.99
Whiskey	Drinks	365	$45.99

Figure 14-13. Using a function to sort data objects

Sorting with Multiple Predicates

AngularJS sorting functions are a little odd. Rather than being asked to compare two objects and determine their relative ranking, you are asked to return a value that the orderBy filter will use to perform the ranking. This means you can end up with something that only approximates the intended effect when you assign weight to values of different properties, as I did in the previous example. I wanted to put the objects with the smallest expiry values at the top of the table—which happened—but the orderBy filter didn't perform any further ranking.

Fortunately, you can configure the orderBy filter to use an array of property names or functions that will be used in sequence to order objects. If two objects have the same value for the first property or function in the array, then the orderBy filter will consider the second value or function, continuing until it can rank the data objects or runs out of properties/functions to try. In Listing 14-16, you can see how I have applied an array in the filters.html file.

Listing 14-16. Using an Array for Sorting with the orderBy Filter in the filters.html File

```
...
<tr ng-repeat="p in products | orderBy:[myCustomSorter, '-price']">
    <td>{{p.name}}</td>
    <td>{{p.category}}</td>
    <td>{{p.expiry}}</td>
    <td class="text-right">{{p.price | currency }}</td>
</tr>
...
```

I have applied the myCustomSorter function from the previous section, followed by the price property in descending order. The myCustomSorter function assigns the same sorting value for objects with a small expiry value, so using the array lets me sort those objects relative to one another, as shown in Figure 14-14.

Name	Category	Expiry	Price
Tuna	Fish	3	$20.45
Salmon	Fish	2	$17.93
Trout	Fish	4	$12.93
Apples	Fruit	10	$1.20
Pears	Fruit	6	$2.02

Figure 14-14. Using an array of sorting instructions

Chaining Filters

I have shown you all of the built-in filters individually, but one of the best filter features is the way you can combine them to create more complex effects. In Listing 14-17, you can see how I have used chaining to combine the limitTo and orderBy filters.

Listing 14-17. Chaining Filters in the filters.html File

```
...
<tr ng-repeat="p in products | orderBy:[myCustomSorter, '-price'] | limitTo: 5">
    <td>{{p.name}}</td>
    <td>{{p.category}}</td>
    <td>{{p.expiry}}</td>
    <td class="text-right">{{p.price | currency }}</td>
</tr>
...
```

▪ **Tip** You *can* chain together filters that operate on single data values, but there isn't much point in doing this with the built-in filters like currency and date, since they are designed to format a specific kind of data. For this reason, you will usually see chaining used with filters rather than with operations on collections, allowing complex transformations to be performed.

Filters are chained together using the bar (|) character and are evaluated in the order in which they are written. In the listing, the orderBy filter is applied first, and then the limitTo filter is applied to the sorted results. The overall effect is that the ng-repeat directive operates on the first five sorted objects, as shown in Figure 14-15.

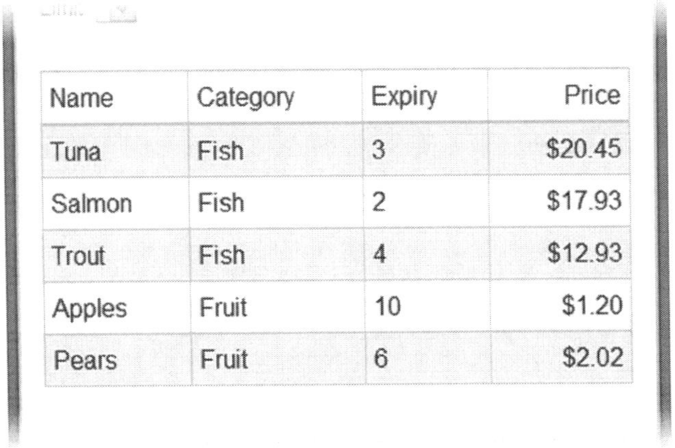

Name	Category	Expiry	Price
Tuna	Fish	3	$20.45
Salmon	Fish	2	$17.93
Trout	Fish	4	$12.93
Apples	Fruit	10	$1.20
Pears	Fruit	6	$2.02

Figure 14-15. *Chaining filters*

Creating Custom Filters

You are not restricted to the built-in filters and can create your own to process data in ways that are specific to your applications. In this section I will show you how to create three different filters: one that formats a single data value, one that processes an array of objects, and one that builds on functionality provided by other filters.

Creating a Filter That Formats a Data Value

Filters are created by the Module.filter method, which takes two arguments: the name of the filter that will be created and a factory function that creates the worker function that will undertake the actual work. To demonstrate how to create a filter, I have added a new JavaScript file called customFilters.js to the angularjs folder. Listing 14-18 shows the contents of the new file.

Listing 14-18. The Contents of the customFilters.js File

```
angular.module("exampleApp")
    .filter("labelCase", function () {
        return function (value, reverse) {
            if (angular.isString(value)) {
                var intermediate =  reverse ? value.toUpperCase() : value.toLowerCase();
                return (reverse ? intermediate[0].toLowerCase() :
                    intermediate[0].toUpperCase()) + intermediate.substr(1);
            } else {
                return value;
            }
        };
    });
```

375

■ **Note**   Notice that I have used the `angular.module` method with only one argument in this example. This retrieves a previously defined module for further configuration—in this case, the module defined in the main `filters.html` file. By retrieving the module, I am able to call the `filter` method to supplement the `exampleApp` module, even though my code is in a separate file.

The filter I have created is called `labelCase`, and it formats a string so that only the first letter is capitalized. The worker function I defined accepts two arguments: The first is the value that is to be filtered (which will be provided by AngularJS when the filter is applied), and the second allows the use of the filter to be reversed so that the first letter is lowercase and the rest of the string is capitalized.

■ **Tip**   Notice that I used the `angular.isString` method to check that the value my filter is formatting is really a string. Although I differentiated between *using* single-value and collection filters in this chapter, there is no real difference when *writing* either kind of filter, and it is always worth checking that you have received the kind of data you are expecting, which can happen when your filter is misapplied in a directive expression. For this filter, I simply return the data value unmodified if it isn't a string, but you may prefer to generate an error that will be detected during testing.

Before I can apply the filter, I need to add a `script` element to the `filters.html` file to bring the code contained in the `customFilters.js` file into the main document, as shown in Listing 14-19.

Listing 14-19. Adding a script Element for the customFilters.js File to the filters.html File

```
...
<head>
    <title>Filters</title>
    <script src="angular.js"></script>
    <link href="bootstrap.css" rel="stylesheet" />
    <link href="bootstrap-theme.css" rel="stylesheet" />
    <script>
        angular.module("exampleApp", [])
            .controller("defaultCtrl", function ($scope) {

                // ...statements omitted for brevity...
            });
    </script>
    <script src="customFilters.js"></script>
</head>
...
```

I have to put the `script` element for the `customFilters.js` file after the one that defines the exampleApp module, since the code in the JavaScript files relies on the module already being defined. The only other change I have to make is to apply the filter to the markup. In Listing 14-20, you can see how I have applied the filter to the Name and Category columns of the table in the `filters.html` file.

Listing 14-20. Applying a Custom Filter to the filters.html File

```
...
<tr ng-repeat="p in products | orderBy:[myCustomSorter, '-price'] | limitTo: 5">
    <td>{{p.name | labelCase }}</td>
    <td>{{p.category | labelCase:true }}</td>
    <td>{{p.expiry}}</td>
    <td class="text-right">{{p.price | currency }}</td>
</tr>
...
```

I have not specified a configuration option when applying the filter to the name property, which means that AngularJS will pass null as the value for the second argument to the filter worker function. I have written the filter so that a false or null value for the second value means that the default behavior is used, and I recommend you take the same approach for your custom filters because it makes them easier to use. I have specified the configuration option true when applying the filter to the category property, which will invert the case transformation applied by the filter. You can see the effect of both filters in Figure 14-16.

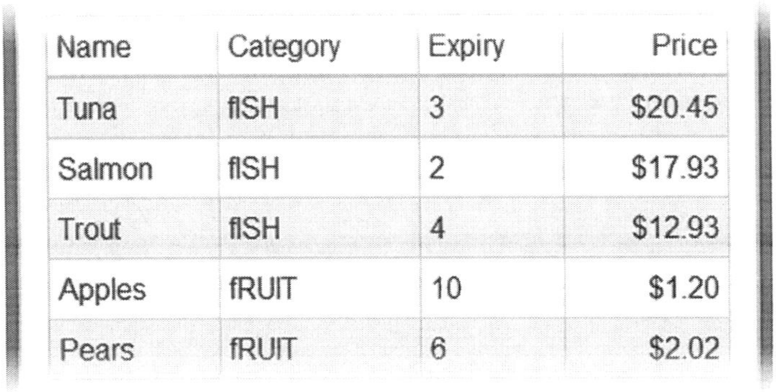

Name	Category	Expiry	Price
Tuna	fISH	3	$20.45
Salmon	fISH	2	$17.93
Trout	fISH	4	$12.93
Apples	fRUIT	10	$1.20
Pears	fRUIT	6	$2.02

Figure 14-16. *Applying a custom filter*

Creating a Collection Filter

The process for creating a filter that operates on a collection of objects is just the same but is worth demonstrating anyway. In this section, I am going to build a skip filter that removes a specified number of items from the head of the array—something that isn't that useful on its own but which I'll build on later in the chapter. Listing 14-21 shows the additions I made to define the skip filter in the customFilters.js file.

Listing 14-21. Defining a Collection Filter in the customFilters.js File

```
angular.module("exampleApp")
    .filter("labelCase", function () {
        return function (value, reverse) {
            if (angular.isString(value)) {
                var intermediate =  reverse ? value.toUpperCase() : value.toLowerCase();
                return (reverse ? intermediate[0].toLowerCase() :
                    intermediate[0].toUpperCase()) + intermediate.substr(1);
```

```
                  } else {
                      return value;
                  }
              };
          })
          .filter("skip", function () {
              return function (data, count) {
                  if (angular.isArray(data) && angular.isNumber(count)) {
                      if (count > data.length || count < 1) {
                          return data;
                      } else {
                          return data.slice(count);
                      }
                  } else {
                      return data;
                  }
              }
          });
```

In the worker function, I check to see that the data is an array and that I have received a numeric value for the count argument. I perform some bounds checking to make sure that the filter can perform the requested transformation on the array, and if all is well, I use the built-in JavaScript slice method to skip over the specified number of objects. In Listing 14-22, you can see how I have applied the skip filter to the expression for the ng-repeat directive in the filters.html file. (I also removed the labelCase filter from the table columns.)

Listing 14-22. Applying a Custom Collection Filter in the filters.html File

```
...
<tr ng-repeat="p in products | skip:2 | limitTo: 5">
    <td>{{p.name}}</td>
    <td>{{p.category}}</td>
    <td>{{p.expiry}}</td>
    <td class="text-right">{{p.price | currency }}</td>
</tr>
...
```

I have chained the skip and limitTo filters to emphasize that custom filters are used in just the same way as the built-in ones. The overall effect of these two filters is to skip over the first two items and then select the next five, as shown in Figure 14-17.

Name	Category	Expiry	Price
Pears	Fruit	6	$2.02
Tuna	Fish	3	$20.45
Salmon	Fish	2	$17.93
Trout	Fish	4	$12.93
Beer	Drinks	365	$2.99

Figure 14-17. *Applying custom and built-in collection filters*

Building on Existing Filters

In this section I am going to combine the functionality of skip and limitTo in a single filter. As Listing 14-20 demonstrated, it is easy to use chaining to apply these filters together, but I want to demonstrate how you can build on existing filter functionality without having to duplicate any code. In Listing 14-23, you can see the additions I made to the customFilters.js file to define the take filter.

Listing 14-23. Defining the take Filter in the customFilters.js File

```
angular.module("exampleApp")
    .filter("labelCase", function () {
        // ...statements omitted for brevity...
    })
    .filter("skip", function () {
        // ...statements omitted for brevity...
    })
    .filter("take", function ($filter) {
        return function (data, skipCount, takeCount) {
            var skippedData = $filter("skip")(data, skipCount);
            return $filter("limitTo")(skippedData, takeCount);
        }
    });
```

My take filter doesn't implement a transformation itself and doesn't even check to see what kind of data it is working with. Instead, it relies on the skip and limitTo filters, which perform their own validation and apply their transformations as though they were being used directly.

In the listing, my filter factory function declares a dependency on the $filter service, which provides access to all of the filters that have been defined in the module. These filters are accessed and invoked in the worker function by name, like this:

```
...
var skippedData = $filter("skip")(data, skipCount);
...
```

This statement invokes the `skip` filter within the worker function, and I store the processed data collection by assigning it to a regular JavaScript variable. I repeat the process with the `limitTo` filter, allowing me to create a filter that builds on other filters. In Listing 14-24, you can see how I have applied this filter to the expression for the `ng-repeat` directive in the `filters.html` file.

Listing 14-24. Applying the take Filter in the filters.html File

```
...
<tr ng-repeat="p in products | take:2:5">
    <td>{{p.name}}</td>
    <td>{{p.category}}</td>
    <td>{{p.expiry}}</td>
    <td class="text-right">{{p.price | currency }}</td>
</tr>
...
```

■ **Tip**   This is the first time I have used a filter whose worker function expects more than one configuration argument; you can see that I provide the values for the arguments by separating them with colons. AngularJS takes care of processing the values and passing them to the worker function.

My `take` filter doesn't offer any real advantage over the filters it builds on, but the example demonstrates how easy it is to build filters that *do* add value without duplicating functionality you have created elsewhere.

Summary

In this chapter I explained how AngularJS supports filters to format or transform data so that it can be displayed as part of a view. I showed you the built-in AngularJS filters that format single data items and transform collections, and I showed you how to create and apply custom filters. I finished the chapter by demonstrating how you can use the `$filter` service to build on other filters so that you don't have to duplicate the same code in multiple places in an application. In the next chapter, I show you how to create custom directives.

CHAPTER 15

■ ■ ■

Creating Custom Directives

In Chapters 10–12, I showed you how to use the built-in directives that AngularJS provides, including directives that handle one- and two-way data bindings (ng-bind and ng-model), generate content from data (such as ng-repeat and ng-switch), manipulate HTML elements (such as ng-class and ng-if), and respond to user interaction (such as ng-click and ng-change). In Chapter 12, I demonstrated the directives that replace the standard HTML form elements to enable data validation and perform common tasks such as generating option elements.

AngularJS comes with a comprehensive range of directives that address most common web application scenarios, but, of course, you can create your own directives when the built-in ones don't work the way you require. In this chapter, I explain the basic process for creating a custom directive and describe *jqLite*, which is used by directives to manage HTML elements. In Chapters 16 and 17, I describe the advanced features that are available to gain greater control over how custom directives work. Table 15-1 summarizes this chapter.

Table 15-1. *Chapter Summary*

Problem	Solution	Listing
Create a custom directive.	Call the Module.directive method, passing in the name of the directive and a factory function.	1–3
Prepare the elements contained by the directive.	Return a link function from the factory function.	4–5
Configure a directive.	Add a support attribute or evaluate an expression.	6–8
Respond to changes in the scope.	Use a watcher function.	9–11
Manipulate elements in the link function.	Use jqLite.	12–19
Replace jqLite with jQuery.	Add a script element for the jQuery library before the one for AngularJS.	20

■ **Note** As you'll learn, writing custom directives depends on functionality that I have described in previous chapters, especially scopes, and this is why I have had to cover other topics before returning to the topic of directives.

Why and When to Create Custom Directives

You can create a custom directive whenever the built-in directives don't meet your needs, when you want to express complex functionality in code rather than in HTML, or when you want to create a self-contained unit of functionality that you can use in multiple AngularJS applications. I'll show you examples of each of these types of directive in this chapter. Table 15-2 summarizes why and when to create custom directives in an AngularJS application.

Table 15-2. *Why and When to Create Custom Directives*

Why	When
Custom directives let you create functionality that goes beyond the built-in directives that AngularJS provides.	You create custom directives when the built-in directives don't do what you want or when you want to create self-contained functionality that you can reuse in different applications.

Preparing the Example Project

To prepare for this chapter, I deleted the contents of the angularjs web server folder and installed the angular.js, bootstrap.css, and bootstrap-theme.css files, as described in Chapter 1. I then created a file called directives.html, which you can see in Listing 15-1.

Listing 15-1. The Contents of the directives.html File

```
<html ng-app="exampleApp">
<head>
    <title>Directives</title>
    <script src="angular.js"></script>
    <link href="bootstrap.css" rel="stylesheet" />
    <link href="bootstrap-theme.css" rel="stylesheet" />
    <script>
        angular.module("exampleApp", [])
            .controller("defaultCtrl", function ($scope) {
                $scope.products = [
                    { name: "Apples", category: "Fruit", price: 1.20, expiry: 10 },
                    { name: "Bananas", category: "Fruit", price: 2.42, expiry: 7 },
                    { name: "Pears", category: "Fruit", price: 2.02, expiry: 6 }
                ];
            });
    </script>
</head>
<body ng-controller="defaultCtrl">
    <div class="panel panel-default">
        <div class="panel-heading">
            <h3>Products</h3>
        </div>
        <div class="panel-body">
            Content will go here
        </div>
    </div>
</body>
</html>
```

This document defines an AngularJS application with a single controller called defaultCtrl. The controller sets up a products array on the scope that contains a subset of the data I used to demonstrate filters in Chapter 14. You can see how the browser displays this file in Figure 15-1.

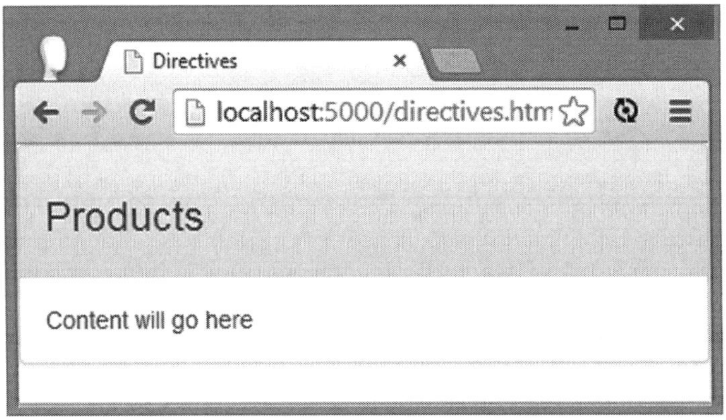

Figure 15-1. *Displaying the initial content of the directives.html file*

Creating a Custom Directive

I am going to start with a simple example to demonstrate how custom directives are created, just to outline the basic features and to set the scene for later examples in the chapter. My initial goal will be to create and apply a directive that will generate an ul element that contains an li element for each object in the products array. I'll walk through the process step-by-step in the sections that follow.

Defining the Directive

Directives are created using the Module.directive method, and the arguments are the name of the new directive and a factory function that creates the directive. In Listing 15-2, you can see how I have added a directive called unorderedList to the directives.html file. This directive doesn't do anything at the moment, but it allows me to explain some important points as I build the functionality in the sections that follow.

Listing 15-2. Adding a Directive to the directives.html File

```
...
<script>
    angular.module("exampleApp", [])
        .directive("unorderedList", function () {
            return function (scope, element, attrs) {
                // implementation code will go here
            }
        })
```

```
        .controller("defaultCtrl", function ($scope) {
            $scope.products = [
                { name: "Apples", category: "Fruit", price: 1.20, expiry: 10 },
                { name: "Bananas", category: "Fruit", price: 2.42, expiry: 7 },
                { name: "Pears", category: "Fruit", price: 2.02, expiry: 6 }
            ];
        })
</script>
...
```

■ **Tip** I have defined the directive before the controller in the listing, but that is not a requirement, and in larger projects you would generally define directives in one or more separate files, much as I did for the SportsStore application in Chapters 6–8.

The first argument that I passed to the directive method set the name of the new directive to unorderedList. Notice that I have used the standard JavaScript case convention, meaning that the u of unordered is lowercase and the L of list is uppercase. AngularJS is particular when it comes to names with mixed capitalization. You can see what I mean in Listing 15-3, which shows how I have applied the unorderedList directive to an HTML element.

Listing 15-3. Applying a Custom Directive in the directives.html File

```
...
<body ng-controller="defaultCtrl">
    <div class="panel panel-default">
        <div class="panel-heading">
            <h3>Products</h3>
        </div>
        <div class="panel-body">
            <div unordered-list="products"></div>
        </div>
    </div>
</body>
...
```

I have applied the directive as an attribute on a div element, but notice how the name of the attribute is different from the argument I passed to the directive method: unordered-list instead of unorderedList. Each uppercase letter in the argument passed to the method is treated as a separate word in the attribute name, where each word is separated by a hyphen.

■ **Tip** I have applied the directive as an attribute in this example, but in Chapter 16 I show you how to create and apply elements that can be used as HTML elements, as values for the class attributes, and even as comments.

I have set the value of the attribute to the name of the array whose objects I want to list, which is products in this case. Directives are intended to be reusable within and across applications, so you avoid creating hardwired dependencies, including references to data created by specific controllers.

Implementing the Link Function

The worker function in the directive I created is called the *link function*, and it provides the means to *link* the directive with the HTML in the document and the data in the scope. (There is another kind of function associated with directives, called the *compile function*, which I describe in Chapter 17.)

The link function is invoked when AngularJS sets up each instance of the directive and receives three arguments: the *scope* for the view in which the directive has been applied, the HTML *element* that the directive has been applied to, and the *attributes* of that HTML element. The convention is to define the link function with arguments called scope, element, and attrs. In the sections that follow, I'll walk through the process of implementing the link function for my example directive.

■ **Tip**   The scope, element, and attrs arguments are regular JavaScript arguments and are not provided via dependency injection. This means the order in which the objects are passed to the link function is fixed.

Getting Data from the Scope

The first step I need to take to implement my custom directive is to get the data I am going to display from the scope. Unlike AngularJS controllers, directives don't declare a dependency on the $scope service; instead, they are passed the scope created by the controller that supports the view in which the directive is applied. This is important because it allows a single directive to be applied multiple times in an application, where each application may be operating on a different scope in the hierarchy (I explained the scope hierarchy in Chapter 13).

In Listing 15-3, I applied my custom directive to a div element as an attribute and used the attribute value to specify the name of the array in the scope that I wanted to process, like this:

```
...
<div unordered-list="products"></div>
...
```

To get the data from the scope, I need first to get the value of the attribute. The third argument to the link function is a collection of attributes, indexed by name. There is no special support for getting the name of the attribute used to apply the directive, which means I use the incantation in Listing 15-4 to get the data from the scope.

Listing 15-4. Getting the Data from the Scope in the directives.html File

```
...
angular.module("exampleApp", [])
    .directive("unorderedList", function () {
        return function (scope, element, attrs) {
            var data = scope[attrs["unorderedList"]];
            if (angular.isArray(data)) {
                for (var i = 0; i < data.length; i++) {
                    console.log("Item: " + data[i].name);
                }
            }
        }
    })
...
```

I get the value associated with the unorderedList key from the attrs collection and then pass the result to the scope object to get the data, like this:

```
...
var data = scope[attrs["unorderedList"]];
...
```

■ **Tip**   Notice that I use unorderedList to get the value of the unordered-list attribute. AngularJS automatically maps between the two naming formats. The form unorderedList is an example of a *normalized name* and is used because of the different ways in which directives can be applied to HTML.

Once I get the data, I use the angular.isArray method to check that I really am working with an array and then use a for loop to write the name property of each object to the console. (This would be a poor design in a real project because it assumes that all of the objects that the directive will process have a name attribute, which hampers reuse. I'll show you how to be more flexible in the "Evaluating Expressions" section.) If you load the directives.html file into the browser, you'll see the following output in the JavaScript console:

```
Item: Apples
Item: Bananas
Item: Pears
```

Generating the HTML Elements

The next step is to generate the elements I need from the data objects. AngularJS includes a cut-down version of jQuery called *jqLite*. It doesn't have all of the features of jQuery, but it has sufficient functionality for working with directives. I describe jqLite in detail in the "Working with jqLite" section later in the chapter, but for now I am just going to show you the changes I need to make for my custom directive, as shown in Listing 15-5.

Listing 15-5.   Generating Elements in a Custom Directive in the directives.html File

```
...
angular.module("exampleApp", [])
    .directive("unorderedList", function () {
        return function (scope, element, attrs) {
            var data = scope[attrs["unorderedList"]];
            if (angular.isArray(data)) {
                var listElem = angular.element("<ul>");
                element.append(listElem);
                for (var i = 0; i < data.length; i++) {
                    listElem.append(angular.element('<li>').text(data[i].name));
                }
            }
        }
    })
...
```

The jqLite functionality is exposed through the element argument that is passed to the link function. First, I call the angular.element method to create a new element and use the append method on the element argument to insert the new element into the document, like this:

```
...
var listElem = angular.element("<ul>");
element.append(listElem);
...
```

The result from most jqLite methods is another object that provides access to the jqLite functionality, much as the methods in the full jQuery library return jQuery objects. AngularJS doesn't expose the DOM API provided by the browser, and any time you are working with elements, you can expect to receive a jqLite object. I'll refer to the results that jqLite methods return as jqLite objects.

If you don't have a jqLite object but need one—because you want to create a new element, for example—then you can use the angular.element method, like this:

```
...
angular.element('<li>').text(data[i].name)
...
```

Both approaches return jqLite objects, which you can then use to call other jqLite methods, a technique known as *method chaining*. I included an example of method chaining in the example when I create the li elements and then call the text method to set their contents, like this:

```
...
angular.element('<li>').text(data[i].name)
...
```

A library that provides support for method chaining is said to provide a fluent API, and jQuery, from which jqLite is derived, is one of the most widely used fluent APIs.

■ **Tip** You will recognize the purpose and nature of the jqLite methods if you have used jQuery, but don't worry if they don't make sense. I'll introduce jqLite properly in the "Working with jqLite" section shortly.

The result of my jqLite additions is that my custom directive will add an ul element to the element to which it has been applied—the div in this case—and create a nested li element for each object in the data array obtained from the scope, as shown in Figure 15-2.

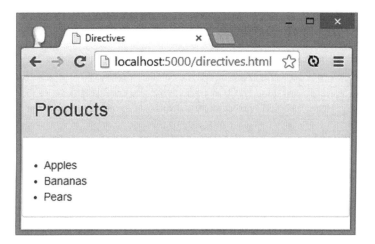

Figure 15-2. *The effect of using jqLite in the custom directive*

Breaking the Data Property Dependency

My custom directive works, but it has a dependency on the objects in the array that it uses to generate list items:
It assumes that they have a name property. This kind of dependency ties the directive to a specific set of data objects
and means that it can't be used elsewhere in the application or in other applications. There are several ways that I can
address this, which I describe in the following sections.

Adding a Support Attribute

The first approach is the simplest and requires defining an attribute that specifies the property whose values will be
displayed in the li items. This is easy to do, because the link function is passed a collection of all the attributes that
have been defined on the element to which the directive has been applied. In Listing 15-6, you can see how I have
added support for a list-property attribute.

Listing 15-6. Adding Support for a Directive Attribute in the directives.html File

```
<html ng-app="exampleApp">
<head>
    <title>Directives</title>
    <script src="angular.js"></script>
    <link href="bootstrap.css" rel="stylesheet" />
    <link href="bootstrap-theme.css" rel="stylesheet" />
    <script>
        angular.module("exampleApp", [])
            .directive("unorderedList", function () {
                return function (scope, element, attrs) {
                    var data = scope[attrs["unorderedList"]];
                    var propertyName = attrs["listProperty"];
                    if (angular.isArray(data)) {
                        var listElem = angular.element("<ul>");
                        element.append(listElem);
```

```
                    for (var i = 0; i < data.length; i++) {
                        listElem.append(angular.element('<li>')
                            .text(data[i][propertyName]));
                    }
                }
            }
        })
        .controller("defaultCtrl", function ($scope) {
            $scope.products = [
                { name: "Apples", category: "Fruit", price: 1.20, expiry: 10 },
                { name: "Bananas", category: "Fruit", price: 2.42, expiry: 7 },
                { name: "Pears", category: "Fruit", price: 2.02, expiry: 6 }
            ];
        })
    </script>
</head>
<body ng-controller="defaultCtrl">
    <div class="panel panel-default">
        <div class="panel-heading">
            <h3>Products</h3>
        </div>
        <div class="panel-body">
            <div unordered-list="products" list-property="name"></div>
        </div>
    </div>
</body>
</html>
```

I obtain the value of the list-property attribute through the attrs argument to the link function, using the key listProperty. Once again, AngularJS has normalized the attribute name. I use the value of the listProperty attribute to obtain a value from each of the data objects, like this:

```
...
listElem.append(angular.element('<li>').text(data[i][propertyName]));
...
```

■ **Tip**   If you prefix your property name with data-, then AngularJS will remove the prefix when it builds the set of attributes passed to the link function. This means, for example, that an attribute of data-list-property and list-property will both be presented as listProperty when the name is normalized and passed to the link function.

Evaluating Expressions

Adding another attribute has helped, but I still have some problems. For example, consider the effect of the change in Listing 15-7, in which I apply a filter to the property I want to display.

Listing 15-7. Adding a Filter to the Attribute Value in the directives.html File

```
...
<body ng-controller="defaultCtrl">
    <div class="panel panel-default">
        <div class="panel-heading">
            <h3>Products</h3>
        </div>
        <div class="panel-body">
            <div unordered-list="products" list-property="price | currency"></div>
        </div>
    </div>
</body>
...
```

This change breaks my custom directive because I read the value of the attribute and use the value as the name of the property I am going to display in each li element I generate. The solution to this problem is to have the scope evaluate the attribute value as an expression, which is done through the scope.$eval method, the arguments to which are the expression to evaluate and any local data required to perform the evaluation. In Listing 15-8, you can see how I have used $eval to support the kind of expression shown in Listing 15-7.

Listing 15-8. Evaluating Expressions in the directives.html File

```
...
angular.module("exampleApp", [])
    .directive("unorderedList", function () {
        return function (scope, element, attrs) {
            var data = scope[attrs["unorderedList"]];
            var propertyExpression = attrs["listProperty"];

            if (angular.isArray(data)) {
                var listElem = angular.element("<ul>");
                element.append(listElem);
                for (var i = 0; i < data.length; i++) {
                    listElem.append(angular.element('<li>')
                        .text(scope.$eval(propertyExpression, data[i])));
                }
            }
        }
    })
...
```

I obtain the value of the listProperty attribute, which gives me the string that I need to evaluate as an expression. When I create the li elements, I call the $eval method on the scope argument passed to the link function, passing in the expression and the current data object as a source for the properties required to evaluate the expression. AngularJS takes care of the rest, and you can see the effect in Figure 15-3, which illustrates how the li elements contain the value of the price property for each data object, formatted by the currency filter.

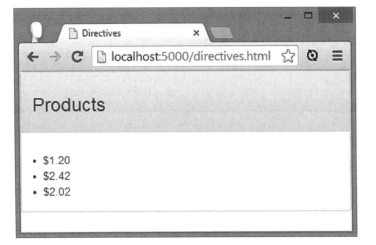

Figure 15-3. Evaluating expressions

Handling Data Changes

The next feature I am going to add to this introductory directive is the ability to respond to data changes in the scope. At the moment, the contents of the li elements are set when the HTML page is processed by AngularJS and don't automatically update when the underlying data values change. In Listing 15-9, you can see the changes that I have made to the directives.html file to change the price properties of the product objects.

■ **Tip**   I am going to break down the process of handling changes because I want to demonstrate a common problem that arises between AngularJS and JavaScript in directives and explain the solution.

Listing 15-9. Changing Values in the directives.html File

```
<html ng-app="exampleApp">
<head>
    <title>Directives</title>
    <script src="angular.js"></script>
    <link href="bootstrap.css" rel="stylesheet" />
    <link href="bootstrap-theme.css" rel="stylesheet" />
    <script>
        angular.module("exampleApp", [])
            .directive("unorderedList", function () {
                return function (scope, element, attrs) {
                    var data = scope[attrs["unorderedList"]];
                    var propertyExpression = attrs["listProperty"];

                    if (angular.isArray(data)) {
                        var listElem = angular.element("<ul>");
                        element.append(listElem);
```

391

```
                    for (var i = 0; i < data.length; i++) {
                        listElem.append(angular.element('<li>')
                            .text(scope.$eval(propertyExpression, data[i])));
                    }
                }
            }
        })
        .controller("defaultCtrl", function ($scope) {
            $scope.products = [
                { name: "Apples", category: "Fruit", price: 1.20, expiry: 10 },
                { name: "Bananas", category: "Fruit", price: 2.42, expiry: 7 },
                { name: "Pears", category: "Fruit", price: 2.02, expiry: 6 }
            ];

            $scope.incrementPrices = function () {
                for (var i = 0; i < $scope.products.length; i++) {
                    $scope.products[i].price++;
                }
            }
        })
    </script>
</head>
<body ng-controller="defaultCtrl">
    <div class="panel panel-default">
        <div class="panel-heading">
            <h3>Products</h3>
        </div>
        <div class="panel-body">
            <button class="btn btn-primary" ng-click="incrementPrices()">
                Change Prices
            </button>
        </div>
        <div class="panel-body">
            <div unordered-list="products" list-property="price | currency"></div>
        </div>
    </div>
</body>
</html>
```

I have added a button and applied the ng-click directive so that the incrementPrices controller behavior is invoked. This behavior is pretty simple; it uses a for loop to enumerate the objects in the products array and increments the value of the price property of each of them. A value of, say, 1.20 will become 2.20 the first time the button is clicked, 3.20 for the second click, and so on.

Adding the Watcher

Directives use the $watch method that I described in Chapter 13 to monitor the scope for changes. The process is more complicated for my custom directive because I am obtaining the expression that is to be evaluated from an attribute value, and as you'll see, that requires an extra preparatory step. In Listing 15-10, you can see the changes I made to the directive to monitor the scope and update the HTML elements when the property values change.

■ **Caution**   The code in this listing doesn't work. I explain why in the next section.

Listing 15-10. Handling Data Changes in the directives.html File

```
...
angular.module("exampleApp", [])
    .directive("unorderedList", function () {
        return function (scope, element, attrs) {
            var data = scope[attrs["unorderedList"]];
            var propertyExpression = attrs["listProperty"];

            if (angular.isArray(data)) {
                var listElem = angular.element("<ul>");
                element.append(listElem);
                for (var i = 0; i < data.length; i++) {
                    var itemElement = angular.element('<li>');
                    listElem.append(itemElement);
                    var watcherFn = function (watchScope) {
                        return watchScope.$eval(propertyExpression, data[i]);
                    }
                    scope.$watch(watcherFn, function (newValue, oldValue) {
                        itemElement.text(newValue);
                    });
                }
            }
        }
    })
...
```

In Chapter 13, I show you how to use the $watch method with a string expression and a handler function. AngularJS evaluated the expression each time that the scope changed and called the handler function when the evaluation produced a different result.

In this case, I am using two functions. The first function—the *watcher function*—calculates a value based on data in the scope and is called by AngularJS each time the scope changes. If the value returned by the function changes, then the handler is called, just as for a string expression.

Being able to provide a function lets me deal with the fact that my expression contains a data value that may be filtered. Here is the watcher function that I defined:

```
...
var watcherFn = function (watchScope) {
    return watchScope.$eval(propertyExpression, data[i]);
}
...
```

The watcher function is passed the scope as an argument each time it is evaluated, and I use the $eval function to evaluate the expression I am working with, passing in one of the data objects as a source of property values. I can then pass this function to the $watch method and specify the callback function, which uses the jqLite text function to update the text content of the li elements to reflect a value change:

```
...
scope.$watch(watcherFn, function (newValue, oldValue) {
    itemElement.text(newValue);
});
...
```

The effect is that the directive monitors the property values that are displayed by the li elements and updates the content of the elements when they change.

■ **Tip**   Notice that I don't have to set the content of the li elements outside of the $watch handler function. AngularJS calls the handler when the directive is first applied; the newValue argument gives the initial evaluation of the expression, and the oldValue argument is undefined.

Fixing the Lexical Scope Problem

If you load the directives.html file into the browser, the directive won't keep the li elements up-to-date. If you look at the HTML elements in the DOM, you will see that the li elements don't contain any content. This is a problem that is so common that I want to demonstrate how to fix it even though it results from a JavaScript, rather than AngularJS, feature. The problem is this statement:

```
...
var watcherFn = function (watchScope) {
    return watchScope.$eval(propertyExpression, data[i]);
}
...
```

JavaScript supports a feature called *closures*, which allows a function to refer to variables outside of its scope. This is a great feature, and it makes writing JavaScript a more pleasant experience. Without closures, you would have to make sure to define arguments for every object and value that your function needed to access.

The point of confusion is that the variable that a function accesses is evaluated when the function is invoked rather than when it is defined. In the case of my watcher function, that means the variable i isn't evaluated until AngularJS calls the function. This means the sequence of events goes like this:

1. AngularJS calls the link function to set up the directive.

2. The for loop starts to enumerate the objects in the products array.

3. The value of i is 0, which corresponds to the first object in the array.

4. The for loop increments i to 1, which corresponds to the second object in the array.

5. The for loop increments i to 2, which corresponds to the third object in the array.

6. The for loop increments i to 3, which is greater than the length of the array.

7. The for loop terminates.

8. AngularJS evaluates the three watcher functions, which refer to data[i].

By the time step 8 happens, the value of i is 3, and this means that all three watcher functions try to access an object in the data array that doesn't exist, and that's why the directive doesn't work.

To address this problem, I need to control the closure feature so that I refer to the data objects using a *fixed* or *bound* variable, which just means that the value assigned to the variable is set during steps 3–5 and not when AngularJS evaluates the watcher function. You can see how I have done this in Listing 15-11.

Listing 15-11. Fixing the Value of a Variable in the directives.html File

```
...
angular.module("exampleApp", [])
    .directive("unorderedList", function () {
        return function (scope, element, attrs) {
            var data = scope[attrs["unorderedList"]];
            var propertyExpression = attrs["listProperty"];

            if (angular.isArray(data)) {
                var listElem = angular.element("<ul>");
                element.append(listElem);
                for (var i = 0; i < data.length; i++) {
                    (function () {
                        var itemElement = angular.element('<li>');
                        listElem.append(itemElement);
                        var index = i;
                        var watcherFn = function (watchScope) {
                            return watchScope.$eval(propertyExpression, data[index]);
                        }
                        scope.$watch(watcherFn, function (newValue, oldValue) {
                            itemElement.text(newValue);
                        });
                    }());
                }
            }
        }
    })
...
```

I have defined an *immediately invoked function expression* (IIFE) inside the for loop, which is a function that is evaluated immediately (and, as a consequence, is often called a self-executing function). Here is the basic structure of an IIFE:

```
...
(function() {
    // ...statements that will be executed go here...
}());
...
```

The IIFE allows me to define a variable called index to which I assign the current value of i. Since the IIFE is executed as soon as it is defined, the value of index won't be updated by the next iteration of the for loop, and this means I can access the right object in the data array from within the watcher function, like this:

```
...
return watchScope.$eval(propertyExpression, data[index]);
...
```

395

The result of adding the IIFE is that the watcher function uses a valid index to get hold of the data object it is working with, and the directive works the way it is supposed to, as shown in Figure 15-4.

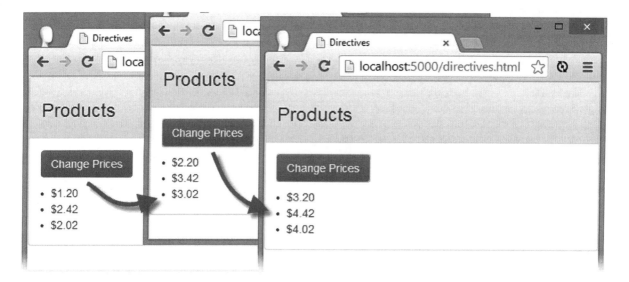

Figure 15-4. *Handling data changes*

Working with jqLite

Now that I have shown you how to create a custom directive, I am going to step back and show you jqLite, which is the cut-down version of jQuery that AngularJS comes with and that is used within directives to create, manipulate, and manage HTML elements. In this part of this chapter, I will describe the methods that jqLite provides and demonstrate the most important.

I don't demonstrate every method that jqLite provides because the implementation of each method corresponds to a jQuery method of the same name. See http://jquery.com for the jQuery API documentation, or see my book *Pro jQuery 2.0*, which is also published by Apress.

Navigating the Document Object Models

The first area that I am going to describe is the jqLite support for locating elements in the Document Object Model (DOM). You usually won't need to navigate around the DOM for simple directives because the link function is passed the element argument, which is the jqLite object that represents the element to which the directive has been applied. You may have to manage a set of elements in more complex directives, and that can require the ability to traverse the element hierarchy to locate and select one or more elements on which to operate. Table 15-3 describes the jqLite methods that deal with DOM navigation.

Table 15-3. *The jqLite Methods for DOM Navigation*

Name	Description
children()	Returns the set of child elements. The jqLite implementation of this method does not support the selectors feature that jQuery provides.
eq(index)	Returns an element at the specified index from a collection of elements.
find(tag)	Locates all of the descendant elements with the specified tag name. The jQuery implementation provides additional options for selecting elements, which are not available in the jqLite implementation of this method.
next()	Gets the next sibling element. The jqLite implementation of this method does not support the selectors feature that jQuery provides.
parent()	Returns the parent element. The jqLite implementation of this method does not support the selectors feature that jQuery provides.

These methods and their descriptions may appear a little odd if you have not used jQuery. The object that AngularJS uses to represent HTML elements, which I will call the jqLite object, can actually represent zero, one, or multiple HTML elements. That's why some of the jqLite methods, such as eq, treat the jqLite object as a collection or—like children—return a collection of elements. To give you a sense of how this works, I have added a new HTML file called jqlite.html to the angularjs folder and used it to define a directive that uses jqLite to perform some simple DOM navigation. You can see the contents of the new file in Listing 15-12.

Listing 15-12. The Contents of the jqlite.html File

```
<html ng-app="exampleApp">
<head>
    <title>Directives</title>
    <script src="angular.js"></script>
    <script>
        angular.module("exampleApp", [])
            .directive("demoDirective", function () {
                return function (scope, element, attrs) {
                    var items = element.children();
                    for (var i = 0; i < items.length; i++) {
                        if (items.eq(i).text() == "Oranges") {
                            items.eq(i).css("font-weight", "bold");
                        }
                    }
                }
            })
            .controller("defaultCtrl", function ($scope) {
                // controller defines no data or behaviors
            })
    </script>
</head>
```

```
<body ng-controller="defaultCtrl">
    <h3>Fruit</h3>
    <ol demo-directive>
        <li>Apples</li>
        <li>Oranges</li>
        <li>Pears</li>
    </ol>
</body>
</html>
```

The directive in this example is called, obviously enough, demoDirective, and it processes the children of the element it is applied to, looking for any element that contains Oranges as its content. This isn't something you often need to do in a real project, but it lets me demonstrate the basics of using jqLite.

The starting point for this—and for all—directives is the element argument that is passed to the link function. The element argument is a jqLite object that supports all of the methods in Table 15-3 and the other sections in this part of the chapter. The element object represents the element to which the directive has been applied. I start by calling the children method, like this:

```
...
var items = element.children();
...
```

The result returned by the children method is another jqLite object, but this one contains all of the child elements defined by the element to which the directive has been applied. Child elements are immediate descendants of an element, which in this example is the set of li elements.

I use a standard for loop to enumerate the elements that the items object contains, using the length property to figure out how many there are. For each element, I use the text method, which returns the text content of an element (as I describe in the "Modifying Elements" section) to look for the term Oranges:

```
...
if (items.eq(i).text() == "Oranges") {
...
```

Notice that I get the element at the current index using the eq method and not by treating the jqLite object as a JavaScript array (i.e., items[i]). The eq method returns a jqLite object that contains the element at the specified index and that supports all of the jqLite methods. Using a JavaScript array index returns an HTMLElement object, which is what the browser uses to represent elements in the DOM. You can work directly with HTMLElement objects if you want, but they don't support the jqLite methods, and the DOM API is pretty verbose and painful to work with compared to jqLite/jQuery.

To complete my explanation of this example, I use the css method (which sets a CSS property directly on an element, as I explain in the "Modifying Elements" section) so that the browser displays the text of the element in bold, like this:

```
...
items.eq(i).css("font-weight", "bold");
...
```

Once again, notice that I access the element I want via the eq method. Figure 15-5 shows the effect of the directive.

Figure 15-5. *Navigating the DOM using jqLite*

Locating Descendants

The children method returns all of the elements that are directly the element or elements represented by the jqLite object. If you want to go further down the hierarchy of elements, then you need to use the find method, which will look for elements of a specified type in the children, the children's children, and so on, through all the descendants of an element. You can see the limitation of the children method if I add some additional elements to the list in the jqlite.html file, as shown in Listing 15-13.

Listing 15-13. Adding Elements to the jqlite.html File

```
...
<ol demo-directive>
    <li>Apples</li>
    <ul>
        <li>Bananas</li>
        <li>Cherries</li>
        <li>Oranges</li>
    </ul>
    <li>Oranges</li>
    <li>Pears</li>
</ol>
...
```

The children method will return the direct descendants of the ol element only, which includes the newly added ul element but excludes the new li elements. You can see the problem this causes in Figure 15-6 where only one of the elements that contains Oranges has been marked in bold.

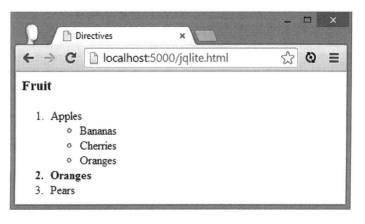

Figure 15-6. *The limitation of the children method*

By contrast, I can use the `find` method to locate all of the `li` elements that are descendants of the `ol` element, including those further down the hierarchy. You can see how I have applied the `find` element in Listing 15-14.

Listing 15-14. Applying the find Element in the jqlite.html File

```
...
angular.module("exampleApp", [])
    .directive("demoDirective", function () {
        return function (scope, element, attrs) {
            var items = element.find("li");
            for (var i = 0; i < items.length; i++) {
                if (items.eq(i).text() == "Oranges") {
                    items.eq(i).css("font-weight", "bold");
                }
            }
        }
    })
...
```

It isn't just that jqLite implements a subset of the methods supported by the full jQuery library; the methods that are supported often have a subset of the features that jQuery provides. This includes the `find` method, which can locate elements based only on their tag name. The full jQuery implementation of the `find` method can locate descendants in a range of flexible ways. In this listing, I have specified that the `find` method should locate all of the `li` elements that are descendants of the `ol` element, and this will include the ones that I added in Listing 15-13. You can see the effect of this change in Figure 15-7.

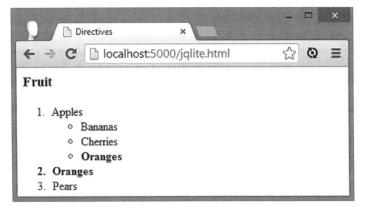

Figure 15-7. *Using the find method*

■ **Caution**   You can use the jqLite methods to navigate anywhere in the DOM, even outside of the element that the directive has been applied to. As tempting as it can be to roam the document, my advice is to stick with the children and descendants of the element passed to the link function because operating on other elements just causes confusion and runs the risk of interfering with the operation of other directives.

Modifying Elements

One of the most common reasons for navigating the DOM in a directive link function is so you can modify one or more elements. jqLite provides a set of methods for modifying the content and attributes of elements, as described in Table 15-4.

Table 15-4. *The jqLite Methods for Modifying Elements*

Name	Description
addClass(name)	Adds all of the elements in the jqLite object to the specified class.
attr(name) attr(name, value)	Gets the value of the specified attribute for the first element in the jqLite object or sets the specified value for all of the elements.
css(name) css(name, value)	Gets the value of the specified CSS property from the first element or sets the property to the specified value for all the elements in the jqLite object.
hasClass(name)	Returns true if *any* of the elements in the jqLite object belong to the specified class.
prop(name) prop(name, value)	Gets the value of the specified property for the first element in the jqLite object or sets the specified value for all of the elements.
removeAttr(name)	Removes the attribute from all of the elements in the jqLite object.
removeClass(name)	Removes the elements in the jqLite object from the specified class.

(*continued*)

Table 15-4. (*continued*)

Name	Description
text() text(value)	Gets the concatenated text content from all the elements or sets the text content for all the elements in the jqLite object.
toggleClass(name)	Toggles membership of the specified class for all the elements in the jqLite object. Those elements that were not in the class will be added to it, and those that were in the class will be removed from it.
val() val(value)	Gets the value attribute for the first element or sets the value attribute for all the elements in the jqLite object.

Some of these methods come in two forms, and you can use them to get a value or set a value. The form of the method with the fewest arguments will get a value from the first element represented by the jqLite object. So, for example, if you call the css method with one argument, you will receive the value of the property you specified from the first element in the jqLite object—all of the other elements will be ignored. As a demonstration, I have called the css method on the jqLite object returned by the find method in the example directive in the jqlite.html file, as shown in Listing 15-15.

Listing 15-15. Calling the get Version of a jqLite Method in the jqlite.html File

```
...
angular.module("exampleApp", [])
    .directive("demoDirective", function () {
        return function (scope, element, attrs) {
            var items = element.find("li");

            for (var i = 0; i < items.length; i++) {
                if (items.eq(i).text() == "Oranges") {
                    items.eq(i).css("font-weight", "bold");
                } else {
                    items.eq(i).css("font-weight", "normal");
                }
            }
            console.log("Element count: " + items.length);
            console.log("Font: " + items.css("font-weight"));
        }
    })
...
```

■ **Tip** An exception to this pattern is the text method, which, when called without arguments, returns a string that concatenates the text content of *all* the elements represented by the jqLite object and not just the first one.

I have written the number of elements represented by the `item` object and the result of calling the `css` method with one argument to the JavaScript console. I specified the `font-weight` property, which produced the following result:

```
...
Element count: 6
Font: normal
...
```

The result displays the font weight of the first element only, which is `normal` in this example. By contrast, when you use the method to set a value, it applies to all of the elements that the `jqLite` object represents. You can see a demonstration of this in Listing 15-16, where I have used the `css` method to set the CSS `color` property.

Listing 15-16. Calling the set Version of a jqLite Method in the jqlite.html File

```
...
angular.module("exampleApp", [])
    .directive("demoDirective", function () {
        return function (scope, element, attrs) {
            var items = element.find("li");

            items.css("color", "red");

            for (var i = 0; i < items.length; i++) {
                if (items.eq(i).text() == "Oranges") {
                    items.eq(i).css("font-weight", "bold");
                }
            }
        }
    })
...
```

This has the effect of changing the `color` property for all the `li` elements that are descendants of the directive element, as shown in Figure 15-8.

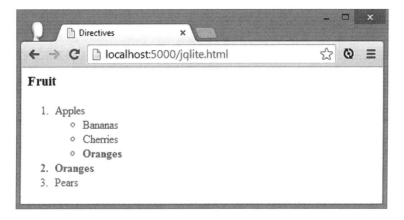

Figure 15-8. *Setting values for a CSS property*

■ **Tip** If you want to target specific elements, then use the DOM navigation methods, described in Table 15-3, to create a jqLite object that represents just the elements you want to modify.

ATTRIBUTES VERSUS PROPERTIES

In Table 15-4, you will see that the attr and removeAttr methods deal with attributes while the prop method operates on properties—a difference that is not always understood. The difference is that the prop method deals with properties defined by the DOM API HTMLElement object, rather than attributes defined by the HTML element in markup. Often, the attributes and properties are the same, but this isn't always the case. A simple example is the class attribute, which is represented in the HTMLElement object using the className property.

In general, the prop method is the one you should use because it returns objects that are easier to work with than attribute values. These objects are defined by the DOM API, which is detailed at www.w3.org/TR/html5.

Creating and Removing Elements

You won't always want to locate and modify existing elements in your directive, of course. You will often want to create new content or remove outdated content from the DOM. In Table 15-5, I have described the methods that jqLite provides for creating and removing elements.

Table 15-5. *The jqLite Methods for Creating and Removing Elements*

Name	Description
angular.element(html)	Creates a jqLite object that represents the element specified by the HTML string
after(elements)	Inserts the specified content after the element on which the method is called
append(elements)	Inserts the specified elements as the last child of each element in the jqLite object on which the method has been called
clone()	Returns a new jqLite object that duplicates the elements from the object on which the method is called
prepend(elements)	Inserts the specified elements as the first child of each element in the jqLite object on which the method has been called
remove()	Removes the elements in the jqLite object from the DOM
replaceWith(elements)	Replaces the elements in the jqLite object on which the method is called with the specified elements
wrap(elements)	Wraps each element in the jqLite object with the specified elements

Those methods that receive elements as argument can process jqLite objects or fragments of HTML, which makes it easy to create new content dynamically. The angular.element method bridges the gap between these two approaches and takes an HTML fragment or an HTMLElement object from the DOM and packages it as a jqLite object.

The main issue to watch out for here is that the jQuery fluent API means that many of the methods return a jqLite object containing the original set of elements that were in the jqLite object on which the method was called and not those in the argument. I know that sentence is hard to parse, so I'll demonstrate the trap that awaits the unwary. In Listing 15-17, you can see that I have updated the jqlite.html file so that the example directive generates a set of list elements.

Listing 15-17. Generating List Elements in the jqlite.html File

```
<html ng-app="exampleApp">
<head>
    <title>Directives</title>
    <script src="angular.js"></script>
    <script>
    angular.module("exampleApp", [])
        .directive("demoDirective", function () {
            return function (scope, element, attrs) {
                var listElem = element.append("<ol>");
                for (var i = 0; i < scope.names.length; i++) {
                    listElem.append("<li>").append("<span>").text(scope.names[i]);
                }
            }
        })
        .controller("defaultCtrl", function ($scope) {
            $scope.names = ["Apples", "Bananas", "Oranges"];
        })
    </script>
</head>
<body ng-controller="defaultCtrl">
    <h3>Fruit</h3>
    <div demo-directive></div>
</body>
</html>
```

I have changed the element to which the directive is applied to a div, updated the controller so that it defines a data array in the scope, and revised the directive link function so that it uses jqLite to create an ol element that contains a set of li elements, each of which contains a span element that, in turn, contains a value from the array. The set of elements I want to generate looks like this:

```
...
<div demo-directive="">Oranges</div>
    <ol>
        <li><span>Apples</span></li>
        <li><span>Bananas</span></li>
        <li><span>Oranges</span></li>
    </ol>
</div>
...
```

This isn't what the example really produces, however, and you can see the real outcome in Figure 15-9.

Figure 15-9. *Trying (and failing) to generate a set of list items*

Using the F12 tools to look at the HTML elements in the DOM shows that the HTML I generated looks like this:

```
...
<div demo-directive="">Oranges</div>Oranges</div>
...
```

What went wrong? The answer is that I am operating on the wrong elements in the DOM, right from the start. Here is the first jqLite operation in the example:

```
...
var listElem = element.append("<ol>");
...
```

I append an ol element as a child of the element argument passed to the link function, which represents the div element. The problem is signaled in the name I use in the variable to which I assign the result of the append operation: listElem. In fact, the append method—like all the methods that take element arguments in Table 15-5—returns a jqLite object representing the elements on which the operation was performed, which is, in this example, the div element and *not* the ol element. That means the other jqLite statement in the example has an unexpected effect:

```
...
listElem.append("<li>").append("<span>").text(scope.names[i]);
...
```

There are three operations in this statement—two calls to the append method and a call to the text method—and all of these operations are being applied to the div element. First, I add a new li element as a child of the div element; then, I add a span element. Finally, I call the text method, which has the effect of replacing all the child elements I added to the div with a text string, and since I am performing these operations in a for loop, I repeat them for each value in the array. This is why the div element ends up containing Oranges; it is the last value in the array.

This is an incredibly common mistake to make, even for developers experienced in jQuery. I do it all the time, including when I sketched out the custom directive that I started the chapter with. You must keep an eye on which set of elements you are performing operations on—something that jqLite makes harder than jQuery by omitting some methods that are helpful in keeping track of what's going on.

I find that the most reliable way of avoiding this problem is to use the angular.element method to create jqLite objects and perform operations on them in separate statements. You can see how I have done this in Listing 15-18, in which I demonstrate how to properly generate the list elements.

Listing 15-18. Fixing the Problem in the jqlite.html File

```
...
angular.module("exampleApp", [])
    .directive("demoDirective", function () {
        return function (scope, element, attrs) {
            var listElem = angular.element("<ol>");
            element.append(listElem);
            for (var i = 0; i < scope.names.length; i++) {
                listElem.append(angular.element("<li>")
                    .append(angular.element("<span>").text(scope.names[i])));
            }
        }
    })
...
```

The effect is the hierarchy of ol, li, and span elements that I described at the start of this section, as shown by Figure 15-10.

Figure 15-10. *Correctly creating a set of elements using jqLite*

Handling Events

jqLite includes support for handling events emitted by elements, using the methods described in Table 15-6. These are the same methods that built-in event directives (described in Chapter 11) use to receive and handle events.

Table 15-6. *The jqLite Methods for Handling Events*

Name	Description
on(events, handler)	Registers a handler for one or more events emitted by the elements represented by the jqLite object. The jqLite implementation of this method does not support the selectors or event data features that jQuery provides.
off(events, handler)	Removes a previously registered handler for the specified events from the elements represented by the jqLite object. The jqLite implementation of this method does not support the selectors feature that jQuery provides.
triggerHandler(event)	Triggers all of the handlers for the specified event registered on the elements represented by the jqLite object.

In Listing 15-19, you can see how I have added a button element to the markup in the jqlite.html file and use the on method to set up a handler function that is invoked when the element emits the click event.

Listing 15-19. Adding an Event Handler in the jqlite.html File

```
<html ng-app="exampleApp">
<head>
    <title>Directives</title>
    <script src="angular.js"></script>
    <style>
        .bold { font-weight: bold; }
    </style>
    <script>
        angular.module("exampleApp", [])
            .directive("demoDirective", function () {
                return function (scope, element, attrs) {
                    var listElem = angular.element("<ol>");
                    element.append(listElem);
                    for (var i = 0; i < scope.names.length; i++) {
                        listElem.append(angular.element("<li>")
                            .append(angular.element("<span>").text(scope.names[i])));
                    }
                    var buttons = element.find("button");
                    buttons.on("click", function (e) {
                        element.find("li").toggleClass("bold");
                    });
                }
            })
            .controller("defaultCtrl", function ($scope) {
                    $scope.names = ["Apples", "Bananas", "Oranges"];
                })
    </script>
</head>
<body ng-controller="defaultCtrl">
    <h3>Fruit</h3>
    <div demo-directive>
        <button>Click Me</button>
    </div>
</body>
</html>
```

Within the directive link function, I use the find method to locate all the button elements that are descendants of the element to which the directive has been applied. I call the on method on the jqLite object that I receive from the find method to register a function as a handler for the click event.

When invoked, the handler function locates the descendant li elements and uses the toggleClass method to add and remove them from the bold class, which corresponds to the simple CSS style I added to the document. The effect is that clicking the button switches the list items between regular and bold text, as shown in Figure 15-11.

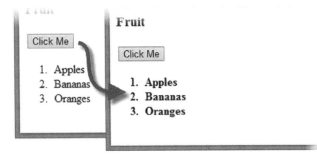

Figure 15-11. *Handling an event*

Other jqLite Methods

There are a few other jQuery methods that jqLite provides that don't fit into the other categories, and I describe them in Table 15-7. I have listed these methods for completeness, but I do not demonstrate them because they are not widely used in AngularJS directives; see my *Pro jQuery 2.0* book for details.

Table 15-7. *Other jqLite Methods*

Name	Description
data(key, value) data(key)	Associates arbitrary data with all the elements or retrieves a value for the specified key from the first element represented by the jqLite object
removeData(key)	Removes data associated with the specified key from the elements represented by the jqLite object
html()	Returns an HTML representation of the content of the first element represented by the jqLite object
ready(handler)	Registers a handler function that will be invoked once the contents of the DOM are fully loaded

Accessing AngularJS Features from jqLite

In addition to the jQuery methods that I described in previous sections, jqLite offers some extra methods that provide access to features that are specific to AngularJS. Table 15-8 describes these methods.

Table 15-8. *jqLite Methods That Access AngularJS Features*

Name	Description
controller() controller(name)	Returns the controller associated with the current element or its parent. See Chapter 17 for details of how controllers and directives can interact.
injector()	Returns the injector associated with the current element or its parent. I describe injectors in Chapter 24.
isolatedScope()	Returns an isolated scope if there is one associated with the current element. I describe isolated scopes in Chapter 16.
scope()	Returns the scope associated with the current element or its parent. See Chapter 16 for details of how directives can manage scopes.
inheritedData(key)	This method performs the same function as the jQuery data method but will walk up the element hierarchy looking for a value to match the specified key.

■ **Note**   You won't need to use these methods in most projects. I have listed them here for completeness, but they are rarely required.

Replacing jqLite with jQuery

jqLite implements only some of the methods that the full jQuery library provides, and some of those methods—as I noted in the tables in earlier sections—don't offer all of the options that jQuery programmers are used to.

The emphasis of jqLite is on speed, simplicity, and size, and once you get used to the limited set of methods available, you will find that you can achieve everything you need to do in a directive, even if the result is less elegant than it would be with the full range of jQuery methods and features available. Consider that all of the built-in AngularJS directives are built using jqLite, and you will understand that all of the essential features are available.

If, however, you really can't stand to work with jqLite, then you can replace it with the full jQuery library. In Listing 15-20, you can see how I have done this in the `directives.html` file and used some of the jQuery methods that are not available in jqLite to simplify the custom directive.

■ **Tip**   If you use the full jQuery library, you will require browsers to download and process a second JavaScript file, and any application that reuses your directive will also be dependent on jQuery. My advice is to spend some time getting used to jqLite and see whether you really need to make the switch to jQuery.

Listing 15-20. Replacing jqLite with jQuery in the directives.html File

```
...
<head>
    <title>Directives</title>
    <script src="http://code.jquery.com/jquery-1.10.1.min.js"></script>
    <script src="angular.js"></script>
    <link href="bootstrap.css" rel="stylesheet" />
    <link href="bootstrap-theme.css" rel="stylesheet" />
    <script>
        angular.module("exampleApp", [])
            .directive("unorderedList", function () {
                return function (scope, element, attrs) {
                    var data = scope[attrs["unorderedList"]];
                    var propertyExpression = attrs["listProperty"];
                    if (angular.isArray(data)) {
                        var listElem = angular.element("<ul>").appendTo(element);
                        for (var i = 0; i < data.length; i++) {
                            (function () {
                                var itemElement =
                                    angular.element("<li>").appendTo(listElem);
                                var index = i;
                                var watcherFn = function (watchScope) {
                                    return watchScope.$eval(propertyExpression,
                                        data[index]);
                                }
```

```
                        scope.$watch(watcherFn, function (newValue, oldValue) {
                            itemElement.text(newValue);
                        });
                    }());
                }
            }
        }
    }).controller("defaultCtrl", function ($scope) {
        $scope.products = [
            { name: "Apples", category: "Fruit", price: 1.20, expiry: 10 },
            { name: "Bananas", category: "Fruit", price: 2.42, expiry: 7 },
            { name: "Pears", category: "Fruit", price: 2.02, expiry: 6 }
        ];

        $scope.incrementPrices = function () {
            for (var i = 0; i < $scope.products.length; i++) {
                $scope.products[i].price++;
            }
        }
    })
    </script>
</head>
...
```

I have added a script element that loads the jQuery library file from a content delivery network (CDN), which means that I can demonstrate the effect without having to add any files to the angularjs folder. First, notice that the jQuery script element appears *before* the one for AngularJS. AngularJS checks to see whether jQuery has been loaded before installing jqLite and so the script elements must appear in this order. If you don't add jQuery until after AngularJS, then jqLite will be used.

The method that I miss most of all when working with jqLite is appendTo, which is one of the ways that I avoid the problems I described in the "Creating and Removing Elements" section. This method lets me create some new elements, add them to the document, and then call other jQuery methods to modify the new elements. I find the effect helpful, and it lets me replace multiple jqLite statements like this:

```
...
var itemElement = angular.element('<li>');
listElem.append(itemElement);
...
```

with a single jQuery statement like this one:

```
...
var listElem = angular.element("<ul>").appendTo(element);
...
```

■ **Tip** As much as I rely on this method when working with jQuery, I rarely replace jqLite with jQuery in my own AngularJS projects. I have learned to adjust to the limitations of jqLite, and I recommend you try to do the same.

411

Summary

In this chapter, I showed you the techniques required for creating basic custom directives. I showed you how to use the `directive` method to define a new directive and define its link function and how a directive can be used to process expressions and observe the scope for changes. I also described jqLite, which is the cut-down version of jQuery that is included with AngularJS for use in directives and which can be replaced with jQuery if required (although I encouraged you to try to get used to jqLite first to reduce the amount of JavaScript your application requires and to ease the reuse of directives). In the next chapter, I show you some more advanced techniques that you can use to create more sophisticated directives.

CHAPTER 16

■ ■ ■

Creating Complex Directives

In the previous chapter, I showed you the techniques required to create a custom directive, including using jqLite to manipulate and manage HTML elements. In this chapter, I am going to show you techniques that let you take more control over how your custom directives work. You won't always need these techniques (the basic ones I showed you in Chapter 15 cover a surprisingly wide range of situations), but if you require something more complex or sophisticated, then they become invaluable and are complemented by the truly advanced techniques I describe in Chapter 17. Table 16-1 summarizes this chapter.

Table 16-1. *Chapter Summary*

Problem	Solution	Listing
Define a complex directive.	Return a definition object from the directive factory function.	1
Specify how the directive can be applied.	Set the restrict property	2–6
Express the directive content as HTML (rather than using jqLite).	Set the template property.	7–8
Use an external template file.	Set the templateUrl property.	9–12
Specify whether the template contents replace the element to which the directive has been applied.	Set the replace property.	13–15
Create a separate scope for each instance of a directive.	Set the scope property to true.	16–19
Prevent the scope created for a directive from inheriting objects and properties from the parent scope.	Create an isolated scope.	20
Create a one-way binding in an isolated scope.	Add a property to the scope object whose value is prefixed with @.	21–22
Create a two-way binding in an isolated scope.	Add a property to the scope object whose value is prefixed with =.	23
Evaluate an expression in the context of a parent scope.	Add a property to the scope object whose value is prefixed with &.	24

Preparing the Example Project

For this chapter, I am going to continue working on the unorderedList directive that I created in Chapter 15. Before I start, I am going to return the directive to a more basic state and remove the dependency on the full jQuery library, as shown in Listing 16-1.

Listing 16-1. Preparing the directives.html File

```html
<html ng-app="exampleApp">
<head>
    <title>Directives</title>
    <script src="angular.js"></script>
    <link href="bootstrap.css" rel="stylesheet" />
    <link href="bootstrap-theme.css" rel="stylesheet" />
    <script>
        angular.module("exampleApp", [])
            .directive("unorderedList", function () {
                return function (scope, element, attrs) {
                    var data = scope[attrs["unorderedList"]];
                    var propertyExpression = attrs["listProperty"];
                    if (angular.isArray(data)) {
                        var listElem = angular.element("<ul>");
                        element.append(listElem);
                        for (var i = 0; i < data.length; i++) {
                            var itemElement = angular.element("<li>")
                                .text(scope.$eval(propertyExpression, data[i]));
                            listElem.append(itemElement);
                        }
                    }
                }
            }).controller("defaultCtrl", function ($scope) {
                $scope.products = [
                    { name: "Apples", category: "Fruit", price: 1.20, expiry: 10 },
                    { name: "Bananas", category: "Fruit", price: 2.42, expiry: 7 },
                    { name: "Pears", category: "Fruit", price: 2.02, expiry: 6 }
                ];
            })
    </script>
</head>
<body ng-controller="defaultCtrl">
    <div class="panel panel-default">
        <div class="panel-heading">
            <h3>Products</h3>
        </div>
        <div class="panel-body">
            <div unordered-list="products" list-property="price | currency"></div>
        </div>
    </div>
</body>
</html>
```

Defining Complex Directives

In Chapter 16, I showed you how to create custom directives by using a factory function that returns a *link function*. This is the simplest approach, but it means that defaults are used for many of the options that directives can define. To customize those options, the factory function must return a *definition object*, which is a JavaScript object that defines some or all of the properties described in Table 16-2. In the sections that follow, I show you how to apply some of these properties to take control of the way your custom directives are used; the others I describe in Chapter 17.

Table 16-2. *The Properties Defined by Directive Definition Objects*

Name	Description
compile	Specifies a compile function. See Chapter 17.
controller	Creates a controller function for the directive. See Chapter 17.
link	Specifies the link function for the directive. See the "Defining How the Directive Can Be Applied" section in this chapter.
replace	Specifies whether the contents of the template replace the element that the directive has been applied to. See the "Replacing the Element" section in this chapter.
require	Declares a dependency on a controller. See Chapter 17.
restrict	Specifies how the directive can be applied. See the "Defining How the Directive Can Be Applied" section in this chapter.
scope	Creates a new scope or an isolated scope for the directive. See the "Managing Directive Scopes" section in this chapter.
template	Specifies a template that will be inserted into the HTML document. See the "Using Template Directives" section in this chapter.
templateUrl	Specifies an external template that will be inserted into the HTML document. See the "Using Template Directives" section in this chapter.
transclude	Specifies whether the directive will be used to wrap arbitrary content. See Chapter 17.

Defining How the Directive Can Be Applied

When you return just a link function, you create a directive that can be applied only as an attribute. This is how most AngularJS directives are applied, but you can use the restrict property to change the default and create directives that can be applied in different ways. In Listing 16-2, you can see how I have updated the unorderedList directive so that it is defined with a definition object and uses the restrict property.

Listing 16-2. Setting the restrict Option in the directives.html File

```
...
<script>
    angular.module("exampleApp", [])
        .directive("unorderedList", function () {
            return {
                link: function (scope, element, attrs) {
                    var data = scope[attrs["unorderedList"] || attrs["listSource"]];
                    var propertyExpression = attrs["listProperty"] || "price | currency";
                    if (angular.isArray(data)) {
                        var listElem = angular.element("<ul>");
                        if (element[0].nodeName == "#comment") {
                            element.parent().append(listElem);
                        } else {
                            element.append(listElem);
                        }
```

```
                    for (var i = 0; i < data.length; i++) {
                        var itemElement = angular.element("<li>")
                            .text(scope.$eval(propertyExpression, data[i]));
                        listElem.append(itemElement);
                    }
                }
            },
            restrict: "EACM"
        }
    }).controller("defaultCtrl", function ($scope) {
        $scope.products = [
            { name: "Apples", category: "Fruit", price: 1.20, expiry: 10 },
            { name: "Bananas", category: "Fruit", price: 2.42, expiry: 7 },
            { name: "Pears", category: "Fruit", price: 2.02, expiry: 6 }
        ];
    })
</script>
...
```

LINK VS. COMPILE FUNCTIONS

Strictly speaking, you should use a compile function, specified by the compile definition property, only to modify the DOM and use the link function only to perform tasks such as creating watchers and setting up event handlers. The compile/link separation can improve performance for directives that are especially complex or deal with large amounts of data, but I tend to put everything in the link function in my own projects and suggest that you do the same. I use compile functions only for creating functionality similar to the ng-repeat directive, which I demonstrate in Chapter 17.

I have changed the factory function method so that it returns an object, which is my definition object, rather than just the link function. I still need a link function for my directive, of course, so I assign the function to the link property of the definition object, as described in Table 16-2. The next change is to add the restrict property to the definition object. This tells AngularJS which of the four ways that I want to allow my custom directive to be used, with each kind of use represented by one of the letters described in Table 16-3.

Table 16-3. *The Letters That Configure the restrict Definition Option*

Letter	Description
E	Allows the directive to be applied as an element
A	Allows the directive to be applied as an attribute
C	Allows the directive to be applied as a class
M	Allows the directive to be applied as a comment

I specified all four letters in Listing 16-2, which means that my custom directive can be applied in all four ways: as an element, as an attribute, as a class, and as a comment. You can see the directive applied in all four ways in the sections that follow.

■ **Tip**   It is rare that a directive in a real project would be applicable in all four ways. The most common values for the `restrict` definition property are `A` (the directive can be applied only as an attribute), `E` (the directive can be applied only as an element), or `AE` (the directive can be applied as an element or an attribute). As I explain in the following sections, the `C` and `M` options are rarely used.

Applying the Directive as an Element

The AngularJS convention is to use elements for directives that manage a template through the `template` and `templateUrl` definition properties and that I describe in the "Using Directive Templates" section. That's just a convention, however, and you can apply any custom directive as an element by including the letter E in the value for the `restrict` definition property. In Listing 16-3, you can see how I have applied my example directive as an element.

Listing 16-3. Applying a Directive as an Element in the directives.html File

```
...
<div class="panel-body">
    <unordered-list list-source="products" list-property="price | currency" />
</div>
...
```

I apply the directive as an `unordered-list` element, which I configure using attributes. This requires me to make a change to the link function for the directive because the source of the data has to be defined with a new attribute. I have selected the name `list-source` for the new attribute, and you can see how I check for the value of the attribute if there is no `unordered-list` attribute value available:

```
...
var data = scope[attrs["unorderedList"] || attrs["listSource"]];
...
```

Applying the Directive as an Attribute

The AngularJS convention is to apply most directives as attributes, which is why this is the approach that I demonstrated in Chapter 15. But for completeness, Listing 16-4 shows how I apply the custom directive as an attribute.

Listing 16-4. Applying a Directive as an Attribute in the directives.html File

```
...
<div class="panel-body">
    <div unordered-list="products" list-property="price | currency"></div>
</div>
...
```

No changes were needed to the link function to support applying the directive in this way, of course, since I wrote the original code with this approach in mind.

Applying the Directive as a Class Attribute Value

Wherever possible, you should apply directives as elements or attributes, not least because these approaches make it easy to see where the directives have been applied. You can, however, also apply directives as the value for the class attribute, which can be helpful when you are trying to integrate AngularJS into HTML that is generated by an application that can't easily be changed. Listing 16-5 shows how I applied the directive using the class attribute.

Listing 16-5. Applying a Directive as a class Attribute Value in the directives.html File

```
...
<div class="panel-body">
    <div class="unordered-list: products" list-property="price | currency"></div>
</div>
...
```

I set the value of the class attribute to the directive name. I want to supply a configuration value for the directive, so I follow the name with a colon (the : character) and the value. AngularJS will present this information as though there were an unordered-list attribute on the element, just as though I had applied the directive as an attribute.

I have cheated slightly in this example and defined a list-property attribute on the element to which the directive has been applied. Of course, if I were able to do that in a real project, then I wouldn't need to apply the directive through the class attribute in the first place. In a real project, I would have to do something like this:

```
...
<div class="panel-body">
    <div class="unordered-list: products, price | currency"></div>
</div>
...
```

This would cause AngularJS to provide the directive link function with a value for the unorderedList attribute of "products, price | currency", and I would then be responsible for parsing the value in the link function. I have skipped over this because I want to remain focused on AngularJS, rather than on JavaScript string parsing for a feature that I recommend you avoid when possible.

Applying the Directive as a Comment

The final option is to apply the directive as an HTML comment. This is the last resort, and you should try to use one of the other options whenever possible. Using comments to apply a directive makes it harder for other developers to read the HTML, who won't be expecting comments to have an effect on application functionality. It can also cause problems with build tools that strip out comments to reduce file size for deployment. In Listing 16-6, you can see how I applied the custom directive as a comment.

Listing 16-6. Applying a Directive as a Comment in the directives.html File

```
...
<div class="panel-body">
    <!-- directive: unordered-list products -->
</div>
...
```

The comment must start with the word `directive`, followed by a colon, the name of the directive, and an optional configuration argument. Just as in the previous section, I don't want to get sucked into the world of string parsing, so I have used the optional argument to specify the source of the data and updated the link function to set a default for the property expression, like this:

```
...
var propertyExpression = attrs["listProperty"] || "price | currency";
...
```

I had to change the way that the link function operates to support the comment approach. For the other approaches, I add the content to the element that the directive has been applied to, but that won't work for a comment. Instead, I use jqLite to locate and operate on the parent of comment elements, like this:

```
...
if (element[0].nodeName == "#comment") {
    element.parent().append(listElem);
} else {
    element.append(listElem);
}
...
```

This code is a bit of a hack and relies on the fact that jQuery/jqLite objects are presented as an array of HTMLElement objects, which are the browser's DOM representations of HTML elements. I get the first element in the jqLite object using an array index of zero and call the nodeName property, which tells me what kind of element the directive has been applied to. If it is a comment, then I use the jqLite parent method to get the element that contains the comment and add my ul element to it. This is a pretty ugly approach and is another reason why using comments to apply directives should be avoided.

Using Directive Templates

So far, my custom directive has been generating elements using jqLite or jQuery. This works, but it is essentially an imperative approach to generating declarative content, and for complex projects this mismatch of approaches becomes apparent in complex blocks of jqLite statements that can be hard to read and maintain.

An alternative approach is to generate content from an HTML template, which is used to replace the content of the element to which the directive is applied. In Listing 16-7, you can see how I have created a simple template using the `template` definition property.

Listing 16-7. Using a Template to Generate Content in the directives.html File

```
<html ng-app="exampleApp">
<head>
    <title>Directives</title>
    <script src="angular.js"></script>
    <link href="bootstrap.css" rel="stylesheet" />
    <link href="bootstrap-theme.css" rel="stylesheet" />
    <script>
        angular.module("exampleApp", [])
            .directive("unorderedList", function () {
                return {
```

```
                    link: function (scope, element, attrs) {
                        scope.data = scope[attrs["unorderedList"]];
                    },
                    restrict: "A",
                    template: "<ul><li ng-repeat='item in data'>"
                        + "{{item.price | currency}}</li></ul>"
                }
            }).controller("defaultCtrl", function ($scope) {
                $scope.products = [
                    { name: "Apples", category: "Fruit", price: 1.20, expiry: 10 },
                    { name: "Bananas", category: "Fruit", price: 2.42, expiry: 7 },
                    { name: "Pears", category: "Fruit", price: 2.02, expiry: 6 }
                ];
            })
    </script>
</head>
<body ng-controller="defaultCtrl">
    <div class="panel panel-default">
        <div class="panel-heading">
            <h3>Products</h3>
        </div>
        <div class="panel-body">
            <div unordered-list="products">
                This is where the list will go
            </div>
        </div>
    </div>
</body>
</html>
```

The result is a simpler directive. Using code to generate HTML statements in any language can be verbose, even when using a library as tightly focused as jQuery/jqLite. There are two areas of change in the listing. The first is that I create a scope property called data and use it to set the source of the data, which I get from the directive attribute. (To keep the example simple, I changed the restrict definition property to A so that the directive can be applied only as an attribute, which means that I don't have to check different attribute names to find the source of the data.)

That's all I have to do in the link function, which is no longer responsible for generating the HTML elements used to present the data to the user. Instead, I have used the template definition property to specify a fragment of HTML that will be used as the content of the element to which the directive has been applied, like this:

```
...
template: "<ul><li ng-repeat='item in data'>{{item.price | currency}}</li></ul>"
...
```

I concatenated two strings together to create the template in the listing, but that was just so that I could fit the code on the printed page. My HTML fragment consists of an ul element and an li element to which I have applied the ng-repeat directive and used an inline binding expression.

When AngularJS applies the custom directive, it will replace the contents of the div element to which it is applied with the value of the template definition property and then evaluate the new content to look for other AngularJS directives and expressions. The result is that the div element is transformed from this:

```
...
<div unordered-list="products">
    This is where the list will go
</div>
...
```

into this:

```
...
<div unordered-list="products">
    <ul><!-- ngRepeat: item in data -->
        <li ng-repeat="item in data" class="ng-scope ng-binding">$1.20</li>
        <li ng-repeat="item in data" class="ng-scope ng-binding">$2.42</li>
        <li ng-repeat="item in data" class="ng-scope ng-binding">$2.02</li>
    </ul>
</div>
...
```

Using a Function as a Template

In the previous section, I expressed my template content as a literal string, but the template property can also be used to specify a function that produces templated content. The function is passed two arguments (the element to which the directive has been applied and the set of attributes) and returns the fragment of HTML that will be inserted into the document.

■ **Caution**   Don't use the template function feature to generate the content you require programmatically. Use the link function instead, as demonstrated in Chapter 15 and at the start of this chapter.

I find this feature useful for separating out my template content from the rest of the directive. In Listing 16-8, you can see how I have created a script element that contains my template and the way that I use a function assigned to the template property to obtain that content for the directive.

Listing 16-8. Separating Template Content in the directives.html File

```
...
<head>
    <title>Directives</title>
    <script src="angular.js"></script>
    <link href="bootstrap.css" rel="stylesheet" />
    <link href="bootstrap-theme.css" rel="stylesheet" />
```

```
<script type="text/template" id="listTemplate">
    <ul>
        <li ng-repeat="item in data">{{item.price | currency}}</li>
    </ul>
</script>
<script>
    angular.module("exampleApp", [])
        .directive("unorderedList", function () {
            return {
                link: function (scope, element, attrs) {
                    scope.data = scope[attrs["unorderedList"]];
                },
                restrict: "A",
                template: function () {
                    return angular.element(
                        document.querySelector("#listTemplate")).html();
                }
            }
        }).controller("defaultCtrl", function ($scope) {
            $scope.products = [
                { name: "Apples", category: "Fruit", price: 1.20, expiry: 10 },
                { name: "Bananas", category: "Fruit", price: 2.42, expiry: 7 },
                { name: "Pears", category: "Fruit", price: 2.02, expiry: 6 }
            ];
        })
</script>
</head>
...
```

I added a script element that contains the template content I want to use and set the template definition object function. jqLite doesn't support selecting elements by their id attribute (and I don't want to use the full jQuery library for such a simple directive), so I have used the DOM API to locate the script element and wrap it in a jqLite object, like this:

```
...
return angular.element(document.querySelector("#listTemplate")).html();
...
```

I use the jqLite html method to get the HTML content of the template element and return it as the result from the template function. I'd rather not break into the DOM API like this, but I find it the least bad option when I want to go outside of the features that jqLite provides for such simple tasks.

■ **Tip** You can also get the contents of an element using just the DOM. You can see examples of this in Chapter 17.

Using an External Template

Using a script element is a useful way of separating out the template content, but the elements remain part of the HTML document, and this can be hard to manage in complex projects when you want to share templates freely between different parts of the application or even between applications. An alternative approach is to define the template content in a separate file and then use the `templateUrl` definition object property to specify the file name. In Listing 16-9, you can see the contents of a new HTML file called `itemTemplate.html` that I added to the angularjs folder.

Listing 16-9. The Contents of the itemTemplate.html File

```
<p>This is the list from the template file</p>
<ul>
    <li ng-repeat="item in data">{{item.price | currency}}</li>
</ul>
```

The file contains the same simple template I used in previous examples, with some additional text to make the source of the content clear. In Listing 16-10, I have set the `templateUrl` definition property to reference the file.

Listing 16-10. Specifying an External Template File in the directives.html File

```
...
<script>
    angular.module("exampleApp", [])
        .directive("unorderedList", function () {
            return {
                link: function (scope, element, attrs) {
                    scope.data = scope[attrs["unorderedList"]];
                },
                restrict: "A",
                templateUrl: "itemTemplate.html"
            }
        }).controller("defaultCtrl", function ($scope) {
            $scope.products = [
                { name: "Apples", category: "Fruit", price: 1.20, expiry: 10 },
                { name: "Bananas", category: "Fruit", price: 2.42, expiry: 7 },
                { name: "Pears", category: "Fruit", price: 2.02, expiry: 6 }
            ];
        })
</script>
...
```

Selecting an External Template with a Function

The `templateUrl` property can be set as a function that specifies the URL that is used by the directive, which provides the means to dynamically select the template based on the element to which the directive has been applied. To demonstrate how this works, I have added a new HTML file called `tableTemplate.html` in the angularjs folder, the contents of which are shown in Listing 16-11.

Listing 16-11. The Contents of the tableTemplate.html File

```
<table>
    <thead>
        <tr><th>Name</th><th>Price</th></tr>
    </thead>
```

```
    <tbody>
        <tr ng-repeat="item in data">
            <td>{{item.name}}</td>
            <td>{{item.price | currency}}</td>
        </tr>
    </tbody>
</table>
```

This template is based around a `table` element to make it easy to tell which template file is used to generate content. In Listing 16-12, you can see how I have used a function for the `templateUrl` property to select the template based on an attribute defined on the element to which the directive is applied.

Listing 16-12. Dynamically Selecting a Template File in the directives.html File

```
<html ng-app="exampleApp">
<head>
    <title>Directives</title>
    <script src="angular.js"></script>
    <link href="bootstrap.css" rel="stylesheet" />
    <link href="bootstrap-theme.css" rel="stylesheet" />
    <script>
        angular.module("exampleApp", [])
            .directive("unorderedList", function () {
                return {
                    link: function (scope, element, attrs) {
                        scope.data = scope[attrs["unorderedList"]];
                    },
                    restrict: "A",
                    templateUrl: function (elem, attrs) {
                        return attrs["template"] == "table" ?
                            "tableTemplate.html" : "itemTemplate.html";
                    }
                }
            }).controller("defaultCtrl", function ($scope) {
                $scope.products = [
                    { name: "Apples", category: "Fruit", price: 1.20, expiry: 10 },
                    { name: "Bananas", category: "Fruit", price: 2.42, expiry: 7 },
                    { name: "Pears", category: "Fruit", price: 2.02, expiry: 6 }
                ];
            })
    </script>
</head>
<body ng-controller="defaultCtrl">
    <div class="panel panel-default">
        <div class="panel-heading">
            <h3>Products</h3>
        </div>
        <div class="panel-body">
            <div unordered-list="products">
                This is where the list will go
            </div>
        </div>
    </div>
```

```
    <div class="panel-body">
        <div unordered-list="products" template="table">
            This is where the list will go
        </div>
    </div>
</div>
</body>
</html>
```

The function assigned to the `templateUrl` property is passed a `jqLite` object that represents the element to which the directive has been applied and the set of attributes defined on that element. I check for a `template` attribute, and if it is present and set to table, I return the URL of the `tableTemplate.html` file. I return the URL of the `itemTemplate.html` file if there is no `template` attribute or if it has any other value. In the body section of the `directives.html` file, I apply the directive to two `div` elements, one of which has the attribute and value that I check for. Figure 16-1 shows the result.

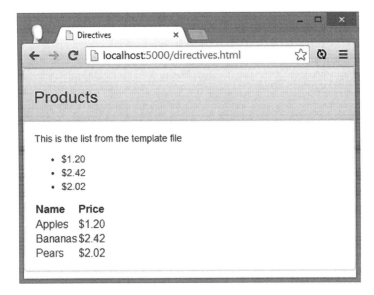

Figure 16-1. *Dynamically selecting a template in a directive*

Replacing the Element

By default, the contents of the template are inserted within the element to which the directive has been applied. You can see this in the previous example, where the `ul` element is added as a child to the `div` element. The `replace` definition property can be used to change this behavior such that the template replaces the element. Before I demonstrate the effect of the `replace` property, I have simplified the directive and added some CSS styling so that I can emphasize an important effect. Listing 16-13 shows the revised `directives.html` file.

Listing 16-13. Preparing for the replace Property in the directives.html File

```html
<html ng-app="exampleApp">
<head>
    <title>Directives</title>
    <script src="angular.js"></script>
    <link href="bootstrap.css" rel="stylesheet" />
    <link href="bootstrap-theme.css" rel="stylesheet" />
    <script>
        angular.module("exampleApp", [])
            .directive("unorderedList", function () {
                return {
                    link: function (scope, element, attrs) {
                        scope.data = scope[attrs["unorderedList"]];
                    },
                    restrict: "A",
                    templateUrl: "tableTemplate.html"
                }
            }).controller("defaultCtrl", function ($scope) {
                $scope.products = [
                    { name: "Apples", category: "Fruit", price: 1.20, expiry: 10 },
                    { name: "Bananas", category: "Fruit", price: 2.42, expiry: 7 },
                    { name: "Pears", category: "Fruit", price: 2.02, expiry: 6 }
                ];
            })
    </script>
</head>
<body ng-controller="defaultCtrl">
    <div class="panel panel-default">
        <div class="panel-heading">
            <h3>Products</h3>
        </div>
        <div class="panel-body">
            <div unordered-list="products" class="table table-striped">
                This is where the list will go
            </div>
        </div>
    </div>
</body>
</html>
```

I changed the templateUrl property so that the tableTemplate.html file is always used and added a class attribute to the div element to which I applied the directive. I added the div element to two bootstrap classes: table and table-striped. You can see the effect in Figure 16-2.

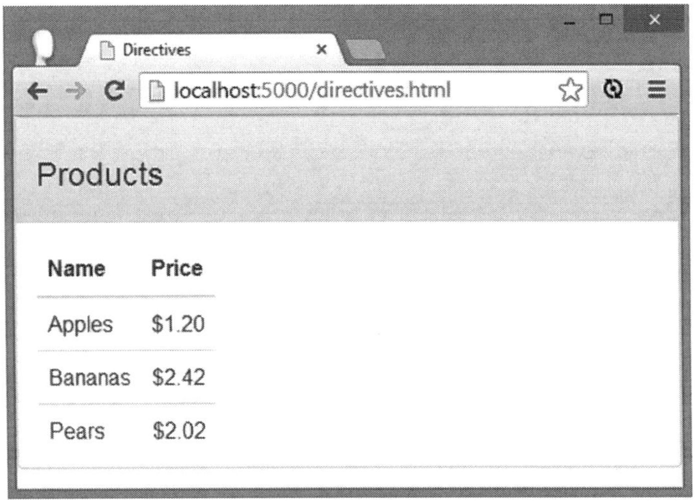

Figure 16-2. *The effect of a class applied to a wrapper element*

The table class has worked because Bootstrap defines it in such a way that it doesn't need to be applied directly to a table element—but that's not the case for the table-striped class, so my table lacks contrasting color rows. Here is the first part of the HTML that the directive generated:

```
...
<div class="panel-body">
    <div unordered-list="products" class="table table-striped">
        <table>
            <thead>
                <tr><th>Name</th><th>Price</th></tr>
        </thead>
...
```

In Listing 16-14, you can see how I have applied the replace property.

Listing 16-14. Applying the replace Property in the directives.html File

```
...
.directive("unorderedList", function () {
    return {
        link: function (scope, element, attrs) {
            scope.data = scope[attrs["unorderedList"]];
        },
        restrict: "A",
        templateUrl: "tableTemplate.html",
        replace: true
    }
...
```

The effect of setting the `replace` property to `true` is that the template content replaces the `div` element to which the directive has been applied. Here is the first part of the HTML that the directive generates:

```
...
<div class="panel-body">
    <table unordered-list="products" class="table table-striped">
        <thead>
            <tr><th>Name</th><th>Price</th></tr>
        </thead>
...
```

The `replace` property doesn't just replace the element with the template; it also transfers the attributes from the element to the template content. In this case, this means the `table` and `table-striped` Bootstrap classes are applied to the `table` element, creating the result shown in Figure 16-3. 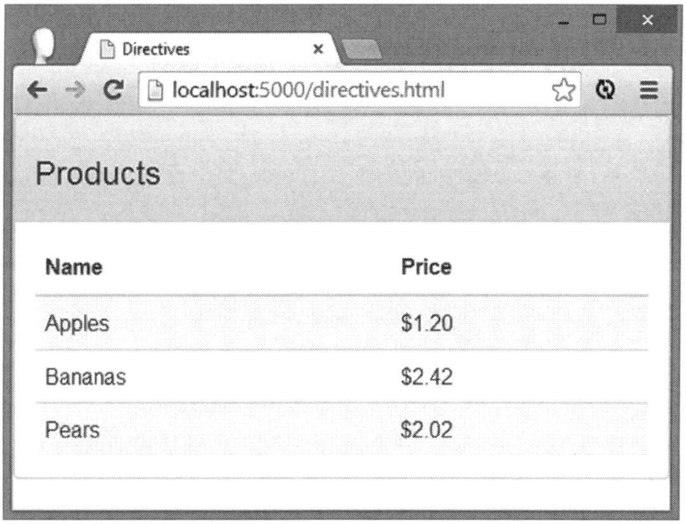

Figure 16-3. *Transferring classes via the replace definition property*

This is a useful technique that allows the content a directive generates to be configured by the context in which the directive is applied. I can use my custom directive in different parts of the application and apply different Bootstrap styles to each table, for example.

You can also use this feature to transfer other AngularJS directives directly to the template content of a directive. In Listing 16-15, you can see how I have applied the `ng-repeat` directive to the `div` element in the example.

Listing 16-15. Using the replace Definition Property to Transfer Directives in the directives.html File

```
...
<div class="panel-body">
    <div unordered-list="products" class="table table-striped"
            ng-repeat="count in [1, 2, 3]">
        This is where the list will go
    </div>
</div>
...
```

This has the same effect as applying the ng-repeat directive to the table element in the template file, without needing to reproduce the containing div element.

Managing Directive Scopes

The relationship between a directive and its scope means that some care is required if you want to create a directive that can be reused throughout an application. By default, the link function is passed the scope of the controller that manages the view that contains the element to which the directive has been applied. I know that last sentence sounds like a tongue-twister nursery rhyme—but if you read it again, you'll make sense of the relationship between some of the major components of an AngularJS application. A simple example will help give context, and Listing 16-16 shows the content of the directiveScopes.html file that I added to the angularjs directory.

Listing 16-16. The Contents of the directiveScopes.html File

```
<!DOCTYPE html>
<html ng-app="exampleApp">
<head>
    <title>Directive Scopes</title>
    <script src="angular.js"></script>
    <link href="bootstrap.css" rel="stylesheet" />
    <link href="bootstrap-theme.css" rel="stylesheet" />
    <script type="text/javascript">
        angular.module("exampleApp", [])
            .directive("scopeDemo", function () {
                return {
                    template:
                        "<div class='panel-body'>Name: <input ng-model=name /></div>",
                }
            })
        .controller("scopeCtrl", function ($scope) {
            // do nothing - no behaviours required
        });
    </script>
</head>
<body>
    <div ng-controller="scopeCtrl" class="panel panel-default">
        <div class="panel-body" scope-demo></div>
        <div class="panel-body" scope-demo></div>
    </div>
</body>
</html>
```

This is such a simple directive that I don't even need to define a link function—just a template that contains an input element to which the ng-model directive has been applied. The ng-model directive creates a two-way binding for a scope property called name, and I have applied the directive to two separate div elements in the body section of the document.

Even though there are two instances of the directive, they are both updating the same name property on the scopeCtrl controller. You can see the effect this creates by loading the directivesScopes.html file into the browser and entering some characters into either input element. The two-way data bindings ensure that both input elements are in sync, as shown in Figure 16-4.

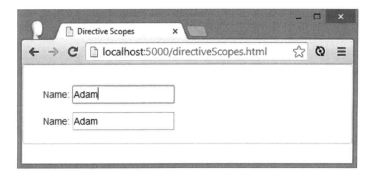

Figure 16-4. *The effect of two instances of a directive updating the same scope*

This behavior can be useful, and it is a nice demonstration of how the scope can be used to keep elements coordinated and capture or display the same data. But you will often want to reuse a directive to capture or display *different* data, and that's where the management of scopes comes in.

It can be hard to get your head around the different ways that directives and scopes can be set up, so I am going to diagram each of the different configurations that I created in this part of the chapter. In Figure 16-5, you can see the effect created by Listing 16-16, shown before and after the input elements have been edited.

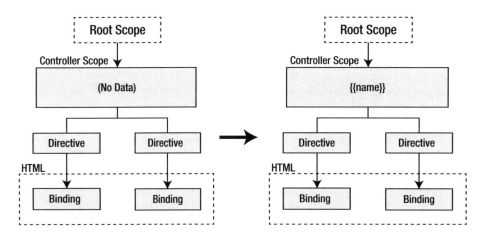

Figure 16-5. *Multiple instances of a directive operating on the controller scope*

There is no scope data in this example when the application first starts, but the ng-model directive that I included in the directive template means that AngularJS will dynamically create a name property when the contents of either input element are changed. Since there is only one scope in this example—well, aside from the root scope, which I am not directly using in this chapter—both directives bind to the same property, and that's why they are synchronized.

■ **Tip** In this chapter, I only describe the scopes used by the controller and the directives I create. In fact, there can be a lot more scopes because directives can use other directives in their templates or even explicitly create scopes. I am focused on controller/directive scopes in this chapter, but the same rules and behaviors apply throughout the scope hierarchy.

Creating Multiple Controllers

The simplest but least elegant way to reuse directives is to create a separate controller for each instance of the directive so that each gets its own scope. This is an inelegant technique, but it can be useful when you don't control the source code for the directive you are using and so can't change the way that the directive works. In Listing 16-17, you can see how I have added an additional controller to the directiveScopes.html file.

Listing 16-17. Adding a Second Controller to the directiveScopes.html File

```
<!DOCTYPE html>
<html ng-app="exampleApp">
<head>
    <title>Directive Scopes</title>
    <script src="angular.js"></script>
    <link href="bootstrap.css" rel="stylesheet" />
    <link href="bootstrap-theme.css" rel="stylesheet" />
    <script type="text/javascript">
        angular.module("exampleApp", [])
            .directive("scopeDemo", function () {
                return {
                    template:
                        "<div class='panel-body'>Name: <input ng-model=name /></div>",
                }
            })
        .controller("scopeCtrl", function ($scope) {
            // do nothing - no behaviours required
        })
        .controller("secondCtrl", function($scope) {
            // do nothing - no behaviours required
        });
    </script>
</head>
<body>
    <div class="panel panel-default">
        <div ng-controller="scopeCtrl" class="panel-body" scope-demo></div>
        <div ng-controller="secondCtrl" class="panel-body" scope-demo></div>
    </div>
</body>
</html>
```

The effect of using two controllers is that there are two scopes, each of which has its own name property, and this allows the input elements to operate independently. Figure 16-6 shows how the scopes and data in this example are arranged.

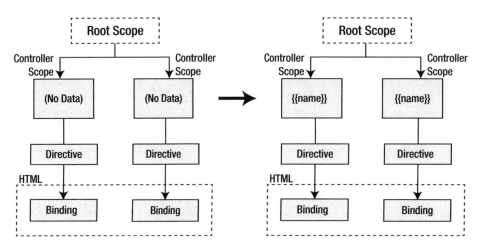

Figure 16-6. *The effect of creating a controller for each instance of the directive*

There are two controllers, each of which contains no data when the application starts. Editing the input elements dynamically creates a name property in the scope of the controller that contains the directive instance the input element is managed by, but these properties are completely separate from one another.

Giving Each Directive Instance Its Own Scope

You don't have to create controllers to give directives their own scopes. A more elegant approach is to ask AngularJS to create a scope for each instance of the directive by setting the scope definition object property to true, as shown in Listing 16-18.

Listing 16-18. Creating a New Scope for Each Instance of a Directive in the directiveScopes.html File

```
<!DOCTYPE html>
<html ng-app="exampleApp">
<head>
    <title>Directive Scopes</title>
    <script src="angular.js"></script>
    <link href="bootstrap.css" rel="stylesheet" />
    <link href="bootstrap-theme.css" rel="stylesheet" />
    <script type="text/javascript">
        angular.module("exampleApp", [])
            .directive("scopeDemo", function () {
                return {
                    template:
                        "<div class='panel-body'>Name: <input ng-model=name /></div>",
                    scope: true
                }
            })
            .controller("scopeCtrl", function ($scope) {
                // do nothing - no behaviours required
            });
    </script>
</head>
```

```
<body ng-controller="scopeCtrl">
    <div class="panel panel-default">
        <div class="panel-body" scope-demo></div>
        <div class="panel-body" scope-demo></div>
    </div>
</body>
</html>
```

Setting the scope property true allows me to reuse the directive within the same controller, and that means I am able to remove the second controller and simplify the application. The simplification isn't enormously significant in a simple example like this one, but large projects are complex enough without having to create endless controllers just to stop your directives from sharing data values.

The scopes that are created when the scope property is set to true are part of the regular scope hierarchy that I described in Chapter 13. This means the rules I described about inheritance of objects and properties apply, giving you flexibility about how you set up the data used—and potentially shared—by instances of a custom directive. As a quick demonstration, I have expanded my example in Listing 16-19 to show the most commonly used permutations.

Listing 16-19. Expanding the Example Directive in the directiveScopes.html File

```
<!DOCTYPE html>
<html ng-app="exampleApp">
<head>
    <title>Directive Scopes</title>
    <script src="angular.js"></script>
    <link href="bootstrap.css" rel="stylesheet" />
    <link href="bootstrap-theme.css" rel="stylesheet" />
    <script type="text/ng-template" id="scopeTemplate">
        <div class="panel-body">
            <p>Name: <input ng-model="data.name" /></p>
            <p>City: <input ng-model="city" /></p>
            <p>Country: <input ng-model="country" /></p>
        </div>
    </script>
    <script type="text/javascript">
        angular.module("exampleApp", [])
            .directive("scopeDemo", function () {
                return {
                    template: function() {
                        return angular.element(
                            document.querySelector("#scopeTemplate")).html();
                    },
                    scope: true
                }
            })
            .controller("scopeCtrl", function ($scope) {
                $scope.data = { name: "Adam" };
                $scope.city = "London";
            });
    </script>
</head>
```

```
<body ng-controller="scopeCtrl">
    <div class="panel panel-default">
        <div class="panel-body" scope-demo></div>
        <div class="panel-body" scope-demo></div>
    </div>
</body>
</html>
```

I have reached the limits of using a string as the template, so I used a `script` element to define the markup I require and select its contents through a `template` function, as I described in the "Using a Function as a Template" section earlier in the chapter. The template contains three `input` elements, each of which is bound through the `ng-model` directive to a data value in the scope. Figure 16-7 shows the arrangement of scopes and data in the example.

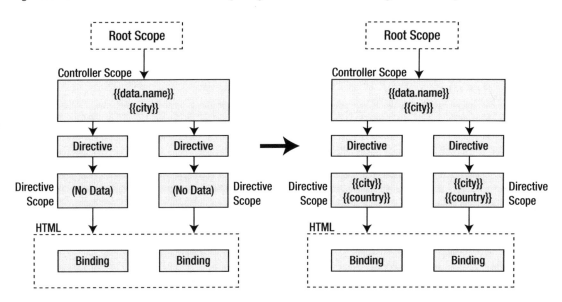

Figure 16-7. *Giving each instance of the directive its own scope within a single controller*

The disposition of the data in this example is a step up in complexity, so I have described what happens to each of the three data values in Table 16-4, just to provide some additional detail.

Table 16-4. *The Data Properties in the directiveScopes.html File*

Name	Description
data.name	This property is defined on an object, which means a single value will be shared between instances of the directive and all of the `input` elements bound to this property will be kept in sync.
city	This property is assigned a value directly on the controller's scope, which means that all of the directive scopes will start with the same value but create and modify their own version in their own scopes when the `input` element is modified.
country	This property is not assigned a value. Each instance of the directive will create separate `country` properties when the corresponding `input` element is modified.

Creating Isolated Scopes

In the previous example, you saw how creating a separate scope for each instance of the directive allowed me to remove the redundant controllers and mix together the different ways that objects and properties are inherited from one level to the next in the scope hierarchy (which I described in Chapter 13).

The advantage of this approach is that it is simple and consistent with the rest of AngularJS, but the disadvantage is that the behavior of your directive is at the mercy of the controller in which it is applied because the default rules for scope inheritance are always used. It is easy to get into a situation where one controller defines a scope property called count as 3 and another defines count as Dracula. You may not want to inherit the value at all, and you may end up modifying the controller scope in an unexpected way if your changes are made to properties defined on scope objects, something that is likely to cause problems if your directive is being applied by other developers.

The solution to this problem is to create an *isolated scope*, which is where AngularJS creates a separate scope for each instance of the directive but the scope *doesn't* inherit from the controller scope. This is useful if you are creating a directive that you intend to reuse in a range of different situations and don't want any interference caused by the data objects and properties defined on by the controller or elsewhere in the scope hierarchy. An isolated scope is created when the scope definition property is set to an object. The most basic kind of isolated scope is represented by an object with no properties, as shown in Listing 16-20.

Listing 16-20. Creating an Isolated Scope in the directiveScopes.html File

```
...
<script type="text/javascript">
    angular.module("exampleApp", [])
        .directive("scopeDemo", function () {
            return {
                template: function() {
                    return angular.element(
                        document.querySelector("#scopeTemplate")).html();
                },
                scope: {}
            }
        })
    .controller("scopeCtrl", function ($scope) {
        $scope.data = { name: "Adam" };
        $scope.city = "London";
    });
</script>
...
```

You can see the effect of the isolated scope if you load the directiveScopes.html file into the browser—although this is one of the dullest examples to test, since all six input elements are empty. This is the consequence of the isolated scope; because there is no inheritance from the controller's scope, there are no values defined for any of the properties specified by the ng-model directive. AngularJS will dynamically create these properties if you edit the input elements, but the properties will only be part of the isolated scope of the directive that the modified input element is associated with. Figure 16-8 shows the disposition of the scopes in Listing 16-20 so that you can compare an isolated scope with previous examples.

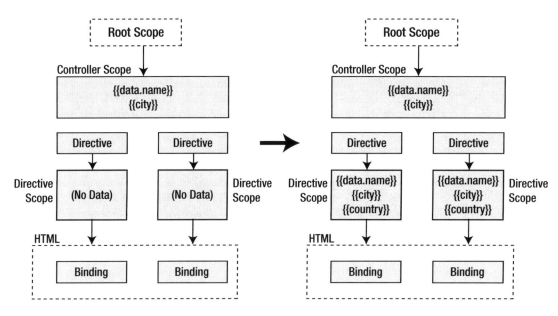

Figure 16-8. *The effect of an isolated scope*

Each instances of the directive has its own scope but does not inherit any data values from the controller scope. Because there is no inheritance, changes to properties that are defined via objects are not propagated to the controller scope. In short, an isolated scope is cut off from the rest of the scope hierarchy.

Binding via an Attribute Value

Isolated scopes are an important building block when you are creating a directive that you intend to reuse in different situations because it avoids *unexpected* interactions between the controller scope and the directive. But totally isolating a directive makes it hard to get data in and out, so AngularJS provides a mechanism by which you can break through the isolation to created *expected* interactions between the controller scope and the directive.

Isolated scopes allow you to bind to data values in the controller scope using attributes applied to the element alongside the directive. It makes more sense when you see a demonstration, and in Listing 16-21 you can see how I have created a one-way binding between a data value in the controller scope and the directive's local scope.

Listing 16-21. Creating a One-Way Binding for an Isolated Scope in the directiveScopes.html File

```
<!DOCTYPE html>
<html ng-app="exampleApp">
<head>
    <title>Directive Scopes</title>
    <script src="angular.js"></script>
    <link href="bootstrap.css" rel="stylesheet" />
    <link href="bootstrap-theme.css" rel="stylesheet" />
    <script type="text/ng-template" id="scopeTemplate">
        <div class="panel-body">
            <p>Data Value: {{local}}</p>
        </div>
    </script>
```

```
    <script type="text/javascript">
        angular.module("exampleApp", [])
            .directive("scopeDemo", function () {
                return {
                    template: function() {
                        return angular.element(
                            document.querySelector("#scopeTemplate")).html();
                    },
                    scope: {
                        local: "@nameprop"
                    }
                }
            })
        .controller("scopeCtrl", function ($scope) {
            $scope.data = { name: "Adam" };
        });
    </script>
</head>
<body ng-controller="scopeCtrl">
    <div class="panel panel-default">
        <div class="panel-body">
            Direct Binding: <input ng-model="data.name" />
        </div>
        <div class="panel-body" scope-demo nameprop="{{data.name}}"></div>
    </div>
</body>
</html>
```

There are three changes in this example, and together they created a binding between the controller and directive scopes. The first change is in the scope definition object, where I set up a one-way mapping between an attribute and a property in the directive scope, as follows:

```
...
scope: {
    local: "@nameprop"
}
...
```

I have defined a property called local on the object assigned to the scope definition object, and this tells AngularJS that I want to define a new property in the directive scope by that name. The value of the local property is prefixed with an @ character, which specifies that the value for the local property should be obtained as a one-way binding from an attribute called nameprop.

The second change is to define the nameprop attribute on the elements to which I apply my custom directive, as follows:

```
...
<div class="panel-body" scope-demo nameprop="{{data.name}}"></div>
...
```

I specify the value for the local property in the directive scope by providing an AngularJS expression in the nameprop attribute. In this case, I selected the data.name property, but any expression can be used. The final change is to update the template so that it displays the value of the local property:

```
...
<script type="text/ng-template" id="scopeTemplate">
    <div class="panel-body">
        <p>Data Value: {{local}}</p>
    </div>
</script>
...
```

I have used an inline binding expression to display the value of the local property. I added an input element to the view that modifies the data.name property in the controller scope, and you can see the result in Figure 16-9.

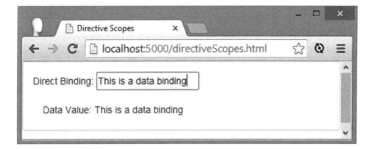

Figure 16-9. *Adding a one-way data binding to an isolated scope*

It is worth reiterating what is happening in this example because it is an important concept in advanced directive development and one that causes a lot of confusion. I have used an isolated scope so that my directive doesn't inherit the data in the controller's scope and end up working with data that it wasn't expecting—something that can happen because there is no way to selectively control how a regular nonisolated scope inherits data values from its parent.

■ **Caution** One-way bindings on isolated scopes are always evaluated to string values. You must use a two-way binding if you want to access an array, even if you don't intend to modify it. I explain how to create two-way bindings in the next section.

But my directive *does* need to access a data value in the controller's scope, so I told AngularJS to create a one-way binding between an expression I specified as an attribute value and a property on the local scope. Figure 16-10 shows how the scopes and data in this example are arranged.

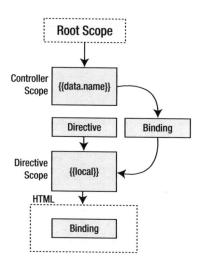

Figure 16-10. *The effect of a one-way data binding on an isolated scope*

As the diagram shows, there are two data bindings. The first binds the data.name property in the controller scope to the local property in the isolated scope, as specified by the attribute value. The second binds the local property in the isolated scope to the inline binding expression in the directive template. AngularJS keeps everything organized so that changes to the data.name property update the value of the local property.

■ **Caution**   You will notice that I removed the input element with the ng-model directive from the template for this example. I did this because I created a one-way data binding, which means that updates to the data.name property in the controller's scope will update the local property in the directive's scope—but not the other way around. You will need a two-way binding if you want your directive to be able to modify the data in the controller's scope, which I describe in the next section.

This gives me the selective control over the scope inheritance that I need and, as a bonus, allows that selection to be configured when the directive is applied, which is key to allowing a single directive to be reused in different ways without needing any code or markup changes. You can see a demonstration of this reuse in Listing 16-22.

Listing 16-22. Reusing a Directive with a One-Way Data Binding in the directiveScopes.html

```
<!DOCTYPE html>
<html ng-app="exampleApp">
<head>
    <title>Directive Scopes</title>
    <script src="angular.js"></script>
    <link href="bootstrap.css" rel="stylesheet" />
    <link href="bootstrap-theme.css" rel="stylesheet" />
    <script type="text/ng-template" id="scopeTemplate">
        <div class="panel-body">
            <p>Data Value: {{local}}</p>
        </div>
    </script>
```

```
    <script type="text/javascript">
        angular.module("exampleApp", [])
            .directive("scopeDemo", function () {
                return {
                    template: function() {
                        return angular.element(
                            document.querySelector("#scopeTemplate")).html();
                    },
                    scope: {
                        local: "@nameprop"
                    }
                }
            })
            .controller("scopeCtrl", function ($scope) {
                $scope.data = { name: "Adam" };
            });
    </script>
</head>
<body ng-controller="scopeCtrl">
    <div class="panel panel-default">
        <div class="panel-body">
            Direct Binding: <input ng-model="data.name" />
        </div>
        <div class="panel-body" scope-demo nameprop="{{data.name}}"></div>
        <div class="panel-body" scope-demo nameprop="{{data.name + 'Freeman'}}"></div>
    </div>
</body>
</html>
```

I created a second instance of my custom directive and set the nameprop attribute to bind to an expression based on the data.name property. What's important in this example is what I did *not* do, which is to make changes to the directive. I used the same (admittedly simple) functionality to display two different data values just by changing the expression specified in the attribute on the element to which the directive is applied. This is a powerful technique and one that is invaluable for creating complex directives.

Creating a Two-Way Binding

The process for creating two-way bindings in isolated scope is similar to that for a one-way binding, as shown by Listing 16-23.

Listing 16-23. Creating a Two-Way Binding in the directiveScopes.html File

```
<!DOCTYPE html>
<html ng-app="exampleApp">
<head>
    <title>Directive Scopes</title>
    <script src="angular.js"></script>
    <link href="bootstrap.css" rel="stylesheet" />
    <link href="bootstrap-theme.css" rel="stylesheet" />
```

```
        <script type="text/ng-template" id="scopeTemplate">
            <div class="panel-body">
                <p>Data Value: <input ng-model="local" /></p>
            </div>
        </script>
        <script type="text/javascript">
            angular.module("exampleApp", [])
                .directive("scopeDemo", function () {
                    return {
                        template: function() {
                            return angular.element(
                                document.querySelector("#scopeTemplate")).html();
                        },
                        scope: {
                            local: "=nameprop"
                        }
                    }
                })
                .controller("scopeCtrl", function ($scope) {
                    $scope.data = { name: "Adam" };
                });
        </script>
</head>
<body ng-controller="scopeCtrl">
    <div class="panel panel-default">
        <div class="panel-body">
            Direct Binding: <input ng-model="data.name" />
        </div>
        <div class="panel-body" scope-demo nameprop="data.name"></div>
    </div>
</body>
</html>
```

To create a two-way binding, I replace the @ character with the = character when I create the isolated scope so that this definition from the previous example:

```
...
scope: { local: "@nameprop" }
...
```

becomes this:

```
...
scope: { local: "=nameprop" }
...
```

This isn't the only change, however. When using a one-way binding, I provided a binding expression complete with the {{ and }} characters, but AngularJS needs to know which property to update with changes in a two-way binding, so I have to set the attribute value to a property name, like this:

```
...
<div class="panel-body" scope-demo nameprop="data.name"></div>
...
```

441

These changes create the two-way binding and allow me to update my directive template so that I can include content that modifies the data value. For this simple example, that just means an input element that uses the ng-model directive, like this:

```
...
<div class="panel-body" scope-demo nameprop="data.name"></div>
...
```

The effect this example creates is that the flow of updates goes in both directions between the scopes—updates to the data.name property in the controller scope update the local property in the isolated scope *and* changes to the local property cause data.name to be updated, as shown in Figure 16-11. It is impossible to capture this relationship in a figure, and I recommend you load the directiveScopes.html file into the browser to see firsthand how the contents of the input elements are synchronized.

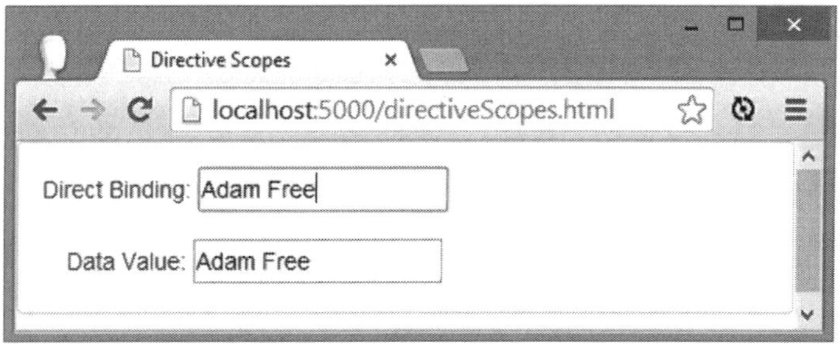

Figure 16-11. *Adding a one-way data binding to an isolated scope*

■ **Tip** The arrangement for the scopes in this example is just the same as in Figure 16-10, except that the data bindings are two-way.

Evaluating Expressions

The final isolated scope feature is the ability to specify expressions as attributes and have them evaluated in the controller's scope. This is another feature that is easier to understand with an example, such as the one shown in Listing 16-24.

Listing 16-24. Evaluating an Expression in the Controller Scope in the directiveScopes.html File

```
<!DOCTYPE html>
<html ng-app="exampleApp">
<head>
    <title>Directive Scopes</title>
    <script src="angular.js"></script>
    <link href="bootstrap.css" rel="stylesheet" />
    <link href="bootstrap-theme.css" rel="stylesheet" />
    <script type="text/ng-template" id="scopeTemplate">
        <div class="panel-body">
            <p>Name: {{local}}, City: {{cityFn()}}</p>
        </div>
    </script>
```

```
    <script type="text/javascript">
        angular.module("exampleApp", [])
            .directive("scopeDemo", function () {
                return {
                    template: function () {
                        return angular.element(
                            document.querySelector("#scopeTemplate")).html();
                    },
                    scope: {
                        local: "=nameprop",
                        cityFn: "&city"
                    }
                }
            })
        .controller("scopeCtrl", function ($scope) {
            $scope.data = {
                name: "Adam",
                defaultCity: "London"
            };

            $scope.getCity = function (name) {
                return name == "Adam" ? $scope.data.defaultCity : "Unknown";
            }
        });
    </script>
</head>
<body ng-controller="scopeCtrl">
    <div class="panel panel-default">
        <div class="panel-body">
            Direct Binding: <input ng-model="data.name" />
        </div>
        <div class="panel-body" scope-demo
            city="getCity(data.name)" nameprop="data.name"></div>
    </div>
</body>
</html>
```

This technique is slightly convoluted, but it is worth unwinding it because it can be useful, especially when you need to create a directive that takes advantage of the behavior and data defined by the controller in a reusable and predictable way.

The first change I made was to define a simple controller behavior that checks a first name argument and returns the name of the city associated with it; the default city is defined as a scope property. It doesn't matter what the behavior does for this demonstration, only that the behavior and the data it depends on are defined in the controller scope, which would not be available by default in the directives isolated scope.

The name of the behavior is getCity, and to make this available to the directive, I added a new attribute to the element the directive is applied to, as follows:

```
...
<div class="panel-body" scope-demo city="getCity(data.name)" nameprop="data.name"></div>
...
```

The value of the `city` attribute is an expression that calls the `getCity` behavior and passes the value of the `data.name` property as the argument to process. To make this expression available in the isolated scope, I have added a new property to the `scope` object, as follows:

```
...
scope: {
    local: "=nameprop",
    cityFn: "&city"
}
...
```

The & prefix tells AngularJS that I want to bind the value of the specified attribute to a function. In this case, the attribute is `city`, and I want to bind it to a function called `cityFn`. All that remains is to call the function to evaluate the expression in the directive template, like this:

```
...
<div class="panel-body">
    <p>Name: {{local}}, City: {{cityFn()}}</p>
</div>
...
```

Notice that I call `cityFn()`, with the parentheses, to evaluate the expression specified by the attribute, This is required even when the expression is itself a call to a function. You can see the effect in Figure 16-12: When the value of the `data.name` property is Adam, the data binding in the template displays the city name of London.

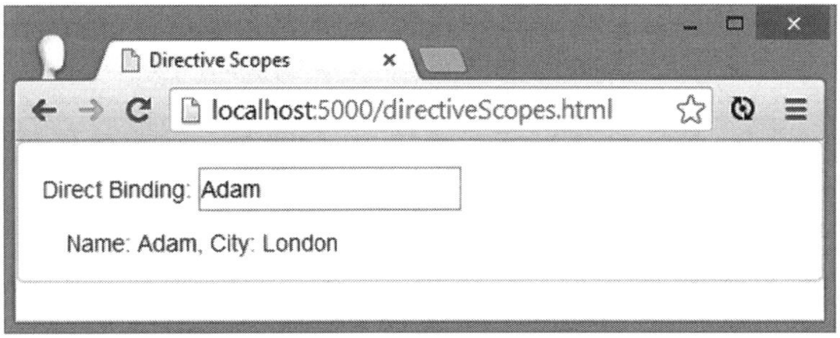

Figure 16-12. *Evaluating an expression in the controller's scope*

Using Isolated Scope Data to Evaluate an Expression

A variation on this previous technique allows you to pass data from the isolated scope to be evaluated as part of the expression in the controller's scope. To do this, I modify the expression so that the argument passed to the behavior is the name of the property that has not been defined on the controller's scope, as follows:

```
...
<div class="panel-body" scope-demo city="getCity(nameVal)" nameprop="data.name"></div>
...
```

I selected `nameVal` as the name for the argument in this case. To pass data from the isolated scope, I have updated the binding in my template that evaluates the expression, passing in an object that provides values for the expression arguments, like this:

```
...
<div class="panel-body">
    <p>Name: {{local}}, City: {{cityFn({nameVal: local})}}</p>
</div>
...
```

This has the effect of creating a data binding that evaluates an expression using a mix of data defined in the isolated scope and the controller scope. You have to be careful to make sure that the controller scope doesn't define a property whose name corresponds to the argument in the expression; if it does, the value from the isolated scope will be ignored.

Summary

In this chapter, I continued showing you the features that are available to create custom directives, moving from the basic to more advanced topics. I showed you how to create directives with definition objects, how to use templates, and how to create and manage the scopes that directives use. I finish explaining directive features in the next chapter, showing you the extremely advanced features that you probably won't need on a regular basis but that are valuable for especially complex projects.

Advanced Directive Features

In this chapter, I complete my coverage of custom directives by showing you the most advanced features. These are not features you will need often, but they are powerful and flexible and can help you build complex and fluid directives. Table 17-1 summarizes this chapter.

Table 17-1. *Chapter Summary*

Problem	Solution	Listing
Wrap elements.	Create a directive that uses transclusion.	1
Repeat transcluded content.	Use a compile function.	2
Communicate between directives.	Use directive controllers.	3–5
Create custom form elements.	Use the ngModel controller.	6
Handle external data changes in a custom form directive.	Redefine the $render method.	7
Handle internal data changes in a custom form directive.	Call the $setViewValue method.	8
Format a value in a custom form directive.	Use the $formatters array.	9, 10
Validate a value in a custom form directive.	Use the $parsers array and call the $setValidity method.	11, 12

▓ **Note**   Don't worry if not all of these techniques make sense the first time you read this chapter. I recommend you come back and read through again after you have completed your first few AngularJS applications; you will find that the experience provides some helpful context.

Preparing the Example Project

For this chapter, I continue to work with the angularjs folder that I created in Chapter 15 and added to in Chapter 16. I'll add new HTML files to demonstrate features in each section of this chapter.

Using Transclusion

The term *transclusion* means to insert one part of a document into another by reference. In the context of directives, it is useful when you are creating a directive that is a wrapper around arbitrary content. To demonstrate how this works, I have added a new HMTML file called `transclude.html` to the `angularjs` folder and used it to define the example application shown in Listing 17-1.

Listing 17-1. The Contents of the transclude.html File

```
<!DOCTYPE html>
<html ng-app="exampleApp">
<head>
    <title>Transclusion</title>
    <script src="angular.js"></script>
    <link href="bootstrap.css" rel="stylesheet" />
    <link href="bootstrap-theme.css" rel="stylesheet" />
    <script type="text/ng-template" id="template">
        <div class="panel panel-default">
            <div class="panel-heading">
                <h4>This is the panel</h4>
            </div>
            <div class="panel-body" ng-transclude>
            </div>
        </div>
    </script>
    <script type="text/javascript">
        angular.module("exampleApp", [])
            .directive("panel", function () {
                return {
                    link: function (scope, element, attrs) {
                        scope.dataSource = "directive";
                    },
                    restrict: "E",
                    scope: true,
                    template: function () {
                        return angular.element(
                            document.querySelector("#template")).html();
                    },
                    transclude: true
                }
            })
            .controller("defaultCtrl", function ($scope) {
                $scope.dataSource = "controller";
            });
    </script>
</head>
<body ng-controller="defaultCtrl">
    <panel>
        The data value comes from the: {{dataSource}}
    </panel>
</body>
</html>
```

My goal in this example is to create a directive that can be applied to arbitrary content in order to wrap it in a set of elements that are styled as a Bootstrap panel. I have called my directive panel and used the restrict definition property to specify that it can be applied only as an element (this isn't a requirement for using transclusion but rather a convention I use when I write directives that wrap other content). I want to take content like this:

```
...
<panel>
    The data value comes from the: {{dataSource}}
</panel>
...
```

and generate markup like this:

```
...
<div class="panel panel-default">
    <div class="panel-heading">
        <h4>This is the panel</h4>
    </div>
    <div class="panel-body">
        The data value comes from the: controller
    </div>
</div>
...
```

The term *transclusion* is used because the content that is inside the panel element will be inserted into the template. Two specific steps are required to apply transclusion. The first is to set the transclude definition property to true when creating the directive, like this:

```
...
transclude: true
...
```

The second step is to apply the ng-transclude directive in the template at the point where you want the wrapped elements inserted.

■ **Tip** Setting transclude to true will wrap the contents of the element to which the directive has been applied, but not the element itself. If you want to include the element, then set the translude property to 'element'. You can see a demonstration of this in the "Using Compile Functions" section.

I want the elements inserted into the one template div element that is styled as the panel body, like this:

```
...
<div class="panel panel-default">
    <div class="panel-heading">
        <h4>This is the panel</h4>
    </div>
    <div class="panel-body" ng-transclude>
    </div>
</div>
...
```

Any content that is contained by the `panel` element will be inserted into the highlighted `div` element, and you can see the result in Figure 17-1.

Figure 17-1. *Using transclusion to wrap arbitrary content*

You will notice that I included an inline data binding in the content that I transclude:

```
...
The data value comes from the: {{dataSource}}
...
```

I did this to show an important aspect of the transclusion feature, which is that expressions in the transcluded content are evaluated in the controller's scope, not the scope of the directive. I defined values for the `dataSource` property in the controller factory function and the directive link function, but AngularJS has done the sensible thing and taken the value from the controller. I say *sensible* because this approach means that content that is going to be transcluded doesn't need to try to work out which scope its data is defined in; you just write expressions as though transclusion were not an issue and let AngularJS work it out.

However, if you *do* want to take the directive scope into account when evaluating transcluded expressions, then make sure you set the `scope` property to `false`, as follows:

```
...
restrict: "E",
scope: false,
template: function () {
...
```

This ensures that the directive operates on the controller scope and any values you define in the link function will affect the transcluded expressions. You can see the result of this change in Figure 17-2, which demonstrates that the data value for the inline binding expression is the one defined in the link function.

Figure 17-2. *The effect of sharing a scope during transclusion*

Using Compile Functions

In Chapter 16, I explained that directives that are especially complex or deal with a lot of data can benefit by using a compile function to manipulate the DOM and by leaving the link function to perform other tasks. I rarely use compile functions in my own projects, and I tend to approach performance problems by simplifying my code or optimizing the data I am working with, but in this section I'll explain how compile functions work.

Aside from performance, there is one advantage to using compile functions, and that is the ability to use transclusion to repeatedly generate contents, much as ng-repeat does. You can see an example in Listing 17-2, which shows the content of the compileFunction.html file I added to the angularjs folder.

Listing 17-2. The Contents of the compileFunction.html File

```
<!DOCTYPE html>
<html ng-app="exampleApp">
<head>
    <title>Compile Function</title>
    <script src="angular.js"></script>
    <link href="bootstrap.css" rel="stylesheet" />
    <link href="bootstrap-theme.css" rel="stylesheet" />
    <script type="text/javascript">
        angular.module("exampleApp", [])
            .controller("defaultCtrl", function ($scope) {
                $scope.products = [{ name: "Apples", price: 1.20 },
                    { name: "Bananas", price: 2.42 }, { name: "Pears", price: 2.02 }];

                $scope.changeData = function () {
                    $scope.products.push({ name: "Cherries", price: 4.02 });
                    for (var i = 0; i < $scope.products.length; i++) {
                        $scope.products[i].price++;
                    }
                }
            })
```

```
        .directive("simpleRepeater", function () {
            return {
                scope: {
                    data: "=source",
                    propName: "@itemName"
                },
                transclude: 'element',
                compile: function (element, attrs, transcludeFn) {
                    return function ($scope, $element, $attr) {
                        $scope.$watch("data.length", function () {
                            var parent = $element.parent();
                            parent.children().remove();
                            for (var i = 0; i < $scope.data.length; i++) {
                                var childScope = $scope.$new();
                                childScope[$scope.propName] = $scope.data[i];
                                transcludeFn(childScope, function (clone) {
                                    parent.append(clone);
                                });
                            }
                        });
                    }
                }
            }
        });
    </script>
</head>
<body ng-controller="defaultCtrl" class="panel panel-body" >
    <table class="table table-striped">
        <thead><tr><th>Name</th><th>Price</th></tr></thead>
        <tbody>
            <tr simple-repeater source="products" item-name="item">
                <td>{{item.name}}</td><td>{{item.price | currency}}</td>
            </tr>
        </tbody>
    </table>
    <button class="btn btn-default text" ng-click="changeData()">Change</button>
</body>
</html>
```

This example contains a directive called simpleRepeater that uses transclusion to repeat a set of elements for each object in an array, like a simple version of ng-repeat. The real ng-repeat directive goes to great lengths to avoid adding and removing elements from the DOM, but my example just replaces all of the transcluded elements and so isn't as efficient. Here is how I applied the directive to an HTML element:

```
...
<tbody>
    <tr simple-repeater source="products" item-name="item">
        <td>{{item.name}}</td><td>{{item.price | currency}}</td>
    </tr>
</tbody>
...
```

I specify the source of the data objects using the source attribute and the name that can be used to refer to the current object in the transcluded template using the item-name attribute. For this example, I specified the products array created by the controller and a name of item (which allows me to refer to item.name and item.currency in the transcluded content).

My goal is to repeat the tr element for each product object, so I have set the transclude definition property to element, which means that the element itself will be included in the transclusion, as opposed to its contents. I could have applied my directive to the tbody element and set the transclude property to true, but I wanted to demonstrate both configuration values.

The centerpiece of the directive is the compile function, which is specified using the compile property. The compile function is passed three arguments: the element to which the directive has been applied to, the attributes on that element, and a function that can be used to create copies of the transcluded elements.

The most important thing to realize about compile functions is that they return a link function (the link property is ignored when the compile property is used). This may seem a little odd, but remember that the purpose of a compile function is to modify the DOM, so returning a link function from the compile function can be helpful because it provides an easy way to pass data from one part of the directive to the next.

The compile function is supposed to manipulate the DOM only, so it is not provided with a scope, but a link function returned by a compile function can declare dependencies on $scope, $element, and $attrs arguments, which correspond to their regular link function counterparts.

Don't worry if this doesn't make sense; the reason that I used a compile function is solely so I can get a link function that has a scope *and* can call the transclusion function. As you'll see, that's the key combination to creating a directive that can repeat content.

Understanding the Compile Function

Here is the compile function and—within it—the link function:

```
...
compile: function (element, attrs, transcludeFn) {
    return function ($scope, $element, $attr) {
        $scope.$watch("data.length", function () {
            var parent = $element.parent();
            parent.children().remove();
            for (var i = 0; i < $scope.data.length; i++) {
                var childScope = $scope.$new();
                childScope[$scope.propName] = $scope.data[i];
                transcludeFn(childScope, function (clone) {
                    parent.append(clone);
                });
            }
        });
    }
}
...
```

The first thing I do in the link function is set up a watcher on the scope for the data.length property so that I can respond when the number of data item changes. I use the $watch method, which I described in Chapter 13. (I don't have to worry about the individual properties of the data objects since they will be data bound in the transcluded template.)

Within the watcher function I use jqLite to locate the parent of the element to which the directive has been applied and then remove its children. I have to work with the parent element because I set the transclude property to element, which means that I want to add and remove copies of the directive's element.

The next step is to enumerate the data objects. I create a new scope by calling the $scope.$new method. This allows me to assign a different object to the item property for each instance of the transcluded content, which I clone like this:

```
...
transcludeFn(childScope, function (clone) {
    parent.append(clone);
});
...
```

This is the most important part of the example. For each data object, I call the transclude function that is passed to the compile function. The first argument is the child scope that contains the item property set to the current data item. The second argument is a function that is passed a cloned set of the transcluded content, which I append to the parent element using jqLite. The result is that I generate a copy of the tr element that my directive has been applied to—and its contents—for each data object and create a new scope that allows the transcluded content to refer to the current data object as item.

So that I can test that the directive responds to changes in the data, I added a Change button that calls the changeData behavior in the controller. This behavior adds a new item to the data array and increments the value of the price property on all of the data objects. You can see the result of my directive and of clicking the Change button in Figure 17-3.

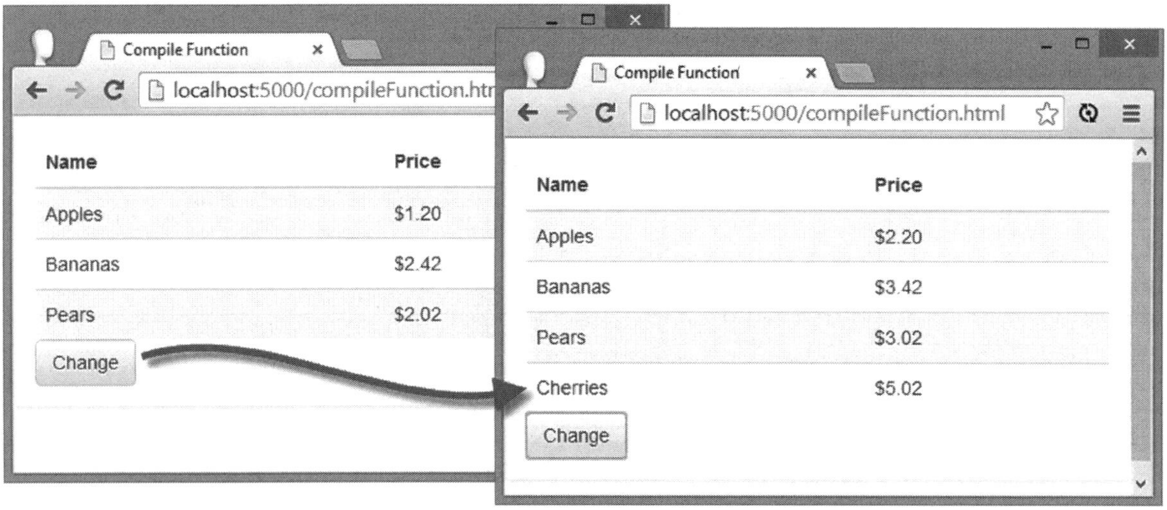

Figure 17-3. *Using transclusion and a compile function to duplicate content*

Using Controllers in Directives

Directives can create controllers, which can then be used by other directives. This allows directives to be combined to create more complex components. To demonstrate this feature, I added a new HTML file called directiveControllers.html to the angularjs folder and used it to define the AngularJS application shown in Listing 17-3.

Listing 17-3. The Contents of the directiveControllers.html File

```html
<!DOCTYPE html>
<html ng-app="exampleApp">
<head>
    <title>Directive Controllers</title>
    <script src="angular.js"></script>
    <link href="bootstrap.css" rel="stylesheet" />
    <link href="bootstrap-theme.css" rel="stylesheet" />
    <script type="text/ng-template" id="productTemplate">
        <td>{{item.name}}</td>
        <td><input ng-model='item.quantity' /></td>
    </script>
    <script>
        angular.module("exampleApp", [])
        .controller("defaultCtrl", function ($scope) {
            $scope.products = [{ name: "Apples", price: 1.20, quantity: 2 },
                { name: "Bananas", price: 2.42, quantity: 3 },
                { name: "Pears", price: 2.02, quantity: 1 }];
        })
        .directive("productItem", function () {
            return {
                template: document.querySelector("#productTemplate").outerText
            }
        })
        .directive("productTable", function () {
            return {
                transclude: true,
                scope: { value: "=productTable", data: "=productData" },
            }
        });
    </script>
</head>
<body ng-controller="defaultCtrl">
    <div class="panel panel-default">
        <div class="panel-body">
            <table class="table table-striped" product-table="totalValue"
                    product-data="products" ng-transclude>
                <tr><th>Name</th><th>Quantity</th></tr>
                <tr ng-repeat="item in products" product-item></tr>
                <tr><th>Total:</th><td>{{totalValue}}</td></tr>
            </table>
        </div>
    </div>
</body>
</html>
```

This example is based around two directives. The productTable directive is applied to a table element and uses transclusion to wrap a series of tr elements, one of which contains an inline binding for a value called totalValue. The other directive, productItem, is applied within the table using the ng-repeat directive to generate table rows for each of the data objects defined by the standard AngularJS controller; this isn't the directive controller feature, just a regular one.

455

The value for the property is the name of the directive and an optional prefix, as described in Table 17-2.

Table 17-2. *The Prefixes Used for the Value of the require Property*

Prefix	Description
None	Assumes that both directives are applied to the same element
^	Looks for the other directive on the parent elements of the element to which this directive was applied
?	Does not report an error if the directive cannot be found—use with caution

I specified the name productTable (since that is the name of the directive with the controller I want to use) and prefixed the value with ^, which I need to use because the productTable directive is applied to a parent of the element to which the productItem directive is applied.

I specify an additional parameter on the link function in order to use the capabilities defined by the controller, like this:

```
...
link: function (scope, element, attrs, ctrl) {
...
```

The controller argument isn't dependency injected, so you can call it whatever you want; my personal convention is to use the name ctrl. With these changes, I can then call the functions on the controller object as though they had been defined within the local directive:

```
...
ctrl.updateTotal();
...
```

I am invoking a controller method as a signal to perform a calculation, which doesn't require any arguments, but you can pass data from one controller to another, just as long as you remember that the $scope argument passed to the controller function is the scope of the directive that *defines* the controller, not the scope of the directive that requires it.

Adding Another Directive

The value of defining controller functions comes from the ability to separate and reuse functionality without having to build and test monolithic components. In my previous example, the productTable controller has no knowledge of the design or implementation of the productItem controller, which means I can test them separately and make changes freely as long as the productTable controller continues to provide the updateTotal function.

This approach also allows you to mix and match directive functionality to create different combinations of functionality within an application, and to demonstrate this, I have added a new directive to the directiveControllers.html file, as shown in Listing 17-5.

Listing 17-5. Adding a New Directive to the directiveControllers.html File

```html
<!DOCTYPE html>
<html ng-app="exampleApp">
<head>
    <title>Directive Controllers</title>
    <script src="angular.js"></script>
    <link href="bootstrap.css" rel="stylesheet" />
    <link href="bootstrap-theme.css" rel="stylesheet" />
    <script type="text/ng-template" id="productTemplate">
        <td>{{item.name}}</td>
        <td><input ng-model='item.quantity' /></td>
    </script>
    <script type="text/ng-template" id="resetTemplate">
        <td colspan="2"><button ng-click="reset()">Reset</button></td>
    </script>
    <script>
        angular.module("exampleApp", [])
        .controller("defaultCtrl", function ($scope) {
            $scope.products = [{ name: "Apples", price: 1.20, quantity: 2 },
                { name: "Bananas", price: 2.42, quantity: 3 },
                { name: "Pears", price: 2.02, quantity: 1 }];
        })
        .directive("productItem", function () {
            return {
                template: document.querySelector("#productTemplate").outerText,
                require: "^productTable",
                link: function (scope, element, attrs, ctrl) {
                    scope.$watch("item.quantity", function () {
                        ctrl.updateTotal();
                    });
                }
            }
        })
        .directive("productTable", function () {
            return {
                transclude: true,
                scope: { value: "=productTable", data: "=productData" },
                controller: function ($scope, $element, $attrs) {
                    this.updateTotal = function () {
                        var total = 0;
                        for (var i = 0; i < $scope.data.length; i++) {
                            total += Number($scope.data[i].quantity);
                        }
                        $scope.value = total;
                    }
                }
            }
        })
```

```
        .directive("resetTotals", function () {
            return {
                scope: { data: "=productData", propname: "@propertyName" },
                template: document.querySelector("#resetTemplate").outerText,
                require: "^productTable",
                link: function (scope, element, attrs, ctrl) {
                    scope.reset = function () {
                        for (var i = 0; i < scope.data.length; i++) {
                            scope.data[i][scope.propname] = 0;
                        }
                        ctrl.updateTotal();
                    }
                }
            }
        });
    </script>
</head>
<body ng-controller="defaultCtrl">
    <div class="panel panel-default">
        <div class="panel-body">
            <table class="table table-striped" product-table="totalValue"
                    product-data="products" ng-transclude>
                <tr><th>Name</th><th>Quantity</th></tr>
                <tr ng-repeat="item in products" product-item></tr>
                <tr><th>Total:</th><td>{{totalValue}}</td></tr>
                <tr reset-totals product-data="products" property-name="quantity"></tr>
            </table>
        </div>
    </div>
</body>
</html>
```

The new directive is called resetTotals, and it adds a Reset button to the table that zeros all of the quantities, which it locates using data bindings on an isolated scope that provide the data array and the name of the property to set to zero. After the values are reset, the resetTotals directive calls the updateTotal method provided by the productTable directive.

This is still a simple example, but it demonstrates that the productTable neither knows nor cares which directives, if any, will use its controllers. You can create productTable instances that contain as many or as few instances of the resetTotals and productItem directives, and everything will continue to work without modification.

Creating Custom Form Elements

I introduced the ng-model directive in Chapter 10 when I showed you two-way data binding and again in Chapter 12 when I described the way that AngularJS supports HTML forms. The way that the ng-model directive is structured allows you to go beyond the standard form elements and capture data input in any way you want, giving you complete freedom about the components that you create and present to your users. As a demonstration, I added a file called customForms.html to the angularjs folder and used it to create the example shown in Listing 17-6.

Listing 17-6. The Contents of the customForms.html File

```html
<!DOCTYPE html>
<html ng-app="exampleApp">
<head>
    <title>CustomForms</title>
    <script src="angular.js"></script>
    <link href="bootstrap.css" rel="stylesheet" />
    <link href="bootstrap-theme.css" rel="stylesheet" />
    <script type="text/ng-template" id="triTemplate">
        <div class="well">
            <div class="btn-group">
                <button class="btn btn-default">Yes</button>
                <button class="btn btn-default">No</button>
                <button class="btn btn-default">Not Sure</button>
            </div>
        </div>
    </script>
    <script>
        angular.module("exampleApp", [])
        .controller("defaultCtrl", function ($scope) {
            $scope.dataValue = "Not Sure";
        })
        .directive("triButton", function () {
            return {
                restrict: "E",
                replace: true,
                require: "ngModel",
                template: document.querySelector("#triTemplate").outerText,
                link: function (scope, element, attrs, ctrl) {
                    var setSelected = function (value) {
                        var buttons = element.find("button");
                        buttons.removeClass("btn-primary");
                        for (var i = 0; i < buttons.length; i++) {
                            if (buttons.eq(i).text() == value) {
                                buttons.eq(i).addClass("btn-primary");
                            }
                        }
                    }
                    setSelected(scope.dataValue);
                }
            }
        });
    </script>
</head>
<body ng-controller="defaultCtrl">
    <div><tri-button ng-model="dataValue" /></div>
    <div class="well">
            Value:
            <select ng-model="dataValue">
```

```
                <option>Yes</option>
                <option>No</option>
                <option>Not Sure</option>
            </select>
    </div>
</body>
</html>
```

This listing defines the structure of my custom form element but doesn't yet use the API. I am going to explain how my control will work and then apply the new techniques. As it stands, this example doesn't contain anything new. I have created a directive called triButton that can be applied as an element and presents the user with three button elements that have been styled using Bootstrap. I have declared a dependency on the ngModel controller (which is the controller defined by the ng-model directive since AngularJS normalizes names), and I have added the ctrl argument to the link function.

I defined a function called setSelected within the link function that I use to highlight the button element that represents the form value that my directive displays. I do this by using jqLite to add and remove a Bootstrap class; you can see the effect in Figure 17-5.

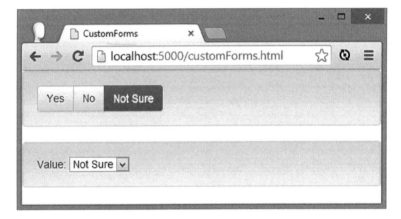

Figure 17-5. *The initial state of the example*

Notice that I applied the ng-model directive to my tri-button element, as follows:

```
...
<div><tri-button ng-model="dataValue" /></div>
...
```

This applies the directive to my custom element and sets up a two-way binding to the dataValue property on the scope. My goal is to use the ngModel controller API to implement that binding within my triButton directive.

I included a select element that is bound to the dataValue property as well. This isn't part of my custom directive, but since I am implementing a two-way data binding, I need to be able to show the effect of the user changing the dataValue value through the custom directive and how to receive and handle notification that the value has been changed elsewhere.

Handling External Changes

The first feature I am going to add is the ability to change the highlighted button when the dataValue property is modified outside of my directive, which in this example means through the select element (but could be from any number of sources in a real project). You can see the changes I made to the link function in Listing 17-7.

Listing 17-7. Handling Changes to the Data Value in the customForms.html File

```
...
link: function (scope, element, attrs, ctrl) {

    var setSelected = function (value) {
        var buttons = element.find("button");
        buttons.removeClass("btn-primary");
        for (var i = 0; i < buttons.length; i++) {
            if (buttons.eq(i).text() == value) {
                buttons.eq(i).addClass("btn-primary");
            }
        }
    }

    ctrl.$render = function () {
        setSelected(ctrl.$viewValue || "Not Sure");
    }
}
...
```

The change is minor, but it has a big impact. I have replaced the $render function defined by the ngModel controller with one that calls my setSelected function. The $render method is called by the ng-model directive when the value has been modified outside the directive and the display needs to be updated. I get the new value by reading the $viewValue property.

■ **Tip**   Notice that I removed the explicit call to setSelected that was present in Listing 17-6. The ngModel controller will call the $render function when the application first starts so that you can set the initial state of your directive. The value of the $viewValue will be undefined if you are using dynamically defined properties, and that's why it is good practice to provide a fallback value, as I have done in the listing.

You can see the effect by loading the customForms.html file into the browser and using the select element to change the value of the dataValue property, as shown in Figure 17-6. Notice that my directive code doesn't reference the dataValue property directly; the data binding and the data property are managed through the NgModel controller API.

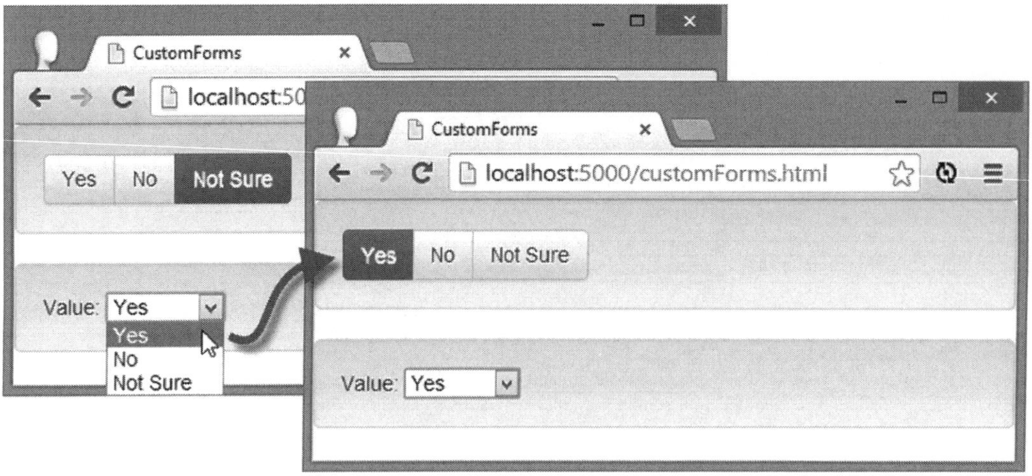

Figure 17-6. *Changing the dataValue property from outside the custom directive*

The $render method and the $viewValue properties are the mainstays of the API provided by the NgModel controller, but I have described the complete set of basic methods and properties in Table 17-3. I say *basic* because there are some others that relate to form validation that I describe in a later section.

Table 17-3. *The Basic Methods and Properties Provided by the NgModel Controller*

Name	Description
$render()	This is the function that the NgModel controller calls to update the UI when the data-bound value changes. It is usually overridden by custom directives.
$setViewValue(value)	Updates the data-bound value.
$viewValue	Returns the formatted value that should be displayed by the directive.
$modelValue	Returns the unformatted value from the scope.
$formatters	An array of formatter functions that transform $modelValue into $viewValue.

I'll show you how to use the remaining methods and properties in the sections that follow.

Handling Internal Changes

The next addition to my custom directive is the ability to propagate changes through the ng-model directive to the scope when the user clicks one of the buttons. You can see how I have done this in Listing 17-8.

Listing 17-8. Adding Support for Propagating Changes in the customForms.html File

```
...
link: function (scope, element, attrs, ctrl) {
    element.on("click", function (event) {
        setSelected(event.target.innerText);
```

```
        scope.$apply(function () {
            ctrl.$setViewValue(event.target.innerText);
        });
    });

    var setSelected = function (value) {
        var buttons = element.find("button");
        buttons.removeClass("btn-primary");
        for (var i = 0; i < buttons.length; i++) {
            if (buttons.eq(i).text() == value) {
                buttons.eq(i).addClass("btn-primary");
            }
        }
    }

    ctrl.$render = function () {
        setSelected(ctrl.$viewValue || "Not Sure");
    }
}
...
```

I have used the jqLite on method, described in Chapter 15, to register a handler function for the click event on the button elements in the directive template. When the user clicks one of the buttons, I notify the NgModel controller by calling the $setViewValue method, like this:

```
...
scope.$apply(function () {
    ctrl.$setViewValue(event.target.innerText);
});
...
```

I introduced the scope.$apply method in Chapter 13 and explained that it is used to push updates into the data model. In Chapter 13, I pass the $apply method an expression for the scope to evaluate, but I have used a function as the argument in this example. The scope will execute the function and then update its state; using a function allows me to notify the NgModel controller of the change and have the scope update its state in a single step.

To update the data-bound value, I call the $setViewValue method, which accepts the new value as its argument. For this example, I get the value from the text content of the button that has been clicked, such that clicking the Yes button causes the dataValue property to be set to Yes.

■ **Caution** Calling the $setViewValue method doesn't cause the NgModel controller to call the $render method. This means you are responsible for updating the state of the directive elements to reflect the new value, and it is why I made a call to the setSelected function in the click event handler.

Formatting Data Values

In Table 17-3, I described the $viewValue and $modelValue properties. The NgModel controller provides a simple mechanism for formatting values in the data model so that they can be displayed by a directive. The application of these formatters, which are expressed as functions, transforms the $modelValue property into the $viewValue. Listing 17-9 shows the use of a formatter that maps an additional value defined by the select value to the buttons provided by the directive.

Listing 17-9. Using a Formatter in the customForms.html File

```
...
link: function (scope, element, attrs, ctrl) {

    ctrl.$formatters.push(function (value) {
        return value == "Huh?" ? "Not Sure" : value;
    });

    // ...other statements omitted for brevity...
}
...
```

The $formatters property is an array of functions that are applied in order. The result from the previous formatter is passed as the argument, and the function returns its formatted result. The formatter I created in this instance maps a new value, Huh?, to Not Sure. To make use of the formatter, I have added the new value to the select element, as shown in Listing 17-10.

Listing 17-10. Adding a Value to the select Element in the customForms.html File

```
...
<div class="well">
    Value: <select ng-model="dataValue">
        <option>Yes</option>
        <option>No</option>
        <option>Not Sure</option>
        <option>Huh?</option>
    </select>
</div>
...
```

You can see the effect in Figure 17-7. The select element is set to Huh?, but my custom directive has highlighted the Not Sure button. The key point to note is that the result of the formatting is assigned to the $viewValue property but that you can get the unformatted value if you need it from the $modelValue property.

Figure 17-7. The effect of using a formatter

Validating Custom Form Elements

The ngModel controller also provides support for integrating custom directives into the AngularJS form validation system. To demonstrate how this works, Listing 17-11 shows how I have updated my triButton directive so that only the Yes and No values are valid.

Listing 17-11. Adding Validation in the customForms.html File

```
<!DOCTYPE html>
<html ng-app="exampleApp">
<head>
    <title>CustomForms</title>
    <script src="angular.js"></script>
    <link href="bootstrap.css" rel="stylesheet" />
    <link href="bootstrap-theme.css" rel="stylesheet" />
    <style>
        *.error { color: red; font-weight: bold; }
    </style>
    <script type="text/ng-template" id="triTemplate">
        <div class="well">
            <div class="btn-group">
                <button class="btn btn-default">Yes</button>
                <button class="btn btn-default">No</button>
                <button class="btn btn-default">Not Sure</button>
            </div>
            <span class="error" ng-show="myForm.decision.$error.confidence">
                You need to be sure
            </span>
        </div>
    </script>
    <script>
        angular.module("exampleApp", [])
        .controller("defaultCtrl", function ($scope) {
            $scope.dataValue = "Not Sure";
        })
        .directive("triButton", function () {
            return {
                restrict: "E",
                replace: true,
                require: "ngModel",
                template: document.querySelector("#triTemplate").outerText,
                link: function (scope, element, attrs, ctrl) {

                    var validateParser = function (value) {
                        var valid = (value == "Yes" || value == "No");
                        ctrl.$setValidity("confidence", valid);
                        return valid ? value : undefined;
                    }

                    ctrl.$parsers.push(validateParser);
```

```
                    element.on("click", function (event) {
                        setSelected(event.target.innerText);
                        scope.$apply(function () {
                            ctrl.$setViewValue(event.target.innerText);
                        });
                    });

                    var setSelected = function (value) {
                        var buttons = element.find("button");
                        buttons.removeClass("btn-primary");
                        for (var i = 0; i < buttons.length; i++) {
                            if (buttons.eq(i).text() == value) {
                                buttons.eq(i).addClass("btn-primary");
                            }
                        }
                    }

                    ctrl.$render = function () {
                        setSelected(ctrl.$viewValue || "Not Sure");
                    }
                }
            }
        });
    </script>
</head>
<body ng-controller="defaultCtrl">
    <form name="myForm" novalidate>
        <div><tri-button name="decision" ng-model="dataValue" /></div>
    </form>
</body>
</html>
```

Most of the changes in this listing are for the standard form validation techniques that I described in Chapter 12. I have added a span element to the directive template whose visibility is keyed to a validation error called confidence, and I have added a form element to wrap the triButton directive and applied the name attribute.

To perform the validation, I have defined a new function called validateParser, as follows:

```
...
var validateParser = function (value) {
    var valid = (value == "Yes" || value == "No");
    ctrl.$setValidity("confidence", valid);
    return valid ? value : undefined;
}
...
```

Parser functions are passed the data-bound value and are responsible for checking to see whether it is valid. The validity of a value is set with a call to the $setValidity method defined by the NgModel controller, where the arguments are the key (used to display the validation message) and the validation status (expressed as a Boolean). The parser function is also required to return undefined for invalid values. Parsers are registered by adding the function to the $parsers array, defined by the NgModel controller, as follows:

```
...
ctrl.$parsers.push(validateParser);
...
```

A directive can have multiple parser functions, just as it can have multiple formatters. You can see the result of the validation by loading the customForms.html file into the browser and clicking the Yes button and then the Not Sure button, as shown in Figure 17-8.

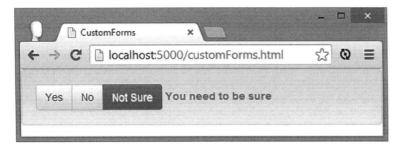

Figure 17-8. *Performing validation on a custom form control*

The NgModel controller provides a range of methods and properties that are useful for integrating a custom directive into the validation process, as described in Table 17-4.

Table 17-4. *The Validation Methods and Properties Provided by the NgModel Controller*

Name	Description
$setPristine()	Returns the validation state of the control to pristine, which prevents validation from being performed.
$isEmpty()	Can be set to the directive to indicate when the control has no value. The default implementation is intended for standard form elements and looks for values that are the empty string, null, or undefined.
$parsers	An array of functions used to validate the model value.
$error	Returns an object whose properties correspond to validation errors.
$pristine	Returns true if the control has not been modified by the user.
$dirty	Returns true if the control has been modified by the user.
$valid	Returns true if the model value is valid.
$invalid	Returns true if the model valid is invalid.

You may have wondered why you had to click the Yes button before clicking Not Sure to reveal the validation message. The issue is that validation is not performed until the user interacts with the UI presented by the directive (or more, accurately, when a new value is passed to the NgModel controller), so the parsers are not used until the model changes.

This isn't always what is required and doesn't make sense for my example directive, but the problem can be addressed by explicitly calling the parser function in the $render function, as shown in Listing 17-12.

Listing 17-12. Explicitly Calling a Parser Function in the customForms.html File

```
...
ctrl.$render = function () {
    validateParser(ctrl.$viewValue);
    setSelected(ctrl.$viewValue || "Not Sure");
}
...
```

This is a bit of a hack, but it does the job, and the validation message is displayed as soon as the HTML file is loaded.

Summary

In this section, I finished describing custom AngularJS directives by showing you the most advanced features. I showed you how to wrap content using transclusion, how to use transclusion and a compile function to generate repeating content, how to create directives that communicate with one another using controllers, and—my favorite feature—how to create custom form elements by building on the API provided by the NgModel controller. In Part 3 of this book, I turn to modules and services, including the extensive set of built-in services that AngularJS provides.

PART 3

AngularJS Services

CHAPTER 18

■ ■ ■

Working with Modules and Services

In this chapter, I recap the role that modules play in AngularJS and show you how to can use modules to organize the components in an application. I also introduce the *service* component, show you the different ways to create and use services, and briefly describe the many built-in services that AngularJS includes. I say *briefly* because I dive into the detail of the built-in services in the chapters that follow. Table 18-1 summarizes this chapter.

Table 18-1. *Chapter Summary*

Problem	Solution	Listing
Split an application into multiple files.	Extend an existing module or create a new one.	1–5
Create a service by defining an object.	Use the `Module.factory` method.	6–8
Create a service by defining a constructor.	Use the `Module.service` method.	9–10
Create a service that can be configured via a provider.	Use the `Module.provider` method.	11–13

Why and When to Use and Create Services and Modules

Services are used to encapsulate functionality that you want to reuse in an application but that don't fit neatly into the Model-View-Controller pattern that I described in Chapter 3. Services are commonly used to implement *cross-cutting concerns*, which is a catchall term for any functionality that is affected by more than one component or affects more than one component. Typical examples are logging, security, and networking. They are not part of the model (unless your business *is* logging, security, or networking), they don't belong to the controllers because they don't respond to user interaction or perform operations on the model, and they are not part of the view or a directive because they don't present the model to the user. In short, if you need to create functionality that doesn't go elsewhere, then you create a service.

Modules have two roles in AngularJS. The first is they define the application functionality that is applied to the HTML elements using the `ng-app` directive. I have done this in every example application in this book, and defining a module is the starting point for AngularJS development. The second use of a module is to define functionality, such as services, directives, and filters, in a way that makes it easy to reuse it in different applications. Table 18-2 summarizes why and when to create services and modules.

Table 18-2. *Why and When to Create Modules and Services*

Why	When
Services allow you to package up reusable functionality so that it can be used across the application. Modules allow you to package up reusable functionality so that it can be used across multiple applications.	Create a service when functionality doesn't fit into one of the other MVC building blocks and is a cross-cutting concern. Create a module to package functionality so that it can be used in multiple applications.

AngularJS includes a number of built-in modules services that provide important functionality. In this chapter, I'll show you the different ways to create and use modules and services before describing the built-in services in depth in the following chapters.

Preparing the Example Project

To prepare for this chapter, I deleted the contents of the angularjs web server folder and installed the angular.js, bootstrap.css, and bootstrap-theme.css files, as described in Chapter 1. I then created a file called example.html, which you can see in Listing 18-1.

Listing 18-1. The Contents of the example.html File

```
<!DOCTYPE html>
<html ng-app="exampleApp">
<head>
    <title>Services and Modules</title>
    <script src="angular.js"></script>
    <link href="bootstrap.css" rel="stylesheet" />
    <link href="bootstrap-theme.css" rel="stylesheet" />
    <script>
        angular.module("exampleApp", [])
        .controller("defaultCtrl", function ($scope) {
            $scope.data = {
                cities: ["London", "New York", "Paris"],
                totalClicks: 0
            };

            $scope.$watch('data.totalClicks', function (newVal) {
                console.log("Total click count: " + newVal);
            });
        })
        .directive("triButton", function () {
            return {
                scope: { counter: "=counter" },
                link: function (scope, element, attrs) {
                    element.on("click", function (event) {
                        console.log("Button click: " + event.target.innerText);
```

```
                            scope.$apply(function () {
                                scope.counter++;
                            });
                        });
                    }
                }
            });
        </script>
    </head>
    <body ng-controller="defaultCtrl">
        <div class="well">
            <div class="btn-group" tri-button
                 counter="data.totalClicks" source="data.cities">
                <button class="btn btn-default"
                        ng-repeat="city in data.cities">
                    {{city}}
                </button>
            </div>
            <h5>Total Clicks: {{data.totalClicks}}</h5>
        </div>
    </body>
</html>
```

This example is based around three button elements, which are generated by the ng-repeat directive from a list of city names defined on the scope by the controller. There is a triButton directive that handles click events from the button elements and updates a counter that is defined by the controller and is data bound via an isolated scope.

This is a totally pointless example in and of itself, but it has some key characteristics that will allow me to demonstrate some important features in the sections that follow. You can see how the example appears in the browser in Figure 18-1.

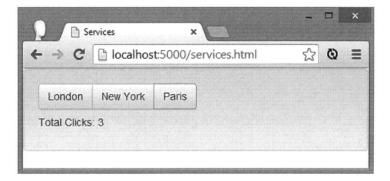

Figure 18-1. *The three buttons and counter of the simple example*

Each time a button is clicked, messages are written to the JavaScript console (which you can access through your browser's F12 developer tools) by the controller and the directive, like this:

```
Button click: London
Total click count: 1
```

The total number of clicks is also displayed via an inline binding expression in the HTML markup (and can be seen in the figure).

■ **Tip** A message will also be written to the console by the controller when the application is first loaded into the browser. This is because I have used the scope `$watch` method (described in Chapter 13) whose handler function is triggered when the watcher is first set up.

Using Modules to Structure an Application

As I explained in Chapter 3, AngularJS shines when it is used to implement complicated applications, and that tends to mean that AngularJS applications have lots of components such as controllers, directives, filters, and services that work together to deliver functionality to the user. Most of the examples I have created to show you features in this book have contained all of the code and markup in a single HTML file, but that just doesn't work in real projects. Not only does a single file become unwieldy, but it also makes it hard for several developers to work on the project at the same time.

The solution is to organize the application's components into separate files and use `script` elements to reference those files in a central HTML file. You can name and organize your files in any way that makes sense to your project; common approaches include putting all of the components of a given type together (controllers in one file, directives in another) and putting all of the components related to a particular part of the application together (components for user management in one file, components for content management in another).

■ **Tip** You can similarly break the HTML markup in your application into multiple files and load the fragments you need as the application runs. I explain how this is done in Chapter 22.

For especially large .0 applications, it is common to create hierarchies of folders for one level of organization (function or component) and then have multiple files for the other level. Whatever approach you settle on, you will need to use modules to organize your code. In the sections that follow, I'll show you two approaches to using modules to structure an application.

■ **Tip** If you are new to AngularJS, then I recommend you start organizing by component type because it is what tends to be at the front of the mind when trying to figure out whether you should express some code as a controller or a directive, for example. You can switch to another organizational style once you have become familiar with the way that AngularJS works.

Maintaining a Single Module

The simplest way to move a component to another file is to do so within the same module. To demonstrate this, I have created a file called directives.js and moved the triButton directive from Listing 18-1 to it, as shown in Listing 18-2.

Listing 18-2. The Contents of the directives.js File

```
angular.module("exampleApp")
.directive("triButton", function () {
    return {
        scope: { counter: "=counter" },
        link: function (scope, element, attrs) {
            element.on("click", function (event) {
                console.log("Button click: " + event.target.innerText);
                scope.$apply(function () {
                    scope.counter++;
                });
            });
        }
    }
});
```

I call the angular.module method and pass in the name of the module defined in the script element of the example.html file. Calling the module method with a single argument tells AngularJS that you want to obtain the Module object that represents a previously defined module, on which you can call methods such as directive to define new functionality. I have already described many of the methods defined by the Module object, and I describe the rest in this chapter. As a reminder, Table 18-3 summarizes the Module methods.

Table 18-3. The Members of the Module Object

Name	Description
animation(name, factory)	Supports the animation feature, which I describe in Chapter 23.
config(callback)	Registers a function that can be used to configure a module when it is loaded. See Chapter 9.
constant(key, value)	Defines a service that returns a constant value. See Chapter 9.
controller(name, constructor)	Creates a controller. See Chapter 13 for details.
directive(name, factory)	Creates a directive. See Chapters 15–17 for details.
factory(name, provider)	Creates a service. See the "Using the Factory Method" section later in this chapter for details.
filter(name, factory)	Creates a filter that formats data for display to the user. See Chapter 14 for details.
provider(name, type)	Creates a service, as described in the "Using the Provider Method" section of this chapter.

(*continued*)

Table 18-3. (*continued*)

Name	Description
name	Returns the name of the module.
run(callback)	Registers a function that is invoked after AngularJS has loaded and configured all of the modules. See Chapter 9.
service(name, constructor)	Creates a service, as described in the "Using the Service Method" section of this chapter.
value(name, value)	Defines a service that returns a constant value. See Chapter 9.

■ **Tip** The constant and value methods also create services—just services that are limited in what they can be used for. This doesn't have any real bearing on how you use these methods, but I think it is a nice insight into how widely AngularJS uses services.

To bring the contents of the new JavaScript file into the application, I need to add a script element to the example.html file, as shown in Listing 18-3.

Listing 18-3. Adding a script Element to the example.html File

```
...
<head>
    <title>Services and Modules</title>
    <script src="angular.js"></script>
    <link href="bootstrap.css" rel="stylesheet" />
    <link href="bootstrap-theme.css" rel="stylesheet" />
    <script>
        angular.module("exampleApp", [])
        .controller("defaultCtrl", function ($scope) {
            $scope.data = {
                cities: ["London", "New York", "Paris"],
                totalClicks: 0
            };

            $scope.$watch('data.totalClicks', function (newVal) {
                console.log("Total click count: " + newVal);
            });
        });
    </script>
    <script src="directives.js"></script>
</head>
...
```

I have to add the script element for the directives.js file after the inline script element because the directive is being added to the module that is defined in the example.html file. AngularJS will report an error if the directives.js file is imported before the exampleApp module is defined.

Creating a New Module

Keeping everything in a single module is fine for simple applications, but for more complex applications it can be helpful to define multiple modules, especially if you intend to reuse functionality in several projects. In Listing 18-4, you can see how I have changed the `directives.js` file so that the directive is defined in a new module.

Listing 18-4. Defining a New Module in the directives.js File

```
angular.module("customDirectives", [])
.directive("triButton", function () {
    return {
        scope: { counter: "=counter" },
        link: function (scope, element, attrs) {
            element.on("click", function (event) {
                console.log("Button click: " + event.target.innerText);
                scope.$apply(function () {
                    scope.counter++;
                });
            });
        }
    }
});
```

The difference is the way that I have called the `angular.module` method. I have provided two arguments, which tells AngularJS that I want to create a new module. The first argument is the name of the new module, which is `customDirectives` in this example, and the second is an array containing the names of the modules that my new module depends on. I have used an empty array to indicate that there are no dependencies. In Listing 18-5, you can see how I use my new module in the `example.html` file.

Listing 18-5. Using the New Module in the example.html File

```
...
<head>
    <title>Services and Modules</title>
    <script src="angular.js"></script>
    <script src="directives.js"></script>
    <link href="bootstrap.css" rel="stylesheet" />
    <link href="bootstrap-theme.css" rel="stylesheet" />
    <script>
        angular.module("exampleApp", ["customDirectives"])
        .controller("defaultCtrl", function ($scope) {
            $scope.data = {
                cities: ["London", "New York", "Paris"],
                totalClicks: 0
            };

            $scope.$watch('data.totalClicks', function (newVal) {
                console.log("Total click count: " + newVal);
            });
        });
    </script>
</head>
...
```

To use the directive in the `directives.js` file, I have added the name of the `customDirectives` module as a dependency of the `exampleApp` module. I need to declare this dependency because a directive in the new module has been applied to one of the elements in the view managed by the `defaultCtrl` controller.

■ **Tip**   Although I moved the `script` element for the `directives.html` file in this listing, the application would have worked quite happily if I had left it at the bottom of the `head` element as in Listing 18-3. AngularJS loads all of its modules before processing dependencies; ordering matters only when you are trying to modify a module defined in another `script` element.

Creating and Using a Service

The AngularJS Module defines three methods for defining services: `factory`, `service`, and `provider`. The result of using these methods is the same—a *service object* that provides functionality that can be used throughout the AngularJS application—but the way that the service object is created and managed by each method is slightly different, as I explain and demonstrate in the sections that follow.

Using the Factory Method

The simplest way to create a service is to use the `Module.factory` method, passing as arguments the name of the service and a factory function that returns the service object. To demonstrate how this works, I have created a new file called `services.js` in the angularjs folder and used it to create a new module that defines a service. You can see the contents of the `services.js` file in Listing 18-6.

Listing 18-6. The Contents of the services.js File

```
angular.module("customServices", [])
    .factory("logService", function () {
        var messageCount = 0;
        return {
            log: function (msg) {
                console.log("(LOG + " + messageCount++ + ") " + msg);
            }
        };
    });
```

I have defined a new module called `customServices` and called the `factory` method to create a service called `logService`. My service factory function returns an object that defines a `log` function, which accepts a message as an argument and writes it to the console.

■ **Tip**   I am creating a custom logging service, but there is a built-in one that I could have used instead. The built-in service is called `$log`, and I describe it in Chapter 19.

The object returned by the factory function is the *service object* and will be used by AngularJS whenever the `logService` is requested. The factory function is called only once because the object it creates and returns is used whenever the service is required within the application. A common error is to assume that each consumer of the service will receive a different service object and assume that variables like counters will be modified by only one AngularJS component.

■ **Caution**   Be careful not to reuse the name of a service. If you do, your service will replace the existing one. One of the reasons that the built-in services that I describe in the following chapters all begin with $ is to help avoid naming conflicts. In Chapter 19, I show you the one built-in service that is intended to be replaced by a custom implementation—but otherwise, keep your service names unique.

I have defined a variable called messageCount that is included in the messages written to the JavaScript console to emphasize the fact that services objects are singletons. The variable is a counter that is incremented each time a message is written to the console, and it will help demonstrate that only one instance of the object is created. You will see the effect of this counter when I test the service shortly.

■ **Tip**   Notice that I defined the messageCount variable in the factory function, rather than as part of the service object. I don't want consumers of the service to be able to modify the counter, and placing it outside of the service object means that it isn't accessible to service consumers.

Having created the service, I can now apply it to the main application module, as shown in Listing 18-7.

Listing 18-7. Consuming the Service in the example.html File

```
<!DOCTYPE html>
<html ng-app="exampleApp">
<head>
    <title>Services and Modules</title>
    <script src="angular.js"></script>
    <script src="directives.js"></script>
    <script src="services.js"></script>
    <link href="bootstrap.css" rel="stylesheet" />
    <link href="bootstrap-theme.css" rel="stylesheet" />
    <script>
        angular.module("exampleApp", ["customDirectives", "customServices"])
        .controller("defaultCtrl", function ($scope, logService) {
            $scope.data = {
                cities: ["London", "New York", "Paris"],
                totalClicks: 0
            };

            $scope.$watch('data.totalClicks', function (newVal) {
                logService.log("Total click count: " + newVal);
            });
        });
    </script>
</head>
```

```
<body ng-controller="defaultCtrl">
    <div class="well">
        <div class="btn-group" tri-button
            counter="data.totalClicks" source="data.cities">
            <button class="btn btn-default"
                    ng-repeat="city in data.cities">
                {{city}}
            </button>
        </div>
        <h5>Total Clicks: {{data.totalClicks}}</h5>
    </div>
</body>
</html>
```

I have added a script element to import the services.js file into the HTML document, which ensures that the service is available for use. After that, it is simply a matter of adding an argument to the factory function of the controller to declare its dependency on the service. The name of the argument *must* match the name used to create the service because AngularJS inspects the arguments of factory functions and uses them to perform dependency injection. That means you can define the argument in any order, but it does prevent you from picking your own argument names. I can also consume the service in my custom directive, as shown in Listing 18-8.

Listing 18-8. Consuming the Service in the directives.js File

```
angular.module("customDirectives", ["customServices"])
    .directive("triButton", function (logService) {
        return {
            scope: { counter: "=counter" },
            link: function (scope, element, attrs) {
                element.on("click", function (event) {
                    logService.log("Button click: " + event.target.innerText);
                    scope.$apply(function () {
                        scope.counter++;
                    });
                });
            }
        }
    });
```

Once the dependencies on the module and the service have been declared, I call the logService.log method to access the simple functionality provided by the service. If you load the example HTML file into the browser and click the buttons, you will see output like this in the JavaScript console:

```
(LOG + 0) Total click count: 0
(LOG + 1) Button click: London
(LOG + 2) Total click count: 1
(LOG + 3) Button click: New York
(LOG + 4) Total click count: 2
```

You might be wondering why using a service is better than the original example where I called console.log directly. There are a couple of benefits. The first is that I can disable logging throughout the entire application by commenting out one line in the services.js file, rather than having to search through the application looking for console.log calls. This is not a big deal in my simple example application, but it is a big deal in a real project made up of many large and complex files.

The second benefit is that the consumers of the service have no insight into or dependency on its implementation. The controller and directive in this example know that there is a logService, and they know that it defines a method called log, but that's all—and that means I can completely change the way that logging is performed without having to make any changes outside of the service object.

The final benefit is that I can isolate and test the logging functionality separately from the rest of the application, using the techniques I describe in Chapter 25.

In short, services let you build common functionality without breaking the MVC pattern—something that becomes increasingly important as your projects grow in scale and complexity. And, as you will learn, some important AngularJS features are provided through a set of built-in services.

Using the Service Method

The Module.service method also creates service objects, but in a slightly different way. When AngularJS needs to satisfy a dependency for a service defined by the factory method, it simply uses the object returned by the factory function, but for a service defined with the service method, AngularJS uses the object returned by the factory function as a constructor and uses the JavaScript new keyword to create the service object.

The new keyword isn't widely used in JavaScript development, and when it is used, it causes a lot of confusion because most developers are familiar with the class-based inheritance used by languages such as C# and Java and not the prototype-based inheritance used by JavaScript. A demonstration will help explain what the new keyword does and how it is used by the Module.service method. In Listing 18-9, I have updated the contents of the services.js file to take advantage of the service method.

Listing 18-9. Using the service Method in the service.js File

```
var baseLogger = function () {
    this.messageCount = 0;
    this.log = function (msg) {
        console.log(this.msgType + ": " + (this.messageCount++)  + " " + msg);
    }
};

var debugLogger = function () { };
debugLogger.prototype = new baseLogger();
debugLogger.prototype.msgType = "Debug";

var errorLogger = function () { };
errorLogger.prototype = new baseLogger();
errorLogger.prototype.msgType = "Error";

angular.module("customServices", [])
    .service("logService", debugLogger)
    .service("errorService", errorLogger);
```

The first thing I have done is create a *constructor function*, which is essentially a template for defining functionality that will be defined on new objects. My constructor function is called baseLogger, and it defines the messageCount variable and the log method you saw in the previous section. The log method passes an undefined variable called msgType to the console.log method, which I'll set when I use the baseLogger constructor function as a template.

The next step I take is to create a new constructor function called debugLogger and set its prototype to a new object created using the new keyword and the baseLogger keyword. The new keyword creates a new object and copies the properties and functions defined by the constructor function to the new object. The `prototype` property is used to alter the template. I call it once to ensure that the `debugLogger` constructor inherits the property and method from the `baseLogger` constructor and again to define the `msgType` property.

The whole point of using constructors is that you can define functionality in the template once and then have it applied to multiple objects—and to that end, I have repeated the process to create a third constructor function called `errorLogger`. The use of the `new` keyword in both cases means that I define the `messageCount` property and the `log` method once but have it apply to both to objects that are created by the `debugLogger` and `errorLogger` constructors and the objects that are created from them. To finish the example, I register the `debugLogger` and `errorLogger` constructors as services, like this:

```
...
angular.module("customServices", [])
    .service("logService", debugLogger)
    .service("errorService", errorLogger);
...
```

Notice that I pass the constructors to the `service` method. AngularJS will call the new method to create the service objects. To test the new service, simply load the `example.html` file into the browser. I don't need to make any changes to the controller or directive because AngularJS presents all service objects to consumers in the same way, hiding the details of how they were created. If you click the city buttons, you will see output like the following:

```
...
Debug: 0 Total click count: 0
Debug: 1 Button click: London
Debug: 2 Total click count: 1
Debug: 3 Button click: New York
Debug: 4 Total click count: 2
...
```

As I said, the `new` keyword isn't widely used, prototype-based inheritance can be confusing, and I am just touching the surface of what's possible. The advantage of this approach is that I defined my `log` method in one place but was able to use it in two services. The disadvantage is that the code is verbose and won't be readily understood by many JavaScript programmers.

You don't have to use prototypes with the `service` method. You can treat it as being equivalent to the factory method, and I recommend you do exactly that when you are new to AngularJS because you have enough to keep track of without remembering which methods use a specific technique to create service objects. In Listing 18-10, you can see how I have updated the `services.js` file to define a service with the `service` method, but without the use of the JavaScript prototype features.

Listing 18-10. Using the service Method Without Prototypes in the services.js File

```
angular.module("customServices", [])
    .service("logService", function () {
        return {
            messageCount: 0,
            log: function (msg) {
                console.log("Debug: " + (this.messageCount++) + " " + msg);
            }
        };
    });
```

This isn't as flexible, and AngularJS will still use the new keyword behind the scenes, but the overall effect is to allow the service method to be used as an interchangeable replacement for the factory method but with a more immediately meaningful name.

Using the Provider Method

The Module.provider method allows you to take more control over the way that a service object is created or configured. In Listing 18-11, you can see how I have updated my logging service so that it is defined using the provider method.

Listing 18-11. Using the provider Method to Define a Service in the services.js File

```
angular.module("customServices", [])
    .provider("logService", function() {
        return {
            $get: function () {
                return {
                    messageCount: 0,
                    log: function (msg) {
                        console.log("(LOG + " + this.messageCount++ + ") " + msg);
                    }
                };
            }
        }
    });
```

The arguments to the provider method are the name of the service that is being defined and a factory function. The factory function is required to return a *provider object* that defines a method called $get, which in turn is required to return the service object.

When the service is required, AngularJS calls the factory method to get the provider object and then calls the $get method to get the service object. Using the provider method doesn't change the way that services are consumed, which means that I don't need to make any changes to the controller or directive in the example. They continue to declare the dependence on the logService service and call the log method of the service object they are provided with.

The advantage of using the provider method is that you can add functionality to the provider method that can be used to configure the service object. This is best explained with an example, and in Listing 18-12 I have added a function to the provider object that controls whether the message counter is written out as part of the log message and another to control whether messages are written at all.

Listing 18-12. Adding Functions to the provider Object in the services.js File

```
angular.module("customServices", [])
    .provider("logService", function () {
        var counter = true;
        var debug = true;
        return {
            messageCounterEnabled: function (setting) {
                if (angular.isDefined(setting)) {
                    counter = setting;
                    return this;
                } else {
                    return counter;
                }
            },
```

485

```
        debugEnabled: function(setting) {
            if (angular.isDefined(setting)) {
                debug = setting;
                return this;
            } else {
                return debug;
            }
        },
        $get: function () {
            return {
                messageCount: 0,
                log: function (msg) {
                    if (debug) {
                        console.log("(LOG"
                            + (counter ? " + " + this.messageCount++ + ") " : ") ")
                            + msg);
                    }
                }
            };
        }
    }
});
```

I have defined two configuration variables, counter and debug, that are used to control the output from the log method. I expose these variables through two functions called messageCounterEnabled and debugEnabled, which I added to the provider object. The convention for provider objects methods is to allow them to be used to set the configuration when an argument is provided and query the configuration when there is no argument. When the configuration is set, the convention is to return the provider object as the result from the method in order to allow multiple configuration calls to be chained together.

AngularJS makes the provider object available for dependency injection, using the name of the service combined with the word Provider, so for the example the provider object can be obtained by declaring a dependency on logServiceProvider. The most common way to obtain and use the provider object is in a function passed to the Module.config method, which will be executed when AngularJS has loaded all of the modules in the application, as described in Chapter 9. In Listing 18-13, you can see how I have used the config method to obtain the provider object for the logging service and change the settings.

Listing 18-13. Configuring a Service via Its Provider in the example.html File

```
...
<script>
    angular.module("exampleApp", ["customDirectives", "customServices"])
    .config(function (logServiceProvider) {
        logServiceProvider.debugEnabled(true).messageCounterEnabled(false);
    })
    .controller("defaultCtrl", function ($scope, logService) {
        $scope.data = {
            cities: ["London", "New York", "Paris"],
            totalClicks: 0
        };
```

```
        $scope.$watch('data.totalClicks', function (newVal) {
            logService.log("Total click count: " + newVal);
        });
    });
</script>
...
```

You don't have to configure services using the Module.config method, but it is sensible to do so. Remember that service objects are singletons and any changes you make once the application has started will affect all of the components that are consuming the service—something that often causes unexpected behaviors.

Using the Built-in Modules and Services

AngularJS provides a comprehensive set of services that can be used to perform common tasks. I explain each of them in depth in the chapters that follow, but as a quick reference, Table 18-4 briefly describes what they do and tells you where I provide more information.

Table 18-4. *The Built-in AngularJS Services*

Name	Description
$anchorScroll	Scrolls the browser window to a specified anchor. See Chapter 19.
$animate	Animates the content transitions. See Chapter 23.
$compile	Processes an HTML fragment to create a function that can be used to generate content. See Chapter 19.
$controller	A wrapper around the $injector service that instantiates controllers. See Chapter 25.
$document	Provides a jqLite objects that contains the DOM window.document object. See Chapter 19.
$exceptionHandler	Handles exceptions that arise in the application. See Chapter 19.
$filter	Provides access to filters, as described in Chapter 14.
$http	Creates and manages Ajax requests. See Chapter 20.
$injector	Creates instances of AngularJS components. See Chapter 24.
$interpolate	Processes a string that contains binding expressions to create a function that can be used to generate content. See Chapter 19.
$interval	Provides an enhanced wrapper around the window.setInterval function. See Chapter 19.
$location	Provides a wrapper around the browser location object. See Chapter 19.
$log	Provides a wrapper around the global console object. See Chapter 19.
$parse	Processes an expression to create a function that can be used to generate content. See Chapter 19.
$provide	Implements many of the methods that are exposed by Module. See Chapter 24.
$q	Provides deferred objects/promises. See Chapter 20.
$resource	Provides support for working with RESTful APIs. See Chapter 21.

(*continued*)

Table 18-4. (*continued*)

Name	Description
$rootElement	Provides access to the root element in the DOM. See Chapter 19.
$rootScope	Provides access to the top of the scope hierarchy, as described in Chapter 13.
$route	Provides support for changing view content based on the browser's URL path. See Chapter 22.
$routeParams	Provides information about URL routes. See Chapter 22.
$sanitize	Replaces dangerous HTML characters with their display-safe counterparts. See Chapter 19.
$sce	Removes dangerous elements and attributes from HTML strings in order to make them safe to display. See Chapter 19.
$swipe	Recognizes swipe gestures. See Chapter 23.
$timeout	Provides an enhanced wrapper around the window.setITimeout function. See Chapter 19.
$window	Provides a reference to the DOM window object. See Chapter 19.

Summary

In this chapter, I recapped the role that modules play in an AngularJS application and showed you how you can use them to organize the components in your code. I also showed you role that services play and the three different ways that the module class provides to create them. In the next chapter, I describe the first set of built-in services that AngularJS provides.

CHAPTER 19

■ ■ ■

Services for Global Objects, Errors, and Expressions

In this chapter, I show you the built-in services that AngularJS provides for accessing global objects, dealing with exceptions, displaying dangerous data, and processing expressions. These are some of the most useful services that AngularJS provides, and using them directly gives you the ability to control some of the fundamental AngularJS features that I demonstrated in earlier chapters. Table 19-1 summarizes this chapter.

Table 19-1. *Chapter Summary*

Problem	Solution	Listing
Access global objects in a way that eases unit testing.	Use the $document, $interval, $log, $timeout, $window, $location, and $anchorScroll services.	1–9
Handle exceptions.	Redefine the $exceptionHandler service.	11–13
Display dangerous data.	Use the ng-bind-html binding.	14–16
Explicitly sanitize data values.	Use the $sanitize service.	16
Trust data values.	Use the $sce services.	17
Process expressions.	Use the $parse, $interpolate, and $compile services.	18–22

Preparing the Example Project

For this chapter, I am going to continue working with the files I created in Chapter 18. I will be adding new HTML files as I demonstrate different features, but I will also enhance the example application that I used to demonstrate the basic use of modules and services.

Accessing the DOM API Global Objects

The simplest built-in services expose aspects of the browser's DOM API in a way that is consistent with the rest of AngularJS or with jqLite. Table 19-2 describes these services.

Table 19-2. *The Services That Expose DOM API Features*

Name	Description
$anchorScroll	Scrolls the browser window to a specified anchor
$document	Provides a jqLite object that contains the DOM `window.document` object
$interval	Provides an enhanced wrapper around the `window.setInterval` function
$location	Provides access to the URL
$log	Provides a wrapper around the `console` object
$timeout	Provides an enhanced wrapper around the `window.setITimeout` function
$window	Provides a reference to the DOM `window` object

Why and When to Use the Global Object Services

The main reason that AngularJS includes these services is to make testing easier. I get into testing in Chapter 25, but an important facet of unit testing is the need to isolate a small piece of code and test its behavior without testing the components it depends on—in essence, creating a focused test. The DOM API exposes functionality through global objects such as document and window. These objects make it hard to isolate code for unit testing without also testing the way that the browser implements its global objects. Using services such as $document allows AngularJS code to be written without directly using the DOM API global objects and allows the use of AngularJS testing services to configure specific test scenarios.

Accessing the Window Object

The $window service is simple to use, and declaring a dependency on it gives you an object that is a wrapper around the global window object. AngularJS doesn't enhance or change the API provided by this global object, and you access the methods that the window object defines ust as you would if you were working directly with the DOM API. To demonstrate this service—and the others in this category—I have added an HTML file called domApi.html to the angularjs folder, the contents of which are shown in Listing 19-1.

Listing 19-1. The Contents of the domApi.html File

```
<!DOCTYPE html>
<html ng-app="exampleApp">
<head>
    <title>DOM API Services</title>
    <script src="angular.js"></script>
    <link href="bootstrap.css" rel="stylesheet" />
    <link href="bootstrap-theme.css" rel="stylesheet" />
    <script>
        angular.module("exampleApp", [])
        .controller("defaultCtrl", function ($scope, $window) {
            $scope.displayAlert = function(msg) {
                $window.alert(msg);
            }
        });
    </script>
</head>
```

```
<body ng-controller="defaultCtrl" class="well">
    <button class="btn btn-primary" ng-click="displayAlert('Clicked!')">Click Me</button>
</body>
</html>
```

I have declared a dependency on the $window service in order to define a controller behavior that calls the alert method. The behavior is invoked by the ng-click directive when a button element is clicked, as shown in Figure 19-1.

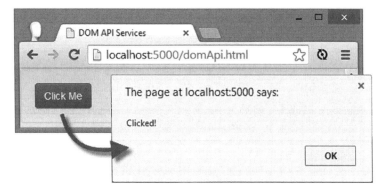

Figure 19-1. Using the $window service

Accessing the Document Object

The $document service is a jqLite object containing the DOM API global window.document object. Since the service is presented via jqLite, you can use it to query the DOM using the methods I described in Chapter 15. In Listing 19-2, you can see the $document service applied.

Listing 19-2. Using the $document Service in the domApi.html File

```
<!DOCTYPE html>
<html ng-app="exampleApp">
<head>
    <title>DOM API Services</title>
    <script src="angular.js"></script>
    <link href="bootstrap.css" rel="stylesheet" />
    <link href="bootstrap-theme.css" rel="stylesheet" />
    <script>
        angular.module("exampleApp", [])
        .controller("defaultCtrl", function ($scope, $window, $document) {
            $document.find("button").on("click", function (event) {
                $window.alert(event.target.innerText);
            });
        });
    </script>
</head>
<body ng-controller="defaultCtrl" class="well">
    <button class="btn btn-primary">Click Me</button>
</body>
</html>
```

491

Using Intervals and Timeouts

The $interval and $timeout services provide access to the window.setInterval and window.setTimeout functions, with some enhancements that make it easier to work with AngularJS. Table 19-3 shows the arguments that are passed to these services.

Table 19-3. *The Arguments Used with the $interval and $timeout Services*

Argument	Description
fn	A function whose execution will be delayed.
delay	The number of milliseconds before fn will be executed.
count	The number of times that the delay/execute cycle will be repeated ($interval only). The default value is zero, which means there is no limit.
invokeApply	When set to true, which is the default value, fn will be executed within the scope.$apply method.

These functions work in the same way, in that they defer the execution of a function for a specified period of time. The difference is that the $timeout service delays and executes the function only once, whereas $interval does so periodically. Listing 19-3 shows the use of the $interval service.

Listing 19-3. Using the $interval Service in the domApi.html File

```
<!DOCTYPE html>
<html ng-app="exampleApp">
<head>
    <title>DOM API Services</title>
    <script src="angular.js"></script>
    <link href="bootstrap.css" rel="stylesheet" />
    <link href="bootstrap-theme.css" rel="stylesheet" />
    <script>
        angular.module("exampleApp", [])
        .controller("defaultCtrl", function ($scope, $interval) {
            $interval(function () {
                $scope.time = new Date().toTimeString();
            }, 2000);
        });
    </script>
</head>
<body ng-controller="defaultCtrl">
    <div class="panel panel-default">
        <h4 class="panel-heading">Time</h4>
        <div class="panel-body">
            The time is: {{time}}
        </div>
    </div>
</body>
</html>
```

▓ **Tip** Exceptions thrown by the function passed to these services are passed to the $exceptionHandler service, which I describe in the "Dealing with Exceptions" section.

I use the $interval service to execute a function that updates a scope variable with the current time every two seconds. I omitted the final two arguments, which means the default values are applied.

Accessing the URL

The $location service is a wrapper around the location property of the global window object and provides access to the current URL. The $location service operates on the part of the URL following the first # character, which means it can be used for navigation within the current document but not to navigate to new documents. This may seem odd, but you rarely want the user to navigate away from the main document because it unloads your web application and discards your data and state. Consider the following URL, which is typical of an AngularJS application:

```
http://mydomain.com/app.html#/cities/london?select=hotels#north
```

The $location service lets you change the part of the URL I have emphasized, which it calls the *URL* and is the combination of three components: the *path*, the *search term*, and the *hash*. These are all terms that refer to parts of the URL before the # character, which is unfortunate but understandable because AngularJS is re-creating a complete URL after the # so that we can navigate within the application—something that is made easier using the service I describe in Chapter 22. Here is the same URL with the path emphasized:

```
http://mydomain.com/app.html#/cities/london?select=hotels#north
```

And here it is with the search term emphasized:

```
http://mydomain.com/app.html#/cities/london?select=hotels#north
```

And, finally, here it is with the hash emphasized:

```
http://mydomain.com/app.html#/cities/london?select=hotels#north
```

In Table 19-4, I have described the methods that the $location service provides.

Table 19-4. *The Methods Defined by the $location Service*

Name	Description
absUrl()	Returns the complete URL of the current document, including the parts before the first # character (`http://mydomain.com/app.html#/cities/london?select=hotels#north`).
hash()hash(target)	Gets or sets the hash section of the URL—see earlier.
host()	Returns the hostname component of the URL (`mydomain.com`).
path()path(target)	Gets or sets the path component of the URL—see earlier.
port()	Returns the port number. This is implied in my example URL and defaults to 80.
protocol()	Returns the protocol component of the URL (`http`).
replace()	When called on an HTML5 browser, the change in the URL replaces the most recent entry in the browser history rather than creating a new one.
search()search(term, params)	Gets or sets the search term—see earlier.
url()url(target)	Gets or sets the path, query string, and hash together—see earlier.

■ **Tip** These are messy URLs. I'll show you how to enable support for HTML5 features in the "Using HTML5 URLs" section.

In addition to the methods shown earlier, the $location service defines two events that you can use to receive notification when the URL changes, either because of user interaction or programmatically. I have described the events in Table 19-5. Handler functions for these events are registered using the scope $on method (which I described in Chapter 15) and are passed an event object, the new URL, and the old URL.

Table 19-5. *The Events Defined by the $location Service*

Name	Description
$locationChangeStart	Triggered before the URL is changed. You can prevent the URL from changing by calling the preventDefault method on the Event object.
$locationChangeSuccess	Triggered after the URL has changed.

In Listing 19-4, you can see how I have updated the domApi.html file to demonstrate the use of the $location service. This example uses all of the read-write methods so that you can see how the changes to the URL are applied.

Listing 19-4. Using the $location Service in the domApi.html File

```
<!DOCTYPE html>
<html ng-app="exampleApp">
<head>
    <title>DOM API Services</title>
    <script src="angular.js"></script>
    <link href="bootstrap.css" rel="stylesheet" />
    <link href="bootstrap-theme.css" rel="stylesheet" />
```

```
<script>
    angular.module("exampleApp", [])
    .controller("defaultCtrl", function ($scope, $location) {

        $scope.$on("$locationChangeSuccess", function (event, newUrl) {
            $scope.url = newUrl;
        });

        $scope.setUrl = function (component) {
            switch (component) {
                case "reset":
                    $location.path("");
                    $location.hash("");
                    $location.search("");
                    break;
                case "path":
                    $location.path("/cities/london");
                    break;
                case "hash":
                    $location.hash("north");
                    break;
                case "search":
                    $location.search("select", "hotels");
                    break;
                case "url":
                    $location.url("/cities/london?select=hotels#north");
                    break;
            }
        }
    });
</script>
</head>
<body ng-controller="defaultCtrl">
    <div class="panel panel-default">
        <h4 class="panel-heading">URL</h4>
        <div class="panel-body">
            <p>The URL is: {{url}}</p>
            <div class="btn-group ">
                <button class="btn btn-primary" ng-click="setUrl('reset')">Reset</button>
                <button class="btn btn-primary" ng-click="setUrl('path')">Path</button>
                <button class="btn btn-primary" ng-click="setUrl('hash')">Hash</button>
                <button class="btn btn-primary"
                    ng-click="setUrl('search')">Search</button>
                <button class="btn btn-primary" ng-click="setUrl('url')">URL</button>
            </div>
        </div>
    </div>
</body>
</html>
```

This example contains buttons that let you set the four writable components of the URL: the path, the hash, the query string, and the URL. You can see how each component is changed and how, since the changes happen after the # character, the navigation doesn't cause the browser to load a new document.

Using HTML5 MURLs

The standard URL format that I showed you in the previous section is messy because the application is essentially trying to duplicate the component parts of a URL after the # character so that the browser doesn't load a new HTML document.

The HTML5 History API provides a more elegant approach to dealing with this, and the URL can be changed without causing the document to reload. All recent versions of the mainstream browsers support the History API, and support for it can be enabled in AngularJS applications through the provider for the $location service, $locationProvider. In Listing 19-5, you can see how I have enabled the History API in the domApi.html file.

Listing 19-5. Enabling the HTML5 History API in the domApi.html File

```
...
<script>
    angular.module("exampleApp", [])
    .config(function($locationProvider) {
        $locationProvider.html5Mode(true);
    })
    .controller("defaultCtrl", function ($scope, $location) {

        $scope.$on("$locationChangeSuccess", function (event, newUrl) {
            $scope.url = newUrl;
        });

        $scope.setUrl = function (component) {
            switch (component) {
                case "reset":
                    $location.path("");
                    $location.hash("");
                    $location.search("");
                    break;
                case "path":
                    $location.path("/cities/london");
                    break;
                case "hash":
                    $location.hash("north");
                    break;
                case "search":
                    $location.search("select", "hotels");
                    break;
                case "url":
                    $location.url("/cities/london?select=hotels#north");
                    break;
            }
        }
    });
</script>
...
```

■ **Caution** The History API is relatively new and is not consistently implemented by browsers. Use this feature with caution and test thoroughly.

Calling the html5Mode method with true as the argument enables the use of the HTML5 features, which has the effect of changing the parts of the URL that the methods of the $location service operate on. In Table 19-6, I have summarized the changes that the buttons in the example have on the URL displayed in the browser's navigation bar, pressed in sequence.

Table 19-6. *The Effect of the Buttons in the Example on the URL*

Name	Effect
Reset	http://localhost:5000
Path	http://localhost:5000/cities/london
Hash	http://localhost:5000/cities/london#north
Search	http://localhost:5000/cities/london?select=hotels#north
URL	http://localhost:5000/cities/london?select=hotels#north

This is a much cleaner URL structure, but, of course, it relies on HTML5 features that are not available on older browsers, and your application will fail to work if you enable the $location HTML5 mode for a browser that doesn't support the History API. You can work around this by testing for the History API, either using a library like Modernizr or manually, as I have shown in Listing 19-6.

Listing 19-6. Testing for the Presence of the History API in the domApi.html File

```
...
<script>
    angular.module("exampleApp", [])
    .config(function ($locationProvider) {
        if (window.history && history.pushState) {
            $locationProvider.html5Mode(true);
        }
    })
    .controller("defaultCtrl", function ($scope, $location) {
...
```

I have to access two global objects directly because only constant values and providers can be injected into config functions, which means I can't use the $window service. If the browser has defined the window.history object and the history.pushState method, then I enable the HTML5 mode for the $location service and benefit from the improved URL structure. For other browsers, the HTML5 mode will be disabled, and the more complex URL structure will be used.

Scrolling to the $location Hash Location

The $anchorScroll service scrolls the browser window to display the element whose id corresponds to the value returned by the $location.hash method. Not only is the $anchorScroll service convenient to use, but it means you don't have to access the global document object in order to locate the element to display or the global window object to perform the scrolling. Listing 19-7 shows the $anchorScroll service being used to display an element in a long document.

Listing 19-7. Using the $anchorScroll Service in the domApi.html File

```
<!DOCTYPE html>
<html ng-app="exampleApp">
<head>
    <title>DOM API Services</title>
    <script src="angular.js"></script>
    <link href="bootstrap.css" rel="stylesheet" />
    <link href="bootstrap-theme.css" rel="stylesheet" />
    <script>
        angular.module("exampleApp", [])
        .controller("defaultCtrl", function ($scope, $location, $anchorScroll) {
            $scope.itemCount = 50;
            $scope.items = [];

            for (var i = 0; i < $scope.itemCount; i++) {
                $scope.items[i] = "Item " + i;
            }

            $scope.show = function(id) {
                $location.hash(id);
            }
        });
    </script>
</head>
<body ng-controller="defaultCtrl">
    <div class="panel panel-default">
        <h4 class="panel-heading">URL</h4>
        <div class="panel-body">
            <p id="top">This is the top</p>
            <button class="btn btn-primary" ng-click="show('bottom')">
                Go to Bottom</button>
            <p>
                <ul>
                    <li ng-repeat="item in items">{{item}}</li>
                </ul>
            </p>
            <p id="bottom">This is the bottom</p>
            <button class="btn btn-primary" ng-click="show('top')">Go to Top</button>
        </div>
    </div>
</body>
</html>
```

In this example, I use the ng-repeat directive to generate a series of li elements so that one of the p elements with the id values top and bottom cannot be seen on the screen. The button elements use the ng-click directive to invoke a controller behavior called show, which accepts an element id as an argument and uses it to call the $location.hash method.

The $anchorScroll service is unusual because you don't have to use the service object; you just declare a dependency. When the service object is created, it starts to monitor the $location.hash value and scrolls automatically when it changes. You can see the effect in Figure 19-2.

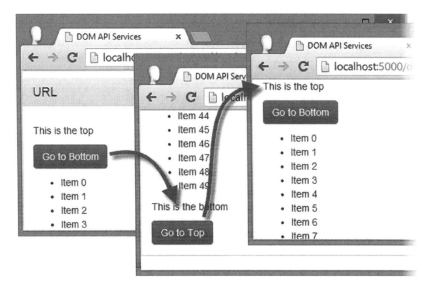

Figure 19-2. *Scrolling to elements using the $anchorScroll service*

You can disable the automatic scrolling through the service provider, which allows you to selectively scroll by invoking the $anchorScroll service as a function, as shown in Listing 19-8.

Listing 19-8. Selectively Scrolling in the domApi.html File

```
...
<script>
    angular.module("exampleApp", [])
    .config(function ($anchorScrollProvider) {
        $anchorScrollProvider.disableAutoScrolling();
    })
    .controller("defaultCtrl", function ($scope, $location, $anchorScroll) {

        $scope.itemCount = 50;
        $scope.items = [];

        for (var i = 0; i < $scope.itemCount; i++) {
            $scope.items[i] = "Item " + i;
        }
```

```
        $scope.show = function(id) {
            $location.hash(id);
            if (id == "bottom") {
                $anchorScroll();
            }
        }
    });
</script>
...
```

I use a call to the Module.config method (as described in Chapter 9) to disable automatic scrolling, which I do by calling the disableAutoScrolling method on the $anchorScrollProvider. Changes to the $location.hash value will no longer trigger automatic scrolling. To explicitly trigger scrolling, I invoke the $anchorScroll service function, which I do when the argument passed to the show behavior is bottom. The effect is that the browser scrolls when the Go to Bottom button, but not the Go to Top button, is clicked.

Performing Logging

I built my own simple logging service in Chapter 18, but AngularJS provides the $log service, which is a wrapper around the global console object. The $log service defines debug, error, info, log, and warn methods that correspond to those defined by the console object. As the examples in Chapter 18 demonstrate, you don't have to use the $log service, but it does make unit testing easier. In Listing 19-9, you can see how I have modified my custom logging service to make use of the $log service to write its messages out.

Listing 19-9. Using the $log Service in the services.js File

```
angular.module("customServices", [])
    .provider("logService", function () {
        var counter = true;
        var debug = true;
        return {
            messageCounterEnabled: function (setting) {
                if (angular.isDefined(setting)) {
                    counter = setting;
                    return this;
                } else {
                    return counter;
                }
            },
            debugEnabled: function (setting) {
                if (angular.isDefined(setting)) {
                    debug = setting;
                    return this;
                } else {
                    return debug;
                }
            },
```

```
    $get: function ($log) {
        return {
            messageCount: 0,
            log: function (msg) {
                if (debug) {
                    $log.log("(LOG"
                        + (counter ? " + " + this.messageCount++ + ") " : ") ")
                        + msg);
                }
            }
        };
    }
}
});
```

Notice that I declare the dependency on the service on the $get function. This is a peculiarity of using the provider function and something you don't encounter when working with the service or factory methods. To demonstrate this, Listing 19-10 shows the $log service used in the version of the custom service I created using the factory method in Chapter 18.

Listing 19-10. Consuming $log in a Service Defined Using the Factory Method in the services.html File

```
angular.module("customServices", [])
    .factory("logService", function ($log) {
        var messageCount = 0;
        return {
            log: function (msg) {
                $log.log("(LOG + " + this.messageCount++ + ") " + msg);
            }
        };
    });
```

■ **Tip** The default behavior of the $log service is not to call the debug method to the console. You can enable debugging by setting the $logProvider.debugEnabled property to true. See Chapter 18 for details of how to set provider properties.

Dealing with Exceptions

AngularJS uses the $exceptionHandler service to handle any exceptions that arise during the execution of an application. The default implementation calls the error method defined by the $log service, which in turn calls the global console.error method.

Why and When to Use the Exception Service

I think of exceptions in two broad categories. The first category includes those that occur during coding and testing, which are a natural part of the development cycle and help you shape the application you are building. The other category includes those that the user sees after you have released the application to the world.

The way that you deal with these categories is different, but what's needed in both situations is a consistent way of capturing those exceptions so that they can be responded to and, ideally, logged for future analysis. That's where the $exceptionHandler service comes in. By default, it simply writes details of exceptions to the JavaScript console and allows the application to continue running (if that's possible), but, as you'll see, it can also be used to perform more sophisticated tasks, such as the ones you'll need to keep your users happy and frustration-free when things go wrong after deployment.

■ **Tip** The $exceptionHandler service deals only with uncaught exceptions. You can catch an exception using a JavaScript try...catch block, and it will not be handled by the service.

Working with Exceptions

To demonstrate the $exceptionHandler service, I have added a new HTML file called exceptions.html to the angularjs folder, as shown in Listing 19-11.

Listing 19-11. The Contents of the exceptions.html File

```
<!DOCTYPE html>
<html ng-app="exampleApp">
<head>
    <title>Exceptions</title>
    <script src="angular.js"></script>
    <link href="bootstrap.css" rel="stylesheet" />
    <link href="bootstrap-theme.css" rel="stylesheet" />
    <script>
        angular.module("exampleApp", [])
        .controller("defaultCtrl", function ($scope) {
            $scope.throwEx = function () {
                throw new Error("Triggered Exception");
            }
        });
    </script>
</head>
<body ng-controller="defaultCtrl">
    <div class="panel panel-default">
        <div class="panel-body">
            <button class="btn btn-primary" ng-click="throwEx()">Throw Exception</button>
        </div>
    </div>
</body>
</html>
```

This example contains a button element that uses the ng-click handler to trigger a controller behavior called throwEx, which throws an exception. If you load the exceptions.html file into the browser and click the button, you will see output in the JavaScript console, as follows:

```
Error: Triggered Exception
```

Depending on the browser you are using, you will also see a stack trace that includes the line number and file name of the throw statement.

Working Directly with the Exception Service

Although AngularJS will automatically pass exceptions to the $exceptionHandler service, you can provide more context information by working directly with the service in your code. In Listing 19-12, you can see how I have declared a dependency on the $exceptionHandler service so that I can pass my exception directly to the service.

Listing 19-12. Working Directly with the $exceptionHandler Service in the exceptions.html File

```
<!DOCTYPE html>
<html ng-app="exampleApp">
<head>
    <title>Exceptions</title>
    <script src="angular.js"></script>
    <link href="bootstrap.css" rel="stylesheet" />
    <link href="bootstrap-theme.css" rel="stylesheet" />
    <script>
        angular.module("exampleApp", [])
        .controller("defaultCtrl", function ($scope, $exceptionHandler) {
            $scope.throwEx = function () {
                try {
                    throw new Error("Triggered Exception");
                } catch (ex) {
                    $exceptionHandler(ex.message, "Button Click");
                }
            }
        });
    </script>
</head>
<body ng-controller="defaultCtrl">
    <div class="panel panel-default">
        <div class="panel-body">
            <button class="btn btn-primary" ng-click="throwEx()">Throw Exception</button>
        </div>
    </div>
</body>
</html>
```

The $exceptionHandler service object is a function that takes two arguments: the exception and an optional string describing the exception's cause. There can be only one cause of the exception in my example, so the cause argument isn't that useful, but if you catch an exception in a loop processing data items, for example, it can be helpful to pass details of the data item that causes the problem as the cause. Here is the output shown in the console when the button in the example is clicked:

```
Triggered Exception Button Click
```

Implementing a Custom Exception Handler

In Chapter 18, I cautioned you to pick distinctive service names to avoid overriding those defined by AngularJS or other packages you might be using. In this section, I am going to deliberately override the AngularJS implementation of the $errorHandler service in order to define a custom exception handling policy. In Listing 19-13, you can see how I have implemented the replacement service.

Listing 19-13. Replacing the $errorHandler Service in the exceptions.html File

```
<!DOCTYPE html>
<html ng-app="exampleApp">
<head>
    <title>Exceptions</title>
    <script src="angular.js"></script>
    <link href="bootstrap.css" rel="stylesheet" />
    <link href="bootstrap-theme.css" rel="stylesheet" />
    <script>
        angular.module("exampleApp", [])
        .controller("defaultCtrl", function ($scope, $exceptionHandler) {
            $scope.throwEx = function () {
                try {
                    throw new Error("Triggered Exception");
                } catch (ex) {
                    $exceptionHandler(ex, "Button Click");
                }
            }
        })
        .factory("$exceptionHandler", function ($log) {
            return function (exception, cause) {
                $log.error("Message: " + exception.message + " (Cause: " + cause + ")");
            }
        });
    </script>
</head>
<body ng-controller="defaultCtrl">
    <div class="panel panel-default">
        <div class="panel-body">
            <button class="btn btn-primary" ng-click="throwEx()">Throw Exception</button>
        </div>
    </div>
</body>
</html>
```

I have used the factory method, which I described in Chapter 18, to redefine the $errorHandler service object so that it better formats the message from the exception and the cause.

■ **Tip** You can replace the default behavior with something much more complex, but I recommend caution. Error handling code needs to be bullet-proof because if it contains bugs, then you won't see the real problems in the application. The simplest error handling is generally best.

If you load the exceptions.html file into the browser and click the button, you will see the formatted output:

```
Message: Triggered Exception (Cause: Button Click)
```

Working with Dangerous Data

A common attack on web applications is to try to get them to display data crafted to fool either the browser or another user. This usually involves getting the browser to execute JavaScript code that the attacker has provided, but attacks can also involve trying to alter the application layout with some carefully crafted CSS styles. The types of attack are endless, but one common thread is injecting malicious content into the application through forms, either so it will be displayed back to the attacker or so it will be presented to other users. AngularJS has some nice built-in support for mitigating the risk of this kind of attack, and in this section I describe how it works and explain the built-in facilities that allow you to take control of the mitigation process. Table 19-7 shows the services that AngularJS provides for working with dangerous data.

Table 19-7. *The Services That Operate on Dangerous Data*

Name	Description
$sce	Removes dangerous elements and attributes from HTML
$sanitize	Replaces dangerous characters in HTML strings with their escaped counterparts

Why and When to Use the Dangerous Data Services

AngularJS has a good default policy for dealing with potentially dangerous content, but you will need to work directly with the services I describe in this section when you need a little more flexibility. This can be needed when you are writing an application that allows users to generate HTML content (such as an online HTML editor, for example) or where you are dealing with content that is generated from a legacy system that mixes data and presentation in HTML fragments (old content management systems and portals are terrible for this).

Displaying Dangerous Data

AngularJS uses a feature called *strict contextual escaping (SCE)* that prevents unsafe values from being expressed through data bindings. This feature is enabled by default, and to demonstrate how it works, I have added a new HTML file called htmlData.html to the angularjs folder, the contents of which are shown in Listing 19-14.

Listing 19-14. The Contents of the htmlData.html File

```
<!DOCTYPE html>
<html ng-app="exampleApp">
<head>
    <title>SCE</title>
    <script src="angular.js"></script>
    <link href="bootstrap.css" rel="stylesheet" />
    <link href="bootstrap-theme.css" rel="stylesheet" />
```

```
    <script>
        angular.module("exampleApp", [])
        .controller("defaultCtrl", function ($scope) {
            $scope.htmlData
                = "<p>This is <b onmouseover=alert('Attack!')>dangerous</b> data</p>";
        });
    </script>
</head>
<body ng-controller="defaultCtrl">
    <div class="well">
        <p><input class="form-control" ng-model="htmlData" /></p>
        <p>{{htmlData}}</p>
    </div>
</body>
</html>
```

The controller scope in this example contains an input element bound to a property called htmlData, which is then displayed using an inline binding expression. I have set the property to a dangerous HTML string so that you don't have to enter the text manually into the input element, but the idea is that an attacker will try to get the browser to execute some JavaScript code from the input element that isn't part of the application—in this case, to display the alert dialog box, but in most of the attacks that I have seen in the wild, attackers try to get the application to display the data they enter as HTML to other users, most often to prompt them for their credentials or simply as a destructive act.

To help mitigate the risk, AngularJS automatically replaces dangerous characters (like < and > in HTML content) with their display-safe escaped counterparts, as shown in Figure 19-3.

Figure 19-3. *AngularJS automatically escapes the data value displayed in bindings*

AngularJS has transformed this HTML string from the input element:

```
<p>This is <b onmouseover=alert('Attack!')>dangerous</b> data</p>
```

into this string, which is safe to display:

```
&lt;p&gt;This is &lt;b onmouseover=alert('Attack!')&gt;dangerous&lt;/b&gt; data&lt;/p&gt;
```

Each of the characters that would lead the browser to treat the string as HTML has been replaced with a safe alternative.

■ **Tip** The process of escaping content doesn't affect the original values in the scope—just the way that the data is displayed by the binding. This means you can continue to safely work with HTML data behind the scenes and allow AngularJS to render it safely in the browser.

For most applications, the default AngularJS behavior is exactly what is required to prevent dangerous data from being displayed. If, however, you find yourself in one of rare situations where you need to display HTML content without it being escaped, then there are a range of techniques available.

Using an Unsafe Binding

The first technique is to use the `ng-bind-html` directive, which allows you to specify that a data value is trusted and should be displayed without being escaped. The `ng-bind-html` directive depends on the `ngSanitize` module, which isn't included in the main AngularJS library. Go to `http://angularjs.org`, click Download, select the version you require (version 1.2.5 is the latest version as I write this), and click the Extras link in the bottom-left corner of the window, as shown in Figure 19-4.

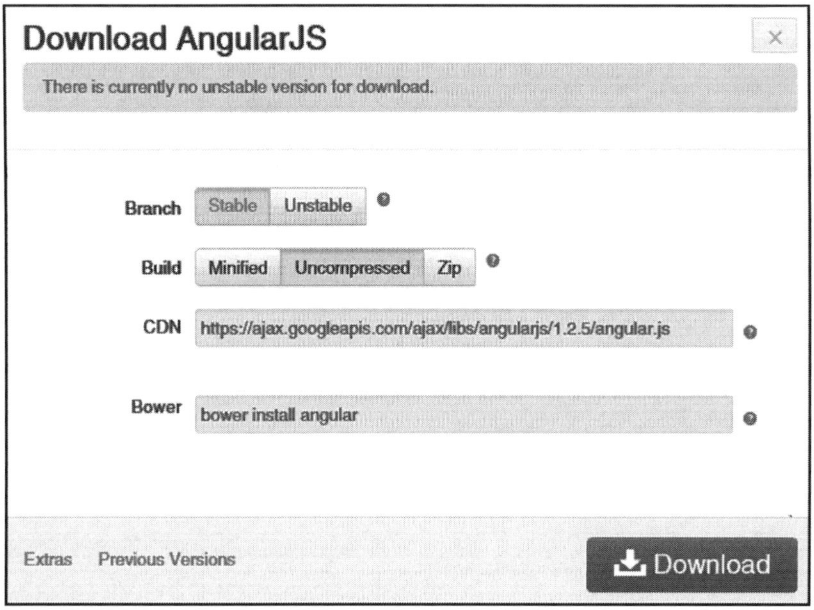

Figure 19-4. *Downloading an optional AngularJS module*

Download the `angular-sanitize.js` file into the `angularjs` folder. In Listing 19-15, you can see how I have added a dependency on the `ngSanitize` module and applied the `ng-bind-html` directive to display a dangerous data value.

Listing 19-15. Displaying Trusted Data in the htmlData.html File

```
<!DOCTYPE html>
<html ng-app="exampleApp">
<head>
    <title>SCE</title>
    <script src="angular.js"></script>
    <script src="angular-sanitize.js"></script>
    <link href="bootstrap.css" rel="stylesheet" />
    <link href="bootstrap-theme.css" rel="stylesheet" />
    <script>
        angular.module("exampleApp", ["ngSanitize"])
        .controller("defaultCtrl", function ($scope) {
            $scope.htmlData
                = "<p>This is <b onmouseover=alert('Attack!')>dangerous</b> data</p>";
        });
    </script>
</head>
<body ng-controller="defaultCtrl">
    <div class="well">
        <p><input class="form-control" ng-model="htmlData" /></p>
        <p ng-bind-html="htmlData"></p>
    </div>
</body>
</html>
```

There is no inline binding expression for the ng-bind-html directive, so I have added a span element so that I can apply it to the content. You can see the effect in Figure 19-5.

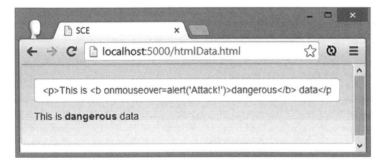

Figure 19-5. The effect of the ng-bind-html directive

Although the content is displayed at HTML, the onmouseover event handler that I applied to the b element doesn't work, and that's because there is a second security measure in place that strips out dangerous elements and attributes from HTML strings. Here is what the htmlData value has been transformed into:

```
<p>This is <b>dangerous</b> data</p>
```

This process removes script and css elements, inline JavaScript event handlers and style attributes, and anything else that might cause problems. The process is known as *sanitization* and is provided by the $sanitize service in the ngSanitize module. The $sanitize service is used automatically by the ng-bind-html directive and is the reason that I had to add the module to the example.

Performing the Sanitization Directly

You can rely on AngularJS to use the $sanitize service on the values it displays unless you specifically disable the safety measures (which I describe later in this chapter). However, you may want to go further and sanitize values that you store in your application. Making display values safe is good practice, but if you store unsafe HTML in a database, for example, you can easily make your application the attack vector for any other application that reads that data and doesn't benefit from the AngularJS protections. In Listing 19-16, you can see how I sanitize my HTML content before I added to the scope by using the $sanitize service directly.

Listing 19-16. Explicitly Sanitizing Content in the htmlData.html File

```
<!DOCTYPE html>
<html ng-app="exampleApp">
<head>
    <title>SCE</title>
    <script src="angular.js"></script>
    <script src="angular-sanitize.js"></script>
    <link href="bootstrap.css" rel="stylesheet" />
    <link href="bootstrap-theme.css" rel="stylesheet" />
    <script>
        angular.module("exampleApp", ["ngSanitize"])
        .controller("defaultCtrl", function ($scope, $sanitize) {
            $scope.dangerousData
                = "<p>This is <b onmouseover=alert('Attack!')>dangerous</b> data</p>";

            $scope.$watch("dangerousData", function (newValue) {
                $scope.htmlData = $sanitize(newValue);
            });
        });
    </script>
</head>
<body ng-controller="defaultCtrl">
    <div class="well">
        <p><input class="form-control" ng-model="dangerousData" /></p>
        <p ng-bind="htmlData"></p>
    </div>
</body>
</html>
```

I have changed the ng-model directive on the input element to set an implicitly defined variable called dangerousData. In the controller, I use a scope watcher function to monitor the defaultData property for changes and, when there is a new value, use the $sanitize service object to process the value. The $sanitize object is a function that takes the potentially dangerous value and returns the sanitized result. To demonstrate the effect, I have reverted to a standard ng-bind directive to display the sanitized htmlData value, as shown in Figure 19-6.

Figure 19-6. *Explicitly sanitizing data*

You can see that the sanitization process has removed the JavaScript event handler from the string I entered into the input element. The value isn't displayed as HTML because the ng-bind directive is still escaping the dangerous characters.

Explicitly Trusting Data

There are some—incredibly rare—circumstances under which you may need to display potentially dangerous content without escaping or sanitizing it. You can declare content to be trustworthy by using the $sce service.

■ **Caution**   I have worked on countless web application projects over the years, and the number of times that I have needed to display raw untrusted data values is still in single digits. There was a trend in the mid-2000s for delivering applications as portals, and each piece of content tended to come with its own JavaScript and CSS. When the portal movement died out, the applications that replaced them inherited a database of content fragments that had to be rendered without interference, which meant that the features loosely equivalent to AngularJS SCE had to be disabled. In every other project that I have worked on, I have been at pains to achieve the opposite effect, which is to safely escape every piece of data that the application displays—and that's especially true for data provided by users. The bottom line is: Don't mess around with this stuff unless you have a truly compelling need.

The $sce service object defines the trustAsHtml method, which returns a value that will be displayed with the SCE process being applied, as demonstrated in Listing 19-17.

Listing 19-17. Displaying Dangerous Content in the htmlData.html File

```
<!DOCTYPE html>
<html ng-app="exampleApp">
<head>
    <title>SCE</title>
    <script src="angular.js"></script>
    <script src="angular-sanitize.js"></script>
    <link href="bootstrap.css" rel="stylesheet" />
    <link href="bootstrap-theme.css" rel="stylesheet" />
```

```
    <script>
        angular.module("exampleApp", ["ngSanitize"])
        .controller("defaultCtrl", function ($scope, $sce) {
            $scope.htmlData
                = "<p>This is <b onmouseover=alert('Attack!')>dangerous</b> data</p>";

            $scope.$watch("htmlData", function (newValue) {
                $scope.trustedData = $sce.trustAsHtml(newValue);
            });
        });
    </script>
</head>
<body ng-controller="defaultCtrl">
    <div class="well">
        <p><input class="form-control" ng-model="htmlData" /></p>
        <p ng-bind-html="trustedData"></p>
    </div>
</body>
</html>
```

I use a watcher function to set a trustedData property with the result from the $sce.trustAsHtml method. I still have to use the ng-bind-html directive to display the value as HTML rather than escaped text. Trusting the data value prevents the JavaScript event handler from being removed, and using the ng-bind-html directive prevents character escaping. The result is that the browser displays the content from the input element and processes the JavaScript. If you move the mouse over the bold text, you will see the alert window displayed, as illustrated by Figure 19-7.

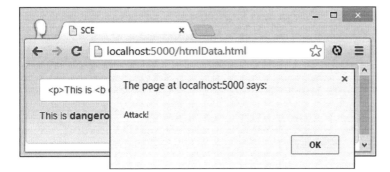

Figure 19-7. *Displaying trusted, unescaped data*

Working with AngularJS Expressions and Directives

AngularJS provides a set of services that are used to work with AngularJS content and binding expressions. I have described these services in Table 19-8. These services process content into functions that you can then invoke to generate content in your applications, ranging from simple expressions to fragments of HTML that contain bindings and directives.

Table 19-8. *The Services That Operate on AngularJS Expressions*

Name	Description
$compile	Converts an HTML fragment that contains bindings and directives into a function invoked to generate content
$interpolate	Converts a string that contains inline bindings into a function that can be invoked to generate content
$parse	Converts AngularJS expressions into functions that can be invoked to generate content

Why and When to Use the Expression and Directive Services

These services can be useful when writing directives because they let you take explicit control of the process used to generate and render content. You won't need these services in basic directives, but you will find them invaluable when you get into problems that require precise management of templates.

Converting Expressions into Functions

The $parse service takes an AngularJS expression and converts it into a function that you can use to evaluate the expression using a scope object. This can be useful in custom directives, allowing the expression to be provided via attributes and evaluated without the directive needing to know the details of the expression. To demonstrate the use of the $parse service, I have added an expressions.html HTML file to the angularjs folder, the contents of which are shown in Listing 19-18.

Listing 19-18. The Contents of the expressions.html File

```
<!DOCTYPE html>
<html ng-app="exampleApp">
<head>
    <title>Expressions</title>
    <script src="angular.js"></script>
    <link href="bootstrap.css" rel="stylesheet" />
    <link href="bootstrap-theme.css" rel="stylesheet" />
    <script>
        angular.module("exampleApp", [])
        .controller("defaultCtrl", function ($scope) {
            $scope.price = "100.23";
        })
        .directive("evalExpression", function ($parse) {
            return function(scope, element, attrs) {
                scope.$watch(attrs["evalExpression"], function (newValue) {
                    try {
                        var expressionFn = $parse(scope.expr);
                        var result = expressionFn(scope);
                        if (result == undefined) {
                            result = "No result";
                        }
```

```
                } catch (err) {
                    result = "Cannot evaluate expression";
                }
                element.text(result);
            });
        }
    });
</script>
</head>
<body ng-controller="defaultCtrl">
    <div class="well">
        <p><input class="form-control" ng-model="expr" /></p>
        <div>
            Result: <span eval-expression="expr"></span>
        </div>
    </div>
</body>
</html>
```

This example contains a directive called evalExpression that is configured with a scope property that contains an expression that will be evaluated with the $parse service. I have applied the directive to a span element and configured it to use a scope property called expr, which is bound to an input element, allowing an expression to be entered and evaluated dynamically. You can see the effect in Figure 19-8.

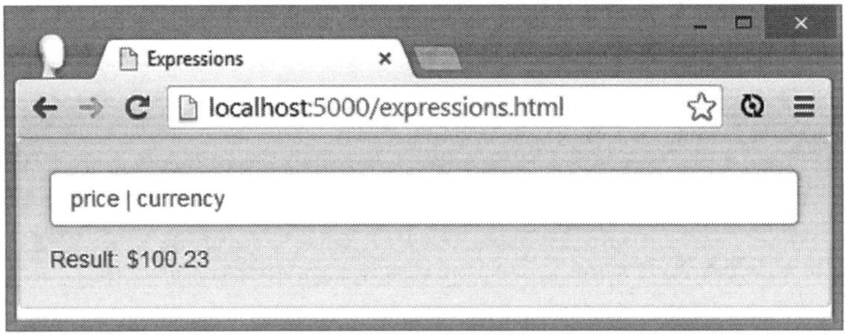

Figure 19-8. Using the $parse service to evaluate expressions

So that there is data to work with, I used the controller to add a scope property called price that is set to a numeric value. The figure shows the effect when I enter price | currency in the input element: The price property is processed by the currency filter and the result is displayed as the text content of the span element to which the directive was applied.

You wouldn't usually expect your users to enter AngularJS expressions into the application (and I'll show you a more typical use of $parse shortly), but I wanted to demonstrate how deeply you can dive into the internals of AngularJS and deal with changing expressions and not just changing data values.

The process for using the $parse service is simple—the service object is a function whose sole argument is the expression that will be evaluated and that returns a function that you use when you are ready to perform the evaluation. That is to say that the $parse service doesn't evaluate expressions itself; it is a factory for functions that do the actual work. Here is the statement from the example in which I use the $parse service object:

```
...
var expressionFn = $parse(scope.expr);
...
```

I pass the expression—which is whatever the user has entered into the input element in this example—to the $parse function and assign the function that I get back to a variable called expressionFn. I then invoke the function, passing in the scope as the source of the data values for the expression, like this:

```
...
var result = expressionFn(scope);
...
```

You don't have to use a scope as the source for the values in the expression, but it is usual to do so. (In the next section I show you how to use the scope and local data for the expression.) The result of invoking the function is the evaluated expression, which in the case of my example is the value of the price property after it has been processed by the currency filter, as shown in the figure.

When you are evaluating expressions that the user has provided, you need to deal with the possibility that the expression is invalid. If you delete a couple of characters from the filter name in the input element so that the expression specifies a nonexistent filter, then you will see a message that indicates that the expression cannot be evaluated. This is because I have caught the exception that arises when trying to parse and evaluate an invalid expression.

You must also be prepared to deal with an undefined result when evaluating the expression, which can happen when the expression refers to nonexistent data values. The AngularJS binding directives automatically display an undefined value as the empty string, but you need to deal with this yourself when working directly with the $parse service. In my example, I display the string No result when the expression evaluates to undefined, as follows:

```
...
if (result == undefined) {
    result = "No result";
}
...
```

Providing Local Data

The previous example isn't the way that the $parse service is usually used because it is rare that you can expect the user to enter expressions to be evaluated. It is much more common to have an expression defined within the application for which the user provides data values. In Listing 19-19, you can see how I have rewritten the contents of the expression.html file for this scenario.

Listing 19-19. Evaluating User Values Against a Fixed Expression in the expressions.html File

```
<!DOCTYPE html>
<html ng-app="exampleApp">
<head>
    <title>Expressions</title>
    <script src="angular.js"></script>
    <link href="bootstrap.css" rel="stylesheet" />
    <link href="bootstrap-theme.css" rel="stylesheet" />
    <script>
        angular.module("exampleApp", [])
        .controller("defaultCtrl", function ($scope) {
            $scope.dataValue = "100.23";
        })
```

```
        .directive("evalExpression", function ($parse) {
            var expressionFn = $parse("total | currency");
            return {
                scope: {
                    amount: "=amount",
                    tax: "=tax"
                },
                link: function (scope, element, attrs) {
                    scope.$watch("amount", function (newValue) {
                        var localData = {
                            total: Number(newValue)
                                + (Number(newValue) * (Number(scope.tax) /100))
                        }
                        element.text(expressionFn(scope, localData));
                    });
                }
            }
        });
    </script>
</head>
<body ng-controller="defaultCtrl">
    <div class="well">
        <p><input class="form-control" ng-model="dataValue" /></p>
        <div>
            Result: <span eval-expression amount="dataValue" tax="10"></span>
        </div>
    </div>
</body>
</html>
```

In this example, I have defined the directive using a definition object (as described in Chapter 16) for variety. The expression is parsed into a function by the $parse service in the directive factory function. I parse the expression only once, and then I invoke the function to evaluate the expression each time the amount property changes.

The expression includes a reference to a total property that does not exist in the scope and that is, in fact, calculated dynamically in the watcher function using two properties bound to an isolated scope, like this:

```
...
var localData = {
    total: Number(newValue) + (Number(newValue) * (Number(scope.tax) /100))
}
element.text(expressionFn(scope, localData));
...
```

The key point to note in these statements is the way that I pass an object containing a total property as an argument to the expression function. This supplements any values that are taken from the scope and provides a value for the total reference in the expression. The effect is that you can enter a value in the input element, and the total value, including a configurable a tax rate, is displayed as the contents of the span element to which the directive was applied, as shown in Figure 19-9.

Figure 19-9. *Providing local data when evaluating an expression*

Interpolating Strings

The $interpolate service and its provider, $interpolateProvider, are used to configure the way that AngularJS performs interpolation, which is the process of inserting expressions into strings. The $interpolate service is more flexible than $parse because it can work with strings that contain expressions rather than just expressions themselves. In Listing 19-20, you can see how I have used the $interpolate service in the expressions.html file.

Listing 19-20. Performing Interpolation in the expressions.html File

```
<!DOCTYPE html>
<html ng-app="exampleApp">
<head>
    <title>Expressions</title>
    <script src="angular.js"></script>
    <link href="bootstrap.css" rel="stylesheet" />
    <link href="bootstrap-theme.css" rel="stylesheet" />
    <script>
        angular.module("exampleApp", [])
        .controller("defaultCtrl", function ($scope) {
            $scope.dataValue = "100.23";
        })
        .directive("evalExpression", function ($interpolate) {
            var interpolationFn
                = $interpolate("The total is: {{amount | currency}} (including tax)");
            return {
                scope: {
                    amount: "=amount",
                    tax: "=tax"
                },
                link: function (scope, element, attrs) {
                    scope.$watch("amount", function (newValue) {
                        var localData = {
                            total: Number(newValue)
                                + (Number(newValue) * (Number(scope.tax) /100))
```

```
                }
                element.text(interpolationFn(scope));
            });
        }
    }
});
    </script>
</head>
<body ng-controller="defaultCtrl">
    <div class="well">
        <p><input class="form-control" ng-model="dataValue" /></p>
        <div>
            <span eval-expression amount="dataValue" tax="10"></span>
        </div>
    </div>
</body>
</html>
```

As the listing shows, using the $interpolate service is similar to using $parse, although there are a couple of important differences. The first—and most obvious—difference is that the $interpolate service can operate on strings that contain non-AngularJS content mixed with inline bindings. In fact, the {{ and }} characters that denote an inline binding are known as the *interpolation characters* because they are so closely associated with the $interpolate service. The second difference is that you can't provide a scope and local data to the interpolation function that the $interpolate service creates. Instead, you must ensure that the data values your expression requires are contained within the object you pass to the interpolation function.

Configuring Interpolation

AngularJS isn't the only library that uses the {{ and }} characters, and this can be a problem if you are trying to mix AngularJS with another package. Fortunately, you can change the characters that AngularJS uses for interpolation through the provider for the $interpolate service, $interpolateProvider, using the methods described in Table 19-9.

Table 19-9. *The Methods Defined by the $interpolate Provider*

Name	Description
startSymbol(symbol)	Replaces the start symbol, which is {{ by default
endSymbol(symbol)	Replaces the end symbol, which is }} by default

Some care must be taken when using these methods because they will affect all AngularJS interpolation, including inline data bindings in the HTML markup. You can see a demonstration of changing the interpolation characters in Listing 19-21.

Listing 19-21. Changing the Interpolation Characters in the expressions.html File

```html
<!DOCTYPE html>
<html ng-app="exampleApp">
<head>
    <title>Expressions</title>
    <script src="angular.js"></script>
    <link href="bootstrap.css" rel="stylesheet" />
    <link href="bootstrap-theme.css" rel="stylesheet" />
    <script>
        angular.module("exampleApp", [])
        .config(function($interpolateProvider) {
            $interpolateProvider.startSymbol("!!");
            $interpolateProvider.endSymbol("!!");
        })
        .controller("defaultCtrl", function ($scope) {
            $scope.dataValue = "100.23";
        })
        .directive("evalExpression", function ($interpolate) {
            var interpolationFn
                = $interpolate("The total is: !!amount | currency!! (including tax)");
            return {
                scope: {
                    amount: "=amount",
                    tax: "=tax"
                },
                link: function (scope, element, attrs) {
                    scope.$watch("amount", function (newValue) {
                        var localData = {
                            total: Number(newValue)
                                + (Number(newValue) * (Number(scope.tax) / 100))
                        }
                        element.text(interpolationFn(scope));
                    });
                }
            }
        });
    </script>
</head>
<body ng-controller="defaultCtrl">
    <div class="well">
        <p><input class="form-control" ng-model="dataValue" /></p>
        <div>
            <span eval-expression amount="dataValue" tax="10"></span>
            <p>Original amount: !!dataValue!!</p>
        </div>
    </div>
</body>
</html>
```

I have changed the start and the end symbols to !!. My example application will no longer recognize {{ and }} as denoting an inline binding expression and will operate only on my new character sequence, as follows:

```
...
$interpolate("The total is: !!amount | currency!! (including tax)");
...
```

I added an inline expression to the body section of the expressions.html document to demonstrate that the effect is wider than just the direct use of the $interpolate service:

```
...
<p>Original amount: !!dataValue!!</p>
...
```

Regular inline bindings are processed by AngularJS using the $interpolate service, and since service objects are singletons, any configuration changes are applied throughout the module.

Compiling Content

The $compile service processes an HTML fragment that contains bindings and expressions to create a function that can then be used to generate content from a scope. This is rather like the $parse and $interpolate services, but with support for directives. In Listing 19-22, you can see that using the $compile service is slightly more complex than the other services in this section—but only slightly.

Listing 19-22. Compiling Content in the expressions.html File

```
<!DOCTYPE html>
<html ng-app="exampleApp">
<head>
    <title>Expressions</title>
    <script src="angular.js"></script>
    <link href="bootstrap.css" rel="stylesheet" />
    <link href="bootstrap-theme.css" rel="stylesheet" />
    <script>
        angular.module("exampleApp", [])
        .controller("defaultCtrl", function ($scope) {
            $scope.cities = ["London", "Paris", "New York"];
        })
        .directive("evalExpression", function($compile) {
            return function (scope, element, attrs) {
                var content = "<ul><li ng-repeat='city in cities'>{{city}}</li></ul>"
                var listElem = angular.element(content);
                var compileFn = $compile(listElem);
                compileFn(scope);
                element.append(listElem);
            }
        });
    </script>
</head>
```

```
<body ng-controller="defaultCtrl">
    <div class="well">
        <span eval-expression></span>
    </div>
</body>
</html>
```

The controller in this example defines an array of city names. The directive uses the $compile service to process a fragment of HTML that uses the ng-repeat directive to populate an ul element with the city data. I have broken down the process of using the $compile service into individual statements so I can explain what I am doing step-by-step. First I define a fragment of HTML and wrap it in a jqLite object like this:

```
...
var content = "<ul><li ng-repeat='city in cities'>{{city}}</li></ul>"
var listElem = angular.element(content);
...
```

I am working with a simple fragment in this example, but you can pull in more complex content from template elements, just as I demonstrated when working with directives in Chapters 15–17. The next step is to use the $compile service object, which is a function, to create the function that will be used to generate the content:

```
...
var compileFn = $compile(listElem);
...
```

Once I have the compilation function, I can invoke it to process the content in the fragment. This will cause the expressions and directives that the fragment contains to be evaluated and executed, but notice that there is no return value from invoking the compilation function:

```
...
compileFn(scope);
...
```

Instead, the processing of the content updates the elements in the jqLite object, which is why I finish by adding those elements to the DOM:

```
...
element.append(listElem);
...
```

The effect is an ul element that contains one li element for each value in the cities scope array, as shown in Figure 19-10.

Figure 19-10. *Compiling content*

Summary

In this chapter, I showed you the built-in services that can be used to manage elements, handle errors, display dangerous data, and process expressions. These are services that underpin AngularJS, and by using them you are able to take control of some of the core application features—something that can be useful when writing custom directives in particular. In the next chapter, I show you the services that provide asynchronous HTTP requests and, *promises*, the objects required to handle their responses.

CHAPTER 20

■ ■ ■

Services for Ajax and Promises

In this chapter, I describe the built-in AngularJS services for making Ajax requests and representing asynchronous activities. These are important services, not just in their own right but because they provide the underpinnings for services that I describe in later chapters. Table 20-1 summarizes this chapter.

Table 20-1. *Chapter Summary*

Problem	Solution	Listing
Make Ajax requests.	Use the $http service.	1–3
Receive data from an Ajax request.	Register callback functions using the success, error, or then method on the object returned by the $http method.	4
Process non-JSON data.	Receive the data via a success or then callback function. You can use jqLite to process the data if it is XML.	5–6
Configure a request or preprocess response.	Use transform functions.	7–8
Set defaults for Ajax requests.	Use the $httpProvider.	9
Intercept requests or responses.	Register an interceptor factory function with $httpProvider.	10
Represent an activity that will be completed at an unspecified time in the future.	Use a promise, which is made up of a deferred object and a promise object.	11
Obtain a deferred object.	Call the defer method provided by the $q service.	12
Obtain a promise object.	Use the promise value defined by a deferred object.	13
Chain promises together.	Use the then method to register callbacks. The then method returns another promise that will be resolved when the callback function has been executed.	14
Wait for multiple promises.	Use the $q.all method to create a promise that isn't resolved until all of its input promises are resolved.	15

Why and When to Use the Ajax Services

Ajax is the foundation of the modern web application, and you will use the services that I describe in this chapter every time that you need to communicate with a server without causing the browser to load new content and, in doing so, dump your AngularJS application.

That said, if you are consuming data from a RESTful API, then you should use the $resource service. I describe REST and $resource in Chapter 21, but the short version is that $resource provides a higher-level API that is built on the services I describe in this chapter and makes it easier to perform common data operations.

Preparing the Example Project

For this chapter, I am going to make an addition to the angularjs folder. I need a data file for many of the examples in this chapter, and for this reason I added a file called productData.json to the angularjs folder, the content of which is shown in Listing 20-1.

Listing 20-1. The Contents of the productData.json File

```
[{ "name": "Apples", "category": "Fruit", "price": 1.20, "expiry": 10 },
{ "name": "Bananas", "category": "Fruit", "price": 2.42, "expiry": 7 },
{ "name": "Pears", "category": "Fruit", "price": 2.02, "expiry": 6 },
{ "name": "Tuna", "category": "Fish", "price": 20.45, "expiry": 3 },
{ "name": "Salmon", "category": "Fish", "price": 17.93, "expiry": 2 },
{ "name": "Trout", "category": "Fish", "price": 12.93, "expiry": 4 }]
```

This file contains some product information, similar to the data I used in earlier chapters, expressed in the JavaScript Object Notation (JSON) format, which I introduced in Chapter 5.

JSON is a language-independent way of expressing data that emerged from JavaScript but that has since taken on a life of its own and is supported by every major programming language—so much so that it has displaced other data formats, especially in web applications. XML used to be the data exchange format of choice (the *X* in Ajax stands for XML), but JSON has largely replaced it because it is more concise and easier for developers to read. As a bonus for web applications, JSON is easy to generate and parse with JavaScript, and AngularJS takes care of formatting and parsing automatically.

Making Ajax Requests

The $http service is used to make and process Ajax requests, which are standard HTTP requests that are performed asynchronously. Ajax is at the heart of modern web applications, and the ability to request content and data in the background while the user interacts with the rest of the application is an important way of creating a rich user experience. To demonstrate making an Ajax request using the $http service, I have created a simple example application that, as yet, doesn't have any data. Listing 20-2 shows the contents of the ajax.html file, which I added to the angularjs folder.

Listing 20-2. An Application Without Data in the ajax.html File

```
<!DOCTYPE html>
<html ng-app="exampleApp">
<head>
    <title>Ajax</title>
    <script src="angular.js"></script>
    <link href="bootstrap.css" rel="stylesheet" />
```

```
        <link href="bootstrap-theme.css" rel="stylesheet" />
        <script>
            angular.module("exampleApp", [])
            .controller("defaultCtrl", function ($scope) {
                $scope.loadData = function () {


                }
            });
        </script>
    </head>
    <body ng-controller="defaultCtrl">
        <div class="panel panel-default">
            <div class="panel-body">
                <table class="table table-striped table-bordered">
                    <thead><tr><th>Name</th><th>Category</th><th>Price</th></tr></thead>
                    <tbody>
                        <tr ng-hide="products.length">
                            <td colspan="3" class="text-center">No Data</td>
                        </tr>
                        <tr ng-repeat="item in products">
                            <td>{{name}}</td>
                            <td>{{category}}</td>
                            <td>{{price | currency}}</td>
                        </tr>
                    </tbody>
                </table>
                <p><button class="btn btn-primary"
                    ng-click="loadData()">Load Data</button></p>
            </div>
        </div>
    </body>
</html>
```

The example consists of a table with a placeholder row that uses the ng-hide directive to control its visibility, based on the number of items in a scope array called products. The data array is not defined by default and so the placeholder is displayed. The table includes a row to which I have applied the ng-repeat directive, which will generate a row for each product data object when the array is defined.

I have added a button that uses the ng-click directive to call a controller behavior called loadData. The behavior is currently defined as an empty function, but this is where I will make the Ajax request using the $http service. You can see the initial state of the example application in Figure 20-1; currently, clicking the button has no effect.

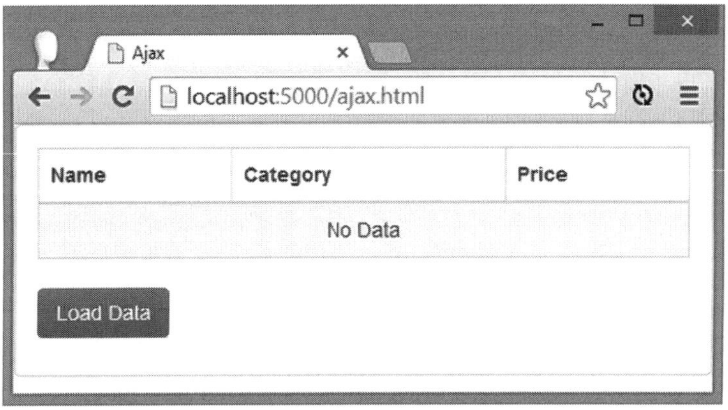

Figure 20-1. *The initial state of the example application*

I want to show the application before and after I use the $http service to emphasize just how little additional code is required to make the Ajax request and process the response. Listing 20-3 shows the ajax.html file after I used the $http service.

Listing 20-3. Using the $http Service to Make an Ajax Request in the ajax.htm File

```
<!DOCTYPE html>
<html ng-app="exampleApp">
<head>
    <title>Ajax</title>
    <script src="angular.js"></script>
    <link href="bootstrap.css" rel="stylesheet" />
    <link href="bootstrap-theme.css" rel="stylesheet" />
    <script>
        angular.module("exampleApp", [])
        .controller("defaultCtrl", function ($scope, $http) {
            $scope.loadData = function () {
                $http.get("productData.json").success(function (data) {
                    $scope.products = data;
                });
            }
        });
    </script>
</head>
<body ng-controller="defaultCtrl">
    <div class="panel panel-default">
        <div class="panel-body">
            <table class="table table-striped table-bordered">
                <thead><tr><th>Name</th><th>Category</th><th>Price</th></tr></thead>
                <tbody>
                    <tr ng-hide="products.length">
                        <td colspan="3" class="text-center">No Data</td>
                    </tr>
```

```
            <tr ng-repeat="item in products">
                <td>{{item.name}}</td>
                <td>{{item.category}}</td>
                <td>{{item.price | currency}}</td>
            </tr>
        </tbody>
    </table>
    <p><button class="btn btn-primary"
            ng-click="loadData()">Load Data</button></p>
        </div>
    </div>
</body>
</html>
```

I have declared a dependency on the $http service and added three lines of code. One of the differences in working with Ajax in an AngularJS application as opposed to, say, jQuery, is that you apply the data that you obtain from the server to the scope, which then automatically refreshes its bindings to update the HTML elements in the application. As a consequence, the code that would be required in a jQuery application to process the data and manipulate the DOM to display it is not required. Despite this, the basic mechanism for making Ajax requests will be familiar to you if you have used jQuery. There are two stages—making the request and receiving the response—that I describe in the following sections.

Making the Ajax Request

There are two ways to make a request using the $http service. The first—and most common—is to use one of the convenience methods that the service defines, which I have described in Table 20-2 and which allows you to make requests using the most commonly needed HTTP methods. All of these methods accept an optional configuration object, which I describe in the "Configuring Ajax Requests" section later in this chapter.

Table 20-2. *The Methods Defined by the $http Service for Making Ajax Requests*

Name	Description
get(url, config)	Performs a GET request for the specified URL.
post(url, data, config)	Performs a POST request to the specified URL to submit the specified data.
delete(url, config)	Performs a DELETE request to the specified URL.
put(url, data, config)	Performs a PUT request with the specified data and URL.
head(url, config)	Performs a HEAD request to the specified URL.
jsonp(url, config)	Performs a GET request to obtain a fragment of JavaScript code that is then executed. JSONP, which stands for *JSON with Padding*, is a way of working around the limitations that browsers apply to where JavaScript code can be loaded from. I do not describe JSONP in this book because it can be incredibly dangerous; see http://en.wikipedia.org/wiki/JSONP for details.

The other way to make an Ajax request is to treat the $http service object as a function and pass in a configuration object. This is useful when you require one of the HTTP methods for which there is not a convenience method available. You pass in a configuration object (which I describe later in this chapter) that includes the HTTP method you want to use. I'll show you how to make Ajax requests in this way in Chapter 21 when I talk about RESTful services, but in this chapter I am going to focus on the convenience methods.

From the table, you can see that I made a GET request without a configuration object in Listing 20-3, as follows:

```
...
$http.get("productData.json")
...
```

For the URL, I specified productData.json. A URL like this will be a requested relative to the main HTML document, which means that I don't have to hard-code protocols, hostnames, and ports into the application.

GET AND POST: PICK THE RIGHT ONE

The rule of thumb is that GET requests should be used for all read-only information retrieval, while POST requests should be used for any operation that changes the application state. In standards-compliance terms, GET requests are for *safe* interactions (having no side effects besides information retrieval), and POST requests are for *unsafe* interactions (making a decision or changing something). These conventions are set by the World Wide Web Consortium (W3C), at www.w3.org/Protocols/rfc2616/rfc2616-sec9.html.

GET requests are *addressable*—all the information is contained in the URL, so it's possible to bookmark and link to these addresses. Do not use GET requests for operations that change state. Many web developers learned this the hard way in 2005, when Google Web Accelerator was released to the public. This application prefetched all the content linked from each page, which is legal within HTTP because GET requests should be safe. Unfortunately, many web developers had ignored the HTTP conventions and placed simple links to "delete item" or "add to shopping cart" in their applications. Chaos ensued.

One company believed its content management system was the target of repeated hostile attacks because all its content kept getting deleted. The company later discovered that a search engine crawler had hit upon the URL of an administrative page and was crawling all the delete links.

Receiving Ajax Responses

Making a request is only the first part of the Ajax process, and I also have to receive the response when it is ready. The *A* in Ajax stands for asynchronous, which means that the request is performed in the background, and you will be notified when a response from the server is received at some point in the future.

AngularJS uses a JavaScript pattern called *promises* to represent the result from an asynchronous operation, such as an Ajax request. A promise is an object that defines methods that you can use to register functions that will be invoked when the operation is complete. I'll get into promises in more detail when I describe the $q service later in this chapter, but the promise objects returned from the $http methods in Table 20-2 define the methods shown in Table 20-3.

Table 20-3. *The Methods Defined Promise Objects Returned by $http Service Methods*

Name	Description
success(fn)	Invokes the specified function when the HTTP request has successfully completed
error(fn)	Invokes the specified function when the request does not complete successfully
then(fn, fn)	Registers a success function and an error function

The success and error methods pass their functions a simplified view of the response from the server. The success function is passed the data that the server sends, and the error function is passed a string that describes the problem that occurred. Further, if the response from the server is JSON data, then AngularJS will parse the JSON to create JavaScript objects and pass them to the success function automatically.

It is this feature that I used in Listing 20-3 to receive the data in the productData.json file and add it to the scope, as follows:

```
...
$http.get("productData.json").success(function (data) {
    $scope.products = data;
});
...
```

Within my success function, I assign the data object that AngularJS has created from the JSON response to the products property on the scope. This has the effect of removing the placeholder row in the table and causing the ng-repeat directive to generate rows for each item received from the server, as shown in Figure 20-2.

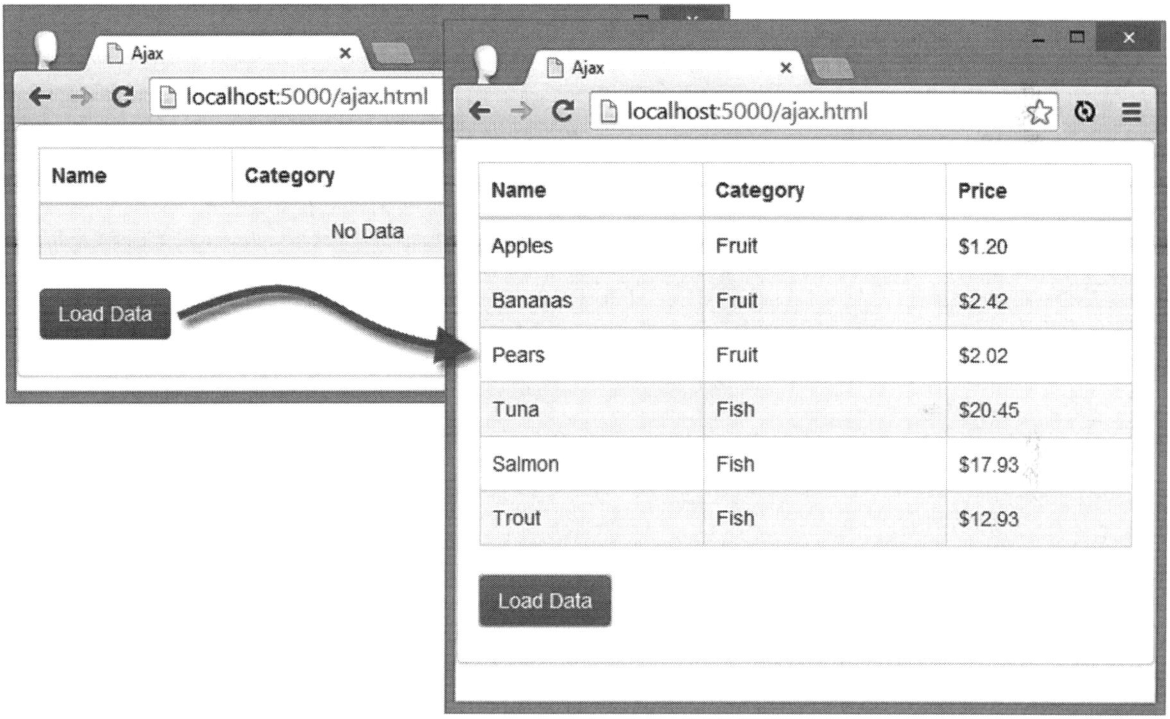

Figure 20-2. *Loading JSON data via Ajax*

■ **Tip**   The result from both the success and error methods is the promise object itself, which allows calls to these methods to be chained together in a single statement.

Getting More Response Details

Using the then method on the promise object allows you to register both a success and error function in a single method call. But also, more importantly, it provides access to more detailed information about the response from the server. The object that the then method passes to its success and error functions defines the properties I have described in Table 20-4.

Table 20-4. *The Properties of the Object Passed by the then Method*

Name	Description
data	Returns the data from the request
status	Returns the HTTP status code returned by the server
headers	Returns a function that can be used to obtain headers by name
config	The configuration object used to make the request (see the "Configuring Ajax Requests" section for details)

In Listing 20-4, you can see how I have used the then method to register a success function (the error function is optional) and write some of the response details to the console.

Listing 20-4. Using the promise.then Method in the ajax.html File

```
...
<script>
    angular.module("exampleApp", [])
    .controller("defaultCtrl", function ($scope, $http) {
        $scope.loadData = function () {
            $http.get("productData.json").then(function (response) {
                console.log("Status: " + response.status);
                console.log("Type: " + response.headers("content-type"));
                console.log("Length: " + response.headers("content-length"));
                $scope.products = response.data;
            });
        }
    });
</script>
...
```

In this example, I write the HTTP status code and the Content-Type and Content-Length headers to the console, which produces the following output when the button is clicked:

```
Status: 200
Type: application/json
Length: 434
```

AngularJS still automatically processes JSON data when using the then method, which means I can simply assign the value of the data property from the response object to the products property on the controller scope.

Processing Other Data Types

Although obtaining JSON data is the most common use for the $http service, you may not always have the luxury of working with a data format that AngularJS will process automatically. If this is the case, then AngularJS will pass the success function an object containing the properties shown in Table 20-4, and you will be responsible for parsing the data. To give you a simple example of how this works, I created a simple XML file called productData.xml that contains the same product information as the previous example, but expressed as a fragment of XML. You can see the contents of the productData.xml file in Listing 20-5.

Listing 20-5. The Contents of the productData.xml File

```
<products>
  <product name="Apples" category="Fruit" price="1.20" expiry="10" />
  <product name="Bananas" category="Fruit" price="2.42" expiry="7" />
  <product name="Pears" category="Fruit" price="2.02" expiry="10" />
  <product name="Tuna" category="Fish" price="20.45" expiry="3" />
  <product name="Salmon" category="Fish" price="17.93" expiry="2" />
  <product name="Trout" category="Fish" price="12.93" expiry="4" />
</products>
```

The XML fragment defines a products element that contains a set of product elements, each of which uses attribute values to describe a single product. This is typical of the kind of XML that I find myself handling when dealing with older content management systems: The XML is expressed as schema-less fragments, but it is well-formed and consistently generated. In Listing 20-6, you can see how I have updated the ajax.html file to request and process the XML data.

Listing 20-6. Working with an XML Fragment in the ajax.html File

```
...
<script>
    angular.module("exampleApp", [])
    .controller("defaultCtrl", function ($scope, $http) {
        $scope.loadData = function () {
            $http.get("productData.xml").then(function (response) {
                $scope.products = [];
                var productElems = angular.element(response.data.trim()).find("product");
                for (var i = 0; i < productElems.length; i++) {
                    var product = productElems.eq(i);
                    $scope.products.push({
                        name: product.attr("name"),
                        category: product.attr("category"),
                        price: product.attr("price")
                    });
                }
            });
        }
    });
</script>
...
```

XML and HTML are closely related—so much so that there is a version of the HTML specification that complies with XML called XHTML. The practical effect of this similarity is that you can use jqLite to process XML fragments as though they were HTML, which is the technique that I have used in this example.

The `data` property of the object passed to the `success` function returns the contents of the XML file, which I wrap in a jqLite object using the `angular.element` method. I then use the `find` method to locate the `product` elements and use a `for` loop to enumerate them and extract the attribute values. I described all of the jqLite methods in this example in Chapter 15.

Configuring Ajax Requests

The methods defined by the `$http` service all accept an optional argument of an object containing configuration settings. For most applications, the default configuration used for Ajax requests will be fine, but you can adjust the way the requests are made by defining properties on the configuration object corresponding to Table 20-5.

***Table 20-5.** The Configuration Properties for $http Methods*

Name	Description
data	Sets the data sent to the server. If you set this to an object, AngularJS will serialize it to the JSON format.
headers	Used to set request headers. Set `headers` to an object with properties whose names and values correspond to the headers and values you want to add to the request.
method	Sets the HTTP method used for the request.
params	Used to set the URL parameters. Set `params` to an object whose property names and values correspond to the parameters you want to include.
timeout	Specifies the number of milliseconds before the request expires.
transformRequest	Used to manipulate the request before it is sent to the server (see the later text).
transformResponse	Used to manipulate the response when it arrives from the server (see the later text).
url	Sets the URL for the request.
withCredentials	When set to `true`, the `withCredentials` option on the underlying browser request object is enabled, which includes authentication cookies in the request. I demonstrated the use of this property in Chapter 8.
xsrfHeaderNamexsrfCookieName	These properties are used to response to cross-site request forgery tokens that can be demanded by servers. See `http://en.wikipedia.org/wiki/Cross-site_request_forgery` for details.

The most interesting configuration feature is the ability to transform the request and response through the aptly named `transformRequest` and `transformResponse` properties. AngularJS defines two built-in transformations; outgoing data is serialized into JSON, and incoming JSON data is parsed into JavaScript objects.

Transforming a Response

You can transform a response by assigning a function to the transformResponse property of the configuration object. The transform function is passed the data from the response and a function that can be used to obtain header values. The function is responsible for returning a replacement version of the data, which is usually a deserialized version of the format sent by the server. In Listing 20-7, you can see how I have used a transform function to automatically deserialize the XML data contained in the productData.xml file.

Listing 20-7. Transforming a Response in the ajax.html File

```
...
<script>
    angular.module("exampleApp", [])
    .controller("defaultCtrl", function ($scope, $http) {
        $scope.loadData = function () {
            var config = {
                transformResponse: function (data, headers) {
                    if(headers("content-type") == "application/xml"
                            && angular.isString(data)) {
                        products = [];
                        var productElems = angular.element(data.trim()).find("product");
                        for (var i = 0; i < productElems.length; i++) {
                            var product = productElems.eq(i);
                            products.push({
                                name: product.attr("name"),
                                category: product.attr("category"),
                                price: product.attr("price")
                            });
                        }
                        return products;
                    } else {
                        return data;
                    }
                }
            }

            $http.get("productData.xml", config).success(function (data) {
                $scope.products = data;
            });
        }
    });
</script>
...
```

I check the value of the Content-Type header to make sure I am working with XML data and check to see that the data value is a string. It is possible to assign multiple transform functions using an array (or via the provider for the $http service, which I describe later in this chapter), so it is important to ensure that a transform function is dealing with the data format it expects.

■ **Caution** I am taking a shortcut to make a simpler demonstration in this listing. My code assumes that all XML data received by the request will contain `product` elements with `name`, `category`, and `price`. This is reasonable in the closed world of book examples, but you should be more careful in real projects and check that you received the kind of data you expected.

Once I am confident that there is XML data to process, I use the jqLite technique I demonstrated earlier to process the XML into an array of JavaScript objects, which I return as the result of the transform function. The effect of the transformation is that I don't have to process the XML data in the `success` function.

■ **Tip** Notice that I return the original data if the response doesn't contain XML data or if the data is not a string. This is important because whatever is returned from the transform function will eventually be passed to your `success` handler functions.

Transforming a Request

You can transform a request by assigning a function to the `transformRequest` property of the configuration object. The function is passed the data that will be sent to the server and a function that returns header values (although many headers will be set by the browser just before it makes the request). The result returned by the function will be used for the request, which provides the means for serializing data. In Listing 20-8, you can see how I have written a transform function that will serialize product data as XML.

■ **Tip** You don't need to use a transform function if you want to send JSON data because AngularJS will serialize it for you automatically.

Listing 20-8. Applying a Request Transformation Function in the ajax.html File

```
<!DOCTYPE html>
<html ng-app="exampleApp">
<head>
    <title>Ajax</title>
    <script src="angular.js"></script>
    <link href="bootstrap.css" rel="stylesheet" />
    <link href="bootstrap-theme.css" rel="stylesheet" />
    <script>
        angular.module("exampleApp", [])
        .controller("defaultCtrl", function ($scope, $http) {

            $scope.loadData = function () {
                $http.get("productData.json").success(function (data) {
                    $scope.products = data;
                });
            }
```

```
            $scope.sendData = function() {
                var config = {
                    headers: {
                        "content-type": "application/xml"
                    },
                    transformRequest: function (data, headers) {
                        var rootElem = angular.element("<xml>");
                        for (var i = 0; i < data.length; i++) {
                            var prodElem = angular.element("<product>");
                            prodElem.attr("name", data[i].name);
                            prodElem.attr("category", data[i].category);
                            prodElem.attr("price", data[i].price);
                            rootElem.append(prodElem);
                        }
                        rootElem.children().wrap("<products>");
                        return rootElem.html();
                    }
                }
                $http.post("ajax.html", $scope.products, config);
            }
        });
    </script>
</head>
<body ng-controller="defaultCtrl">
    <div class="panel panel-default">
        <div class="panel-body">
            <table class="table table-striped table-bordered">
                <thead><tr><th>Name</th><th>Category</th><th>Price</th></tr></thead>
                <tbody>
                    <tr ng-hide="products.length">
                        <td colspan="3" class="text-center">No Data</td>
                    </tr>
                    <tr ng-repeat="item in products">
                        <td>{{item.name}}</td>
                        <td>{{item.category}}</td>
                        <td>{{item.price | currency}}</td>
                    </tr>
                </tbody>
            </table>
            <p>
                <button class="btn btn-primary" ng-click="loadData()">Load Data</button>
                <button class="btn btn-primary" ng-click="sendData()">Send Data</button>
            </p>
        </div>
    </div>
</body>
</html>
```

I have added a button element that uses the ng-click directive to call a controller behavior called sendData when clicked. This behavior, in turn, defines a configuration object with a transform function that uses jqLite to generate XML from the request data. (You will have to click the Load Data button first in order to pull in the data so that it can be sent back to the server.)

USING JQLITE TO GENERATE XML

You probably won't want to use jqLite to generate XML in a real project because there are some nice JavaScript libraries around that are designed specifically for the purpose. But if you do need to create a small amount of XML and don't want to add a new dependency to your project, then jqLite can do the job as long as you are aware of a couple of tricks. The first trick is that you must use the < and > characters for tag names when you create a new element, like this:

```
...
angular.element("<product>")
...
```

If you omit < and >, then jqLite will throw an exception that explains you can't search for elements using selectors.

The other trick is related to getting the finished XML data. jqLite makes it easy to get the contents of an element, but not the element itself. To work around this, create a dummy element, like this:

```
...
var rootElem = angular.element("<dummy>");
...
```

I usually use the xml tag, but that's just my preference—the element you specify won't be included in the final output. When you are ready to get the XML string from your data, use the wrap method to insert the top-level element that you require and then call the html method on the dummy element:

```
...
rootElem.children().wrap("<products>").html();
return rootElem.html();
...
```

You'll end up with an XML fragment that contains a products element that contains multiple product elements. The xml element won't be included in the output.

I submit the data to the server using the $http.post method. I target the ajax.html URL, but the data will be ignored by the server, which will just send the content of the ajax.html file again. I don't want the contents of the HTML file, so I have not specified a success (or error) function.

■ **Tip**   Notice that I explicitly set the Content-Type header to application/xml in the configuration object. AngularJS has no way of knowing how a transform function has serialized data, so you must take care to correctly set the header. If you do not, the server may not process the request properly.

Setting Ajax Defaults

You can define default settings for Ajax requests through the provider for the $http service, $httpProvider. The provider defines the properties shown Table 20-6.

Table 20-6. *The Properties Defined by the $httpProvider*

Name	Description
defaults.headers.common	Defines the default headers used for all requests.
defaults.headers.post	Defines the headers used for POST requests.
defaults.headers.put	Defines the headers used for PUT requests.
defaults.transformResponse	An array of transform functions that are applied to all responses.
defaults.transformRequest	An array of transform functions that are applied to all requests.
interceptors	An array of interceptor factory functions. Interceptors are a more sophisticated form of transform function. I explain how they work in the next section.
withCredentials	Sets the withCredentials option for all requests. This property is used to address cross-origin requests that require authentication, and I demonstrated its use in Chapter 8.

■ **Tip**   The defaults object on which many of these properties are defined can also be accessed through the $http.defaults property, which allows the global Ajax configuration to be changed through the service.

The defaults.transformResponse and defaults.transformRequest properties are useful for applying transform functions to all of the Ajax requests made in an application. These properties are defined as arrays, meaning that additions must be made using the push method. In Listing 20-9, you can see how I have applied my XML deserialize function from an earlier example using the $httpProvider.

Listing 20-9. Setting a Global Response Transform Function in the ajax.html File

```
...
<script>
    angular.module("exampleApp", [])
    .config(function($httpProvider) {
        $httpProvider.defaults.transformResponse.push(function (data, headers) {
            if (headers("content-type") == "application/xml"
                                    && angular.isString(data)) {
                products = [];
                var productElems = angular.element(data.trim()).find("product");
                for (var i = 0; i < productElems.length; i++) {
                    var product = productElems.eq(i);
                    products.push({
                        name: product.attr("name"),
                        category: product.attr("category"),
                        price: product.attr("price")
                    });
                }
                return products;
            } else {
                return data;
            }
        });
    })
```

```
    .controller("defaultCtrl", function ($scope, $http) {
        $scope.loadData = function () {
            $http.get("productData.xml").success(function (data) {
                $scope.products = data;
            });
        }
    });
</script>
...
```

Using Ajax Interceptors

The $httpProvider also provides a feature called *request interceptors,* which is best thought of as sophisticated alternatives to transform functions. In Listing 20-10, you can see how I have used an interceptor in the ajax.html file.

Listing 20-10. Using an Interceptor in the ajax.html File

```
<!DOCTYPE html>
<html ng-app="exampleApp">
<head>
    <title>Ajax</title>
    <script src="angular.js"></script>
    <link href="bootstrap.css" rel="stylesheet" />
    <link href="bootstrap-theme.css" rel="stylesheet" />
    <script>
        angular.module("exampleApp", [])
        .config(function ($httpProvider) {
            $httpProvider.interceptors.push(function () {
                return {
                    request: function (config) {
                        config.url = "productData.json";
                        return config;
                    },
                    response: function (response) {
                        console.log("Data Count: " + response.data.length);
                        return response;
                    }
                }
            });
        })
        .controller("defaultCtrl", function ($scope, $http) {
            $scope.loadData = function () {
                $http.get("doesnotexit.json").success(function (data) {
                    $scope.products = data;
                });
            }
        });
    </script>
</head>
```

```
<body ng-controller="defaultCtrl">
    <div class="panel panel-default">
        <div class="panel-body">
            <table class="table table-striped table-bordered">
                <thead><tr><th>Name</th><th>Category</th><th>Price</th></tr></thead>
                <tbody>
                    <tr ng-hide="products.length">
                        <td colspan="3" class="text-center">No Data</td>
                    </tr>
                    <tr ng-repeat="item in products">
                        <td>{{item.name}}</td>
                        <td>{{item.category}}</td>
                        <td>{{item.price | currency}}</td>
                    </tr>
                </tbody>
            </table>
            <p><button class="btn btn-primary"
                    ng-click="loadData()">Load Data</button></p>
        </div>
    </div>
</body>
</html>
```

The $httpProvider.interceptor property is an array into which you insert factory functions that return objects with properties from Table 20-7. Each property corresponds to a different type of interceptor, and the functions assigned to the properties have the opportunity to change the request or response.

Table 20-7. *The Interceptor Properties*

Name	Description
request	The interceptor function is called before the request is made and is passed the configuration object, which defines the properties described in Table 20-5.
requestError	The interceptor function is called when the previous request interceptor throws an error.
response	The interceptor function is called when the response is received and is passed the response object, which defines the properties described in Table 20-4.
responseError	The interceptor function is called when the previous response interceptor throws an error.

In the example, the object that my factory method produces defines request and response properties. The function I have assigned to the request property demonstrates how an interceptor can alter a request by forcing the requested URL to be productData.json, irrespective of what was passed to the $http service method. To do this, I set the url property on the configuration object and return it as the result from the function so that it can be passed to the next interceptor or, if my interceptor is the last in the array, so that the request can be made.

For the response interceptor, I have demonstrated how a function can be used to debug the responses received from the server—which is how I find interceptors most useful—by looking at the data property of the response object and writing out how many objects it contains.

My response interceptor relies on the fact that AngularJS uses an interceptor to parse JSON data, which is why I check for an array of objects, rather than a string. This isn't something you would do in a real project, but I wanted to demonstrate that AngularJS processes the response before the interceptors are applied.

Working with Promises

Promises are a way of registering interest in something that will happen in the future, such as the response sent from a server for an Ajax request. Promises are not unique to AngularJS, and they can be found in many different libraries, including jQuery, but there are variations between implementations to accommodate differences in design philosophy or the preferences of the library developers.

There are two objects required for a promise: a promise object, which is used to receive notifications about the future outcome, and a deferred object, which is used to send the notifications. For most purposes, the easiest way to think of promises is to regard them as a specialized kind of event; the deferred object is used to send events via the promise objects about the outcome of some task or activity.

I am not being needlessly vague when I talk about "some task or activity" because promises can be used to represent anything that will happen in the future. And the best way to demonstrate this flexibility is with an example—but rather than show you another Ajax request, I am going to keep things simple and use button clicks. Listing 20-11 shows the contents of the promises.html file that I added to the angularjs folder. This is the initial implementation of an application to which I will add promises but which for the moment is just a regular AngularJS application.

Listing 20-11. The Contents of the promises.html File

```html
<!DOCTYPE html>
<html ng-app="exampleApp">
<head>
    <title>Promises</title>
    <script src="angular.js"></script>
    <link href="bootstrap.css" rel="stylesheet" />
    <link href="bootstrap-theme.css" rel="stylesheet" />
    <script>
        angular.module("exampleApp", [])
        .controller("defaultCtrl", function ($scope) {

        });
    </script>
</head>
<body ng-controller="defaultCtrl">
    <div class="well">
        <button class="btn btn-primary">Heads</button>
        <button class="btn btn-primary">Tails</button>
        <button class="btn btn-primary">Abort</button>
        Outcome: <span></span>
    </div>
</body>
</html>
```

This is a trivially simple application that contains buttons marked Heads, Tails, and Abort and inline data binding for a property called outcome. My goal will be to use deferred and promise objects to wire up the buttons such that clicking one of them will update the outcome binding. Along the way, I'll explain why promises are not like regular events. Figure 20-3 shows how the browser displays the promises.html file.

Figure 20-3. *The initial state of the promises example application*

AngularJS provides the $q service for obtaining and managing promises, which it does through the methods that I have described in Table 20-8. In the sections that follow, I'll show you how the $q service works as I build out the example application.

Table 20-8. *The Methods Defined by the $q Service*

Name	Description
all(promises)	Returns a promise that is resolved when all of the promises in the specified array are resolved or any of them is rejected
defer()	Creates a deferred object
reject(reason)	Returns a promise that is always rejected
when(value)	Wraps a value in a promise that is always resolved (with the specified value as a result)

Getting and Using the Deferred Object

I am showing you both sides of a promise in this example, and that means I need to create a deferred object, which I will use to report on the eventual outcome when the user clicks one of the buttons. I obtain a deferred object through the $q.defer method, and a deferred object defines the methods and properties shown in Table 20-9.

Table 20-9. *The Members Defined by deferred Objects*

Name	Description
resolve(result)	Signals that the deferred activity has completed with the specified value
reject(reason)	Signals that the deferred activity has failed or will not be completed for the specified reason
notify(result)	Provides an interim result from the deferred activity
promise	Returns a promise object that receives the signals from the other methods

The basic pattern of use is to get a deferred object and then call the resolve or reject method to signal the outcome of the activity. You can, optionally, provide interim updates through the notify method. Listing 20-12 shows how I have added a directive to the example that uses a deferred object.

Listing 20-12. Working with deferred Objects in the promises.html File

```html
<!DOCTYPE html>
<html ng-app="exampleApp">
<head>
    <title>Promises</title>
    <script src="angular.js"></script>
    <link href="bootstrap.css" rel="stylesheet" />
    <link href="bootstrap-theme.css" rel="stylesheet" />
    <script>
        angular.module("exampleApp", [])
        .directive("promiseWorker", function($q) {
            var deferred = $q.defer();
            return {
                link: function(scope, element, attrs) {
                    element.find("button").on("click", function (event) {
                        var buttonText = event.target.innerText;
                        if (buttonText == "Abort") {
                            deferred.reject("Aborted");
                        } else {
                            deferred.resolve(buttonText);
                        }
                    });
                },
                controller: function ($scope, $element, $attrs) {
                    this.promise = deferred.promise;
                }
            }
        })
        .controller("defaultCtrl", function ($scope) {

        });
    </script>
</head>
<body ng-controller="defaultCtrl">
    <div class="well" promise-worker>
        <button class="btn btn-primary">Heads</button>
        <button class="btn btn-primary">Tails</button>
        <button class="btn btn-primary">Abort</button>
        Outcome: <span></span>
    </div>
</body>
</html>
```

The new directive is called promiseWorker, and it relies on the $q service. Within the factory function I call the $q.defer method to obtain a new deferred object so that I can access it within both the link function and the controller.

The link function uses jqLite to locate button elements and register a handler function for the click event. On receipt of the event, I check the text of the clicked element and call either the deferred object's resolve method (for the Heads and Tails buttons) or reject method (for the Abort button). The controller defines a promise property that maps to the deferred object's promise property. By exposing this property through the controller, I can allow other directives to obtain the promise object associated with the deferred object and receive the signals about the outcome.

▪ **Tip** You should expose the `promise` object only to other parts of the application and keep the `deferred` object out of reach of other components, which would otherwise be able to resolve or reject the promise unexpectedly. This is partially why I assign the `deferred` object in Listing 20-12 within the factory function and provide the `promise` property only through the controller.

Consuming the Promise

The example application works at the point, in that the `deferred` object is used to signal the result of the user button click, but there is no one to receive those signals. The next step is to add another directive that will monitor the outcome through the promise created in the previous example and update the contents of the span element in the example. In Listing 20-13, you can see how I have created the required directive, which I have named promiseObserver.

Listing 20-13. Consuming a Promise in the promises.html File

```
<!DOCTYPE html>
<html ng-app="exampleApp">
<head>
    <title>Promises</title>
    <script src="angular.js"></script>
    <link href="bootstrap.css" rel="stylesheet" />
    <link href="bootstrap-theme.css" rel="stylesheet" />
    <script>
        angular.module("exampleApp", [])
        .directive("promiseWorker", function($q) {
            var deferred = $q.defer();
            return {
                link: function(scope, element, attrs) {
                    element.find("button").on("click", function (event) {
                        var buttonText = event.target.innerText;
                        if (buttonText == "Abort") {
                            deferred.reject("Aborted");
                        } else {
                            deferred.resolve(buttonText);
                        }
                    });
                },
                controller: function ($scope, $element, $attrs) {
                    this.promise = deferred.promise;
                }
            }
        })
        .directive("promiseObserver", function() {
            return {
                require: "^promiseWorker",
                link: function (scope, element, attrs, ctrl) {
                    ctrl.promise.then(function (result) {
                        element.text(result);
```

```
                }, function (reason) {
                    element.text("Fail (" + reason + ")");
                });
            }
        }
    })
    .controller("defaultCtrl", function ($scope) {

    });
</script>
</head>
<body ng-controller="defaultCtrl">
    <div class="well" promise-worker>
        <button class="btn btn-primary">Heads</button>
        <button class="btn btn-primary">Tails</button>
        <button class="btn btn-primary">Abort</button>
        Outcome: <span promise-observer></span>
    </div>
</body>
</html>
```

The new directive uses the `require` definition property to obtain the controller from the other directive and get the `promise` object. The `promise` object defines methods shown in Table 20-10.

Table 20-10. *The Methods Defined by Promise Objects*

Name	Description
then(success, error, notify)	Registers functions that are invoked in response to the deferred object's resolve, reject, and notify methods. The functions are passed the arguments that were used to call the deferred object's methods.
catch(error)	Registers just an error handling function, which is passed the argument used to call the deferred object's reject method.
finally(fn)	Registers a function that is invoked irrespective of the promise being resolved or rejected. The function is passed the argument used to call the deferred object's resolve or reject method.

■ **Tip** Notice that `promise` objects do not define the `success` and `error` methods that I used in the Ajax examples earlier in the chapter. These are convenience methods added to make using the `$http` service easier.

In the listing, I use the then method to register functions that will be called in response to the associated deferred object's `resolve` and `reject` methods being called. Both of these functions update the contents of the element to which the directive has been applied. You can see the overall effect by loading the `promises.html` file into the browser and clicking one of the buttons, as shown in Figure 20-4.

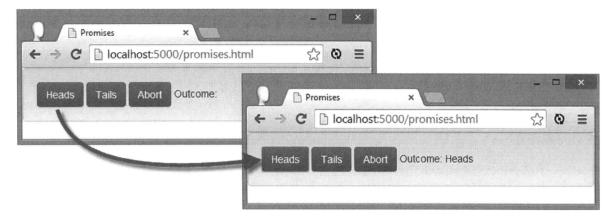

Figure 20-4. *Using deferred objects and promises*

Understanding Why Promises Are Not Regular Events

At this point, you might be wondering why I have gone to all the trouble of creating deferred and promise objects just to achieve something that could as easily be done with a regular JavaScript event handler.

It is true that promises perform the same basic function: They allow a component to indicate that it would like to be notified when something specific happens in the future, be that a button click or an Ajax result arriving from the server. Promises and regular events both provide the features required to register functions that will be invoked when the future thing happens (but not before). And, yes, I could have easily handled my button example using regular events—or even the ng-click directive, which relies on regular events but hides away the details.

It is only when you start to dig into the details that the differences between promises and events and the roles they play in an AngularJS application become apparent. In the sections that follow, I'll describe the ways in which promises differ from events.

Use Once, Discard

Promises represent a single instance of an activity, and once they are resolved or rejected, promises cannot be used again. You can see this if you load the promises.html file into the browser and click the Heads button and then the Tails button. When you click the first button, the display is updated so that the outcome is shown as Heads. The second button click has no effect, and that's because the promise in the example has already been resolved and can't be used again; once set, the outcome is immutable.

This is important because it means that the signal sent to the observer represents "the first time that the user choses Heads or Tails or Aborts." If I used regular JavaScript click events, then each single would be simply "the user has clicked a button," without any context about whether this is the first or tenth time that the user has clicked or what those clicks represented in terms of a user's decision.

This is an important difference, and it makes promises suitable for signaling the outcome of specific activities, while events signal outcomes that can recur and even differ. Or, put another way, promises are more precise because they signal the outcome or result of a single activity, be that a user's decision or the response for a particular Ajax requests.

Signals for Outcomes and Results

Events allow you to send a single when something happens—when a button is clicked, for example. Promises can be used in the same way, but they can also be used to signal when there is no outcome, either because the activity wasn't performed or because the activity failed through the reject method in the deferred object, which triggers the error callback function registered with the promise object. You can see this in the example, where clicking the Abort button calls the reject button, which in turn updates the display to show that the user didn't make a decision.

Being able to signal that the activity didn't happen or that something went wrong ensures that you have a definite view of the outcome, which is important for activities such as making Ajax requests where you want to notify the user if there is a problem.

Chaining Outcomes Together

Having a definite view of the outcome, even when the activity wasn't performed, allows for one of the best features of promises—the ability to chain promises together to create more complex arrangements of outcomes. This is possible because the methods defined by the promise object, such as then, return another promise, which is resolved when the callback function has completed execution. In Listing 20-14, you can see a simple example using the then method to chain promises together.

Listing 20-14. Chaining Promises in the promises.html File

```
...
<script>
    angular.module("exampleApp", [])
    .directive("promiseWorker", function($q) {
        var deferred = $q.defer();
        return {
            link: function(scope, element, attrs) {
                element.find("button").on("click", function (event) {
                    var buttonText = event.target.innerText;
                    if (buttonText == "Abort") {
                        deferred.reject("Aborted");
                    } else {
                        deferred.resolve(buttonText);
                    }
                });
            },
            controller: function ($scope, $element, $attrs) {
                this.promise = deferred.promise;
            }
        }
    })
    .directive("promiseObserver", function() {
        return {
            require: "^promiseWorker",
            link: function (scope, element, attrs, ctrl) {
                ctrl.promise
                    .then(function (result) {
                        return "Success (" + result + ")";
                    }).then(function(result) {
                        element.text(result);
                    });
            }
        }
    })
```

```
        .controller("defaultCtrl", function ($scope) {

        });
</script>
...
```

Within the `link` function of the `promiseObserver` directive, I obtain the promise and call the `then` method to register a callback function that will be invoked when the promise is resolved. The result from the `then` method is another `promise` object, which will be resolved when the callback function has been executed. I use the `then` method again to register a callback with the second `promise`.

■ **Tip**   For simplicity, I have not included a handler for dealing with the promise being rejected, which means that this example will respond only to the Heads and Tails buttons being clicked.

Notice that the first callback function returns a result, as follows:

```
...
ctrl.promise.then(function (result) {
    return "Success (" + result + ")";
}).then(function(result) {
    element.text(result);
});
...
```

When you chain promises together, you can manipulate the result that is passed along to the next promise in the chain. In this case, I do some simple formatting of the result string, which is then passed as the result to the next callback in the chain. Here is the sequence that occurs when the user clicks the Heads button:

1. The `promiseWorker` link function calls the resolve method on the deferred object, passing in Heads as the outcome.

2. The promise is resolved and invokes its `success` function, passing the Heads value.

3. The callback function formats the Heads value and returns the formatted string.

4. The second promise is resolved and invokes its success function, passing in the formatted string to the callback function as the outcome.

5. The callback function displays the formatted string in the HTML element.

This is important when you want to set up a domino-effect of actions, where each action in the chain depends on the result of the previous outcome. My string formatting example is not compelling in this regard, but you can imagine making an Ajax request to obtain a URL of a service and passing this as the outcome to the next promise in the chain, whose callback will use the URL to request some data.

Grouping Promises

Chains of promises are useful when you want to perform a sequence of actions, but there are occasions when you want to defer an activity until the several other outcomes are available. You can do this through the `$q.all` method, which accepts an array of promises and returns a promise that isn't resolved until all of the input promises are resolved. In Listing 20-15, I have expanded the example to use the `all` method.

Listing 20-15. Grouping Promises in the promises.html File

```html
<!DOCTYPE html>
<html ng-app="exampleApp">
<head>
    <title>Promises</title>
    <script src="angular.js"></script>
    <link href="bootstrap.css" rel="stylesheet" />
    <link href="bootstrap-theme.css" rel="stylesheet" />
    <script>
        angular.module("exampleApp", [])
        .directive("promiseWorker", function ($q) {
            var deferred = [$q.defer(), $q.defer()];
            var promises = [deferred[0].promise, deferred[1].promise];
            return {
                link: function (scope, element, attrs) {
                    element.find("button").on("click", function (event) {
                        var buttonText = event.target.innerText;
                        var buttonGroup = event.target.getAttribute("data-group");
                        if (buttonText == "Abort") {
                            deferred[buttonGroup].reject("Aborted");
                        } else {
                            deferred[buttonGroup].resolve(buttonText);
                        }
                    });
                },
                controller: function ($scope, $element, $attrs) {
                    this.promise = $q.all(promises).then(function (results) {
                        return results.join();
                    });
                }
            }
        })
        .directive("promiseObserver", function () {
            return {
                require: "^promiseWorker",
                link: function (scope, element, attrs, ctrl) {
                    ctrl.promise.then(function (result) {
                        element.text(result);
                    }, function (reason) {
                        element.text(reason);
                    });
                }
            }
        })
        .controller("defaultCtrl", function ($scope) {

        });
    </script>
</head>
```

```
<body ng-controller="defaultCtrl">
    <div class="well" promise-worker>
        <div class="btn-group">
            <button class="btn btn-primary" data-group="0">Heads</button>
            <button class="btn btn-primary" data-group="0">Tails</button>
            <button class="btn btn-primary" data-group="0">Abort</button>
        </div>
        <div class="btn-group">
            <button class="btn btn-primary" data-group="1">Yes</button>
            <button class="btn btn-primary" data-group="1">No</button>
            <button class="btn btn-primary" data-group="1">Abort</button>
        </div>
        Outcome: <span promise-observer></span>
    </div>
</body>
</html>
```

In this example, there are two groups of buttons, allowing the user to choose Heads/Tails and Yes/No. In the promiseWorker directive, I create an array of deferred objects and an array of the corresponding promise objects. The promise that I expose via the controller is created using the $q.all method, like this:

```
...
this.promise = $q.all(promises).then(function (results) {
    return results.join();
});
...
```

The call to the all method returns a promise that won't be resolved until *all* of the input promises are resolved (which is the set of promise objects in the promises array) but will be rejected if *any* of the input promises are rejected. This is the promise object that the promiseObserver directive obtains and observes by registering success and error callback functions. To see the effect, load the promises.html file into the browser and click the Heads or Tails button followed by the Yes or No button. After you make the second selection, the overall result will be displayed, as shown in Figure 20-5.

Figure 20-5. *Grouping promises*

The promise that I created with the $q.all method passes an array to its success function containing the results from each of the input elements. The results are arranged in the same order as the input promises, meaning that Heads/Tails will always appear first in the array of results. For this example, I use the standard JavaScript join method to concatenate the results and pass them to the next stage in the chain. If you look closely at this example, you will see that there are five promises:

1. The promise that is resolved when the user selects Heads or Tails

2. The promise that is resolved when the user selects Yes or No

3. The promise that is resolved when promises (1) and (2) are both resolved

4. The promise whose callback uses the join method to concatenate the results

5. The promise whose callback displays the concatenated results in the HTML element

I don't want to labor the point, but complex chains of promises can cause a lot of confusion, so here is the sequence of actions in the example, referencing the previous list of promises (I am assuming that the user choses Heads/Tails first, but the sequence is much the same if Yes/No is selected first):

1. The user clicks Heads or Tails, and promise (1) is resolved.

2. The user clicks Yes or No, and promise (2) is resolved.

3. Promise (3) is resolved without any further user interaction and passes an array containing the results from promises (1) and (2) to its success callback.

4. The success function uses the join method to create a single result.

5. Promise 4 is resolved.

6. Promise 5 is resolved.

7. The success callback for promise (5) updates the HTML element.

You can see how a simple example can lead to complex combinations and chains of promises. This may seem overwhelming at first, but as you get used to working with promises, you will come to appreciate the precision and flexibility that they offer, which is especially valuable in complex applications.

Summary

In this chapter, I described the $http and $q services, which are used to make Ajax requests and manage promises, respectively. These two services are closely related because of the asynchronous nature of Ajax requests, but they also form the foundation for some of the higher-level services that I describe in the following sections, including the service that provides access to RESTful services, which I describe in the next chapter.

CHAPTER 21

■ ■ ■

Services for REST

In this chapter, I show you how AngularJS supports working with RESTful web services. *Representational State Transfer* (REST) is a style of API that operates over HTTP requests, which I introduced in Chapter 3. The requested URL identifies the data to be operated on, and the HTTP method identifies the operation that is to be performed.

REST is a style of API rather than a formal specification, and there is a lot of debate and disagreement about what is and isn't RESTful, a term used to indicate an API that follows the REST style. AngularJS is pretty flexible about how RESTful web services are consumed, and I show you how you can tailor AngularJS to work with specific REST implementations.

Don't worry if you are not familiar with REST or if you have not worked with a RESTful web service before. I start by building a simple REST service and then provide plenty of examples to show you how to use it. Table 21-1 summarizes this chapter.

Table 21-1. *Chapter Summary*

Problem	Solution	Listing
Consume a RESTful API through explicit Ajax requests.	Use the $http service to request the data from the server and perform operations on it.	1–8
Consume a RESTful API without exposing the Ajax requests.	Use the $resource service.	9–14
Tailor the Ajax requests used by the $resource service.	Define custom actions or redefine the default ones.	15–16
Create components that can work with RESTful data.	Ensure that you can optionally enable support for working with the $resource service and remember to allow the actions that must be used to be configured when the component is applied.	17–18

Why and When to Use the REST Services

You should use the services that I describe in this chapter when you are performing data operations on a RESTful API. You may initially prefer to use the $http service to make Ajax requests, especially if you are coming from a jQuery background. To that end, I describe the use of $http at the start of the chapter, before explaining its limitations when used with REST and the advantages of using the $resource service as an alternative.

Preparing the Example Project

I need a back-end service to demonstrate the different ways in which AngularJS can be used to consume a RESTful web service, so I will be using Deployd once again. If you have not downloaded and installed Deployd, then see the instructions in Chapter 1.

■ **Caution** I reuse the name of the products data collection from the SportsStore example in Part 1 of this book. If you created the SportsStore example, be sure to remove the Deployd directory before following the instructions in this chapter.

Creating the RESTful Service

To create the new service, I typed the following at the command prompt:

```
dpd create products
```

To start the new service, I entered the following commands to start Deployd and show the service console:

```
dpd -p 5500 products\app.dpd
dashboard
```

The Deployd dashboard will be displayed in the browser, as shown in Figure 21-1.

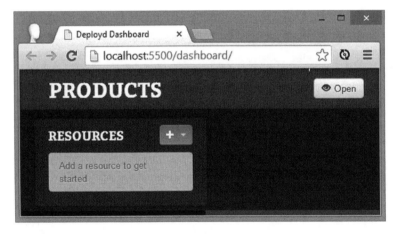

Figure 21-1. *The initial state of the Deployd dashboard*

Creating the Data Structure

Having created the back-end service, it is time to add the data structure data. Click the green button in the Deployd dashboard and select Collection from the pop-up menu. Set the name of the collection to /products, as shown in Figure 21-2, and then click the Create button.

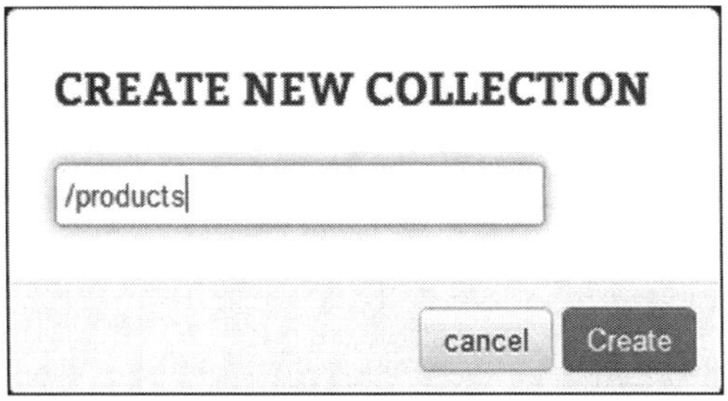

CREATE NEW COLLECTION

/products

cancel   Create

Figure 21-2. *Creating the products collection*

Deployd will prompt you to define the properties that the objects in the collection will have. Enter the properties I have listed in Table 21-2.

Table 21-2. *The Properties Required for the products Collection*

Name	Type	Required
name	string	Yes
category	string	Yes
price	number	Yes

When you have finished, the dashboard should match Figure 21-3. Make sure you have spelled the property names correctly and that you selected the right type for each property.

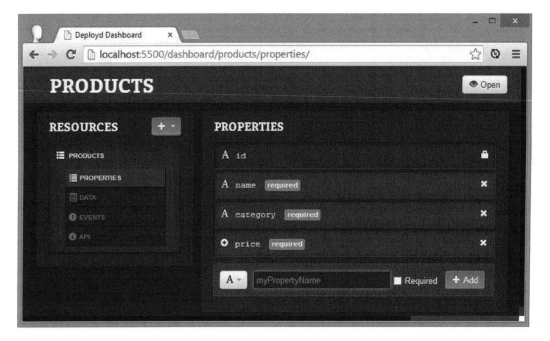

Figure 21-3. *The set of properties in the Deployd dashboard*

Adding the Initial Data

I am going to populate Deployd with some initial data to make creating the example simple. Click the Data link in the Resources section of the dashboard screen and use the table editor to add the data items I have listed in Table 21-3.

Table 21-3. *The Initial Data Items*

Name	Category	Price
Apples	Fruit	1.20
Bananas	Fruit	2.42
Pears	Fruit	2.02
Tuna	Fish	20.45
Salmon	Fish	17.93
Trout	Fish	12.93

When you have added the data, the dashboard should look like the one shown in Figure 21-4.

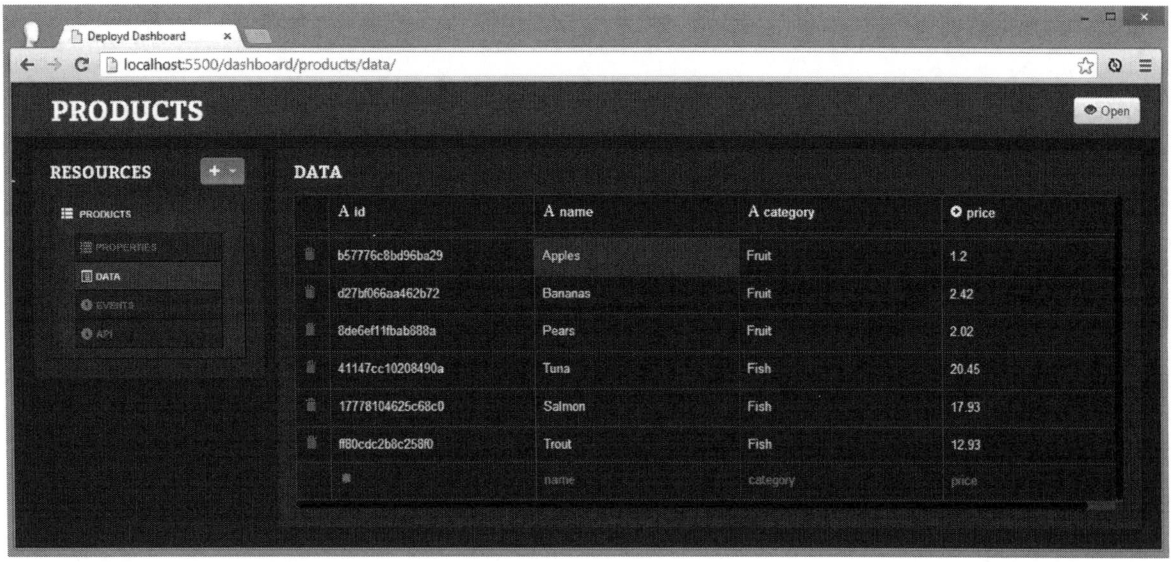

Figure 21-4. *Adding the data*

Testing the API

If you click the API link in the Deployd dashboard, you will be shown a table that lists the URLs and HTTP methods that can be used to manipulate the data, which is the essence of a RESTful service. My goal in this chapter is to show you the different facilities that AngularJS provides to combine these URLs and HTTP methods to drive the data from an application. In Table 21-4, I have repeated the key details from the API table.

Table 21-4. *The HTTP Methods and URLs That the RESTful Service Supports*

Task	Method	URL	Accepts	Returns
List products	GET	/products	Nothing	An array of objects
Create an object	POST	/products	A single object	The saved object
Get an object	GET	/products/<id>	Nothing	A single object
Update an object	PUT	/products/<id>	A single object	The saved object
Delete an object	DELETE	/products/<id>	A single object	Nothing

■ **Tip**   It is always worth checking the API that your RESTful service provides because there isn't complete consistency about the way that HTTP methods are combined with URLs to manipulate data. As an example, some services support using the PATCH method to update individual properties for an object, whereas others, including Deployd, use the PUT method.

The command I used to start Deployd set the port that the server uses to 5500, which means you can manually list the products by opening a browser and navigating to the following URL (assuming you are running Deployd on the local machine):

```
http://localhost:5500/products
```

When this URL is requested, the Deployd server returns a JSON string that contains the details entered from Table 21-3. If you are using Google Chrome, then the JSON will be displayed in the browser window, but other browsers, including Internet Explorer, will ask you to save the JSON data to a file. The JSON from Deployd is similar to the JSON I manually created in Chapter 20, but with one difference: Since the data is being stored in a database, each product object is assigned a unique key on a property called id. The value of the id property is used to identify individual product objects in the RESTful URLs, as shown in Table 21-4. Here is the JSON that Deployd sent to represent just one of the product objects:

```
...
{"name":"Apples",
 "category":"Fruit",
 "price":1.2,
 "id":"b57776c8bd96ba29"
}
...
```

The id value b57776c8bd96ba29 uniquely identifies the product object whose name property is set to Apples. To delete this object via REST, I would use the HTTP DELETE method to invoke the following URL:

```
http://localhost:5500/products/b57776c8bd96ba29
```

Creating the AngularJS Application

Now that the RESTful API is set up and populated with data, I am going to create a skeletal AngularJS application. This application will display the content and present the user with the means to add, modify, and delete product objects.

I started by clearing the contents of the angularjs directory and reinstalling the AngularJS and Bootstrap files, as described in Chapter 1. I then created a new HTML file called products.html, the contents of which you can see in Listing 21-1.

Listing 21-1. The Contents of the products.html File

```
<!DOCTYPE html>
<html ng-app="exampleApp">
<head>
    <title>Products</title>
    <script src="angular.js"></script>
    <link href="bootstrap.css" rel="stylesheet" />
    <link href="bootstrap-theme.css" rel="stylesheet" />
    <script src="products.js"></script>
</head>
```

```
<body ng-controller="defaultCtrl">
    <div class="panel panel-primary">
        <h3 class="panel-heading">Products</h3>
        <ng-include src="'tableView.html'" ng-show="displayMode == 'list'"></ng-include>
        <ng-include src="'editorView.html'" ng-show="displayMode == 'edit'"></ng-include>
    </div>
</body>
</html>
```

I am going to break this example into a series of smaller files, much as you would do in a real project. The products.html file contains the script element for AngularJS and the link elements for Bootstrap. The main content for this application is contained in two view files, tableView.html and editorView.html, which I will create shortly. These are imported into the products.html file using the ng-include directive, and the visibility of the elements is controlled using the ng-show directive tied to a scope variable called displayMode.

The products.html file also contains a script element for a file called products.js, which I have used to define the behaviors that the application will need. I have started by using dummy local data, which I will replace with data obtained via REST later in the chapter. Listing 21-2 shows the contents of the products.js file.

Listing 21-2. The Contents of the products.js File

```
angular.module("exampleApp", [])
.controller("defaultCtrl", function ($scope) {

    $scope.displayMode = "list";
    $scope.currentProduct = null;

    $scope.listProducts = function () {
        $scope.products = [
            { id: 0, name: "Dummy1", category: "Test", price: 1.25 },
            { id: 1, name: "Dummy2", category: "Test", price: 2.45 },
            { id: 2, name: "Dummy3", category: "Test", price: 4.25 }];
    }

    $scope.deleteProduct = function (product) {
        $scope.products.splice($scope.products.indexOf(product), 1);
    }

    $scope.createProduct = function (product) {
        $scope.products.push(product);
        $scope.displayMode = "list";
    }

    $scope.updateProduct = function (product) {
        for (var i = 0; i < $scope.products.length; i++) {
            if ($scope.products[i].id == product.id) {
                $scope.products[i] = product;
                break;
            }
        }
        $scope.displayMode = "list";
    }
```

```
    $scope.editOrCreateProduct = function (product) {
        $scope.currentProduct =
            product ? angular.copy(product) : {};
        $scope.displayMode = "edit";
    }

    $scope.saveEdit = function (product) {
        if (angular.isDefined(product.id)) {
            $scope.updateProduct(product);
        } else {
            $scope.createProduct(product);
        }
    }

    $scope.cancelEdit = function () {
        $scope.currentProduct = {};
        $scope.displayMode = "list";
    }

    $scope.listProducts();
});
```

The controller in the listing defines all the functionality I need to operate on the product data. The behaviors I have defined fall into two categories. The first category consists of behaviors that manipulate the data in the scope: the listProducts, deleteProduct, createProduct, and updateProduct functions. These behaviors correspond to the REST operations I described in Table 21-4, and most of this chapter is spent showing you different ways to implement those methods. For the moment, the application uses some dummy test data, just so I can separate showing you how the application works from showing you how to consume restful services.

The other behaviors, editOrCreateProduct, saveEdit, and cancelEdit, all support the user interface and are invoked in response to user interaction. In Listing 21-1, you will see that I used the ng-include directive to import two HTML views. The first of these is called tableView.html, and I use it to display the data and provide buttons that will allow the user to reload the data and create, delete, and edit a product. Listing 21-3 shows the contents of the tableView.html file.

Listing 21-3. The Contents of the tableView.html File

```
<div class="panel-body">
    <table class="table table-striped table-bordered">
        <thead>
            <tr>
                <th>Name</th>
                <th>Category</th>
                <th class="text-right">Price</th>
                <th></th>
            </tr>
        </thead>
        <tbody>
            <tr ng-repeat="item in products">
                <td>{{item.name}}</td>
                <td>{{item.category}}</td>
                <td class="text-right">{{item.price | currency}}</td>
                <td class="text-center">
```

```
                <button class="btn btn-xs btn-primary"
                        ng-click="deleteProduct(item)">
                    Delete
                </button>
                <button class="btn btn-xs btn-primary"
                        ng-click="editOrCreateProduct(item)">
                    Edit
                </button>
            </td>
        </tr>
    </tbody>
</table>
<div>
    <button class="btn btn-primary" ng-click="listProducts()">Refresh</button>
    <button class="btn btn-primary" ng-click="editOrCreateProduct()">New</button>
</div>
</div>
```

This view uses AngularJS features that I have described in earlier chapters. I use the ng-repeat directive to generate rows in a table for each product object, and I use the currency filter to format the price property on the product objects. Finally, I use the ng-click directive to respond when the user clicks a button, calling the behaviors defined in the controller defined in the products.js file.

The other view file is called editorView.html, and I use it to allow the user to create new product objects or edit existing ones. You can see the contents of the editorView.html file in Listing 21-4.

Listing 21-4. The Contents of the editorView.html File

```
<div class="panel-body">
    <div class="form-group">
        <label>Name:</label>
        <input class="form-control" ng-model="currentProduct.name" />
    </div>
    <div class="form-group">
        <label>Category:</label>
        <input class="form-control" ng-model="currentProduct.category" />
    </div>
    <div class="form-group">
        <label>Price:</label>
        <input class="form-control" ng-model="currentProduct.price" />
    </div>
    <button class="btn btn-primary" ng-click="saveEdit(currentProduct)">Save</button>
    <button class="btn btn-primary" ng-click="cancelEdit()">Cancel</button>
</div>
```

This view uses the ng-model directive to create two-way bindings with the product being edited or created, and it uses the ng-click directive to respond to the user clicking the Save or Cancel button.

Testing the Application

To test the AngularJS application, simply load the products.html file into the browser. All of the other files will be imported, and you will see the list of dummy data, as illustrated in Figure 21-5.

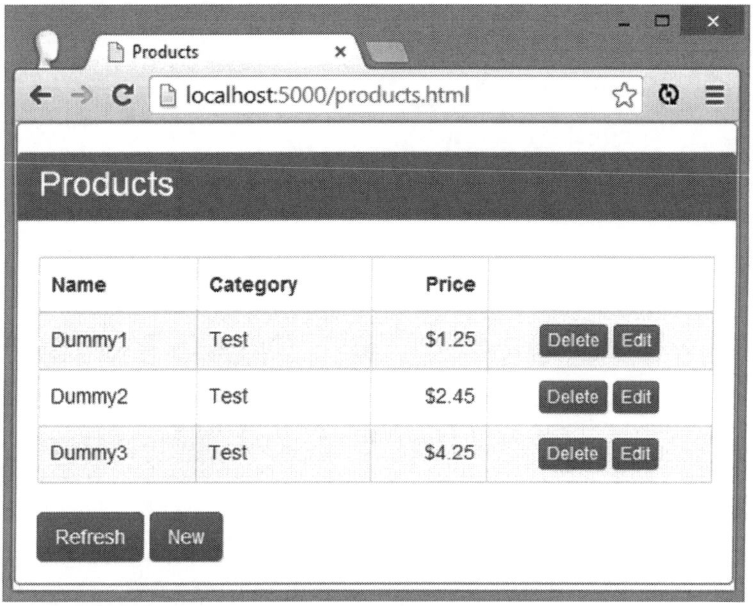

Figure 21-5. Displaying dummy data

If you click the Delete button, the deleteProduct behavior will be invoked, and the product in the corresponding row will be removed from the data array. If you click the Refresh button, the listProducts behavior will be invoked, and the data will be reset because this is where the dummy data is defined; the data won't be reset when I start making Ajax requests.

Clicking the Edit or New button will invoke the editOrCreateProduct behavior, which causes the contents of the editorView.html file to be displayed, as shown in Figure 21-6.

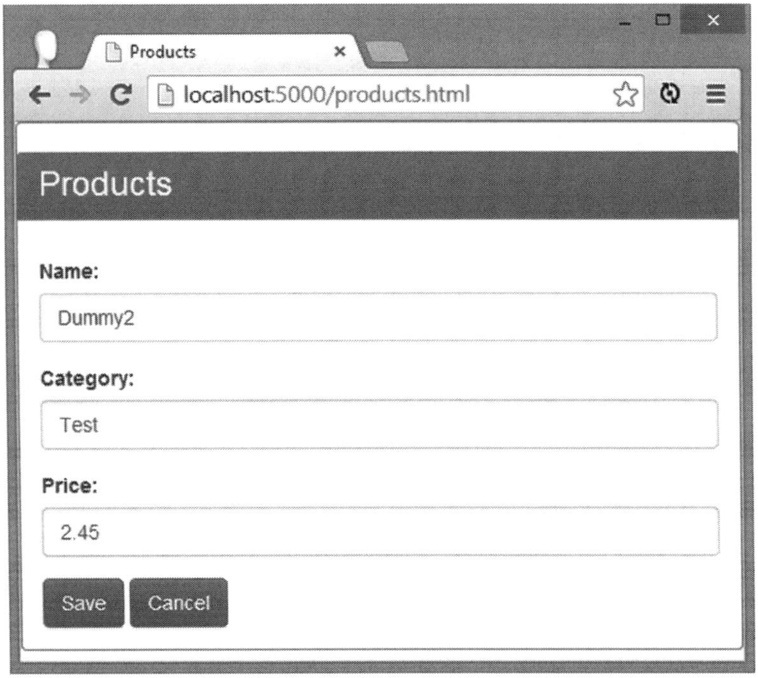

Figure 21-6. *Editing or creating a product*

If you click the Save button, the changes made to an existing item will be saved or a new product will be created. I rely on the fact that data objects that are being edited will have an `id` attribute. The Cancel button returns to the list view without saving any changes, which I handle by using the `angular.copy` method to create a copy of the `product` object so that I can discard it when needed.

> ■ **Note** One shortcoming of the current implementation is that I don't add an `id` attribute when I create new `product` objects. This is because the RESTful service will set the `id` value for me when a new `product` is stored in the database and will be resolved when I add support for real network requests.

Using the $http Service

The first service that I am going to use to complete the implementation of the example application is `$http`, which I described in Chapter 20. RESTful services are consumed using standard asynchronous HTTP requests, and the `$http` service provides all of the features that are required to bring the data into the application and write changes to the server. In the sections that follow, I'll rewrite each of the data manipulation behaviors to use the `$http` service.

Listing the Product Data

None of the changes that I have to make to use Ajax is especially complex, and in Listing 21-5, you can see how I have changed the definition of the controller factory function to declare its dependencies.

I don't want to embed the URL for the RESTful service throughout the application, so I have defined a constant called baseUrl for the root URL that provides access to the data. (You will need to change this URL if you have used a different port for Deployd or have installed it on a separate computer.) I then declare a dependency on baseUrl (which is possible because, as I explained in Chapter 18, constants are just simple services).

Listing 21-5. Declaring Dependencies and Listing Data in the products.js File

```
angular.module("exampleApp", [])
.constant("baseUrl", "http://localhost:5500/products/")
.controller("defaultCtrl", function ($scope, $http, baseUrl) {

    $scope.displayMode = "list";
    $scope.currentProduct = null;

    $scope.listProducts = function () {
        $http.get(baseUrl).success(function (data) {
            $scope.products = data;
        });
    }

    $scope.deleteProduct = function (product) {
        $scope.products.splice($scope.products.indexOf(product), 1);
    }

    $scope.createProduct = function (product) {
        $scope.products.push(product);
        $scope.displayMode = "list";
    }

    $scope.updateProduct = function (product) {
        for (var i = 0; i < $scope.products.length; i++) {
            if ($scope.products[i].id == product.id) {
                $scope.products[i] = product;
                break;
            }
        }
        $scope.displayMode = "list";
    }

    $scope.editOrCreateProduct = function (product) {
        $scope.currentProduct =
            product ? angular.copy(product) : {};
        $scope.displayMode = "edit";
    }

    $scope.saveEdit = function (product) {
        if (angular.isDefined(product.id)) {
            $scope.updateProduct(product);
        } else {
            $scope.createProduct(product);
        }
    }
```

```
    $scope.cancelEdit = function () {
        $scope.currentProduct = {};
        $scope.displayMode = "list";
    }

    $scope.listProducts();
});
```

The implementation of the listProduct method relied on the $http.get convenience method that I described in Chapter 20. I make a call to the base URL, which, as Table 21-4 noted, obtains the array of product objects from the server. I use the success method to receive the data that the server sends and assign it to the products property in the controller scope.

The last statement in the controller's factory function calls the listProduct behavior to ensure that the application starts with some data. You can see the effect by loading products.html into the browser and using the F12 developer tools to look at the network requests that are made. You will see a GET request being made to the base URL, and the data will be displayed in the table element, as shown in Figure 21-7.

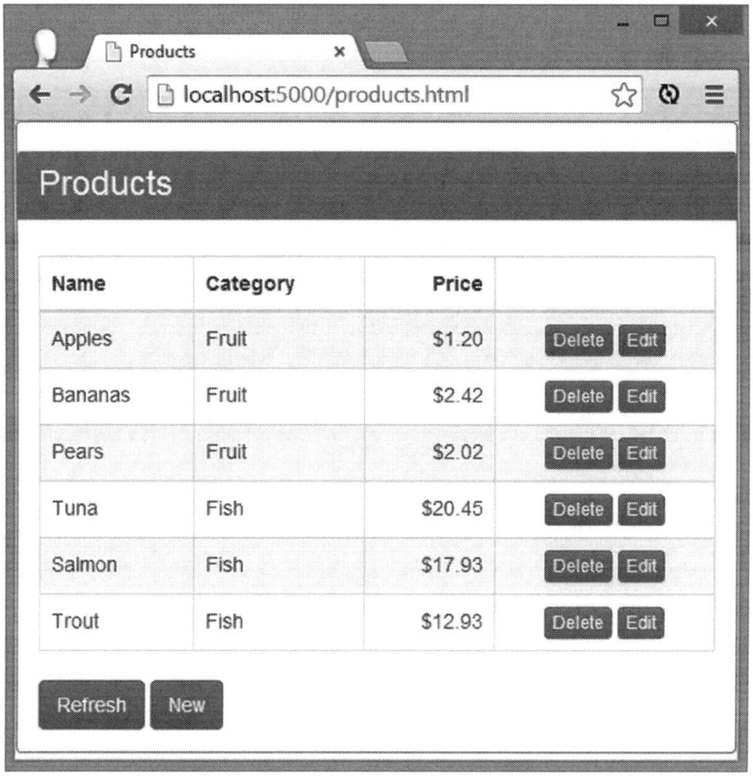

Figure 21-7. *Listing the data from the server using Ajax*

> ■ **Tip** You may notice a small delay between the contents of the `tableView.html` file being displayed and the `table` element being populated. This is the time taken for the server to process the Ajax request and send the response, and it can be quite pronounced when the network or the service is busy. In Chapter 22, I show you how you can use the URL routing feature to prevent the view from being shown until the data has arrived.

Deleting Products

The next behavior I am going to reimplement is deleteProduct, which you can see in Listing 21-6.

Listing 21-6. Adding Ajax Requests to the deleteProduct Function in the products.js File

```
...
$scope.deleteProduct = function (product) {
    $http({
        method: "DELETE",
        url: baseUrl + product.id
    }).success(function () {
        $scope.products.splice($scope.products.indexOf(product), 1);
    });
}
...
```

There is no $http convenience method for the HTTP DELETE method, so I have to use the alternative technique of treating the $http service object as a function and pass in a configuration object. I described the properties that can be set on a configuration object in Chapter 20, but I need only the method and url properties for this example.

I set the URL to be the base URL plus the id of the product I want deleted following the URL pattern I listed in Table 21-4. The $http service object returns a promise, and I use the success method to delete the corresponding product from the local array so that the server data and the local copy of it remain in sync.

The effect of this change is that clicking a Delete button removes the corresponding product from the server and the client. You can see the change both in the Deployd dashboard and, of course, in the browser that is running the example AngularJS application.

Creating Products

Adding support for creating new product objects requires the use of the HTTP POST method, for which there is an $http convenience method. You can see the changes I made to the createProduct behavior in Listing 21-7.

Listing 21-7. Creating Products in the products.js File

```
...
$scope.createProduct = function (product) {
    $http.post(baseUrl, product).success(function (newProduct) {
        $scope.products.push(newProduct);
        $scope.displayMode = "list";
    });
}
...
```

The RESTful service responds to my create request by returning the object that it has created in the database from the data I sent. It is this object—and not the one passed as the argument to the behavior—that I add to the products array because the object returned by the server will have been assigned an id property. If I had stored the product object created from the ng-model directives, I would not have been able to edit or delete the object later because the server handles those operations based on the id. Once I have added the new object to the array, I set the displayMode variable so that the application displays the list view.

Updating Products

The last behavior I have to revise is updateProduct, which you can see in Listing 21-8.

Listing 21-8. Using Ajax in the updateProduct Behavior Defined in the product.json File

```
...
$scope.updateProduct = function (product) {
    $http({
        url: baseUrl + product.id,
        method: "PUT",
        data: product
    }).success(function (modifiedProduct) {
        for (var i = 0; i < $scope.products.length; i++) {
            if ($scope.products[i].id == modifiedProduct.id) {
                $scope.products[i] = modifiedProduct;
                break;
            }
        }
        $scope.displayMode = "list";
    });
}
...
```

Updating an existing product object requires the HTTP PUT method for which there is no $http convenience method, meaning that I have to invoke the $http service object as a function and pass in a configuration object with the method and URL. The response from the server is the modified object, which I put into the local data array by checking each object in turn and comparing id values. Once I have added the modified object to the array, I set the displayMode variable so that the application displays the list view.

Testing the Ajax Implementation

You can see from the previous sections that implementing the Ajax calls to integrate the RESTful service into the application is a relatively simple task. I have skipped over some details that would be required in a real application, such as form validation and handling errors, but you get the idea: With just a little care and thought, it is easy to use the $http service to consume a RESTful service.

Hiding the Ajax Requests

Using the $http service to consume a RESTful API is easy, and it provides a nice demonstration of how different AngularJS features can be combined to create applications. In terms of features, it works just fine, but there are serious problems when it comes to the design of the application that it produces.

The problem is that the local data and the behaviors that manipulate the data on the server are separate and care has to be taken to make sure that they stay synchronized. This runs counter to the way that AngularJS usually work, where data is propagated throughout the application via scopes and can be updated freely. To demonstrate the problem, I have added a new file to the angularjs folder called increment.js, which contains the module shown in Listing 21-9.

Listing 21-9. The Contents of the increment.js File

```
angular.module("increment", [])
    .directive("increment", function () {
        return {
            restrict: "E",
            scope: {
                value: "=value"
            },
            link: function (scope, element, attrs) {
                var button = angular.element("<button>").text("+");
                button.addClass("btn btn-primary btn-xs");
                element.append(button);
                button.on("click", function () {
                    scope.$apply(function () {
                        scope.value++;
                    })
                })
            },
        }
    });
```

The module in this file, called increment, contains a directive, also called increment, that updates a value when the button is clicked. The directive is applied as an element and uses a two-way binding on an isolated scope to get its data value (a process that I described in Chapter 16). To use the module, I had to add a script element to the products.html file, as shown in Listing 21-10.

Listing 21-10. Adding a script Element to the products.html File

```
<!DOCTYPE html>
<html ng-app="exampleApp">
<head>
    <title>Products</title>
    <script src="angular.js"></script>
    <link href="bootstrap.css" rel="stylesheet" />
    <link href="bootstrap-theme.css" rel="stylesheet" />
    <script src="products.js"></script>
    <script src="increment.js"></script>
</head>
<body ng-controller="defaultCtrl">
    <div class="panel panel-primary">
        <h3 class="panel-heading">Products</h3>
        <ng-include src="'tableView.html'" ng-show="displayMode == 'list'"></ng-include>
        <ng-include src="'editorView.html'" ng-show="displayMode == 'edit'"></ng-include>
    </div>
</body>
</html>
```

I also had to add a dependency for the module in the `products.js` file, as shown in Listing 21-11.

Listing 21-11. Adding a Module Dependency in the products.js File

```
angular.module("exampleApp", ["increment"])
.constant("baseUrl", "http://localhost:5500/products/")
.controller("defaultCtrl", function ($scope, $http, baseUrl) {
...
```

And, finally, I had to apply the directive to the `tableView.html` file so that each row in the table has an increment button, as shown in Listing 21-12.

Listing 21-12. Applying the increment Directive to the tableView.html File

```
...
<tr ng-repeat="item in products">
    <td>{{item.name}}</td>
    <td>{{item.category}}</td>
    <td class="text-right">{{item.price | currency}}</td>
    <td class="text-center">
        <button class="btn btn-xs btn-primary"
                ng-click="deleteProduct(item)">
            Delete
        </button>
        <button class="btn btn-xs btn-primary"
                ng-click="editOrCreateProduct(item)">
            Edit
        </button>
        <increment value="item.price" />
    </td>
</tr>
...
```

The effect is shown in Figure 21-8. Clicking the + button increments the `price` property of the corresponding product object by 1.

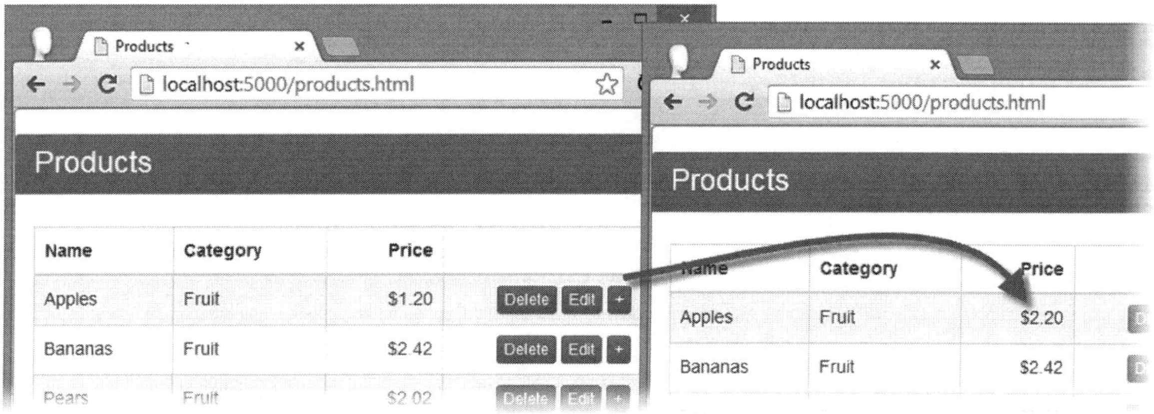

Figure 21-8. *Incrementing prices*

The problem can be seen by clicking the Reload button, which replaces the local product data with fresh data from the server. The increment directive didn't perform the required Ajax update when it incremented the price property, so the local data fell out of sync with the server data.

This may seem like a contrived example, but it arises frequently when using directives written by other developers or provided by a third-party. Even if the author of the increment directive knew that Ajax updates were required, they could not be performed because all of the Ajax update logic is contained in the controller and not accessible to a directive, especially one in another module.

The solution to this problem is to make sure that any changes to the local data automatically cause the required Ajax requests to be generated, but this means that any component that needs to work with the data has to know whether the data needs to be synchronized with a remote server *and* know how to make the required Ajax requests to perform updates.

AngularJS offers a partial solution to this problem through the $resource service, which makes it easier to work with RESTful data in an application by hiding away the details of the Ajax requests and URL formats. I'll show you how to apply the $resource service in the sections that follow.

Installing the ngResource Module

The $resource service is defined within an optional module called ngResource that must be downloaded into the angularjs folder. Go to http://angularjs.org, click Download, select the version you require (version 1.2.5 is the latest version as I write this), and click the Extras link in the bottom-left corner of the window, as shown in Figure 21-9.

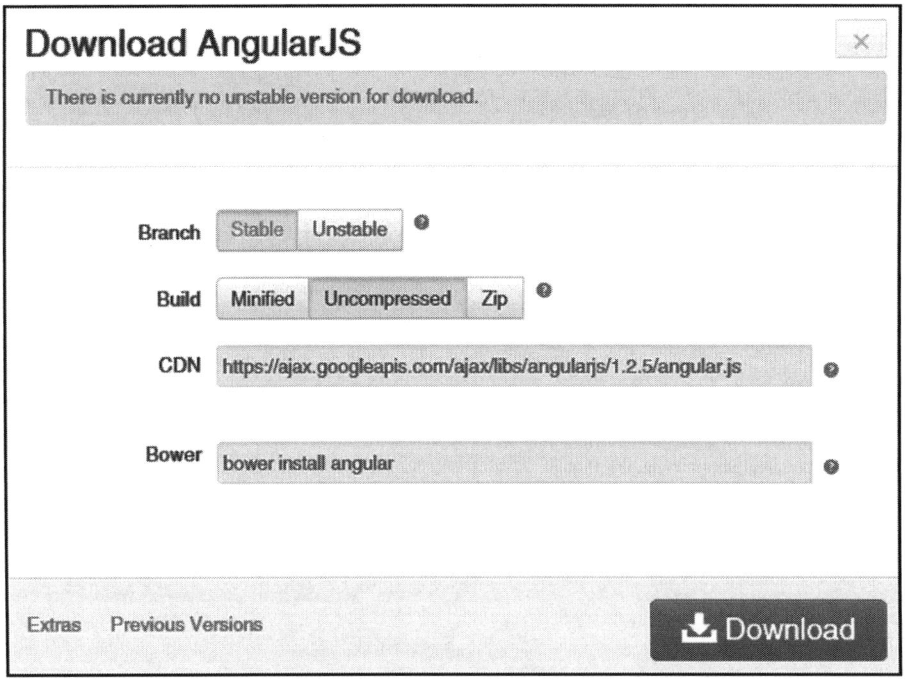

Figure 21-9. *Downloading an optional module*

Download the `angular-resource.js` file into the `angularjs` folder. In Listing 21-13, you can see how I have added a `script` element for the new file to the `products.html` file.

Listing 21-13. Adding a Reference to the products.html File

```
...
<head>
    <title>Products</title>
    <script src="angular.js"></script>
    <script src="angular-resource.js"></script>
    <link href="bootstrap.css" rel="stylesheet" />
    <link href="bootstrap-theme.css" rel="stylesheet" />
    <script src="products.js"></script>
    <script src="increment.js"></script>
</head>
...
```

Using the $resource Service

In Listing 21-14, you can see how I have used the $resource service in in the `products.js` file to manage the data that I get from the server without directly creating Ajax requests.

Listing 21-14. Using the $resource Service in the products.js File

```
angular.module("exampleApp", ["increment", "ngResource"])
.constant("baseUrl", "http://localhost:5500/products/")
.controller("defaultCtrl", function ($scope, $http, $resource, baseUrl) {

    $scope.displayMode = "list";
    $scope.currentProduct = null;

    $scope.productsResource = $resource(baseUrl + ":id", { id: "@id" });

    $scope.listProducts = function () {
        $scope.products = $scope.productsResource.query();
    }

    $scope.deleteProduct = function (product) {
        product.$delete().then(function () {
            $scope.products.splice($scope.products.indexOf(product), 1);
        });
        $scope.displayMode = "list";
    }

    $scope.createProduct = function (product) {
        new $scope.productsResource(product).$save().then(function(newProduct) {
            $scope.products.push(newProduct);
            $scope.displayMode = "list";
        });
    }
```

```
    $scope.updateProduct = function (product) {
        product.$save();
        $scope.displayMode = "list";
    }

    $scope.editOrCreateProduct = function (product) {
        $scope.currentProduct = product ? product : {};
        $scope.displayMode = "edit";
    }

    $scope.saveEdit = function (product) {
        if (angular.isDefined(product.id)) {
            $scope.updateProduct(product);
        } else {
            $scope.createProduct(product);
        }
    }

    $scope.cancelEdit = function () {
        if ($scope.currentProduct && $scope.currentProduct.$get) {
            $scope.currentProduct.$get();
        }
        $scope.currentProduct = {};
        $scope.displayMode = "list";
    }

    $scope.listProducts();
});
```

The function signature for the behaviors defined by the controller have remained the same, which is good because it means I don't have to change any of the HTML elements in order to use the $resource service. The implementation of every behavior has changed, not only because the way that I obtain the data has changed but also because the assumptions that can be made about the nature of the data are different. There is a lot going on in this listing, and the $resource service can be confusing, so I am going to break down what's going on step-by-step in the sections that follow.

Configuring the $resource Service

The first thing I have to do is set up the $resource service so that it knows how to work with the RESTful Deployd service. Here is the statement that does this:

```
...
$scope.productsResource = $resource(baseUrl + ":id", { id: "@id" });
...
```

The $resource service object is a function that is used to describe the URLs that are used to consume the RESTful service. The URL segments that change per object are prefixed with a colon (the : character). If you look back to Table 21-4, you will see that for my example service there is only one variable part of the URL, and that is the id of the product object, which is required when deleting or modifying an object. For the first argument I combine the value of the `baseUrl` constant with `:id` to indicate a URL segment that will change, producing a combined value of the following:

```
http://localhost:5500/products/:id
```

The second argument is a configuration object whose properties specify where the value for the variable segment will come from. Each property must correspond to a variable segment from the first argument, and the value can be fixed or, as I have done in this example, bound to a property on the data object by prefixing a property name with the @ character.

■ **Tip** Most real applications will need multiple segment parts to express more complex data collections. The URL passed to the $resource service can contain as many variable parts as you require.

The result from calling the $resource service function is an *access object* that can be used to query and modify the server data using the methods that I have described in Table 21-5.

Table 21-5. *The Default Actions Defined by an Access Object*

Name	HTTP	URL	Description
delete(params, product)	DELETE	/products/<id>	Removes the object with the specified ID
get(id)	GET	/products</id>	Gets the (single) object with the specified ID
query()	GET	/products	Gets all of the objects as an array
remove(params, product)	DELETE	/products</id>	Removes the object with the specified ID
save(product)	POST	/products</id>	Saves modifications to the object with the specified ID

■ **Tip** The delete and remove methods are identical and can be used interchangeably.

Notice that the combination of HTTP methods and URLs in Table 21-5 is similar, but not identical, to the API defined by Deployd that I described in Table 21-4. Fortunately, Deployd is flexible enough to work around the differences, but later in the chapter, I'll show you how to customize the configuration of the $resource service so that it matches exactly.

■ **Tip** I have shown the delete and remove methods as requiring a params argument. This is an object that contains additional parameters to be included in the URL sent to the server. All of the methods shown in the table can be used with an initial object like this, but because of an oddity in the $resource code, the delete and remove methods must be called this way, even if the params object has no properties and values.

Don't worry if you don't understand the role of actions at the moment; it will become clear soon.

Listing the REST Data

I assigned the access object returned from invoking the $resource service object to a variable called productResource, which I then use to get the initial snapshot of data from the server. Here is the definition of the listProducts behavior:

```
...
$scope.listProducts = function () {
    $scope.products = $scope.productsResource.query();
}
...
```

The access object provides me with the means to query and modify data on the server, but it doesn't automatically perform any of these actions itself, which is why I call the query method to get the initial data for the application. The query method requests the /products URL provided by my Deployd service to get all of the data objects available.

The result from the query method is a *collection* array that is initially empty. The $resource service creates the result array and then uses the $http service to make an Ajax request. When the Ajax request completes, the data that is obtained from the server is placed into the collection. This is such an important point that I am going to repeat it as a caution.

■ **Caution**   The array returned by the query method is initially empty and is populated only when an asynchronous HTTP request to the server has completed.

┌──┐
│   **RESPONDING TO DATA LOADING**   │
└──┘

For many applications, loading the data asynchronously works perfectly well, and the changes in the scope caused the data arrives ensure that the application responds correctly. Even though the example in this chapter is simple, it illustrates the way that many, if not most, AngularJS applications are structured: The data arrives, causing a change in the scope that refreshes the bindings and displays the data in a table.

Sometimes you need to respond more directly at the moment when the data arrives. To support this, the $resource service adds a $promise property to the collection array returned by the query method. The promise is resolved when the Ajax request for the data is complete. Here is an example of how you would register a success handler with the promise:

```
...
$scope.listProducts = function () {
    $scope.products = $scope.productsResource.query();
    $scope.products.$promise.then(function (data) {
        // do something with the data
    });
}
...
```

The promise is fulfilled after the result array is populated, which means you can access the data through the array or through the argument passed to the success function. See Chapter 20 for details of promises and how they work.

The asynchronous delivery of the data works nicely with data bindings because they automatically update when the data arrives and the collection array is populated.

Modifying Data Objects

The query method populates the collection array with Resource objects, which define all of the properties specified in the data returned by the server and some methods that allow manipulation of the data without needing to use the collections array. Table 21-6 describes the methods that Resource objects define.

Table 21-6. *The Methods Supported by Resource Objects*

Name	Description
$delete()	Deletes the object from the server; equivalent to calling $remove()
$get()	Refreshes the object from the server, clearing any uncommitted local changes
$remove()	Deletes the object from the server; equivalent to calling $delete()
$save()	Saves the object to the server

The $save method is the simplest to work with. Here is how I used it in the updateProduct behavior:

```
...
$scope.updateProduct = function (product) {
    product.$save();
    $scope.displayMode = "list";
}
...
```

All of the Resource object methods perform asynchronous requests and return promise objects that you can use to receive notifications when the request completes or fails.

■ **Note**   I am blithely assuming that all of my Ajax requests succeed in this example for the sake of simplicity, but you should take care to respond to errors in real projects.

The $get method is also pretty straightforward. I used it in this example to back out from abandoned edits in the cancelEdit behavior, as follows:

```
...
$scope.cancelEdit = function () {
    if ($scope.currentProduct && $scope.currentProduct.$get) {
        $scope.currentProduct.$get();
    }
    $scope.currentProduct = {};
    $scope.displayMode = "list";
}
...
```

Before I call the $get method, I check to see that it is available for me to call and the effect is to reset the edited object to the state stored on the server. This is a different approach to editing from the one I took when using the $http service, where I duplicated local data in order to have a reference point to which I could return when editing was cancelled.

Deleting Data Objects

The $delete and $remove methods generate the same requests to the server and are identical in every way. The wrinkle in their use is that they send the request to remove an object from the server but don't remove the object from the collection array. This is a sensible approach, since the outcome of the request to the server isn't known until the response is received and the application will be out of sync with the server if the local copy is deleted and the request subsequently returns an error.

To work around this, I have used the promise object that these methods return to register a callback handler that synchronizes the local data upon the successful deletion at the server in the deleteProduct behavior, as follows:

```
...
$scope.deleteProduct = function (product) {
    product.$delete().then(function () {
        $scope.products.splice($scope.products.indexOf(product), 1);
    });
    $scope.displayMode = "list";
}
...
```

Creating New Objects

Using the new keyword on the access object provides the means to apply the $resource methods to data objects so that they can be saved to the server. I use this technique in the createProduct behavior so that I can use the $save method and write new objects to the database:

```
...
$scope.createProduct = function (product) {
    new $scope.productsResource(product).$save().then(function (newProduct) {
        $scope.products.push(newProduct);
        $scope.displayMode = "list";
    });
}
...
```

Rather like the $delete method, the $save method doesn't update the collection array when new objects are saved to the server. I use the promise returned by the $save method to add the object to the collection array if the Ajax request is successful.

Configuring the $resource Service Actions

The get, save, query, remove, and delete methods that are available on the collection array and the $-prefixed equivalents on individual Resource objects are known as *actions*. By default, the $resource service defines the actions I described in Table 21-5, but these are easily configured so that the methods correspond to the API provided by the server. In Listing 21-15, you can see how I have changes the actions to match the Deployd API that I described in Table 21-4.

Listing 21-15. Modifying the $resource Actions in the products.js File

```
...
$scope.productsResource = $resource(baseUrl + ":id", { id: "@id" },
        { create: { method: "POST" }, save: { method: "PUT" }});
...
```

The $resource service object function can be invoked with a third argument that defines actions. The actions are expressed as object properties whose names correspond to the action that is being defined, or redefined, since you can replace the default actions if need be.

Each action property is set to a configuration object. I have used only one property, method, which sets the HTTP method used for the action. The effect of my change is that I have defined a new action called create, which uses the POST method, and I have redefined the save action so that it uses the PUT method. The result is to make the actions supported by the productsResoures access object more consistent with the Deployd API, separating the requests for creating new objects from those that modify existing objects. Table 21-7 shows the set of configuration properties that can be used to define or redefine actions.

Table 21-7. The Configuration Properties Used for Actions

Name	Description
method	Sets the HTTP method that will be used for the Ajax request.
params	Specifies values for the segment variables in the URL passed as the first argument to the $resource service function.
url	Overrides the default URL for this action.
isArray	When true, specifies that the response will be a JSON data array. The default value, false, specifies that the response to the request will be, at most, one object.

In addition, you can use the following properties to configure the Ajax request that the action will generate (I described the effect of these options in Chapter 20): transformRequest, transformResponse, cache, timeout, withCredentials, responseType, and interceptor.

Actions that are defined in this way are just like the defaults and can be called on the collection array and on individual Resource objects. In Listing 21-16, you can see how I updated the createProduct behavior to use my new create action. (No change is required for the other action I defined since it just changes the HTTP method used by the existing save action.)

Listing 21-16. Using a Custom Action in the products.js File

```
...
$scope.createProduct = function (product) {
    new $scope.productsResource(product).$create().then(function (newProduct) {
        $scope.products.push(newProduct);
        $scope.displayMode = "list";
    });
}
...
```

Creating $resource-Ready Components

Using the $resource service lets me write components that can operate on RESTful data without needing to know the details of the Ajax requests that are required to manipulate the data. In Listing 21-17, you can see how I have updated the increment directive from earlier in the chapter so that it can be configured to use data obtained from the $resource service.

AVOIDING THE ASYNCHRONOUS DATA TRAP

The $resource service provides a partial solution to disseminating RESTful data throughout an application: It hides the details of the Ajax requests, but it still requires that the components that use the data know that the data is RESTful and should be manipulated with methods like $save and $delete.

At this point, you might be thinking of ways of completing the process and using scope watchers and event handlers to create a wrapper around the RESTful data that monitors for changes and automatically writes changes to the server.

Don't be tempted to try this. It is a trap, and it doesn't—in fact, it *can't*—ever work properly because you will be trying to hide the asynchronous nature of the Ajax requests that underpin REST from the components that use the data. Code that doesn't know that RESTful data is being used will assume that all operations take effect immediately and that the data in the browser is the authoritative reference, neither of which is true when there are Ajax requests being fired off in the background.

Things fall apart completely when the server returns an error, which will reach the browser long after the synchronous operation on the data has completed and execution of the code has moved on. There is no compelling way of dealing with errors: You can't unwind the operation without risking causing an inconsistent state application (because execution of the synchronous code has continued), and you lack the means to signal the original code so that it can try again (because that would require awareness of the Ajax requests). The best thing you can do is dump the application state and reload the data from the server, which will come as a nasty surprise to the user.

Instead, accept that components have to be rewritten or adapted to understand the methods that the $resource service adds to data objects and, as I demonstrate in the updated increment directive, make the use of these methods configurable.

Listing 21-17. Working with RESTful Data in the increment.js File

```
angular.module("increment", [])
    .directive("increment", function () {
        return {
            restrict: "E",
            scope: {
                item: "=item",
                property: "@propertyName",
                restful: "@restful",
                method: "@methodName"
            },
            link: function (scope, element, attrs) {
                var button = angular.element("<button>").text("+");
                button.addClass("btn btn-primary btn-xs");
```

```
                element.append(button);
                button.on("click", function () {
                    scope.$apply(function () {
                        scope.item[scope.property]++;
                        if (scope.restful) {
                            scope.item[scope.method]();
                        }
                    })
                })
            },
        }
});
```

When creating components that may operate on data provided by the $resource service, you need to provide configuration options not only to enable the RESTful support but also to specify the action method or methods that are required to update the server. In this example, I use the value of an attribute called restful to configure the REST support and method to get the name of the method that should be called when the value is incremented. In Listing 21-18, you can see how I apply these changes in the tableView.html file.

Listing 21-18. Adding Configuration Attributes in the tableView.html File

```
<div class="panel-body">
    <table class="table table-striped table-bordered">
        <thead>
            <tr>
                <th>Name</th>
                <th>Category</th>
                <th class="text-right">Price</th>
                <th></th>
            </tr>
        </thead>
        <tbody>
            <tr ng-repeat="item in products">
                <td>{{item.name}}</td>
                <td>{{item.category}}</td>
                <td class="text-right">{{item.price | currency}}</td>
                <td class="text-center">
                    <button class="btn btn-xs btn-primary"
                            ng-click="deleteProduct(item)">
                        Delete
                    </button>
                    <button class="btn btn-xs btn-primary"
                            ng-click="editOrCreateProduct(item)">
                        Edit
                    </button>
                    <increment item="item" property-name="price" restful="true"
                        method-name="$save" />
                </td>
            </tr>
        </tbody>
    </table>
```

```
    <div>
        <button class="btn btn-primary" ng-click="listProducts()">Refresh</button>
        <button class="btn btn-primary" ng-click="editOrCreateProduct()">New</button>
    </div>
</div>
```

The result is that when you click the + button in a table row, the local value is updated, and the $save method is then called to send the update to the server.

Summary

In this chapter I showed you how to work with RESTful services. I showed you how to manually form the Ajax requests using the $http service and explained why this can cause problems when the data is used beyond the component that creates it. I demonstrated how the $resource service can be used to hide the details of the Ajax requests, and I gave a stern warning about the dangers of trying to hide the asynchronous nature of RESTful data from the components that operate on it. In the next chapter, I describe the service that provides URL routing.

■ ■ ■

CHAPTER 22

Services for Views

In this chapter, I describe the set of services that AngularJS provides for working with views. I introduced views in Chapter 10 and showed you how to use the ng-include directive to import them into an application. In this chapter, I demonstrate how to use *URL routing*, which uses views to enable sophisticated navigation within an application. URL routing can be a difficult topic to understand, so I introduce the functionality gradually in this chapter, slowly revising the example application to introduce individual features. Table 22-1 summarizes this chapter.

Table 22-1. *Chapter Summary*

Problem	Solution	Listing
Enable navigation within the application.	Define URL routes using the $routeProvider.	1–4
Display the view from the active route.	Apply the ng-view directive.	5
Change the active view.	Use the $location.path method or use an a element whose href attribute matches the route path.	6–7
Pass information via the path.	Use route parameters in the route URL. Access the parameters using the $routeParams service.	8–10
Associate a controller with the view displayed by the active route.	Use the controller configuration property.	11
Define dependencies for the controller.	Use the resolve configuration property.	12–13

Why and When to Use the View Services

The services I describe in this chapter are useful for simplifying complex applications by allowing multiple components to control the content that the user sees. You won't need these services in small or simple applications.

Preparing the Example Project

For this chapter, I am going to continue to work with the example I created in Chapter 21 to demonstrate the different ways in which AngularJS applications can consume RESTful APIs. In the previous chapter, the focus was on managing the Ajax for the RESTful data, so you may not have noticed a rather nasty hack, which I will explain before showing how to resolve it.

Understanding the Problem

The application contains two view files, tableView.html and editorView.html, which I imported into the main products.html file using the ng-include directive.

The tableView.html file contains the default view for the application and lists the data from the server in a table element. I switch to the contents of the editorView.html file when the user is creating a new product or editing an existing one. When the operation is complete—or cancelled—I return to the contents of the tableView.html file again. The problem is the way that I manage the visibility of the contents of the view files. Listing 22-1 shows the products.html file.

Listing 22-1. The Contents of the products.html File

```
<!DOCTYPE html>
<html ng-app="exampleApp">
<head>
    <title>Products</title>
    <script src="angular.js"></script>
    <script src="angular-resource.js"></script>
    <link href="bootstrap.css" rel="stylesheet" />
    <link href="bootstrap-theme.css" rel="stylesheet" />
    <script src="products.js"></script>
    <script src="increment.js"></script>
</head>
<body ng-controller="defaultCtrl">
    <div class="panel panel-primary">
        <h3 class="panel-heading">Products</h3>
        <ng-include src="'tableView.html'" ng-show="displayMode == 'list'"></ng-include>
        <ng-include src="'editorView.html'" ng-show="displayMode == 'edit'"></ng-include>
    </div>
</body>
</html>
```

The issue is the use of the ng-show directive to control the visibility of the elements. To work out whether the contents of the view should be shown to the user, I check the value of a scope variable called displayMode and compare it to a literal value, like this:

```
...
<ng-include src="'tableView.html'" ng-show="displayMode == 'list'"></ng-include>
...
```

I set the value of displayMode in the controller behaviors defined in the products.js file to display the content I require. Listing 22-2 highlights how I set displayMode in the products.js file to switch between the views.

Listing 22-2. Setting the displayMode Value in the products.js File

```
angular.module("exampleApp", ["increment", "ngResource"])
.constant("baseUrl", "http://localhost:5500/products/")
.controller("defaultCtrl", function ($scope, $http, $resource, baseUrl) {

    $scope.displayMode = "list";
    $scope.currentProduct = null;
```

```
$scope.productsResource = $resource(baseUrl + ":id", { id: "@id" },
        { create: { method: "POST" }, save: { method: "PUT" } });

$scope.listProducts = function () {
    $scope.products = $scope.productsResource.query();
}

$scope.deleteProduct = function (product) {
    product.$delete().then(function () {
        $scope.products.splice($scope.products.indexOf(product), 1);
    });
    $scope.displayMode = "list";
}

$scope.createProduct = function (product) {
    new $scope.productsResource(product).$create().then(function (newProduct) {
        $scope.products.push(newProduct);
        $scope.displayMode = "list";
    });
}

$scope.updateProduct = function (product) {
    product.$save();
    $scope.displayMode = "list";
}

$scope.editOrCreateProduct = function (product) {
    $scope.currentProduct = product ? product : {};
    $scope.displayMode = "edit";
}

$scope.saveEdit = function (product) {
    if (angular.isDefined(product.id)) {
        $scope.updateProduct(product);
    } else {
        $scope.createProduct(product);
    }
}

$scope.cancelEdit = function () {
    if ($scope.currentProduct && $scope.currentProduct.$get) {
        $scope.currentProduct.$get();
    }
    $scope.currentProduct = {};
    $scope.displayMode = "list";
}

$scope.listProducts();
});
```

This approach works, but it presents a problem, which is that any component that needs to change the layout of the application needs access to the displayMode variable, which is assigned to the controller scope. This isn't too much of a burden in such a simple application where the view is always managed by a single controller, but it doesn't scale up when additional components need to control what the user sees.

What's needed is a way to separate the view selection from the controller so that the application content can be driven from any part of the application, and that's what I will show you in this chapter.

Using URL Routing

AngularJS supports a feature called *URL routing*, which uses the value returned by the $location.path method to load and display view files without the need for nasty literal values embedded throughout the markup and code in an application. In the sections that follow, I'll show you how to install and use the $route service, which provides the URL routing functionality.

Installing the ngRoute Module

The $route service is defined within an optional module called ngRoute that must be downloaded into the angularjs folder. Go to http://angularjs.org, click Download, select the version you require (version 1.2.5 is the latest version as I write this), and click the Extras link in the bottom-left corner of the window, as shown in Figure 22-1.

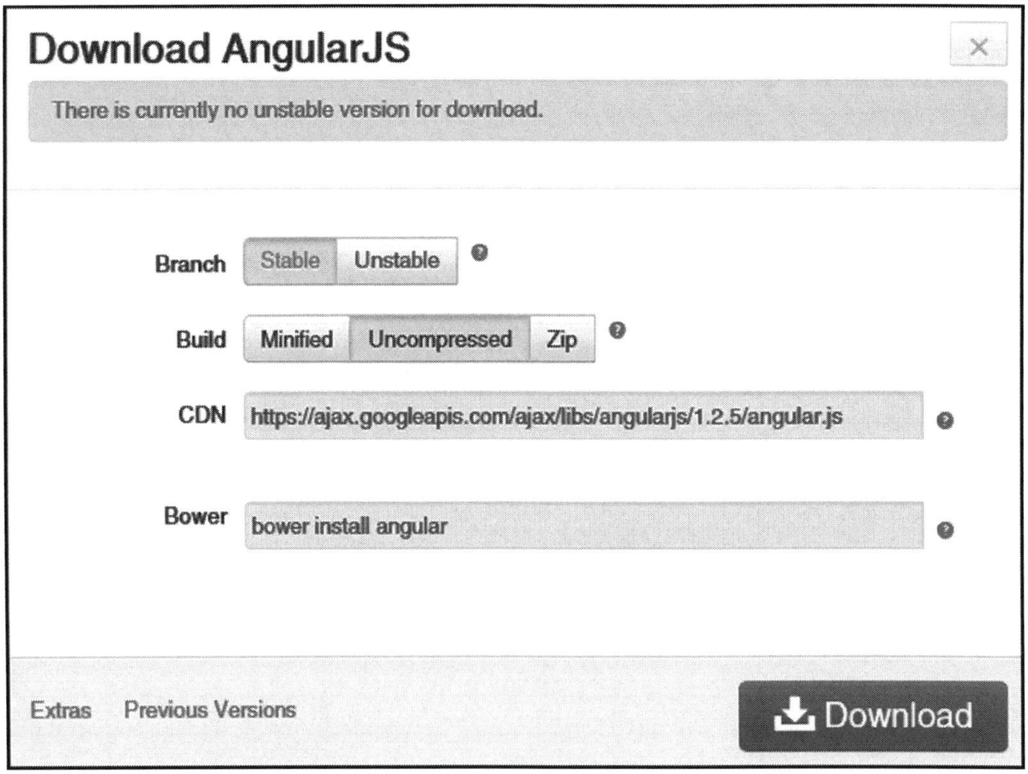

Figure 22-1. Downloading an optional module

Download the angular-route.js file into the angularjs folder. In Listing 22-3, you can see how I have added a script element for the new file to the products.html file.

Listing 22-3. Adding a Reference to the products.html File

```
<!DOCTYPE html>
<html ng-app="exampleApp">
<head>
    <title>Products</title>
    <script src="angular.js"></script>
    <script src="angular-resource.js"></script>
    <script src="angular-route.js"></script>
    <link href="bootstrap.css" rel="stylesheet" />
    <link href="bootstrap-theme.css" rel="stylesheet" />
    <script src="products.js"></script>
    <script src="increment.js"></script>
</head>
<body ng-controller="defaultCtrl">
    <div class="panel panel-primary">
        <h3 class="panel-heading">Products</h3>
        <ng-include src="'tableView.html'" ng-show="displayMode == 'list'"></ng-include>
        <ng-include src="'editorView.html'" ng-show="displayMode == 'edit'"></ng-include>
    </div>
</body>
</html>
```

Defining the URL Routes

At the heart of the functionality provided by the $route service is a set of mappings between URLs and view file names, known as *URL routes* or just *routes*. When the value returned by the $location.path method matches one of the mappings, the corresponding view file will be loaded and displayed. The mappings are defined using the provider for the $route service, $routeProvider. Listing 22-4 shows how I have defined routes for the example application.

Listing 22-4. Defining Routes in the product.js File

```
angular.module("exampleApp", ["increment", "ngResource", "ngRoute"])
.constant("baseUrl", "http://localhost:5500/products/")
.config(function ($routeProvider, $locationProvider) {

    $locationProvider.html5Mode(true);

    $routeProvider.when("/list", {
        templateUrl: "/tableView.html"
    });

    $routeProvider.when("/edit", {
        templateUrl: "/editorView.html"
    });
```

```
$routeProvider.when("/create", {
    templateUrl: "/editorView.html"
});

$routeProvider.otherwise({
    templateUrl: "/tableView.html"
});
})
.controller("defaultCtrl", function ($scope, $http, $resource, baseUrl) {
    // ...controller statements omitted for brevity...
});
```

I have added a dependency on the ngRoute module and added a config function to define the routes. My config function declares dependencies on providers for the $route and $location services, the latter of which I use to enable HTML5 URLs.

■ **Tip**   I am going to use HTML5 URLs in this chapter because they are cleaner and simpler and I know that the browser I will be using supports the HTML5 History API. See Chapter 19 for details of the $location service support for HTML5, how to detect that the browser provides the required features, and the potential for problems.

Routes are defined using the $routeProvider.when method. The first argument is the URL that the route will apply to, and the second argument is the route configuration object. The routes I have defined are the simplest possible because the URLs are static and I have provided the minimum configuration information, but later in the chapter I'll show you more complex examples. I'll describe all of the configuration options later in the chapter, but for now it is enough to know that the templateUrl configuration option specifies the view file that should be used when the path of the current browser URL matches the first argument passed to the when method.

■ **Tip**   Always specify the value of the templateUrl with a leading / character. If you do not, the URL will be evaluated relative to the value returned by the $location.path method, and changing this value is one of the key activities required when using routing. Without the / character, you will quickly generate a Not Found error as you navigate within the application.

The otherwise method is used to define a route that is used when no other one matches the current URL path. It is good practice to provide such a fallback route, and I have summarized the overall effect of the routes I have defined in Table 22-2.

Table 22-2. *The Effect of the Routes Defined in the products.js File*

URL Path	View File
/list	tableView.html
/edit	editorView.html
/create	editorView.html
All other URLs	tableView.html

■ **Tip**   I didn't really need to define the route for /list since the route defined with the otherwise method displays the tableView.html view if no other route matches the current path. I like to be explicit when defining routes because they can become quite complex, and anything that makes them easier to read and understand is worth doing.

Displaying the Selected View

The ngRoute module includes a directive called ng-view that displays the contents of the view file specified by the route that matches the current URL path returned by the $location service. In Listing 22-5, you can see how I am able to use the ng-view directive to replace the troublesome elements in the products.html file, removing the literal values that I dislike so much.

Listing 22-5. Using the ng-view Directive in the products.html File

```
<!DOCTYPE html>
<html ng-app="exampleApp">
<head>
    <title>Products</title>
    <script src="angular.js"></script>
    <script src="angular-resource.js"></script>
    <script src="angular-route.js"></script>
    <link href="bootstrap.css" rel="stylesheet" />
    <link href="bootstrap-theme.css" rel="stylesheet" />
    <script src="products.js"></script>
    <script src="increment.js"></script>
</head>
<body ng-controller="defaultCtrl">
    <div class="panel panel-primary">
        <h3 class="panel-heading">Products</h3>
        <div ng-view></div>
    </div>
</body>
</html>
```

When the value returned by the $location/path changes, the $route service evaluates the routes defined through its provider and changes the content of the element to which the ng-view directive has been applied.

Wiring Up the Code and Markup

All that remains is to update the code and the markup to change the URL rather than the displayMode variable to change the layout of the application. In JavaScript code, this means I need to use the path method provided by the $location service, as shown in Listing 22-6.

Listing 22-6. Using the $location Service to Change Views in the products.js File

```
angular.module("exampleApp", ["increment", "ngResource", "ngRoute"])
.constant("baseUrl", "http://localhost:5500/products/")
.config(function ($routeProvider, $locationProvider) {

    $locationProvider.html5Mode(true);

    $routeProvider.when("/list", {
        templateUrl: "/tableView.html"
    });

    $routeProvider.when("/edit", {
        templateUrl: "/editorView.html"
    });

    $routeProvider.when("/create", {
        templateUrl: "/editorView.html"
    });

    $routeProvider.otherwise({
        templateUrl: "/tableView.html"
    });

})
.controller("defaultCtrl", function ($scope, $http, $resource, $location, baseUrl) {

    $scope.currentProduct = null;

    $scope.productsResource = $resource(baseUrl + ":id", { id: "@id" },
            { create: { method: "POST" }, save: { method: "PUT" } });

    $scope.listProducts = function () {
        $scope.products = $scope.productsResource.query();
    }

    $scope.deleteProduct = function (product) {
        product.$delete().then(function () {
            $scope.products.splice($scope.products.indexOf(product), 1);
        });

        $location.path("/list");
    }

    $scope.createProduct = function (product) {
        new $scope.productsResource(product).$create().then(function (newProduct) {
            $scope.products.push(newProduct);
            $location.path("/list");
        });
    }
```

```
    $scope.updateProduct = function (product) {
        product.$save();
        $location.path("/list");
    }

    $scope.editProduct = function (product) {
        $scope.currentProduct = product;
        $location.path("/edit");
    }

    $scope.saveEdit = function (product) {
        if (angular.isDefined(product.id)) {
            $scope.updateProduct(product);
        } else {
            $scope.createProduct(product);
        }
        $scope.currentProduct = {};
    }

    $scope.cancelEdit = function () {
        if ($scope.currentProduct && $scope.currentProduct.$get) {
            $scope.currentProduct.$get();
        }
        $scope.currentProduct = {};
        $location.path("/list");
    }

    $scope.listProducts();
});
```

This isn't a huge change. I have added a dependency on the $location service and replaced the calls that changed the displayMode value with equivalent calls to the $location.path method. There is a more interesting change, however: I replaced the editOrCreateProduct behavior with one called editProduct, which is slightly simpler. Here is the old behavior:

```
...
$scope.editOrCreateProduct = function (product) {
    $scope.currentProduct = product ? product : {};
    $scope.displayMode = "edit";
}
...
```

And here is its replacement:

```
...
$scope.editProduct = function (product) {
    $scope.currentProduct = product;
    $location.path("/edit");
}
...
```

The old behavior was the start point for both the editing and creation process, which were differentiated by the product argument. If the product argument wasn't null, then I used the object to set the currentProduct variable, which populates the fields in the editorView.html view.

■ **Tip** There is one other change highlighted in the listing. I have updated the saveEdit behavior to reset the value of the currentProduct variable. Without this change, the values from an edit operation are displayed to the user if they subsequently create a new product. This is a temporary problem that will be resolved as I expand the support for routing in the application.

The reason I am able to simplify the behavior is that the routing feature allows me to initiate the process of creating a new product object just by changing the URL. In Listing 22-7, you can see the changes I have made to the tableView.html file.

Listing 22-7. Adding Support for Routes to the tableView.html File

```html
<div class="panel-body">
    <table class="table table-striped table-bordered">
        <thead>
            <tr>
                <th>Name</th>
                <th>Category</th>
                <th class="text-right">Price</th>
                <th></th>
            </tr>
        </thead>
        <tbody>
            <tr ng-repeat="item in products">
                <td>{{item.name}}</td>
                <td>{{item.category}}</td>
                <td class="text-right">{{item.price | currency}}</td>
                <td class="text-center">
                    <button class="btn btn-xs btn-primary"
                            ng-click="deleteProduct(item)">
                        Delete
                    </button>
                    <button class="btn btn-xs btn-primary" ng-click="editProduct(item)">
                        Edit
                    </button>
                    <increment item="item" property-name="price" restful="true"
                            method-name="$save" />
                </td>
            </tr>
        </tbody>
    </table>
    <div>
        <button class="btn btn-primary" ng-click="listProducts()">Refresh</button>
        <a href="create" class="btn btn-primary">New</a>
    </div>
</div>
```

I have replaced the button element whose ng-click directive invoked the old behavior and replaced it with an a element whose href attribute specifies the URL that matches the route that displays the editorView.html view. Bootstrap allows me to style button and a elements to look the same, so there is no discernable difference in the layout to the user. However, when the a element is clicked, the URL changes to /create and the editorView.html view is displayed, as shown in Figure 22-2.

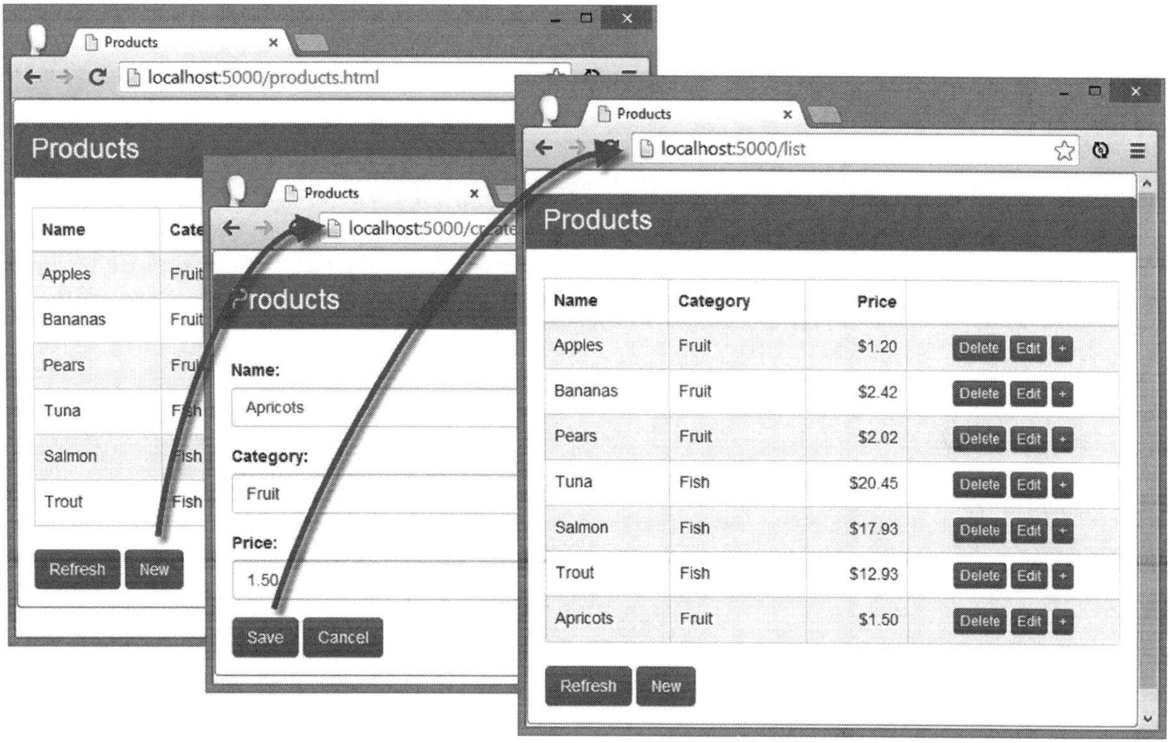

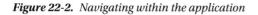

Figure 22-2. *Navigating within the application*

To see the effect, load the products.html file into the browser and click the New button. The URL displayed by the browser will change from http://localhost:5000/products.html to http://localhost:5000/create. This is the magic of HTML5 URLs managed through the HTML5 Browser History API, and the contents of the editorView.html view will be displayed. Enter details of a new product and click the Save button (or Cancel if you prefer), and the contents of the tableView.html view are shown again, with a URL of http://localhost:5000/list.

■ **Caution**   Routing works when the application changes the URL, but it doesn't work if the user changes it; the browser takes any URL that the user enters as being a literal request for a file and tries to request the corresponding content from the server.

589

Using Route Parameters

The URLs I used to define the routes in the previous section were *fixed* or *static*, meaning that the value passed to the `$location.path` method or set in an a element's href attribute has to exactly match the value I used with the `$routeProvider.when` method. As a reminder, here is one of the routes that I defined:

```
...
$routeProvider.when("/create", {
    templateUrl: "editorView.html"
});
...
```

This route will be activated only when the path component of the URL matches /create. This is the most basic kind of URL that routes can be used with and, as a consequence, the most limited.

Route URLs can contain *route parameters*, which match one or more *segments* in the path displayed by the browser. A segment is the set of characters between two / characters. As an example, the segments in the URL http://localhost:5000/users/adam/details are users, adam, and details. There are two kinds of route parameters: *conservative* and *eager*. A conservative route parameter will match one segment, and an eager one will match as many segments as possible. To demonstrate how this works, I have changed the routes in the products.js file, as shown in Listing 22-8.

Listing 22-8. Defining Routes with Route Parameters in the products.js File

```
...
.config(function ($routeProvider, $locationProvider) {

    $locationProvider.html5Mode(true);

    $routeProvider.when("/list", {
        templateUrl: "/tableView.html"
    });

    $routeProvider.when("/edit/:id", {
        templateUrl: "/editorView.html"
    });

    $routeProvider.when("/edit/:id/:data*", {
        templateUrl: "/editorView.html"
    });

    $routeProvider.when("/create", {
        templateUrl: "/editorView.html"
    });

    $routeProvider.otherwise({
        templateUrl: "/tableView.html"
    });
})
...
```

The first highlighted route URL, /edit/:id, contains a conservative route parameter. The variable is denoted by a colon character (:) and then a name, which is id in this case. The route will match a path such as /edit/1234, and it will assign the value of 1234 to a route parameter called id. (Route variables are accessed through the $routeParams service, which I describe shortly.)

Routes that use only static segments and conservative route parameters will match only those paths that contain the same number of segments as their URL. In the case of the /edit/:id URL, only URLs that contain two segments where the first segment is edit will be matched. Paths with more or less segments won't match and nor will paths whose first segment isn't edit.

You can extend the range of paths that a route URL will match by including an eager route parameter, like this:

```
...
$routeProvider.when("/edit/:id/:data*", {
...
```

An eager route parameter is denoted by a colon, followed by a name, followed by an asterisk. The example will match any path that has at least three segments where the first segment is edit. The second segment will be assigned to the route parameter id, and the remaining segments will be assigned to the route parameter data.

■ **Tip** Don't worry if segment variables and route parameters don't make sense at the moment. You will see how they work as I develop the examples in the following sections.

Accessing Routes and Routes Parameters

The URLs I used in the previous section process paths and assign the contents of segments to route parameters, which can then be accessed in code. In this section, I am going to demonstrate how to access those values using the $route and $routeParams services, both of which are contained in the ngRoute module. My first step is to change the button that edits product objects in the tableView.html file, as shown in Listing 22-9.

Listing 22-9. Using Routing to Trigger Editing in the tableView.html File

```
<div class="panel-body">
    <table class="table table-striped table-bordered">
        <thead>
            <tr>
                <th>Name</th>
                <th>Category</th>
                <th class="text-right">Price</th>
                <th></th>
            </tr>
        </thead>
        <tbody>
            <tr ng-repeat="item in products">
                <td>{{item.name}}</td>
                <td>{{item.category}}</td>
                <td class="text-right">{{item.price | currency}}</td>
                <td class="text-center">
                    <button class="btn btn-xs btn-primary"
                            ng-click="deleteProduct(item)">
                        Delete
                    </button>
```

```
                <a href="/edit/{{item.id}}" class="btn btn-xs btn-primary">Edit</a>
                    <increment item="item" property-name="price" restful="true"
                            method-name="$save" />
                </td>
            </tr>
        </tbody>
    </table>
    <div>
        <button class="btn btn-primary" ng-click="listProducts()">Refresh</button>
        <a href="create" class="btn btn-primary">New</a>
    </div>
</div>
```

I have replaced the button element with an a element whose href element corresponds to one of the routing URLs I defined in Listing 22-9, which I achieve using a standard inline binding expression within the ng-repeat directive. This means that each row in the table element will contain an a element like this one:

```
<a href="/edit/18d5f4716c6b1acf" class="btn btn-xs btn-primary">Edit</a>
```

When this link is clicked, the route parameter called id that I defined in Listing 22-8 will be assigned the value 18d5f4716c6b1acf, which corresponds to the id property of the product object that the user wants to edit. In Listing 22-10, you can see that I have updated the controller in the products.js file to respond to this change.

Listing 22-10. Accessing a Route Parameter in the products.js File

```
...
.controller("defaultCtrl", function ($scope, $http, $resource, $location,
    $route, $routeParams, baseUrl) {

    $scope.currentProduct = null;

    $scope.$on("$routeChangeSuccess", function () {
        if ($location.path().indexOf("/edit/") == 0) {
            var id = $routeParams["id"];
            for (var i = 0; i < $scope.products.length; i++) {
                if ($scope.products[i].id == id) {
                    $scope.currentProduct = $scope.products[i];
                    break;
                }
            }
        }
    });

    $scope.productsResource = $resource(baseUrl + ":id", { id: "@id" },
            { create: { method: "POST" }, save: { method: "PUT" } });

    $scope.listProducts = function () {
        $scope.products = $scope.productsResource.query();
    }
```

```
    $scope.deleteProduct = function (product) {
        product.$delete().then(function () {
            $scope.products.splice($scope.products.indexOf(product), 1);
        });

        $location.path("/list");
    }

    $scope.createProduct = function (product) {
        new $scope.productsResource(product).$create().then(function (newProduct) {
            $scope.products.push(newProduct);
            $location.path("/list");
        });
    }

    $scope.updateProduct = function (product) {
        product.$save();
        $location.path("/list");
    }

    $scope.saveEdit = function (product) {
        if (angular.isDefined(product.id)) {
            $scope.updateProduct(product);
        } else {
            $scope.createProduct(product);
        }
        $scope.currentProduct = {};
    }

    $scope.cancelEdit = function () {
        if ($scope.currentProduct && $scope.currentProduct.$get) {
            $scope.currentProduct.$get();
        }
        $scope.currentProduct = {};
        $location.path("/list");
    }

    $scope.listProducts();
});
...
```

There is a lot going on in the highlighted code, so I am going to break down each major part and explain them in turn in the sections that follow.

■ **Note**   I have removed the `editProduct` behavior from the controller, which was previously invoked to initiate the editing process and displayed the `editorView.html` view. The behavior is no longer required since editing is not initiated through the routing system.

Table 22-5. *The Route Configuration Options*

Name	Description
controller	Specifies the name of a controller to be associated with the view displayed by the route. See the "Using Controllers with Routes" section.
controllerAs	Specifies an alias to be used for the controller.
template	Specifies the content of the view. This can be expressed as a literal HTML string or as a function that returns the HTML.
templateUrl	Specifies the URL of the view file to display when the route matches. This can be expressed as a string or as a function that returns a string.
resolve	Specifies a set of dependencies for the controller. See the "Adding Dependencies to Routes" section.
redirectTo	Specifies a path that the browser should be redirected to when the route is matched. Can be expressed as a string or a function.
reloadOnSearch	When true, the default value, the route will reload when only the values returned by the $location search and hash methods change.
caseInsensitiveMatch	When true, the default value, routes are matched to URLs without case sensitivity (e.g., /Edit and /edit are considered to be the same).

Using Controllers with Routes

If you have lots of views in an application, having them share a single controller (as I have been doing so far in this chapter) becomes unwieldy to manage and test. The controller configuration option allows you to specify a controller that has been registered through the Module.controller method for the view. The effect is to separate out the controller logic that is unique to each view, as shown in Listing 22-11.

Listing 22-11. Using a Controller with a View in the products.js File

```
angular.module("exampleApp", ["increment", "ngResource", "ngRoute"])
.constant("baseUrl", "http://localhost:5500/products/")
.config(function ($routeProvider, $locationProvider) {

    $locationProvider.html5Mode(true);

    $routeProvider.when("/edit/:id", {
        templateUrl: "/editorView.html",
        controller: "editCtrl"
    });

    $routeProvider.when("/create", {
        templateUrl: "/editorView.html",
        controller: "editCtrl"
    });

    $routeProvider.otherwise({
        templateUrl: "/tableView.html"
    });
})
.controller("defaultCtrl", function ($scope, $http, $resource, $location, baseUrl) {
```

596

```
    $scope.productsResource = $resource(baseUrl + ":id", { id: "@id" },
            { create: { method: "POST" }, save: { method: "PUT" } });

    $scope.listProducts = function () {
        $scope.products = $scope.productsResource.query();
    }

    $scope.createProduct = function (product) {
        new $scope.productsResource(product).$create().then(function (newProduct) {
            $scope.products.push(newProduct);
            $location.path("/list");
        });
    }

    $scope.deleteProduct = function (product) {
        product.$delete().then(function () {
            $scope.products.splice($scope.products.indexOf(product), 1);
        });

        $location.path("/list");
    }

    $scope.listProducts();
})
.controller("editCtrl", function ($scope, $routeParams, $location) {

    $scope.currentProduct = null;

    if ($location.path().indexOf("/edit/") == 0) {
        var id = $routeParams["id"];
        for (var i = 0; i < $scope.products.length; i++) {
            if ($scope.products[i].id == id) {
                $scope.currentProduct = $scope.products[i];
                break;
            }
        }
    }

    $scope.cancelEdit = function () {
        if ($scope.currentProduct && $scope.currentProduct.$get) {
            $scope.currentProduct.$get();
        }
        $scope.currentProduct = {};
        $location.path("/list");
    }

    $scope.updateProduct = function (product) {
        product.$save();
        $location.path("/list");
    }
```

```
    $scope.saveEdit = function (product) {
        if (angular.isDefined(product.id)) {
            $scope.updateProduct(product);
        } else {
            $scope.createProduct(product);
        }
        $scope.currentProduct = {};
    }
});
```

I have defined a new controller called editCtrl and moved the code from the defaultCtrl controller that is unique to supporting the editorView.html view. I then associate this controller with the routes that display the editorView.html file using the controller configuration property.

A new instance of the editCtrl controller will be created each time that the editorView.html view is displayed, which means I don't need to use the $route service events to know when the view has changed. I can just rely on the fact that my controller function is being executed.

One of the nice aspects of using controllers in this way is that the standard inheritance rules that I described in Chapter 13 apply, such that the editCtrl is nested within the defaultCtrl and can access the data and behaviors defined in its scope. This means I can define the common data and functionality in the top-level controller and just define the view-specific features in the nested controllers.

Adding Dependencies to Routes

The resolve configuration property allows you to specify dependencies that will be injected into the controller specified with the controller property. These dependencies can be services, but the resolve property is more useful for performing work required to initialize the view. This is because you can return promise objects as dependencies, and the route won't instantiate the controller until they are resolved. In Listing 22-12, you can see how I have added a new controller to the example and used the resolve property to load the data from the server.

Listing 22-12. Using the resolve Configuration Property in the products.js File

```
angular.module("exampleApp", ["increment", "ngResource", "ngRoute"])
.constant("baseUrl", "http://localhost:5500/products/")
.factory("productsResource", function ($resource, baseUrl) {
    return $resource(baseUrl + ":id", { id: "@id" },
            { create: { method: "POST" }, save: { method: "PUT" } });
})
.config(function ($routeProvider, $locationProvider) {

    $locationProvider.html5Mode(true);

    $routeProvider.when("/edit/:id", {
        templateUrl: "/editorView.html",
        controller: "editCtrl"
    });

    $routeProvider.when("/create", {
        templateUrl: "/editorView.html",
        controller: "editCtrl"
    });
```

```javascript
    $routeProvider.otherwise({
        templateUrl: "/tableView.html",
        controller: "tableCtrl",
        resolve: {
            data: function (productsResource) {
                return productsResource.query();
            }
        }
    });
})
.controller("defaultCtrl", function ($scope, $location, productsResource) {

    $scope.data = {};

    $scope.createProduct = function (product) {
        new productsResource(product).$create().then(function (newProduct) {
            $scope.data.products.push(newProduct);
            $location.path("/list");
        });
    }

    $scope.deleteProduct = function (product) {
        product.$delete().then(function () {
            $scope.data.products.splice($scope.data.products.indexOf(product), 1);
        });

        $location.path("/list");
    }
})
.controller("tableCtrl", function ($scope, $location, $route, data) {
    $scope.data.products = data;

    $scope.refreshProducts = function () {
        $route.reload();
    }
})
.controller("editCtrl", function ($scope, $routeParams, $location) {

    $scope.currentProduct = null;

    if ($location.path().indexOf("/edit/") == 0) {
        var id = $routeParams["id"];
        for (var i = 0; i < $scope.data.products.length; i++) {
            if ($scope.data.products[i].id == id) {
                $scope.currentProduct = $scope.data.products[i];
                break;
            }
        }
    }
```

```
    $scope.cancelEdit = function () {
        $location.path("/list");
    }

    $scope.updateProduct = function (product) {
        product.$save();
        $location.path("/list");
    }

    $scope.saveEdit = function (product) {
        if (angular.isDefined(product.id)) {
            $scope.updateProduct(product);
        } else {
            $scope.createProduct(product);
        }
        $scope.currentProduct = {};
    }
});
```

There are a lot of changes in the listing, so I'll walk you through them in turn. The most important is the change of the definition of the /list route so that it uses the controller and resolve properties, like this:

```
...
$routeProvider.otherwise({
    templateUrl: "/tableView.html",
    controller: "tableCtrl",
    resolve: {
        data: function (productsResource) {
            return productsResource.query();
        }
    }
});
...
```

I have specified that the route should instantiate a controller called tableCtrl, and I have used the resolve property to create a dependency called data. The data property is set to a function that will be evaluated before the tableCtrl controller is created, and the result will be passed as an argument called data.

For this example, I use the $resource access object to obtain the data from the server, which means that the controller won't be instantiated until it is loaded and that, as a consequence, the tableView.html view won't be displayed until then either.

To be able to access the access object from the route dependency, I have to create a new service, as follows:

```
...
.factory("productsResource", function ($resource, baseUrl) {
    return $resource(baseUrl + ":id", { id: "@id" },
            { create: { method: "POST" }, save: { method: "PUT" } });
})
...
```

This is the same code that I used to create the `productResource` object in the controller in previous listings, just moved to a service through the `factory` method (described in Chapter 18) so that it is accessible more widely in the application.

The `tableCtrl` controller is rather simple, as follows:

```
...
.controller("tableCtrl", function ($scope, $location, $route, data) {

    $scope.data.products = data;

    $scope.refreshProducts = function () {
        $route.reload();
    }
})
...
```

I receive the product information from the server via the `data` argument and simply assign it to the `$scope.data.products` property. As I explained in the previous sections, the controller/scope inheritance rules that I described in Chapter 13 apply when using controllers with routes, so I had to add an object to which the data property belongs to ensure that the product data is available to all of the controllers in the applications and not just the scope belonging to the `tabelCtrl` controller.

The effect of adding the dependency in the route is that I no longer need the `listProducts` behavior, so I removed it from the `defaultCtrl` controller. That stranded the Refresh button in the `tableView.html` view without a way to force reload the data, so I defined a new behavior called `refreshProducts`, which uses the `$route.reload` method I described in Table 22-3. The final JavaScript change was to simplify the `cancelEdit` behavior, which no longer needs to reload a single product object from the server when editing is cancelled because all of the data will be refreshed when the `/list` route is activated:

```
...
$scope.cancelEdit = function () {
    $scope.currentProduct = {};
    $location.path("/list");
}
...
```

To reflect the changes in the controller, I had to update the `tableView.html` file, as shown in Listing 22-13.

Listing 22-13. Updating the tableView.html File to Reflect Controller Changes

```
<div class="panel-body">
    <table class="table table-striped table-bordered">
        <thead>
            <tr>
                <th>Name</th>
                <th>Category</th>
                <th class="text-right">Price</th>
                <th></th>
            </tr>
        </thead>
```

Why and When to Use the Animation Service

Animations can be a useful means of drawing the user's attention to an important change in the layout of an application, making the transition from one state to another less jarring.

Many developers treat animations as an outlet for their frustrated artistic ambition and ladle on as many as possible. The results can be annoying, especially for the user who has to endure endless special effects every time they perform a task. For a line-of-business application, where the user could be repeating the same set of actions all day, the effect is demoralizing beyond description.

Animations should be subtle, brief, and quick. The goal is to draw the user's attention to the fact that something has changed. Use animations consistently, cautiously, and—above all—sparingly.

Installing the ngAnimation Module

The $animation service is defined within an optional module called ngAnimate that must be downloaded into the angularjs folder. Go to http://angularjs.org, click Download, select the version you require (version 1.2.5 is the latest version as I write this), and click the Extras link in the bottom-left corner of the window, as shown in Figure 23-1.

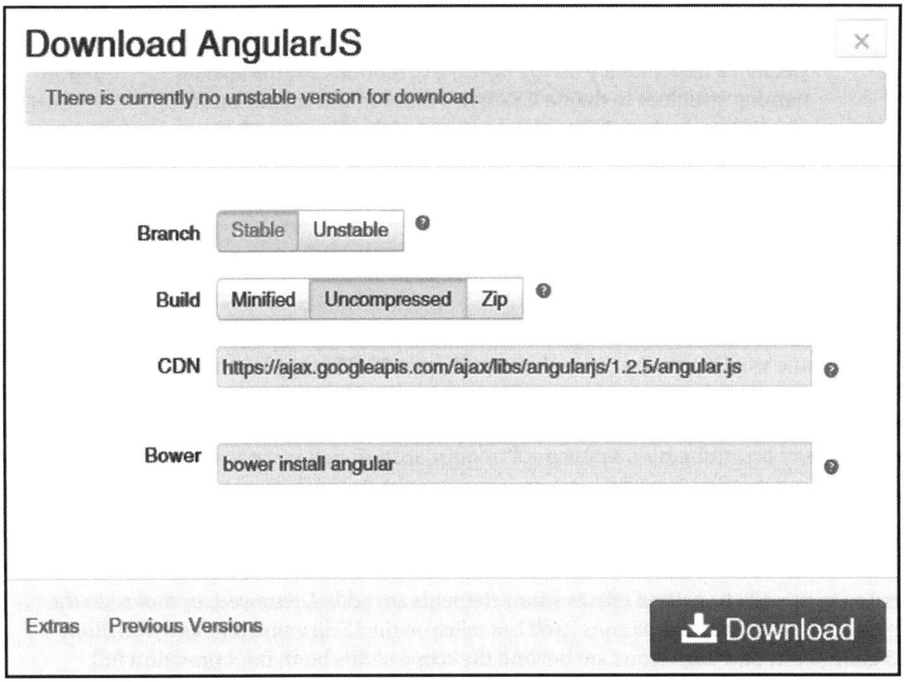

Figure 23-1. *Downloading an optional module*

Download the angular-animate.js file into the angularjs folder. In Listing 23-1, you can see how I have added a script element for the new file to the products.html file.

Listing 23-1. Adding a Reference to the products.html File

```
<!DOCTYPE html>
<html ng-app="exampleApp">
<head>
    <title>Products</title>
    <script src="angular.js"></script>
    <script src="angular-resource.js"></script>
    <script src="angular-route.js"></script>
    <script src="angular-animate.js"></script>
    <link href="bootstrap.css" rel="stylesheet" />
    <link href="bootstrap-theme.css" rel="stylesheet" />
    <script src="products.js"></script>
    <script src="increment.js"></script>
</head>
<body ng-controller="defaultCtrl">
    <div class="panel panel-primary">
        <h3 class="panel-heading">Products</h3>
        <div ng-view></div>
    </div>
</body>
</html>
```

In Listing 23-2, you can see the module dependency that I added to the products.js file for ngAnimate.

Listing 23-2. Adding the Module Dependency in the products.js File

```
angular.module("exampleApp", ["increment", "ngResource", "ngRoute", "ngAnimate"])
.constant("baseUrl", "http://localhost:5500/products/")
.factory("productsResource", function ($resource, baseUrl) {
    return $resource(baseUrl + ":id", { id: "@id" },
            { create: { method: "POST" }, save: { method: "PUT" } });
})
.config(function ($routeProvider, $locationProvider) {
...
```

Defining and Applying an Animation

You don't work directly with the $animate service to apply animations. Instead, you define animations or transitions with CSS, following a special naming convention, and then apply those names as classes to elements, which also have AngularJS directives. The best way to explain is with an example, and Listing 23-3 shows the changes I have made to the products.html file to animate the transition between views.

Listing 23-3. Animating View Transition in the products.html File

```
<!DOCTYPE html>
<html ng-app="exampleApp">
<head>
    <title>Products</title>
    <script src="angular.js"></script>
    <script src="angular-resource.js"></script>
    <script src="angular-route.js"></script>
```

```
<script src="angular-animate.js"></script>
<link href="bootstrap.css" rel="stylesheet" />
<link href="bootstrap-theme.css" rel="stylesheet" />
<script src="products.js"></script>
<script src="increment.js"></script>
<style type="text/css">
    .ngFade.ng-enter { transition: 0.1s linear all;  opacity: 0; }
    .ngFade.ng-enter-active { opacity: 1; }
</style>
</head>
<body ng-controller="defaultCtrl">
    <div class="panel panel-primary">
        <h3 class="panel-heading">Products</h3>
        <div ng-view class="ngFade"></div>
    </div>
</body>
</html>
```

The key to understand what's happening in this example is the knowledge that some of the built-in directives support animations when they change their content. Table 23-2 lists directives and the names given to those changes for the purposes of animation.

Table 23-2. *The Built-in Directives That Support Animation and the Names Associated with Them*

Directive	Names
ng-repeat	enter, leave, move
ng-view	enter, leave
ng-include	enter, leave
ng-switch	enter, leave
ng-if	enter, leave
ng-class	add, remove
ng-show	add, remove
ng-hide	add, remove

The name enter is used when content is shown to the user. The name leave is used when content is hidden from the user. The name move is used when content is moved within the DOM. The names add and remove are used when content is added and removed from the DOM.

With Table 23-2 as a reference, you can get a sense of the contents of the style element I added to the example:

```
...
<style type="text/css">
    .ngFade.ng-enter { transition: 0.1s linear all;  opacity: 0; }
    .ngFade.ng-enter-active { opacity: 1; }
</style>
...
```

I have defined two CSS classes, ngFade.ng-enter and ngFade.ng-enter-active, and the names of these classes is important. The first part of the name—ngFade in this case—is the name used to apply the animations or transitions to the element, like this:

```
...
<div ng-view class="ngFade"></div>
...
```

■ **Tip**   There is no requirement to prefix the top-level class name with ng, as I have done, but this is something that I have taken to doing to avoid conflicts with other CSS classes. The transition I have defined in the example causes elements to fade into view, and you might reasonably be tempted to use the name fade. However, Bootstrap, which I am also using in this example, also defines a CSS class fade, and that kind of conflict can cause problems. This has happened to me often enough that I now prefix my AngularJS animation classes with ng, just to make sure that the names are unique within the application.

The second part of the name tells AngularJS what the CSS style is to be used for. There are two names in this example: ng-enter and ng-enter-active. The ng- prefix *is* required, and AngularJS won't process the animation without it. The next part of the name corresponds to the details in Table 23-2. I am using the ng-view directive, which will perform animations when a view is displayed to the user and hidden from the user. My styles use the prefix ng-enter, which tells AngularJS that they should be used when a view is shown to the user.

The two styles define the start and end points for the transition that I want the ng-view directive to use. The ng-enter style defines the start point and details of the transition. I have specified that the CSS opacity property is initially 0 (meaning that the view is initially transparent and not visible to the user) and that the transition should be performed over a tenth of a second (I was serious when I said that animations should be brief). The ng-enter-active style defines the end point for the transition. I have specified that the CSS opacity property should be 1, meaning that the view will be entirely opaque and so visible to the user.

The overall effect is that when the view changes, the ng-view directive will apply the CSS classes to the new view, which will transition it from transparent to opaque—basically, fading in the new view.

Avoiding the Perils of Parallel Animation

It is natural to assume you have to animate both the departure of old content and the arrival of new content, but doing so can be troublesome. The problem is that under normal circumstances, the ng-view directive adds the new view to the DOM and then removes the old one. If you try to animate the showing of the new content *and* the hiding of the old, then you will end up with both displayed at once. Listing 23-4 shows additions to the products.html file that will demonstrate the problem.

Listing 23-4. Adding Leave Animations to the products.html File

```html
<!DOCTYPE html>
<html ng-app="exampleApp">
<head>
    <title>Products</title>
    <script src="angular.js"></script>
    <script src="angular-resource.js"></script>
    <script src="angular-route.js"></script>
    <script src="angular-animate.js"></script>
    <link href="bootstrap.css" rel="stylesheet" />
    <link href="bootstrap-theme.css" rel="stylesheet" />
    <script src="products.js"></script>
    <script src="increment.js"></script>
    <style type="text/css">
        .ngFade.ng-enter { transition: 0.1s linear all;  opacity: 0; }
        .ngFade.ng-enter-active { opacity: 1; }
        .ngFade.ng-leave { transition: 0.1s linear all; opacity: 1;  }
        .ngFade.ng-leave-active { opacity: 0; }
    </style>
</head>
<body ng-controller="defaultCtrl">
    <div class="panel panel-primary">
        <h3 class="panel-heading">Products</h3>
        <div ng-view class="ngFade"></div>
    </div>
</body>
</html>
```

The result is a brief moment when both views are visible, which is unappealing and confusing to the user. The ng-view directive doesn't worry about trying to position views over one another, and the new content is just displayed beneath the old, as illustrated in Figure 23-2.

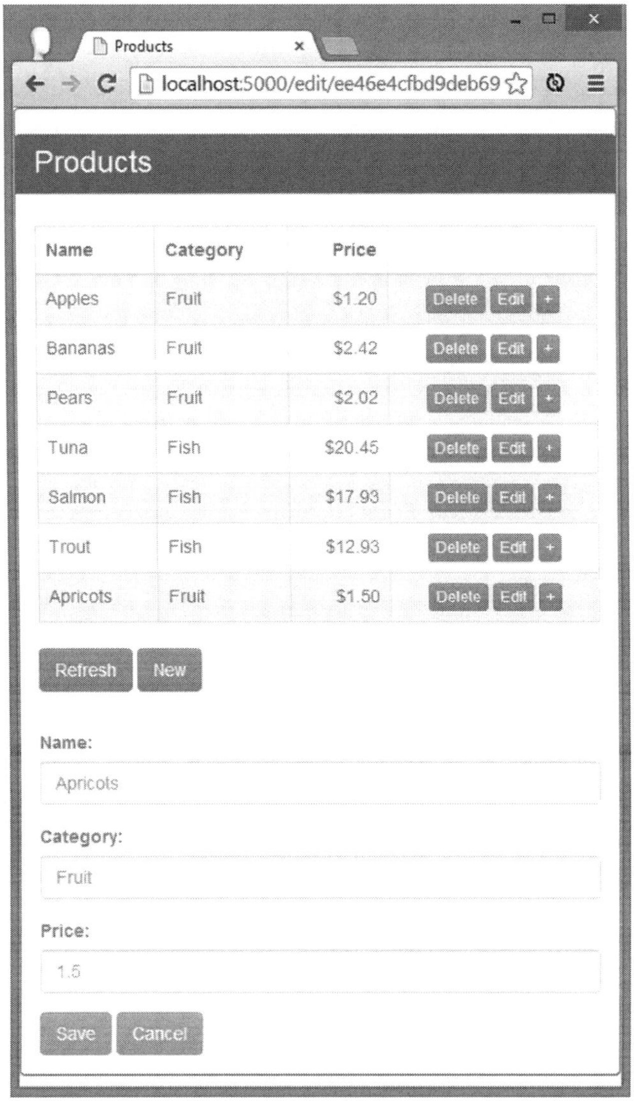

Figure 23-2. *The effects of parallel animation*

The content is faded because I took the screenshot at the midpoint in the transition and the opacity value of both views is about 0.5. A better effect is achieved by just animating the incoming view using enter. It is subtle, but it makes the view transition less jarring and still draws the user's attention to the change.

Supporting Touch Events

The ngTouch module contains the $swipe service, which is used to improve support for touchscreen devices beyond the basic events I described in Chapter 11. The events in ngTouch module provide notification of swipe gestures and a replacement for the ng-click directive, which addresses a common event problem on touch-enabled devices.

Why and When to Use Touch Events

The swipe gestures are useful whenever you want to improve support for touchscreen devices. The ngTouch swipe events can be used to detect left-to-right and right-to-left swipe gestures. To avoid confusing the user, you must ensure that the actions you perform in response to these gestures are consistent with the rest of the underlying platform—or at the very least, the default web browser for that platform. For example, if the right-to-left gesture usually means "go back" in the web browser, then it is important that you do not interpret the gesture in your application in a different way.

The replacement for the ng-click directive is useful for touch-enabled browsers because they synthesize click events for compatibility for JavaScript code that has been written with mouse events in mind. Touch browsers generally wait for 300 milliseconds after the user has tapped the screen to see whether another tap occurs. If there is no second tap, then the browser generates the touch event to represent a tap *and* a click event to simulate a mouse—but that 300-millisecond delay is just enough of a lag to be noticeable to the user, and it can make an application appear unresponsive. The ng-click replacement in the ngTouch module doesn't wait for a second tap and issues the click event much faster.

Installing the ngTouch Module

The ngTouch module must be downloaded from http://angularjs.org. Follow the same procedure as for the ngAnimate module earlier in the chapter, but select the angular-touch.js file and download it into the angularjs folder.

Handling Swipe Gestures

To demonstrate swipe gestures, I have created an HTML file called swipe.html in the angularjs folder. Listing 23-5 shows the contents of the new file.

Listing 23-5. The Contents of the swipe.html File

```
<!DOCTYPE html>
<html ng-app="exampleApp">
<head>
    <title>Swipe Events</title>
    <script src="angular.js"></script>
    <script src="angular-touch.js"></script>
    <link href="bootstrap.css" rel="stylesheet" />
    <link href="bootstrap-theme.css" rel="stylesheet" />
    <script>
        angular.module("exampleApp", ["ngTouch"])
        .controller("defaultCtrl", function ($scope, $element) {
            $scope.swipeType = "<None>";
            $scope.handleSwipe = function(direction) {
                $scope.swipeType = direction;
            }
        });
    </script>
</head>
<body ng-controller="defaultCtrl">
    <div class="panel panel-default">
        <div class="panel-body">
            <div class="well"
                ng-swipe-right="handleSwipe('left-to-right')"
                ng-swipe-left="handleSwipe('right-to-left')">
```

```
                <h4>Swipe Here</h4>
            </div>
            <div>Swipe was: {{swipeType}}</div>
        </div>
    </div>
</body>
</html>
```

I start by declaring a dependency on the ngTouch module. The event handlers are applied through the ng-swipe-left and ng-swipe-right directives. I have applied these directives to a div element and set them to call a controller behavior that updates a scope property that is displayed using an inline binding expression.

The swipe gestures will be detected on touch-enabled devices or when the gesture is made using the mouse. The best way to test touch events is with a touch-enabled device, of course. But if you don't have one on hand, then I find the ability of Google Chrome to simulate touch input to be useful. Click the gear icon in the bottom-right corner of the F12 tools window, select the Overrides tab, and enable the Emulate Touch Events option. Google seems to redesign the layout of the F12 tools every now and again, so you may have to hunt around to find the right option. Once touch events are enabled, you can use the mouse to swipe left and right using the mouse, and the browser will generate the required touch events, as shown in Figure 23-3.

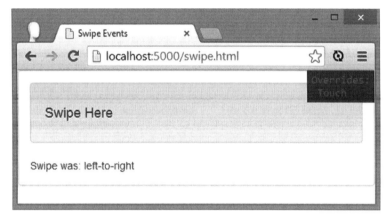

Figure 23-3. *Detecting swipe gestures*

Using the Replacement ng-click Directive

I am not going to demonstrate the replacement ng-click directive because it is a like-for-like replacement for the one I described in Chapter 11.

Summary

In this chapter, I described the services that AngularJS provides for animating elements and detecting gestures. In the next chapter, I describe some services that are used internally by AngularJS but that set the foundation for how unit testing functions.

Table 24-2. *The Methods Defined by the $provide Service*

Name	Description
constant(name, value)	Defines a constant value, as described in Chapter 9
decorator(name, service)	Defines a service decorator, as explained in a moment
factory(name, service)	Defines a service, as described in Chapter 18
provider(name, service)	Defines a service, as described in Chapter 18
service(name, provider)	Defines a service, as described in Chapter 18
value(name, value)	Defines a value service, as described in Chapter 9

The method that is not exposed via the Module type is decorator, which is used to intercept requests for a service in order to provide different or additional functionality. In Listing 24-1, you can see how I have used a decorator to alter the behavior of the $log service in a new HTML file called components.html that I added to the angularjs folder.

Listing 24-1. The Contents of the components.html File

```
<!DOCTYPE html>
<html ng-app="exampleApp">
<head>
    <title>Components</title>
    <script src="angular.js"></script>
    <link href="bootstrap.css" rel="stylesheet" />
    <link href="bootstrap-theme.css" rel="stylesheet" />
    <script>
        angular.module("exampleApp", [])
        .config(function($provide) {
            $provide.decorator("$log", function ($delegate) {
                $delegate.originalLog = $delegate.log;
                $delegate.log = function (message) {
                    $delegate.originalLog("Decorated: " + message);
                }
                return $delegate;
            });
        })
        .controller("defaultCtrl", function ($scope, $log) {
            $scope.handleClick = function () {
                $log.log("Button Clicked");
            };
        });
    </script>
</head>
<body ng-controller="defaultCtrl">
    <div class="well">
        <button class="btn btn-primary" ng-click="handleClick()">Click Me!</button>
    </div>
</body>
</html>
```

This example application consists of a button that uses the ng-click directive to trigger a scope behavior called handleClick, which writes a message to the console using the $log service that I described in Chapter 19.

I have highlighted the important part of this example, which is contained in a call to the Module.config method (described in Chapter 9). My configuration function declares a dependency on the $provide service, which allows me to call the decorator method.

The arguments to the decorator method are the name of the service that you want to decorate (expressed as a literal string) and a *decorator function* that must declare a dependency on $delegate, which is used to pass the original service to your function.

■ **Tip**   You must use a string value for the first argument to the decorator method, such as "$log" and not just $log. This argument tells AngularJS which service you want to decorate and is not used to declare a dependency.

In my example, I set the first argument to "$log", which tells AngularJS that I want to decorate the $log service that I described in Chapter 19. This means AngularJS will instantiate the $log service object and pass it as the $delegate argument of the decorator function. Within the decorator function, I am free to make whatever changes I want to the $delegate object, and the result that I return will be used to resolve dependencies on the $log service when it is required in other parts of the application.

■ **Tip**   Your decorator function must return the object you want used to resolve dependencies for the service you specified. If you don't return a value, then dependencies will be resolved with the JavaScript undefined value.

Here are the decorations I made to the service in this example:

```
...
$provide.decorator("$log", function ($delegate) {
    $delegate.originalLog = $delegate.log;
    $delegate.log = function (message) {
        $delegate.originalLog("Decorated: " + message);
    }
    return $delegate;
});
...
```

I rename the log method so that it is called originalLog and add a new log method that prepends the word Decorated to the log message. You can see the effect by starting the application, clicking the button, and looking at the output in the JavaScript console:

```
Decorated: Button Clicked
```

You can change a service in any way that you want, but you must remember that the object you return from your decorator function will be passed to components that already have an expectation about the nature of the service object. There is no point, for example, in renaming the log method in the $log service so that it is called detailedLog because no component that declares a dependency on the $log service will expect a method of that name and will continue to use the original method name. As a consequence, I find that decorating services is most useful for making small adjustments—most often for writing a message to the JavaScript console when a service method is called, which can be helpful when debugging complex problems.

Managing Injection

The $injector service is responsible for determining the dependencies that a function declares and resolving those dependencies. Table 24-3 lists the methods supported by the $injector service.

Table 24-3. *The Methods Defined by the $injector Service*

Name	Description
annotate(fn)	Gets the arguments for the specified function, including those that do not correspond to services
get(name)	Gets the service object for the specified service name
has(name)	Returns true if a service exists for the specified name
invoke(fn, self, locals)	Invoked the specified function, using the specified value for this and the specified nonservice argument values.

The $injector service is right at the core of the AngularJS library, and there is rarely a need to work directly with it, but it can be useful for understanding and customizing how AngularJS works. However, these are the kind of customizations that should be considered carefully and tested thoroughly.

▓ **Tip** AngularJS includes a related service called $controller, which creates instances of controllers. The only time you need to create controllers directly is when writing unit tests, and I demonstrate the use of the $controller service in Chapter 25.

Determining Function Dependencies

JavaScript is a fluid and dynamic language, and there is a lot to recommend it, but it lacks the ability to annotate functions to manage their execution and behavior. Other languages, such as C#, support features such as attributes that are used to express instructions or metadata about a function.

The lack of annotations means that AngularJS has to go to some extraordinary lengths to implement dependency injection, which is handled by matching the names of function arguments to services. Usually the person writing a function gets to decide the names of arguments, but in AngularJS the names take on a special significance. The annotate method defined by the $injector service is used to get the set of dependencies that a function has declared, as shown in Listing 24-2.

Listing 24-2. Getting Function Dependencies in the components.html File

```
<!DOCTYPE html>
<html ng-app="exampleApp">
<head>
    <title>Components</title>
    <script src="angular.js"></script>
    <link href="bootstrap.css" rel="stylesheet" />
    <link href="bootstrap-theme.css" rel="stylesheet" />
```

```
    <script>
        angular.module("exampleApp", [])
        .controller("defaultCtrl", function ($scope, $injector) {
            var counter = 0;

            var logClick = function ($log, $exceptionHandler, message) {
                if (counter == 0) {
                    $log.log(message);
                    counter++;
                } else {
                    $exceptionHandler("Already clicked");
                }
            }

            $scope.handleClick = function () {
                var deps = $injector.annotate(logClick);
                for (var i = 0; i < deps.length; i++) {
                    console.log("Dependency: " + deps[i]);
                }
            };
        });
    </script>
</head>
<body ng-controller="defaultCtrl">
    <div class="well">
        <button class="btn btn-primary" ng-click="handleClick()">Click Me!</button>
    </div>
</body>
</html>
```

In this example, I have defined a function called logClick that depends on the $log and $exceptionHandler services as well as a regular argument called message. Neither of the services is declared as dependencies by the controller factory function, and my goal in this part of the chapter will be to provide the logClick function with its dependencies so that I can execute it.

■ **Note**   This is not something you are likely to need to do in a real project, and I am demonstrating the use of the $injector service solely so you can see how AngularJS works internally. You can readily skip these examples if you want to stay focused on day-to-day techniques.

My first step is to get the set of dependencies from the function itself, which I do using the $injector.annotate method, like this:

```
...
var deps = $injector.annotate(logClick);
for (var i = 0; i < deps.length; i++) {
    console.log("Dependency: " + deps[i]);
}
...
```

If you load the `components.html` file into the browser and click the button twice, you will see output from the `$log` and `$exceptionHandler` services written to the JavaScript console, like this:

```
Button Clicked
Already Clicked
```

Simplifying the Invocation Process

I have taken the long way around to the point where I can invoke the function because the `$injector.invoke` method will take care of locating the services and managing the additional values that I need to provide to the function. In Listing 24-5, you can see how I have used the `invoke` method in the example.

Listing 24-5. Using the invoke Method in the components.html File

```
...
<script>
    angular.module("exampleApp", [])
    .controller("defaultCtrl", function ($scope, $injector) {
        var counter = 0;

        var logClick = function ($log, $exceptionHandler, message) {
            if (counter == 0) {
                $log.log(message);
                counter++;
            } else {
                $exceptionHandler("Already clicked");
            }
        }

        $scope.handleClick = function () {
            var localVars = { message: "Button Clicked" };
            $injector.invoke(logClick, null, localVars);
        };
    });
</script>
...
```

The arguments to the `invoke` method are the function that will invoked, the value for `this`, and an object whose properties correspond to the function arguments that are not service dependencies.

Getting the $injector Service from the Root Element

The `$rootElement` service provides access to the HTML element to which the `ng-app` directive is applied and which is the root of the AngularJS application. The `$rootElement` service is presented as a `jqLite` object, which means you can use jqLite to locate elements or modify the DOM using the jqLite methods I described in Chapter 15. Of interest in this chapter, the `$rootElement` service object has an additional method called `injector`, which returns the `$injector` service object. You can see how I replaced the dependency on the `$injector` service with the `$rootElement` service in Listing 24-6.

Listing 24-6. Using the $rootElement Service in the components.html File

```
...
<script>
    angular.module("exampleApp", [])
    .controller("defaultCtrl", function ($scope, $rootElement) {
        var counter = 0;

        var logClick = function ($log, $exceptionHandler, message) {
            if (counter == 0) {
                $log.log(message);
                counter++;
            } else {
                $exceptionHandler("Already clicked");
            }
        }

        $scope.handleClick = function () {
            var localVars = { message: "Button Clicked" };
            $rootElement.injector().invoke(logClick, null, localVars);
        };
    });
</script>
...
```

■ **Tip**   I have yet to find a compelling reason to access the $injector service via the $rootElement service, and I am including the information in this chapter just for completeness.

Summary

In this chapter, I described the services that are responsible for managing services and injecting them into functions to resolve dependencies. These are not services that you will use every day, but they can provide interesting insights into the way that AngularJS operates. In the next chapter, I describe the facilities that AngularJS provides for unit testing.

■ ■ ■

Unit Testing

In this chapter, I describe the facilities that AngularJS provides for unit testing and, in particular, the services that make it easy to isolate a piece of code from the rest of the AngularJS framework to enable thorough and consistent testing. Table 25-1 summarizes this chapter.

Table 25-1. *Chapter Summary*

Problem	Solution	Listing
Write a basic Jasmine unit test.	Use the Jasmine describe, beforeEach, it, and expect functions.	1–4
Prepare an AngularJS test.	Use the angular.mock.module method to load the module you want to test, and use the angular.mock.inject method to resolve dependencies.	5
Mock HTTP requests.	Use the $httpBackend service in the ngMocks module.	6–7
Mock timeouts and intervals.	Use the $interval and $timeout services in the ngMocks module.	8–9
Test logging.	Use the $log service in the ngMocks module.	10–11
Test a filter.	Instantiate the filter using the $filter service.	12–13
Test a directive.	Use the $compile service to generate a function that can be invoked with a scope argument to generate HTML that can then be evaluated using jqLite.	14–15
Test a service.	Use the angular.mock.inject method to resolve a dependency on the service that is to be tested.	16–17

Why and When to Unit Testing

Unit testing is the technique of isolating a single small piece of functionality and testing it independently of the rest of the application and AngularJS. Carefully applied, unit testing can reduce the number of software defects that show up later in the development process, especially those that the user encounters when the application is deployed.

Unit testing works best with teams that have strong design skills and a good understanding of what and who the finished product is for. Without those skills and the broader perspective, the narrow focus that unit testing creates can put too much emphasis on the quality of individual bricks at the cost of the overall structure of the house they are being used to build. The worst possible environment for unit testing is the one in which I encounter it most often: large corporate projects with thousands of developers. In these projects, individual developers have little visibility of the overarching objectives in anything other than the broadest terms, and passing arbitrary unit tests quickly becomes the sole measure of quality, which requires developers to make assumptions about external inputs to their code that turn out to be wrong. In these situations, a project whose unit test results are positive will get bogged down in integration testing as all of those individual assumptions are discovered and found wanting.

Even so, unit testing can be a powerful tool when applied carefully. Just be sure that you are able to measure the benefit that it brings, that you understand that unit testing triggers the natural inclination of many developers to turn their focus inward, and that passing unit tests doesn't mean that those units are going to work well together. Use unit testing as part of a broader strategy of end-to-end testing. The AngularJS project recommends Protractor for end-to-end testing, which you can learn about and download from `https://github.com/angular/protractor`.

Preparing the Example Project

For this chapter, I removed the contents of the `angularjs` folder and reinstalled the AngularJS and Bootstrap files as described in Chapter 1.

■ **Caution**   In previous chapters, it didn't really matter if you ignored my instruction to clear out the contents of the `angularjs` folder and start over. It *does* make a difference in this chapter, and you won't get the right results unless you remove the JavaScript files from previous chapters.

Installing the ngMocks Module

AngularJS provides an optional module called `ngMock`, which provides useful tools for unit testing. Go to `http://angularjs.org`, click Download, select the version you require, and click the Extras link in the bottom-left corner of the window, as shown in Figure 25-1.

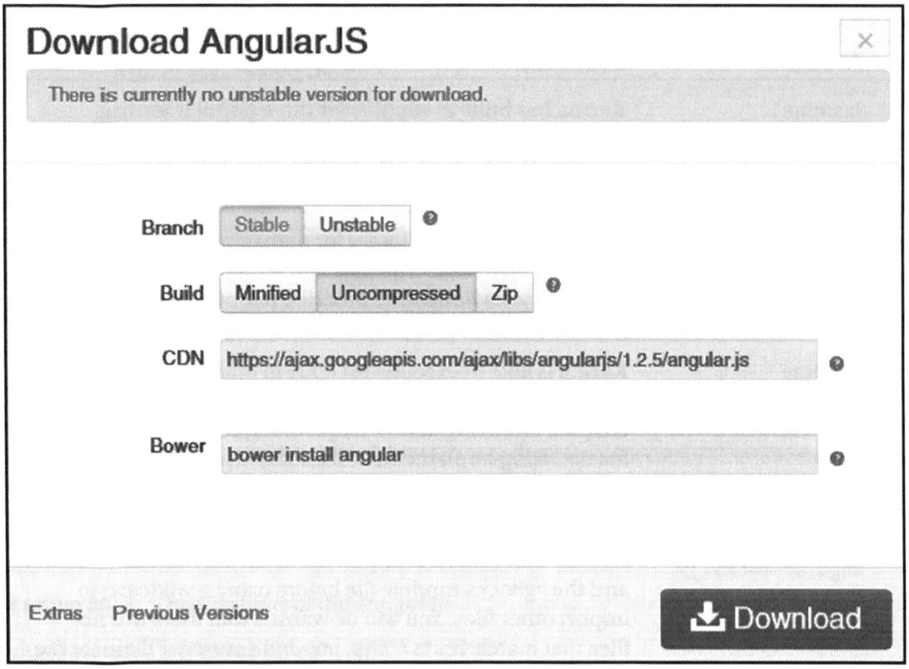

Figure 25-1. *Downloading an optional module*

Download the angular-mocks.js file into the angularjs folder.

Creating the Test Configuration

During the initial preparation steps in Chapter 1, I installed the Karma test runner. Karma needs to be configured for each new project. Run the following from the command line within the angularjs folder:

```
karma init karma.config.js
```

The Karma setup process will begin, and you will be prompted to answer a number of questions. I have listed the questions and the answers that are required for this chapter in Table 25-2.

```
it("Preserves the data order", function () {
    expect(mockScope.products[0].name).toEqual("Apples");
    expect(mockScope.products[1].name).toEqual("Bananas");
    expect(mockScope.products[2].name).toEqual("Pears");
});
...
```

These are simple tests to ensure that the controller doesn't mangle or rearrange the data, although in a real project the emphasis of HTTP testing is generally focused on the requests rather than the data handling.

Mocking Periods of Time

The mock $interval and $timeout services define extra methods that allow you to explicitly trigger the callback functions registered by the code being tested. In Listing 25-8, you can see how I have used the real services in the app.js file.

Listing 25-8. Adding Intervals and Timeouts to the app.js File

```
angular.module("exampleApp", [])
    .controller("defaultCtrl", function ($scope, $http, $interval, $timeout) {

        $scope.intervalCounter = 0;
        $scope.timerCounter = 0;

        $interval(function () {
            $scope.intervalCounter++;
        }, 5000, 10);

        $timeout(function () {
            $scope.timerCounter++;
        }, 5000);

        $http.get("productData.json").success(function (data) {
            $scope.products = data;
        });

        $scope.counter = 0;

        $scope.incrementCounter = function() {
            $scope.counter++;
        }
    });
```

I have defined two variables, intervalCounter and timerCounter, that are incremented by functions passed to the $interval and $timeout services. These functions are called after five-second delays, which isn't ideal in unit testing when the idea is to run a lot of tests quickly and often. Table 25-9 shows the additional methods defined by the mock versions of these services.

Table 25-9. *The Additional Methods Defined by the Mock $timeout and $interval Services*

Service	Method	Description
$timeout	flush(millis)	Advances the timer by the specified number of milliseconds
$timeout	verifyNoPendingTasks()	Checks to see whether there are callbacks that have yet to be invoked
$interval	flush(millis)	Advances the timer by the specified number of milliseconds

The flush method can be used to skip ahead, and Listing 25-9 shows the contents of the tests/controllerTest.js file, which I have extended to demonstrate this feature.

Listing 25-9. Adding Tests to the controllerTest.js File

```
describe("Controller Test", function () {

    // Arrange
    var mockScope, controller, backend, mockInterval, mockTimeout;

    beforeEach(angular.mock.module("exampleApp"));

    beforeEach(angular.mock.inject(function ($httpBackend) {
        backend = $httpBackend;
        backend.expect("GET", "productData.json").respond(
        [{ "name": "Apples", "category": "Fruit", "price": 1.20 },
        { "name": "Bananas", "category": "Fruit", "price": 2.42 },
        { "name": "Pears", "category": "Fruit", "price": 2.02 }]);
    }));

    beforeEach(angular.mock.inject(function ($controller, $rootScope,
            $http, $interval, $timeout) {
        mockScope = $rootScope.$new();
        mockInterval = $interval;
        mockTimeout = $timeout;
        $controller("defaultCtrl", {
            $scope: mockScope,
            $http: $http,
            $interval: mockInterval,
            $timeout: mockTimeout
        });
        backend.flush();
    }));

    // Act and Assess
    it("Creates variable", function () {
        expect(mockScope.counter).toEqual(0);
    })

    it("Increments counter", function () {
        mockScope.incrementCounter();
        expect(mockScope.counter).toEqual(1);
    });
```

```
                { name: "Apples", category: "Fruit", price: 1.20, expiry: 10 },
                { name: "Bananas", category: "Fruit", price: 2.42, expiry: 7 },
                { name: "Pears", category: "Fruit", price: 2.02, expiry: 6 }];
    }));

    it("Generates list elements", function () {

        var compileFn = compileService("<div unordered-list='data'></div>");
        var elem = compileFn(mockScope);

        expect(elem.children("ul").length).toEqual(1);
        expect(elem.find("li").length).toEqual(3);
        expect(elem.find("li").eq(0).text()).toEqual("Apples");
        expect(elem.find("li").eq(1).text()).toEqual("Bananas");
        expect(elem.find("li").eq(2).text()).toEqual("Pears");
    });

});
```

I use the `inject` method to obtain the $rootScope and $compile services. I create a new scope and assign the data that the directive will use to the data property. I keep a reference to the $compile service so that I can use it in the test.

Following the approach that I described in Chapter 19, I compile a fragment of HTML to which the directive has been applied, specifying that the source of the data is the scope data array. This produces a function that I invoked with the mock scope to get the HTML output from the directive. To assess the results, I use jqLite to check the structure and the order of the elements that the directive has produced.

Testing a Service

Obtaining an instance of a service to test is easy because the `inject` method can be used, just as I have been doing to get the built-in and mocked services in earlier tests. In Listing 25-16, I have added a simple service to the app.js file.

Listing 25-16. Adding a Service to the app.js File

```
angular.module("exampleApp", [])
    .controller("defaultCtrl", function ($scope, $http, $interval, $timeout, $log) {

        $scope.intervalCounter = 0;
        $scope.timerCounter = 0;

        $interval(function () {
            $scope.intervalCounter++;
        }, 5, 10);

        $timeout(function () {
            $scope.timerCounter++;
        }, 5);

        $http.get("productData.json").success(function (data) {
            $scope.products = data;
            $log.log("There are " + data.length + " items");
        });

        $scope.counter = 0;
```

```
        $scope.incrementCounter = function () {
            $scope.counter++;
        }
    })
    .filter("labelCase", function () {
        return function (value, reverse) {
            if (angular.isString(value)) {
                var intermediate = reverse ? value.toUpperCase() : value.toLowerCase();
                return (reverse ? intermediate[0].toLowerCase() :
                    intermediate[0].toUpperCase()) + intermediate.substr(1);
            } else {
                return value;
            }
        };
    })
    .directive("unorderedList", function () {
        return function (scope, element, attrs) {
            var data = scope[attrs["unorderedList"]];
            if (angular.isArray(data)) {
                var listElem = angular.element("<ul>");
                element.append(listElem);
                for (var i = 0; i < data.length; i++) {
                    listElem.append(angular.element('<li>').text(data[i].name));
                }
            }
        }
    })
    .factory("counterService", function () {
        var counter = 0;
        return {
            incrementCounter: function () {
                counter++;
            },
            getCounter: function() {
                return counter;
            }
        }
    });
```

I used the `factory` method, described in Chapter 18, to define a service that maintains a counter and that defines methods that increment and return the counter value. This isn't a useful service in its own right, but it lets me demonstrate the process for testing a service. Listing 25-17 shows the contents of the `tests/serviceTest.js` file.

Listing 25-17. The Contents of the serviceTest.js File

```
describe("Service Tests", function () {

    beforeEach(angular.mock.module("exampleApp"));

    it("Increments the counter", function () {
        angular.mock.inject(function (counterService) {
            expect(counterService.getCounter()).toEqual(0);
            counterService.incrementCounter();
            expect(counterService.getCounter()).toEqual(1);
        });
    });
});
```

Just for some variety, I use the `inject` function to obtain the service object within the Jasmine `it` function. I then test the counter value, increment it, and then test again. The tools that AngularJS provides for unit testing are heavily oriented toward instantiating services, which make them simple and easy to test.

Summary

In this chapter, I have shown you the tools that AngularJS provides to aid in unit testing. I explained their use and demonstrated the basic approach for testing each major component in an AngularJS application.

And that is all I have to teach you about AngularJS. I started by creating a simple application and then took you on a comprehensive tour of the different components in the framework, showing you how they can be configured, customized, or replaced entirely. I wish you every success in your AngularJS projects, and I can only hope that you have enjoyed reading this book as much as I enjoyed writing it.

Index

■ T

Get the eBook for only $10!

Now you can take the weightless companion with you anywhere, anytime. Your purchase of this book entitles you to 3 electronic versions for only $10.

This Apress title will prove so indispensible that you'll want to carry it with you everywhere, which is why we are offering the eBook in 3 formats for only $10 if you have already purchased the print book.

Convenient and fully searchable, the PDF version enables you to easily find and copy code—or perform examples by quickly toggling between instructions and applications. The MOBI format is ideal for your Kindle, while the ePUB can be utilized on a variety of mobile devices.

Go to www.apress.com/promo/tendollars to purchase your companion eBook.

28138370R00382

Made in the USA
Middletown, DE
03 January 2016